Controversies in the Epistles

A Comparative Analysis of Controversies in the Epistles

Controversies in the Epistles

A Comparative Analysis of Biblical Controversies

Copyright © David Criswell 2014

David Criswell

FORTRESS

ADONAI
PRESS

North Charleston, S.C.

Controversies in the Epistles

A Comparative Analysis of Biblical Controversies

David Criswell

ISBN NUMBER 978-0692290217

Cover Design by David Criswell
Cover Art is from Rembrandt

FORTRESS

ADONAI
PRESS

Dallas, TX

Printed in the United States of America

Dedication

For my *filmi* friends. I pray that we may make a difference.

"Be always ready to make a defense to everyone who asks you to give an account for the hope that is in you" (1 Peter 3:15).

"We demolish arguments and every pretension that sets itself up against the knowledge of God, and we take captive every thought to make it obedient to Christ." (2 Corinthians 10:5 NIV).

Preface

Why a series of books about Biblical controversies? The answer is to be found in the Bible itself. Peter said, "Be always ready to make a defense to everyone who asks you to give an account for the hope that is in you" (1 Peter 3:15). I have always been a seeker. I do not object the notion of being critically minded, but I do object to the notion that being critically minded means being critical of one thing, but uncritical of another. Lest anyone believe that this is not the case with so-called Bible critics I will note that one of professors once scolded me for not being "critically minded" but when I told her that she was only mad because I *was* being critical ... of *her* beliefs, she became strangely silent.

Studying controversies is a way of strengthening our understanding of the Bible and of God's Word. It is way of getting closer to the Word of God; not further from it. If a war begins, you flee to the safety of the strongest bunker, and yet it is that bunker which the enemy most wants to eliminate. So it is with the Word of God. The Bible is attacked *because* of its strength. To be fearful of controversies is to be fearful that the Bible does not have all the answer we claim, and yet it does. It is our strength, because it is the Word of our Strength, the Lord God.

Sir Robert Anderson once said, "for the Christian to solve difficulties by repudiating the teaching of Christ, is like committing suicide to escape from danger."[1] Unfortunately, this is exactly what many Christians do. They hear that "science as disproven" X, Y, or Z, and instead of delving into the science and issues to debate and refute such attacks, they retreat, thinking to themselves that no harm will come to them if they just concede, "well, maybe it is just a story meant to tell a story." But of what inspiration can I draw from Cinderella if I know in my heart that I will always be a servant girl who can never be anything more than that. I can only draw inspiration from stories that are true because I know that it *can* be true in my life. I draw inspiration from the story of Joseph in Genesis because I know *it is* a true story, and not a fairy tale. I have hope in eternal life because I know Jesus *was* resurrected from the dead!

David Criswell, August 2114

> "We demolish arguments and every pretension that sets itself up
> against the knowledge of God, and we take captive every thought
> to make it obedient to Christ." (2 Corinthians 10:5 NIV).

Table of Contents

✝   ✝   ✝

1
—
Introduction

Seven is a holy number, It was not my intention to make seven books in the Controversies series, but as the books kept growing, I found it necessary to divide the series into more and more books. Eventually I wound up with seven; three in the Old Testament and four in the New. Even so, this volume was actually divided, for two of my Appendices eventually became separate books; *The Apostles After Jesus* and *Anonymous*. The first of those is a history of the apostles after the time of Jesus, including my attempt to separate the traditions of the apostles from their true history. The second is a short book about the author of Hebrews. These may be considered companion pieces to *Controversies in the Epistles*.

For those who are new to my series, Controversies in the Epistles is an attempt to study, analyze, and refute attacks upon the Bible, as well as to gain a better understanding of the proper exegesis and interpretation of the Bible. I address issues ranging from critics' claims that the apostles did not write the Bible to various theological debates. In previous books I dealt with Biblical archaeology and issues in science, as well as historical research and textual criticism. The epistles are doctrinal letters from the apostles, so there is not as much debate involving archaeology or the like, but there is no shortage of controversy. Most of the controversies in this volume involve theology. As always I attempt to present the evidence and argument from both sides before drawing a conclusion. I try to be fair, as I believe that the truth will always prevail when it is given an open and fair platform. Some may disagree with my conclusions, but hopefully will accept that I have endeavored to present all facts for or against by own conclusions. Of course, there is ample discussion of critical attacks upon the Bible and its authenticity as well. The reader will be allowed to examine all sides of the issue and draw his own conclusions, but hopefully will do so with a better understanding of those issues.

Types of Controversies Addressed

Because the controversies in the epistles are different from those found in the gospels and the Old Testament, I will not repeat many of those issues here. In some cases, however, I will refer the reader to a previous volume. For example, when Paul quotes from Genesis I will debate the relevant issues, but will refer the reader to Controversies in the Pentateuch for more information on the debate over said passage in Genesis. This is regretable but is the only way to keep the size of this volume from becoming over burdensome and repeated too much of what I have said elsewhere. Consequently, when there is overlap I will give a brief summary of the debate or issue, but will try not to repeat too much of what has been said previous.

Below is a brief list of the types of controversies I endeavor to discuss.

Historical Controversies
Since the epistles are doctrinal letters one would not expect to find a great deal of historical controversies, but some Bible critics will continue to claim that the authors either erred in history or that the epistles could not have been written when they claim to have been written based on some alleged historical error. Such issues are fewer than in my previous volumes but will still appear. I will endeavor to respond to these when they arise.

Apostlic Authorship
Closely related to the historical criticism are the accusations of the "higher critics" in which the epistles were not written by whom they claimed to have been written. I will refute these theories with facts and evidence, showing that the authors were exactly who they claim to have been.

In some cases the author is not named. In such cases I will debate the question of authorship, as well as the date and circumstances which led to the composition of said epistle.

Alleged Contradictions
As usual critics will claim that the epistles either contradict some other passage (or at least their interpretation of it does) or that historical references in the epistles are contradictory to the facts. As Chief Inspector Sir Robert Anderson once said, "when in my official life I have found a conflict of testimony between persons of known integrity, I have always sought some way of reconciling them."[2] To do so is not bias, as the critic suggests, but common sense. If two witnesses give two entirely different descriptions of a perpetrator then the police may begin to look into the question of whether or not there were more than one perpetrator. To *ignore* this possibility is bias, not to *explore* the possibility.

Continuing the criminal justice analogy, I again refer to Sir Anderson who noted that "when I set myself to investigate the case against Daniel [of the Bible], I did so in the same spirit in which I have not infrequently prosecuted criminal charges against persons, whom, though I greatly wished to save, I was determined to bring to justice if guilty."[3] His conclusion was that the Bible was historically accurate in every facet in which it is able to examined, and even commented somewhat sarcastically that, "I owe much to the Higher Critics for settling my faith in Scripture; and I confess that my full acceptance of the [Biblical books] dates from my study of their reasons for rejecting it."[4] So also a fair objective examination of the alleged "contradictions" will render the same conclusions in the epistles of the New Testament.

2

Textual Errors

Another issue of importance to the inerrantist is that of textual errors. No one seems to deny that copyists occasionally made minor mistakes in transcribing manuscripts, but the extent of those errors and their impact upon the Biblical doctrine of inerrancy is in question, and remains, among conservatives, a major controversy. The liberal scholar seems content to argue that our manuscripts are but shadows of the original, while the conservative points to textual apparatii to demonstrate that we have faithful copies of the originals.

Having said this, there is no doubt that occasional questions arise as to what the original writing said and whether or not the original manuscript, if different from ours, would have had any real impact upon the meaning of the text. Because the evangelical seeks to truly understand the Word of God he must walk a careful line between seeking to understand the original meaning of the text and simply discarding one reading for another that he may like better. These controversies will not be neglected.

Theological and Exegetical Controversies

Of course the most numerous of all controversies are those that emerge from theological arguments. This is especially true of the epistles. Many theologians (although they will never admit it) tend to read *into* the text what they want to be there. This has sometimes been called *eisogesis* as opposed to *exegesis*. Obviously, many of the controversies addressed will be of this nature. What do the Biblical authors seek to say versus what we want to hear.

A final word should be said as to what my own personal approach will be. Let me, therefore, state that while I am an evangelical who believes in the inerrancy and accuracy of the Bible in everything of which it speaks, including history, science, and all other matters which may be reflected in it, I was by no means raised to believe these things. I was raised in a liberal church with a pastor who not only denied the reality of hell, but upon his deathbed he conveyed to me a fear that there was no heaven. He did not teach me anything that I have come to learn. I was taught that the Bible was myth; that it was stories told to promote a "moral" but that had no real historical meaning. That also meant that it had no practical meaning. My belief in the inerrancy of the Scriptures, therefore, was not a belief I inherited or was taught, but one that I came to me by personal study. I believed only that the Bible should be treated with the same respect that all other works of antiquity receive, and that the authors were not liars or fools. Beyond that my personal bias was not to accept all things. This I have come to believe by faith; but that faith is grounded in the fact that the Biblical authors have *proven* themselves reliable, honest, inspired, and trustworthy. Fact and faith have always been brothers. It is a myth to present them as enemies for, as Sir Robert Anderson would have said, the testimony of the eyewitness is accepted on good faith provided he is proven honest in all other matters which can be verified. This is my approach to the

Scriptures and their interpretations thereof. My conclusion is that there is no other work in human history as trustworthy as that of the Bible.

My final word is that I entrust this volume to the reader so that he might be better able to comply with the command of the apostle Peter:

> Be always "ready to make a defense to everyone who asks you to give an account for the hope that is in you" (1 Peter 3:15).

> To this I add Paul's plea in Corinthians:

> "We demolish arguments and every pretension that sets itself up against the knowledge of God, and we take captive every thought to make it obedient to Christ." (2 Corinthians 10:5 NIV).

2
—
Romans

The book of Romans is often considered a primer, so-to-speak, for the gospel. It offers a basic systematic theology of the gospel like no other. If I were to take a recently convert through the Bible, I begin with the gospel of John and the book of Romans. Together these two books offer any young believer a solid foundation and understanding of his new faith.

Unlike most of Paul's epistles, Romans was not written to correct some specific error or to address a schism but to instruct an apparently young church in his absence.[5] The book of Romans is not, however, without controversy. Indeed, where the gospel is clear many will attempt to make hazy. Some of the controversies in Romans are contextual, some are cultural, and some are fabricated by critics. Among the most prevalent are those controversies revolving around Israel and the Jews. Some Christians wish to make Israel a part of the old dispensation and of no value in the new. Others wish to continue Israel's dominance into the new. Still others believe that Israel is to be chastised during the "times of the gentiles" (Luke 21:24), but will be restored in the End of Days. Other debates involve the question of election and its relationship to Calvinism. Are the elect predestined by God, and for what purpose? The reader may be surprised to find that even Calvinists are not in agreement. Finally, Paul gives advice to the church of Rome regarding their submission to government, the role of family and marriage, and other issues which were of particular relevance both then and today. As with all things, many take such passages out of their context to read one assumption or another into them. What are we to make of such passages and their application in the modern world?

These are the dominant issues which arise in Romans. As is my usual practice, I will outline all the various views and their evidence before stating my own conclusions. The reader must then make his own decision between himself and God, for in the in end it is always between us and God, and never between each other.

The Date and Occasion of the Epistle

Obviously the epistle was written to the church of Rome. However, most believe that it was written before Paul had ever been to Rome (1:10-11). Clearly Paul was longing to come to Rome in order that he might "impart some spiritual gift to you, that you may be established" (1:11). Since the book of Acts makes it clear that Paul did not arrive in Rome until he was brought to Rome in chains around 60 A.D., this epistle had to have been written either before this time, or after his initial release from prison in early 63 A.D. (see *Controversies in Acts* for a debate over these dates). Nonetheless, we may easily reject the post imprisonment date for three reasons. First, the entire precept of the letter implies that the church in Rome was fairly new and in need of basic doctrinal instruction. Second, it is strongly inferred that Paul had never been to Rome, or else they would not have needed a spiritual gift in order to be established (1:11). Third, Romans 15:25 states that Paul was about to depart for Jerusalem. Since there is little doubt that he never returned to Jerusalem after his first imprisonment, for it was under seige by Rome, then this must have been before his first, second, or third trip to Jerusalem (Acts 9:26; 15:2; 19:21). However, we may eliminate the first two trips to Jerusalem, for in Romans 15:26 Paul says "Macedonia and Achaia have been pleased to make a contribution for the poor among the saints in Jerusalem" and in Acts 19:21 it is stated that Paul had just passed through Macedonia and Achaia on his way to Jerusalem.[6] This then establishes the timeline of Romans sometime shortly after his visit to Macedonia and Achaia en route to Jerusalem.

Many believe that it was written in Corinth based on the mention of Gaius (Romans 16:23) who was a member of the Corinthian church (1 Corinthians 1:14).[7] Since Paul states that he is a "host" of Gaius this is probable. Furthermore, Phoebe was the apparent courier of the epistle, and she was from Cenchrea which is a municipality of modern day Corinth.[8] Unfortunately, there is some debate as to the exact date that Paul was at Corinth. Merrill Tenney places the writing of Romans in the spring of 56 A.D.[9] Merrill Unger placed much it later in 56 A.D.[10] and Everett Harrison believes it was written in early 57 A.D.,[11] but these theories are based primarily on the belief that Paul arrived in Jerusalem on May 20, 57 A.D.[12] However, I concluded in *Controversies in the Acts of the Apostles* that Paul probably did not arrive in Jerusalem until 58 A.D.[13] Consequently, Romans was probably written from Corinth sometime late in 57 A.D.

Now one question regarding the writing of this epistle is in regard to its emphasis upon basic doctrinal instruction. As aforementioned, Paul wrote the epistle because he could not be there in person. He had longed to go to Rome (Acts 19:21; Romans 1:11) in order to help "establish" them (1:11). This begs the question. Who founded Rome and why did they need basic instruction? Why did they need to be "established"? A long standing tradition says that Peter and Paul were the co-founders of the church in Rome,[14] but this is probable only the spiritual sense of the word for the Roman church appears to have come into existence by at least 49 or 50 A.D. since Aquila and Priscilla had come from the Roman church around that time (see notes under Acts 18:2 in *Controverseies in the Acts of the Apostles*). Since Peter had never left Israel until after the Council of Jerusalem in 49 A.D. and Paul had not yet been to Rome, it is likely that the church had come into being through some disciples and not an apostle. Conversely, some argue that because Paul had previously been hindered from going to Rome "the only conclusion we can draw from his statement is that the Church in Rome had already been founded by some other apostle."[15] However, this is not likely for why would Paul feel the need for the church to be "established" by an apostle (cf. 1:11) if an apostle had founded Rome. Moreover, the book of Acts makes it fairly certain that none of the apostles but Paul ventured beyond Israel and Syria until after the Council of Jerusalem. Consequently, most have concluded that "the congregation of Rome was not founded by any apostle"[16] in the strict sense of the word. Thus, the tradition of Peter and Paul as its founders can only be accepted in a spiritual sense.

First to the Jew?
Roman 1:16

"I am not ashamed of the gospel, for it is the power of God for salvation to everyone who believes, to the Jew first and also to the Greek."

"The Jew first." This simple statement is controversial in many ways. Does it imply Jewish preeminence? Some might even say it wreaks of racism! Why does Paul, who elsewhere speaks of equality before God (Galatians 3:28), say that the Jews comes first? To this three different interpretations have been given. The first is that this is a simple statement of fact. I.e. the Jews were the first to whom the gospel was preached in time. The second is that the Jews do have a priority in regard to the promises made to the Israelites. A third view of recent origin distinguishes Greeks from gentiles, and assigns priority to the Greeks alongside Jews.

First in Time
Peter Abelard, the medieval scholar, echoed the medieval Catholic view that this was simply the historical order, and not one of preference.[17] This view is echoed by modern Protestant scholars like Albert Barnes[18] who said that it is merely "the order in which the gospel was actually preached."[19] He is followed by men like Donald Barnhouse,[20] James Montgomery Boice,[21] and Charles Hodges who claims that "πρωτον [first] must have reference to time."[22] However, it is interesting to note that famous anti-Semite Martin Luther conveniently ignored this verse in this commentary[23] while the *Liberty Bible Commentary* amends its acceptance of this view with the addendum that "it was through the Jews that Christ Jesus came,"[24] but this is the point. If Jesus came through the Jews, then should not the Jews, like a mother, have priority over others in regard to her child? This leads to the second view.

First in Priority
The Renaissance scholar Erasmus believed that the gospel "was offered first to the Jews for the sake of honor, but soon, through the preaching of the gospel,

was to be spread among the Greeks, and all the nations of the world."[25] He declared that the Jews were "especially" called "because Christ was promised to the Jews, from whom he sprung."[26] Leon Morris calls this "an electing purpose."[27] It is not that the Jews are better than gentiles so much as the fact that the Jews are "God's own chosen people, so the gospel must first be preached to them."[28] Even the early church father Ambrosiaster said that "Paul puts Jews first because of their ancestors."[29] However, many have had a problem with this, because they see the Jews as those who rejected Christ, ignoring that we too rejected Him. A General is not inferior to his soldiers, but he is preeminent over them. So also the Jews were chosen, not by their own merit but because of God's grace, to prepare the way for the Messiah.

This topic cannot be solved here in this passage but is repeated throughout Romans, especially in chapter eleven. So this issue will be picked up again repeatedly in Romans as Paul devotes a great deal of space to the place of Jews in this age, and of the relationship of gentiles to Christ. Of this relationship a rather strange third alternative explanation has been offered. That of Greek preeminence.

Greek Preeminence
A somewhat odd offshoot of the second view is one that attempts to distinguish the Greek from the barbarian and then places the Greeks alongside the Jews in preeminence. Men like Frederick Godet have argued that the Bible distinguishes between Greek and barbarian.[30] He then argues that they are completely separate and states that "first" should be read as "in preference to."[31] Nonetheless, the only passage in Romans that speak of barbarians is Romans 1:14 which has no bearing upon the doctrine of salvation or covenants, but is couple with "the wise and the foolish" (1:14). The Greeks were considered "wise" in their own eyes, but Paul follows this up by saying that they, "professing to be wise, they became fools" (Romans 1:22). Two more times in Romans he warns us not to become wise in our own eyes (Romans 11:25; 12:16). So contextually, Paul is actually proving that there is no difference in the Greek and barbarian, nor the wise and foolish (cf. 1 Corinthians 1:20). This is also apparent in Colossians 3:11 where Paul says "there is no *distinction between* Greek and Jew, circumcised and uncircumcised, barbarian, Scythian, slave and freeman." Hence, Godet's assersion that the Greek and barbarian are a different class of people in regard to the gospel seems weak. Moreover, although the Jew and gentile are equal in the eyes of God and share the gospel, this passage seems to contrast the Jews with Greeks, so how is this possible?

Richard Lenski suggested that πρωτον [first] modifies *both* Jews and Greek, hence it is "in the first place for both Jews and Greek" because "the two stood highest among men."[32] Lenski goes so far as to seemingly deny that Greeks are gentiles[33] and repeatedly sees Greeks as superior.[34] Once again, this is reading Greek superiority into the text. Jews are only distinguished from

8

gentiles because of their special covenants with God, not because of any moral or spiritual superiority, so how can anyone claim that the Greeks were superior to other gentiles? Because of their civilization? Is salvation based upon our education or learning? Of course not. Paul is speaking here of the gospel and distinguishes between Jews and gentiles only in the context of their special position in God's covenant and providence. No other class of people exist.

An even more odd derivation of this idea is that of David Martyn Lloyd-Jones who believed that Jews did not need the gospel.[35] He seemed to imply that the gospel was only intended to bring gentiles into the saving grace of the Messiah, but Jews did not need any special dispensation. Since he does not elaborate or defend this view, it is hard to ascertain his exact meaning, for I am giving him the benefit of the doubt. Nevertheless, in all cases it seems unbiblical to assume that there are more than two classes of people among God. Many even deny that there are more than one. Whether or not the Jew has a special place in God's providence will be debated throughout Romans, but one thing is certain. Nowhere does the Bible create three (or more) classes of people to whom God ministers in three (or more) different ways. God has made covenants with the Jews and with gentiles (even this is debated), but nowhere does he make a separate covenant for Jews, Greeks, and barbarians. There is only Jew and gentile. The theory of Greek preminence is nothing more than (south) European pride.

Conclusion

Throughout the book of Romans Paul speaks of two classes of people; the Jew and the gentile. Sometimes he uses the word "Greek" generically, since they had reached the then pinacle of civilization among the gentiles, but nowhere does he create three or more classes of people. Romans speaks of God's special covenants with the Jews and of gentile salvation offered through Jesus the Messiah.

As the reader can see, Romans immediately opens up a debate in regard to the difference between Jews and gentiles. If we are all equal in the eyes of God, then how can Jews be "first." This topic will be discussed repeatedly by Paul with the pinacle of his arguments appearing in Romans 11. It is sufficient at this point to say that Paul recognizes the special covenant and position of the Jews in God's providence. The gospel is no different for the Jew than for the gentile, but was promised first to the Jews and so it is to them first that the gospel should be offered. When we hold a wedding, we invite first our immediate family and closest friends. Only then do we invite the extended family and friends (cf. Matthew 22:2-14). So also the Jews are the first to whom the gospel must be offered, and then it is presented to us as well.

Salvation and the Law of Conscience
Roman 2:11-16

"All who have sinned without the Law will also perish without the Law,
and all who have sinned under the Law will be judged by the Law."

Probably every believer has heard the question, "what happens to all
those who have never heard the gospel throughout history?" Our answers have
ranged vastly, and poorly. The Bible is not silent on this issue, but neither is it
of particular importance in the Bible for our duty is to spread the gospel and
those who hear it are accountable to it. Nevertheless, Paul touches upon the
issue in these next few chapters, but nowhere more so than in Romans 2;
particularly 2:14-16. In full it reads:

> "For when Gentiles who do not have the Law do instinctively the
> things of the Law, these, not having the Law, are a law to themselves, in
> that they show the work of the Law written in their hearts, their
> conscience bearing witness and their thoughts alternately accusing or
> else defending them, on the day when, according to my gospel, God
> will judge the secrets of men through Christ Jesus" (Romans 2:14-16).

Now it is important to note that this passage is not so much about the
salvation or damnation of the lost among the world as about the nature of the
law and the coming judgment. Consequently, it is best to look at these passages
in context. The purpose of Paul's epistle is to explain the necessity of salvation
and the purpose of the law, not to comfort those who have lost family or to warn
those whose family members are lost. Let us then look at the basic context and
meaning of the passages first.

The Nature of Law
"Ignorance of the law is no excuse." This legal precedence once held meaning
in our courts, for it came directly from Romans 2:15, "the Law [is] written in
their hearts, their conscience bearing witness" so that the criminal is without
excuse. Centuries before John Calvin said that "ignorance is in vain pretended
as an excuse."[36] Of course this precedent was supposed to apply only to felony
crimes which are by their very nature immoral. Now that laws are amoral the
line has become fuzzy and immorality has increased, but I shall not debate the
decadence and decay of our society. The point is that all men know right from
wrong whether they admit it or not. Paul is affirming that even the pagan has
the law written in his heart. This then begs the question, "why have a written
law?" "What is the purpose of the Mosaic Law?" That question is answered in
Romans 3:20. Here I will restrict the debate to the nature of the law.

Most theologians throughout the centuries have distinguished "the
difference between '*law*' and '*the* Law.'"[37] Generally the term was "natural

10

law"[38] as "distinct from 'revealed' religion."[39] As the term "natural law" came to means the laws of science by which nature is governed, most modern scholars have adopted the term "the unwritten law."[40] As Tertullian said, "affirming that the heathen do by nature those things which the law requires, he suggests both natural law and a law-revealing nature."[41] Desiderius Erasmus noted that the Greek word for "without law" is literally "lawlessly,"[42] but he was careful to affirm that "there is no one, however, who is entirely without the law."[43] This is the law of conscience.

According to Peter Abelard, the medieval Catholic, "that rule of natural law" is to do unto others as you would have them do unto you.[44] To an extent this is apparent in that most cultures have a similar rule or code, although none fully practice it. Thus Paul's point is that all have sinned and stand convicted through their conscience, but there is more to it than just this, for the Law of Moses is clearly distinguished from this natural unwritten law. Many say that "the Jews only were under *the* (Mosaic) Law"[45] and Constantius said that "the Jew is given priory over the greek because in addition to the natural law, he has the law of Moses as well."[46] However, this is only partly true, for the Jews were chosen not only to carry the Law, but through whom the Messiah would come. The Law thus points to Christ, but we are getting far ahead of ourselves. Paul is following a logical argument point by point. His point here is that all men were given a conscience by which they know right and wrong. His next point then involves judgment.

God's Judgment

A criminal is judged for his crimes. No matter how much good he has done, if he is convicted of a crime he will pay the price. So also all men are sinners (Romans 3:23) and all men stand convicted either before the Law or before their own conscience. This is Paul's second point.

Nevertheless, some have tried to distinguish between the pagan "perishing" and the Jew being "judged." Saint Augustine said that "it seems that it is worse to perish than to be judged"[47] but other have argued the reverse. John MacArthur, for example, says that the pagan's "eternal tribulation and distress will be less than that of the Jews, who have the immeasureable advantage of possessing God's law."[48] On this issue, however, Pelagius is probably correct when he says, "perish means the same thing as will be judged, for the man who perishes perishes by God's judgment, and the man who is judged a sinner perishes."[49] Paul is not trying to distinguish between perishing and judgment. Rather he is pointing out that all face the same eternal fate ... unless there be a savior.

The Need of Salvation

Having established that all know right from wrong and all are guilty before God, it is now clear that man needs a savior. We all stand condemned. Therefore we all need saving. This is the point of Paul's argument. Man is need of a savior.

Despite such an obvious implication, however, some controversy still exist for Karl Barth sees this not as a passage about conscience and conviction but about the Christian.[50] He saw this as an allegory for the Christian whose conscience is superior to the Law. Such an argument takes this passage entirely out of context and applies the same hypocrisy and self-righteousness to the Christian that Paul condemns in the Pharisee. Contextually Paul says nothing here about the Christian, for he has only now established in his line of reasoning that we are in need of a savior. To strip the passage of this simple context destroys the entire argument.

Salvation for Unbelievers?
The reader will have noted that nowhere is the question of salvation of those who have never heard the gospel even discussed. There is a reason for this. We are not to be distracted from out job. Our job is to tell the lost that there is a savior. What has happened to those who have never heard the gospel? Some argue that since all are convicted of sin, all perish. Others argue that they cannot be condemned without having heard and rejected the gospel (cf. Romans 5:13). Both arguments have merit, but neither can be substantiated for Paul simply is not concerned with this argument. Therefore, my answer is best. It may seem a "cop out" but is a 100% true regardless of what position one takes. What is that answer? Simply this : God knows whether or not someone would or would not have accepted the gospel. God judges by the heart. God will decide. This simple answer is true no matter which position a theologian takes and it is preferable because it neither side tracks us from our duty, not destroys the hope of those whose family members passed on without having heard the gospel. Our job is simply to spread the good news that there is a savior so that no more may die without having heard. Our motto should be "evangelize as if few may be saved, but love as if all will be saved."

Conclusion
The typical Jew understood the Law as the ultimate key to righteousness, but Paul here demonstrates that the Law does not make the Jew superior to the gentile, for they too have the law of conscience. Nonetheless, "being moral is insufficient to be righteous. They are not synonymous."[51] All have failed. As R.C. Sproul said, "he isn't saying that the Gentiles, who do not have the law, in fact keep the law. He is saying that they do things required by the law. That is quite different from saying that they keep the law perfectly."[52] On the contrary, the point is that, as Paul states in 3:23, "all have sinned and fall short of the glory of God." All men, Jew or gentile, know right from wrong and stand condemned either before the Law or before our own conscience. No man can claim ignorance. It is for this reason that man needs a savior. We cannot save ourselves.

"My" Gospel
Romans 2:16

"According to my gospel ..."

There are some extreme theologies and cults which alternately reject that the gospel is intended for Jews or that Paul was a true apostle. These sects occasionally appear and point to verses like Romans 2:16 where Paul refers to the gospel as "my gospel," implying that it is "his" and not Jesus's, or so the argument goes. In fact, "gospel" in Greek is ευαγγελιος (*evangelios*) from which we get the word "evangelism." It literally means "good news" from ευ (*eu*), a prefix meaning good, and αγγελιος (*angelios*), meaning message or news. Consequently, grammatically speaking it is "our" good news *about* Jesus. The use of the possessive pronoun in no way negates the fact that the gospel is about Jesus. It is *our* good news *about* Him.

Is a Jew a Jew?
Roman 2:28-29

"He is not a Jew who is one outwardly ... but he is a Jew who is one inwardly."

It is not unusual to hear some misquote this passage to imply that Christians are now "Jews" in the eyes of God. This is an ironic argument since it implies a superiority of the Jew to which the interpreter is denying! Yet this specific passage is addressed to the Jews (cf. Romans 2:17). In the previous passage Paul was affirming both Jew and gentile stand condmended. He is now saying that being a Jew does not insure salvation. Paul is not saying that Jews are not Jews or that Christians have supplanted the Jews in all of God's covenants, for that would be entirely outside of the context of his argument. His argument is that neither the Jew nor the gentile has any advantage over the other in regard to salvation. Being a Jew has no advantage over being a gentile in *this* regard (but cf. Romans 3:1). *Both* need a savior.

The Purpose of the Law
Romans 3:20

"Because by the works of the Law no flesh will be justified in His sight; for through the Law *comes* the knowledge of sin."

The previous chapter made clear that all men understand right from wrong and all men stand condemned. Thus the Law does not save. If the Law was the ultimate means of salvation then why did not God give the Ten Commandments to Adam and Eve after their Fall? Perhaps it is because they could not even keep the one and only commandment that God had given them. No, there is far more to it than this, for our conscience, as Paul stated in Romans 2, existed from the beginning so that no man can claim ignorance. Why then was the Law given? What is the purpose of the Law?

Salvation or Conviction?

Robert Govett said that the Law's purpose is "the recognition of *sin*, not of *salvation*."[53] Among most Christians this is universally recognized. Catholics, liberal scholars, fundamentalists, and evangelicals of all persuasions agree, although some disgree on the nature of works, which is distinguished from the Law.

The church father Clement of Alexandria stated that "the law did not create sin, it revealed it."[54] The Tübingen theologian Karl Barth also concurred, saying that "by the law [we] are placed under indictment."[55] Another liberal theologian, Dean Farrar of Canterbury, said "this is the way in which the sinner is converted; the more closely and faithfully the law is preached, the more it will condemn him, and show him that he needs some other plan of salvation."[56] On the other end of the spectrum is the evangelical Warren Wiersbe who also believes that our inability to obey all the law demands is how we know we are sinners.[57]

Thus on the surface this fundamental doctrine is universally agreed, but that is only the surface, for some distinguish between the Law and works. Catholics, for example, have often been criticized for emphasizing works as a process. Some Protestants go to the other extreme condemning all emphasis on works. This is where the real controversy erupts. If the Law does not save, what use is it after our conversion? Do works enter the picture? Is the Law abolished? These two issues will reoccur throughout the epistles, and will be cursorily addressed here inasmuch as it is relevant to the topic.

Are Works and the Law Synonymous?

Believing something in theory and in practice are not the same. If all Christians agree that no man is saved by the works of the Law, not all are agreed on what the works of the Law means. For example, Theodoret and others believe the "works" by which we are not justified properly refers only to "*ceremonial* works" as opposed to "moral obedience."[58] They argue that if Paul said "*it is* not the hearers of the Law *who* are just before God, but the doers of the Law will be justified" (2:13), then works do justify after all. However, these same men admit that there are none who truly and wholly are "doers of the Law." That is the point Paul is making. We have "all sinned and we all fall short of the glory of God" (Romans 3:22).

Why then does Paul emphasize circumcision so many times in these passages? Are these not part of the "*ceremonial* works"?[59] Can we compare murder to being uncircumcised? Certainly not, but this misses the entire point and stretches Paul's argument beyond the context. Circumcision was hotly debated at that time, hence Paul's emphasis upon it, but Paul nowhere distinguishes in these passages between ceremonial law and other laws. He only distinguishes between the Mosaic Law and the law of conscience. That is explicitly clear in Romans 3:28 where Paul says, "we maintain that a man is justified by faith apart from works of the Law." There is no qualifier attached to the Law. We are justified "by faith *apart* from the works of the Law."

Lenski believes the "opposite" of Theodoret's proposition, declaring that "not only does God *not* justify because of works of law, law itself bring us realization of sin."[60] This was Paul's point. Charles Hodge summarizes the Biblical position by saying, "His whole design is to prove that men cannot be justified by their own righteousness."[61]

So then is it okay to break the Law? Such a query is often used to attack the Biblical doctrine of justification by faith, but it is best answered under "Works and Faith – James 2:14-26" where James addresses the same issues. I will devote many pages to the subject there. The only question remaining here is whether or not Paul is abolishing the Law.

Is the Law Abolished?
If the Law does not save, then many ask whether or not it has any application to the believer. To that end many Christians believe that the Law has no authority over believers at all. Others distinguish between generic law, the principles of the law, Old Testament or Mosaic Law,[62] and ritual law. Pelagius, for example, believed that only ritual law is of no avail and believed that we were still bound to the rest of the Law.[63] Peter Abelard argued similarly that the natural law still applied, but rejected Jewish law.[64]

Each of these views is flawed in its own way. As this debate reoccurs elsewhere in the epistles I save a fuller discussion under passages like Hebrews 7:18-19. Nevertheless, let us look quickly at the logic of these arguments.

Jesus said in Matthew 5:17, "Do not think that I came to abolish the Law or the Prophets; I did not come to abolish but to fulfill," so it is clear on one level that the Law still exists, but does this bind the believer to the Law? Consider the facts. If I do not kill people I have no need to know that murder is against the law. If I murder, then I am guilty before the law. If the Law was intended to convict man of sin and we continue to break the Law (at this point I am speaking generically) then we have placed ourselves voluntarily under the Law. In other words, Jesus saves us from the punishment of the Law, but that does not mean that Law ceases. Murder, rape, stealing, and other crimes are obviously still immoral sins and one who continues to do these things is mocking Christ. Perhaps the quote by Benjamin Disraeli best summarizes Paul's point, for he said "when men are pure, laws are useless; when men are corrupt, laws are broken."

Now it is clear that not all law is the same. Many speak of ceremonial, or ritual, law. These laws, however, had their application to the Temple and

15

temple purity. Obviously if there is no Temple in Jerusalem then not even the Jews can properly obey all these laws. In this context it is true that ceremonial law has only limited application even to the Jew.

Consequently, the Law exist for the lawbreaker. As Christians we may continue to sin (see Romans 7:18) but we do not continue *in* sin (see 1 John 1:8-10; 3:9; 5:18). If we continue to live in sin then we place ourselves under the Law. However, if we place ourselves under Christ then He becomes our advocate and the Law cannot convict us when we do sin. The Law serves it purpose and will continue to exist, but the believer places himself under Christ. The Law still exist and still convicts us when we sin, but it no longer rules over us, for the man who does what is right does not need to be concerned with what is wrong.

Conclusion

Donald Barnhouse phrased it best when he said, "the law of God is like a mirror. Now the purpose of a mirror is to reveal to you that your face is dirty ... not to wash your face."[65] The Law convicts us of sin. We know that we need a savior because we know we are condemned under the Law.

The Law does not save, it condemns. When we are brought before a court of justice the judge does not ask how many laws we have obeyed or how much good we have done, but whether or not we are guilty of breaking the law. Good deeds may be taken into consideration during the punishment phase of a court of law, but it never acquits a guilty man. The guilty man *must* be punished. Thus the Law is only useful in demonstrating to us that we are in need of a savior. Obeying the law 99% of the time will not save us from judgment for that 1%. Only a savior can save us from the damnation we properly deserve. So here Paul is saying that the Law points us toward the need for a savior. He is not saying that the Law serves no purpose.

"Did not Sin in the Likeness of Adam"
Romans 5:13-18

> "For until the Law sin was in the world, but sin is not imputed when there is no law. Nevertheless death reigned from Adam until Moses, even over those who had not sinned in the likeness of the offense of Adam."

This statement has caused much debate and division among Christians. What does it mean to sin the likeness of Adam? Would we be living in Paradise today if Adam and Eve had not sinned? Is sin genetic? All these questions have been asked by commentators and critics alike. The debate crosses typical boundaries and crosses into many snake paths beyond the context of Paul's epistles.

Some are not even agreed upon whether the "likeness" refers to Adam or his sin. Desiderius Erasmus, for example, argued that it is "unto the likeness," not "in the likeness," and thus may refer back to death, not Adam. In other words, it is either a likeness to the sin of Adam or likeness unto death which comes from sin, and not Adam's alone.[66]

John MacArthur is another example of one who breaks from the traditional mold to some degree since he concedes that it is "impossible" to sin in the likeness of Adam because of the eviction from the Garden of Eden.[67] None of us can commit the same sin for none of us were born into a world without sin. Yet this begs the question, if none of us can sin in the likeness of Adam's sin, then Paul could not be referring to our sins at all. His point is that death exist because of Adam's sin, not ours. But this is another controversy, for some hold that sin is inherent while others hold that sin is inherited, or genetic. Can we be held responsible for sin which is not our own?

Once again it is best to break down the arguments to their most basic elements and examine them on this level. We must also be careful not to go beyond the scope of Paul's original remarks, as many have done. The context of Paul's arguments here are sin, the Law, and its punishment upon sin, being death. To go beyond this context is doomed to create poor theology.

The Sin of Adam
The first question is what was that sin of Adam? It cannot simply be disobedience for we have all disobeyed God at one time or another. It is a sin which apparently few, if any, have repeated since the expulsion from the Garden of Eden, for Paul makes it clear that "death reigned from Adam until Moses" before the Law was given *even over those who had not sinned in the likeness* of the offense of Adam" (5:14).

Albert Barnes argued that "Adam had a revealed and positive law."[68] This "positive command"[69] being God's spoken Word. It was "a direct command of God."[70] Since Paul is specifically talking about those who lived between Adam and the Law of Moses, it may well be that he is referring to, as John Wesley believed, those who had not "sinned against an expressed law."[71] These men had only the "natural law."[72]

This is generally agreed. They "transgressed knowingly"[73] against the Law of God. Adam and Eve "wickedly sinned against God's precept"[74] whereas those since Adam sinned against their conscience and the natural law. They did not sin against the Law of Moses.[75]

This is brought out clearly in the NIV translation which reads, "those who did not sin by breaking a command" (5:14). While this is more of a paraphrase than an actual translation of this passage, it is clear from the context of Paul's remarks that he is talking about the Law. From Origen to Ambrose to Jerome to the modern day scholar, most agree that Paul's statement here, simply put, is that death reigned from Adam up to the coming of Law even though men

17

had not broken any expressed commandments.[76] He is reaffirming his belief that death is the consequence of sin, and that all men die. Conscience has always existed even if the Law of Moses had not.

So what does this mean then? Were men condemned for Adam's sin rather than our own? Are we all damned for the sins of another? This is exactly what some believe. They argue that Paul is blaming all sin upon Adam. Some even argue that sin has been genetically passed down through our parents unto us. But is this really what Paul meant?

The Effect Upon the Human Race
Romans 5:15 states that "by the transgression of the one the many died." This statement, isolated from context, tends to imply that "*all* were constituted sinners in his sin."[77] It would suggest that, as Luther and Augustine believed, men "had not yet sinned through their own personal volition."[78] This concept has been called "original sin" and is debated throughout the centuries by heretics, Catholics, and Protestants alike, and yet even Catholicism is not wholly united on its meaning. Nevertheless, these debates upon "original sin" go far beyond the scope of Paul's arguments here. They tend to envelop philosophy more than theology. Consequently, it is best to begin, as always. with the scope of Paul's epistles.

First, it is clear that "all have sinned and fall short of the glory of God" (Romans 3:23). This much is apparent. No one, save Jesus Himself, can claim to have never sinned. Second, death reigns over all men. Every man ever born has died, and death was the curse God placed upon man for sin. Third, even innocent children die, some before they are even old enough to speak or walk. This is the paradox. A child is generally considered innocent, and yet the child dies seemingly for no sin of his own. Why then is even the child called a sinner? This is the crux of the debate. Is sin inherent or inherited, and what does that mean?

Sin as Inherent or Inherited?
It has long been held that sin is inherent in the human race, but inherent is not the same as inherited. Some scholars use the two interchangeably but this is dangerous, and even heretical. Consider that Douglas Moo says that all men "inherit a sinful nature from Adam."[79] This seems innocent enough, but Charles Hodge takes it one step further saying, "all are tainted with the hereditary corruption derived from Adam."[80] So we have moved from inherent to inherited to hereditary and even genetic determinism. What is the difference?

First, psychiatry is notorious for its failure to distinguish between cause and effect, or physiology and etiology.[81] This is why psychiatry has a reputation for labeling sin as disease. One time a professional psychiatrist was invited to speak at a neuro-pharmocology course I was taking in college. She was arguing that alchoholism is a disease, but when the students began to press her for proof of etiology (genetic cause) she finally tossed up her hands and said, "well, all I

18

know is ... either it is a disease or I am a sinner, and I don't know about you, but I'm no sinner!" So there a professional psychiatrist admitted that there is no genetic evidence, it is simply a choice; either sin is genetic or she is a willful sinner and she chose the former. Are modern day evangelicals doing the same?

Warren Wiersbe said that the "condemn[ation of] the whole human race [came] through one man."[82] Notice however the subtle shift from Paul's statement. Paul actually said "by the transgression of the one, death reigned through the one" (5:17). Now death is the judgment for sin, and it came through the one, but we must complete the sentence. Paul is comparing the first Adam to the second Adam. If sin is genetic, why not salvation?

Most, including the authors cited above, would agree that sin is not genetic. My point is not to suggest that Wiersbe, Moo, and Hodge believe sin is genetic, but to illustrate the dangers inherent (but not inherited) in our language and how we perceive things. The doctrine of "original sin" is so polluted with philosophy and extra-Biblical conceptions that we subliminally read these concepts into the Bible. Consequently, let us look at the doctrine of original sin more closely.

Original Sin

The term "original sin" refers to the sin in the Garden of Eden through which death was introduced into the world. Because of that sin, we are born into a world of death. However, the doctrine of original sin is a philosophical doctrine extrapolated from Romans 5:16-17. Although none agree completely on it, the general gist of the doctrine as it has come to be understood is that "the death of men after Adam cannot have been occasioned by their own individual sins, but only in Adams."[83] Frederick Godet even argued that it is "obvious" that all "individuals died, not for their own sin, but because of Adam's."[84] Even my own Seminary taught that Adam's sin was imputed to us in that God reckoned and counted to us "what he or she has not personally done" for "Adam's sin was not his alone, it was ours as well."[85] All this is taken from two brief comments by Paul. He said that "judgment *arose* from one *transgression* resulting in condemnation" (5:16) and that "by the transgression of the one, death reigned through the one" (5:17). What does this mean?

Paul's statement is a matter of fact. Following the sin in Eden the earth was cursed and death came to the world. So it is quite literally acurate to say that "by the transgression of the one, death reigned through the one" (5:17). So also judgment arose from that day which has resulted in condemnation. Notice however that nothing is said of our innocence. There is nothing in the context which implies, infers, or insinuates that *any* of us would have done anything different had we been in the Garden of Eden. God does not condemn the innocent for the sins of the guilty. If He did then Paul could never have said, "all have sinned and fall short of the glory of God" (3:23), and yet many argue that we are only sinners because of the Fall as if we would have chosen a different path from Adam had we been given the opportunity. Such an argument echoes the excuses made by Adam and Eve in the Garden. Eve blamed the serpent, Adam blamed Eve, and none took responsibility for their own sins.

What then is Paul's point? Consider two facts. First, Adam and Eve were created into a direct relationship with God in the Garden. God was there with them in the Garden personally interacting with them. Mankind was made to share his soul with the Creator. Today, because of the Fall, we are born alone. From the time we open our eyes we see the world through our own eyes and no one else's. We cannot understand another man's pain except by emphathy of a common experience. We cannot truly know another man's mind. We are alone unless the Holy Spirit of God indwells within us. So Paul is correct to say that judgment and death are the result of one man's sin. However, the second fact is equally clear. Our sin is the result of our own selfish thoughts and actions. Sin is not imputed by another, nor does Paul say so. Sin is within our nature because we born apart from God, but at the same time *none* of us would have chosen differently in the Garden. *That* is why we need a savior.

Abbey Alston – Adam and Eve Expelled – 19th Cetnury

Imputation of Sin

One of the arguments for the theological concepts of original sin is Paul's statement that "sin is not imputed when there is no law" (5:13). He then follows by saying that death has reigned despite this fact, even over those who did not sin against a spoken commandment of God (5:14). Does this not mean that Adam's sin was imputed to us? Not entirely. Let us consider what imputation means, especially in the context of Romans.

20

Imputation means to "take into account" or count against (NIV, NLV, ESV). Thus it is argued that since death has reigned over those to whom sin is not imputed then death "was executed on [Adam's] descendants" on account of his sins.[86] The problem with this conclusion is two fold. First, if Adam's sin was imputed upon us, as many argue, then Paul could definitely *not* say "sin is not imputed when there is no law" (5:13),[87] for sin would be imputed regardless of whether or not there is Law. Thus the height of irony is to attribute imputation where the Bible says there is no imputation.

Second, Paul's argument is consistent. He is not saying that those without the Law are sinless but judged for another's sin. On the contrary he has already established that the law of conscience condemns us all (2:12) and that all men sin (3:23). He cannot then here say that we are condemned for another's sins. Rather the sins against conscience are imputed against them, not the sins against the Law.

Let us look at Paul's reasoning point by point and see how this remarks fits with his logic. He has already established the follow:

1. All men know right from wrong (2:12-16).
2. The Law reveals sin (3:20).
3. All men sin (3:23).
4. Even those without the Law are guilty of sin before their conscience (5:13).
5. All men die (5:14).
6. All men will be judged either according their conscience or the Law (2:12).

So once again, Paul has established the need for a savior. He is here comparing and contrasting the first Adam with the second Adam. Logically, if all were condemned for Adam's sin then all would be saved by Christ. If we truly believe that Adam's sin was imputed to us then we must also believe in universalism. If, however, Adam's sin was that which introduced sin into a fallen world then Christ was the One who offered salvation to the world. Nevertheless, note that it is now a fallen world, whereas once it was a Paradise. Adam's sin did more than just introduce sin into the world. On that much we agree. What impact then has sin had upon our fallen world? What did the curse of Eden (Genesis 3:17-19) bring?

Sin in the World
Lloyd-Jones argues that the death of innocent children is proof of original sin,[88] but it is really proof only that death has come to the world, not that children are executed for Adam's sin. We call children innocent because they are far more innocent than us, but were not Adam and Eve children of a sort? How many days had they been alive before they rebelled against God? R.C. Sproul is more accurate when he says that "because Adam sinned, we all suffer the consequences of sin."[89] This is so. The world into which we were

born is cursed (Genesis 3:17-19). All men will die so that "the sin of one had entailed spiritual and physical death upon all."[90]

What then does the death of children in this world truly mean? Why do the (relatively speaking) innocent die? Let us consider what has happened. Through Adam death has come to the world. The earth is cursed. All men are born apart from God. We are all alone in a world without God. We will all die. These facts stand alone. We cannot leap to the conclusion that men are innocent and being punished for another man's sin. We sin. We rebel. We choose the same sin as Adam when we reject the Lord, which *all* of us has done at some point in our lives.

The question here is what aspects of the earth are cursed by God and in what aspects of the world are we ourselves the curse? When a hurricane or tornado kills people we hear the atheist blame the God they don't believe in. When men murder, rape, and create poverty, despair, and war, the atheist is silent unless he can somehow blame religion. Nonetheless, these two examples do reflect two different aspects of sin in the world. Hurricanes and natural disasters are a result of God's curse upon nature. Regardless of what sins we have or have not committed we can die at any time. We will die someday. This is does not mean that we are innocent, for the curse applies to us all. Only Jesus was without sin. Conversely, most evil in the world is the result of the curse called mankind. Poverty is not the result of a lack of resources, but of governments refusal and/or inability to utilize resources and work for them. Even desert countries have thrived for thousands of years in places like Egypt, but famine results when their governments fail to store food and resources for the inevitable droughts which come. Crime, war, and sin rage because of mankind; because we are sinners who live only for ourselves. Family offsets a small amount of that selfish sin nature, but even families suffer from sin.

In short, sin is the real curse upon the earth. The curse of nature is a result of sin, and all men sin. Much of the evil on the earth is not the result of nature or nature's curse, but our own actions. These actions alone prove that the curse upon nature is deserved. Death is both a punishment and a blessing to those who trust in Christ. Someone once said, "this world is either the only heaven you will ever know, or the only hell you will ever know." This is true. Death is both a curse and a blessing, depending on our eternal choice. If we repent of our sins, instead of blaming others, and turn to Christ we will never be touched by the second death. If we cling to the belief in our own innocence, we will die not once, but twice, eternally (cf. Revelation 2:11; 20:6, 14; 21:8).

Conclusion

Paul makes a simple line of argument. All men sin. All men die. The Law gives us no advantage over those who do not have the Law, for we all stand condemned. He then compares the first Adam, through whom sin was introduced into the world, to the second Adam, through whom salvation was introduced. To go beyond this, as many have done, is to trivialize Christ. If sin is genetic, so is salvation. If sin is inherited, so is salvation. But if sin is inherent, then so also the offer of salvation is inherent to all who turn from their sins and trust in Him.

Man was made to be with God, but we are all born without God. Because of Adam's sin none of us are born into a direct relationship with God as he and Eve were. In this sense it is literally true that all sin came into the world through Adam. However, nowhere does Paul impute all men's sins to Adam. This largely medieval doctrine of "original sin" is a gross misrepresentation of Paul's remarks. Adam was the first man through whom sin was introduced into the world. Christ is likened to a second Adam through whom eternal life is introduced. This is Paul's statement and to go beyond it as if to pass our own deserved condemnation upon another, it is wrong. The earth is under a curse. That curse began with Adam, but none save Christ have demonstrated that we do not *deserve* the same condemnation. Death is the result of our sins. Eternal life is the result of Christ's righteousness. It is a contrast and comparison of two Adams. One brought death. The other life.

Does Sin Abide in Believers
Romans 7:14-22

"For I know that nothing good dwells in me, that is, in my flesh; for the willing is present in me, but the doing of the good *is* not."

If the doctrine of original sin is controversial then no less controversial is the question of sin in the believer's heart. Here in these passages Paul describes in excruciating detail the sinful desires of the flesh at war with the Spirit ... or does he? Some argue that Paul could not possibly be referring to himself in his Christian life. One professor of mine sarcastically retorted that if this was our idea of the Christian life then there is something wrong, but is there a difference in the Christian life and the Christian struggle? Do we still struggle with sin? If so, to what degree. This topic is addressed under 1 John 1:8-10; 3:9; and 5:18, but this passage deserves special attention by itself, so I will examine the four dominant interpretations represented by various Christian scholars throughout the ages.

The first view is that Paul is referring to the unregenerate man who has yet to become reborn. It, they say, is a reference to unbelievers. The second view argues that this is the man convicted of sin, but not yet regenerated. A third attributes this passage to the carnal believer who is not living as he should. Finally, is the controversial opinion that Paul is referring to himself, and to all Christians by extension.[91]

View # 1 : The Unbeliever

The early medieval church appeared to favor the belief that Paul was speaking of unbelievers.[92] The arguments are largely theological rather than exegetical. They object to the notion that a Christian could ever be called a "slave to sin" or say that there is "nothing good in me."

On the surface this sounds good, at least from a strictly theological standpoint. The problems, however, are also theological as well as exegetical. Consider the context of Paul's remarks. He does not call the Christian a "slave to sin," but rather says, "the Law is spiritual, but I am of flesh, sold into bondage to sin" (7:14). In other words, Paul appears to be speaking of two natures in man. This doctrine, that of two natures, is denied by some, like John MacArthur,[93] but held by most Christians across theological boundaries. Obviously, Paul is contrasting the spiritual with the carnal, and yet this does not answer whether Paul is referring to an unregenerate man or not.

One problem is that Paul repeatedly uses "I" and "me" in these verses. How then can he be referring to unbelievers? Some have argued that this is the just the "editorial" use of "I" and "me" while others have argued that Paul is referring to himself only in his "unrenewed nature."[94] This, however, cannot be so for Paul repeatedly uses the present tense,[95] and only shifts to the aorist (simple past) tense in verse fourteen when he refers to himself as being *sold* into bondage of sin.[96] This is significant, for it implies that he had been sold into slavery in the past. Everywhere else Paul uses the present tense. Hence, Christ has ransomed us from slavery although it still holds sway upon us.

The greatest proof that Paul cannot be referring to unbelievers, is the simple fact that the unbeliever does not generally see himself as a sinner. The unregenerate Pharisee sees himself as obedient to the law and righteous.[97] Yet here Paul is clearly struggling with his sin. He recognizes his failures and sins. Moreover, Donald Barnhouse has suggested that the this *cannot* be an unregenerate man because the unregenerate sinner does not truly *desire* good as Paul does in verses eighteen through twenty-two.[98] He says, "the good that I want, I do not do, but I practice the very evil that I do not want" (7:19). This proves that the one of whom Paul is speaking desires to do good and serve the Lord. He struggles with sin, but his heart is with God. So we must look elsewhere for the answer.

View # 2 : The Man Convicted

A second view improves upon the first. It denies that this is simply an unbeliever, arguing instead that this is the man convicted of his sins, but not yet born again.[99] In one sense it is a vast improvement, for the man convicted of his sins does indeed seek good and seeks God, but this still inherits many of the same problems as the previous view. Paul's use of the present tense and first person pronoun is inconsistent with the idea that this is a past experience before conversion. In fact, Paul's only use of the past tense (or more specifically the aorist tense) is his reference to having been sold as a slave to sin. The analogy is

24

clearly that while we are no longer slaves to sin, it still wars with our spirit. It is thus an analogy of the war between flesh and spirit, but some reject the notion of the two parts of man while others, like Frederick Godet, see Freudian overtones in *ego, I, and flesh*![100]

Another problem with this entire line of reasoning is apparent in John Brown's commentary where he argues that this passage applies only to children and mentally diseased who do not know right and wrong![101] In trying to deny that the believer is still tempted by sin, the war of the flesh is trivialized. Both of these views imply that the Christian is free from temptation and sin, and that is one of the most dangerous doctrines to hold, for when we deny the temptation exist, we become all the more susceptible to it. Still, many argue that this passage describes far more than mere temptation. They argue that the dark overtones describe a man in darkness and therefore a man without the Holy Spirit. Is this so?

View # 3 : The Carnal Christian

If it is not the unbeliever then perhaps it is the carnal Christian. This is the popular modernist view shared in particular among the Lordship-Salvation crowd.[102] This is ironic indeed since John MacArthur denies what we have two natures,[103] and yet admits that the sin nature "resides ... residual dwelling in his flesh."[104] He apparently tries to split hairs, arguing that sinful nature of man no longer resides in the believer except in a "residual" sense of the word. Nevertheless, Paul's entire line of reasoning assumes two natures at war with one another.

According to Desiderius Erasmus there are "two men in one, a carnal and gross men, the second the internal man. The one, subject to passions, is inclined to vices; the other retaining some seeds of goodness."[105] Note that in Erasmus's thesis the good seed is not the Holy Spirit. Rather it is the seed that God planted in all men. Without God that seed will never blossom or grow, but it exist nevertheless. God did not create man to be evil, but "very good" (Genesis 1:31). This enters into a debate I discuss in greater detail under "Trichotomy or Dichotomy? 1 Thessalonians 5:23 – Hebrew 4:12." As usual, I will restrict my arguments to Romans 7:14-22 and the war between the two natures.

Thomas Aquinas saw flesh as "a cage"[106] but Pelagius, Ambrosiaster, and Chrysostom all rejected that physical flesh is evil.[107] This is the controversy. Sproul said that "nothing good" refers to flesh, not the Holy Spirit.[108] Certainly this is so, but if God had made nothing good in man then there could be no conscience, no inner conflict, and God would have made evil rather than good (Genesis 1:31). Our sinful nature stems from our being born apart from God, as Paul established in Romans 5:13-18. Remember that Paul is continuing a line of arguments. He is not throwing random theologies at the Romans but continuing a point by point logical and systematic theology. Romans 7 is then continuing Paul's arguments concering the nature and purpose

25

of the Law and man's need for a savior. Here then he is not discussing disobedient Christians, for he clearly includes himself as among those described, but illustrating the spiritual war and inner conflict which rages within us. To relegate this conflict simply to the "carnal Christian" is fall into self-righteousness and leave us open to temptation and sin. Indeed, it is no small irony (or surprise) that those preachers who fall into sin and scandal are usually those who deny that the believer is still subject to the temptations and sins described herein.

View # 4 : The Believer Undergoing Sanctification
"Understanding the conflict in personal sanctification involves seeing the relationship between a believer and his indwelling sin."[109] This has traditionally been the Reformed position,[110] although hyper-Calvinists tend to reject it, opting for the first or second view.

J.I Packer believes that ultimate sanctificion is a "future redemption" which takes place at our resurrection.[111] Our current life, however, is one of struggle. Martin Luther compared it to a horse whose rider pulls the reigns.[112] In this case, sin is pulling back on our reigns, trying to stop us. This is our sinful nature which still exist in us all. This is not a liberal versus conservative issue, but generally a Christian consensus. Karl Barth, for example, stated that "to know that *in me dwelleth no good thing* is the second requirement of a religious man."[113] On the other end of the spectrum, John Calvin (in contrast to most hyper-Calvinists) stated that Paul spoke of "the faithful who are divided in two parts – the relics of the flesh, and grace."[114]

This war of the two natures of men is of what Paul speaks.[115] Some call it a "duallality"[116] but more simply, and accurately, it is better said that "the Christian is made up of two parts; the flesh and the spirit. These two are of opposite origins and qualities, and hence the perpetual combat."[117] This "fallen Adamic nature"[118] does not cease to exist because we trust in Christ. "All men continue to possess it."[119] As Robert Govett said the difference between the unbeliever and the believer is that the the the old flesh is "not the ruling one."[120]

One scholar commented that Paul was being refreshingly honest.[121] unlike those who maintain that they are Holy and pure in spirit, Paul delivers a humble and somber picture of what lies beneath our spirit. The Holy Spirit allows us to triumph over that nature, but it still exist. Charles Spurgeon put it best when he said, "there is in each one of us a law of sin ... there is within our nature that which would send the best saint to hell if sovereign grace did not prevent ... there is a little hell within the heart of every child of God, and only the great God of heaven can overmaster" it.[122]

Conclusion
The context of Paul's remarks is still consistent with his discussion of the law and its purpose. As Charles Hodge points out, Paul stated that "the law is spiritual" because it wars with our bondage to sin.[123] The difference between

Paul and most of the Pharisees is that they believed that they obeyed the Law and were made righteous by that obedience. Paul has argued that the Law convicts us of our sins, but cannot save us. He is now describing the spiritual warfare which rages in every believer. To that end the Law continues to convict us and show us which path we need to take. The Law does not lord over us, it convicts us. The Holy Spirit is what helps us lord over sin.

"He is a defeated Christian when he is controlled by sin."[124] This is the warning of Paul. As usual he shows the danger of both legalism and libertinism. On the one side is the danger of believing that the Law makes us righteous and that salvation comes by observing the Law. On the other is the danger of believing that we are no longer at war with our sinful nature. *Both* result in self righteousness and both end in defeat. Here Paul shows us humility. He does not deny that his "flesh" still desires sin and the picture he paints is not a pretty one. Nevertheless, the Holy Spirit allows us to overcome the selfish desires of the "flesh" nature. Throught Christ we alone can overcome the sinful nature and be what God intended us to be, but this is a process called sanctification which will never be complete in our lifetimes. To deny this is to become self-righteous and give the victory to the enemy.

Romans 8:29-33 – See Romans 9:11-13 and Ephesians 1:1-12

Election and Love
Romans 9:11-13

> Before Jacob and Esau were "yet born and had not done anything good or bad, so that God's purpose according to *His* choice ... it was said to her, 'The older will serve the yonger.' Just as it is written, 'Jacob I loved, but Esau I hated.'"

Two debates rage over this passage. The first is the question of election, which is tied to the Calvinist debate over God's sovereignty and man's free will. The second is closely connected to this debate. It is the question of whether or not God truly hates anyone, especially one whom had not yet even been "born and had not done anything good or bad" (9:11).

The question of election is addressed in detail under Ephesians 1:1-12. Many Calvinists set up a false trichotomy, arguing that there are only three positions. One being the denial of the doctrine of election, the second being the belief that election entails foreknowledge only, and third being the traditional Calvinist view which rejects any and all elements of free will.[125] By setting up this false straw man argument, the Calvinist hopes to tear down the first two views (which is easy enough to do) and then leave the reader with the false assumption that Calvinism is the only option remaining. In fact, nothing could be further from the truth. If I offer a guest in my house a choice between Coke and Pepsi, it does not mean that I have lost sovereignty over my refrigerator. I neither had to give him the choice, nor did I make the offer without knowing the possible outcomes of either choice. I did not give him the option of Dr. Pepper, so his choices were limited to my will. Such a simple and amusing analogy is the best way to summarize this debate in a way that even a child can understand. Nevertheless, an extensive debate of election and predestination is given under Ephesians 1:1-12. Having said this, it is necessary first to distinguish between election and predestination. As Lewis Sperry Chafer said, "*election* and *predestination* do not indicate the same thing"[126] but rather predestination is a "plan and purpose" whereas election represents God's selections in fulfilling that purpose.[127]

So the question is why was Esau selected for bad, and Jacob for good? First, let us consider the context of the passage to which Paul refers. It is found in Malachi 1:3. Now within Malachi's context the passage is really a prophecy about the Edomites, who are the descendants of Esau. It reads, "I have hated Esau, and I have made his mountains a desolation and *appointed* his inheritance for the jackals of the wilderness" (Malachi 1:3). The prophecy then describes the fall of Edom. Thus the blessings of the Jews, descendants of Jacob, are contrasted with the fall of the Edomites, the descendants of Esau. Consequently, most agree that neither the prophecy nor Paul's comment are about God actually hating Esau as a person, but rather that "in his sovereignty God chose Jacob over Esau, a choice that was tantamount to 'hating' Esau."[128] John Walvoord puts it best by saying, "it must be understood as a relative statement in the sense that God, choosing between the two, chose Jacob."[129]

Thus Paul is making a point about election, not about Esau's eternal destiny. The context of Paul's remark is that Israel was chosen by God not because Jews are inherently better than others, but because of God's sovereign will and love. Paul was emphasizing that the Jew is blessed not through any worthy merit of his own, but through God's election and purpose. Thus they should count themselves blessed, not worthy. This passage does not stand alone. It is still a continuation of his previous line of reasoning wherein Paul is rebuking the mindset of the Pharisetical Jew who believed that the Law made them worthy and that their blessings were the result of their worthiness. On the contrary, says Paul, God had chosen Jacob before he was even born and Esau, the edler brother through whom an inheritance was usually bequeathed, was rejected before he had "done anything good or bad" (9:11) so that the question of merit does not even enter into the picture.

We are the beneficiaries of grace, not works. It is nothing less than the abuse of Scripture to apply this passage to eternal salvation. The hyper-Calvinist, like the Bible critic, rips this passage out of context to apply God's election of nations to individual salvation. In so doing, he is stripping Paul of his context and altering the line of argument which Paul has established. Election to salvation or damnation is another debate which is not even touched upon here in this passage. It is not a passage about not damnation and hatred but about grace and election.

Israel's Jealousy
Romans 10:18-21

"I will make you jealous by that which is not a nation, by a nation without understanding will I anger you."

Paul has previously been speaking primarily about the Law and the Jew. Now Paul is beginning to shift his argument toward the gentiles. He is still talking to the Jew at this point, but with an emphasis upon God's will for the gentiles. If the Jew was blessed through no merit of his own, then what will happen to the gentile?

This passage is actually a quote from Deuteronomy 32:21. It is a prophecy following the Deuteronomic covenant in which the Lord declares that the Israelites "have made Me jealous with *what* is not God; They have provoked Me to anger with their idols. So I will make them jealous with *those who* are not a people; I will provoke them to anger with a foolish nation." Paul applies this prophecy to the gentile's conversion to Christ, for through the Church God has worked many miracles and wonders and brought about great change to the world. Europe was once the bastion of barbarians, cannibals, human sacrifice, and paganism. In the nineteenth century it was the home of churches, schools, libraries, colleges, art, literature, science, and democracy. Only the radical revisionist historian can deny the fingerprints of the gospel on all these institutions.

Now the fact is that the Jews are the chosen people. It is they to whom the Messiah was first promised and it is through them that the Messiah came. The Jew was entrusted with the Law (Romans 3:2). Paul himself was a Jew. However, with being chosen comes a great responsibility and burden. Among those is great punishment for sin. Twice Israel has been sent into exile for their sins, and twice God has restored His people, but there is something else. There is this jealousy which was intended to provoke the Jews to faithfulness. How does this work? What does it mean?

Who Are Those that Are not a Nation?
Let us start with the obvious question. Who are those who are simultaneously called "not a nation" and "a nation"? What does this imply? Robert Govett is correct to point out that "the Gentiles were not by the Jews regarded as nations rightly constituted."[130] Even though the gentiles had many nations the Jewish people always looked down upon them as mere tribes.

The full prophecy of Deuteronomy also refers to these as "no people." Albert Barnes believed that this was a reference to the barbarians who had no nation or "people."[131] They were literally tribals and yet history has shown that

29

these barbaric savages, as such we were, grew to become great nations. Wierbse notes that "Jewish believers were shocked when Peter went to the Gentiles (Acts 11:1-18)."[132] How much more shocked would the Jews be when they found these barbarians, tribals, and savages accepting the Messiah and forging great nations. The focal point of history moved from the Middle East and Israel to the nations of Christian Europe and eventually America. How then does this make the Jews jealous, and to what purpose?

The Purpose
The actual verb usually translated "make jealous" literally means to provoke.[133] In Romans the Greek word is παραζηλωσω (*parazeloso*). In Deuteronomy the Hebrew word is קִנְאָה (*qinnah*). קִנְאָה (*qinnah*) means jealousy or envy, but also has the meaning of "ardent zeal."[134] Παραζηλωσω (*parazeloso*) means to "provoke to jealousy" or "provoke to anger,"[135] but once again its root lies with the word ζηλος (*zelos*) from which we get the word "zeal."[136] Hence, the jealous man pursues those he loves with more zeal, fearing loss. So also God provokes the Jews to faithfulness by letting them fear that He has turned to another people, to a people once considered mere tribal barbarians.

So there is irony here. God created the church (in part) to fill the vacancy left by an unbelieving Jewish nation, but in so doing, God is making the Jews jealous, and stirring some to repentance. They are more eagerly and zealously seeking to return the Lord, secretly fearing that God has turned to another. Yet some gentiles wish to claim that God truly *has* turned away from the Jews and transferred all the promises to the church! This has become one of the greatest controversies in the New Testament, and will frequently reoccur throughout the epistles.

Some, like Martin Luther, argue that the Jews "have been rejected."[137] John MacArthur is more charitable, comparing this to the parable of the banquet.[138] He thus suggest that the Jews were invited, but gentiles took their place when the Jews refused the invitation. Although the application to the parable itself is valid to a degree, it is misplaced here. Paul is not speaking of a permament displacement or diaspora, but of the redemption of the Jewish people (see chapter 11). Thus while the Church could be equated with those who came to the banquet dinner, we cannot agree with Luther that the Jews "have been rejected."[139] That would be an entirely different thing, and would contradict Paul's belief in the redemption of the *Jew*.

Conclusion
Once again Paul is continuing his argument and not starting a new one. Any interpretation of the jealousy of the Jews which ignores the previous and subsequent passages is out of context. With the church father Ambosiaster we can say that "the jealousy of the Jews arose from their envy at seeing a people which earlier had been without God and barbarous claim the Jewish God as their

own,"[140] but we cannot agree with Peter Abelard's statement that through "unbelieveing Romans, I will cause you to be not a people."[141] There is nothing either here or in Deuteronomy which declares the Jews will no longer be a "people" in either the national sense or in the special sense.

Paul has continued his line of reasoning regarding the purpose of God in both Jews and gentiles. Here he is arguing that Deuteronomy's prophecy of the jealousy of the Jews applies to the rise of the church and the gentile converts, but it is clear in the subsequent passages that God has not disolved the Jews as a special and distinct people. Their purpose in God's plan is not yet finished. The church age is not the last age, but a pivotal age. It is an age in which gentiles are brought into the people of God while the chosen people reject the Messiah, but Paul, realizing the possible implications of this argument, immediately rebuts all those who deny the Jews have a distinct place as a people. The purpose of the jealousy is to lead the Jews to repentance and zeal, not to disinherit them. To this end he illustrates his argument with a parable of an Olive Tree.

Has the Church Replaced Israel?
Romans 11:17

> "If some of the branches were broken off, and you, being a wild olive, were grafted in among them and became partaker with them of the rich root of the olive tree, but do not be arrogant toward the branches; but if you are arrogant, *remember that* it is not you who supports the root, but the root *supports* you."

Now if the Jews were chosen through no action of their own, and God has now bestowed His blessings upon the hated gentiles through no merit of our own, then has the Church replaced Israel? This question is one of the most controversial in Christian history. The relationship between the Jews and gentiles in the ancient church is evident even in Paul's epistles, and all the more clear in history as the unbelieving Jews soon came to view Christianity not as a sect, but as a cult. They resented the domination of gentiles in the church and disavowed any connection to Christanity. This in turn led to animosity between Christians and Jews over the years and eventual persecution; first by the Jews and then, for centuries, by "Christians."

Part of the problem was that the early Christians attended Jewish synagogues on Saturday and had private services on Sundays. Since the synagogues were not Christian the Jews came to view these gentiles with suspicion, especially when debates over Jesus erupted. One such eruption apparently led to riots in Rome (see *Controversies in the Acts of the Apostles* on Acts 18:2). It is, therefore, no surprise that many Christians began to view the Jews as cast outs. Here Paul provides a perfect illustration for the question of Jews and gentiles, and yet few passages have been misrepresented and distorted as this one. The passage itself seems self-evident, but this has never stopped controversy before.

Here Paul likens God's people in history to an Olive tree. The tree trunk is firmly rooted in the ground and grows, but many of its branches are dead. New branches are then grafted into the tree. He then warns the newly graftly branches not to be arrogant for "if God did not spare the natural branches, He will not spare you, either" (11:21) and reminds us that "it is not you who supports the root, but the root *supports* you." (11:18). Despite this dire warning, many of us have become just that ... arrogant against the branches.

Now in Paul's analogy are three parts. There is the tree trunk, there are the natural branches, and there grafted branches. Any sincere interpretation of these passages must interpret these three parts consistently and logically. Here I will list the main views, and then I will discuss the strengths and weaknesses of each.

Replacement Theology

Although by no means the universal view of the early church, many read the Church into the tree trunk. They correctly see the natural branches as Jews and the grafted branches as gentile church members, but then inexplicably see the tree trunk as the church in general! One German Tübingen scholar argues that the "collective body of the Gentiles is conceived as an entire tree"![142] John Calvin also implied that gentiles are a part of the "blessed trunk."[143] One modern evangelical shifts Israel from the root to the natural branches, saying, "Israel was broken off"[144] and declaring that the "tree stands for God's place of blessing."[145]

Such analogies defy logic as is evident in the words of Replacement Theologian Karl Barth who argues that it is Paul, and not himself, who "defies correct and natural analogy"![146] This conflict is obvious only because Barth sees the trunk as the church and yet the church did not give birth to the Jews, nor to Israel, but rather the church and gentile believers sprang forth out of Israel!

Strictly in terms of Paul's analogy here and the context of the passage, replacement theology is incompatible. The words of Karl Barth himself prove that if we attempt to make the tree trunk synonymous with the church, then the analogy fails. This is also clear in Paul's unheeded warning to gentiles found in verses 18-21. It is Israel from which the church sprang. The root of the tree cannot be the church as it is commonly understood, for the branches are the Jews and gentiles. The church is the body of believers which strang forth from the promised root. Understanding this, and Paul's analogy, is critical to understanding the church and its role in history.

Dispensational Theology

Dispensationalists generally represent the polar opposite of the replacement theologians. Many see the tree as "nation of Israel."[147] Others more generically as Abraham and his physical descendents. Charles Hodge said, "it is plain from this verse, that *the root* in this passage cannot be the early converts from among the Jews, but the ancient covenant people of God."[148] R.C. Sproul declared that "the roots are in Abraham, in Isaac, and in Jacob."[149]

Since "there is only one olive tree"[150] it is clear that the olive tree existed *before* the church. It cannot, therefore, *be* the church. The tree must be rooted in the promise to Abraham. "The ancient root or stock ... was good."[151] "The tree of Abraham has not been removed."[152] The promises made to Abraham, to Isaac, and to Jacob are "without condition."[153] The conditional promises of Deuteronomy do not enter into this picture.

This analogy appears to be borrowed in part from Hosea[154] where he says, "I will be like the dew to Israel; He will blossom like the lily, and he will take root like *the cedars of* Lebanon. His shoots will sprout, and his beauty will be like the olive tree and his fragrance like *the cedars of* Lebanon" (Hosea 14:5-6).

So dispensationalism sees Israel and/or the Abrahamic covenant as central to the image of the olive tree. This makes sense, but begs the question as to nature of the church. This is the fundamental debate. Is the church nothing more than branches? If the church are branches, then is the olive tree superior to the church? The answer to this question is central to understanding Paul's analogy, as we shall discuss forthwith.

Other Views
There are others who interpret the olive tree in a different manner. However, each of these views is similar to one of the two previous theories. Desiderius Erasmus, for example, equates the olive tree with the Jews.[155] In this respect he is on similar ground with dispensationalists, yet distinguishes between Israel and the Jews. He would fit more closely with those dispensationalists who see the promise of Abraham, Isaac, and Jacob. With him stands the controversial medieval scholar Peter Abelard who acknowledged that the Jews gave "birth to the Gentile people in faith."[156] Obviously, neither can be called dispensationalists, and yet both see the Jews, if not Israel, in the olive tree.

Conversely Irenaeus made this a symbol of our conversion and ignores the whole issue of Israel and the church altogether.[157] Although by no means replacement theologians, these scholars see "Christian Israelites"[158] and not Jews.

In each case it is clear that scholars throughout the ages have been divided over the role of Israel and the Jews in the root of the olive tree. All acknoweldge that the bad branches are unbelieving Jews and the grafted branches are gentile Christians, but where does the church fit into this analogy. This is the question that plagues and divides Christians. It is the question that must be answered to understand Paul's argument.

Evaluation

Everyone, it seems, from replacement theologians to dispensationalists are guilty of trying to read the church into this passage, but it is not surprising that Paul nowhere mentions the church in chapter eleven. In fact, despite the fact that Paul is debating the role of gentiles and Jews in the church throughout Romans the word "church" appears *only* in chapter sixteen, referring to local assemblies!

In *Controversies in the Acts of the Apostles* I spent considerable time refuting the teaching of some dispensationalists who argue that the "church" was created in Acts 2 at Pentecost. I also refute those who argue that the church as replaced Israel. It seems that we (collectively) are guilty of reading theology into the text, rather than exegeting the text and drawing our theology out of it! I will not repeat all of what I said there, but it is clear that the word "church" as used in the Bible is not distinct in and of itself from the ancient "assembly of God" found in the Old Testament. In fact, the Greek *Septuagint* translates this very phrase as "church of God" in the Old Testament!

It is obvious that the "church" of this age is different from the "church" of the Old Testament. In that we are all agreed. I personally count myself as a dispensationalist, but of the older traditional variety. I reject both "progressive dispensationalism" and the ultradispensationalism that has been wedded to many traditional dispensationalists. So also the covenant theology and replacement theologians also have tried to read something into the church which is never found in the Bible, thus arguing that the church has replaced Israel, or has it replaced itself? Such a paradox explains why theologians of all persuasions have backed themselves into a corner.

Are Israel and the church synonymous? No? What then? To summarize much of what I said in *Controversies in the Acts of the Apostles*, the debate may be broken down into three issues:

1. The "Church" in the Bible

Today most define church as synoymous with the third entity (described below). However, in the Bible the word "church" is generally used in a different sense. The word "church" is found approximately 77 times in the New Testament. It comes from the Greek word εκκλησια (*ekklesia*). That word is variously translated as "congregation, assembly, gathering (of religious, political, or unofficial groups)."[159] Its most literal meaning is, therefore, an assembly or gathering of the Christian community. However, there is no doubt that the Bible uses this term, at times, in a larger sense of the word, as applying to all believers whether they are gathered together or not. In this sense, they are a congregation of God's children (both natural and adopted). This is the case when the word church is coupled with God, as in "the church of God" (cf. Acts 12:5; 1 Corinthians 10:32, 11:22; Galatians 1:13; etc.). Thus church can be synonymous with all believers or it may refer to a local assembly.

In the Old Testament, the equivalent of "church" is "congregation" or "assembly" and the Greek *Septuagint* translation of the Old Testament uses the word εκκλησια (*ekklesia*) in place of congregation. Moreover, the NAS Bible (and others) sometimes translates εκκλησια (*ekklesia*) in the New Testament as "congregation" (cf. Acts 7:38) when it is speaking about the time of Moses. Thus the "church" of the New Testament and the "congregation" of Israel are uses in the same way. Sometimes it is a "assembly of Israel" gathering to meet with Moses, and at other times it is used to refer to the entire "congregation" or "assembly" of God. The two terms are therefore virtually identical, save that the "church" now consist of many gentiles. It is for this very reason that some translations, like Darby, refuse to translate εκκλησια (*ekklesia*) as church anywhere in the Bible, preferring instead "assembly."

2. National Israel

The nation of Israel was made up of the physical descendants of Abraham, Isaac, and Jacob in accordance with God's promises. It is through the nation of Israel that the Messiah was promised, but this is not all. Israel was established as "a nation of priests" (Exodus 19:6). The Jewish people have a very special place in God's plan, and contrary to what many teach most of the promises made to Abraham, Isaac, and Jacob were *unconditional*. The conditional promises of the Deuteronomic covenant are usually appealed to as proof that God has "broken off" Israel,[160] but this is selective interpretation, for the Palestinian covenant, the Davidic covenant, and many others are still in effect, and to gloss over these covenants is poor exegesis. It is true that Abrahamic covenant prophesies gentile blessings to all of us who believe and the Deuteronomic covenant resulted in the diasporas of history, but the Palestinian covenant and several others affirm that the Jews will *always* retain a special role in the priesthood of God. God does not violate his oaths or alter his contracts. His Word is gold. Believing Israel is therefore a part of the church, but it is a sort of priestly caste within the church. What then of the gentile priesthood? What of the "church" which exist today?

3. Gentile priesthood (commonly called "the church" today)

Twice Israel was driven into exile for its sins, in accordance with the Deuteronomic covenant. Twice Israel has been restored according to God's promise. However, the second diaspora lasted nearly two thousand years during which time gentiles have served the role as God's priesthood (cf. Revelation 1:6). This is the root of the controversy and its crux. Has the "church," or gentile priesthood, replaced Israel? The answer must be "no." As per Paul's analogy we are all grafted into the tree, which is Jacob's root, but the natural branches remain (Romans 11:21). We serve as priest during the time of Israel's chastisement, but the Jewish people will be preserved and retain their special role as Israelites (see below). This is the gist of much of Paul's debate.

35

Let us look carefully at Paul's analogy. Borrowing from Hosea 14:5-6 and Jeremiah 11:16[161] Paul compares the root of Jacob to a tree root. In Jeremiah many branches are deemed worthless. Here Paul says that God grafts gentile believers into the tree, but as Charles Swindoll noted, "the graft does not change the nature of the branch."[162] A pear is still pear, not an apple. No matter how hard it tries, a branch from an apple tree will never produce pears, nor will pears produce apples. So also Jews forever remain Jews, a part of the priesthood and a natural branch. Gentiles are grafted into the tree, but we remain gentiles, blessed through the Abrahamic covenant, but we do not, never have, and never will replace Israel.

Conclusion

It is no small irony that gentiles have not heeded Paul explicitly warnings to gentiles. "Do not be arrogant toward the branches; but if you are arrogant, *remember that* it is not you who supports the root, but the root *supports* you" (11:18). He further warns "do not be conceited, but fear; for if God did not spare the natural branches, He will not spare you, either" (11:20-21).

Despite such clear and explicit warning many Christians continue to hold that "Israel was broken off"[163] and that the tree is the church, despite the fact that the tree gave birth to the church, and not vice-versa. As John Darby said, "the dispensation of the Gentiles has been found unfaithful ... as the Jewish dispensation was cut off, the Christian dispensation will be also."[164] Our arrogance and unfaithfulness as a whole is no different that that of Israel. Our salvation is assured, but as an entity the gentile church has failed, even as the nation of Israel failed. It is God who upholds us, and it is God who is faithful to His promises.

Israel's Redemption
Romans 11:25-26

> "A partial hardening has happened to Israel until the fullness of the gentiles has come in, and so all Israel will be saved."

The line of Paul's arguments should be clear at this point. He has been discussing Israel and the Jewish people's role in God's plan for the ages. Nevertheless, as we have seen, many have read the church into these passages. Certainly no one (barring Universalists) believes that every Jew will be saved! Indeed not. What then does this mean? Naturally, the views and opinions tend to follow a pattern. Replacement theologians argue that the church is the "New Israel" or "Spiritual Israel" while most dispensationalists assign this to national Israel, but beyond this the reader may be surprised to find that there is no universal agreement among Catholics, Protestants, evangelicals, or other sects. In fact, there were famed medeival Catholic theologians who saw the redemption of the Jews and there are evangelicals today who reject any role for national Israel. The divisions are not as clear as we might assume.

Historical Overview

Consider the antagonism which had developed early in church history between Jew and gentile. We might expect that the early Church fathers all saw the Church as a new Israel, and indeed, many did. Theodoret of Cyr, for example, believed that this "spiritual" Israel consisted of "all those who believe" whether they were Jews or Gentiles.[165] Origen, however, was not so sure. He could merely say, "only God knows."[166] Conversely, Cyril of Alexandria saw this as Jews, but not necessarily a national Israel.[167] Chrysostom and Theodoret followed this line of reasoning.[168] Some, however, like Irenaeus, one of the earliest of the church fathers, seemed to believe in the future conversion of Israel as a nation.[169]

By the Middle Ages anti-semitism was at its fevered pitch and yet medieval scholars were not so blind as many believe. Although most did favor either the church alone, like Jerome,[170] or a mixture of Jews and gentiles, like Augustine[171] there were men even of such stature as Thomas Aquinas who saw a future salvation for Jewish people.[172] So also the controversial Peter Abelard declared "many [Jews] will be converted in the end, by the preaching of Enoch and Elijah."[173] Although not speaking of the nation of Israel itself, which he appears to have rejected, Abelard acknowledged God's providence in the redemption of the Jews in Last Days.

The Reformation saw no less contention. Martin Luther, a notorius anti-semite, saw only the "elect Jews" within the church and saw no future for Israel as a nation.[174] He was naturally followed in this by John Calvin who saw this as "all the people of God."[175] Alternately, Desiderius Erasmus believed that "all Israelites will be restored to salvation."[176]

In the modern church the debate has been fairly, but not solely, divided between covenant theologians (especially replacement theologians) and dispensationalists. Indeed, despite the heavy handed rhetoric which is often spread about, covenant theologians and dispensationalists are primarily divided on this one issue, and not so much on other issues. Namely; is there a role for national Israel and the Jewish people outside of the traditional "church" (as defined by most theologians today)?

The Arguments and Evaluation on Israel

There are essentially three major interpretations of this passage throughout the ages. Some have tried to distinguish as many as five, but they seem to be splitting hairs as they are all essentially derivations of three. The view of replacement theologians and many other covenant theologians is that this passage speaks of "spiritual Israel" and not literal Israel. A second view held by other covenant theologians and a few dispensationalists is that it speaks of the Jewish "remnant" within the modern day church. Finally, the view of most dispensationalists is that this passage is about national Israel. Let us examine these views.

1. "Spiritual Israel"

Every person raised in a church today has probably heard this term countless times in sermons and Bible commentaries. The only problem is that the term "spiritual Israel" does not exist anywhere in the Bible. It is a term applied to a certain interpretation of "Israel" found in the New Testament. This is one of the primary passages where the idea of a "spiritual Israel" is implanted. They argue that not all Jews are saved and that since Paul himself declares that "he is not a Jew who is one outwardly ... but he is a Jew who is one inwardly" (Romans 2:28-29) then this "must" refer to "spiritual Israel."

When we look at this argument isolated by itself, it appears sound. However, when we examine the passages before and after 11:26 it becomes completely untenable. Romans 11:25 reads, "a partial hardening has happened to Israel until the fullness of the gentiles has come in." It is then that Paul says "and so all Israel shall be saved." Note that Paul connects the events together, "and so." He further continues this argument by quoting Isaiah 59:20, "the Deliverer will come from Zion, He will remove ungodliness from Jacob." Finally, he reminds us that "the calling of God [is] irrevocable" (11:29)! Let us put this all together.

First, how can Israel be contrasted with the gentile church in 11:25 if it is synonymous in 11:26? As F.F. Bruce (who is no dispensationalist) states, "it is impossible to entertain any exegesis which understands 'Israel' here in a different sense from 'Israel' in verse 25."[177] Moreover, the prophecy of Isaiah 59:20 is specifically about the redemption of the people of "Jacob" from their sins. There are prophecies that make it clear that Jesus redeemed all men, Jew or gentile, but Isaiah 59:20 is not one of those. It is about Israel and the Jewish people. Consequently, to read "spiritual Israel" into this passage makes no sense. Try to read the passage by substituting the word "spiritual Israel" in place of Israel. It would say, "a partial hardening has happened to spiritual Israel until the fullness of the gentiles has come in, and so all spiritual Israel will be saved." This makes no sense! It would be saying, "the saved will be hardened so all the saved will be saved"!

So it clear that contrary to the view of Karl Barth, Israel cannot be "the whole Church."[178] The Post-millennial hope of men like Jonathan Edwards, who declared that "the whole world shall one day be brought into the Christian Church,"[179] cannot hold up against proper exegesis, nor has history shown the world to be becoming better. The last century has been the most savage in human history and persecutions of Christians have actually been more oppressive outside of the western world than ever. Even in the west Christianity is being marginalized in much the same way that Europe marginalized the Jews. "Spiritual Israel" cannot be the meaning of this passage.

2. The Jewish Remnant

A better argument made by some covenant theologians, and even a few dispensationalists, is that this refers to the "remnant" of Israel within the church.[180]   One dispensational Bible commentary even declares that the "remnant of Israel has been paired with elect Genties."[181]   However, while a better argument, and one consistent with Romans 2:28-29, it falls apart for a reason that should be obvious. Perhaps too obvious. Like one of those riddles whose answer is so obvious, people never even think to look at it. If "all Israel" means "saved Jews,"[182] as Lenski believed, then would this not be redundant? Let us apply again the same logic we did to the previous view. Paul would be saying, " a partial hardening has happened to all saved Jews until the fullness of the gentiles has come in, and so all saved Jews will be saved"! Paul is much more meticulous and logical in his reasoning, and so should we.

3. National Israel

A third view is that Paul is speaking of national Israel. A couple of derivations exist, but since they are extensions of this view I have grouped them together.   According to this view it is "not every Israelite, but Israel as a nation"[183] Albert Barnes even says, "he does not mean to say *every* Jew ... but .. as a people ... as a nation."[184]   It is the Jews "as a people,"[185] but "not necessarily including every 'individual Israelite.'"[186]

Obviously this view has the strength of being a literal reading of Romans 11, but it does have some drawbacks as well. For one thing, if we speak of "the nation of Israel"[187] as R.C. Sproul does, then we speak of a corporate entity. Israel must then be distinguished from the Jews who make up Israel. In so doing there is a risk that "all Israel" becomes an oxymoron, for Israel as a nation is a single entity and there can be only one. "All" implies more than one, thus affirming that Israel is probably intended to refers to Jews as a whole and not only the nation of Israel.

Having said this, there should be little doubt that Paul is using Israel in a literal sense of the word. Israel refers to the sacred nation made up of the descendants of Abraham, Isaac, and Jacob. Thus Barnhouse argued that "Israel's deliverance will be not only spiritual but political as well."[188]   Certainly the role of Israel in history could only be questioned by the most atheistic of men. Consider that when Frederick the Great asked a chaplain to explain "in one word" proof of the Bible's inspiration, the chaplain answered "Israel."[189] Napoleon is alleged to have made a similar remark.   Thomas Chalmers also commented once that "the evidence of their singular preservation unprecedented in other history ... bespeaking the special providence of God."[190]   Clearly Israel and the Jews have a role to play in history beyond that in antiquity. God is not through with the Jews yet.

How then can we resolve the minor difficulties with this issue?   Once again the answer must be to take it at its most literal sense. This derivation view

39

believes that Paul is specifically talking about the Jews of the Tribulation in the Last Days.[191] John MacArthur believes that this refers to the Jews who are under the preaching of the 144,000 in Revelation.[192] Warren Wiersbe says that it is the "Jews living when the Redeemer returns."[193] Thus in the most literal sense of the word "every Jew" alive at the Second Coming will be saved. It is both Israel as a nation, and every surviving Jew at the end of the age.

The "Hardening" of Israel

One of the primary reasons that we cannot accept this as "spiritual Israel" is the fact that Paul has coupled this with a "partial hardening" of Israel. What does this mean and what does it have to do with the "fullness of the gentiles" (v. 25)?

The answer to this is implicit in Paul's entire discourse. God has a plan which involves both Jews and gentiles, but each has a specific role to fill. Israel, a nation of priests, *will* be redeemed, but the gentiles will also enjoy the blessings of Abraham through Christ Jesus. The "time of the gentiles" (Luke 21:24) is a part of that plan, but not its finality. It will end (cf. Luke 21:24). After that time Israel will enjoy all the promises God made to his covenant people for, as Paul says in 11:29, "God's calling is irrevocable."

The partial hardening of the Jews was intended to allow the gentile dominated church "to provoke the Jews to jealousy,"[194] but it was also intended to prove that gentiles are no more faithful as an entity than was Israel. Just as corporate Israel fell into sin many times, so also the "church" has failed in its faithfulness. The Whore of Babylon (Revelation 17) is a prophecy of such a church which began in faithfulness and ended like a harlot (see *Controversies in Revelation*). In the end, both Jew and gentile believers will be redeemed, but not before God has fulfilled all His promises. Consider Jesus's oft repeated belief that "many of the first will be last, and many of the last will be first" (Matthew 19:30; Mark 10:31; Luke 13:30). These passages have multiple applications, but one of the most overlooked applications is of God's providence in history. Who were the first chosen? The Jews? Who were the last? Pagan gentiles? Yet Isaiah 65:1 is quoted by Paul in this same discourse (10:20) reading, "I permitted Myself to be sought by those who did not ask *for Me; I* permitted Myself to be found by those who did not seek Me." Thus the first chosen, the Jews, will also be the last to accept the Messiah, Christ. That will take place in the End Times when God will redeem the Jews before the Second Coming.

Conclusion

Too many of these passages are taken in isolation, but they constitute a continued argument and line of reasoning by Paul regarding the role of the Jews, gentiles, and the nation of Israel in God's plan for redemption. All involve Jesus Christ, but not all accept Christ at the same time. The times of the gentile (Luke 21:24) coincide, in part, with the "church," but Luke clearly says that time will end, after which the Jews will be restored to the blessings God promised. In a literal sense of the word all surviving Jews at the time of the Second Coming will be saved. The nation of Israel will survive and fulfill its role as a "nation of priests" (Exodus 19:6). Then all will be blessed, and all God's promises (to the Jew and to the gentile) will be kept, for God does not lie.

Government Subservience?
Romans 13:1-5

> "Therefore it is necessary to be in subjection, not only because of wrath, but also for conscience' sake."

Paul's view of goverment submission is both complicated and, not surprisingly, controversial. Paul has been repeatedly misquoted throughout history, often by those who seek to persecute us and deny us the very liberties that we helped to create. It reoccurs throughout Paul's epistles, and will therefore, be repeated in this volume. However, I will attempt to restrict my arguments to that which is most explicitly relevant to the said passage. For example, the subject of slavery does not appear in these passages at all, nor in the book of Romans. It will, therefore, be addressed in Ephesians 6:5; Galatians 3:22; 1 Timothy 6:1, etc. Here Paul is only speaking of government submission in a general and generic way, which is perhaps best since it is best to begin with the general, before looking at specific issues which may crop up, for I can think of few issues where interpreters are more divided.

The Historical Context
I once knew an atheist who criticized Christians for always talking about "context." To him it seemed a cop-out, but by definition, anything which is not in context is out of context. Context is the key to understanding anything. Without context isolated passages can be easily twisted and manipulated for personal gain or agendas. It is best, therefore, to look specifically at the overall context of Paul's comments of the place Christians had in ancient Rome and its society.

First, we must remember the political climate in the time of Jesus and the apostles. Rome was not Christian. Rome was not just. Rome was a corrupt empire which brutally persecuted Christians. Israel at the time was near rebellion, and that would eventually erupt into a real war which ended in the destruction of Jerusalem. Charles Hodge noted that many Jewish converts had Zealot sentiments and feelings which they had carried over into the Christian faith.[195] Thus this was the reason that Paul needed to debate to issue.

Second, Paul is not giving a glowing endorsement of the Romans persecution of Christians. Paul called Satan the "god of this world" (2 Corinthians 4:4). Consequently, our hope is not in salvation from the government (as socialists believe), but from God through Jesus Christ. It was at this very time that Christians were being persecuted and killed. As Robert

Govett said, "so much said on this point to the Christians ... because there was danger."[196]

Fedor Andreevich Bronnikov – Exit the Circus – 1869

How then does Paul say that governments are instituted by God? Why are we told to submit? These are the questions which entail the debate, but there are no simple answers, for they involve the very question of church and state, which have sparred with other in one way or another since the beginning of history.

Church and State
Church is a distinctly Christian word, but if we substitute the word "religion" then the distinction between the religious establishment and the state has been debated since the beginning of history when ancient kings claimed to be gods to the modern world where Marxist states seek to overthrow religion and make the state a substitute for God (as Marx himself strongly implies in the Communist Manifesto).

Most would be surprised to learn that is the Paul who distinguished between the Church and state. This distinction, however, is not a one way street. Paul does not say that we are to violate the tenants of Christ because the state so orders, or he would have sacrificed to Caesar and not been executed, for the early emperors allowed all Christians to live who offered up sacrificial offerings to them. Many would say that this is a simple and unimportant gesture. They would say that God would forgive us and that sacrificing an animal to Caesar does not harm anyone, but Paul, the apostles, and hundreds of thousands of Christians chose to die before sacrificing to anyone but Christ.

Tertullian, the early church father, who saw several persecutions in his lifetime, said that "man is the property of God alone ... the king indeed must be honored, yet so that the king be honored *only* when he keeps to his own sphere, when he is far from assuming divine honors."[197] So, as William Newell said, "it is only when 'Caesar' interferes with the things that belong to God, that God's saints 'obey *God* rather than man.'"[198]

If the Church is to obey earthly laws then the state must not interfere with heavenly laws, but this is only one small piece of the puzzle. It is not enough to say that we must defy unrighteous laws, for the early Christians died in arenas and not in battlefields. Paul was executed on the road to Ostia and not in the civil war that erupted to overthrow Nero. In fact, while there may have been Christians fighting in that civil war, there is no record of it. The civil war was politically motivated and resulted in new Caesars, but not in the propagation of the gospel. Why? What is the reason that Paul urged Christ's followers not to rebel?

The Purpose for Governments

Another piece of the puzzle is the role of governments in the world. Governments do not always serve the purpose for which they were created, but they do serve a purpose. Anarchy has never succeeded in history, and yet even corrupt governments often lend some stability. Here Paul discusses the purposes and uses of government without exhonerating or endorsing everything they do (for they were persecuting Christians and Jews alike).

Paul says that "rulers are not a cause of fear for good behavior, but for evil" (Romans 13:3). This statement is, of course, a general rule which applies even to many corrupt leaders. Anarchy has never succeeded in doing anything but allowing crimes of the worst kind to run rampant. Murder, rape, theft, torture, and all manner of evil run wild in anarchy. When the French Revolution overturned the French monarchy, the result was not a free democratic republic as they dreamed (and as many erroneously believed happened), but anarchy, the reign of terror, the rise of the dictator Napoleon, and ultimately the return of the French monarchy. Thus as bad and corrupt as the French monarchy was, it helped create a certain stability and fear among criminals. So also even under Nero crime was not unrestrained, but restrained. The people were generally protected from invasion by neighboring countries and criminals were severely punished. So even the worst of governments provide stability and prevent anarchy.

Jonathan Edwards, whose followers participated in the American Revolution, said that "civil government was at first a thing of divine institution."[199] John Wesley believed that this was true and that governments "in general, not withstanding some particular exceptions, [are] a terror to evil works only."[200] Righteousness has rarely been outlawed. To do a good work only seldom is prohibited even by corrupt governments. Hence, obedience to civil rulers, even bad ones, is generally required. As R.C. Sproul said, if "God is the Lord of History," and He is, then even evil rulers could not rule "without the Lord's permission"[201]

These statements again provide a general summary, but is this all? Once again we must ask why Paul defied the law and was executed as a criminal and traitor against Rome? Was Paul innocent of the charges, as Jesus was false accused? No. Although there were many false accusations against Christians, ultimately most of the early Christians were executed for refusing to obey a law requiring citizens to offer sacrifices to Caesar. So Paul, who wrote these words, was a criminal according to the laws of Rome! How can we reconcile this? What was Paul's purpose in these words?

Submission and Rebellion
The paradox is that Paul urged submission while refusing to submit to Roman law concerning sacrificing to Caesar. Christians were fed to lions and executed under the most absurd charges (accusations included cannibalism) rather than denying Christ. How then can we reconcile these remarks? Was Paul wrong? Are Christians to submit to injustice?

First, while Paul acknowledged the necessity of governments and of law and order he nowhere subscribes to the myth that governments are the solution to man's problems or that the Messianic age will be ushered in through worldly governments. This is one of the fundamental difference between socialism and Christian charity. Charities are run by the church. Socialism places the government (and bureaucracy) in charge of "helping" people. Ronald Reagan used to joke that the most frightening words in the English language were "I'm from the government and I'm here to help." Neither Christ nor Paul believed the government was the answer to the world's problems. How could they? They were both executed by the governing authorities!

If government is not the solution to man's problems then this leads to the second point; government reform is not the solution to man's problems either. *This* is the crux of the issue. The Spartacus revolt did not end slavery, but resulted in the deaths of hundreds of thousands of slaves and harsher treatment of slaves. Paul did not want Christians to fall into the trap of what is today called the "social gospel." As Christians we certainly have the right to stand up for what is right, but Paul did not want Christians to become revolutionaries. The Israeli Zealots were sparking a revolt that would end with the fall of ancient Israel. If Christianity was to survive it *could not* be a *political movement*. *This* is what is forgotten in most all commentaries on the Bible.

Submission in History
Let us look at history and see exactly how it is that Christianity grew from a tiny Jewish sect to the dominant religion of the world. Polycarp, the disciple of the Apostle John, even as he was sent to die, professed obedience to the authorities ordained by God.[202] Likewise, Irenaeus, the early church father,

died under the persecution of Serverus and yet urged his followers to obey the earthly government which executed him for "disobeying" its edicts.[203] Theodoret of Cyr explained the limitations of our obedience. He said that we "must [obey] insofar as obeidience is consistent with godliness."[204] Beyond this we were quite willing to die, and for two and a half centuries we did just that.

For more than two centuries after Christ the faith grew and increased beyond the bounds of any religion in history, and yet this was done while ten great persecutions butchered countless believers. Christianity survived because it was a God movement, not a political movement.

This all began to change after Constantine legalized Christianity. Now contrary to what many believe Constantine did not make Christianity the state religion.[205] Rather he passed the "Edict of Tolerance" which established religious freedom for all.[206] Nevertheless, Christianity did rise to prominence and become the religion of most emperors until it eventually was declared the state religion about a hundred years later.[207] This shift was in part because of the attractiveness of worldly power, but also because of the prominence of the theologian Augustine. It is with Saint Augustine that theologians first began to believe that the the Kingdom of God was to be ruled through the earthly church, and its kingdom thereby fell under the domain of the emperor.[208] Church and state were deemed to be separate, but the shift was in that the church now saw the state as means to solve man's problems and change the world. It is no surprise that it is with the rise of this earthly view that Christianity began a spiritual decline. No longer was Christianity a Godly movement. Now it was a political movement.

The Middle Ages cannot be so simply stereotyped as many do, but it is true that the medieval church was a worldly church which supressed religious freedom and sought to enhance its earthly power. The depths of the medieval church's depravity became so severe that the Reformation erupted into civil wars. Would Paul have approved of such a revolution? Let us consider briefly what happened, quoting Erasmus, the Catholic scholar who had deep sympathies with the Protestants. While clinging to the hope that the Catholic church could be reformed from within, he acknowledged that "if they order impious things, God must be obeyed rather than men."[209] Jesus said "no one can serve two masters" (Matthew 6:24; Luke 16:13). When a leader, whomever it may be, sets himself up against, in place of, or in opposition to God, we must do as Peter did. "We must obey God rather than men" (Acts 5:29).

The end result of the Reformation was an extended, but not complete, move toward religious freedom. Sometimes Reformers oppressed Catholics as Catholics oppressed Protestants, but the ultimate result was the church's "purification" from worldly powers. It is for this very reason that the Puritans (whose name came from the idea of "purifying" the Church of England) fled to America where they brought their democratic and abolitionist ideals. This then leads to the question of the American Revolution. Was it truly a Biblical revolution? Would Paul have approved? John MacArthur even rejected the American revolution, calling it a violation of the Scriptures, saying, "much like liberal Christians ... many evangelicals have lost their focus on eternal values and become enamored of termporal issues."[210] Let us first look at the facts strictly from a historical perspective.

When the revolution began our forefathers did not seek to overthrow the crown of England, nor invade it. Rather we stood upon English law itself and the *Magna Carta*. The Declaration of Independence issues a long list of violations made by the crown against its own law, against the laws of God, and against religious freedom. The American Revolution was unique in many ways, and it is perhaps unfair to consider it a model for the Christian, since the circumstances of it may never be seen again, but it is no small thing to point out that the French Revolution which followed on the heals of the American Revolution ended not in democracy, but in anarchy, the Reign of Terror, the dictatorship of Napoleon, and ultimately a return to the French monarchy. The differences between the French and American Revolutions are glossed over, and even ignored, by revisionists today, but they are important. The most obvious of which is that the American Revolution was founded by Christian abolitionists, reformers, and the like. The French Revolution was founded by deists who believed in the autonomy of man. The one suceeded. The other failed.

Now what can we learn from this brief excursion into history? Only this. Man centered revolutions ultimately fail. Revolutions which were grounded in religious freedom succeed. Paul did not want the early Christians to become a political movement similar to the Jewish Zealots who sought to overthrow Rome. However, he did not order Christians to submit to laws which put them over and against God. In those instances we gave up our lives, and changed the world ... often without even lifting a single sword. Still, this issue goes beyond this. Let us examine God's providence.

God's Ordination?

When Jesus stood before Pilate being condemned for a crime of which Pilate himself admitted Jesus was innocent, our Lord quietly answered Pilate's asertion of authority by saying, "you would have no authority over Me, unless it had been given you from above" (John 19:11). Thus even as Jesus was standing and awaiting execution orders He acknowledged God's hand of Providence.

Here then is a paradox for many. If nothing happens except "by God's permission"[211] and evil rules while persecuting Christians, then how can there be a contradiction between God and man? How is it that Rome persecuted Christians at all? How can we be told to submit to them? This paradox comes from a misunderstanding of this world and God's future kingdom. God bequeethed the earth to Adam, but in his sin, he bequeethed it to Satan (cf. Matthew 4:9; Luke 4:6; 2 Corinthians 4:4). Still, in His love God has never yet permitted unrestrained evil such as will exist in the days of the anti-Christ. Even

Satan must obtain permission before doing evil, and that evil is restricted to this world. Only God can punish men eternally, or save them. In short, *this* world is not Christ's (John 18:36). When Jesus returns He will claim the world and take it from Satan. Until that time, Satan is the "god of this world" (2 Corinthians 4:4). Consequently, we submit as good citizens. George Washington himself said that "good Christians will always be good citizens." This citizenship requires submission, but "the words used here [in Romans] does not designate the *extent* of the submission."[212] If submission were absolute then we would ourselves be in rebellion against God. As Thomas Chalmers said, "by this doctrine of an entire unconditional passivenesss, oppression and injustice must at length have unlimited sway upon the earth."[213] What then can we conclude from all these facts?

General Summary and Conclusion
"The obedience which the Christian owes to the government is never absolute and must be carefully weighed in light of his subjection to God."[214] As the apostles chose to "obey God rather than men"[215] so we are also sometimes left to make that difficult choice. It is true that we are not to seek salvation or expect justice through worldly institutions, and as such we are not called to be political revolutionaries. This is the context of Paul's epistles. As "the proud love of freedom of the Jews"[216] led many to become Zealot revolutionaries, so also there is a desire in all Christians to seek social change through government institutions, but Paul warned that any such actions must be tempered with reality. This is a sinful world ruled by sinful men. Government is not the solution to our problems; Christ is. In this world we will face conflicts between our faith and our governments.

John Knox said that "religion took neither [its] origin nor authority from worldly princes, but from the Eternal God alone."[217] It is true that governments have received their authority from God, but it is for this very reason that when they go beyond that authority and tresspass upon religion we must disobey.[218] The context of Paul's discourse was to refute those Jews who pledged national loyalty for Israel as a justification for rebellion against Rome.[219] Paul discouraged the riots and rebellions which had become common place among the Jews.[220] He does not, however, say that the government is always right, righteous, or even just. Nor does he say that we must always submit. Our submission is not absolute. We are to be good citizens in order that the world may see our light, but a good citizen does not turn a deaf ear or blind eye to evil, nor disobey Jesus. It is impossible to serve two masters (Matthew 6:24; Luke 16:13) and so there are times that we will have to choose between the good master in Christ and the wicked ones who serve another master.

The Weaker Brother
Romans 14:1-23

"Now accept the one who is weak in faith, *but* not for *the purpose of* passing judgment on his opinions."

It is popular for some to refer to this verse whenever they are in a debate. The "weak" one is always the one with whom you disagree. As Charles Spurgeon said, "while the strong looked down upon the weak, almost doubting whether they could have come to the liberty of Christ at all, the weak condemned the strong, almost charging them with turning their liberty into license."[221] John Calvin said both parties were at fault,[222] and to an extent this is true. Both have a tendancy to look down upon the other. I personally do not drink beer, but I have known some friends who feel obligued to make me drink beer as if it is sin not to. They want my acceptance by seeing that I am doing the same thing. Thus the issues Paul faces here have not died. They continue on in differing forms to this very day.

First and foremost it must be clear that "this does not refer to *saving faith.*"[223] The faith to which Paul refers is one of sanctification and maturity. It is not *can* a Christian eat meat, but *should* a Christian eat meat? The same can be said of many issue today from alcohol to immoral movies to choice of music. Let us then look at the instance to which Paul refers.

Maturity, by definition, comes with time. No one is born an adult, nor is any born again Christian instantaneously sanctified. The more I grow in my faith, the less sanctified I feel, for I see my own sins and shortcomings more readily and easily than I did when I was young and immature. Each man must resolve in his own mind not only what is permissible but what is useful. It is no sin to drink, unless one cannot hold their liquor, and if one cannot drink in moderation it is best not to drink at all, nor tempt your friends to drink. These were the issues which Paul also faced in his day, and here in Romans he deals primarily with the question of food, similar (although not exactly the same) as that of *kosher* food law today.

The readers in Rome knew exactly what the issues to which Paul was referring were, but today we only know that it involved questions concerning the eating of meat, and drinking wine. Some believe that "by 'the weak' he means the Jews, who were not yet able to disregard the choice of foods."[224] Peter Abelard argued that "Jewish converts still having weak, that is, imperfect faith"[225] and Thomas Chalmers pointed out that "the church at Rome was made up partly of Jews and partly of Gentiles."[226] However, this cannot be. As Robert Govett pointed out "Jews were never confined to eating vegetables."[227] Alternately, Lenski said that "there were a few pagan vegetarians, but none of them abstained from the use of wine."[228] Who then could these men have been? Charles Hodge believes they may have been Essenes,[229] but it is not clear that the Essenes were vegetarians either.

Two viable alternatives exist. It is apparent that gentile asceticism would eventually envelop the church over the next few centuries, and some ascetics may have already existed.[230] Another option is the theory of Constantius who believes some ate only vegetables because they thought the meat market might have been tainted from food sacrificed to idols.[231] This is discussed in depth under 1 Corinthians 8.

In any case, it does not matter so much who the people were so much as Paul's resolution of the issue. He states clearly that "I know and am convinced in the Lord Jesus that nothing is unclean in itself; but to him who thinks anything to be unclean, to him it is unclean" (14:14). It is a matter of conscience. For this reason Paul concludes that "if because of food your brother is hurt, you are no longer walking according to love. Do not destroy with your food him for whom Christ died" (14:15). In other words, it does not *per se* matter whether the vegetarian is right or wrong. What matters is that you bear with him in his faith. "It is good not to eat meat or to drink wine, or *to do anything* by which your brother stumbles" (14:21). Our purpose should be to bear one another up, not tear one another down.

The same is true today. Some expect the Messianic Jew to eat pork, while many still adhere to *kosher* law. The question should not be whether we can eat pork, but should we eat pork if is a stumbling block to the Jew? But food and alcohol are not the only issues which are parallel. Indeed, today we may have many instances where music, movies, and other influences (and they are influences) are tolerated by some, reveled in by others, and shunned by still others. Amish and most Mennonites will not even watch television at all. On the other extreme there are Christians who will watch all manner of immoral television and movies, oblivious to its influence upon our thinking and mind set. Some watch "in moderation" (such as myself), some will not watch at all, and others watch everything. As we read through the Bible we will realize that while entertainment is acceptable, most things either build us up or break us down. If something is not edifying to Christ, it is best to avoid it, and yet this does not mean that we cannot watch entertainment to relax. We can, but can we do it without it harming our relationship to God? This must ultimately be settled in each man's own mind. It is a "question of personal conscience"[232] Is the weaker brother the one who does or does not watch television? Is the "strong" one tearing down the "weak" or building him up?

Desiderius Erasmus said that "it is better sometimes to abstain from that which is in itself does not improve."[233] We are not to "put a stumbling block in a brother's way" (14:13) for if someone believes it is wrong to eat meat and we make them eat meat then have sinned (14:14), not because there was sin in the eating itself but because they did what they believed was wrong. Thus it is better for us to "abandon it altogether"[234] then to cause a brother to stumble.

Douglas Moo noted that "the weak condemned the strong for cavalierly dismissing God's law, while the strong pooh-poohed the weak, looking down on them"[235] but Paul tell us not to "pass judgment on disputable matters."[236] "If because of food your brother is hurt, you are no longer walking according to love. Do not destroy with your food him for whom Christ died" (Rom 14:15).

A Sabbath Argument?
Romans 14:5

> "One person regards one day above another, another regards every day *alike*."

There has been a long standing debate about whether or not the apostolic age Christians worshipped on Saturday (traditional Jewish Sabbath) or Sunday. In *Controversies in the Acts of the Apostles* under Acts 20:7 I debated this subject in depth. Here I will summarize my conclusions found therein. The apostles and the apostolic age Christians worshipped in Jewish Synagogues on Saturday as per custom, but had memorial services for Jesus on Sunday which were held for Christians only. As time passed and the divide between Jews and Christians increased the church began to abandon synagogues altogether but retained the Sunday services. Eventually Sunday became a sort of Christian Sabbath to honor the resurrection of our Lord and Savior.

Now the issue here is not whether we should worship on Saturday or Sunday, but rather does it matter? Paul notes that already in his day some Christians were divided on Sabbath worship. Why, after all, would one day be more holy than another? Some probably held that we should retain the Saturday Sabbath as practiced by the Jews since the time of Moses, while others held that the day of resurrection was more holy. Paul, however, connects this with same issue of the "weaker brother." He does not say which side he supported, but that neither side is worth creating an obstacle to a brother in Christ.

I have known Christians who think it akin to legalistic heresy to worship on Saturday and I have known Christians who think it is a violation of the fourth commandment, but I have discussed in *Controversies in the Gospels* the fact that even the ancient Jews did not begin days at the same time. One sect began the new day at sundown (as modern Orthodox Jews do), another began the new day at sunrise, and the Romans began the new day at midnight as we do. That means one sect actually honored the Sabbath from 6 A.M. Friday to 6 A.M. Saturday whereas another honored it from 6 P.M. Friday to 6 P.M. Saturday. One could argue that some Jews had a Friday Sabbath! Of course, they would deny this, for they simply began Saturday (*Sabbath*) 16 hours earlier than we do today. Thus God is not so much concerned with the 24 hour time period as that we set aside a day to worship the Lord and honor Him. We should not create obstacles to another brother based on the exact day.

Was Phoebe a Deaconess?
Romans 16:1

"I commend to you our sister Phoebe, who is a servant of the church which is at Cenchrea."

The word here used by Paul to describe Phoebe is διακονον (*diakonon*) from which we get the office title of "deacon." Consequently, some have actually translated this as "deaconess" (RSV, NLT). However, it literally means "servant." One dictionary defines it as "servant" or "helper" as well as being a title for some "ministers" and "deacons."[237] The question is whether or not Phoebe was a "helper" of Paul or held an official office. The debate, of course, peripherally concerns the question of women in ministry.

Now it should be said from the outset that *no one* denies that woman can, and *should*, serve in the church. However, the official office of "deacon" is believed by most conservatives to be restricted to men. Some have argued that Phoebe was of the women who served the sick and needy, such as found in 1 Timothy 5:9. Matthew Henry, for example, saw this as some official position but "not to preach the word (that was forbidden to women), but in acts of charity and hospitality."[238] Others argue that she is proof that women can be deaconesses.

First, let us begin with the passage itself. Some older translations have rendered this as "in the ministry of the church" or similarly (Douay-Rheims, Darby, Tyndale). The word is διακονον (*diakonon*) sometimes used of the office of deacon (Philippians 1:1; 1 Timothy 3:8, 10, 12),[239] but it is often used in a generic sense as "servant" (Romans 15:8; 1 Corinthians 3:5).[240] It is of interest to note that one of these passages is just a few sentences before in Romans 15:8 where Paul calls himself a "servant." Now one scholar argued that 1 Timothy 3:11 "suggest [women] held such an office in the church" but admits "the word 'deaconess' is not used in that passage."[241] Nevertheless, the "use of the word with the phrase 'of the church' strongly suggests some recognized position."[242] So should this be accepted as a generic title or as a specific office? The fact that she was sent as a messenger by Paul is more than sufficient to explain its use in connection with the church, but also implies that she was probably not an actual deacon whom we would not expect to be acting as couriers.

The real problem here is not with the translations or words but with Paul's own prohibition against women teaching and preaching in church (cf. 1 Timothy 2:12; etc.). Paul had no problem with women serving in ministry, but they served in a different capacity from men. Mother Teresa was a nun. She was not a bishop. She was not inferior to most bishops in the eyes of God or the church, but she served a different (and equally important) duty. So also Paul held that women served in one capacity and men in another; equally important but different capacities. Consequently, most doubt Phoebe actually held the

51

church office which has since come to be called the "deacon." Paul's use of the word is usually more generic as he called himself a διακονον (*diakonon*) or "servant" (Romans 15:8) even though he was never a "deacon."

In short, while this passage is often used by some to "prove" that women can preach and serve as deacons, elders, and pastors, there is nothing here to prove such. Paul's explicit comments elsewhere prohibit this and the Greek word is properly "servant." Phoebe doubtless served in the church in some official capacity and she was an associate of Paul who was acting as a courier for him to Rome. Such duties are noble, but are not those of a deacon.

3
—

1 & 2 Corinthians

The Corinthian church may most be likened to many western churches. They were materialistic and worldly people who focused on the external rather than the internal. Even their spirituality focused on external signs. 1 and 2 Corinthians therefore deal with the practical application of theology to the world in contrast to Romans' apologetics.

Corinth itself was located in ancient Achaia, which is a part of Greece today. As such the Corinthians resided in a place of high decadence. Ancient Greece was always known for their promicuity and immorality. Fidelidy was not honored highly and homosexuality as well as most every other sexually deviant acts was accepted. Obviously the parallels to the modern western culture are strong.

The epistles were written in the mid to late 50s during Paul's Second Missionary Journey. Most believe that they were written from Ephesus (cf. Acts 19). However, there are questions about missing letters as well. It is apparent in at least two verses that Paul may have written more than the two epistles we have in our possession. 1 Corinthians 5:9, for example, refers to a previous letter and 2 Corinthians 7:8 is believed by some to refer to yet another letter, although it probably refers back to 1 Corinthians (see notes there). This troubles a few who believe that all the writings of Paul must be inspired, but the inspiration of the Holy Spirit does not work that way. We have what the Lord deemed necessary and appropriate to ensure the sacred Scriptures, so the fact that Paul may have written other letters (he certainly did) does not prove that these are "lost Scriptures." They are lost only because they never were Scripture. The Scriptures are infallible. The apostles were not. They all had failings, weaknesses, and made mistakes, but God inspired them to write some works that were infallible for our sake. The distinction is important in understanding historical passages such as those where Peter and Paul collided (cf. Galatians 2:11-21).

Paul's Quote of Eliphaz
1 Corinthians 3:19 (Job 5:13)

"He captures the wise by their own craftiness."

This brief quotation is from Eliphaz from the book of Job. Contextually Eliphaz was largely giving Job poor advice and blaming Job for his own condition. Eliphaz was wrong to suggest that the poor and suffering are being punished for their own bad karma. Here, however, Paul quotes Eliphaz in a seemingly positive manner. He even speaks as if Eliphaz was inspired in this passage. How can this be resolved?

Ilya Repin – Job and His Friends – 19th Century

The truth is that this is not as difficult as some present. The great Stoic senator and philosopher Seneca once said, "whatever is well said by another, is mine" and also, "I shall never be ashamed of citing a bad author if the line is good." The same can be said of anyone. Did not God speak through Pharaoh in Genesis 41 or through Nebuchadnezzar in Daniel 2-4? Gleason Archer points out that even Caiaphas, the lead conspirator against Christ, was inspired to prophesy about Jesus (John 11:51)![243] How can this be?

We like to think of inspiration as being from great men, and certainly the closer we are to God, the more easily we may be inspired by Him, but the truth is that God can, and does, inspire whomever He wants for whatever purpose He desires. As with Pharaoh and Nebuchadnezzar God used them for His purpose. Many times, such as with Caiaphas, the person being inspired may actually understand the exact opposite of what God intended. As the Scriptures say, what man intends for evil, God intends for good. As Joseph's brothers intended harm to him out of jealousy, God intended that Joseph prepare the way for the preservation of Israel (cf. Genesis 50:20). So also Caiaphas prophesied that "it is better for one man to die for the people, and for the whole nation not perish" (John 11:50), but he understood that killing Jesus would save their people from a false Messiah whereas God meant for Jesus to become the sacrificial Lamb for the salvation of all Israel (and the world).

Consequently, Paul's quote of Eliphaz is not problematic at all. Even a fool can say a wise thing. Even sinners can be inspired on occasion. Moreover, while Job's friends were known for bad advice and unfair criticism of Job, much of what they said was good. We should not, as some do, look to fools and

54

atheists for inspiration, but neither should we assume that God cannot work in the sinner as well as in the saint.

"Beyond What is Written"
1 Corinthians 4:6

"Learn not to exceed what is written."

Paul here warns the Corinthians "not to go beyond what is written" in regard to spiritual matters. Many Protestants believe that Paul is referring to nothing less than the Scriptures themselves. "The Apostle Paul is enjoining the Corinthians not to beyond Scripture."[244] However, some argue that Paul is "probably referring to what he had said in chap. iii."[245] Lenski argued that "this could not be the Scriptures" but does not explain why.[246] Such an argument is weak for several reasons. First, "would not Paul have said ... what has been written before?"[247] This would make more grammatical sense and remove any doubt as to what he was saying. Second, "'what is written' is used thirty more times by Paul, always referring to a citation from Scripture."[248] It is a common way of citing Scripture, so that "what is written" could be translated simply as "the Bible." In fact, the New Living Translation renders this somewhat freely as "pay attention to what I have quoted from the Scriptures." Others prefer "live according to Scripture."[249] Charles Hodge believes that it means "the Corinthians were not to think of their ministers more hightly than the Bible."[250] Perhaps this is the reason that some do not want to render this as a reference to Scripture for there are many who hold their teachers, "prophets", and priests to be modern day apostles. To this end they have argued that this refers back only to 1 Corinthians 3:5-9![251]

Another weak argument used to discount this verse is the argument that this passage is a "gloss" (un-Scriptural addition) based on the unusual Greek use of the word "the."[252] In other words, the Greek actually reads, α γεγραπται (*ha gegraptai*) or "the, what is written." This is obviously an unusual use of the word "the" which is left untranslated. Based on this it is assumed that the entire passage is suspect, but "the solution is defeated by its very ingenuity and complexity."[253] Moreover, the use of "the" normally introduced a noun, hence this actually supports the fact that "what is written" is an idiom for "His written word."[254]

Finally, some argue this is a proverb, but cannot find this proverb in Scripture or out of Scripture.[255] The NIV even reads, "learn from us the meaning of the saying, 'Do not go beyond what is written.'" While this is not particularly important one way or another, it is an argument worth knowing. In either case, it is clear that the reference is to all Scripture, as J.A. Bengal believed.[256] F.F. Bruce equated this solely with the gospel,[257] but the best interpretation is to take it as all Scripture. "What is written" is used sixty-seven times in Greek in the New Testament. In all but two of those verses it refers to Scripture. Moreover, the only two verses where it does not refer to Scripture are both found in Revelation and refer to "what is written" in the "Book of Life" (Revelation 13:8; 17:8)! Therefore it is obvious that Paul is enjoining them not to go beyond the Scriptures in spiritual matters or to elevate men above the Word of God.

Discipline in the Church
1 Corinthians 5:1-13

"For what have I to do with judging outsiders? Do you not judge those who are within *the church?* But those who are outside, God judges. Remove the wicked man from among yourselves."

There are two extremes within the church today. I have personally experienced both of them. On the one side is libertarianism where there is no discipline and church members feel they have a license to sin. The other is legalism and judgmentalism where church leadership play God and pass judgment with little or no trial and no real desire to see repentance or restoration. In short, apathy and judgmentalism. The Corinthian church obviously leaned toward the libertarian view. Here Paul stresses the need for correction and discipline, but his words are, not surprisingly, controversial for both extremes misrepresent Paul's words.

The first thing we need to examine in understanding Paul's words is the specific context and the individual in question. According to Paul there was an individual who was having sexual relations with his "father's wife" (5:1). He expressed outrage that such things were not even acceptable among the pagans and yet apparently being tolerated by the Corinthian church. Now some have argued that "father's wife" is actually a reference to a step-mother,[258] since "mother" would normally be used. Moreover, Dan Mitchell assumes that the woman was a pagan or else Paul would have included her in his discipline.[259]

John Calvin said that this reminds us of Reuben (Genesis 35:22).[260] It is indeed a sad reminder of just how far even the believer can sink into sin when he is neither guarded nor disciplined. To this end, John MacArthur argues that "the chapter is not directed at believer, or 'so-called' believers (v. 11), who were committing the sins but, at the rest of the church who stood by doing nothing about it."[261] Thus, the apathy and libertarian license which the church was practicing may have helped to contribute to the sin.

The second thing we need to understand is what Paul meant by "deliver such a one to Satan for the destruction of his flesh" (5:5). This harsh punishment has been taken several ways. Some have argued that it was "a secret execution,"[262] but this seems extreme speculation without merit. The *Pastor of Hermas* alludes to an "angel of punishment"[263] which may refer to this passage. Others argue that "within the church a person enjoys a certain right of santuary from Satan becase the church is the temple of God, and the Holy Spirit dwells there (3:16). To be excluded is to be deprived of that protection and therefore vulnerable to the attacks of Satan, which God allows for punishment."[264] This is the traditional Catholic view of excommunication. Nevertheless, John Darby argued that only an apostle may deliver "unto Satan" and thus "there is no such thing now."[265] He, therefore, denied that churches have the power to inflict this sort of punishment. He furthered argued that the man was not literally "delievered to Satan, though in result he might possibly come under Satan" to destroy flesh but save soul.[266]

What then can we make of these facts? First, this passage may be referenced by Paul in 2 Corinthians 2:7, in which Paul urges the church to accept him back into the fold (see notes there). Second, this passage must be tempered with 1 Timothy 5:21 and Mattthew 7:1. I was once censored by a church based on mere rumor and gossip for which I was not even permitted to defend myself. They accepted rumor and innuendo and denied me a right to defend myself or present witnesses on my behalf. In fact, the individual in question was under psychological stress due to something which had happened recently. I was just the object of ventilation. This is not what Paul intended. On the contrary, Desiderius Erasmus noted that discipline is intended as a means to heal.[267] Its purpose is not to get rid of those we do not like or to keep out "undesireables" but to insure "that his spirit may be saved in the day of the Lord Jesus" (1 Corinthians 5:5). Moreover, as Warren Wiersbe remarks, "Christians are not to judge one another's motives" but sins.[268] We are called to be separate from the world and not a part of it. Discipline should never be used to remove people from the church body, but to preserve people within the church body. This was Paul's ultimate goal.

Homosexual or Male Prostitute?
1 Corinthians 6:9-10

> "Or do you not know that the unrighteous will not inherit the kingdom of God? Do not be deceived; neither fornicators, ... nor adulterers, nor effeminate, nor homosexuals ... will inherit the kingdom of God."

There are two controversies involving the appearance of homosexuality in this passage. For convenience I will address them separately. The first is whether or not this is properly translated as "homosexual" or "male prostitute" or something else. The second, addressed separately, is the question of whether or not homosexuality is genetic; therefore negating any guilt associated with it.

As to the first issue, there are two words here at the heart of the issue. The first word is μαλακοι (*malakoi*) which is usually translated as "effeminate" (KJV, NAS, ASV, RV). It has also been translated as "abusers" (MKJV), "male prostitutes" (NIV, NLT) and "homosexuals" (NKJV). The second word is αρσενοκοιτης (*arsenokoites*) which is usually translated as "homosexual"

(MKJV, NAS, NIV, NLT, ESV), but the NKJV reads "sodomites" and the older Geneva translation reads "buggerers." Oddly enough, the RSV simply combines the two words as one, translating them into "sexual perverts" while the NRSV renders them as "revilers."

It is no coincidence that recent modern translations have been influenced by the myth of the homosexual gene (see below) and therefore chosen suspect translations to minimize the Bible's condemnation of homosexual behavior. At this point whether or not homosexuality is "normal" or harmful will not be debated. Only an honest translation will be discussed in this section.

The first word, μαλακοι (*malakoi*), is the more difficult of the two, but only because it is used idiomatically. Its natural meaning is simply "soft."[269] Obviously this is an idiomatic use referring to something else. Translations have varied over the centuries from "effeminate" to "those who make women of themselves" (Darby) to "male prostitutes" (NIV). Contextually, the term refers to one who acts "soft" like a woman, as opposed to a man. Although William Tyndale rendered it as "weakling" it is apparent from its context that it was a derogatory term for "effeminate" or "catamite" men (men who practice anal intercourse).[270] Ironically, even though this is the more debateable of the two terms, those who reject the homosexual translations in this passage do not challenge the definition of μαλακοι (*malakoi*) so much as they do αρσενοκοιτης (*arsenokoites*).

Αρσενοκοιτης (*arsenokoites*) is a compound word formed from αρσην (*arsen*) and κοιτης (*koite*).[271] Αρσην (*arsen*) means "male" and κοιτης (*koite*) is the word from which we get "coitus" meaning to lie with, or copulate.[272] Together it means "homosexual" or "sodomite."[273] Nevertheless, some have tried to argue that if μαλακοι (*malakoi*) means "catamite" or a "passive male prostitute" then αρσενοκοιτης (*arsenokoites*) could refer to an "active male prostitute."[274] It is further argued that the term is not used in "homoerotic" Greek literature of the day to refer to homosexuals,[275] but this is misleading for two reasons. First, "homoerotic Greek literature" is by definition favorable toward homosexual practices, so it is hardly surprising that a technical or negative word associated with homosexuals would be used in Greek poetry or literature. The argument is, therefore, disingenuous. Secondly, and more importantly, it is generally believed that the word did not come into use until the first century so its absence from Herodotus, Plato, and Aristotle is irrelevant.[276]

That this is the word used in the Greek *Septuagint* translation of Leviticus 18:22 and 20:13 is acknowledged by all. The response is simply to argue that Leviticus does not in fact refer to homosexual acts at all, but rather Temple Prostitutes. The argument is not only weak, but inconceivable. The Hebrew literally reads "one who lies with a man as one lies with a woman." There can be no reasonable doubt that this refers to homosexual acts.

Is Homosexuality Genetic?
1 Corinthians 6:9-10

"Or do you not know that the unrighteous will not inherit the kingdom of God? Do not be deceived; neither fornicators, ... nor adulterers, nor effeminate, nor homosexuals ... will inherit the kingdom of God."

Here is a clear and explicit verse which condemns homosexuality and other sexual practices outside of marriage. In recent years, however, we have heard over and over that homosexuality is genetic; that they are "born that way." If true then it would make us question what kind of God would condemn someone for how they were born! Is this true? Is there any evidence of genetic disposition for sexually deviant behavior?

The Diagnostic and Statistical Manual of Mental Disorders (DSM) admits that there is "no empircal evidence" to show that any sexually deviant activity has genetic origins in nature.[277] Nazi Minister of Propaganda Joseph Goebels is famous for saying, "if you repeat a lie often enough, people will believe it, and you will even come to believe it yourself." Various spins off of this phrase have also been spread around over time. All are true. When I confronted a professor in college about the genetic theory of homosexuality he admitted that there was no "proof" but that it was possible. Later in that same conversation he was again saying that it is a "fact." When one examines the myth of a homosexual gene he will find that in scientific literature it is always admitted to be an unproven theory, but in textbooks it is all of the sudden passed off as scientific fact, despite the fact that no genetic research has ever been done on the "homosexual gene." Why?

Genetic research is expensive and time consuming. It is so expensive that *no* genetic research can or is done without first passing some prelimilary tests. The main test is whether or not something runs in families. For example, if breast cancer runs in the same family then researchers have good reason to believe that it may be genetic. They can only then justify the expensive and time consuming research necessary to discover this cancer gene and effect a cure. No such cure has yet been discovered, illustrating how difficult and time consuming the research is. In regard to homosexual activity it is no secret that homosexual do not have natural children unless they are engaging in a heterosexual act. The argument that homosexuality runs in families is based on adopted families, not natural families. Consequently, this is actually strong evidence that homosexual conduct is learned, and not genetic. How would an adopted child receive the genes of his adopted parents? He could not. His behavior was taught to him by homosexual couples.

One might ask how we got to this stage at all. I am old enough to remember when homosexuality was first called a "sickness" or disease. The subtle idea is that it was not their fault and it was something that could be corrected. Actor Anthony Perkins gained some notoriety for going to see a psychiatrist to be cured of homosexuality. Eventually before his death he had settled down and married a woman with whom he had two children. We are now told that he was "denying his true self." From "sickness" we began to move to genetics, and now we are told that people are "born" this way. Notice how the shift is subtle. In each case the sinful choice is trivialized to make the sinner feel less responsible for his sin. Finally, we are told that his act is not wrong and the Bible is portrayed as intollerant and bigotted.

On a related issue, we might ask the same question repeated by advocates of homosexual acts. "Why is wrong to love whomever we wish?" The question is itself based on a lie. Since when are sex and love the same? If you love someone you will not sin with them by commiting an unnatural, and harmful act. Homosexual acts are by nature unnatural, and physically harmful. Indeed, they now teach in sex education courses in school how to avoid tearing the anus during homosexual acts. Does this not prove that such an act can be physically dangerous. One can even be hospitalized under certain circumstances. In fact, a woman who died from a gang rape actually died form injuries caused by anal sex. This does not even count veneral diseases like AIDs, but cannot heterosexual couples contract venereal diseases? True, and this leads to the final point.

Paul does not condemn homosexuality alone. In this respect the critic is correct. Homosexuality is placed alongside heterosexual acts outside of marriage such as adultery and even fornication. It would, therefore, be wrong for a philandering man to condemn the homosexual when his acts are placed equally alongside by God. This then ties in with the previous passages about judgment and discipline. Our objective is not to condemn the homosexual, nor to justify or turn a blind eye to his sinful acts. Our objective, whether with the philandering heterosexual or the homosexual, is lead them to repentance and help them acknowledge their sins before God. Alleged bisexual Oscar Wilde became a born-again Christian (or at least Catholic) before his death, presumeably repenting of all his deviant acts. His writings make clear that he struggled with sin but recognized Christ as the true source of change. So also we must seek to lead the sinner to Christ and help him turn away from sin. In order for this to happen, however, one must acknowledging his sin, and we cannot make someone else acknowledge their sin if we ourselves do not recognize it as sin. That people are "born" into unnatural desires is a lie that is repeated over and over again until we ourselves have come to believe it.

Paul and Marriage
1 Corinthians 7:1-16, 25-40

"It is good for a man not to touch a woman. But because of immoralities, each man is to have his own wife, and each woman is to have her own husband."

After dicsussing deviant sexual acts, Paul now discusses the sanctified act of marriage. However, his words are extremely controversial since many take them to imply that celebacy is superior to chasity. These words are also used by those churches, such as the Catholic church, which forbid their priests from marrying. What was Paul's view of marriage? Did he hate marriage? Was he a misogynist? What of divorce?

Celibacy or Chasity
As usual we must start with context. It is clear that Paul is actually answering a specific question. 1 Corinthians 7:1 begins with the words, "Now concerning the things about which you wrote." He then says immediately thereafter "it is good for a man not to touch a woman." Consequently, while we do not know exactly what the Corinthians were asking, it is apparent that Paul's remark is in direct answer to that question. Moreover, it follows Paul's chastisement of their immorality within the church. This is also implied in the next verse where Paul says, "because of immoralities, each man is to have his own wife, and each woman is to have her own husband" (7:2). Therefore, while we do not know what the question may have been, it is obvious that Paul was not requiring celibacy, although he concedes its virtue to the Corinthians who had asked concerning it.

One commentator argued that this is "like listening to only one side of a telephone conversation."[278] Another notes that "it is forgotten that the apostle is not here framing a theory of marriage in general; he is answering precise questions."[279] Moreover, "Paul writes to Corinth ... and such as were living in the worst pagan surroundings."[280] Consequently, we cannot forget the larger context even if we are not acutely aware of what they were asking. Nevertheless, there are hints within the passage which help us to identify the larger context and help us frame his response.

Is Celibacy Best?
"It is good for a man not to touch a woman" (7:1). Few words have been as controversial. Some, like Saint Jerome, argue that celebacy is nearer to spiritual perfection,[281] while others, like John Calvin, call "admiration of celibacy" a "superstition."[282] Additionally, the Catholic church requires its priests and nuns to remain celibate based in part upon these very passages, but what is Paul saying?

Charles Hodge notes that "the word *good* (καλον) here means expedient, profitable."[283] In this way it is argued that Paul's reply means "it is good for a man or a woman to have the gift of celibacy, but the celibate state is not better than marriage."[284] John MacArthur reminds us that "he does not say ... singleness is the only good condition."[285]

Conversely, some argue with Saint Jerome that "if it is good not to touch, then it is bad to touch."[286] However, this is a logical fallacy. Eating fried chicken is good, but this does not lead to the assumption that eating something

61

else is bad. Not touching something may be good, but it is does necessarily follow that touching it is always bad. This is a basic logic fallacy. Morever, as one Catholic commentator noted, "for the Apostle, marriage is a *charism*, a gift of God (7:7), as much as celibacy is."[287] Another logic fallacy used to support celibacy is the interpretation that Paul is saying "celibacy is best."[288] Severian, for example, claims that "he praised chasity as more perfect."[289] This is not correct. To say "the movie was good" does not mean "the movie was the best." This would be false. Surely there is more than one good movie, and celibacy is never said by Paul to be superior to chasity and marriage. Before examing Paul's intended meaning, it is necessary to show how some church fathers, like Pelagius, twisted these words to promote celibacy as a requirement for ministry.

Pelagius argued that "people who want to be promiscuous argue that God commanded us to have sexual relations, so that the earth would be filled with human beings. But God is quite capable of making humans out of the earth, as he did at the beginning, so this is not excuse."[290] He then nullifies the command of Genesis 1:22 (a command repeated about a dozen times). Fortunately, Irenaeus and other church fathers reminded the early church that Paul did not make abstinence a commandment.[291] Paul was merely answering a question. What exactly was that question?

We must remember that the early church was a mixture of converted gentiles and Jews. "Orthodox Jews were opposed to celibacy, regarding marriage as a duty."[292] In fact, there was an "extreme Jewish view which held that it was a sin if a man reached the age of twenty without being married."[293] The *Mishnah* even makes marriage obligatory (*Niddah* 5:9). Hence it seems that "Paul was waging a campaign on two fronts." On the one side was the libertine sex discussed and condemned in chapter six and on the other side is was an ascetic view[294] ... or was it? In light of the "extreme" Jewish view cited above, it may not be that some Corinthians were actually promoting celibacy so much as resisting the arranged marriage alliances which many Jews required before reaching the age of twenty. This then leads to the next question.

Why Marry?

Paul's statement, "because of immoralities, each man is to have his own wife, and each woman is to have her own husband" (7:2) does not exactly appear on the surface to provide a glowing endorsement of the reasons for marriage. In speaking about widows he further says, "if they do not have self-control, let them marry; for it is better to marry than to burn" (7:9). These remarks, divorced from context, have let many to believe that Paul viewed marriage only as an "expedient alternative to sexual immorality."[295] Chrysostom said that "the very fact that it is designed to avoid fornication shows that he is really trying to encourage virginity."[296] The problem with these interpretations that we are again "listening to only one side of a telephone conversation."[297]

John William Godward – "Yes" or "No" – 1893

We don't know what was said on the other end of the line, but we do know that Paul summarizes his discourse with these words; it "is good in view of the present distress, that it is good for a man to remain as he is" (7:26). The key to understanding his view then is to understand "the present distress." If we understand what this distress is then we will have a better understanding of what was being said on the other end of the line.

"Present Distress"

It is clear that Paul's entire discourse is premised upon "the present distress" (7:9). His advice therefore depends on this factor and is based on that context, but was the "present distess"? There are two prevalent views.

Tertullian believed that Paul's command was "because 'the time is short.'"[298] It is assumed that Paul believed the end would come within a generation, but this argument has several fundamental flaws. First, it is Paul himself who warns against quiting jobs or abandoning our duties. Second, although urging believers to be ready, he also stresses that the time has not yet arrived and that many things must happen first (cf. 1 Thessalonians). In short, the idea that Paul advised against marriage because the Second Coming was imminent is a false assumption and bad theology.

The second view is stronger, although not without problems. This is the idea that "the existing condition of the church, [w]as exposed to trials and perscutions."[299] John Wesley said it was the church "under persecution."[300] The strengths of this view are obvious. As H.A. Ironside noted, Paul "wrote in a day when to become a Christian ... meant to put one's very life in jeopardy."[301] It is natural that when one has a wife and family he has others whom he must protect. Therefore to sacrifice one's life is never as easy when you have a family. This is one reason that Roman soldiers were actually forbidden to marry. Caesar wanted people who were totally committed. So also Paul believed that a single man was more committed to ministry in a time of danger than someone who had a family to protect. Nevertheless, this view does have some drawbacks.

One problem is that Corinthians was written in the mid 50s, almost a decade before Nero's brutal persecution began. Some therefore question this theory, but it cannot be forgotten that persecution was not restricted to Nero. Paul himself bore the brunt of persecution throughout his ministry life. In fact, it is in 2 Corinthians 11:24 that Paul boast that "five times I received from the Jews thirty-nine *lashes*." Persecution, therefore, was never restricted to Nero's time and at least three of the apostles were martyred before Nero's reign.[302] A second problem is that Paul defends the right of even an apostle to take a wife in this same epistle (1 Corinthians 9:5). Of course the answer to this is that Paul does not forbid anyone from marrying, and even encourages it in certain circumstances.

Weighing all these facts together, it is apparent that some in the Jewish community chastized the Corinthians for not being married at age twenty or having arranged marriages. Paul defended the right of a man to not marry or wait until later in life. The church itself faced persecution not only from the Romans but also from Jewish radicals. Paul's comments must, therefore, be weighed in light of this context.

Widows

Here Paul continues his discourse upon the state of married and single people. Both history and *midrash* give us a much more clear picture of the full context. In those days women were not generally able to get jobs and work, especially if they were older. Widows, therefore, were often supported by the local communities (cf. 1 Timothy 5:13-14) or else they were encouraged to marry another man. Since communities, even churches, felt the burden of supporting widows it was not uncommon to marry widows off as soon as possible to another man. Here Paul is again speaking against arranged marriages.

John Calvin stated that "the Lord does not in any part of the Scripture declare what persons ought to remain unmarried."[303] Neither is Paul saying that the widow must remain unmarried. In fact, in 1 Timothy 5:13-14 (and here in 1 Corinthians 7:39) he freely permits widows to marry, but only of their own will and "in the Lord" (7:39).

Divorce and Remarriage

Paul's advice regarding the unmarried he identified as his own opinion and advice. However, in regard to divorce and remarriage Paul now says, "not I, but the Lord" (7:10). Jesus Himself forbade divorce "except for immorality" (Matthew 19:9). Here Paul elaborates beyond adultery, indicating that divorce could be permissible in other rare instances, but this is where the controversy lies.

Grounds for Divorce

First, there are many misconceptions about divorce in the Old Testament. Because Jesus's enemies asked "is it lawful *for a man* to divorce his wife for any reason at all?" (Matthew 19:3) and then followed up the question by asking "why then did Moses command to give her a certificate of divorce and send her away?" (Matthew 19:7) it has been assumed that there were no restrictions upon obtaining a divorce. In fact, the enemies of Jesus were misquoting the Scriptures. The passage actually reads in full, "because he has found some indecency in her he may give her a certificate of divorce and send her away" (Deuteronomy 24:1). Thus "indecency" or immorality has always been a prerequisite to divorce.

The question here goes beyond adultery. In fact, Paul does not specifically address the grounds for divorce here at all. Rather he urges the following:

"To the married I give instructions, not I, but the Lord, that the wife should not leave her husband (but if she does leave, she must remain unmarried, or else be reconciled to her husband), and that the husband should not divorce his wife" (1 Corinthians 7:10-11).

Notice first that unlike the previous passages regarding celibacy, Paul now says specifically, "not I, but the Lord." This is therefore a command, not an opinion. Second, Paul does not actually address the grounds for divorce. Third, although Paul addresses those married to unbelievers separately, his advice remains the same:

"To the rest I say, not the Lord, that if any brother has a wife who is an unbeliever, and she consents to live with him, he must not divorce her. And a woman who has an unbelieving husband, and he consents to live with her, she must not send her husband away" (1 Corinthians 7:12-13).

What can we draw from this? For one thing the grounds for divorce were well known and accepted in the Jewish community. Adultery was specifically named by Jesus (Matthew 19:9). Additionally, divorce was granted if a man was convicted of serious crime then the woman could be freed from her marriage to him. The Talmudic Law was very specific on the types of crimes. It is sufficient to say that if a man was sentenced to prison for certain serious crimes then the women was free to divorce him. In early American law the grounds for divorce were similar, and beating a woman was a crime. Nevertheless, it is still evident that Paul is saying that even under such circumstances where divorce is legal, it is preferable to reconcile. Moreover, it appears that the divorced person is not to remarry unless reconciled to their spouse (1 Corinthians 7:11).

Now some have argued that divorce should never be an option.[304] Paul seems to be suggesting that it is better to stay celibate than to marry and divorce. Jesus said that it was only because of the hardness of our hearts that divorce was ever permitted (Matthew 19:8). As Erasmus said, "people are naturally vengeful and stubborn, if denied the right of divorce, might commit offences more horrid than divorce."[305] Divorce is preferable to executing an adulterous spouse, but reconciliation and forgiveness are better still.

Yet Paul is not actually discussing the grounds for divorce at all. Rather he is encouraging those married to unbelievers not to divorce. This is the real controversy. Why were they married to unbelievers at all? Is it permissible to marry an unbeliever? Is it permissible to divorce someone because they are unbelievers? This is the real subject of debate.

Unbelievers
The first question is then whether or not it is permissible to marry an unbeliever. On the surface it appears that the answer is "no." 2 Corinthians

66

6:14 states clearly, "do not be bound together with unbelievers; for what partnership have righteousness and lawlessness, or what fellowship has light with darkness?" However, the answer here is not so simple. Most believe that this simply refers to those who were unbelievers when they got married and later converted to the faith. John Wesley, for example, said that "the persons here spoken of were married, while both in a state of heathenism."[306] Nevertheless, this is only one instance. There are reasons to believe that there were other reasons that interfaith marriages existed, and still do. For example, to this very day arranged marriages exist in countries like India. Arranged marriages were very common in the ancient world, and in Israel. In such instances, a believer may be married to an unbeliever.

So *should* believers marry unbelievers? Tertullian said that "by understanding *generally* this monition regarding *married* believers, they think that licence is granted (thereby) to marry even *un*believers. God forbid that he who this interprets (the passage) by *wittingly* ensnaring himself!"[307] He then list a variety of problems which can result from willingly marrying outside the faith. One, he suggest that submission to a man who is not in submission to God will create conflicts. Two, a heathen may require his wife to participate in acts which are not acceptable for Christians. Three, the pagan may wish the spouse to participate in religious rituals and festivals which are in violation of the Christian faith.[308] Nonetheless, Tertullian shifts dramatically when speaking of those converted after marriage. These he calls "hopeful" arguing that the pagan spouse has observed God's work in them and may come to salvation themselves one day.[309] To that end some have argued that history has shown interfaith marriages to make a profound difference in history. One scholar, for example, said that if such marriages "rendered possible such epoch-making marriages as that of Clotilda with Clovis, and of Bertha with Ethelbert ... [which] had a direct influence on the conversion of the two great kingdoms of France and England"[310] then it must be acceptable. To this he might have added Constantine's mother who was a Christian woman married to a pagan lord and heir. The counterpoint to this argument is that neither Constantine nor Clovis in particular truly changed hearts. They were tools used by God for His purpose, but certainly few, if any, believe that Clovis was true Christian. What then is my conclusion?

The truth is that we should ideally marry those who love and obey God and will help to strengthen our faith. However, it is naive to deny that interfaith marriage can and do happen for a variety of reasons. Arranged marriages, insincere converts (Matthew 13:20-21), or even naive young believers are examples of instances where a believer and unbeliever have becomed joined. Such an arrangement may create unnecessary complications, but do occur in the real world. Should they divorce when they realize they made a "mistake"? On this the answer is even more clear; "*no.*"

The Bible does *not* permit divorce because of religious differences (1 Corinthians 7:12-15). If the unbelievers leaves then the believer is free in such instances (7:15) but they cannot use religion or faith as a grounds for divorce. To do so would be to negate the entire gospel which is based on love and commitment! Paul is clear on this, and even provides hope.

"For the unbelieving husband is sanctified through his wife, and the unbelieving wife is sanctified through her believing husband; for otherwise your children are unclean, but now they are holy" (1 Corinthians 7:14). What does this mean? First, is does not refer to salvation. Sanctification and salvation are not the same things. Sanctification comes from the Greek word meaning to be made holy. "Holy" ('αγια – *hagia*) and "sanctification" ('ηγιασται– *hagiastai*) both come from the root word 'αγιος (*hagios*). If an unbelievers is willing to stay with a believing, then they are made more holy. This does not mean they will necessarily be saved, but by witnessing your holiness, they too become more holy and, therefore, draw closer to God.

Gordon Fee says, "it is not the believer who is *defiled*, but the unbeliever who is *sanctified*."[311] This is actually only part true. In the real world friends influence us. It is mutual and reciprocal. The believer sanctifies the unbeliever, which gives us ground for hope, but the unbeliever still pulls the believer down. Even among believers, the one who is more spiritual will elevate the less spiritual one, while the less spiritual one pulls down the more spiritual one. It is like magnetism. The two magnetized objects are drawn toward one another. The stronger of the two (which will always be the believer) will yield the highest pull, but the attraction will always work both ways. That is why "evangelical dating" does not work. Paul grants the sanctifying power of the believer over their spouse, but if the believer were never harmed by such a relationship then there would be no prohibition against marrying an unbeliever. Such marriages take place out of culture, law, and circumstances, but are ideally discouraged, if not prohibited. Having said that, we cannot forget that divorce is *never* to be granted upon ground of religion or faith.

Summary
The entire premise behind Paul's discussion is based on "the present distress" and the culture of arranged marriages. Paul expressly defends the right of marriage in 1 Corinthians 9:5. Moreover, in 1 Timothy 4:3 he declares that those who "forbid marriage" are heretics. Marriage is sacred, and many believe that Paul himself had been married at one time based on his status as a Pharisee and Rabbi. This is because Pharisees required Rabbis to marry and the *Mishnah* also requires that religious teachers be married to resist temptation and impropriety as well as to fulfill the command of Genesis 1:22 (cf. *Ninnah* 5:9). Hence, it is generally assumed that Paul was a widower.

In any case, his comments must be taken in the context of the "present distress." A man who must protect his family is more vulnerable than a man who has no attachments. The choice of dying for your faith is much harder when you know you are leaving someone behind. Moreover, it allows the persecutors of the faith to theaten your family. This was part of the "present distess" to which Paul was alluding.

Additionally, Paul was dealing with a culture where arranged marriages were normal. It was not uncommon to have young children engaged and marriage off at sixteen years of age. Paul was therefore defending the virtue of those who wanted to wait until later in life. He was not rejecting the holy institution of marriage, and he was certainly not requiring celibacy for priests as he defends the right of even apostles to marry (1 Corinthians 9:5).

When we take all these factors into consideration, Paul upholds the sanctity of marriage, but is dealing with the problems of marriage, divorce, and celibacy on a practical level. Corinthians, unlike Romans, is not a theological discourse *per se*, but an response to practical queries involving everyday life. It involves the application of theology to daily life and present situations which may not always be ideal. This is the context by which we must understand Paul's words. Paul says celibacy is good, but he does not say it is the best. Likewise, he wants believers to marry believers but where mixed marriage occur they should not divorce, but remain together, if possible, their whole life.

Food Sacrificed to Idols
1 Corinthians 8:1-13; 10:25-32

"Now concerning things sacrificed to idols, we know that we all have knowledge. Knowledge makes arrogant, but love edifies."

In Romans 14 we discussed the issue of supporting the man of weak faith in questionable issues. One of the things mentioned was food. Here Paul is answering a specific question from the Corinthians involving food sacrificed to idols. This same issue was addressed at the Council of Jerusalem where the apostles concluded that we should "abstain from meat sacrificed to idols" (Acts 21:25).[312] Is Paul contradicting that admonition? On the contrary Paul concludes that "if food causes my brother to stumble, I will never eat meat again" (8:13). The question is, why?

Paul actually begins his discourse in what seems a defense of eating meat sacrificed to idols, but he concludes that for the sake of those weak in conscience it is best never to eat food sacrificed to idols. This is an issue which exist today in Israel and India. In Israel Jews have been taught their whole life to obey *kosher* food laws, and think it a great sin to violate it.[313] If they see a Christian convert eating unkosher food, they think less of them and damage the reputation of Jesus's followers. So also Hindus in India have been taught that animals are almost as important as men, being living souls (and possibly reincarnations of men). Beef is especially forbidden as the cow is sacred to the Hindu. When a Hindu converts to Christ it is natural for them to still want to refrain from eating beef. In these instances Christians sometimes argue with converts, but Paul pleads that if they do eat such foods "their conscience being weak is defiled" (1 Corinthians 8:7). We should not put obstacles in the way of Christ that are not necessary to the gospel.

Perhaps a better understanding of the issue is needed to fully appreciate Paul's point of view. First, it is generally believed that meat was sometimes obtained from the bodies of animals which had been sacrificed to idols.[314] Although some of the meat was eaten at the sacrificial ritual, much meat was left over. That was then sold to various markets. Second, "there were two sources of meat in the ancient world : the regular market (where the prices were higher) and the local temple (where meat from the sacrifices was always available)."[315] These lower priced meat market took the food from the temples.[316]

Others believe, as Lenski did, that "the desire to participate in [pagan religious] feast as the obligations of family connections or friendships raised the question as to how far a Christian might go in"[317] eating meat. In other words, "invitations to take part in idolatrous banquets"[318] was common. In either case, like the issue of *kosher* food, there was always a danger that one might be eating forbidden food without even knowing it.

Obviously this proved a difficult issue for many. "The basic problem that confronted the Corinthians faces all of us. The issue is : How far does Christian freedom go in regard to behavior not specifically forbidden in Scripture?"[319] This is why Paul argues both sides of the point. He begins by affirming that "we know that there is no such thing as an idol in the world, and that there is no God but one" (8:4). Therefore, eating food sacrificed to nothing is nothing in and of itself. However, Paul then makes clear that because people have been accustomed to thinking of idols as gods there is not only a danger of defiling the conscience of the weak (8:7) but also unnecessarily looking like hypocrites to the world at large. Godet believed that eating such food was "repugnant of Jewish Christians"[320] and set up an unnecessary obstacle. For this reason Erasmus argued that we must "adhere to the dictates of charity rather than the dictates of knowledge."[321] Even though we know there is no sin in eating food sacrificed to idols we should avoid it for the sake of love. The same should be said of issues which exist today. We should not pressure believers into drinking alcohol nor Jewish converts to eating cheeseburgers. Even the converted Hindu should not be pressured into eating beef until their conscience is clear, and even then it is best to avoid eating beef in front of their unconverted family members. We must do all things in love.

Was Peter Married?
1 Corinthians 9:5

"Do we not have a right to take along a believing wife, even as the rest of the apostles and the brothers of the Lord and Cephas?"

It may be remembered that Cephas is the Aramaic rendering of Peter. It was the Lord Himself who gave Peter this nickname (John 1:42) and there can, therefore, be no denying that Cephas and Peter are one and the same. Indeed, "this is the name by which Peter is called whenever he is mentioned by Paul, except in the epistle to the Galatians."[322] The problem is that many Catholics believe that Peter, like the popes of today, was celibate. Nevertheless, many Catholic scholars conceded that Peter was married, but argue that he was a widower before becoming an apostle and thus remained celibate thereafter. Protestants, of course, hold that Peter was married until his very death as recorded in the traditions of Peter's martyrdom. Which are we to believe?

Historical Interpretations
Historically it is hard to say exactly which view was dominant in the early church. Ignatius as the earliest of church fathers to allude to this passage. He was himself a pupil of the apostle John and it is certain that he believed Peter had been married,[323] but since he also believed that Paul had been married we cannot definitely say whether or not Peter, like Paul, was a widower. By the time of Saint Augustine, however, many Catholics had come to believe that the Greek word for woman was "mistranslated" as "wife." Let us examine these positions closely.

View # 1 : Mistranslation
A common argument made among some Catholics is that the word is mistranslated and should be understood as "woman" and not "wife." This is reflected as early as Tertullian who seemed to imply that these were women "who used to minister in the same way as they did when accompanying the Lord."[324] At the same time he believed that bishops were required to be monogomous, but not necessarily celibate.[325] It was Saint Augustine who best represented the view when he said, "the Greek word deceived them, since, in Greek, the same word is used for wife and woman."[326] This is, however, misleading. The word γυναικα (*gynaika*) can be translated as either woman or wife depending of the context. That much is true. Nevertheless, it is not true that the words are interchangeable. Any possessive use of γυναικα (*gynaika*) is necessarily translated as "wife." It is literally "my woman" or "my man" meaning wife or husband. There is, therefore, rarely any ambiguity. Here it is a different matter.

The Greek literally reads "μη ουκ εχομεν εξουσιαν αδελφην γυναικα περιαγειν" (*me ouk echomen exousian adelphen gynaika periagein*). Literally translated without regard for English, it says, "is not we have power sister women/wife lead around?" Notice how "sister" is joined to γυναικα (*gynaika*). In order to translate the word correctly we must understand the relationship of sister to woman/wife.

The Catholic translation Douay-Rheims Bible renders this as "have we not power to carry about a woman, a sister?" This infers that sister is used to refer to a spiritual sister or believing woman. In one respect this is true. The term "sister" is used to imply a spiritual state. On that we agree. "Sister" confirms that the γυναικα (*gynaika*) is a believer in Christ, but it remains unclear from this whether or not the γυναικα (*gynaika*) is simply a generic woman or a wife. Nonetheless, there are three reasons to beleive that γυναικα (*gynaika*) can only refer to a wife here.

Contextually Paul has been discussing marriage and Christian freedom in the Lord. It makes little sense that Paul would shift to a generic woman here when he has been discussing marriage in the previous sections. This is a continuation of that discourse, not a new discourse. Moreover, Mark 1:30 affirms that Peter had a mother-in-law, so he was obviously married at one time.

Additionally, there is grammatical difficulty in making "sister" an adjective of "woman" in the general sense. If Paul wished to refer to a believing woman he would likely have used the idiom "sister in Christ" or even left "sister" standing as a noun since the context would have made clear that he was referring to a Christian woman. The addition of γυναικα (*gynaika*) indicates that "sister" is adjectival and that γυναικα (*gynaika*) refers to the wives of the apostles.

Finally, on a historically level the church father Clement of Alexandria reflects the tradition that the apostles "took their wives around as Christian sisters rather than as spouses" so as not to be "causing scandal."[327] Thus he believed that this is to what Paul was referring.

Although this might seem a viable theory it rips the passage from the context of marriage which Paul has spent so much time discussing. He was answering the Corinthians' query about marriage and food sacrificed to idols. He is still answering those questions here and has not shifted topics. Moreover, it is grammatically suspect and ignores the fact that Peter had a mother-in-law. This latter fact alone indicates that Peter was at least married at some point in his life. The question is then whether or not he was a widower like Paul.

View # 2 : A Widower

Ignatius was the student of the apostle John. He also served at one time as one of the first bishops of Antioch.[328] Since Antioch was the center of the church after the early persecutions by Saul (cf. Acts 11) it is highly likely that Ignatius also knew Peter and Paul. As one of the earliest apostolic fathers who certainly knew some of the apostles his word carries great weight and Ignatius stated that both Peter and Paul had been married.[329] Now in fairness to the Catholic commentators it is to be conceded that "Paul probably was a widower"[330] and, therefore, we cannot say based on Ignatius' comment alone that Peter was not also a widower. It is for that reason that many Catholics hold to this second opinion. Still, this option hinges upon the first view and is therefore still suspect.

Paul does not appear to be referring to some female secretary but to wives. The entire section of 1 Corinthians 7:1 to 10:33 addresses the question of marriage and eating food sacrificed to idols. It is poor exegesis to isolate this passage from those topics. Thus by referring to Peter's wife in 1 Corinthians 9:5 Paul was making an example to the Corinthians of a great apostle who was at that time married. This is further supported by the early tradition of Peter's martyrdom in which Peter witnesses his wife being led to away to execution shortly before his own crucifixion.[331] Let us examine those traditions and the evidence.

View # 3 : Married Until His Death

According to Clement of Alexandria Peter had at least one child.[332] The tradition he cited read that under Nero's persecution "Peter, on seeing his wife led to death, rejoiced on account of her call and conveyance home, and called very encouragingly and comfortingly, addressing her by name, 'Remember thou the Lord.' Such was the marriage of the blessed and their perfect disposition towards those dearest to them."[333] The name of his wife is disputed among tradition, being either Concordia or Pertetua.[334] In either case, history seems to record that Peter was still married "after he became an apostle."[335] He apparently travelled with his wife,[336] as a loving husband would.

This has been the view not only of Protestants and most of the church fathers, but Erasmus also believed Peter to be married.[337] Tertullian believed that bishops were only required to be monogmous, not celibate.[338] Peter "was the example *par excellence.*"[339] He worked with and travelled with his wife. They were one body and one flesh as Scripture declares. There is no disgrace in such a thing.

Conclusion

A commentator once said, "it is right and proper for ministers and missionaries to be married."[340] In fact, the ancient Pharisees *required* Rabbis so that they would not fall under temptation and into sin. The scandals of the Middle Ages, and even many in the modern church, are proof that it is neither natural nor right to deny the right of marriage to bishops. Paul even calls "those who forbid marriage" heretics (1 Timothy 4:3). That Peter was married is attested in Mark 1:30 as well as this passage. That she did not die until the same time as Peter is recorded in all ancient tradition and no writer of antiquity denies Peter's marital status until centuries later. This not to be shamed, but revered. If even Peter was married and travelled with his wife, should we not also have the right to take a wife? This is what Paul says to shame those very people who believed that celibacy should be a requirement of some kind, and it is in this context in which Paul's instructions are given.

Is Twenty-Three Thousand an Error?
1 Corinthians 10:8

"Nor let us act immorally, as some of them did, and twenty-three
thousand fell in one day."

Here Paul alludes to the death of twenty-three thousand Jews who had
engaged in sin and idolatry. The problem is that the only place in the Bible
where such an incident appears in close promixity to the number twenty-three
thousand is in Numbers 25:8-9 and there it is said to be twenty-four thousand
who died. Some Syrian and Latin manuscripts as well as medeival manuscript
81 amend the epistle to read twenty-four thousand, but every ancient reliable
text reads twenty-three. It is clear that Paul wrote twenty-three and not
twenty-four, so how can we explain this apparent discrepancy?

Four possibilities have been suggested. The first is simply that the
numbers were variously rounded up or down.[341] Another is that "Paul was
speaking about how may died in that one day; he does not include others who
were killed subsequently."[342] Alternately it has been suggested that Numbers
included the leaders who died whereas Paul omitted the leaders[343] although it is
unclear why he would do so.

A fourth possibility is that Paul was not referring to Numbers at all but
to the incident with the Golden Calf in Exodus 32:27-28. In that passage Moses
mentions three thousand who were killed by the Levites in punishment for
idolatry (32:28). However, Gleason Archer believes that "twenty thousand ...
died by the plague"[344] which followed in Exodus 32:35. There it is said only
that "the LORD smote the people, because of what they did with the calf which
Aaron had made." No specific number is given as to how many died.

Support for this latter view is found in 1 Corinthians 10:7 where he
quotes Exodus 32:6. He then pleads with the Corinthians "nor let us act
immorally, as some of them did, and twenty-three thousand fell in one day."
One might assume that he is referring to the same event. Since Exodus does not
tell us how many died in the plague it is possible that this was a number found in
Jewish tradition. Since Josephus completely omits the story of the Golden Calf
it is impossible to verify this but it seems slightly stronger than the other
theories. I, therefore, tentatively favor this view.

1 Corinthians 10:25-32 – See 1 Corinthians 8:1-3

Headship
1 Corinthians 11:3

"I want you to understand that Christ is the head of every man, and the
man is the head of a woman, and God is the head of Christ."

This is one of those passages that the modern feminist uses to attack the Bible as a misogynistic sexist work. The evangelical feminist in turn dismisses or "reinterprets" the passage. Conversely there are some men who likewise twist the passage to their own liking. All misrepresent the text based on their own false perseptions about equality and personal goals.

What do I mean by personal goals? Just this. Both the modern feminist and the male chauvinist believe that fame and forture are the ultimate goals of life. Family takes a back seat to these aspirations. Yet the Bible places the family second after God alone. In fact this is why Christianity was long considered to be a *liberating* force for women in history. Because it *elevated* the role of women and mothers. Because it *elevated* the importance of family and a woman's role in the family the code of chivalry and respect for women (whether it was always practiced or not) was the result of Christianity's rise in the western world. Only in the post-industrial revolution did the world see women declaring their unhappiness with domestic duties for only in the post-industrial revolution did the average man (royalty and the upper class excluded) see "career" replace *work*. Money replaced family and with it came the end of chivalry, the rise of modern feminism, and an increased disrespect for women among men.

Here Paul provides a perfect analogy for the roles of men and women. Both need each other. Neither is independent of one another. Neither can succeed or thrive without the other, and yet each hold different positions in the family and the church. As Paul said, "the eye cannot say to the hand, 'I have no need of you'; or again the head to the feet, 'I have no need of you.' On the contrary, it is much truer that the members of the body which seem to be weaker are necessary and those *members* of the body which we deem less honorable, on these we bestow more abundant honor, and our less presentable members become much more presentable" (1 Corinthians 12:21-23).

The Issues Broken Down
As always it is best to break down the individual issues and examine them one by one before putting them all together. In this case there are five issues. The first is the actual meaning of "headship." What does it mean and what does it designate? The second and third are related as they both relate to the question of "man" whom is intended. The fourth and fifth then relate to the woman and her role in the church and society as well as the question of equality in Christ.

The Meaning of Headship
Everyone, it seems, wants to be the head because the head gets all the glory, but a head without a body is parapelegic. Nothing in life, it seems, is as excruciating as being paralized and unable to do anything, and yet people always seek to be the head. This despite the fact that most workers consider the head of their business to be incompetent and stupid! The real question is, what does the Bible mean by "headship"?

It has been said that "the word *head*, in the Scriptures, is designed often to denote *master, ruler, chief.*"[345] That is the same in our own culture as the head of a corporation or government is its chief or ruler, but on a practical level what does it mean? What does freedom in Christ, to which Paul refers in Corinthians, actually mean in regard to headship?

Some argue that the women "is subordinate to him; and in all circumstances – in her demeanor, her dress, her conversation, in public and in the family circle – should recognizes her subordination to him."[346] Others argue that it is a voluntary submission, although this seems somewhat of an oxymoron. The *Liberty Bible Commentary* says that "it is important to note the concept of headship does not connote qualitative or essential difference. It connotes a functional subordination."[347] In other words, an army functions and exist because of its enlisted men. The Sergeants and officers have no use or function without them. No war is won without enlisted men and it is they who do the hard work, pay the price, and ultimately will earn the glory for their sacrifices, but without a Sergeant and officers the enlisted men would have no missions and no goals. The army would be defeated overnight. In the family the man is the "head" of the household but without a woman the home is broken. The same goes for a household without a father. No house is complete without a mother and a father. Every son loves his mother, even above his father. She serves a vital role.

So if the body does not obey the head then it is called epilepsy and the body ceases to function properly. Conversely, a head without a body is parapelegic. The "head" here does not imply superiority but functional command of a given entity. The next question is then, what is that entity and how does it fit with Paul's discussion?

"Man" or "Husband"?

Just as γυναικα (*gynaika*) can mean either "woman" or "wife" depending on the context and adjectival modifiers, so also ανδρος (*andros*) can mean either "man" or "husband" given the context and adjectival modifiers. So some translations have tried to soften the perceived "sexism" of the verse by mistranslating this as "the head of the wife is a husband" (cf. RSV, NRSV, ESV). Politically correct or not, the argument is inherently weak. While it is true that ανδρος (*andros*) can mean "husband"[348] it is clear that this is not the case here.

First is the grammatical argument. Without the adjectival modifier "her" (i.e. "her man" = "her husband") ανδρος (*andros*) and γυναικα (*gynaika*) should always be translated as "man" and "woman" except where the context is explicit and clear. Here, however, the context is explicitly *not* a husband or wife.

Second is the context which throughout chapter eleven is about men and women. *Men* should not have their head covered, women should (11:4-7).

"Man did not come from woman but woman from man" (11:8). Man should not have long hair, women should have long hair (11:14-15). In each and every case, it is man and woman, not husband and wife. It would make no sense to shift the subject here and then shift back again.[349]

Third, 1 Corinthians 11:3 states clearly that Christ is the head of "every man." Can we read this as "every husband"? Is the gospel only for the married men? Clearly not, as Paul previously defended the right of celibacy. So this must be "every man," and not "every husband."[350]

Now it should be noted that Paul prefaces this on the fact that it is "in the Lord, neither is woman independent of man, nor is man independent of woman" (11:11). We both need one another. As the body needs a head, so also the head needs a body. Both are useless alone, and neither are self sufficient. The head does not abuse its own body, nor the body abuse its head. They work together as one. As "Christ is the head of every man, and the man is the head of a woman, and God is the head of Christ" (11:3), but this then begs a theologican question. Is Christ the head of the unbelieving man?

"Every Man"

"We must take 'of every man' as it stands. The fact that only Christian men accept Christ as their head while others do not does not change the truth 'that of every man the head is Christ.'"[351] This simple statement sums up the truth. Whether we acknowledge Christ is our head or not does not change the fact that he is our head.

John MacArthur takes this as a "general principle"[352] but it is far more than that. It illustrates that headship does not depend upon recognition. A leader is a leader whether or not the people see him that way or not. It is an insecure and poor leader who needs approval. These are the men who abuse their authority. They toss around their power and authority like a weapon just to prove that they have that power, but great leaders need not prove anything. Moses was often scorned and mocked by his own people. He did not seek power and did not have to prove himself to the people. It was God who proved Moses's leadership and God who granted him the power.

On a sidenote, Cyril of Jerusalem noted that "the Head suffered in the 'place of the skull.'"[353] Jesus, the true head of all, died in a place named after a skull. God is God of ironies. He makes foolish the wisdom of men and mocks the "wise" leaders of the world, just as the nameplate above the Cross rightly read "Jesus the Nazarene, the King of the Jews" (John 19:19). Jesus did not need the approval of Caiaphas or Pilate to be the king. He was king. Nothing they did or could do would ever change that, and everything they tried to do only played into the plans of the Lord. That is headship. That is leadership.

The Role of Women

A head without a body is paraplegic. A king without an empire is worthless. So also a man is nothing without a woman. A family is not a family without a mother and wife. Women play an important role in God's kingdom, but God's designs are not man's. Mankind desires fame and fortune. For the middle class this becomes respect and career. Both are selfish motivations. Neither is God's desires for man or woman. God created man to revolve around the family. Both the father and mother have vital duties to perform in that task, and while man is the "provider" those provisions do not, and never have, revolved around money. Money can buy the provisions, but money is not the objective as so many believe today. This sin, the love of money (1 Timothy 6:10), has done more damage to the family than almost anything; in both men and women.

Today it has become akin to "slavery" to suggest that women should nurture their child, educate them, and serve their children in a domestic sense of the word. Yet we have seen what happens when children are raised in a home without a mother or without a father. When the "traditional" family (the Biblical family) is abandoned children grow up taking their values from gangs and other peer groups. In one segment of the American population there is a section where as many as 70% of the children grow up without a mother and father. Those same communities are ravaged with gangs, drugs, and a self defeatest mentality that blames others for their problems. They rely on "government aid" because they have no family to speak of. Such is the inevitable result of abandoning God's plan for our own selfish ambitions. We create a selfish hedonistic society that cares for nothing and no one but itself.

In the modern world different roles have been erroneously equated with inquality or inferiority.[354] Such an argument is frivolous. If, as H.A. Ironside said, "it is the responsibility of the husband to care for and protect the wife"[355] then it is equally the responsibility of the mother to care for and protect her children. How is the one superior to, or inferior to, the other? Each is vitally and equally important in the roles to which God has assigned us. It is for that reason that Paul declares elsewhere "there is neither male nor female; for you are all one in Christ Jesus" (Galatians 3:28), but what exactly does this mean?

Equality in Christ?

John Calvin compared these passages to Galatians 3:28 saying that this is "of Christ's spiritual kingdom, in which individual distinctions are not regarded, or made account of, for it has nothing to do with the body."[356] In other words, Galatians does not deny the physical differences or the differing duties but equality in the eyes of the Lord. Just as the law is not supposed to regard one person above another God weighs us all equally in importance. We are to be judged for whether or not we duly and diligently performed the tasks and duties which were assigned to us. To those who fulfilled their obligations, more will be given. To those who shirked their duties "even what they have will be taken away" (Matthew 13:12; 25:29; the Parable of the Virgins).

So let us not look to what the world views as superior or "better," nor let us pay heed to what the world views as equally important, for the priorities of the world are in conflict with the priorities of God. God, faith, family, friends, and lastly ourselves. This is the ideal priorities of God, but in the world these are turned on their heads. We hear that we must love ourselves first. I have even heard a famous Christian charity whose motto is "supply the material needs first, then their spiritual needs."[357] Jesus, however, said, "for what does it profit a man to gain the whole world, and forfeit his soul?" (Mark 8:36). It is time that the church stop letting the world tell us what our priorities should be and start living according to the priorities of God.

The Arguments and an Evaluation
In times past almost everyone remembered and loved their mother, even above their father. Our mother was the one who nurtured us, taught us, and gave birth to us. Our fathers taught us discipline, knowledge, and strength, but our mothers taught is love, compassion, and holiness. Although this is not always true, it is a fair example.

Here in Corinthians Paul is talking not only about women in the family but about the role of women in the church. As John Darby said, "the woman had her place for praying and prophesying, but not in the assembly."[358] Like a business the President of the corporation is not superior to his workers (often he is the very opposite) but the corporation cannot function if each worker is doing his own thing and not following the goals and procedures of the head. If, however, the worker does a good job then he will eventually get promoted and gain new duties. So also God has a purpose for women in the church, but that position is not one which usurps the authority God established. If she does her job and does it well, then she will be rewarded in the kingdom to come.

Does anyone think that Mother Teresa was "inferior" to the men around her who did nothing? She was a nun. She honored her position and did not attempt to usurp the authority of the priests she worked for, but by doing her job in an obedient and sacrificial manner she earned herself great honor.[359]

Many have appealed to women like Deborah in Judges as if to prove that Paul is wrong, but such examples in no way diminish the role and purpose of God anymore than the anointing of a thirteen year old boy (King David) nullifies parental rights, discipline, or respect for elders. Nor have we changed the voting age to thirteen in order to accomodate David's youth. God chooses whom He chooses, but His choices do not nullify His own laws, purpose, priorities, nor the family.

As per Paul's analogy, a head need a body. A head without a body is like a parapelegic and a body which does not obey its head is epileptic. Neither can function. There is no shame or lack of dignity in being a hand. On the contrary, a "helping hand" is often what God desires the most. There is no duty more important than that of a mother. Indeed, it takes a wicked and depraved generation to scorn motherhood. That is why the modern feminist consider child birth a burden rather than a blessing and why abortion has become a sacrosanct sacrifice, akin the child sacrifice of the ancient Caananites. Let us then reject child sacrifice and again elevate children and motherhood to their natural place of honor among God and his church.

Gifts of the Spirit
1 Corinthians 12:4-31

> "Now there are varieties of gifts, but the same Spirit ... But to each one is given the manifestation of the Spirit for the common good."

Surely the most controversial passages in Corinthians, and even among the whole of the New Testament, are these passages about the "gifts of the spirit." Opinions vary greatly and divisively among Christians, even within the evangelical community. Charismatics and Pentecostals see modern day gifts as proof of the Holy Spirit whereas cessationist insist that the gifts of the spirit no longer exist, having existed only for apostolic times. Many lay in between these extremes. Consequently there are many issues to debate.

At this point whether or not the gifts of the spirit have passed away is irrelevant. That topic will be address under 1 Corinthians 13:8. Here the only debate is to how Paul uses this term "gifts of the Spirit" and what these gifts are. Without understanding the meaning of these gifts it is much harder to determine their role in the current church. Were these gifts designed solely to contribute the compilation of the Bible as some cessationist believe? Are they gifts bestowed on all believers? What specifically is/was their purpose? Each must be examined individually before looking at them as a group. Then we can better weigh the options.

What are the Gifts?
I will say at the outset in full disclosure that I have always found it ironic in the highest that the cessationists agree with the Pentecostals and Charismatics in regard to many of the gifts. All have a very specific interpretation of the gifts and their purposes. However, it is suspect whether or not these gifts are to be defined in a techinical sense of the word. Consider how Paul uses the phrase in the Bible. Is it techinical? Can it always be defined specifically? Some believe they can, but many doubt this assumption entirely. D.A. Carson, for example, believes that "Paul is not concerned to define 'spiritual gifts' too narrowly."[360] Instead, these scholars break down the gifts into various kinds of gifts which seem to assist different aspects of Christian life. This makes sense. The Holy Spirit is called by John the Counselor (John 14:26). It is natural that the purpose of the Counselor is help and assist us in various aspects of our spiritual life. To comfort us in times of trouble, to advise us, and to help us in our walk.

Nine gifts are specifically mentioned by Paul. These nine gifts have often been grouped into three different categories, although there is no general agreement on how they fit into these categories. For example, Linksi believes that two gifts (wisdom and knowledge) involve the intellect, five (faith, healing, miracles, prophecy, and discernment) involve faith, and two (tongues and interpretations) involve languages.[361] However, Gordon Fee classifies the last two groups differently, arguing that prophecy and discernment properly fit in with tongues and interpretation as part of "inspired utterances."[362] We might look at them this way:

Insight / Intellect	Faith	Inspired Utterances/Languages
Wisdom	Faith	Tongues
Knowledge	Healing	Interpretation
	Miracles	
	Prophecy	
	Discernment	

Let us look at these gifts individually and see how Paul defines these gifts. Are they generic terms? Do they refer to specific technical miraculous powers? The reader will be suprised to learn that few scholars from any age have come to agree on all the gifts and their meaning; a fact which in itself suggest that Paul did not define these gifts clearly, for he assumed the Corinthians knew to what he was referring.

Gifts of Wisdom

The first gift mentioned is that of the "word of wisdom." I am immediately reminded of Solomon who asked God for wisdom above all other things (1 Kings 3:9-10) and so it is said that "God gave Solomon wisdom and very great discernment and breadth of mind" (1 Kings 4:29). Wisdom is not ordinary. Even those we call wise usually learn their wisdom second hand, by reading the wisdom of others. True wisdom is indeed a rare gift, but in the context of Corinthians there is debate as to what kind of wisdom is intended, as if wisdom may be subdivided.

John Wesley saw this as "a power of understanding and explaining the manifold wisdom of God."[363] Specifically, some see it as "the exposition of wisdom. It is speech that has wisdom as its content."[364] Yet others as "the whole domain of spiritual life."[365] Erasmus said it is "faithful and judicious counsel through wise speech."[366] Still others as "practical counsel."[367] John MacArthur says wisdom "is a broad term. The use of *logos* (word) indicates this is a speaking ability ... practial application of the truth to life situations."[368]

To an extent they may all be correct, for wisdom may apply in all such circumstances, but ultimately Paul's neglectance of an technical definition implies that wisdom should be understand in the most literal sense. It is an all too rare ability to understand and have insight into many things. Solomon is the best example of this uncommon wisdom. When two prostitutes appeared before him with one dead baby and another alive, both claimed the living on was theirs. They had no birth certificates and the fathers were unknown. All Solomon had to go on was the word of two prostitutes and the wisdom of the Lord. He pretended to be like the kings of old; a cruel tyrant and angrily ordered the child to be cut in half so that the two women could each have half of the child. One woman protested and denied the baby was hers, while the other woman, bitter and angry, was quick to accept the king's apparent solution, but Solomon was really only trying to see their reaction, for a true mother would rather surrender her baby then see it killed.[369] The bitter woman was resentful of having lost her own child and Solomon immediately saw into their hearts. He gave the baby to the rightful mother (1 Kings 3:16-27). This is an example of true wisdom.

Wisdom then is discernment of spiritual matters, of human nature, of things both good and evil. It differs from the "discernment of spirits" in that it is more general and wide in scope. The very word wisdom in Hebrew comes from the root word meaning to "judge."[370] Wisdom is the ability judge people, circumstances, events, and spiritual matters sagaciously, fairly, and judiciously. It is an all too rare gift.

Gifts of Knowledge
The word of wisdom is paired with the word of knowledge. This gift is more controversial than the first for some see this in a technical sense as referring to words channeled through a speaker directly from God.[371] This definition, often seen in some charismatic sects, could be compared to mystics who "channel" the voices of the dead through their body. Obviously this view is scorned by a number of Christians and has even been likened to the occult.[372] It appeals to those who see this gift as the product of a prophet or an apostle, and yet this is the very irony of the cessationist for most cessationist *agree* with this hyper-charistmatic definition; one which cannot be found in the Bible. For example, one cessationist author argues that "it was with this gift that Agabus *prophesied* [emphasis added] the famine under Claudius (Acts 11:28),"[373] but when we read that passage we see nothing of the sort. It was *prophecy*; it was not a "word of knowledge." Nowhere is "word of knowledge" used in this sense in the Bible. Despite this, some claim that this is "evidence of overlapping categories."[374]

On the other extreme is the more liberally interpreted "knowledge of God's way of salvation through the cross"[375] and yet this would mean that every believer has the "word of knowledge" which cannot be so since Paul makes clear that not all believers have the same gifts (1 Corinthians 12:29-30). Each has different gifts. Consequently, the knowledge here cannot be general knowledge of salvation which is revealed to all.

Other interpretations have been offered through the years although most make only a slight distinguishment between it and the words of widsom.

John Wesley, for example, said it is "perhaps an extraordinary ability to understand and explain the Old Testament types and prophecies,"[376] and yet this is vitrually the same defition he gave for wisdom. Others have said it is the "exposition of truths"[377] but once again they give wisdom virtually the same definition.

Some interpreters have tried to better distinguish between wisdom and knowledge. One said that "*gnosis* makes the teacher, wisdom, the preacher and pastor."[378] He argued that while wisdom was "the whole domain of spiritual life," knolwedge was "profound insight into certain particular points in this domain."[379] Erasmus placed knowledge more in the realm of teaching, saying that it is to "eruditely explain matters that pertain to the apprehension of the faith."[380] He saw knowledge as "knowledge of liberal learning."[381] MacArthur says it "is also a broad term, which basically refers to perceiving and understanding the truths of God's words."[382] This line of thought sees the word of knowledge as "something more akin to inspired teaching."[383] Some even see it merely as "distinguished knowledge [which is] learned."[384]

Our first step is to decide between the charismatic/cessationist view which sees the word of knowledge as akin to prophecy and the more generic view which sees the word of knowledge more closely associated with pastoring and/or teaching.

One expositor cited the Samaritan woman at the well (John 4:7-29) as an example of words of knowledge.[385] Jesus knew secrets of this woman's life which He could not have known through normal means. Thus the *knowledge* of her life was given directly by divine intervention. The problem is that nowhere in this passage is knowledge or knowing ever mentioned. It is an example of divine revelation but to assume that this is of what Paul's speaks is a leap of logic. Knowledge does not presume secret knowledge, nor prophecy. In fact, this sort of interpretation is more closely associated with prophecy than knowledge for prophecy also reveals information which could not have been known otherwise. Consequently, it is a mistake to confuse prophecy and divine revelation with the word of knowledge.

Whatever this knowledge is Paul pairs it together with wisdom for a reason. If wisdom and knowledge are paired for a reason then we must assume they are closely related. Nevertheless, we must distinguish between the two in a clear fashion. Wisdom involved judgment and discernment. Knowledge involves learning and understanding. The two are not synonymous. Discerment and understanding are related, but good judgment and learning are not. Both involve a godly understanding but that understanding is of different fields. The atheist can often be very learned, but he has no understanding or discernment. He knows that the First Law of Thermodynamics states that matter is not *naturally* created out of nothing, and he knows from Entropy that matter is not eternal, but he has no *understanding* that these facts *prove* that the origin of the universe *must* be supernatural. There is a God. Thus the atheist has learning, but no understanding. He can cite the periodic table but does not understand where it came from. So here is the difference. Words of knowledge involve more than mere learning; they involve a spiritual understanding of what is learned. This spiritual understanding seems all too rare, even among pastors, teachers, and the like. They go to Seminary and learn, but they do not always understand. They lack spiritual insight into what they have learned.

The word of wisdom discerns the facts of life and human nature. Wisdom enables us to see that not everyone is the same. It allows us to look into someone's soul to see how Christ can touch their life. Wisdom helps us understand the world and our spiritual warfare with it. The word of knowledge helps us to understand the Scriptures and what is learned. Knowledge lets us know the spiritual. Wisdom helps us understand it.

Gifts of Faith

What is the gift of faith? Calvinists believe that all faith necessarily comes from God, but this cannot be the kind of faith of which is spoken here, for all believers have that saving faith, but not all believers have the gift of faith (1 Corinthians 12:29). Consequently, this cannot be saving faith.

Others have suggested that this is miraculous faith like that which moves mountains (Matthew 17:20; 21:21; Mark 11:23)[386] or parted the Red Sea, but this cannot be either for if the gift of faith is faith that moves mountains then why does Paul speak about gifts of miracles? Is not moving a mountain as great a miracle as any? Was not the parting of the Red Sea a miracle? Miracles require great faith to be sure, but since Paul list "the effecting of miracles" (12:10) separate from the gift of faith, they cannot be the same.

Next we come to the view of MacArthur who believes it is faith to overcome "overwhelming obstacles and human impossibilities."[387] John Wesley saw this as "extraordinary trust in God."[388] For many this view seems perhaps a little overly simplistic since all faith is trust in God, but what does Wesley mean by "extraordinary"? Perhaps it is the faith of men like Job who performed no great miracles but displayed faith like few have. No matter what the circumstances he trusted that God had a plan. Likewise Abraham showed incredible faith when he believed that God would resurrect Isaac from the dead (Hebrews 11:17-19). Such are examples of faith which performed no miracles and yet changed the world.

Gifts of Healing

The gifts of healings may seem apparent but this has not prevented it from being debated. Most agree that miraculous healing is intended, but some, such as John Wesley also beleive that "it may exert itself also, though in a lower degree, where natural remedies are applied."[389] Hence some see specially skilled doctors as possessing the gift of healing. Certainly the discoveries of devout Christian men like Louis Pasteur and Joseph Lister contributed greatly to the field of medicine and have healed millions over the years,[390] and they themselves did not fail to give credit to God and the Bible, but is this really to what Paul refers? If it is granted that men like Pasteur did have the gift of healing, then we still cannot diminish the obvious fact that miraculous healing such as that done by Jesus and the apostles is what Paul had most in mind.

Many have noted that the Greek words for "gifts of healing" is actually a double plural or "gifts of cures."[391] Frederick Godet said that "gifts and healing are put in the plural as relating to the different classes of sicknesses to be healed"[392] but it has also been argued that "the stress is on results, not on the process. The gift does not produce divine 'healers' but divine 'healing' (cf. Jas. 5:14-15)."[393] This is important. There is a difference in the gift of healing and in a "faith healer." Nowhere does the Bible suggest a career faith healer. Healing by faith is not a profession, it is an act of faith and is only given at God's good pleasure and will. Sometimes sicknesses and handicaps help a person to excel in ways he would never have done before. Consider John Milton or John Henry Newton. What would these men have been had they retained their eyesight? Would they still have achieved as much. *Overcoming obstacles is greater than removing them.* This is a forgotten lesson by so many who claim to be "faith healers."

Obviously it is not the "gifts of healings" that is as controversial as the faux "faith healers." To this end some see this as "the first temporary sign."[394] They argue that faith healing no longer exist but was only for the apostles and their generation. Since I discuss cessationism under 1 Corinthians 13:8 I will not debate this issue here, but the reader should be aware that cesssationists believe that healings no longer exist in this current dispensation. A sidenote, however, is the confusion that some have over the relationship between dispensationism and cessationism. There is no direct correleation between the two. Although many dispensationalists are cessationists, many are not. Conversely, many cessationists are dispensationalists but by no means all of them. The two should not be confused.

Our final question is then how "gifts of healings" is distinguished from miracles, below. Some, like Carson, argue that "the close relationship among the gifts of faith, healings, and miracles again suggests that the entries on the list are not quantum packages, each discrete from the others. Rather, there is considerable overlap." [395] However, given that there is an "overlap" and a general definition, the fact remains that Paul distinguishes between "healings" and "miracles" which follow. Surely there is a reason for this. Perhaps Paul wanted to emphasize physical caring as distinct from other miracles which do not effect health. Hence the caring for the physical needs of church members is a different gift which should be based on compassion.

Gifts of Miracles

We are all familiar with the many miracles performed by Jesus but most people today are unaware that such miracles, performed by Jesus, were rejected in part because they expected greater "signs" like those of Elijah.[396] Many rejected the miracles of Jesus as petty counterfeits wrought by Satan (Matthew 12:22-29). To this Jesus replied "An evil and adulterous generation craves for a sign; and *yet* no sign will be given to it but the sign of Jonah the prophet" (Matthew 12:39; 16:4; Luke 11:29). What then is the "gift of miracles" and what is its purpose?

As with other gifts some see this as a temporary gift reserved the apostles and their companions.[397] This is debated under 1 Corinthians 13:8. The better question here is what purpose do miracles serve? Far too many churches see miracles as a way of "proving" God's favor. It is a "sign" such as those expected by the Pharisees. Thus they fall into the same error and lies as those who rejected Jesus. It is reminiscent of the followers of Marcion, an ancient heretic. The church father Tertullian, refuting Marcion, apply explained that the proof Jesus was Messiah was never in His miracles. On the contrary, he said that Jesus "showed how rash was belief in signs and wonders, which were so very easy of accomplishment by even false christs." [398] Indeed, Jesus warned that "false Christs and false prophets will arise and will show great signs and wonders, so as to mislead, if possible, even the elect" (Matthew 24:24; Mark 13:22). Therefore it is clear that miracles are not, and never were, a means of converting people to the faith. They did not exist to "prove" Jesus' Messianic credentials to believers, for the believer does not need them. What then are the purpose of miracles, and what are these gifts to which Paul refers?

Let us consider Jesus's feeding of the multitudes. With a handful of bread and fish he fed thousands on multiple occasions (cf. Matthew 14:21; Mark 6:44; 8:19-20; Luke 9:14; John 6:10). Such a miracle would have been easy to fake had it just been to "convert" the crowd. In fact many of the people there were probably unaware that a miracle was even taking place unless they were in a position to know how limited the food supply had been. Clearly the purpose of the miracle was to feed the hungry. The Bible says that Jesus had "compassion" (Matthew 14:14) upon the crowd and fed them and healed them.

Consider also the miracle of the Red Sea with Moses. The miracle was not to convert the Jews, but to strike fear into the unbelievers and to deliver the Jews unto safety. Ergo the gift of miracles here is not simply one of signs and wonders, but of compassion and mercy. The miracles to which Paul refers are miracles which may often go unseen. As I allude to in the section on "gifts of healings" there are many "faith healers" who claim to have power from God but there are a great many more medical doctors who will testify to having seen patients they thought were beyond help recover after prayer from family and friends. Miracles should not be confused or confounded with "signs and wonders" which even the heretic can perform (Matthew 24:24; Mark 13:22). They are gifts of God for the comfort and protection of His people in times of need.

Gifts of Prophecy

Prophecy is arguably the most controversial gift in terms of its definition. Some cessationists give prophecy a very specific definition relating to the foretelling of future events or the compilation of the Bible but others define it much more liberally as all "speech inspired by the Holy Spirit."[399] In truth, the answer is somewhere in between.

On the one side is the argument that "the gift was temporary, no longer needed after the canon of the New Testament was completed."[400] However, it is not apparent exactly how *all* prophecy factors into the canon. For example, it is unclear how the prophetess daughters of Philip the Evangelist (Acts 21:9) would have played a role in the formation of New Testament. This is a fatal flaw in the cessationist argument, but not all dispensationists believe this. John Darby is an example of someone who saw prophecy as "all [that] is revealed (that is, in the word)"[401] but he also admitted that prophecy is often "revelation in a lower sense."[402] In other words, prophecy is not exclusive to foretelling the future or forming the Scriptures.

Charles Hodge is another who argued that "the nature of this gift is clearly exhibited in the fourteenth chapter. It consisted in occasional inspiration and revelations, not merely or generally relating to the future, as in the case of Abagus, Acts 11:28, but either in some new communications relating to faith or duty, or simply an immediate impluse and aid from the Holy Spirit."[403] Hence it has been said that prophecy is "not necessaruly predicting the future, but preaching the word with power (xiv. 3, 24, 30)."[404] Even John MacArthur defines prophecy, saying it "simply means 'to speak forth, to proclaim.'"[405] Frederick Godet said it is for "edification, comfort, and consolation."[406]

The same mixed opinions can be dated back throughout history. Erasmus said that "prophecy [is] for explaining things that are either still to come or in some other way difficult to understand."[407] John Calvin saw prophecy was a message between God and man.[408] Notice how both defined prophecy somewhat ambiguously. There is a tendancy to define prophecy solely as the domain of the prophets, but this is not so. It would be a mistake to limit prophecy to prophets. A prime example would be Caiaphas of whom John said "he prophesied that Jesus was going to die for the nation" (John 11:51), and yet this Caiaphas plotted and conspired to kill Jesus! Certainly Caiaphas was no prophet, and yet he made one of the most famous prophecies in the Bible, saying "it is expedient for you that one man die for the people, and that the whole nation not perish" (John 11:50). Prophecy then is not reserved to prophets alone.

Consider also the fact that Paul urged the Corinthians to "desire earnestly spiritual *gifts,* but especially that you may prophesy" (1Corinthians 14:1). Certainly the Corinthians were not packed full of prophets. Indeed, not a single Biblical prophet mentioned in the Bible ever came from Corinth, so how could they prophecy if they had no prophets? The only answer seems to be that

Paul is using prophecy in the "lower sense"[409] of the word. It may refer to foretelling of the future, composing the Word of God for the Scriptures, or simply being the vessel for God to speak to us. This latter sense, sometimes called the "lower sense," is not uncommon. Furthermore, as with Caiaphas, God has even used unbelievers on occasion (Balaam is another example) to prophesy. Prophecy then means allowing God to speak through you, and should not be confused with the "higher sense" of prophecy which we see common in the Biblical prophets and apostles.

Gifts of Discernment
The next gift Paul mentions is that of "distinguishing of spirits." Some have restricted this gift to the ability "to differentiate the Word of God proclaimed by a true prophet from that of a satanic deceiver"[410] but others have argued that this cannot be restricted in such a narrow sense. D.A. Carson reminds us of the magicians of Pharaoh's court who performed counterfeit miracles by the power of Satan[411] and Jesus Himself warned us that "false Christs and false prophets will arise and will show great signs and wonders, so as to mislead, if possible, even the elect" (Matthew 24:24).

Interestingly enough, one cessationist after arguing that this gift was "vital during this period when Scripture was still being formulated" then goes on to admit that "discerning of spirits may be required in any age."[412] Hence the cessationist emphasizes the need for this gift in Biblical times, but does not necessarily consider this a temporary gift.

Once again, the problem is that discernment is not something which should be restricted to a select few. Discernment should be practiced by all, so Paul is not talking about normal discernment. All people should weigh and evaluate spirits (miracles, tongues, healings, etc.) against the Bible and the Word of God. No one should accept a "prophet" simply because he can perform a seeming miracle. Here Paul is speaking of discernment as a gift of God. As with wisdom and knowledge, discernment is more than merely good judgment. It is the ability for God to reveal to someone the very nature of the spirit. You and I, had we been alive in Moses's day, would have judged Moses superior because his serpents swallowed the court magicians and because we know that God is on Moses's side, but one who has a gift of discernment could have recognized the true and false miracles without witnessing the outcome firsthand. This is most likely the definition of the "gift of discernment."

Gifts of Tongues
The term "tongues" has been defined in various ways among theologians. Some define it in light of Acts as the speaking of languages not previously known by the speaker[413] while others see it as a heavenly language. In fact, it becomes readily apparent that the tongues of Acts is different from the tongues spoken of here in Corinthians. Since Paul discusses tongues in greater detail in chapter fourteen I will reserve debate for 1 Corinthians 14:1-19. What

is relevant here is two fold. First, it is clear from 1 Corinthians 12:30 that tongues "were not conferred on all alike."[414] It is not a sign bestowed on all when they receive the Holy Spirit. Second, another gift, the gift of interpretation, is required for its use in church.

Gifts of Interpretation

Here is the dilema. If tongues is merely what is described in Acts where "each one of them was hearing them speak in his own language" (Acts 2:6) then why would the interpretation of tongues be needed at all? Clearly this gift is connected with tongues and is discussed by Paul in 1 Corinthians 14. Its purpose is to insure that church is not filled with incoherent ramblings which edify no one (1 Corinthians 14:26-28). This gift is also discussed more fully below under 1 Corinthians 14.

One final question might be, "are these all the gifts?" Is Paul giving an exhaustive list of gifts? Behind this question lies the very question about the nature of the gifts. In the most literal sense of the word a gift is anything given or done by the Holy Spirit in us. In this sense the gifts cannot pass away as long as the Holy Spirit is at work within us. Nothing we do of our own is of merit to God. It is His work in us which is of value. Consequently, it should be apparent that the "gifts of the Spirit" discussed here by Paul are somewhat general in nature. They should not be viewed as technical designations, although some are more specific than others. They are the outworking of the Spirit within us. Each of us receiving *different* gifts according to God's grace. Each of us being divergent according to God's plan.

The Servants of the Church

Having defined the *gifts*, Paul now mentions the *people* to whom many of these gifts are manifested (1 Corinthians 12:28). Now the gifts are not restricted to these classes of people alone, but it is they to whom the gifts appear to be most prominent. These people make up the leadership and administrators of the church. They are also the helpers and servants for in the Bible there is no distinction. Being a leader is not about being a boss, but about being a servant. Jesus declared "if anyone wants to be first, he shall be last of all and servant of all" (Mark 9:35), yet Jesus humbled Himself unto a servant even washing the disciples' feet. So also a leader in the church must be a servant.

Apostles

Obviously the twelve apostles were building blocks for the church, but Paul is also called an apostle. How many apostles were there? Do apostles still exist? I discussed this debate in depth in *Controversies in the Acts of the Apostles* under "The Thirteenth Apostle – Acts 1:21-26" so I will only briefly address the topic here without repeating too much of what was said there.

Some believe that there were only twelve apostles, not even thirteen. Others believe that apostle is a generic term.[415] John Wesley defined "apostles" as synonymous with missionaries.[416] Evidence exist within the Bible to support both sides of the argument.

Etymologically, apostle comes from αποστολος (*apostolos*) which most literally means "one who is sent," such as a missionary. In the generic sense of the term, it is a missionary or even delegate as in Philippians 2:25 where the word is usually translated as "messenger" (King James, NAS, NIV, NLT, RSV, etc). However, it is obvious that the term is often used in a technical sense as a title in the Bible. The apostle Paul is very clear that the "the signs of a true apostle were performed among you with all perseverance, by signs and wonders and miracles" (2 Corinthians 12:12). Obviously this is not a mere missionary or delegate. A "true apostle" is marked by signs. Additionally, as discussed in *Controversies in the Acts of the Apostles* a true apostle must have seen the resurrected Christ, performed miracles, and been chosen by the Lord Jesus Himself. These three things are all required for a "true apostle" (2 Corinthians 12:12). The real question here is whether or not Paul is referring to a "true apostle" (2 Corinthians 12:12) or falling back on a more generic definition.

While I agree that Paul is using generic terms and definitions in much of this chapter, I also believe it is apparent that Paul does distinguish between terms in such a way as to negate too liberal a definition. Apostles are defined as "first" among the church. Are missionaries really in priority over prophets? Considering that Paul defines the "marks of a true apostle" in another letter to the Corinthians (2 Corinthians 12:12) I at first believed it was unlikely that "apostle" here is to be taken in too liberal a sense. However, when examining the rest of Paul's list here there is no other category in which the missionary and evangelist could be placed. I, therefore, tentatively hold that Paul may here be referring to apostle in a generic sense, but I say this with extreme caution.

Prophets

John Calvin argued that a "prophet is a messenger, as it were, between God and man."[417] Just as prophecy is defined variously, so also a prophet is defined variously. One thing which is clear, however, is that a prophet is one who prophesies. John the Baptist made no prophecies about End Times, nor did he write any of the Bible, but he prophesied about Jesus. He spoke the Word of God concerning the Messiah's coming in their day. He was a mighty prophet (Luke 1:76) and Jesus called him the greatest among men (Luke 7:28). Clearly prophets are more than mere evangelists. They prophesy. Evangelists spread the good news among their own people and hence are closer to missionaries save that they tend to stay among their own culture rather than taking the gospel to other cultures. A prophet should probably not, therefore, be confused or conflated with evangelists.

Teachers

Paul identifies teachers as "third" among those appointed in the church. James 3:1 says that few should teach for as such we bear the greater judgment. Teaching is important because it grooms future generations and plants far more seeds than most others in the church. Bad doctrine results in a bad generation of believers and a watered down gospel. We have all seen the results of poor doctrine over time. Many churches or organizations which began as relatively solid Biblical ministries have naturally degraded over time. Jesus taught that we know a tree by the fruit it bears and we know doctrine by the fruit it bears (Luke 6:43-44). Consequently, sound solid doctrine is necessary from a teacher.

History is filled with churches which have degenerated over time. Even the Catholic Church which Protestants decry so greatly and which reached the depths of weakness during the Middle Ages did not begin as a cult, despite the claims of some. It is not uncommon for some to argue that the Catholic Church was "created" by Constantine or Gregory the Great or some other individual, but a true student of history knows that the doctrine of the church changed slowly over a period of a thousand years until finally the Protestant Reformation forced the church to re-examine itself. I will not pretend that the Catholic Church is wholly reformed, for it continues in many doctrinal errors. The point is merely this. As time passes doctrine becomes polluted. Like the tree which bears good fruit, good doctrine will stand the test of time. Bad doctrine decays. Even atheists understand the importance of schooling. As they have taken control of the National Education Association and the production of school textbooks students have increasingly been taught moral relativity and agnosticism. Teachers carry the future in their words, and so whether we teach the truth or a lie bears impact upon the future generations of the church.

Miracle Workers and Healings

Notice how workers of miracles is placed lower than apostles, prophets, and even teachers. Some wish us to believe that miracles are "proof" that someone is an apostle. They want us to think that miracles authenticate someone's ministry (an error made by both charismatics and cessationists). In fact, miracles, like tongues and other gifts, serve the people of God. We do not serve miracles but rather miracles occur by God's will for His people. The miracle worker is a servant of the church and its people, although it is significant that this word actually refers to a gift or power and not a person. It is literally "miracles," not miracle worker. Does this imply that there actually is no ministry of miracles, signs, and wonders? Miracles stand alone apart from an individuals calling. We are called to serve, not to work miracles. Miracles may accompany our ministries but we cannot build a ministry around miracles. This is not Biblical.

The same can be said of gifts of healings. Like miracles the healings are not specifically identified with a person or calling but are gifts given to some individuals within a ministry. There is no "faith healer" spoken of as if it were an occupation. There is only various ministries and ministers, of whom some have gifts of healings. Again the healings may accompany a ministry but do not appear to be a ministry in and of itself.

Helpers

What are the "helps"? The Greek word αντιλημψεις (*antilempseis*) stems from the root word λημψις (*lempsis*) meaning to "to lay hold of"[418] or "receive."[419] Αντι (*anti*) then shifts the meaning from "receiving" to "giving." It is rendered then as "aid"[420] or "helper."[421] Many beleive that because Paul is speaking of service in the church, this must refer to some church office. Thayer believed that this referred to the duties of deacons,[422] but no such titles are associated with this. Nor can we assume that a specific church office is intended here anymore than we would assume that those who speak in tongues held a specific church office of "tongue speakers." Helpers are those who render aid and assistance, possibly like the seven men elected in Acts 6:5. In fairness, however, many scholars believe that the seven were, in fact, deacons. This is one argument used in favor of the designation here. Against this argument is the fact that Paul mentions deacons and overseers in his epistles, but does not mention either one here in Corinthians where we would expect the titles to be found. This is further support that Paul was not establishing a hierarchy, but expanding on his illustration of the body. *Every* part of the body has a duty. This is not about church offices but about *all* the church members, who are a part of the body. Furthermore, one final piece of evidence that deacons are not intended here is the fact that administrators (listed after helpers) are probably the only reference to actual church governors. Helpers would then be separate from the church government.

Adminstrators

What are the "administrators"? The Greek word is κυβερνησεις (*kuberneseis*) which is often translated as "government" (KJV, Douay Rheims, ASV, RV, etc.). Its root word means "the ability to lead,"[423] hence the NLT translates this as "leadership." Some believe that these administrations "properly denote *ministries*."[424] Others see it as the "preacher's office,"[425] arguing that "the Holy Spirit has developed the *gift* of preaching."[426] However, the general nature of the term suggest that Paul is placing most church offices together. Church ministries, the deacons, pastors, and elders probably all fall under this category.

What is most interesting is that these governing bodies within the church are listed just above tongues. If apostles were "first," prophets "second," teachers "third," then it appears that Paul is listing these in order of their importance. The church governments then fall below teachers, miracles, healings, and helpers. Consequently, while the importance of the local church and its elders, deacons, pastors, etc, should not be minimized it does appear that Paul is far from establishing a hierarchy as many believe. If he is, then bishops and other church officials would be near the bottom of that hierarchy! Once again I am reminded of Jesus's words, "if anyone wants to be first, she shall be last of all and servant of all" (Mark 9:35) for "the last shall be first, and the first last" (Matthew 20:16). So as Jesus became a servant, so we should be servants to one another.

Speakers of Tongues

There is a reason that Paul lists tongues last. The Corinthians were obsessed with the idea that tongues proved their great spirituality and Paul wanted to make sure they knew that tongues was among the least of the gifts. He repeated mocks the Corinthians for their super spiritual attitudes. The nature of tongues, however, is discussed in greater depth below. It is sufficient to say that tongues goes beyond what was experienced at Pentecost and Paul does warn the church leaders not to forbid tongues (14:39). He only wants the Corinthians to understand tongues and keep some semblance of order in a church which had apparently lost order.

The Dispensing of the Gifts

A final issue in chapter twelve is one very controversial to some sects within the Pentecostal church. Now in fairness the Pentecostals have often been falsely accused of teaching that you have to speak in tongues to be saved. This allegation, however, is false and based on a misunderstanding of their teaching. Pentecostals believe that speaking in tongues is a sign of "being filled with the Spirit" which they generally hold is distinct from being born again. Consequently, many Pentecostal sects hold that speaking in tongues is proof that a person is "filled" with the Spirit and those who do not speak in tongues are not "filled" even though we too have the Holy Spirit. The problem is that Paul seems to irrefutably reject his teaching. Let us examine the relevant passage and its meaning.

> "All are not apostles, are they? All are not prophets, are they? All are not teachers, are they? All are not *workers of* miracles, are they? All do not have gifts of healings, do they? All do not speak with tongues, do they? All do not interpret, do they? But earnestly desire the greater gifts. And I show you a still more excellent way" (1 Corinthians 12:29-31).

These verses illustrate three undeniable points. First, not all believers speak in tongues. This is accepted even by most Pentecostals. Not all are apostles, not all are prophets, not all speak in tongues. Lest some doubt this, the Greek makes it clear that the rhetorical questions asked by Paul all end with the answer "no." According to one intermediate Greek textbook, "since rhetorical questions do not expect an answer, the presence of ου or μη in the initial position ... indicate either an affirmative statement or ... a negative statement."[427] In other words, if a sentence begins with ου then we would translate the question "are not all ...?" If, however, the sentence begins with μη then it is translated "not all are ... are they?" The μη indicates a negative answer. Consequently, the answer to all these rhetorical question in 1 Corinthians 12:29-30 is "no."

Second, *all* believers have some gift. No true believer lacks the Holy Spirit and the Holy Spirit gives to all in some way. Third, tongues is spoken of as a lesser gift. "Earnestly disire the greater gifts" (12:31). Tongues is also listed last among the gifts (12:10) and the gifted (12:28). Clearly tongues is not to be counted among the "greater gifts."[428]

When we put all three of these facts together we are left with the inescapable conclusion that tongues cannot be proof of the filling of the Spirit for how can one have a "greater gift" than tongues and not be filled with the Spirit? *Everyone* has a gift. Not everyone speaks in tongues. Tongues is among the least of all the gifts. The conclusion is obviously that tongues cannot be a sign for all "spirit-filled" believers. Some believers speak in tongues, but speaking in tongues does not prove the speaker to be greater, more spiritual, or more "filled" with the Spirit than those who do not. On the contrary, if all have different gifts then it clear that some have gifts greater than tongues without ever having spoken in tongues.

Conclusion

Everything that God does in us is through the Holy Spirit. Jesus works in us through the third person of the Trinity. By definition then everything that is good in our work is gift of God. The gifts of God work in us all until the "perfect" comes (1 Corinthians 13:10), but what is the "perfect"? This is a great controversy indeed and it is answered in 1 Corinthians 13.

Have the Gifts Passed?
1 Corinthians 13:1-13

> "If *there are gifts of* prophecy, they will be done away; if *there are* tongues, they will cease; if *there is* knowledge, it will be done away."

There are two extremes in the Christian church. On the one hand are some sects within the charismatic movement who think of this age as the same as the apostolic age. They envision modern day apostles working signs and wonders and performing great miracles and faith healing services weekly. On the other extreme is a sort of reactionary theology which counters this belief with the doctrine that the gifts of the Spirit (or at least many of them) passed away in the first century and existed only in the apostolic age.

Here Paul clearly says that "if *there are gifts of* prophecy, they will be done away; if *there are* tongues, they will cease; if *there is* knowledge, it will be done away. For we know in part and we prophesy in part" (13:11-12). He then

94

concludes that "when the perfect comes, the partial will be done away" (13:13). In other words, when "the perfect" comes there will be no more need for the imperfect. This is surely the most controversial of all passages in this chapter for this seems to infer that the gifts of the *Holy Spirit* are imperfect!

Let us again look at each passage separately and distinctly so that we may put them together contextually, for as the saying goes, "a text without a context is a pretext."[429]

The Passing of the Gifts

Paul begins by stating simply that the gifts will pass away at some time in the future. At this point he does not indicate when; only that it will happen. However, some have tried to imply that the Greek does indicate time, at least in regard to tongues. John MacArthur, for example, argues that "the Greek middle voice ... [indicates a] reflexive, self-causing action"[430] and thus that "God gave the gift of tongues a built-in stopping place."[431] In more simple terms, it is argued that the Greek middle voice is used with tongues, but not prophecy or knowledge, and that this means "that tongues will cease of themselves. There is something intrinsic to their character that demands they cease – apparently independently of the cessation of prophecy and knowledge."[432] Is this true?

Paul, in making his point, uses prophecy, tongues, and knowledge as examples. "If *there are gifts of* prophecy, they will be done away; if *there are* tongues, they will cease; if *there is* knowledge, it will be done away" (13:8). The fact that prophecy and knowledge both use the same word, while tongues uses a different word in the Greek middle voice is often used to argue that tongues "stopped long ago."[433] Ronald Baxter claims that it "means that the action will come from within, rather than from without ... a fair translation might be, 'tongues shall make themselves to cease.'"[434] Furthermore, the alleged substitution of the word "*to cease*, become silent"[435] in place of "done away with" used in conjunction with prophecy and knowledge also is supposed to indicate the same. While this argument may sound tempting at first, it has many problems grammatically, exegetically, and logically.

Let us begin with grammar. The Greek middle voice cannot be used to imply any "ceasing in its itself" for no other reason than that the word is *deponent!*[436] In simple words, it is an irregular word which commonly appears in the middle voice even when active voice is intended. D.A. Carson cites Luke 8:24 as an example where Jesus commanded the raging waters to "stop."[437] This is the same word in the middle voice, but obviously the waters were not stopping by their own momentum. Jesus commanded them to stop! Consequently, it is poor grammar and exegesis to interpret the middle voice as proof of cessationism.

Second, the reason that Paul prefers "cease" to "be done away with" is simply good writing. To use the same word in all three places would be redundant and poor writing. They are essentially synonyms. No theological implications can be drawn simply based on the choice of "cease" over "done away." Moreover, contextually the "ceasing" of a gift proves nothing in regard to time. If one wanted to make such an argument then they would be better served following Origen's curious intepretation when he said that "'tongues will cease' when I express what I want to say with my mind."[438] Hence Origen concluded that the gift passes away at the moment that the prophecy, knowledge, or tongue has ceased to be spoken! He then believed that the gifts would never cease in history.

Logically, this sentence cannot be isolated from the next sentence. It is that sentence that gives this passage its context and meaning. According to Paul, "we know in part and we prophesy in part; but when the perfect comes, the partial will be done away" (13:9-10). This is the "payoff." Prophesy reveals *part* of the truth. Not even Moses understood all that Jesus was to do. He prophesied in part. Knowledge is likewise in part. Moses had revealed knowledge of God and His Law, but he did not have full knowledge of all of God's plan. He had revealed knowledge of part of God's plan; the giving of the Law and the preparation of a kingdom of priests (Exodus 19:6). Later revelation unfurled the larger plan of God. So Paul is making clear that knowledge, prophecy, and tongues are not complete in themselves. When the "perfect" comes there will be no more need for imperfect, or incomplete, gifts. The gifts point to the "perfect" but are not perfect in themselves. What then is the "perfect"? This is the debate upon which the various factions fight.

The "Perfect"
How we define "the perfect" will define our theology of the gifts to a large degree. Over the centuries there have been three dominant views. The most recent one, and one of the most popular today, is that the "perfect" refers to perfect revelation and therefore the canon of the Scriptures. With the closing of the canon and the death of the apostles and their immediate followers, it is argued there is no more needs for the spiritual gifts (or at least many of the gifts). A second view, arguably the most popular in history, is that the "perfect" refers to heaven. A third view is that it refers to the physical presence of our Lord Jesus on earth in either the Millennial Kindgom or the New Earth (Revelation 20-22). Each view deserves to be discussed individually.

View #1 : Canon of the Scripture
The view dominant among cessationists is that the perfect refers to the canon of Scripture. The argument is that the word "perfect" can also mean "complete" or "finished." Consequently, if prophecy is "partial" in nature, then the "complete revelation" is the Scripture itself.[439] Baxter says that partial revelation is done away with when "it is superseded by the perfect, the complete content of the relvation of God in the scriptures."[440] *Liberty Bible Commentary* adds that "tongues would be 'cut off' as the necessity in the process of New Testament revelation ceased."[441] All these cessationists have in common the

belief in particular that "sign gifts" belonged in a special way to the infancy of the church and no longer exist.[442]

Once again the argument sounds convincing until one examines it closely. Baxter himself admits that even the Scriptures will be superseded "when we meet Christ, according to 1 Cor. 13:12 and we shall be given perfect understanding of all things as opposed to knowledge 'in part' now, even with the Canon of the Holy Scriptures before us."[443] Thus he has effectively negated the majority of his argument. Even Dallas Theological Seminary (which teaches cessationism) professor David Lowery concedes that "verse 12 makes [the Canon] interpretation unlikely."[444] What does 13:12 say? According to Paul, "now we see in a mirror dimly, but then face to face; now I know in part, but then I will know fully just as I also have been fully known." Thus this verse completes the thoughts of verses nine and ten where he is speaking of knowledge and prophecy "in part." It is "face to face" when the partial is replaced by the complete.

Dan Mitchell, a cessationist himself, summarizes the problems with this view when he says, "it cannot be a reference to the completion of the canon of Scripture, since this would imply perfect knowledge in this age. Furthermore, not even the Word of God, which is a mirror, wherein we now behold the glory of the Lord (2 or. 3:18) can compare to seeing Him face to face (cf. v. 12)."[445] So the key to understanding "the perfect" is in relation to verse twelve. What is meant by "face to face"? Two streams of thought remain.

View #2 : Heaven

It seems apparent that when Paul speaks about meeting "face to face" he is referring to the physical presence of the Lord. He is saying "when we see the Lord 'face to face.'"[446] The question is, *when* will we see the Lord "face to face"? It is argued that "the natural interpretation is, to refer it to the future life"[447] but what future life? We are left with three options, which I have divided into two; eternal and/or temporal. In other words, it either "refers to heaven"[448] or it refers to the Second Advent. Alternately, a third view could be that it refers to the New Earth of Revelation 21:1, but this is really an expansion of the Millennial Kingdom into eternity, or the bringing of heaven to earth depending on one's perspective. So we are left with deciding whether or not Paul is speaking of heaven or the *parousia* (Second Coming).

The heaven view is arguably the most popular, earning support from men like Matthew Henry[449] and Charles Hodge,[450] among countless others. Certainly there is an element of truth in this view, for when we meet the Lord "face to face" in heaven we shall have attained that completeness of which Paul speaks, but contextually the argument does not fit. Paul is not speaking of death and resurrection here, but of eschatology. He talking about the plan of God. What is the purpose for the gifts of the Spirit? This was Paul's dialogue. Given that context we should examine the final view in greater detail before deciding.

View #3 : The Millennial Kingdom

The *parousia* or Second Coming is a major theme of Paul throughout his epistles. One author says, "he is so full of the thought of the Second Advent, that he represents this perfection as coming to us."[451] If we are to meet Jesus "face to face" and He will be physically present with us on the earth, then this, it is argued, must be the completion or perfection to which Paul alludes. What need is there for imperfect partial knowledge when the Lord is present in the flesh? So sure of this was Calvin that he, in his usual uncharitable way, said, "it is stupid of people to make the whole of this discussion apply to the intervening time" between the first and second comings.[452]

Ultimately both the second and third view are valid, for if we die before the Second Coming then we shall see the Lord "face to face." Perhaps it is for this reason that Paul is somewhat ambiguous. Nevertheless, the larger context seems to refer to eschatology, and hence the presense of our Lord in the flesh at the Second Advent. It is best therefore to read the Millennial Kingdom but allowing for the intervention of death or rapture when we too shall meet the Lord face to face. The canon of the Scripture is the best that we have in this age, but it is still partial knowledge compared to the full complete knowledge we shall have when the Lord is present with us "face to face" (v. 12).

Other Cessationist Arguments

In addition to these passages cessationists have created a number of other arguments. Since most of those arguments are not exegetical, but rather theological I felt a brief examination of the arguments would best fit here. The reader should bear in mind that not all cessationists hold to these arguments.

Miracles in the Bible

One common argument used by cessationists is the belief that miracles in the Bible only took place in connection with the times of Moses, Elijah and Elisha, and the time of the apostles. Some cessationists amend this argument slightly, accommodating for "minor" miracles elsewhere, but even with this emendation the argument is seriously flawed.

Without even mentioning the miracles laced throughout Genesis, we see in Joshua miracles galore. From the parting of the Jordan river to the fall of Jericho's walls to the sun standing still, we see miracles taking place. Indeed, some might consider the sun standing still to be the greatest miracle in the whole of the Bible! Should we forget the miracles of Gideon, Samson, or even Jonah and the great fish? Did not time fall backward in the days of Hezekiah (2 Kings 20:9-11)? What of Daniel? Have we forgotten about Shadrach, Meshach, and Abednego in the fiery furnace? Or Daniel in the Lion's den? Are these not miracles?[453] Surely to claim that miracles were restricted to Moses, Elijah, Elisha, and the time of the apostles is not only untrue, but wretched exegesis.

H.A. Ironside, a dispensationist, commented that "some insist that some of these gifts have absolutely disappeared, but I do not know of any Scrpiture that tell us that. I do not know of any Scripture that say that the age of miracles has passed and I would not dare to say that the sign gifts all ended with Paul's imprisonment. I know from early church history that this is not true ... I do, however, believe that many of them are not often seen today and I think there is good reason for that."[454] The reason, he argued, is because the Church has strayed from the purity of early church.[455] In other words, miracles require faith. Jesus said "if you have faith the size of a mustard seed, you will say to this mountain, 'Move from here to there,' and it will move; and nothing will be impossible to you" (Matthew 17:20), but no one has ever had that kind of faith. Even Peter wavered when walking on water. Is there anyone today who is truly as faithful and righteous as the apostles, or Moses, or Elijah? This alone is reason to doubt self proclaimed prophets and apostles of this day. We do not need to read into the Bible what is not there.

A Dispensational Argument?

By no means are all dispensationalists cessationists. On the contrary, many are not (myself included). However, some dispensationalists make a "dispensational" argument in regard to the gifts of the Spirit. They argue that miracles were "authenticating" aids to prophets and apostles and that they are no longer needed in this dispensation. This is akin to the argument, discussed above, which relates the passing of the gifts to the canon of Scripture but differs in that it derives its arguments from the belief that "Old Testament prophets" no longer exist. The unspoken assumption is that the New Testament of grace somehow negates miracles in the present age. That this argument is flawed not only Scripturally, but also from a sound dispensational theology, is apparent in that they must make the Tribulation found in the book of Revelation an entirely different seven year dispensation, rather than making it the end of the present dispensation.

This entire line of reasoning is flawed on several levels. First, consider that Peter applied the prophecy of Joel to the whole duration of Last Days from the First Coming to the Second (Acts 2:16-22). Second, are the apostles to be considered "Old Testament saints"? Some will actually debate this very question because they have created an artificially defined barrier between the Testaments (see *Controversies in the Acts of the Apostles* on "Establishing the Church"). Bear in mind that I am a dispensationalist, but I reject such rigid artificial designations which are built on theology rather than exegesis. God has established programs, covenants, and dispensaions with man which all lead toward the reconciliation of man to God (Colossians 1:20), but these should not be artificially or rigidly distinguished. For example, are those who have never heard the gospel still under the law of conscience (see notes on Roman 2:11-16)? Has God restricted Himself so that He cannot work miracles through

His followers today? If so, then perhaps this should be called the dispensation of deism.

Finally, stemming from this same assumption is the straw man argument. Cessationists will cite the hundreds of phony miracles performed by hucksters, frauds, and false prophets, but this is the same logic flaw used by the critics of Jesus (cf. Matthew 9:34). Just because there are false prophets and false signs and wonders (cf. Matthew 24:24) does not negate all signs and wonders, nor all miracles. There will always be more false prophets then true prophets and more false miracles (cf. Exodus 7:22) than true miracles. Proving a negative does not prove a positive. That is a logical flaw.

The Hypothetical Argument

One final argument, which employs exegesis, albeit suspect exegesis, in the hypothetical argument. It is that because Paul speaks "*if* I speak with the tongues of men and of angels ... *if* I have the gift of prophecy" (13:1-2) then the "if" is purely hypothetical, meaning that Paul is not recognizing these are real gifts for today, but rather emphasizing a hypothetical argument.[456]

While this theory at least has the benefit of some form of exegesis, it is poor exegesis. As done elsewhere in the Bible, some use the word "if" to negate the entire purpose of Paul's argument. The point is not that something is impossible, but that it is not essential to whatever the argument is based upon. In other words, here in Corinthians Paul is not saying the gifts of the Spirit do not or shall exist in a short time, or he would not have previously defended the gifts. Rather he is pointing out that the Corinthians lack love which is far more important than tongues or even prophecy! Clearly Paul is not denying the gifts do and shall continue to exist for some time, for in 14:1 he urges these same Corinthians to "earnestly seek the greater spiritual gifts, but especially that you may prophesy." This would be a strange plea indeed if prophesy was intended only for the formation of the Biblical canon, for no Corinthians ever wrote a single word of the Bible!

Conclusion

The doctrine of cessationism is a relatively recent doctrine which appears to have been developed in reaction against the rise in religious cults, "signs and wonders" ministries, and false prophets. The early church fathers, while by no means charismatic in nature, appeared to all accept the validity of the gifts in this age. Tertullian said, "we acknowledge spiritual *charismata*, or gifts, we too have merited the attainment of the prophetic gifts."[457] He accepted all gifts as valid.[458] Irenaeus, who was second generation disciple of John, also did not deny the gifts.[459] It is uncertain when cessationism arose although it may have existed as early as the Reformation.

Regardless of when it arose, it is suspect exegetically. Paul's emphasis is upon love. He does not negate the gifts, but emphasizes their incompleteness. Christ completes our knowledge and gifts. The spiritual gifts of today are partial because Christ is not with us in the flesh. Never does Paul indicate that the gifts are soon to pass away, but rather than they will become unnecessary when we meet the Lord "face to face" (13:12).

True cessationism is the sin of deism. It denies that God intervenes the affairs of man, even today. It paves the way for the very secular myths of the modern age. Why then, asked the critic, are there so few true miracles and so many false prophets, signs, and wonders? First, it is suspect that true miracles were ever the majority. False prophets and false signs always existed even in Jesus's day and in the days of Moses when the court magicians attempted to emulate Moses's miracles. However, there is a second reason, and a better one. As Ironside once commented, there are fewer true miracles and gifts today for the simple reason that we have strayed from the purity of the early church.[460] How many men have ever had the faith of Moses or Elijah? How many men today can claim without hypocrisy to have the faith of Peter or Paul? Yet even Peter denied Christ and began to sink in the sea (Matthew 14:29-31). I would be arrogant and a liar if I claimed to have the faith of Peter. I have performed no great miracles because I am a faithless man, and so it is true of our generation, but this does not mean that God cannot or does not perform miracles even to this very day. He does and he shall continue to do so until Elijah returns and calls forth even greater miracles from God (cf. Matthew 17:11).

Tongues in the Church
1 Corinthians 14:1-40

"Now I wish that you all spoke in tongues, but *even* more that you would prophesy; and greater is one who prophesies than one who speaks in tongues, unless he interprets, so that the church may receive edifying."

Having defended the validity of gifts in the modern age, it is now necessary to examine Paul's restrictions upon those gifts. Yes, Paul does restrict the use of gifts in the church! Why? He does not forbid tongues (14:39), but he does place restrictions upon it. Moreover, the very nature of tongues in Acts is among the great controversies in the Pauline epistles, for it does not appear to be related to the tongues of Acts at all ... or does it? Even this is debated. What is the purpose for tongues? What is its proper use in the church? All these issues are debated among theologians today. So once again it is best to break down the issues piece by piece and examine them individually before putting all the pieces together.

What is the Nature of the Corinthians' Tongues?
Some have argued that tongues is defined only in Acts. Others that the tongues of the Corinthians cannot possibly be the same as that in Acts. Some see tongues as a heavenly language, some as an ecstatic language of praise, others

101

simply as a "a gift of speech."[461] At this point only the nature of tongues will be debated, not its purpose; i.e. is it an edifying tool or an evangelical tool?

Tongues in Relation to Acts

Some have assumed that because the book of Acts is the only place where we see tongues practiced in a historical context, this must be the only real definition of tongues to be found in the Bible. Since "the gift of speaking in tongues in the book of Acts appears to have been limited to speaking in 'known languages' (cf. Acts 2:4; 10:46; & 19:6)"[462] it is then assumed that this tongues must be the same thing spoken of here in Corinthians. This argument is, of course, logically flawed and can be proven incorrect.

The most obvious proof that the tongues of Corinthians cannot be that of Acts is the fact that in 1 Corinthians 14 requires a translator or interpreter be present (14:28) whereas the book of Acts required no such translator or interpreter because "each one of them was hearing them speak in his own language" (Acts 2:6). Another interesting fact overlooked by these expositors is the fact that 1 Corinthians 14:10-11 (where foreign languages are clearly referenced) uses the Greek word φωνη (*phone*) whereas the other references to "tongues" use the word γλωσση (*glossa*).[463] Hence, Paul may be deliberately distinguishing the two things here in Corinthians to avoid confusion.

Finally, Paul says of the tongues in Corinth "one who speaks in a tongue does not speak to men but to God; for no one understands, but in *his* spirit he speaks mysteries" (14:2). This appears almost the polar opposite of the tongues found in Acts where the apostles were clearly speaking *to men* in their own languages (Acts 2:6). In Acts the tongues appears to be for evangelistic purposes. In Corinthians the tongues appears to be a form of prayer.

If there are then two different forms of tongues in the Bible, it is essential to distinguish between the two. That will be done below under "The Purpose for Tongues." This section will merely endeavor to define what the natire of the tongues in Corinth are, and what they are not. One thing is clear. The tongues of Acts cannot be used as the exclusive form of tongues. There is obviously something different about the tongues spoken of here in 1 Corinthians.

Tongues as a Heavenly Language?

Another view, common among some charismatics, is that tongues is actually a "heavenly language." They reject the idea that these are foreign languages and argue that this is a heavenly language. This is based upon 1 Corinthians 13:1 which allegedly speaks of the "tongue of angels." I say allegedly, because it actually reads, "if I speak with the tongue of men and of angels, but do not have love, I have become a noisy gong or a clanging cymbal." Does this really imply that angels have their own language?

Some have argued that Revelation 14:2-3 hints at an angelic language, but the actual passage is about a song which is impossible to sing for any but the elect. It is not unimportant to note those elect are men, not angels. The passage reads, "they sang a new song before the throne and before the four living creatures and the elders; and no one could learn the song except the one hundred and forty-four thousand who had been purchased from the earth" (14:3). Consequently, outside of 1 Corinthians 13:1 there is no indication in the Bible that angels have a distinct language. However, Jewish *apocrypha* and *midrash* may hint at such a belief.

The so-called "Ascension of Isaiah" has sometimes been cited as a parallel,[464] but the text is actually more parallel to Revelation 14:2-3 for it is about angels singing before the throne of God. Once again, there is nothing in the passage to imply a distinct language for angels. Nevertheless, the "Testament of Job" is a much more clear parallel to 1 Corinthians, but it is also ironic for it may shed more light upon Paul's meaning rather than lending credance to the belief in a heavenly tongue. Let us examine the passages in question. According to the "Testament of Job" 11:24-28:

> "And she sang angelic hymns in the voice of angels, and she chanted forth the angelic praise of God while dancing. Then the other daughter, Kassia by name, put on the girdle, and her heart was transformed, so that she no longer wished for worldly things. And her mouth assumed the dialect of the heavenly rulers and she sang the doxology of the work of the High Place and if any one wishes to know the work of the heavens he may take an insight into the hymns of Kassia. Then did the other daughter by the name of Amalthea's Horn gird herself and her mouth spoke in the language of those on high; for her heart was transformed, being lifted above the worldly things. She spoke in the dialect of the Cherubim, singing the praise of the Ruler of the cosmic powers and extolling their glory."

This apocryphal writing may or may not have pre-dated Paul, but it does reflect a belief that may have existed in Paul's days. Nonetheless, while it does imply that angels have different dialects, it is significant to note that it is once again in the context of singing songs of praise. Note then that in Revelation 14:2-3, the "Ascension of Isaiah" 7:15-37, and here in the "Testament of Job" *all* the passages relate to angels singing before the throne of God. Of these only the "Testament of Job" truly indicates that angels have a different dialect or language. What does this mean? Contextually, it is the singing of praises before the Lord. In 1 Corinthians the Paul is speaking about tongues which appears to be related to prayer and/or praise (14:2, 15). Consider verses 14:14-15. "For if I pray in a tongue, my spirit prays, but my mind is unfruitful. What is *the outcome* then? I will pray with the spirit and I will pray with the mind also; I will sing with the spirit and I will sing with the mind also." What is Paul saying? Is he saying that they are praying and singing in the "tongues of angels"? No, but he does draw a "hyperbole" from this.[465] "*If* I speak with the tongue of men and of angels, but do not have love, I have become

103

a noisy gong or a clanging cymbal" (13:1). Paul may be alluding to a tradition common in his day, but the passage does not prove that angels have a different language. The question then must be asked, "Is there evidence that angels *do not* have a different language?"

John Wesley argued that "one language shall prevail upon all the citizens of heaven"[466] but such a statement does not prove *what* language. Indeed, this statement, and true it is, actually contradicts the "Testament of Job" which gives different dialects to different classes of angels. Of course, most Jews believe that Hebrew is the language of heaven. Regardless of whether or not this is so, the best argument against an angelic language distinct from any on earth is the very line of reasoning which Paul employs. If tongues were the language of heaven then "Paul could hardly have said that they will stop."[467] While D.A. Carson calls this argument "pedantic"[468] it is hardly pedantic when the entire line of reasoning for Paul is that our heavenly state with Jesus will render all gifts, tongues is named especially, invalid. We will not need to prophecy for Jesus will be present to tell us what is so. We will not need incomplete knowledge for Jesus will give us complete knowledge. We will not need partial wisdom for Jesus will give us full wisdom. We will not need tongues for there shall be only one language in heaven. If tongues meant "angelic language" than this last statement would be ridiculous!

Let us look lastly at a handful of other views. Matthew Henry, for example, saw the "tongues ... of angels" merely as a metaphor for speaking with "the greatest propriety, elegance, and fluency ... like an angel."[469] This is also the view echoed by Matthew Poole.[470] Erasmus appeared to see tongues solely as foreign language, rejecting the idea of a heavenly language.[471] This seems best. Paul is employing a kind of hyperbole to emphasize that love is superior to any of the gifts of the Spirit. Nowhere in the Bible do angels speak in an angelic language and it is probably they speak one of the same languages which humans speak, such as Hebrew, but this does beg the question. If the tongues of Corinthians is not the same as that of Acts and it is not a heavenly language then what is it?

Tongues as an Ecstatic Language of Praise?

There is one other view of tongues related to the "heavenly language" view, but often separate from it. Some see tongues as an "ecstatic language" of praise based on 1 Corinthians 14:14-16.[472] This differs from the "heavenly language" primarily in that they see the "escatatic language" as a unique language which only the speaker and God can understand. It is "communing with God."[473] Now while this view is often times the most ridiculed, there is some merit it. Let us look first at its strengths.

To begin with "verse after verse shows that speaking in foreign tongues cannot be meant."[474] I have already concluded that the tongues of 1 Corinthians cannot predominantly be the same as that of Acts. Since I have also rejected the idea of a "heavenly language" on might assume that this is the only option left. One author argued that since the tongues of Acts is clearly different from that of the Corinthians "what was spoken of as the gift of tongues at Corinth was an ecstatic utterance."[475] However, this is inference at best. Just because view A or B is false does not automatically lead to the conclusion that view C is true. There may be another view, or perhaps A and B are both partially true. Maybe A, B, and C are all in error or all partially correct. To argue a positive from negatives is another logic flaw.

Slightly stronger support comes from the parallels in Revelation 14:2-3 as well as the *apocrypha* cited above. In each of those instances prayer and/or praise was being used and in several of those instances only the one worshipping appears to have been able to sing. Revelation 14:3 states that "no one could learn the song except the one hundred and forty-four thousand who had been purchased from the earth." Could this not imply an "escatatic language" known only to God and the worshippers?

F.F. Bruce said that "the picture of the whole church assembling (cf. 11:18) suggests that a Corinth *glossalalia* was not so likely to be a feature of private devotion as a manifestation of group fervour."[476] While this is possible, the emphasis upon prayer hints at something personal. In either case, there is no doubt that the tongues of 1 Corinthians 14 are connected in some way to prayer and worship. 1 Corinthians 14:14-15 clearly speaks of both praying and singing. In both cases the Spirit is contrasted the mind. This implies two things. First, the tongues of Corinthians is connected with praying and/or singing "in the Spirit." Second, this same tongues is not equated with the mind. They are distinct from one another. Despite this Paul makes it clear that "the spirits of prophets are subject to prophets" (1 Corinthians 14:32). The Holy Spirit is not like demon possession in the movies. We have control over the gifts which God bestows upon us. Consequently, the use of tongues is subject to the user.

Now having said this the question remains, why is there a need for an interpreter (1 Corinthians 14:27-28)? Indeed, how can there be an interpreter at all if this is a secret language between God and the one praying/singing? This is the main flaw in the argument. Paul explains that an interpreter must be present so that the entire congregation may be edified by the tongues (cf. 14:17 and 14:26-28). This would obviously imply an edifying purpose for tongues which does not fit in well with the theory of ecstatic praise. What then is our answer?

Ultimately how can we choose between foreign language, a heavenly language, and an esctatic language unless we first clearly understand the purpose for tongues? To this end we must understand the purpose for tongues in Corinth. Since Paul and the Corinthians were both aware of what was going on, and we are not, this task is more difficult than at first might be imagined, but it is not impossible. A close study may reveal some clues.

The Purpose for Tongues

Beginning in verse twenty-two Paul debates the effect and purpose for tongues on the believer and unbeliever. He begins with his conclusion, saying:

> "So then tongues are for a sign, not to those who believe but to unbelievers; but prophecy *is for a sign,* not to unbelievers but to those who believe" (1 Corinthians 14:22).

Much controversy revolves around the question of how signs are a sign for unbelievers. Indeed, Paul himself states that "if the whole church assembles together and all speak in tongues, and ungifted men or unbelievers enter, will they not say that you are mad?" (14:23). Such was the state of the church of Corinth and many charismatic churches today. Paul then states, "let all things be done for edification" (14:26). So tongues then are for edifying unbelievers, but how?

The *Liberty University Bible Commentary* suggest that "its purpose was to demonstrate divine power to the unbeliever,"[477] but this is just a restating of the facts. It does not answer the question at all. *How* does it demonstrate divine power? The tongues of Acts is clear in that the apostles were witnessing the gospel to unbelievers in their own language. Once again, however, the tongues of Acts cannot be the same as that of Corinth for there was no interpreter required at Pentecost. In fact, an interpreter would have defeated the entire purpose for tongues at Pentecost!

Lenski offer a different explanation. He claimed that "unintelligible tongues, like the unintelligible language of the Assyrians in Judea, have a certain effect upon unbelievers,"[478] and yet this too is an ambiguous remark. What "certain effect" does this have and why?

Tongues for the Jew?

The answer may be found in Paul's quotation of Isaiah 28:11. It says, "He will speak to this people through stammering lips and a foreign tongue." Paul's paraphrase is "by men of strange tongues and by the lips of strangers I will speak to this people, and even so they will not listen to me" (1 Corinthians 14:21). This passage is significant because it connects the tongues of Corinth with the prophecy of Isaiah. It differs, however, from the tongues of Acts for there "each one of them was hearing them speak in his own language" (Acts 2:6). No interpreter was necessary. Here an interpreter is required (14:26-28). What conclusions can we draw from this?

John MacArthur believes that tongues was a sign "specifically unbelieving Jews."[479] He says, *"the gift of tongues was given soley as a sign to unbelieving Israel"*[480] (emphasis in original). It is on this basis that me makes his cessationist argument, but logic is flawed. For one thing, Israel still exist. Jews still live. If tongues was *solely* for Israel, which is debatable, then we

106

cannot no more say tongues have ceased than we can say that Israel has ceased to exist. Let us look at the cessationist argument in more detail.

The *Liberty Bible Commentary* argues that "tongues would be 'cut off' as the necessity in the process of New Testament revelation ceased."[481] This however assumes that tongues somehow served the same goal as the New Testament revelation. This is suspect. Evangelism is certainly one of the reasons for tongues, as seen in Acts and 1 Corinthians 14:22, but we still evangelize today. Moreover, we cannot dismiss the use of tongues for prayer and praise (cf. 14:15). This too is *one* of the reasons for tongues. Consequently, the canon of the New Testament is not related to the use of tongues. Attempting to tie the two together is an impossible task, so Ronald Baxter argues that tongues ceased in 70 A.D. when the Romans destroyed the Temple.[482] This argument is no better, especially since Israel was been restored in 1948. If tongues is tied directly to the existence of Israel then logically tongues would have returned along with Israel. The argument is therefore inadequate, faulty, and derived from eisogesis rather than exegesis.

Tongues for the Gentile?

Another argument for how tongues can be a sign is a negative inference. It has been argued that "many pagans practiced speaking in other tongues"[483] and hence to see believers speaking in tongues would provide a negative reaction from Jews unless an interpreter translates what is said. While this may be true an extent, it again fails to explain exactly how tongues is a sign to unbelievers about Christ. If pagans spoke in tongues, then how does the Christian speaking in tongues benefit? Perhaps it is similar to Joseph and Daniel's use of dream interpretations. As the pagan kings all had dream interpreters who were incapable of interpreting Pharaoh's and Nebuchadnezzar's dreams, the true man of God was able to interpret and declare the glory of the Lord. Thus, this argument is actually stronger than the previous ones, but only if we reject that tongues was "soley a sign to unbelieving Israel."[484] Was it?

There is no doubt that the tongues of Acts was evangelical in nature, proclaiming the Word of God and Christ to all the nations in their own tongue. However, all the people at Pentecost were clearly Jewish or Jewish proselytes. Does a proselyte constitute a part of Israel? Or does Acts prove that gentiles were part of the target audience? What of Corinth? The population of Corinth was predominantly pagan. In fact, it is that pagan influence which had obviously corrupted the church of Corinth.

The truth is that tongues is never mentioned in the Old Testament except for a few prophecies and John Calvin actually claimed that Paul's quotation was "recontextualing" it![485] He believed that the prophecy did not really relate to the events of Corinth at all. Many believe it is a prophecy of gentile believers or an ambiguous reference to the church, for we are proclaiming the gospel in foreign (strange) languages and yet Israel still does not believe! Thus Paul's application of this prophecy to Corinth was one of analogy according to Calvin.[486]

Now the point of all of this is that the practice of tongues was foreign to Israel. It is a practice found only in the New Testament (excluding, of course, the prophecies concerning it). It is therefore suspect to argue that tongues was a sign solely to Israel as MacArthur believes, and yet all of this still leaves us with the same unanswered question. *How* is tongues a sign?

Summary

The key to understaning the sign is in Paul's quotation of Isaiah 28:11. The actual passage in Isaiah is simply "He will speak to this people Through stammering lips and a foreign tongue." It is prophecy about the Babylonian captivity. Hence the foreign tongue is that of the Babylonian language. God is "speaking" to the Jews through Babylon by using Babylon as a punishment for Israel's idolatry. Paul is thus using this passage somewhat liberally in saying that God is speaking to the Jews *through* gentiles. Consequently, both sides are partly correct here. It is not that tongues was a sign specifically to either Jews or gentiles *per se*, but that the expansion of the church unto gentiles of foreign and strange tongues was a sign to the Jews. God's favor has never left Israel, but has now been extended to the gentiles.

In the context of tongues then the best answer seems to be that of my analogy to the Pharoah and Nebuchadnezzar. Tongues was something known to the pagans of Greece, but to hear men praising Jesus in tongues was unknown to them. If true then it would serve as a sign to them that Jesus was real and the spirit is subject to Him. However, without an interpreter the pagan would not know if Jesus was being praised or cursed. The unbelieving Jew would then see God's favor being bestowed upon gentiles, and be convicted of unfaithfulness, stirring his heart.

If all of this seems a bit confusing, then the reader will understand why Paul was concerned with the mass confusion which the church of Corinth was creating in unrestrained services. This is why Paul instigated rules and regulations upon the use of the gifts in a church service. By bringing some order to the use of gifts in church, the gifts themselves performed an orderly service. It also indicates that the gifts are under the control of the believer (1 Corinthians 14:32). They are gifts to help us, not to control us. It is still within our power to obey or reject God's will.

Regulations on Tongues in the Church

Based on 1 Corinthians 14:23 Paul believed that unrestrained tongues would leave the unbeliever dismayed and even "turned off."[487] The church would appear to be more like a madhouse than a place of worship. To this end Paul wanted order in the church.

1 Corinthians 14:27-35 are all about order in the church. Paul's commands include three things. First, the number of people speaking in tongues is limited to three and they must take turns, each being interpreted. If there is no interpreter then they must remain silent (14:27-28). This passage also indicates that tongues may be for a person to "speak to himself and to God" (14:28). This supports the prayer theory above, but also indicates that public tongues is neither essential nor edifying. If the tongues are for prayer than it should probably be a private affair.

The second regulation is that at most three prophets may speak a revelation, but even then another prophet must make a judgment on their revelation to see if it is truly from God (14:29-33). This is significant. For one thing, a false prophecy was generally punishable by death in the Old Testmanet (cf. Deuteronomy 18:20).[488] Here there is no law, but by letting others pass judgment upon the revelation Paul is indicating that false prophecies existed even among the early church; perhaps even by well meaning believers! Since Paul's topic is order in the church, he does not elaborate so it is best not to infer too much from the words "pass judgment," but it is clear that the church is expected to judge the truth and value of the revelation; not to accept it blindly.

Third, women are forbidden from public speaking in the church assembly (14:34-35). Since I discuss this separately the reader is referred to that debate on the ensuing pages. Here it is important only to note the context; order in the church.

The first thing that should be noted is that most of the problems which cessationists have with some modern charismatic and pentecostal sects would be completely eliminated if churches followed these regulations. Alternately, another rule is found in 1 Corinthians 14:39 where Paul says, "do not forbid speaking in tongues." This indicates that there were those, like the modern cessationists, who opposed the use of tongues in church at all. Paul, however, does not want us to forbid tongues. Thus the regulation Paul imposes upon the Corinthians, if practiced today, would eliminate both extremes; charismania and cessationism.

Conclusion

As the reader can see, this is a difficult issue and there good reason for it. Tongues is mentioned briefly in only two books, Acts and 1 Corinthians. In neither place does tongues occupy a large portion of the dialogue and the relationship between the two is slightly more than nominal. It is dangerous to build an entire theology around a small handful of passages as is done by both cessationists and many charismatic sects.

From my study I have tentatively reached the following conclusions. First, tongues is usually a foreign language not previously known by the speaker. This is certainly the case in the book of Acts. In Corinth the purpose and use of tongues is different, leaving the door open for escatatic praises, but even though the use is different, the probability is high that the tongues of Corinth was also a foreign language.

Second, tongues served multiple purposes in the early church. In Acts it was obviously a tool for evangelism. As missionaries have ventured out into the world this use of tongues has become more infrequent since we have worked to study world languages and reach out to them. Furthermore, tongues served other purposes besides evangelism. In chapter fourteen it is connected with both prayer and praise (14:13-15). I have also likened tongues to the dream interpreters of Pharoah and Nebuchadnezzar. Pagans had their fraudulent imitations, but God provided true interpreters in Joseph and Daniel. It is possible that tongues may have served a similar purpose since pagans also had fraudulent tongues.

Another important factor is the context; particularly that of the tongues at Pentecost. Pentecost signalled the coming of the Holy Spirit. So also the "Samaritan Pentecost" (see notes on Acts 8:15-17 in *Controversies in the Acts of the Apostles*) signalled the Holy Spirit's descent upon gentiles. Consequently, tongues appearance at Pentecost does not prove that this would be a frequent event. It was obviously not a one time event, but neither can it be said, as some have, that it accompanies all baptisms for Paul makes clear that tongues "were not conferred on all alike"[489] (cf. 1 Corinthians 12:30). To draw a cessationist conclusion from this would also be in error. Nevertheless, we cannot assume that tongues was to be the norm, for it is rarely mentioned even in apostolic times.

Next, Paul equates the use of tongues with the Spirit but then contrast it with the mind. He further states that "the spirits of prophets are subject to prophets" (1 Corinthians 14:32). The Holy Spirit is not like demon possession in the movies. We have control over the gifts which God bestows upon us. Consequently, the use of tongues is subject to the user. As one commentator summarized Paul's remarks, "speaking intelligibly, and to the edification of the church, is of more value than the power of speaking a foreign language."[490]

From this we may conclude that the gift of tongues may be more infrequent but not that it has passed away. Should churches obey the rules and regulations which Paul has here established then most of the problems and debates between extreme charismatics and cessationists would disappear. Simply following the Bible thus resolves a great many difficulties.

Prophecy and the Believer
1 Corinthians 14:22

"Prophecy *is for a sign,* not to unbelievers but to those who believe."

Unlike tongues, prophecy is said to be a sign for believers. Considering that the nature of prophecy is often to predict a future event, this statement surprises many, but it should not. Prophecy has often been ridiculed in Hollywood movies and the main stream media. The nature of prophecy is that it is something hidden from unbelieving eyes. In fact, that is what the word prophecy means. It is literally something hidden being revealed. This is why the prophecies of the crucifixion so clearly found in Isaiah 53 are dismissed so easily by the unbeliever. The meaning remains hidden until God reveals it to your heart.

It is also of importance to note that not all prophecy involves the foretelling of future events nor the writing and compilation of the Scriptures. This is evident in several ways. First, note that Philip's four daughters were all said to have been prophetesses (Acts 21:9) and yet there is not a single record or mention of any prophecies they gave. This is inexplicable according to the view that prophecy is a foretelling of future events to be recorded in the Bible. Obviously this is not the case in Acts 21:9.

Some have considered that prophecy is merely a proclamation of God's words. In one sense this is true, but only in the lower sense for we all proclaim God's word if we are being faithful to the Great Commission. No, as discussed under 1 Corinthians 12:4-21 a "prophet is a messenger, as it were, between God and man,"[491] but he is a messenger on the highest order. Godet considered prophecy to be the "first rank" of gifts.[492] What is significant, however, is that Paul desired that the Corinthians would prophecy; "especially prophecy" (1 Corinthians 14:1, 39). Now who ever heard of a prophet from Corinth? What prophet in the Bible hailed from Corinth or even Greece? Thus prophecy cannot be restricted to the canon of Scriptures. It cannot supercede the canon of Scripture, but it would be inaccurate to restrict prophecy to that recorded in the Bible. Prophecy is a communication between God and man, and God never contradicts himself. Any "prophet" who contradicts God's word in the Bible is a heretic and false prophet of whom Jesus warned us many times (cf. Matthew 7:15; 24:24; etc.). The sincerity of the prophet is irrelevant.

So prophecy is a message directed at those who have opened their hearts to the Lord God. The unbeliever will simply dismiss the prophecy and interpret it in an ambiguous manner as false prophets and mystics often do. The prophecy of the Bible is supreme and the standard by which all self proclaimed prophets must be weighed. However, it is of interest to note that most of the Biblical prophets never once called themselves prophets. Humility is one of the marks of a true prophets. John the Baptist denied being a prophet (John 1:21), as did Amos (Amos 7:14), and yet both were among the greatest of prophets so beware of self proclaimed prophets who seek to deceive or magnify themselves. A true prophet points to Jesus. A false prophet points to himself.

Women in Church
1 Corinthians 14:34-35

"The women are to keep silent in the churches; for they are not permitted to speak, but are to subject themselves, just as the Law also says."

This passage is actually the third regulation in a series of regulations about order in the church. The first two restrict the use of tongues and prophecy to an orderly fashion. Now no one suggest that prophecy is "inferior" or degraded because Paul placed restrictions upon its use in church. Here however there is a great controversy over Paul's views of women; especially women in the church.

Views have varied vastly over the years. Some believe that this merely reflected "cultural norms"[493] while others argue that "this rule is positive, explicit, and universal. There is no ambiguity."[494] The problem with both extremes is apparent. On the one side, truth is never effected by "cultural norms." Although cultural norms may be a factor in public life, *truth* is never subject to cultural approval. On the other side, Philip's daughters were prophetesses (Acts 21:9). Likewise, women were allowed to speak and preach the gospel by Paul in certain circumstances. 1 Corinthians 11:13-15, for example, refers to public prayer by women in the synagogue. There is nothing to indicate that Paul or the apostles barred women from ministry *per se*. In fact, it is apparent that some did serve in ministry. So it seems that neither extreme provides a good explanation.

Let us examine both sides more closely. On the cultural side, it is generally believed that men and women were separated in synagogues during the service. Based on 1 Corinthians 14:35 it is then argued that Paul was urging women not to ask questions of their husbands during the service.[495] "If they desire to learn anything, let them ask their own husbands at home; for it is improper for a woman to speak in church" (1 Corinthians 14:35). This is the view of men like John MacArthur who says that "certain women were out of order in asking questions in the church service."[496] While this argument has some merit, it does not seem to be the most logical answer, for it is hard to imagine women standing up and shouting across the room to their husbands, and yet this would be the picture we would have to believe. Certainly the segregation of men and women would have created some problems, which may be in part what Paul has in mind, but the image does not seem realistic.

The other extreme may seem "sexist" to a modern society, but that judgment is ironically influenced just as much by "cultural norms" as the former view. Motherhood is not inferior to fatherhood. In some ways it is superior to fatherhood. The differences between men and women should never be restricted to genitalia as the modern feminist desires. However, it is true that some have interpreted this beyond gender roles in a "sexist" manner. Albert Barnes

112

believed that women are "prone to the vice of garrulousness" and hence "an unseemly disturbance [might] arise."[497] Consequently, he saw this simply as a part of Paul's desire to see order in the church. Upon this same line of reasoning, the anecdote of Licinius Buccio has been circulated. Lincinius was a Roman woman who was so contentious in court that in 48 B.C. Rome made a law barring women from pleading cases for themselves.[498]

The church father Tertullian believed "that women should be under obedience"[499] but prefaced this by making clear that obedience to God is primary. He believed that women occupied an important role "but he does not want women to teach or baptize."[500] Erasmus called "this rule is positive, explicit, and universal."[501] The idea is that "what was recorded in Genesis is not a temporary arrangement" but applied to the church as well.[502]

Now between these two "extremes" (if they are that) is another view. This view acknowledges that men and women have different roles. One role is not inferior to another, but they are different. Consequently, it is argued that "although Deborah was reputed to be a prophetess, there is no indication that she ever corporately addressed the people."[503] In other words, *speaking in the Church* ... can only designate a public speaking."[504] As John Wesley said, Paul was only forbidding "teaching in public assemblies."[505] Women were allowed to prophecy and to participate in various ministries but "it is obvious that the apostle regards speaking in public as an act of authority exercised over the congregation."[506] As Hodge said, "it is only the public exercise [in church] that is prohibited."[507] Ironside believed that it referred only to "regular service."[508]

One final view should be addressed. A minority opinion is that "this must be interpreted in light of 11:15 where it is clear that Paul understand that women were permitted to prophecy and to pray in public worship so long as they were properly dressed. The expression may have reference to speaking in tongues."[509] However, it is unlikely a reference to tongues. In fact, the subject of tongues had not yet even been mentioned by Paul! Tongues was discussed in chapters twelve through fourteen. So this view is not viable.

The best view is that Paul is prohibiting public Biblical teaching by women where men are present. This is consistent with Paul's views in 1 Timothy 2:12 and elsewhere. The other views either exceed Paul's command or find ways to dismiss them. Women can be prophetesses and hold other prominent roles in ministry, but they cannot publicly teach the Bible in a church to men (see notes on 1 Timothy 2:12).

1 Corinthians 14:39 – See 1 Corinthians 14:1-40

"According to the Scriptures"
1 Corinthians 15:3-4

> "Christ died for our sins according to the Scriptures, and that He was buried, and that He was raised on the third day according to the Scriptures."

Critics have mocked this passage, saying that there is no such prophecy "according to the Scriptures." In fairness, even many Christians often wonder where the prophecy of the third day resurrection may be found, for there is no explicit prophecy, and yet the Jews themselves acknowledged that such a prophecy existed. Indeed, there was a certain false messiah, Simon of Perea, mentioned by both Tacitus[510] and Josephus,[511] whose followers believed he would be resurrected in three days time. This prediction is confirmed in the "Hazon Gabriel" or "Gabriel Revelation" inscription which dates to the end of the first century B.C.[512] Hence it is clear that the ancient Jews believed that such a prophecy existed even before Jesus was born! Where then is this prophecy to be found?

Beginning with the first part of the verse, John Calvin stated that Christ's death for our sins is "plainly" seen in Isaiah 53, Daniel 9:26, and Psalm 22.[513] All Christians acknowledge this. Skeptics are referred to my *Controversies in the Prophets* if they doubt these prophecies. Other passages which allude to the death and suffering of Christ include Genesis 22:8,[514] and Ironside even sees an allusion in Leviticus 17:11.[515] The more controversial question is one of the resurrection prophecy.

Regarding the prophecy of a resurrection in general, without regard for the time frame, several passages are cited. Psalm 16:10 is cited in the Book of Acts twice (2:27; 13:35). It says simply "You will not allow Your Holy One to undergo decay." Now the critic argues that this is a metaphor to King David himself, but this is certainly not how the Jewish *midrash* interpreted it, for "Holy One" is used by the Jews as a name for the Messiah and the *Septuagint* translates the meaning as *hosios* (ὅσιός), meaning one "undefiled by sin, free from wickedness, religiously observing every moral obligation, pure, holy, pious."[516] The apostle Peter took this passage quite literally, saying, "David ... was laid among his fathers, and underwent decay, but He whom God raised did not undergo decay" (Acts 13:36-37). Surely this was "foretelling the resrruection of Christ."[517]

What then of the third day? Where is this prophecy? The most commonly accepted passage is Hosea 6:2. The problem is that this prophecy seems to allude to the resurrection of the state of Israel rather than the Messiah. However, there is good reason to believe that this was a dual prophecy. Such dual prophecies are common in the Bible. In dual prophecies there is usually a "near future" application and a "far future" application. The one is often by way of allusion; the other a more literally application. In this case it appears that the

Jews of old long expected a literally application to the Messiah. Not only did the followers of at least one false Messiah, Simon of Perea, claim he would be resurrected in three days, but the very fact that Caiaphas asked Pilate to place guards at the tomb of Jesus on the third day (cf. Matthew 27:63) indicates that the Pharisees were aware of this prophecy even if the disciples did not yet understand it! More importantly, Luke records that when "He opened their minds to understand the Scriptures ... He said to them, 'Thus it is written, that the Christ should suffer and rise again from the dead the third day'" (24:45-46).

John Singer Sargent – Frieze of the Prophets – 1895

That Hosea refers to Christ's resurrection has been accepted by Christian theologians from the earliest of times. From Cyprian[518] to Lactantius[519] and onward to Reformers like Matthew Henry[520] and and the Catholic Church,[521] Hosea is interpreted as a dual prophecy. The proof that this is not mere Christian reinterpretation is found in the Jews' anticipation of a third day resurrection as far back as the first century before Christ, as shown in the "Hazon Gabriel" inscription,[522] and up to the very day that our Lord was risen from the grave.

What is Baptism for the Dead?
1 Corinthians 15:29

"Otherwise, what will those do who are baptized for the dead? If the dead are not raised at all, why then are they baptized for them?"

Undoubtably one of the most debated passages in the whole of the Bible is this passing reference to the "baptism for the dead." Many evangelicals completely reject the concept of a vicarious baptism for the dead while

115

Mormons practice vicarious baptism to this day.[523] In fact, while Paul alludes to a practice which was apparently commonly known to the church of Corinth, he does not engage in debate on the subject, but alludes to it as proof that the resurrection of the dead is commonly accepted even in the practiced rituals of some of the Corinthians.

As to what this ritual was, there are allegedly as many as thirty different views,[524] but most are derivations of one another. Six dominant views have been offered over the centuries. The first view I call the Moniker view. According to this theory "the dead" is a moniker for the Messiah, Jesus. In other words, they are baptized for Jesus (i.e. the Dead One). The second view is what I call the mortician view. This one argues that this is an allusion to the practice of washing and purifying a dead body before burial. The "baptism" is thus not literal. A third view argues that the phrase "baptism for the dead" is actually an idiom for those who have died in persecutions. We are said to be baptized with fire in the persecutions. A fourth view is what I call the Translation view. According to this the passage must be translated in some other way to diminish the obvious implications. Fifth, it is argued that "the dead" refers to our death to sin and resurrection unto the new life. It alleges that Paul is merely alluding to "the hope and expectancy of a resurrection of the dead."[525] Finally, there is the highly controversial theory of vicarious baptism for the dead. Each deserves special individual attention.

The Moniker View
One intriguing, but wrong, view is that "the dead" is a moniker, synonymous with a title, like "the Dead One." In this case "the Dead One" would allegedly be Jesus. So it is argued that "'baptized for the dead' really means, 'baptized for Christ who died.'"[526] Jonathan Edwards, who seems to waver between this view and the Martyrdom view (see below), phrases it best by saying, "they themselves had baptized for Christ. And if Christ be yet dead, what will they do? ... if ... Christ is still dead, why would they go to be baptized for the dead?"[527]

Now while this is intriguing in its ingenuity, it is also completely wrong. First, as Ironside noted, "the word 'dead' is in the plural and therefore cannot refer to Jesus."[528] Whomever the "dead" are, they are more than one. It would not be "the Dead One" but "the Dead Ones." Second, and most importantly, Jesus is *not* dead. Jesus was resurrected from the dead. This is Paul's entire point. The *entire* subject of chapter fifteen is the resurrection of the dead and the victory of Christ over death. Paul insures us that the dead in Christ will be raised even as Christ was raised and those of us who are still alive at the coming of the Lord will be transformed into the resurrected flesh (see 1 Corinthians 15:50-54). Consequently, to suggest that Paul's brief allusion to the practice of "baptizing for the dead" refers to Christ as a "Dead One" is borderline blasphemous, and certainly poor exegesis. We must look for another option.

The Mortician View
Another unique view passed down through the ages is what I call the "Mortician view." According to this Paul is referring to the Jewish practice of washing and purifying a dead body before burial. Theodore Beza believed that Paul was talking about "those who bathe the dead before burying them."[529]

The problem with this argument is multifaceted. For one thing, how could Paul compare this practice to baptism? To call it baptism is more than a stretch. Furthermore, how does such a practice contribute to Paul's argument? Paul is either endorsing a Christian ritual that relates to Christ or he is mocking a non-Christian ritual that is inconsistent with their worldview (see below). The first cannot possibly apply here and neither can the second. It seems that this theory is really just a way of trying to avoid the problems associated with the other views, but exegetically and logically it does not fit the text nor was the view one accepted by the early Church Fathers whom we assume would have understood the context better than a medieval scholar like Beza.

The Martyrdom View
One popular view through the ages has been the application of this passage to persecution. Some call it a "baptism of blood."[530] Like the previous views, this is more the product of ingenuity than exegesis. There is nothing in the context to imply that Paul is talking about persecution. The context is, again, about the resurrection of the dead. What logical connection could persecution have to Paul's discussion? Let us look at the passage, substituting the word "persecution" for "baptism for the dead" and see if it makes sense.

> "Otherwise, what will those do who are persecuted? If the dead are not raised at all, why then are they persecuted for them?"

Notice, the first part makes some sense, but the second part makes none. The argument falls apart. Persecuted for whom? Persecuted for "them"? Who is "them"? Clearly *they* are the dead. It is a practice of baptism *for* the dead, whomever they may be. Persecution does not seem to fit here.

Although apparently supported by such great men as Jonathan Edwards (but he also favored the Moniker view)[531] the fact is that Paul uses no such words as "baptism of blood."[532] He is drawing an argument either about consistence in logic or about a ritual practiced among the Corinthians (or both). This view too must be rejected.

The Translation View
Various scholars have tried to get around the problems of this verse by rendering suspect translations. Gleason Archer, for example, argues that "as older

Christians fell terminally ill and it became apparent that their departure was near, they would summon their loved ones to their bedside and urge those of them who were as yet unconverted to get right with God" and be baptized.[533] He then argues that "the preposition *hyper* is intended to mean 'for the sake of' rather than 'on behalf of.'"[534] Ergo, he claims that this should be translated "baptism for the sake of the dead."[535] Now this fanciful argument may sound good, but it is in fact very weak.

First, conversion to Christ is not and should not be to make someone happy. If I "convert" to Christ because it makes them happy (e.g. to fulfill their death bed wish) then I have not converted at all. Nor is there any evidence of such a thing happening in Corinth. This is pure speculation which could actually imply that they were baptizing faux believers. Second, the Greek preposition ὑπερ (*hyper*), meaning "for," carries the usual meaning of "on behalf of" or "in place of." "For the sake of" is a viable translation given a specific and clear context, but given Archer's rather extravagant proposition, it seems apparent that the context is not obvious in this regard. Paul is talking about the resurrection of the dead. Conversion as a favor for a dying man hardly fits this context.

Other have tried similar ways to retranslate the passage. Linski, for example, argued that they were "baptized with a view to the dead."[536] Such liberal translations allow for wider interpretation, and hence allow the interpreter to get around the thorny problem of "baptism for the dead," but proper exegesis is not concerned with getting around problems but solving them. We must look elsewhere for a solution.

The Christian Baptism View
One of the most popular arguments is that "the dead" refers to the one who is baptized.[537] In other words, it is the spiritually dead.[538] John Calvin said it is those "who are looked upon as already dead."[539] I.e., as Ironside put it, we are "baptized in place of dead ones."[540] Others differ slightly from this, arguing that Paul is explicitly referring to "the hope and expectancy of a resurrection of the dead"[541] as symbolized in the Christian institution of baptism. It is possible to split hairs in regard to these interpretations, but they all have in common that they believe Paul is alluding to the Christian institution of baptism.

John MacArthur believes that "those who we baptized" must be synonymous for Christians,[542] but he then argues that the dead are "deceased believers whose lives were a persuasive testimony leading to the salvation of the baptized."[543] So he is merging the Martyrdom view with the Christian Baptism view, but while it is true that baptism symbolizes the death and resurrection, the statement by Paul goes beyond the death and resurrection of Jesus. This is why MacArthur has attempted to merge the Martyrdom view in with this theory. In so doing, however, he has not merged the two views' strengths but has actually taken the weaknesses from both views and merged them together. If "baptism for the dead" were a mere phrase for Christian baptism then it is unlikely that such controversy would have emerged from it. Indeed, the earliest church fathers rejected this view. Why should Paul's simple allusion be so controversial if it was, in fact, a common phraseology for the symbolism of baptism? Moreover, while MacArthur says that "those who we baptized" must be synonymous for Christians[544] those words are nowhere to be found in Corinthians. If they were he would be correct, but they are absent. Instead Paul refers to "they" and "those" (15:29). It is not "we" who baptize, but "they" who baptize, indicating someone outside of the church, for Paul would have included himself among the church!

The biggest problem with this view is to be found in the very argument that John Calvin makes to defend it. He argued that it *should* be rendered "baptized for dead", rather than "for *the* dead."[545] The problem is that every single Greek text contains the definite article "the." Paul is not saying that baptism is for those of us who are spiritually dead and if he were then it would again loose connection to his discussion which is the resurrection of the actual physically dead! Paul is not speaking of a "spiritual resurrection" as some liberal theologians argue, but of a physical resurrection of the dead even as Jesus was *physically* raised from the dead. The comparison is same to same. It is of a like kind. Jesus was not raised "spiritually," for He was never spiritually dead, but He was raised physically from the grave. The grave cannot hold Him! "Death is swallowed up in victory. O Death, where is your victory? O Death, where is you sting?" (15:54-55).

The Vicarious View
One final view remains. It is the central reason for all the other views, for quite frankly all other views are merely attempts to get around the troublesome idea that Paul was alluding to the practice of vicarious baptism by proxy for those who have already died.

Numerous arguments have been made against this view. The most common is the assumption that "it is extremely doubtful that the apostle would have made reference to this heretical practice without, in the same breath, condening it."[546] John MacArthur even argues that "we can be sure ... that it does not teach vicarious, or proxy, baptism of the dead"[547] for this very reason, but this argument is probably the weakest argument. "Arguments from silence prove nothing."[548] Paul is not attempting to "chase rabbits" or get sidetracked, for all the Corinthians knew that the practice was heretical. Why then does Paul allude to it at all? Here is why, and it is again contextual. Paul is arguing against those who deny the resurrection of the dead. "This method of arguing against others from their own conceptions, is one the apostle frequently empoys,"[549] as Charles Hodge says. Paul is saying quite simply, "if there is no resurrection then what is the point of these cults baptizing on behalf of the dead?" It is a logical inconsistency. Paul employs this tactic throughout his writings, so it is hardly surprising that he should do so here as well, but how do we know that this is what he doing?

The most obvious evidence that Paul is not referring to Christian baptism is his repeated use of "they" and "those" (15:29). When referring to the church Paul always uses either "we" (including himself) or "you" if he chastizing the church of Corinth. This in itself demonstrates that Paul was neither referring to the church in general ("we") nor the church of Corinth ("you") but to some sect outside the church ("they").

That such a practice did exist is mentioned by many ancients such as Tertullian who condemns gnostic sects.[550] So also the Marcionite cult is condemned by Chrysostom for baptizing the dead.[551] Other church fathers who allude to the heretical practice include Gratius, Michaelis, Ambrose, and Didymus the Blind.[552] It is ironic indeed that critics of this view say there is "no evidence" of the practice before the second century. Since the New Testament was completed around 95 A.D. and Corinthians was written in the latter half of the first century it is odd that they acknowledge ancient support for the gnostic cults while arguing that this is evidence *against* such practices!

The fact is, to quote F.F. Bruce, "the *prima facie* meaning of these words points to a practice of baptism by proxy."[553] Nothing in the text suggest that Paul is supporting the practice but rather making "an allusion [to a] wholly unauthorized, and perhaps purely local, custom of having a *survivor baptized by proxy.*"[554] He is making a point about the resurrection of the dead and the gnostic heretics inconsistent practices. If they deny the resurrection then what is the point of baptism for the dead? These cults denied the resurrection and yet "baptized to take the place of those who had died."[555] This is Paul's only point. The hysteria regarding the view is misplaced and based on assumptions about what Paul would or would not say. On the opposint page is a chart in this regard. Let the reader make his own judgment.

Conclusion

John MacArthur declares that "this verse is one of the most difficult in all of Scripture,"[556] but why? The truth is that it is only difficult because the practice of vicarious baptism (which is the most natural interpretation) is heretical and some feel that Paul is silent upon this fact. They react against the notion that Paul might be endorsing a heretical practice. To that end as many as thirty different views have been offered,[557] including Martin Luther's theory that some members were "baptized over the graves of the martyrs."[558] The truth is that Tertullian, the church father, explained it best when he said, "never mind that practice (whatever it may have been)"[559] for the point is "'why are they baptized for the dead,' he asks, unless the bodies rise again which are thus baptized."[560] Paul is proving only that "those" who practice this ritual contradict themselves unless they acknowledge that the dead are resurrected. The entire purpose of chapter fifteen is that there is a resurrection of the dead. This is Paul's point, and this is all that Paul is interested in saying.

Chart on Vicarious Baptism for the Dead [561]

Weaknesses	Answer
The practice is superstitious.	This criticism assumes Paul is endorsing the view, although proof of this exist.
There is allegedly "no evidence" of such a practice before the second century.	The last book of the New Testament was complete at the end of the first century. Second century support is thus strong support given the scarcity of extra-Biblical first century authors.
It is a heretical practice.	As with the superstitious criticism, this assumes that Paul supported the practice, but contextually he was mocking it.
The apostle would never refer to such a practice without condeming it "in the same breath."[562]	Why? Would Paul engage in "chasing rabbits" or diverting from his point when the Corinthians knew full well (whether we do or not) that Paul rejected the practice?

Strength	Answer
Paul uses "they" and "those" rather than "we" or even "you," thus he is referring to those *outside* the church.	It is argued that this is a literary device of some kind and should not be taken too literally.
The context of the passage is a refutation of the gnostic's denial of resurrection. This fits with Paul making an allusion to a heretical gnostic ritual.	Some insist that Paul would still make more clear his disapproval, in case the church did not already know.
Paul often argues points by invalidating the critics' conceptions. It is a common tool in literary logic and criticism.	Some insist that Paul would still make more clear his disapproval, in case the church did not already know.
Paul would not get sidetracked or "chase rabbits." To do so is to loose an argument.	Some still say he would have at least condemned it quickly.

Rapture Defined
1 Corinthians 15:50-54

"We will not all sleep, but we will all be changed. In a moment, in the twinkling of an eye, at the last trumpet; for the trumpet will sound, and the dead will be raised imperishable, and we will be changed. For this perishable must put on the imperishable, and this mortal must put on immortality."

Chapter fifteen is entirely about the resurrection of the dead. Will we live again? To this end the logical question remains, "what of those of us who are alive at the coming of the Lord?" (cf. 1 Thessalonians 4:17). This is the subject of verses 50-58, and without regard to the *timing*, what Paul speaks of is universally called the *rapture*, to distinguish it from the Second Coming with which it is closely associated. This, however, is why the rapture remains arguably the most controversial doctrine among believers. Here in Corinthians Paul only explains the definition of rapture. Aside from a possible allusion in verse fifty-two, Paul does not address the issue of timing, except that it is connected to the coming of our Lord. I will therefore attempt to restrict my discussion to the definition of rapture alone and its meaning. The timing of rapture is discussed in 1 Thessalonians 4.

The word "rapture" comes from the Latin. The root word is found in the parallel passage of 1 Thessalonians 4:17 where Paul is talking about "we who are alive and remain will be caught up together with them in the clouds to meet the Lord in the air." The words "caught up" here in Latin is from the root word rapture. It is also found in the old Wycliff translation. Consequently, those critics who say that the word "rapture" cannot be found in the Bible are simply playing word games. It is a Latin word meaning to be "caught up." According to Paul the resurrected body of Jesus, and of all of the dead to be resurrected, will be immortal and imperishable. Although he calls it a "spiritual body" he also makes it clear that it has substance. It is not some disembodied ghost, but a real substantive glorified and immortal body.

Now the question Paul addresses here is in regard to those of us who "will not sleep" (15:51). Here "sleep" is agreed by all to refer to physical death, or the "first death." The second death is Hell which no believer shall endure (Revelation 20:6). Therefore, Paul refers to "first death" or physical death as "sleep" (cf. 1 Corinthians 11:30). This is universally accepted. In fact, some Latin translations actually read, "we shall not indeed all die, but we shall all be changed."[563] So Paul says that while not everyone will experience death, "we will all be changed" (15:51) from mortal flesh to immortal.

What does it mean to be changed from mortal to immortal? And what is the nature of this imperishable body? Some liberal churches have taken "spiritual body" to mean a disembodied spirit as often seen on Hollywood mythology or even horror films, but Tertuallian asked "if there is to be no flesh, how then shall it put on incorruption and immortality?"[564] He believed, as most have throughout the ages, that Paul is talking about an immortal but corporeal body of some kind. It cannot be compared to our earthly decaying bodies of "flesh and blood" (15:50), but it is real. So when John Wesley said "this animal body shall become spiritual"[565] he did not mean that our bodies would become disembodied spirits as so many of his modern day followers believe, but that the body itself would be incorruptable as Paul said. This, however, is the dilemma for many. If "flesh and blood cannot inherit the kingdom of God" (15:50) then how can we say that we will have bodies in heaven?

First, Paul explicitly says we shall have "bodies" (15:44). "Spiritual bodies" but bodies nevertheless. When Jesus was resurrected from the dead, the tomb was empty! "He is not here. He is risen!" (Luke 24:6). Too many confuse our physical mortal bodies with the heavenly resurrected bodies. The wife of my childhood pastor once mocked the resurrected saying that she did not expect a bunch of zombies to come crawling out of the ground! I did not respond to such an arrogant remark, but it illustrated her fixation with the material world as we know it. Jesus's mortal body was *transformed* into a new body. Although that body was Spiritual Thomas could touch it and feel it (John 20:27). It was capable of eating and drinking (John 21:12-15). However, it was not bound by earthly laws and was not subject to physical decay. Hippolytus, like most believers, said that the raptured bodies were the same as those resurrected from the dead.[566] Our bodies will then be transformed, even as Jesus's was, into a heavenly imperishable body. Our spirit will not be disembodied, but embodied in a new immortal one that transcends the concerns of our "flesh and blood" bodies. This is what Paul says and this is how he defines rapture.

When does this rapture take place? We know that it takes place in close proximity to the coming of the Lord (1 Thessalonians 4:17), but does Corinthians give us any hints as to the specific timing? John Nelson Darby, the famed pretribulational rapture treacher, said that "the moment of the raputre (ver. 54) is not in the scope of the prophets, and Paul merely states the fact, without time."[567] However, others believe that there is a time indication. Verse fifty-two mentions "the last trumpet." Some connect this to Revelation 11:15.[568] Certainly this trumpet is synonymous with the trumpet of 1 Thessalonians 4:16 as John Calvin believed,[569] but it is less clear whether or not Paul's trumpet should be connected with the seventh trumpet of Revelation 11. In fact, such a view would contradict the chronology offered by many of the same people who make this argument, for the seventh trumpet of Revelation does not take place immediately before Christ's return. It is likely at least a year, or more, before the return of Christ (see notes in *Controversies in Revelation*). Consequently, those who connect Paul's trumpet with John's in Revelation are inadvertently admitting that the rapture is separated from the Second Coming by at least a year!

When we look at the imagery of trumpets in the Bible it is clear that trumpets accompany the actions of angels. The trumpets are a signal for an angel to perform a duty (Cf. Zechariah 9:14; Revelation 8-9). In this case the trumpet signals the gathering of believers at rapture. In Revelation the last trumpet signals the release of the final seven plagues. While we cannot exclude the possibility that these are the same, the Bible declares that the sound of angels was "like *the sound* of a trumpet speaking" (Revelation 4:1). What then is the "last trumpet"? John does not even use the words "last trumpet" in Revelation at all. He mentions seven trumpets, but not a "last trumpet." Since angels all speak or sound with trumpets, it is not logical to assume that the seventh trumpet is the "last trumpet." We can only say that it is connected with "the last day" in some form.[570] This then begs the question, last day of what? The last day of this dispensation? The last day of the Tribulation? Both are viable possibilities at this point. Since Paul does not concern himself with a timetable here, it is pointless to speculate based solely on 1 Corinthians.

Interestingly enough, Ambrosiaster believed that the rapture would not take place until *after* the millennial kindgom of Revelation 20:6.[571] He placed the rapture immediately before the eternal kingdom of Revelation 21:1. So this speculation then leads us to one final argument. Some critics, and even some Christians "argue that Paul thought the world would end"[572] in his lifetime. They argue that Paul's "expectations about whether he would live until the Lord's return changed as he grew older."[573] This theory should be dismissed out of hand for many reasons, not the least of which is that Paul did *not* say "I myself shall not die."[574] Indeed, it is Paul who sought to calm those Thessalonians who believed that the end was already upon them (see notes in 1 Thessalonians 4:13-18). Such criticisms are designed only to make people question Paul's authority in the Scriptures. If Paul was wrong, then should we trust the Bible? Yet he was not wrong. He and Peter both taught that we should be prepared for His coming at any time, but that coming may not happen for thousands of years (cf. 2 Peter 3:8).

So in conclusion, Paul has spent all of chapter fifteen defending the resurrection of the dead; not just of Christ, but of us all. Even those of us who are alive in End Times when the Lord returns need not fear, for we shall be transformed from earthly decaying flesh into immortal heavenly bodies and those who have died before us shall be raised from the dead even as Jesus was raised from the dead.

1 Corinthians 16:2 – See Acts 20:7 in *Controversies in the Acts of the Apostles*

The Date and Occasion of 2 Corinthians

As can be deduced by 1 Corinthians, Paul's chastizement of the Corinthians indicates Paul's displeasure with the church at Corinth. 2 Corinthians may have been an attempt to smooth over relations with the church. Indications of the strained relationship between Paul and the church are found not only in Paul's critical tone of 1 Corinthians but in 2 Corinthians 7:8 and elsewhere. In fact, it is in 2 Corinthians 7:8 that Paul alludes to a "sorrowful" letter he wrote the Corinthians. There is much debate as to whether or not Paul is referring to 1 Corinthians or a third, now lost, letter. Was there a third letter by Paul to the Corinthians? If so, was it written before 1 Corinthians or after? This debate is reserved for 2 Corinthians 7:8. The point is that Paul's relationship with the Corinthians was not a smooth one. He was challenged and his authority questioned, but Paul did not give up on the Corinthians. He continued to try to guide them down the right path.

The exact dating of this second letter to the Corinthians is hard to decipher owing to so little information being available to pinpoint it. Obviously it was written after 1 Corinthians and before Paul returned to Jerusalem in 58 A.D.[575] Most place it around 56 A.D.[576] In any case, it was probably written not too long after 1 Corinthians, perhaps within the year, although it is possible that a couple of years had passed.

2 Corinthians 2:4-7 – See notes under 2 Corinthians 7:8

The Veil
2 Corinthians 3:13-16

"But to this day whenever Moses is read, a veil lies over their heart but whenever a person turns to the Lord, the veil is taken away."

Paul compares the unbelief of Israel to the veil of Moses. In Exodus Moses wore a veil when speaking to the people because his face shone with an aora from having spoken to the Lord (34:33-35). So the Jews could not see the glory of his face because he wore a veil. Paul then compares the unbelief of Israel to truth being hidden by a veil; a veil which is removed by Christ (3:14).

The debate here is over the extent of this comparison and what it means specifically for the Jewish people. To understand this we must break down the passage into its various parts. The first of these is the nature of the "veil" itself.

Jonathan Edwards believes that this "alludes to the custom of the Jews, which continues still in the synagogue. When the law is read, they put a veil over their faces."[577] Others see the *law* itself as a veil, arguing that Christian legalists also have the veil.[578] Origen simply called the veil is "a gross understanding, scripture itself is said or thought to be covered."[579] However, Paul expressly mentioned the veil of Moses which is in Exodus 34:33-35. The context of that passage is that the veil was to protect the eyes of the people from the residue of God's full glory, for Moses shone brightly after speaking with God. Consequently, the image Paul uses fits the context of this passage very well. The veil hides the glory of God, so in this context, the truth of Christ is hidden from their eyes when they read the very law that prophesied His coming! John Nelson Darby believed "they know not what they do" could be an allusion to this very veil, for they literally did not understand what they were doing.[580]

So the veil blinded the Jews to their own Messiah, but why and how is it removed? To the first question, John Wesley believed that "Israel could not look steadfastly to the end of that dispensation, which is now abolished."[581] A fuller answer is to be found in the prophecy of Isaiah 65:1 (cf. Romans 10:20). Jesus came not only for the Jews, but for all mankind. The gentiles, who did not seek God, would find Him, while the people of God (and such they are) stubbornly refused to recognize Him. This is the dispensation of the church age, but this is a debate that goes far beyond this passage, so I will refer the reader to my notes on Romans 10:18-21, Isaiah 65:1 in *Controversies in the Prophets*, and *Controversies in Revelation*. The important factor here is that the veil serves a purpose in history. The Jews had to reject Jesus in order that the gentiles might receive His blessings, but does this mean that the Jews cannot be saved or that Israel will not receive its promised blessings? Not at all! The veil will be lifted "when the Jewish people shall be converted."[582] It is "when Irsael turns once again to the Lord" that the veil will be removed and Israel will be restored to its proper place,[583] and yet this begs the very question. How *exactly* is the veil removed?

Erasmus said that the veil "is lifted by evangelical faith."[584] Warren Wiersbe says that it is "after they have been born again."[585] Charles Hodge also notes that it is turning to the Lord that removes veil,[586] and H.A. Ironside said the veil remains "until they turn to God,"[587] but all of these statements, true as they are, ignore the paradox of John Calvin. Yes, this passage is a paradox for the Calvinists and Armenians because it implies both predestined sovereignty and free will. This can be proved by quoting the Calvinists themselves.

John Calvin argued that Paul "lays the whole blame upon" the Jews[588] because the veil "is not removed because it is not done away through Christ,"[589] and yet Calvinists believe that the veil of prophecy was removed at first coming.[590] Calvinist Frederick Danker said that "this hardness of heart can be removed only through conversion to the Lord."[591] Now here is the irony. On the one hand the veil is placed over their hearts and "it is removed by Christ" alone (3:14). This fits the Calvinist narrative, but on the other hand "whenever a person turns to the Lord" (3:16) sounds more compatible with limited free will. This is futher supported by the next passage which explains, "the Lord is the Spirit, and where the Spirit of the Lord is, *there* is liberty" (3:17). But *liberty* means freedom! This is the paradox to which neither Calvinists nor Armenians will ever admit. Calvinists will say that it is God Himself who places the veil over their hearts, and yet in 1 Corinthians 4:4 Paul continues this line of discussion, saying, "the god of this world has blinded the minds of the unbelieving so that they might not see the light of the gospel of the glory of Christ, who is the image of God" (4:4). So God has permitted Satan to place the veil. He has not done so Himself. Instead, Christ removes the veil ... yet they cannot recognize Christ as long as they have the veil! What are we to make of this apparent paradox?

It is not my intention here to get into a protracted debate over Calvinism, but it is sufficient to say that God is not truly sovereign if He cannot give us certain choices. It is not total and complete freedom (and praise the Lord for this) but we do have certain freedoms, particularly in Christ. "Where the Spirit of the Lord is, *there* is liberty" (3:17). There is no contradiction between limited freedom and God's predestined sovereignty. There is a great contradiction between lack of freedom and sovereignty, not to mention the prevalence of evil and God's love if there is indeed no freedom. I will leave this debate at this stage, for it is only important to point out that where God intervenes in our freedom, there is a reason and a plan. What is that plan? Does Paul explain it here?

Paul does not explain God's larger plan at this stage, but has done so elsewhere; most notably Romans 10:18-21. Before the Messianic promises to Israel are fulfilled there was to be an intervening period during which we, gentiles, would receive God's blessings and salvation. This dispensation, the church age, is *not* to last. It is not eternal, although the blessings of salvation are eternal. Instead, in End Times the "times of the gentiles" (Luke 21:24) will come to a close and Israel will return to the Lord as a nation. God will bless Israel and keep all His promises to them as a nation. As the reader can see, this passage touches upon many issues. It touches upon the debate over dispensationalism, the salvation of the Jews, the redemption of Israel, dispensations and covenants, the extent of God's sovereignty, and the nature of free will. It is not hard to see then why the prophecy of the veil is so controversial. Paul is not trying to give a full discourse upon God's plan for the Jews, but rather he is trying to help the Corinthians to see the difference in the law and grace. In order to do this, he touches upon all these different issues without falling into the trap of becoming sidetracked. This is why Paul is sometimes so hard to understand and why his words are so often misrepresented (cf. 2 Peter 3:16).

2 Corinthians 5:21 – See Galatians 3:13

2 Corinthians 6:14 – See 1 Corinthians 7:1-16, 25-40

Third Corinthians?
2 Corinthians 7:8

"For though I caused you sorrow by my letter, I do not regret it; though I did regret it – *for* I see that that letter caused you sorrow, though only for a while –."

Here Paul refers to a letter he wrote that caused much sorrow among the Corinthians. Some believe that this is a reference to 1 Corinthians, but most modern scholars now reject that belief,[592] arguing instead that there is a "lost letter" Paul wrote between 1 and 2 Corinthians. Even though the letter preceded 2 Corinthians it is often called "Third Corinthians" for identification, but if such a letter actually existed it calls into question the nature and meaning of inspiration. Is there some "lost Scripture"? If so, how can we have faith that Scripture is inerrant if some of it is lost? If the letter was intentionally omitted from the canon by God then others ponder why a letter of Paul would not have been inspired. These are questions of interest to the inerrantist, and posed (dishonestly) by those who reject the infallibility of Scripture. How are we to answer these questions?

Was 1 Corinthians the "Sorrowful Letter"?

The view of Matthew Poole and many others at the time of the Reformation was that "the apostle doubtless meaneth the former Epistle to this church."[593] In other words, the letter that caused sorrow was 1 Corinthians itself. Most modern scholars reject this outright, arguing that 1 Corinthians does not fit the description found here.[594] However, it appears to this author that they dismiss it too flippantly. Let us consider the possibility.

There are really only two things mentioned in 2 Corinthians which give us a hint as to what was in this "sorrowful letter." The first is, of course, that it caused grief and sorrow (2:4-5; 7:8-10). Second, that it included instructions on the punishment of someone who had done a great wrong (2:4-7). Although a number of modern commentators assume that this man was the leader of an opposition party who opposed Paul,[595] there is nothing in 2 Corinthians to prove this assumption. Robert Gundry cites 2:5-10 but the description not only says nothing about politics or personal opposition to Paul, but indicates that the individual, whomever he was, should be taken back into the church and forgiven (2:7-8). This does not fit with a cult leader or opposition party, although it is possible that such a man could have repented. The better answer seems to fit with the older commentators, such as Matthew Henry, who believed that this was the same man Paul had cast out of the church in 1 Corinthians 5.[596] Although objections have been drawn to this argument, they are based on assumption. We cannot say definitively whether or not this was the same person as in 1 Corinthians 5, but we can say that 1 Corinthians 5 is the only place in the New Testament where Paul orders the church to take such harsh disciplinary actions. If there was a second, then this would be an anomoly to say the least. Moreover, the apparent repentance of the sinner not only gives us hope when we sin, but fits the context far better than a religious heretic who opposed Paul.

As to the first point, most modern scholars protest that 1 Corinthians is not "sorrowful" and would not have caused grief, but when they say this they say this as someone reading Scripture, not as someone who received the letter. I urge the reader to read through Corinthians on the assumption that it was written to you personally. The letter is quite harsh at times and critical of the Corinthians. Consider, for example, 1 Corinthians 3:1 where Paul begins by saying, "I, brethren, could not speak to you as to spiritual men, but as to men of flesh, as to infants in Christ." When we read this doctrinally, it makes sense. They were young immature believers. When we read this personally, it sounds condescending. I am a child? I am in infant who needs baby food (cf. 1 Corinthians 3:2)? Consider 1 Corinthians 5:2 where Paul says to them, "you have become arrogant." Or 1 Corinthians 14:36 where Paul mockingly asked, "was it from you that the word of God first went forth? Or has it come to you only?" These are a few examples of harsh words that none of us would take without feeling grief, sorrow, or perhaps even anger. Surely the Corinthians reacted in much the same way.

Nevertheless, it must be conceded that while 1 Corinthians is compatible with the "sorrowful letter" it cannot be proven. The strongest evidence on its behalf appears to be the excommunication of 1 Corinthians 5, for it is somewhat doubtful that Paul instigated such a punishment twice in the same church when he did not (to our knowledge) do so even once to any other church. It is for this reason alone that I am inclined to accept that Paul may have been referring to 1 Corinthians. Having said this, it is possible that 1 Corinthians is not the letter to which Paul referred. 2 Corinthians 12:8, for example, is often quoted as proof that Titus is the one who delivered the "sorrowful letter"[597] and yet Titus is not mentioned even once in 1 Corinthians. The evidence is simply not clear. Let us then look at some alternatives.

Is 2 Corinthians 10-13 the "Sorrowful Letter"?

In an age of modern "criticism," speculation has replaced objective analysis. Some have therefore suggested that 2 Corinthians 10-13 is a reproduction of the "lost letter."[598] The first question which comes to mind is, why does 10-13 follow 1-9 if it is truly a letter written before 1-9?

This theory first appeared on the scene around 1870 by a German scholar.[599] Like most of the then trendy scholarship of nineteenth century Germany, it is based on assumption, not fact. It is argued that the "harsh" tone of 10-13 fits the "sorrowful letter" and does not fit with the presumed conciliatory tone of chapters 1-9. It is also argued that Paul must have written from Ephesus (where the "sorrowful letter" was penned) because he refers to "the regions beyond you" which allegedly refers to Italy and Spain.[600] Since Italy and Spain are "beyond" Ephesus, the German rationalists conclude that Paul wrote from Ephesus, nevermind that Italy and Spain are in the "region beyond" everything east of them!

Evidence against this speculative theory are strong. First, no one is excommunicated in chapters 10-13. Since 2 Corinthians 2:4-10 clearly refers to someone cast out of church in the "sorrowful letter" the lack of anyone fitting this description in chapters 10-13 should alone be cause to reject this view. Second, it is ironic that those who insist that 1 Corinthians is not harsh or sorrowful believe that 2 Corinthians 10-13 is harsh. When we compare 10-13 to 1 Corinthians, this seems a stretch. Third, and most convincing, "12:18 mentions a previous visit of Titus, which must have been for delivering the sorrowful letter; but according to the theory of partition, 12:18 is itself part of the sorrowful letter!"[601]

Like most nineteenth century German scholarship the theory is nothing more than idle speculation which neither explains why 10-13 follow 1-9 if indeed it was written before hand, nor offers valid support for its claim. It is merely a part of the trend of the German rationalists to invent multiple authors and divisions in practically every book found in the Bible.[602]

The Lost Letter

A third view, and the most dominant among modern scholarship, is that the "sorrowful letter" is now lost and was written between 1 Corinthians and 2 Corinthians.[603] David Lowery, professor at Dallas Theological Seminary, believes that Paul actually wrote four letters to the Corinthians. The first letter, mentioned in 1 Corinthians 5:9 was actually the first one written around 53 A.D.[604] He then believes that 1 Corinthians was written not too long afterwards to address the questions sent by the Corinthians in response.[605] Next, he argues, was the lost "sorrowful letter" followed by 2 Corinthians.[606]

The evidence for the "sorrowful letter" being written between First and Second Corinthians is essentially simply the rejection of 1 Corinthians as the letter in question. If 1 Corinthians was not the "sorrowful letter" then the letter must be lost. Now it is to be conceded that 1 Corinthians 5:9 alludes to a previous letter written by Paul which is no longer in our possession. Consequently, whether or not the "sorrowful letter" of 2 Corinthians 7:8 refers to 1 Corinthians, as I suspect, or another lost letter, it is clear that there is at least one "lost" letter of Paul to the Corinthians. How does this effect the belief in the inerrancy?

Implications for the Inerrancy

Whether the letter mentioned by Paul in 1 Corinthians 5:9 or the allegedly lost "sorrowful letter" there is no doubt that we do not have every epistle written by Paul. The implications for this in regard to the inerrancy of Scripture are often hyped by Bible critics while fake heretical gnostic documents (usually dating no earlier than the second century) are sometimes distributed as "lost Scripture." However, the truth is that these documents, even if they were genuine (and they are not), are not and never were a part of Scripture. The Bible does not teach that the apostle Paul was inerrant or that Peter was inerrant. In fact, Peter greatly erred when he once taught that you had to be circumcised to be saved (see notes on Galatians 2:11-21)! The doctrine of the inerrancy applies solely to those writings which God acted to canonize in the Holy Scriptures.

Paul Feinberg once commented that the Bible itself distinguishes bewteen the authoritative Word of God and the fallible opinions of its human authors.[607] Evangelicals do not believe that men are infallible, but that God inspired godly men in such a way as to leave an infallible writing to guide us; the Holy Scriptures. The fallible epistles of Paul are lost. There is a reason they are lost. God chose not to preserve them. Should this "lost epistle" ever be found, would it be inerrant? No. It was *never* a part of the Biblical canon even when the letter still existed. I discuss the Biblical canon in the Appendix, but will summarize what I demonstrated there. The canon of the Bible was never formed by councils or the opinions of men. It came to be recognized in a way unparalleled in history. Only the hand of God can adequately explain why the near unanimous voice of history from the apostolic fathers to the latter church fathers all agreed upon what were the true Scriptures. Although some critics have attempted to cast doubt upon this, the fact remains that the twenty seven books which comprise the New Testament were predominantly accepted from the very beginning. "Third Corinthians" was never considered a part of canon even when it existed and its passing into history is further proof that it was never intended to be a part of God's Word.

Conclusion
Soon after Paul established the Corinthian church he had sent them a letter (1 Corinthians 5:9) which is now lost. The letter is of no consequence to the Scriptures as it was probably just a polite correspondence from Paul to insure that the church was progressing and to inquire if there were any problems. The reponse and its questions led to 1 Corinthians (cf. 1 Corinthians 7:1). However, 2 Corinthians 7:8 (also 2:4-10) mentions what some believe is yet another "lost letter." I believe that this is probably a reference to 1 Corinthians itself and not a correspondence written afterwards. In either case, the lost letters have no bearing upon the doctrine of inspiration for not everything in Paul's life was infallible or inspired. God preserved what was to be a guide for us through the ages and any works of apostles not found therein are of historical importance, but not Scriptural importance. God preserved what was necessary.

<h3 style="text-align:center">"Test Yourself"?
2 Corinthians 13:5</h3>

> "Test yourselves *to see* if you are in the faith; examine yourselves! Or do you not recognize this about yourselves, that Jesus Christ is in you – unless indeed you fail the test?"

This passage has created some problems for "Free Grace" advocates. The problem is that Protestantism is based traditionally on the doctrine of *Sola Fide*, meaning salvation is by God's grace alone through faith in Jesus Christ. The Free Grace theologian emphasizes that this grace is offered by God and needs no proof. Every believer is said to have the assurance of salvation. However, here Paul is telling us to test ourselves to see whether or not we are "in the faith"! What does this mean? Is it synonymous with knowing whether or not we are saved?

There are several approaches to this problem. The Catholic church rejects the doctrine of assurance. They believe that salvation can only be known upon meeting the Lord. Pope John Paul II once said that faith is "more than the adherance of the intellect to revealed truth."[608] It must be acted upon. This is also the view of liberal Protestant churches, despite their rejection of Hell.

Rudolf Bultmann, for example, thought said that "faith" means "only the obedience of faith actualized."[609] While it is true that faith produces works, most Protestants object that this emphasizes human works rather than God's grace. The question for most Protestants has always been the *assurance* of savlation. "Once saved, always saved." Of course no one doubts that there are phony believers and those who fall away from the faith, but were they truly believers or perhaps they are just backslidden? This is the gist of the debate.

Charles Hodge said, "Calvin, in his antagonism to the Romanish doctrine that assurance is unattainable in this life, and that all claims to it are unscripture and fanatical, draws the directly opposite conclusion from this passage."[610] To this day Reformed theologians and most evangelicals hold that salvation is assured, but Hodge himself believes that "assurance is not essential to faith."[611] What then does this passage say about assurance? If we are assured of salvation then why do we need to test ourselves?

One approach is the traditional Calvinist one. It says that Paul is not saying "test ourselves to see if we are saved" but "scrutinize ourselves to determine whether our attitudes and decisions can really be called Christian."[612] This argument has merit, for contextually Paul has been talking about his critics who doubtless reminded everyone that Paul used to persecute the faith. He was asking them to "turn the tables" for "Paul's critics were prepared to examine him, to see if he was rightly related to Christ. He asks them to subject themselves to the same scrutiny."[613]

Another solution is to look at this as "objective faith."[614] John Darby said that "it is not my examination of my spiritual state which gives me peace, but faith in the Lord Jesus Christ."[615] Thus some say that this means "all Christians should be often induced to examine the foundation of their hope of eternal salvation."[616] It is not an examination of my salvation, nor even my faith, but of the foundations for our faith.

Beyond this debate the passage has practical significance for it "proves that a true believer may doubt of his good estate."[617] Doubting does not mean that we have lost our salvation or that God has abandoned us. This then returns us to our original question. Why examine ourselves if our salvation is assured? My answer is as follows.

Self examination begins within our own hearts to see if Christ is really a part of it. It is not something we take as a standarized test, for only Christ knows our hearts. Paul was actually chastizing the Corinthians who were questioning his own faith. "Examine yourselves!" I *know* I am saved for the simple reason that Christ said so and He does not lie. Is Christ really in my heart? That is something only I and Jesus know for sure, because it involves my heart. We look too much for external evidences, which falls into the trap of legalism to which the Pharisees had fallen. Jesus always looked to the heart and soul. Will we bear fruit? Yes, but fruit does not prove faith. Charities do many good deeds, but many are not even professed believers and their motives and rewards may be suspect. My point is that there is no external way to examine one's faith. We must simply look to see where our priorities lie and what our motives are. I do not believe that Paul was ordering a simple "test" that could prove whether we know Jesus or not. Only we truly know that *if* we search our own heart. Do we believe in Jesus because we don't want to go to Hell? Is that true faith? Maybe these are the things Paul was telling us to examine.

Frederic Edwin Church – The Parthenon – 1871

4

—

Galatians

Galatia was located in Asia Minor. It was its own small country roughly in the center of modern day Turkey. The central debate which Paul addresses throughout Galatians is the debate between legalism and libertinism. Was the Law of Moses still valid, and if so, to what purpose? Several issues are brought up which were also the subject of the Council of Jerusalem (Acts 15). This council is also mentioned in this very epistle, giving us insight into what happened behind the scenes of that famous council.

Most agree that Galatians was written by Paul sometime between the Council of Jerusalem (see Galatians 2:11-21) and his arrest in Jerusalem,[618] but some argue that "Paul wrote this strong letter prior to attending the Jerusalem Council."[619] The argument is based on the assumption that the Council would have resolved this debate once and for all, but this seems more than a little naive. First, councils have never completely resolved conflicts. Neither do many Christians (particularly Protestants) believe that Council bear the weight of Scripture. Indeed, the Council of Jerusalem and the Council of Nicaea are the only two councils in history that both Catholics and Protestants agree upon. Consequently, the findings of the council would not have immediately settled the debate which was raging in the church at that time. Second, Paul mentions his rebuke of Peter which took place immediately before the council (see notes under Galatians 2:11-21). Donald Campbell believes that Paul wrote the epistle immediately after this encounter and before attending the council, but this is unlikely.[620] Why rush to write a letter to debate an issue that the council was supposed to help resolve in the first place? Why not wait until after the council? It is a virtual certainty that Paul did just that. Nevertheless, we can agree that it was likely written not long after the council. Paul's discussion of the council indicates that the meeting was still fresh in everyone's mind. Consequently, Galatians may probably be dated to around 49 or 50 A.D.[621] If this date is correct, as most believe,[622] then Galatians would actually be the first extant epistle written by Paul.

The Lord's Brother
Galatians 1:19

"I did not see any other of the apostles except James, the Lord's brother."

"James, the Lord's brother." Who is this James? Catholics usually believe that he is James the Less. Protestants usually argue that he is another

James the Just, converted after the resurrection. Now the reader may assume that I will naturally take the side of Protestants, but in this case he would be mistaken. The evidence, although by no means simple, supports that James the Less and James the Just are one and the same. As I debate the subject in detail in *Apostles After Jesus*, which was originally to be an Appendix, I will merely highlight the evidence without prolonged debate.

In the Bible James the son of Alphæus was one of the twelve apostles (Matthew 10:3). There is also a James "the Less" mentioned in Mark 15:40. This is generally believed to distinguish James the son of Alphæus from James the Greater, brother of John. However, tradition calls the first overseer, or bishop, of Jerusalem James the Just. The question is whether or not these are the same person, or two (or even three) different people. With such minimal information, one might consider this a difficult task, when we compare the relevant passages it becomes more clear.

We first encounter a "brother" of Jesus named James in Matthew 13:55-56 and Mark 6:3. There is it said, ""Is not this the carpenter's son? Is not His mother called Mary, and His brothers, James and Joseph and Simon and Judas? And His sisters, are they not all with us? Where then *did* this man *get* all these things?" (Matthew 13:55-56; Cf. Mark 6:3). At this point it seems that James, Joseph, and Simon are the step-brothers of Jesus. Since Jesus's brothers were said to be unbelievers (John 7:5), it is assumed that James must be a later convert and not related to the apostle James, who is a son of Alphæus (Matthew 10:3). This sounds logical, but when we examine it closely there are two problems with it. First, in the near east, to this very day, extended family (including cousins) often live together and are called "brothers" and "sisters." I am not denying that Jesus had step-brothers as indicated in John 7:5 and elsewhere (including the passage in question), but the term in itself cannot prove that James the son of Alphæus is not a cousin. Second, a close examination of the women at the cross reveals that Jesus's extended family included an aunt also named Mary who had children named James, Joseph, Simon, and Judas!

According to Mark 15:40 "Mary the mother of James the Less and Joses" (Mark 15:40 : cf. 16:1) was present at the cross. Joses is the Greek rendition of Joseph, possibly corresponding to the James and Joseph of Mark 6:3. Moreover, it is clear that there are three Marys at the cross, not two. John 19:25 identifies one of the Marys as the wife of Clopas (or Cleophas). Matthew 27:55 further states that "many women were there." Who then is this Mary, wife of Cleophas?

There are at least four different theories on the relationship of James the Less to Jesus. Since I discuss this in detail in *Apostles After Jesus* I will not enter into it here. Instead I will focus briefly on the identity of Cleophas, for in this may lie our answer. According to Calvinist John Gill, Cleophas and Alphæus are different Hellenizations of the same Hebrew names. Consider that Joshua and Jesus are both different Hellenizations of the Hebrew name *Yeshua*

(יֵשׁוּ), which is short for *Yehoshua* (יְהוֹשֻׁעַ). In this case the argument is similar. Gill said that Cleophas was "a name frequently to be met with in Talmudic and Rabbinic writings; and so a Jewish writer observes, that הילפא והוא אילפא, 'Chilpha is the same as Ilpha'; and in Greek may be pronounced either Cleophas, or Alphæus."[623] While this may seem odd to English readers, the fact is that English, Greek, and Hebrew all have entirely different alphabets, making transliteration of names from one language to the next confusing, as is the case with Jesus and Joshua (the same name).

So it would appear that this Mary could be the wife of Alphæus, but why does the Bible use two different transliterations of the same name? This appears to be the only obstacle to this identification. It is an obstacle easily removed, however, when we realize that Matthew, Mark, and Luke all use Alphæus (Matthew 10:3; Mark 2:14, 3:18; Luke 6:15; Acts 1:13) but John never uses this transliteration. It is only in John where the alternate form Clopas (or Cleophas) is found (John 19:25). If so, then James was a cousin of Jesus and a part of the extended family which lived with Jesus and his step-brothers (for further support of this and a suggested family tree for Jesus's extended family, see my book *Apostles After Jesus*).

Finally, here in Galatians 1:19 further indicates that this "brother" of the Lord *was* the apostle James the Less. The exact quote is "I did not see any other of the apostles except James, the Lord's brother." Thus "the Lord's brother" *was* an apostle. This alone seems sufficient proof that James the Less was one and the same as James the Just, overseer of Jerusalem and "pillar" of the church (Galatians 2:9).

Peter Rebuked
Galatians 2:11-21

"When Cephas came to Antioch, I opposed him to his face, because he stood condemned."

Chapter two gives us some insight into the background of the Council of Jerusalem. This council, discussed in Acts 15, is actually of enormous historical significance to the Christian church, and in more than one way. First, the council addressed the very issues that Paul debates here in Galatians. Should gentiles be required to be circumcised? Must Christians keep the whole of the Law of Moses? In short, legalism and libertinism were at the heart of the debate. At stake was the growth of Christianity among the gentiles. Since Paul had been the first to reach out beyond the borders of Israel and Syria, his word of great importance at the council. Although Acts does not discuss the conflict between Peter and Paul, this epistle explains what went on behind the scenes.

The second major impact which the Council of Jerusalem had upon the church was that it led to the dissemination of missions beyond Israel. The Great Commission was now being taken seriously as all but two of the apostles left

Israel soon after this council to begin mission works around the known world. What began as an Appendix expanded into my book, *Apostles After Jesus*, in which I explore the historical evidence of what happened to the apostles after this council.

Here in Galatians Paul concerns himself only with the issue of circumcision and his conflict with Peter. Peter initially took the side of the Judaizers who insisted that gentiles convert to Judaism be circumcised before they could accept Christ. Paul, however, did not hesitate to spare Peter's feelings when he publicly rebuked and insulted Peter. Make no mistake, when Paul "said to Cephas [the Hebrew name for Peter] in the presence of all, 'you, being a Jew, live like the Gentiles'" (2:14), it was a personal insult. To call a Jew a gentile was the equivalent of a racial slur or epithet. Jesus too had been accused of living "unwashed" like a gentile (Mark 7:1-5).

So what then is the controversy? The first, and most debated, is over Paul's harsh treatment of a the man whom Catholics call the first pope, and many others believe was the "head" or leader of the apostles. The other is over the broader issue of legalism itself and of Peter's sin. What was his sin? Was it being wrong? Interestingly enough, although Catholics and Protestants are usually on opposing sides of these issues, it is not always so. John MacArthur, for example, defends Peter's position! Let us again examine the issues and positions.

The Question of Apostolic Authority

This passage is one in which John Calvin gleefully declared "the Roman papacy is struck down by another thunder bolt."[624] He noted that "one man reproves Peter in the presence of the whole Church, and Peter obediently submits."[625] This hardly fits with the doctrine of the primacy of the papacy, so how do Catholics repond?

Some have tried to escape this problem by arguing that this was another Peter, and not the apostle.[626] The argument is, however, inconceivable. For one thing, Galatians 2:9 calls Peter, James, and John "pillars" of the church. If this was another Peter then who is this "pillar" never before mentioned and why is the apostle Peter omitted? Obviously Peter was a member of the inner circle. Peter, James, and John were the three most important apostles. Moreover, Cephas, the name actually found here, is explicitly said to be the Hebrew name for Peter in John 1:42. There can be no doubt that this was the apostle Peter.

A better argument used by Catholics is that Popes are not exempt from rebuke, but that they will eventually come to the true and correct position as "vicars" of Christ. Nevertheless, in so doing they are admitting, as C.I. Scofield said, that "Peter was by no means unfallible."[627]

Yet another argument is that Paul was a unique case. "The Apostle's independence"[628] is emphasized, arguing that Paul "regarded himself as on a level with the chief apostles."[629] Such an argument is not specifically a Catholic one. Even Protestants respect and esteem Peter's position in the church, but believe that Paul "regarded himself ... as on equality with Peter."[630] Certainly Paul did not consider himself beneath Peter, but neither did Peter ever assert any authority over him. In fact, it may be inferred that Peter was following James the Just. Indeed, James seems to have been the spokesperson for the "party of circumcision" (Galatians 2:12) and his prominence and importance at the Council of Jerusalem was arguably the deciding factor in convincing the "party of circumcision" to back down and accept gentiles with but minor reservations, such as abstinence from sexual sin (Acts 15:13-29). It is no accident that James's name is listed before Peter's in (Galatians 2:9). If this same James (see notes above on Galatians 1:19) was the same James who was overseer, or bishop, of Jerusalem then this makes sense, but it also cast more doubt upon any claim to papal supremacy for it was Jerusalem that was the center of the church in those days.

Even if the church of Rome had already existed, and all evidence suggest that it was founded years later, then "St. Paul was in a far truer sense the founder than St. Peter."[631] Even the same church fathers who are quoting in calling Peter Roman's founder, actually call him a co-founder along with Paul. It was Paul who as the "apostle to the gentiles" (1 Timothy 2:7), not Peter whom Paul speaks of having an "apostleship to the circumcised" in Galatians 2:8.

The fact is that "there is no hint of Peter's so-called 'primacy.'"[632] He was certainly one of the Inner Circle and his opinion bore great weight, but nowhere does the Bible speak of Peter having primacy over any of the other apostles, and especially not Paul who did not hesitate to publicly humiliate Peter when he was wrong, and yet this leads to a final question. What was Peter wrong about? Believe it or not, not everyone agrees.

Peter and the Judaizers
John MacArthur, the famed Calvinist preacher, is one of the few who actually defends Peter's position. He argues that "we learn from Peter that it is not enough to believe the gospel – *you must be willing to obey it*."[633] He argues that Peter's sin was not legalism but hypocrisy. He said of Paul, "it is not advantageous to correct in secret an error which occurred publicly."[634] This staggering remark is one that even most Catholics do not make and one which cuts at the heart of the issue. What is the correleation between faith and works? Is obedience to the law a requirement of faith or does faith create good works? This is the debate at the core of Galatians and many other epistles. Since I do not want to repeat the same debate multiple times, I will reserve the larger debate for James 2:14-26. Here it is necessary only to point out that Paul is not condemning Peter for his hyprocisy alone but for his doctrine! The council itself agreed with Paul that gentiles should *not* be required to submit to circumcision. This fact alone is proof that James and Peter had been wrong and only altered their views after being rebuked by Paul.

139

A final comment is necessary. Why did Peter fall into the trap of legalism since he was not accustomed in his own life to such legalism? As Warren Wiersbe put it, "Peter's freedom was threatened by *Peter's fear*."[635] This is true. Compromise of the truth is almost always motivated by a fear of rejection. We want to be accepted. It is human nature to want to be accepted and liked, but Jesus was despised and rejected by men (1 Peter 2:4). We will always be mocked and laughed at for the truth. I remember being sadly amused by all the Flower Children of the '60s who used to say "gotta be me," and yet they all looked, talked, and acted *exactly alike*. Another friend of mine from a certain community in the United States disagreed with my opinions in politics and promptly chastized me by saying, "think for yourself!" The irony is that he was angry because I was thinking for myself and rejecting the talking points of his political party! If we are really independent then we should not all agree. Remember when Christians were mocked for believing that dirt caused disease? Probably not, but it was Joseph Lister who stood out against the Darwinists of his day and the prevailing wisdom. It was he who invented antiseptic surgery which has since saved many lives. Many other examples could be cited as well in both science and theology.[636] Did not many Reformers give their very lives for the right of the common man to read the Bible for himself? Compromise is for politicians. Truth cannot compromise.

Conclusion

Peter asserts no authority here in Galatians. It is to his credit that he accepted Paul's rebuke and submitted to it. Such is the action of humility and character. It is not, however, consistent with a primacy of the Peter, nor does the Bible teach that *any* man, save Christ alone, has spiritual authority over another man. Even a pastor should never be looked upon as having spiritual authority over his members. He is a shepherd; not a cowboy. He is a guiding hand; not a fist. As such he should be willing to accept rebuke from even the lowest of believers.

Was Christ Cursed?
Galatians 3:13

"Christ redeemed us from the curse of the Law, having become a curse for us – for it is written, 'Cursed is everyone who hangs on a tree.'"

"Having become a curse." These words spark strong emotions. Could Jesus be a curse? What does this mean? It is one thing to say that Jesus was cursed, but to say he was a curse is strong language to say the least. The New Living Translation attempts to get around the problem by translating this passage as, "When He was hung on the cross, He took upon Himself the curse for our wrongdoing," but the Greek is γενομενος υπερ ημων καταρα (*genomenos uper amon katara*) which is most literally "having become for us curse." The old Wycliff translation rendered this as "he was maad acursid for vs." This helps resolve the problem by making "a curse" into accursed, but the Greek word is nominative, making the translation suspect. "It is not merely that He has been made accursed for us, but 'a curse'"[637] The truth is that the problem cannot be resolved via translation alone.

Undoubtedly the most bizarre interpretation is that of Martin Luther, who seems to borrow from the old pagan cult of the Sin eater. He declared that "when He took the sins of the whole world upon Himself, Christ was no longer an innocent person. He was a sinner burdened with the sins."[638] Luther presumeably believed that when our sins were imputed to Christ, He Himself became "of all sinners, the greatest"![639] This interpretation goes beyond literalism, for the word "imputed" literally means to "attribute to" or "assign guilt to" someone. It is does not mean they are guilty, but have been attributed with that guilt. Nothing in the Bible suggest that Jesus was ever a sinner, but rather that he was alone among men "without sin" (Hebrews 4:15). Imputation assigns the guilt, *not* the sin.

Another view is to make "a curse" into a title. It is thought to mean "a cursed one"[640] or "*an accursed one*,"[641] similar to Wycliff's translation, but based on context rather than a literal translation. In one sense, this is fair because the passage which Paul quotes from the Hebrew is Deuteronomy 21:23. This passage reads, "his corpse shall not hang all night on the tree, but you shall surely bury him on the same day (for he who is hanged is accursed of God)." However, two things are apparent in this. First, as Jonathan Edwards pointed out, "in the Hebrew it is, 'is the curse of God.'"[642] "Accursed of God" is a necessary translation as "the curse of God" does not make sense in proper English. Nevertheless, John Lightfoot was careful to note that "He was in no literal sense καταρατος υπο Θεου, and St. Paul instinctively omits those words which do not strictly apply."[643] Indeed, Paul omits "of God," leaving it simply as "a curse." This is so, but still does not fully explain what is meant. The answer may be found in a Qumran commentary from the time of Jesus where it is stated that the "hanging" found in Deuteronomy was of dead bodies for "hanging them alive ... was never done in Israel."[644] This actually brings the context of Deuteronomy to life. A dead body cannot be executed. The purpose of the hanging in Deuteronomy was not execution, but a warning ... a *curse* ... to all of the consequences of his crime. So the criminal would be hung during the day, but must be buried before night has fallen so the land will not be defiled (21:23). If this is so, as the Qumran community believed, then the body could literally be called a curse. This opens the door to the theory that Jesus was literally cursed as many believe.

John Calvin remarked that Paul "does not say that Christ was cursed, but something more, that He was a curse, signifying that the curse of all was placed on Him."[645] Another said that "Christ became a curse in that he was the object of divine reprobation."[646] The context of this passage must be Deuteronomy 21:23 for it "is introduced to support the statement that Christ became a curse."[647]   So if "the Eternal One, hung on the cross"[648] then He "took this curse upon Himself."[649]   This was the view of John Wesley,[650] John Darby,[651] H.A. Ironisde [652] and many others.

Despite the apparent context for this, not all believe that Jesus was cursed at all. This is particularly true among many of the early church. Jerome refused to see Jesus as literally cursed at all.[653] Justin Martyr said that "though a curse lies in the law against persons who are crucified, yet no curse lies on the Christ of God."[654]   Tertullian quoted Deuteronomy to show that it refers to "whomever, in *any sin*, has incurred the judgment of Death. Therefore, He did not maledictively adjudge Christ to this Passion."[655]   In other words, Deuteronomy applies to the guilty, but Christ was guiltless. He took the punishment of the guilty upon Himself but remained blameless.

All these views have merit to a degree, except perhaps Luther's. Consequently, one author simpy calls it a "mystery"[656] and does not seek a deeper meaning. However, Paul's meaning is clear. Jesus took the punishment we deserved. We are the ones who should have been cursed and hung upon a tree for *all* of us are sinners guilty before God, and yet God the Son took our place, bearing the punishment for our guilt. He bore the curse that is upon the sinner, and in so doing became our salvation.

Galatians 3:17 – See *Controversies in the Pentateuch* (Genesis 15:13-16)

Who is the Israel of God?
Galatians 6:16

"Peace and mercy *be* upon them, and upon the Israel of God."

Here "Israel" is qualified with "of God." It is not all Israel, but all "the Israel of God." Some have argued that this is a synonym for the Church, and hence the church has replaced Israel, but others say that Israel of God is not contrasted with Israel but with the church. Is the "Israel of God" the Church or is it believing Israelites in contrast to believing gentiles?   The answer is significant for it effects our understanding of God's covenants with Israel and the fulfillment of God's promises.

Probably the most popular understanding is that of Justin Martyr who said that this was "true, spiritual Israel."[657]   This was the view of men like Chrysostom, Theodoret, Martin Luther, John Calvin, Baumgarten, John Lightfoot,[658] and many others.[659]   John Calvin said "Israel of God" is synonymous with "the children of Abraham by faith."[660] Warren Wiersbe calls it "one of many names for the church"[661] and Albert Barnes also concurred that this was "the true church of God."[662] Thus "Israel of God" has in common venacular been equated with Justin Martyr's "spiritual Israel."   The only problem is that "spiritual Israel" is a term never found in the Bible. Despite this, it has become the popular term for Covenant and Replacement theologians to refer to the church. In arguing that "Israel of God" is "the true church of God"[663] they can transplant every promise God ever made to Israel and apply them to the gentile dominated church. However, it is suspect whether or not the term "spiritual Israel" can ever apply to Israel in the Bible at all.

The passage in question reads, "peace and mercy *be* upon them [the church], and upon the Israel of God." Israel of God thus appears to be contrasted with church. This is so obvious that Herman Ridderbas, who believes it does refer to "spiritual Israel" issues the honest statement, "somewhat surprising is the addition : and upon the Israel of God."[664] If it is synonymous with the church, then why say "*and upon* the Israel of God"? "And upon" normally indicates "another body, distinction from"[665] the previous body. However, it has been argued that the less common use of the conjuction καɩ (*kai*) is as an explicative."[666] This would render it "even upon" as stated by Jonathan Edwards.[667] Hence, according to this theory it could be translated, "peace and mercy *be* upon them, even upon the Israel of God." Another more loose translation could be, "*namely*, upon the Israel of God."[668] In this way, Israel of God could be identical with church. This is the translation preference followed by the NIV and the paraphrasistic NLT, which inexplicably paraphrases this as "they are the new people of God."

Despite the overwhelming popularity of this view, it is quite simply wrong. While the *Liberty Bible Commentary* says that "Israel of God is in contrast to Israel after the flesh"[669] it is actually in contrast to the gentile church! Paul has been discussing the issue of circumcising gentile believers. Throughout Galatians he is discussing the division between Jewish believers and gentile converts. Here in his salutation he simply says, "peace and mercy *be* upon them, *and* upon the Israel of God." "Israel of God" is clearly contrasted with "them." Who are they? This is the key to understanding whether or not Paul is using Israel in an allegorical sense or not.

After summarizing his beliefs concerning circumcision to the Galatians, he then says "to those who will walk by this rule, peace and mercy be upon them." So "them" refers to "those who will walk by this rule." What rule? The rules Paul just laid out to the church of Galatia! The rules concerning circumcision and the acceptance of gentile believers without forcing them to convert to Judaism first! In short, to gentile believers. It is "peace and mercy be upon gentile converts and believing Jews."

While not the dominant view of history, this is nevertheless well attested throughout history and is the most natural interpretation. Even the somewhat allegorical Victorinus saw this as Jews.[670] So did Theodore Beza, Ambrosiaster, and J.A. Bengal, to name a few.[671] They are "converted Jews"[672] or, more accurately, "Jewish saints."[673]

To argue any other interpretation is reading into the text. "The phrase occurs nowhere else in the New Testament and so there are no parrallels to which to appeal for a decision."[674] We must appeal to its natural meaning within the text itself. This is especially true since "there is, in fact, no instance of his using Ἰσραηλ except of the Jewish nation."[675] We must, therefore, conclude that "'Israel of God' seems to be used here, not as a general phrase for every saint, but for the believing ones in Israel."[676] Remember that Paul is here only issuing salutation. It is unreasonable to assume that Paul would insert an unparalleled theological symbol with no explanation. He is simply wishing God's grace to both the Jews and gentiles within the church of Galatia. After all, that *was* the entire subject of the epistle.

Summary

The entire epistle of Galatians concerns the topic of Judaizers who believed that circumcision was required before a gentile could convert to Christ. They retained the legalism with which they had been raised and brought it with them to the church, even as many gentiles bring our libertinism with us to the church. Paul then explains the nature of grace and faith. Adult circumcision is painful and a hinderance. The purpose of circumcision was as a sign of the covenant God made with the Jews. Whey should gentiles be forced to accept a covenant sign, at an adult age, which did not strictly apply to them? Jesus came for all men; not only for the Jews. So Paul sought to bring gentile converts together with Jewish believers and unify them in the grace of God.

5

Ephesians

Ephesians and Colossians have been called "twin epistles."[677] The subject matter is very similar in both and each was written while Paul was in prison (Ephesians 3:1, 4:1, 6:20; Colossians 4:10-18). Both were delivered by Tychicus (Ephesians 6:21; Colossians 4:7) and the cities lay approximately 100 miles from one another,[678] making it practical for Tychicus to have delivered both epistles rather than sending two different messengers.

There has been some debate as to the exact date of the epistles because some feel that Paul wrote from prison in Caesarea (between 58-60 A.D.)[679] while others believe this fits Paul's imprisonment in Rome much better (61-63 A.D.).[680] The best evidence revolves around Paul's mention of Aristarchus and Epaphras (Colossians 4:10-12), both of whom died in Rome under the persecution of Nero.[681] While they may have both been released and recaptured after Nero's persecution began, even as Paul was, their appearance in Rome makes it highly likely that they had been to Rome before, probably during Paul's first imprisonment there. Although not certain, it is likely that Paul wrote to both Ephesus and Colossae from Rome, sending Tychicus to deliver both epistles together. They are probably to be dated around 61 A.D.

Pauline Authorship

Liberal scholarship has long had a tradition of assuming that the Bible was forged by later authors and building assumptions to support this view, rather than presenting real evidence. Here in Ephesians the German "rationalist" critic has argued that Ephesians was written under the pseudonym of Paul. In other words, they claim it is a forgery. As usual, they offer no material evidence for this presupposition. Instead they have argued four points.

First, they argue that the vocabulary and style are "non-Pauline" in nature, and therefore were not written by Paul. As I have discussed in *Controversies in the Prophets*, arguments from style and vocabulary are inherently weak. While style will be somewhat consistent with a single author, it varies to some degree depending on the context and situation. Any reader of the epistle can tell that the "style" of Ephesians is not dramatically different from any of Paul's other epistles. They all follow his same style of systematic logic and theology. Superficial differences are unconvincing. Arguments from vocabulary are even more tenuous for the subject matter often dictates what vocabulary is used, and more importantly, thirteen short epistles from Paul (some only a chapter in length) is hardly an extensive enough selection to determine what vocabulary is and is not "Pauline." Consider also that Paul clearly demonstrates a wide vocabulary due to his extensive education. How then can the critic say that phrases like "the heavenly realms" (1:3, 20; 2:6; 3:10; 6:13) could not have been penned by Paul?[682] Such arguments would never hold up in a court of law.

Second, they argue that the similarities between Ephesians and Colossians is not because they were written by the same author but because the one was plagerized by the other![683] Such hypocrisy is laughable. If they are different then it is argued they could not have been written by the same person and if they are too similar then they must have been plagerized! Such is the subjective mindset of the old German critic.

A third agrument used against Pauline authorship is that the personal references are inconsistent with other epistles.[684] Only two examples, however, are given; the absence of his traditional salutations at the end of Ephesians and a contrived interpretation of Ephesians 3:1-8 where Paul is presumeably boastful of his apostleship in Ephesians 3:4, placing himself among the "holy apostles," while humbling in 3:8 where he calls himself "the very least of all saints." Both such arguments are frivolous. While Paul did often send personal salutations at the end of his epistles, this was not always the case. Galatians, for example, does not mention a single church member at Galatia by name. Moreover, Tychicus is mentioned in the brief salutations of Ephesians. As to Paul's "boasting" and humility being mixed in the same letter, such an argument is contrived. Paul could be said to be "boasting" in 1 Corinthians 14:18 but in 1 Corinthians 15:9 Paul calls himself the "least of the apostles." Such arguments only demonstrate the weakness of the critic.

Finally, it is argued that Paul's theology is different in Ephesians. How? Because there are no "references to the preexistence of Christ to the Parousia."[685] This, however, is probably the most absurd of arguments. Ephesians 1:1-12 is all about God's "predestined" Will for us. Ephesians 1:4-5 declares that God "chose us in Him before the foundation of the world" and "predestined us to adoption as sons through Jesus Christ to Himself." While it may not explicitly prove the preexistence of Christ, it is clearly that Christ was in view in eternity past. So the interpretation is again contrived in such a way as to justify the German rationalist's own assumptions. Likewise, the Second Coming, while a prominent theme of Paul, does not appear in every letter he wrote.

Onesimus and Tychicus have been suggested as possible authors,[686] but it is poetic that the same critic who argues against Pauline authorship on such frivolous basis as cited above, consider one of these two men as possible authors with no evidence other than they were admirers of Paul who might have tried to imitate him! The truth is that Ephesians was universally accepted by the early church as Pauline.[687] Moreover, a copy of Ephesians is found in Papyrus 46 ($\mathfrak{P}^{46}$). This manuscript is believed by some to date as early 80 A.D. based on paleographical evidence.[688] While the date is challenged by many, its inclusion in with other Pauline manuscripts so close the first century is a slap in the face to the critic who believes Ephesians was not even written until around 90 A.D.![689] The fact is that Paul wrote Ephesians, probably at the same time he wrote Colossians. He then send Tychicus to deliver both letters. Paul is clearly the author and its composition was probably around 61 A.D., perhaps as little as twenty years before a copy now in our possession.

History Prewritten
Ephesians 1:1-12

> "He chose us in Him before the foundation of the world, that we would be holy and blameless before Him. In love He predestined us to adoption as sons through Jesus Christ to Himself."

There are many passages throughout the Bible where the debate over Calvinism could be discussed. Here, however, is the perfect place for it since two of the six occurences of the word "predestined" appear in these passages. Predestination is thus mentioned by name only six times; two in this passage, two in Romans 8:29-30, once in 1 Corinthians 2:7, and once in Acts 4:28. Five of these were written by Paul's hand.

Traditionally Calvinists and Armenians set up a false dichotomy. They say it is a choice between God's sovereign predestined Will and man's free will. Most believe that the two cannot co-exist. When faced with problems in their theology they either build straw man arguments against one another or make inconsistent exceptions. A prime example is the nature of sin and evil.

R.C. Sproul Jr. has said, "God wills all things that come to pass. *God created sin.*"[690] Such is the view of sovereignty offered by many Calvinists. However, not all agree. John MacArthur, for example, is a Calvinist who freely admits that God is not the author of evil, something with which many Calvinist struggle. He says, "sin is not itself a thing created. Sin is neither substance, being, spirit, nor matter. So it is technically not proper to think of sin as something that was created. Sin is simply a lack of moral perfection in a fallen creature. Fallen creatures themselves bear full responsibility for their sin. And all evil in the universe emanates from the sins of fallen creatures ... [but] ... God is certainly sovereign over evil."[691] The great Jonathan Edwards also conferred that "it would be a reproach and blasphemy, to suppose God to be the author of sin. In this sense, I utterly deny God to be the author of sin."[692] God permits evil, but does not cause it. Such moderate Calvinist voices are correct, but evasive. If there is *no* free will (not even limmitted free will), then God is the author of evil. It is fair to say that God's Will permits evil, but only if we acknowledge that God's Will permits limit choices; free will. If not, then the permission argument falls flat.

Now the nature of evil in this world is discussed more fully under James 1:13. The question here is of the nature of predestination and God's sovereignty. Does God's predestined Will allow *some* choices? Are we completely free? Are we not free at all? Is our will bound by sin? It is not my usual tactic to exceed the parameters of the text in question, and I will try not to do so here, but the very question of predestination and sovereignty touch upon these fundamental questions. This is why almost every Calvinist I have ever met seems to set up a false dichotomy, or even trichotomy. The dichotomy claims that everyone, whether they know it or not, is either Calvinist or Armenian. The false trichotomy offered by others is that we have a choice between the denial of election, equating election with foreknowledge only, or traditional Calvinism.[693] Before these questions can be answered it is necessary to give a brief summary of Calvinism, Armenianism, and the Biblical view.

Joseph Hornung – Death of John Calvin – 19th Century

Calvinism

There is much to be commended in Calvinism. I do not deny this. However, there is much in it that is false, inconsistent, and even heretical. This is even admitted unwittingly by such greats as J. I. Packer who says we must "refuse to regard the apparent inconsistencies as real."[694] Yet there are inconsistencies, and not just inconsistencies with human logic, but inconsistencies with the Bible.

Origins

The first thing to know is that Calvinism did not truly originate with Calvin. In fact, no Calvinist would claim that it did, for to do so would be to admit that it is not fully Biblical. However, they rarely go beyond this to explain its origins. Charles Spuregon admitted that St. Augustine, the "Father of the Middle Ages," had the greatest influence upon Calvin's theology,[695] but few realize that Augustine's theology was influenced heavily from Aristotilianism. Aristotle, of course, was a pagan whose doctrine of fatalism stemmed from his view of the pagan gods who toyed with men like chess pieces. Aristotle once famously said, "What is, necessarily is, when it is; and what is not, necessarily is not, when it is not." [696] This is echoed by Calvinist Heinrich Bullinger when he said, "some are saved and others damned by absolute necessity."[697]

The fundamental assumption which underlies Aristotelianism, Augustinianism, and Calvinism is the idea that sovereignty and predestination cannot coexist with free will, even limitted free will. This is a fundamentally wrong assumption. It is the cornerstone of the problem that even many Calvinists admit exist in "hyper-Calvinists." They reject Biblical apologetics as irrelevant, do not witness, and take no responsibility for sin. Such doctrines were rejected even by Calvin, but are the logical consequence of some of his teachings. Consider the following.

Free Will

A choice is offered to someone either because someone gave him the choice or because of circumstances. Most Christians rightly believe that God is in charge of circumstances. Thus God is sovereign over the circumstances which lay before us, but we *do* have choices ... or do we? John Calvin believed that free will is myth. Both Luther and Calvin, borrowing from Augustine, argued that there is a "bondage of the will" to sin. This may be true, but contradictory to the idea that we have no will. If there be no choices and no will, then how can it be bound?

Consider this remark by Calvinist John Gerstner in *A Primer on Free Will*. "It is your decision to choose or reject Christ, but it is not of your own free will."[698] Such a contradictory remark is one that most Calvinists cannot even resolve in their own mind. John MacArthur, for example, begins by making the correct argument that man "is able to chose God because God has made that choice possible" but he then follows Gerstner in saying it is not of free will.[699] He defends this position by saying, "the problem cannot be resolved by our feeble minds."[700] Nevertheless, God did give us minds. It is logical to say that we cannot fully comprehend an infinite God with finite minds, but it is another thing altogether to say that illogical contradictions must be ignored, and yet this is what the Calvinist must do to maintain the doctrine of Calvinism *and* Biblical Christianity, for they are not the same.

One common argument used by Calvinist is that, as Arthur Pink once wrote, "to say that the sinner's salvation turns upon the action of his own will, is another form of the God-dishonoring dogma of salvation by human efforts. Any movement of the will is a work."[701] The problem with this argument is obvious by the fact that I have, as of yet, not seen a single Calvinist bow down to his son or daughter for accepting a Christmas present! Not one! Sometimes a child may be ingrateful and throw the present away. Sometimes they may whine like a child that it is not what they wanted. Sometimes they accept the present. Was the present not a gift from the Calvinist because the child had to accept it? The very word "grace" in Greek is χαρις (*charis*). The word for "gift" is χαρισμα (*charisma*). Grace is the verb. Gift is the noun. In Greek they are the same root, so accepting a gift does not diminish the gift, but rejecting a gift diminishes the recipient. Likewise, accepting a gift does not elevate the receiver. The argument is faux.

Election

The term "elect" is found only eight times in the Bible; six of those occurences are in the Olivet Discourse. Nevertheless, the term "elect" in Calvinism is a major theme. It is usually considered (by both Calvinists, Armenians, and others) to refer to all believers. Consequently, if all believers are "elect" of God and chosen before the foundations of the world, as implied here in Ephesians 1, then it follows according to Calvin that man has no choice in the matter. He was chosen before he was born and therefore cannot chose otherwise.

On the surface this sounds like a good doctrine, but it rest upon suspect views of election; a word found only eight times in the Bible, and most of those references are in regard to Last Days and the Second Coming. Nevertheless, even if the interpretation is correct (see below), the logical consequences of this doctrine are felt in Heinrich Bullinger's shocking remark, "if I am elect even my most outrageous crimes will not harm me ... because some are saved and others damned by absolute necessity."[702] Obviously such a teaching can be precariously dangerous when taken to its logical end, but the very idea stems from a suspect understanding of election.

Seven times in the gospels Jesus speaks of the "elect." Once Paul speaks of the "elect" (Romans 8:33). Most believe that the "elect" refers to believers in general. This is certainly the most natural interpretation. However, it has been argued that the elect are actually a select group *among* believers, and not inclusive of all believers. Considering the scarcity of the word in the Bible, this view is equally hard to prove. Nonetheless, whether or not the elect constitute all believers, or just some, the fact remains that Calvinism restricts God's predestined plans; yes, restricts. Why is God incapable of placing those he knows will make the right choices in the time and place where they will be most effective? Why is incapable of planning (predetermining or predestining) history around people who will make the choices He wants? Is the Calvinist saying that there is something God *cannot* do? The truth is, he is. Calvinism denies that God can be sovereign if we have any free will at all, even a limited will. So it is the Calvinist who truly denies the sovereignty of God, or does he? What role does foreknowledge have in predestination, if any?

Predestination and Foreknowledge

Calvinist are correct to say that God's "plan is timeless. The fall of man was no surprise to God, and redemption was no afterthought."[703] However, they will then build straw man arguments against those with whom they disagree. D.M. Lloyd-Jones, for example, lies about dispensational theology, claiming that "the Church, say the Dispensationalists, is an afterthought ... not a part of the original plan."[704] Why fabricate lies about other Christians? Because they cannot defend their own position. It reminds me of Oscar Wilde's joke, "if you can't answer a man's arguments, don't panic. You can always call him names." The fact is that all true Christians agree that the Church was planned before the foundations of the world.

Here in Ephesians Paul makes clear that history was written beforehand. God had a plan, but the Calvinist errs in that he rejects the idea that part of that predestined plan could include even limited free will. Like the Armenian they believe that if God gives us free choices in some matters then predestination would be limited to foreknowledge alone. This straw man argument doesn't hold up, however. If I invite someone to my house and offer them a choice between Coke and Pepsi, I have prepared beforehand that I would have both products. If I did not want them to choose between the two then I would have offered them a different choice or none at all. I have not lost my sovereignty over my refrigerator or left myself unprepared for whatever choice they may make. How much greater is God than I? Can God prepare and predestine the future with full cognizance of the choices he offers and the possible outcomes of their choices He Himself gave us? If not, then God could not *really* be sovereign. So it is the Calvinist who ultimately denies God's sovereignty.

Conclusion

Calvinism stemmed from St. Augustine who in turn Christianized Aristotle's fatalism. Its strongest support is in its straw man argument against Armenianism, as if anyone who is not a Calvinist must be an Armenian, but what is Armenianism? Let us examine its tenants as well.

Armenianism

Most Calvinist are completely unaware that Arminius was a disciple of John Calvin.[705] He attended Calvin's university and learned the tenants of Calvinism but broke away over some of the issues mentioned above. However, he did not reject the fundamental errors which led to Calvin's false doctrines. Consequently, he created more false doctrines situated around the same errors!

Free Will

Both Calvin and Armenius believed that free will cannot coexist with God's sovereign will, but each took a different path. Calvin denied free will, whereas Armenius de-emphasized God's sovereignty. He did not actually deny

God's sovereignty but relegated God's will to allowing man's free will to flourish. To an extent Armenianism could be considered a sort of Christian deism. They both see God as a clock maker, but the Armenian does allow God's intervention, such as in sending His Son Jesus. He denies, however, that God is actively in control of our lives. *Both* Calvin and Armenius, therefore, deny the true definition of sovereignty.

A king is sovereign not because his subjects have no will, but because the king's will prevails regardless of whether or not his subjects wish it to. The subjects may resist but they will fail. If they do not fail, then the king is not truly sovereign. Sovereignty involves one person's will reigning supreme over another person's will. This necessitates *both* having wills. Calvin denies human free will whereas Armenius belittled God's sovereign will.

Election

Remember that Armenius was a disciple of Calvin. Consequently, he too believed that the "elect" referred to those who are saved, but saw election solely in terms of foreknowledge. Nevertheless, F.F. Bruce once commented, "what a povery-stricken view of God's predestinating grace is taken by those who think of it solely in terms of being sealed for heaven and delivered from hell."[706] Indeed, many believe that election and grace should not be so narrowly interpreted. It is ironic that Calvin and Armenius wrote thousands of pages upon the word election which only occurs eight times in the Bible.

Marcus Barth, the son of famed liberal theologian Karl Barth, remarked that "Paul seems to depict a despot like God ... the love of God then appears like love only for those elected."[707] This blasphesmous remark stems not so much from Paul as from Barth's own limited understanding of election and predestation. He represents the logical end of Armenianism in the same way that hyper-Calvinist represent the logical end of Calvinism. Both views stem from the same poor understanding. In regard to election, both see election solely as the sealing for heaven, but the one sees it as predestiny alone while the other sees it as foreknowledge alone. This leads to the question of the Armenian view of predestination.

Predestination and Foreknowledge

Since Armenius and Calvin denied the coexistence of predestation, sovereignty, and free will, the Armenian sees predestination, such as that here in Ephesians, solely in terms of foreknowledge. God knows what decisions we will make. Like the Calvinist he restricts the power and sovereignty of God. R.C. Sproul argued that Armenians see God's grace as *conditional* upon the foreseen choices that we make."[708] The alternative Calvinist view is that God's grace is limited (limited atonement). So the Calvinist and Armenian beat up on straw men because neither can defend their position. Findlay, for example, attempts to excuse the inconsistencies of Armenianism by saying "the consistence of foreknowledge with free will is an enigma which the apostle did not attempt to solve."[709]   So just as MacArthur attempted to excuse the inconsistencies of Calvinism by saying it is beyond our understanding,[710] so Findlay excuses the inconsistencies of Armenianism. Note once again, *both* Calvinist and Armenians resort to this type of argument to escape the problems of their system.

Conclusion
Armenianism is the flip side of the Calvinist coin. It is the same coin, but a different side. It is based on the same flawed understanding of God's sovereignty, predestination, and free will. Nevertheless, beating up on straw men is poor way to defend *any* theology, so the real question is, "what is the Biblical view?"

The Biblical View
It is a sad state of affairs when we argue about Calvin and Armenius rather than the Bible. Neither man was even born until almost 1500 years after Jesus. The Scriptures, and the Scriptures alone, should be our guide. So what does the Bible say about predestination? What does Paul mean when he speaks of history being prewritten? To get that answer we should again look at our fundamental assumptions from a Biblical perspective.

Free Will
The Calvinist will ask, "how can God be sovereign if man can rebel against God's will?" This is a two part answer. The first is the very definition of sovereignty which implies the supremacy of one individual's will over another. This in turn suggest that both parties must have free will. Sovereignty is not the absence of free will, but the supremacy of God's will and His plan over our feeble plans. No matter what we choose, it is God's will that will ultimately prevail. The choices we have been given are limited. God's choices are not.

The second part of the answer is found in the application of God's will. Theologians sometimes divide God's will into two distinct types: His active "*sovereign* or *efficacious* will"[711] and His permissive will. The former is when God sent His Son or divided the Red Sea or even when he intervenes on our behalf in our daily lives. God's permissive will is when he *permits* Satan to do something. This is seen in the book of Job wherein Satan must obtain permission from God before persecuting Job. How does this apply to sovereignty?

It is the sovereign will of God that all men worship Him freely and with love, but if man is to be free to love, he must also be free to hate. This is not the denial of sovereignty, but an acknowledgement that free will, as predestined by God, necessiates wrong choices as well as right ones. If this freedom was not a part of God's will, then we would not truly have souls. There would be no evil in this world, but neither would there be any love. This is why Calvinist John

Bunyan declared God "must have sinners to share" His love with.[712] This is part of God's sovereign, predestined, efficacious will.

Election and Predestination

Lewis Sperry Chafer noted that "*election* and *predestination* do not indicate the same thing."[713] He saw predestation as "plan and purpose" whereas election was about selection.[714] Warren Wiersbe says, "election seems to refer to *people*, while predestination refers to *purpose*."[715] Obviously there is a connection, but the two should not be confused as many have. Unfortunately, I must agree with Arno Gaebelein who said that election and predestition have been obscured by the "theories and opinions" of theologians.[716] Calvinists, Armenians, and others have read their own theology into the text, but election and predestination are word found a combined total of fourteen times in the New Testament. That doesn't make the words less important, but it does make rigid definitions more suspect.

Predestination in the New Testament is found six times. Two are in Romans 8:29-30 and two are here in Ephesians 1. In each case, it speaks of what God willed before the creation of the world. It speaks of God's plan for mankind and for the ages. It is noteworthy that Romans 8:29 refers to both foreknowledge and predestination. "Those whom He foreknew, He also predestined," but he continues in the next verse, "these whom He predestined, He also called; and these whom He called, He also justified; and these whom He justified, He also glorified." So foreknowledge, predestination, calling, justification, and glofication are all connected in succession. The Armenian sees foreknowledge as the trigger, the Calvinist sees election as the trigger, and the Biblical student sees God as the trigger. Paul is not speaking of free will in this passage, but of God's plan. That His plan included giving man a choice is evident in that foreknowledge is placed first in this list. Foreknowledge is *not* the trigger, nor can predestination be confused with foreknowledge, but its placement at the beginning here indicates that a choice is involved. If not, why list foreknowledge at all? Why not begin with God's predestined plan? After all, history is prewritten. God predestined history before the creation of the universe. In fact, Ephesians 1:4 says he "chose us in Him before the foundations of the world"! Note, "in Him." The words are vital. It is through Jesus that we were chosen. Hence, Jesus is the trigger.

Now if Jesus is the predestined trigger for our being chosen, and not vice versa, then the question of election arises. The word elect occurs eight times in the New Testament. Six of those times occur in the Olivet Discourse, seven in the gospels. In all the gospel passages "elect" *appears* to be synonymous with all believers. The last passage is Romans 8:33 which follows the discourse concerning predestination, foreknowledge, and our calling. Some have argued that these elect refers to something other than believers, but the argument seems to be heavily influenced by the Millennial Exclusionists (see notes in Hebrew 10:26 and *Controversies in Revelation* for a discussion of this theology; but also see Romans 9:13). The arguments are unconvincing. It is therefore sufficient to say that God's election is done through Jesus and not the other way around. He did not elect us to choose Jesus, for that would diminish Jesus. Rather it is through Jesus that we are chosen.

Conclusion

Calvinism and Armenianism are built on suspect foundations. They echo different sides of the Aristotilian coin. Two anecdotes come to mind.

My old pastor told an anecdote about people attending a Theological conference. Two men came to attend the conference; one Calvinist and the other Armenian. When the Armenian arrived he was asked who had sent him. He replied, "no one, I chose to come" so they kicked him out as an uninvited guest. Then the Calvinist came and they ask him how he came to be here. He replied, "I was sent, I didn't choose to come" so they kicked him out because he didn't really want to be there.[717]

In another anecdote H.A. Ironside, himself a moderate Calvinist, told the story of a poor uneducated country man who explained it in this way. "The Lord done voted for my salvation; the devil done voted for my damnation, and I done voted with the Lord, and so we got into the majority."[718] This was an amusing example of how even the simplest of people can make more sense than some great theologians. Of course, the explanation is not perfect, but neither are Calvin and Armenius. It is the Bible we should pay heed to, and not theologians of any sort.

What Ephesians teaches us is that "the plan was formed before the world."[719] Salvation was no afterthough, as the Calvinist correctly states, but the choice is not between predestination and foreknowledge. The Calvinist set up false choices, such as James Boice who says there are only three views; the denial of election, election as foreknowledge only, or the Calvinist view.[720] Such intellectual dishonesty is perhaps the only way to defend an indefensible position. Election follows Jesus, not the other way around. Yes, we were chosen before the creation of the world, but we were chosen *in* Jesus. Foreknowledge, election, predestination, and salvation are not exclusive terms. Charles Talbert noted that the Greek word is an aorist participle which he takes to mean that "predestination does not follow election."[721] However, we did not need the Greek participle to know that Jesus's death on the cross is predestined. We were chosen in Him.

I have discussed issues in Calvinism and Armenianism throughout the gospels and epistles (see, for example, notes on John 12:32). Far too many in the Christian community read the Bible through theological glasses. Rather than reading the Word of God for what it is, we see it for what Calvin or Armenius saw it to be. Calvinism takes a form of fatalism wherein man is *unable* to repent. However, Biblically speaking man's problem is *not* inability but

155

unwillingness. How can man be judged for not doing something of which he is incapable? If man is not *able* to obey, how can he be condemned for disobeying? Central to the doctrine of Calvinism is the doctrine of the sovereignty of God, and yet it is the very definition of sovereignty which Calvinism threatens, for a God whose Will cannot overcome the free will of man, is not really sovereign at all.

Proverbs 16:9 best summarizes the Biblical view of sovereignty and free will. In a single sentence it explains the truth. "The mind of man plans his way, but the LORD directs his steps." This verse demonstrates the true relationship between God's will and our will; between sovereignty and free will. God's will prevails over our will. This is the first principle we must understand. The second is that our election follows Jesus. Understand these two principles and you will understand predestination.

A Misquote of Psalms?
Ephesians 4:8 – Psams 68:18

"'When He ascended on High, He led captive a host of captives, and he gave gifts to men.' Now this *expression,* 'He ascended,' what does it mean except that He also had descended into the lower parts of the earth?"	"You have ascended on high, You have led captive *Your* captives; You have received gifts among men, even *among* the rebellious also, that the LORD God may dwell *there.*"

The meaning of Jesus's descent into the earth will be discussed in the next section below. Here the issue is over the allegation that Paul is misquoting the Psalms. The primary difference is in that the Psalms speaks of receiving gifts, whereas Paul speaks of Christ giving gifts. John Calvin said bluntly, "Paul has modified the true meaning of this verse."[722] The problem is not just the question of "receiving" or "giving" but the larger context. "Psalm 68 is a psalm of triumph ... it pictures God as having been victorious over his and Israel's enemies."[723] Here, however, Paul clearly attributes it to Christ and the gift of salvation. Can this be resolved?

Some simply argue that "Paul does not intend to quote exactly or to interpret"[724] while others say that "Paul edits Psalm 68 slightly to make his point."[725] In either case, this is not an answer. Why does Paul not quote exactly? What is Paul's purpose in quoting Psalm 68 in the context of Jesus? Typically, there are four ways that theologians have resolved the alleged conflict.[726] The first is via typology. The second is that of comparison. A third argument is the Divinity argument. And the final theory is that Paul is quoting an ancient Christian hymn, not the Psalms.

In the typological view Paul is not attempting to quote Psalms but to use the picture as a "type" signifying Christ. Typological theory is based largely

156

on Hebrews 8-10 where certain historical people and events represent a sort of "prophetic symbol." For example, the Tabernacle in which the ancient Jews worshipped was meant to convey the idea of heaven and God to the people. The Tabernacle thus is a type of heaven in the book of Hebrews. However, some argue that the Tabernacle is actually a type of Jesus Christ Himself.[727] Albert Barnes sees this "as a *beaufitul emblem* of the ascension of the Redeemer to heaven."[728] In this view Paul "quotes general expressions, not by way of dogmatic proof, but freely and illustratively."[729]

The problem with the typological view is that this deviates from normal typology. A good example of typology in the Bible is the feast of Passover. God wanted to teach every generation what happened at Passover. To do this even their feast represented the historical events of Passover. For example, during the first part of the feast the Jews eat *matzo* bread which is called the "poor person's bread." This reminds them of their state of poverty in Egypt. Then they eat *maror* which is a bitter herb symbolizing the bitterness of slavery. Next, they eat *charoset* which is a sweet paste representing the mortar which the Jews used to make bricks. Thus the meal itself is a *type*. "Literalist" therefore do not reject symbolism in the Bible. We only reject making the literal historical events, such as the Exodus, into a meaningless symbol. A symbol represents something real, literal, and historical (or prophetic future history). Here the typological argument has some merit, but it does not strictly apply since the Psalm does not *appear* to reference Christ as the bread references the Passover in the example above.

Another possibility is that this is not so much typological as merely one of comparison. MacArthur calls it a "comparison passage."[730] Psalms is "a call for God to rescue his people"[731] and so Jesus rescued the believer from the grips of Satan. It is said to be an analogy where Psalms speaks of victory over the enemy through the Lord,[732] so here God grants victory through Christ. One intriguing aspect is the verse about where he "led captive a host of captives." In Hebrew this is a poetic form called a "Hebraism" which is literally "captivity captive."[733] In the context of Psalms God is taking the enemy captive, but here in Ephesians it takes on a more literal sense in that we are all captives to sin. It is our captivity itself, our bondage to sin, which God has captured, thereby freeing us from sin, even as the Lord freed Israel from their enemies. So Paul is making a comparison here rather than drawing a specific exegetical argument from it. Another important shift is from God "receiving gifts" in Pslams where in Ephesians God is "giving gifts." According to Paul, Christ is that gift.[734] William Barclay said "in the Old Testament the conquering King *demanded and received* gifts from men : in the New tesament the conquering Christ *offers and gives* gifts to men; That is the essential difference between the two testaments."[735]

A third way to deal with the problem is the divinity view. In this view, because Christ is the second person of the Trinity, God and Christ are not distinguished here. Moreover, the passage in Psalms is taken to be prophetic. Charles Hodge argues "clearly the psalmist referred to the Messiah because the psalm speaks about him ascending."[736] There is merit to this as Paul obviously takes the ascending as proof that He descended (see notes below). Consequently, Psalms can be viewed as having a double meaning; the one applying to David's kingdom, and the other a prophetic image of Christ.

One final argument should be addressed. It is the claim by some that Paul was not quoting the Psalms at all, but rather "some Chritsian hymn based on Ps. lxviii."[737] The differences then are not between Paul and the Psalmist but between the Psalm and the Christian hymn. However, there is no material support for this theory. No evidence has been found of any such hymn, making this pure speculation, and unnecessary speculation as the previous three views all adequately address the issue to one degree or another. The question is, which one is best.

Technically, the second view is superior to the first since typology does not strictly apply to Psalm 68. Proper typology is found in Hebrews but has been misused by many for one reason or another. Paul's quote is more accurately one of comparison rather than of typology. Nevertheless, the literal prophetic application should not be discarded for, as one author asked, "on what principle [did] Paul apply to the ascension"?[738] Obviously Paul took the Psalm literally enough to draw a specific conclusion from the "ascension." That conclusion is a very literal application to the "descent" of Jesus (discussed below). This is an application which would be scarcely possible if Paul did not see some prophetic imagery in the Psalm. Anyone familiar with Jewish interpretation at that time should not doubt this. Symbolism, particularly prophetic symbolism, was not a denial of the literal, as with modern day liberals, but an acknowledgement of God's hand in providence. Even a Psalm of praise could have a literal prophetic application in the future! This is supported by the Aramiac Targum translation which was composed close to the time of Paul. In the Targum the gifts are "given" rather than taken, and the recipients are referred to as "the sons of men." Gleason Archer believes that as a student of "Gamaliel, Paul would have been familiar with this Targumic rendition of Psalm 68:18."[739] Regardless of whether or not Paul was actually quoting the Targum, or paraphrasing it himself, the evidence suggest that Paul took the Psalm as at least partially having a prophetic application to Christ and particularly to the descent of Jesus.

The Descent of Jesus
Ephesians 4:9

"Now this *expression,* 'He ascended,' what does it mean except that He also had descended into the lower parts of the earth?"

This descent of Jesus evokes strong emotions from some. Some believe that Jesus descended into hell itself; a view believed by others to be nothing short of heresy. Still others say that *hades* is not hell, but *Sheol*, an abode of the dead which is divided into two halves; those destined to hell and those who will inherit heaven. Two other dominant views remain, less controversial, but no less debated. One views this as a reference to the incarnation of Jesus while another sees it merely as Jesus's physical death in the grave.

The Major Interpretations
There are four major interpretations of this passage. I present them in logical order, not order of preference. For logical ease, I treat them as if a person is progressing through life, for they could be considered the birth view, death view, hades view, and hell view. Since birth comes first, then death, and then judgment, I will present these views in that order.

The Incarnation
Undoubtebly one of the most popular views in modern times is that the descent refers to the incarnation. They see Jesus as descending from heaven.[740] They argue that "heaven stands opposed to the earth."[741] Charles Hodge calls it the "earthly regions."[742] The problem is that it seems hard to equate "He also had descended into the lower parts of the earth" (4:9) with the earth in general. John Wesley suggested that the "lower parts of the earth" is another name for the womb.[743] To support this he quoted Psalm 58:8-9 and 139:13-15.[744] The former verse is a stretch to say the least, but I will allow the reader to look up the passage for himself. Psalm 139:13-15 provides a little more help. It reads:

> "For You formed my inward parts; You wove me in my mother's womb. I will give thanks to You, for I am fearfully and wonderfully made; Wonderful are Your works, and my soul knows it very well. My frame was not hidden from You, when I was made in secret, *and* skillfully wrought in the depths of the earth."

Thus we were "wove" in our mother's womb and "wrought" in "the depths of the earth." The connection is possible, but not likely. Hebrew poetry, such as that in the Psalms, is based on parallelism.[745] It is a comparison of one thing to another, such as comparing a woman's eyes to the stars. This is the case in Psalm 139, but it is not apparent in Psalm 68 which Paul is quoting quite literally. It is suspect that Paul would make such a veiled allusion to Psalm 139.

Another argument is that of Bishop Abbott who argued that the earth itself is "this lower earth,"[746] but this seems less likely. If there is a "lower earth" then there must be an "upper earth." For that reason Charles Elliot conceded that the Greek genetive ("into") is a genitive of apposition[747] meaning that earth must either stand in apposition to heaven or to hades.[748] Obviously, the incarnation theory sees earth as opposed to heaven. It is the "lowest state of humiliation"[749] for God to become a man. R.C. Sproul is among the most famous theologians in modern times to accept the incarnation view[750] but even some of those who see the incarnation in this passage concede that there is more to this. Robert Govett, for example, sympathizes with this view but noted that Romans 10:7 is a parallel passage which explicitly refers to the death and resurrection of Christ.[751]

Romans 10:6-7 read, "the righteousness based on faith speaks as follows: 'Do not say in your heart, "who will ascend into heaven?" That is, to bring Christ down, or "Who will descend into the abyss?" That is, to bring Christ up from the dead.'" So in Romans Paul also equates the ascension and descent, but he explicitly refers to descending down into order to raise Christ up from the grave. Consequently, Govett admits that "if He was to bear their penalty, He must die. If He die, He must go down into the under world – 'Hades' – the lowest depth of the earth."[752] This leads us to the last three views, which all stem from the more natural meaning.

Death Alone

What does it mean when it says that Christ "descended into the lower parts of the earth"? This is found not only here in Ephesians but also in Romans 10:7 where it is connected with the resurrection of Jesus; not His incarnation. In short, it is connected with Jesus's death and what transpired before His resurrection. To that end three views are offered. The first is that "the lower parts of the earth" refer to the "sepulcre."[753] Lewis Sperry Chafer said it is the grave,[754] and the great Jonathan Edwards called it a euphemism for burial.[755]

Standing in isolation this makes sense, but when we look at 1 Peter 3:18-20 it appears that something else is taking place besides the burial of Jesus. Where was Jesus for the three days before His resurrection? The soul does not die, nor sleep, so where was Jesus's soul? 1 Peter 3:18-20 strongly implies (see notes there) that during those three days "He went and made proclamation to the spirits *now* in prison." What then does this mean? Was Jesus in Hell as some say, or was He in the place called *Sheol*?

Descent into Sheol

Most people have been taught that there is only heaven and hell, or purgatory if you are Catholic. We think in terms of heaven and hell, but the serious Bible student knows that heaven and hell are technically future states. In the present there is only a place called in the Old Testament *Sheol*, which is translated into Greek as *Hades*. However, *Hades* can be misleading for a variety of reasons. One reason is that *Hades* is the same term used in Greek mythology, thus confusing many Christians. In the Bible *Hades* is divided into two halves. The one is for those who are destined to hell. Some call this half alone *Hades*, although Biblically that is not correct. The second half is for those who will inherit salvation and is variously called either *Abraham's Bosom* (Luke 16:22) or *Paradise* (Luke 23:43; 2 Corinthians 12:4).[756] With this in mind, it is logically believed that after Christ died he descended into *Sheol*, where all the dead go to await judgment.

So based on this view, the passage is "an allusion to Christ's descent into Hades."[757] This view is probably the most ancient attested view known to us. It is found in the Creed of Sirmiun (circa 359 A.D.)[758] and probably the Apostle's Creed as well (see *"Descent into Hell"* discussion below). It is expressed multiple times in the second century by Irenaeus,[759] a student of Polycarp, who was in turn the disciple of the apostle John. [760] He declared in one place he said, "for three days He dwelt in the place of the death."[761] He then quoted numerous passages including Ephesians 4:9. So also Tertullian affirms the belief that Jesus resided in *Hades* for those three days, naming specifically *Abraham's Bosom* as the location within *Hades*.[762]

John MacArthur dismisses this view merely by saying that it "cannot be proven to refer to Sheol,"[763] but he presents no real evidence against it. In fact this view, and the following theory, are the only theories that can explain the parallel passages in 1 Peter 3:18-21. If Jesus was not in *Sheol*, then when and how did he preach to the dead (but see notes there)? Logically, when Jesus died His soul went *somewhere*. Since He had not yet been resurrected, He must have gone to *Sheol* where the dead await the resurrection.

Descent into Hell

Some charistmatic preachers argue that it was not *Sheol*, but hell itself to which Jesus went for those three days.[764] They argue that since Jesus paid the price for our sins, that price must include hellfire. This is not a new view, however. In John Calvin's day he lamented that "some foolishly trust this to either Limbo or hell."[765] This is based in part on 1 Peter 3:19. If Jesus preached to those in "prison" then they assume he must have been in prison with them.

Further support for this view is the alleged antiquity of the view as seen in most translations of the Apostles' Creed. If it was a part of the Apostles' Creed then it must be true, or so they say. The problem is two fold. First, the Apostles' Creed was not really written by the apostles. It dates to antiquity, but it is merely names after the Apostles. It was not written by them. Second, the Apostles' Creed probably does not refer to hell at all. Let us look at the creed. It reads in English:

> "I believe in God the Father, Almighty, Maker of heaven and earth: And in Jesus Christ, his only begotten Son, our Lord: Who was conceived by the Holy Ghost, born of the Virgin Mary: Suffered under Pontius Pilate; was crucified, dead and buried: He descended into hell: The third day he rose again from the dead: He ascended into heaven, and sits at the right hand of God the Father Almighty: From thence he shall come to judge the quick and the dead: I believe in the Holy Ghost: I believe in

161

the holy catholic church: the communion of saints: The forgiveness of sins: The resurrection of the body : And the life everlasting. Amen."

"He descended into hell" is the relevant passage, but all our copies are actually in Latin, not Greek. The Latin is *"inferos."* Although it is often associated with hell in later literature, such as Dante's Inferno, the Latin word itself does not refer to hell. It refers to "the lower world" or the land of the dead.[766] In other words, it is synoymous with *Hades*, not hell. So the proper translation of the Apostles' Creed fits the *Hades* theory, rather than the hell theory.

There are several problems with the hell thesis. Some of these are debated under 1 Peter 3:18-20. However, the most obvious problem is that Jesus told the repentant thief on the cross, "Truly I say to you, today you shall be with Me in Paradise" (Luke 23:43). Jesus then declared that He was going, on that very *day*, to Paradise; not to hell. *"Today* you shall be with Me *in Paradise"* (Luke 23:43). These words should settle the matter once and for all.

Conclusion
Although these are the four dominant views, there have of course been other theories. Some argue it is a reference to Pentecost,[767] but Pentecost followed the ascension whereas Paul clearly places the descent before His ascension. Others have simply dismissed the entire passage as "ambiguous."[768] However, Jesus was not ambiguous when he told the repentant thief, *"Today* you shall be with Me *in Paradise"* (Luke 23:43). The context of Paul's epistle should make it clear that he is at the very least alluding to the resurrection if not outright speaking of it. So the descent which precedes this should be seen in the most literal sense as Jesus's descent into the Paradise of *Sheol*.

Appointment of Men
Ephesians 4:11

"And He gave some *as* apostles, and some *as* prophets, and some *as* evangelists, and some *as* pastors and teachers."

In 1 Corinthians 12:4-31 we discussed the gifts of the spirit and the gifts of leadership which included apostles, prophets, teachers, miracle workers, healers, helpers, and administrators (1 Corinthians 12:28). Here Paul again mentions the leadership roles. Since I have discussed much of this in 1 Corinthians 12:4-31 as well as apostleship in *Controversies in the Acts of the Apostles* I will restrict my discussion primarily to that of evangelists and pastors, who were not specifically mentioned in 1 Corinthians.

Like Corinthians Paul list apostles and prophets first. Although some argue that the term apostle can refer to missionaries,[769] it is noteworthy that Paul list evangelists separately from apostles. Now while an evangelist is technically

162

different from a missionary, so also an apostle is different from a missionary. John Calvin felt that "evangelist held a kindred office, but of an inferior rank"[770] to apostles. The apostles were more than missionaries and evangelists. One requirement was that they had to be personally selected by Jesus Christ (see notes in Acts 1:26). Lloyd-Jones argues that the Greek of 4:11 "is emphatic; not 'He' but 'He Himself.'"[771] God personally selected the apostles. So while some include Barnabas, Silvanus, Andronicus, and others as apostles,[772] the more likely answer is that an apostle was "the official title of the Twelve, including Paul."[773] As James Boice said, "here 'apostle' and 'prophet' must be taken in their most technical sense."[774]

What then is an evangelist? Albert Barnes argued that an evangelist is essentially the same as an apostle except "they did not possess the qualifications or the authority of" the apostles.[775] Walter Lock believed that apostles were "for founding new churches"[776] and H.A. Ironside said that "the apostles and prophets were to lay the foundation" of the church.[777] This would be the major difference. Evangelist lack the authority of the apostles and did not establish the church. The apostles were the foundation stones and Jesus was the cornerstone. Peter (and the other apostles) was a πετρος (petros) but Jesus was the λιθος (lithos). The analogy is sound. A building rest upon its cornerstone, without which the building collapses, but the foundation must be solid as well. The cornerstone is the λιθος (lithos). A foundation block is a πετρος (petros), and so all the apostles were rocks.

Now as I discussed prophets previously, I will only briefly address them here. Some believe that, like apostles, prophets "have passed from the scene."[778] They say that prophets are no more.[779] R.C. Sproul argued that "since the Bible is complete, there are not any prophets today."[780] This, however, assumes that prophets were a substitute as it were for the Bible, but did not the Jews have the Scriptures as well? If it argued that the Old Testament was incomplete, then I will remind the reader that Jesus called Abel a prophet (Luke 11:50–51) and yet the Bible records nothing seemingly prophetic about Abel.[781] Moreover, at least two prophets are mentioned in Revelation, and Jesus told us that Elijah would return some day (Matthew 17:11). Nevertheless, prophets were rare even in Biblical times, and most never once called themselves prophets. In fact, John the Baptist even denied being a prophet (John 1:21)!

Other scholars have said that "prophet" is "not only in the more special sense ... but in the more general one of preachers and expounders,"[782] although this is doubtful. Another commentator declared that "we know only a limited amount about New Testament prophets."[783] One thing is certain. Like apostles, prophets were few. While Charles Hodge believes that apostles were "made infallible by the gift of inspiration"[784] Peter was certainly fallible as seen in Galatians 2! No man is infallible, save Christ. The Bible itself is infallible only the hand of the Lord; not because its authors never erred in their daily life. A scientist is fallible and may make many mistakes in his research, but we hope that by the time he finishes his findings and publishes them, there will be no mistakes. The scientist is far from infallible, but his published findings we hope are (I say this by way of analogy only, as many opinions of scientists are flawed and in error, for the only thing "all scientists argee upon" is that only fools say "all scientists agree"). So also when the fallible prophet composes Scripture he is guided by the hand of the Lord.

What then are pastors? The question is more controversial than one might believe. Protestants have been quick to point out that "priests" "are never so much as mentioned"[785] in the epistle. "Had Christian ministers been intended to offer sacrifices, as Jewish priests were, then 'priests' would have been the most obvious and the most natural name by which to call them."[786] The very title "priest" carries with it certain duties which many believe conflicts with the nature of the church. The necessity of sacrifice, a primary duty of priests, is one of those. Nevertheless, it must be conceded in fairness that "those titles are not exactly titles of offices in the Church, but rather express different functions."[787] The Greek word here is actually ποιμενας (*poimenas*) which is a shepherd. It it thus translated either as pastor or shepherd. The title is significant. Unlike a priest, a pastor shepherds a flock. Sheep are easily frightened and run off when treated harshly or scared. A pastor gently herds his flock. He also must know how many sheep he has. A pastor who has too many sheep cannot care for them all, and will necessarily have many sheep stray from the flock and be killed by wolves. The analogy is appropriate. Too many churches are becoming "megachurches." Pastors do not even know the name of all their members, and couldn't if they tried. Paul does not speak of the priesthood, as with Israel, nor of megachurches. He chose the term "pastor" for a reason.

Interestingly enough, although teachers (or doctors as Calvin called them) is listed after pastors, Calvin believed that they "superintend both the education of pastors and the instruction of the whole church."[788] So the role of the teacher has sometimes been considered of more importance than the pastor. Since pastors were not specifically even mentioned in 1 Corinthians 12, this argument has some merit. Teachers were listed third there, but fifth here. Was Paul assigning a specific order of importance here? Probably not. In Corinthians he does specify that it is "first apostles, second prophets, third teachers" (1 Corinthians 12:28), but does not state order elsewhere. A pastor teaches his congregation but a Bible teacher teaches future pastors. This makes his role significant. It is his teaching which should help to insure that "we are no longer to be children, tossed here and there by waves and carried about by every wind of doctrine, by the trickery of men, by craftiness in deceitful scheming" (Ephesians 4:14). Unfortunately, many pastors, preachers, and evangelists are the very ones who promote such crafty, deceitful, doctrines! This is why good Bible teachers are hard to find, but vital. The Scriptures must be the root that binds us to Christ.

164

Is It Okay to Be Angry?
Ephesians 4:26

"Be angry, and *yet* do not sin; do not let the sun go down on your anger."

It is ironic that many people quote this passage to justify anger. They say that Paul is commanding us to "vent." Of course, "venting" is a psychological term invented in recent history and it is term which expresses a philosophy which is at odds with the Bible and, frankly, sets a dangerous precedence.

Three different interpretations exist of this passage. The first is that Paul does not consider anger to be bad at all, but a way of "venting." As long as we "do not sin" they believe that anger should be released. The second view says that this is permissive. We will get angry because we are sinners, but we should control our anger and restrain from sinning externally when we are angry. A third view says that this refers to "righteous indignation." Jesus became angry on occasion, but always with good cause. So this view holds that Paul is not speaking of ordinary anger but righteous indignation.

The first of these interpretations should be rejected. It is based on Freduian grounds, not Biblical grounds, and is a dangerous theology. F.F. Bruce claims that "it is not sinful to be angry,"[789] but this is a blanket statement. While anger against evil may not be sinful, anger is rarely constrained to such things. The emotion of anger is very often triggered by sin in our hearts. Albert Barnes is thus more truthful when he says that there "*may* be anger without sin" but there is "danger in *all* cases."[790] Freud, an atheist, believed that sin was never wrong. The idea of "venting" and "releasing our anger" in an unharmful way is a trendy term for lack of self control. Rather than controlling our anger, as Paul asserts here, we argue that yelling ("venting") is a "harmless" way of releasing "pent up" emotions. In fact, James 3:5-8 warns of us the dangers of such "venting." He declared that "the tongue is a fire, the *very* world of iniquity; the tongue is set among our members as that which defiles the entire body, and sets on fire the course of *our* life, and is set on fire by hell" (v. 6) and "no one can tame the tongue; *it is* a restless evil *and* full of deadly poison" (v. 8). Many other places in the Bible also warn of the bitterness of the tongue and the harm that harshly spoken words may cause (cf. Psalm 34:14, 64:3; Proverbs 12:18, 18:6-8, 18:21, 21:23, 25:23). Lewis Sperry Chafer once said, "words which do not edify are quite sure to injure."[791] Indeed, it is likely that harsh words was the primary meaning of Paul here, although he did not restrict "sin" to this alone.

Now John Calvin saw an allusion to Genesis and the struggles between Jacob and Esau. He saw this as striving or quarreling, noting that God "wants them to be troubled by striving with their own spirits" and adds that "we seek the object of our anger in ourselves rather than in others."[792] So looking inward, rather than outward, is the Biblical appraoch to dealing with anger.

Charles Hodge notes that "the words 'in your anger do not sin' are borrowed from the *Septuagint* version of Psalm 4:4 and can be interpreted in various ways. 1. The original text in Psalms 4:4 can be translated, 'Rage and sin not' – i.e., 'Do not sin by raging'; so the words of the apostle may mean, 'Do not commit the sin of being angry' ... others say the first is conditinal, 'if angry, sin not.'"[793] This is the question. Is sin permissible?

The second view says that because we are sinners we will be angry, but "if you are stirred to sinful anger"[794] then beware. This "is a permissive imperative, rather than a direct command to be angry."[795] Paul is conceding that we will be angry because of our nature, but, to quote Erasmus, "let your anger not only do no harm, but let it also be short lived."[796] Tertullian said, "even if we *must* be angry, our anger, must not be maintained beyond sunset."[797] So it is argued that there is "a distinction between the emotion of anger, for which we may not be responsible, and what we do with it."[798] Still, one criticism of this view exist. "Such a meaning would require αλλα, or the like, instead of και."[799] In other words, it should read "be angry *but* do not sin," rather than "be angry *and* do not sin." However, if this is a quotation of the Greek *Septuagint* then the argument is nullified, and they are word for word the same. This leaves us with one final option.

R.C. Sproul argued that this is "righteous indignation."[800] Rather than being anger in general it is anger "lawfully aroused by injustice."[801] John Wesley said that "anger at sin is not evil; but ... if we are angry at the person, as well as the fault, we sin."[802] MacArthur says, "Jesus was always angered when the Father was maligned or when others were mistreated, but He was never selfishly angry at what was done against Him. That is the measure of righteous anger."[803] Further support for this is allegedly found in Psalms 4:5, a continuation of the passage Paul is quoting.[804] There it says, "Offer the sacrifices of righteousness, And trust in the LORD." However, such a statement may simply reinforce that we should trust the Lord rather than allow anger to consume us.

The truth is that both the second and third views are correct. Anger *may* be righteous indignation, but the middle voice of the Greek suggests that the anger is from within us, and not aroused by outside factors, like evil, alone. Paul is thus making a concession here. It is a "permissive imperative"[805] which allows for both righteous indignation and our sinful nature. The key to this passage is not the anger, but the dangers that anger brings. As Robert Govett said, "anger allowed to settle in the bosom becomes hatred."[806] This is the danger in allowing anger to fester and in "venting" our anger so that we lose self-control over our feelings. Both are sins.

Paul warned that anger opens the door to the devil (4:27). The *Pastor of Hermas*, probably the most ancient non-Biblical writing from New Testament times, states that "the Lord dwells in long-suffering, but the devil in anger."[807] We will all be angry from time to time. Paul acknowledged this was inevitable, but he warns against allowing the devil to get a foothold in our anger. Whether righteous indignation or more selfish reasons, we must never allow our anger to fester nor to sin (which includes "venting"). Two things are urged. Do not sin by opening your mouth, or worse, and second, do not allow anger to linger.

Marriage and Submission
Ephesians 5:22-28

> "Wives, *be subject* to your own husbands, as to the Lord. For the husband is the head of the wife, as Christ also is the head of the church, He Himself *being* the Savior of the body."

Few people remember that it was Christianity that brought more liberty and freedom to women by elevating the status of motherhood and family. Among the ancient Vikings women did all the manual labor and hard work, sometimes even fighting battles, while the men drank beer and ruled the society. Back then there were no modern feminists (which I distinguish from the original suffragettes) demanding the right to til the field. Work meant work in those days. Since the time of Karl Marx, family has increasingly been under attack. Marx himself said that communism seeks the "abolition of the family."[808] "Society" must supercede family. Consequently, liberal socialism invariably undercuts the importance of family and its structure. One of those is the nature of "submission" and the "traditional" role of the wife and mother. Obviously, because we have been trained since childhood to believe that there something "inferior" about motherhood, house wives, and submission, passages such as this one, Colossians 3:18 - 14:1, and many others are highly controversial, so we must again go through the passages step by step to understand what the apostle wanted to say, rather than what we choose to hear.

The Definition of Submission
The first thing we must do is define "submission." The Majority text here uses the word ὑποτασσεσθε (*hypotassesthe*). In the parallel passage in Colossians 3:18 the same word is used. It is "submit" is in the Greek middle voice.[809] This reflects the idea of both inward and outward action in a verb. Interestingly enough, the most ancient text of this passage does not actually use the word "submit" here, but rather supplies the idea of acting. It would technically be "act toward your husbands as to the Lord." Of course this begs many questions which will addressed below. At this stage only the definition at issue. John MacArthur is correct when he says, "Paul says categorically to *all* believing wives: be subject to your own husbands"[810] but notes that the Greek word is different from what is used of children.[811]

Indeed, the verb "submit" (sometimes translated "subject") is different from the word used of children in verse 6:1. That word is "obey" ('υπακουετε – *hypotassesthe*). There is a difference. "Obey" in Greek comes from the root word "to hear" or "listen." The word for "submit" comes from a root word meaning to "under" the authority of another. As John Wesley pointed out, "it is properly a military term."[812] Now the military analogy does not work entirely well with family, but it is appropriate in some ways for no one believes that a soldier is inferior to his commanders. In fact, the Commander in Chief of the U.S. Army is the President of the United States yet I have rarely met anyone who thinks the soldiers who fight on the battle field are inferior to him in way except authority. As Warren Wiersbe said, "the fact that one soldier is a private and another is a colonel does not mean that one man is necessarily *better* than the other."[813] The fact is simply that an army cannot function if everyone is doing their own thing. The 50-50% argument does not work either, for if both partners agree then it is 100%. There must be someone to break the tie. That is why the military has a chain of command. Now, once again, the analogy is limited for a family is not meant to be a battlefield at all. Nor is it meant to be a power struggle. Each has their own duties and responsibilities which can make it work.

Mellick believes that the difference between "submission" and "obedeience" is that submission is voluntary.[814] In any case, all of this defines the word "submission." It does not define the context or the meaning of its relationship to the family *per se*. It does, however, give us a starting point to understand the context in which it is given.

Submission and the Family
The ultimate question is, "what does this all mean?" Straw men arguments have been made on various levels from both sides. One side depicts the traditional family as a sexist abusive patriarchy acting as a tyrant. The other side claims that submission means to obey in everything without question. Our job is to see what submission means within the context of a Biblical marriage and family.

First, I previously alluded to the fact that many ancient Greek texts omit the word "submit," indicating rather "act toward your husbands as to the Lord." Note that the Lord is the center of everything. God is the priority. Erasmus Sarcerius stated that "a husband who acts [abusive] is a tyrant."[815] God is not a tyrant, but when we lived under tyrants, such as the emperor Nero, we do not rebel except under rare and special circumstances. This is why Paul urged us to submit to our governments as well. Rebelling against tyranny can often lead to worse tyranny. The Spartacus revolt did not end slavery, but lead to the deaths of tens of thousands of slaves and more harsh conditions for slaves. Consequently, Paul and the apostles submitted unto death! They died rather than renounce the Lord, but they did not rebel. Even as they were led to execution they could say that they broke no true law of Rome. Thus they were true martyrs.

In the context of the family, the point is that submission does not mean blind obedience. God must be first in our lives in all things, but it does mean that we do not rebel or start fights. Even when the husband is wrong, loving submission will often lead him to the Lord. One secret few women know is that men can be made to do almost anything as long as the women does not act superior or confrontational. Queen Esther did not save her nation and change the world by acting superior, but by acting submissive and loving. She is the ideal of the perfect wife, and in so doing she was able to influence a pagan king into shaping the world in a better way. The woman who derides "traditional women" ignores the fact that it is they who made the saying, "behind every great man is a woman."

Now it is true that men often misrepresent or abuse their priviledge, just as woman do the same with their priviledges. Views have varied from one extreme to the other, but contrary to popular revisionist history, no one generation was starkly different from another, or more repressive. Take, for example, the sixteenth century. Erasmus declared that "the husband takes precedence over his wife not in such a manner as to execrcise tyranny over her, but to take thought for her well-being."[816] In constrast, the words of John Calvin might seem far more strict, saying, "wives cannot obey Christ unless they yield obedience to their husbands."[817] Nevertheless, as Christianity taught to uphold the weak, the idea of the "weaker" sex was what led to chivalry and gallantry. As Findlay remarked, "Christianity ... raises the weaker sex to honor."[818]

Some call the rule on submission "generic."[819] John Wesley said that women should submit "unless where God forbids."[820] In the days of the early church Ignatius, one of the earliest church fathers, declared that women should submit,[821] but also emphasized that husband must love their wives.[822] Men are to cherish their wives as their own bodies (5:29). George Findlay declares that it is "a free and sympathetic obedience – which is true submission – can only subsist between equals."[823] Charles Hodge, however, goes to the extreme of using the oxymoron, "mutual submission."[824] Mutual love is more appropriate, but then the whole idea of submission necessitates that one has a certain measure of authority over the other, so there can be no "mutual submission." Abuse of authority is another issue, discussed below. The importance is not one of shifting blame or creating prerequisites for our own obedience to the Lord, but knowing what our godly role in marriage and family is to be. Prerequisites and the blame game only further aggrevate the problems which do arise in ungodly marriages. If Paul "submitted" to pagan Rome, should be not submit to a godly husband? This is repeated many times in the Scriptures so there is not doubt. Colossians 3:18 – 14:1 and 1 Peter 3:6 are but a few such passages.

Now if motherhood is elevated in the Christian family, and submission is required of her, then what is the role of the man? As with the woman, we must begin with definitions and then look to the context.

The "Head"

Earlier I mentioned that "submission" is often a military term. Here Paul discusses a hierachy. The concept of the man as the "head" of the household has long been accepted in Christianity, but in recent days it has become viewed as a "sexist" institution compared to more barbaric "patriarchal societies." Is this fair?

Warren Wiersbe notes that Jesus washed the feet of his apostles.[825] Indeed, Jesus said that a leader must be a servant (Luke 22:26; Matthew 20:26; Mark 10:43). That does not mean that the leader is any less of a leader, but more of one. Nevertheless, a soldier's obedience to his superior officer is not dependent upon the worthiness of the officer. It is his duty. So also Albert Barnes declared that wives' submission is a "duty" as well.[826] The private is a subordinate of the sergeant, but as R.C. Sproul once commented that suboridination does not mean inferiority.[827] It is necessary to have a chain of command. Here Paul establishes that chain of command beginning with Christ.

Christ is the head of man, and man is the head of woman. So long as the man does not require something in conflict with Christ, the woman should obey even when the man is wrong, but that submission is never absolute. Submission to God alone is absolute. *The Liberty Commentary* says that "submission is not slavish fear, neither is it forced upon her by a demanding domestic despot, but it is voluntary."[828] Perhaps so, but if a soldier violates his orders he must be willing to prove to the General that his disobedience is grounded in chain of command, rules of engagement, or the Constitution. If a wife disrespects her husband she will have to demonstrate to God that if was because he was demeaning something which violates the law of God and Christ.

What then when the man is wrong? I will tell women a secret few in this generation know. The secret to controlling a man is let him think he is right. The secret to controlling a man was known and practiced by Queen Esther who obeyed the king and followed court ettiquette esquisitely. This is in contrast to Queen Vashti who defied her husband's degrading request (and it was demeaning) and was cast out from the King. Esther saved a nation with womanly charms and submissive love. Vashti threw away her crown by her arrogance, even if it was well deserved. Let Esther then be a woman's role model for a less than perfect husband.

One final comment is necessary concerning headship. Verse 24 reads, "But as the church is subject to Christ, so also the wives *ought to be* to their husbands in everything." Now regarding the participle "but," Robert Govett noted that "much questioning has arisen regarding the force of this particle."[829] Some mean that this is in contrast to the previous verse, but this would make little sense in context. Moreover, the Greek word αλλα (*alla*) or "but" does not always means "in contrast to." One basic lexicon says it "adds emphasis" e.g., "not only this but also."[830] Another intermediate Greek text books says, "sometimes αλλα is used as an emphatic particle rather than as a conjuction."[831] That this is the case here is obvious by the fact that verse 24 compliments verse 23. It does not contrast with it. "As the church is subject to Christ, so also the wives *ought to be* to their husbands." Yet one question remains. What is the role of the husband?

The Husband's Role

After declaring the role of the wive, Paul now turns to the husband, declaring, "Husbands, love your wives, just as Christ also loved the church and gave Himself up for her, so that He might sanctify her, having cleansed her by the washing of water with the word, that He might present to Himself the church in all her glory, having no spot or wrinkle or any such thing; but that she would be holy and blameless. So husbands ought also to love their own wives as their own bodies."

This was no new command to the early Christians, for it was Christianity that elevated women's status in society. Ignatius, the famed apostlolic father and martyr, emphasized men's role in loving their wives.[832] Protecting the "weaker sex" was thus a duty and honor for men. Chivarly, now reviled by the lesbian and modern feminist movement, grew out of Christian love and respect. The status of motherhood was also elevated.

The early Reformer David Dickson believed that men were to "defend, cherish, and comfort"[833] women. Such was the doctrine of the Reformation. They emphazied love and goodness, not dominence.[834] F.F. Bruce said that "the wife's subordination to her husband has as its counterpart the husband's obligation to love his wife."[835] This is true, but we must remember that the one is not contigent upon other. We must all do what is right regardless of what others do. In this modern society we all make ourselves out to be victims, blaming others for our problems, and in so doing we victimize ourselves. This is literally true in many of the inner cities where gangs have replaced traditional families, and violence envelops the communities. They made themselves victims by embracing the doctrine of victimization. Those brave enough to reject the heresy invariably leave only to become outcast. The same is true of our society in general. In rejecting godly families and marriages, the Marxists have won their first battle. Where mother and father do not provide for their children's well being someone else, with less noble intentions, will step in to fulfill that role.

Conclusion

In the modern world "submission" has come to be associated with mindless obedience and slavery. Such an absurd definition has ironically enslaved the minds of the very people who promote it. *Everyone* submits to something and to someone. No one is free from this because we do not live alone in the world. In order to get along and survive, we must submit to one another in one way or another. The real question is to whom have we submitted? Have we submitted to God and to godly institutions such as the family? Or have we submitted to the myths and lies of "empowerment" and socialism? It is no coincidence that there were no modern feminist[836] in the day when "equality" meant working in a coal mine.

Throughout these verses Paul establishes Christ and the church as the role model for marriage (5:29-33). Christ Himself is the head of the church, and yet He washed His disciples feet. He is no dictator but a loving God who sacrificed Himself for those He loved. So also the man must love his wife as much, but she must submit even as the church submits to Christ. This is the pattern for marriage. It is a small foretaste the church's marriage with Christ.

Lloyd Ogilvie helps give some historical context by reminding us that Paul "presented a radically new view of marriage which elevated women."[837] Family and motherhood have always been revered in Christianity. This is why Christianity led to the old saying, "behind every great man is a woman." It is doubtful whether or not that is true anymore, but then perhaps that is why there are so few great men anymore.

Self-Esteem?
Ephesians 5:29

"No one ever hated his own flesh, but nourishes and cherishes it."

In the last half century the self-esteem movement has not only encompassed the whole of secular society but has been embraced by the church as well. We are told that we must love ourselves before we can love others, but the underlying assumption here is that self-hatred, not selfishness, is the root of sin. Such a notion is a byproduct of the "Me Generation" and has no basis in fact. Here Paul explicitly says "no one ever hated his own flesh." The "ever" is emphatic. No one. Not one. What then of the rash of suicides and drug addicts? Do they not lack self-esteem? Here is the heart of the problem. Why do they do what they do?

Dave Hunt and T.A. McMahon said that "the person who says, 'I'm so ugly, I hate myself!' doesn't hate himself at all, or he would be *glad* that he was ugly. It is because he loves himself that he is upset with his appearance and the way people respond to him."[838] This is true. Self love is *intrinsic*. We only see the world through our own eyes because we are separated from God. This makes us, by definition, selfish. In another word, it makes us sinners. I can think of no one who has put the "self image" issue more in perspective than Hunt and McMahon when they said:

172

"God made man in His own image. One thinks immediately of a mirror, which has *one purpose only*: to reflect a reality *other than its own*. It would be absurd for a mirror to try to develop a 'good self-image.' It is equally absurd and certainly unbiblical, for humans to attempt to do so. If there is something wrong with the image in the mirror, then the only solution is for the mirror to get back in a right relationship with the one whose image it was designed to reflect."[839]

Jesus is the solution to our problems, not selfishness. I lived in Plano when it was the suicide capital of the world. The people who were committing suicide was often rich, handsome, and popular. It was not enough, because they had no meaning in life. It is only God that gives us meaning, not self fulfillment or inner fulfillments as the trend has become to call such self gratifications. The problem with "self esteem" is the same as the problems with pride. John Piper put it best when he said, "boasting is the voice of pride in the heart of the strong. Self-pity is the voice of pride in the heart of the weak. Boasting sounds self-sufficient. Self-pity sounds self-sacrificing."[840] They are the flip side of the same problem; not self esteem but selfishness.

Paul's appeal here is not put ourselves first, but to love others in the same way we love ourselves. No one has ever starved to death by accident. We do not forget to eat or drink. We do it intrinsicly because we love our bodies. We do not neglect our bodies when hunger pangs start except by the most rigid self discipline practiced in hunger strikes. Such strikes are not easy because we naturally love ourselves. It is impossible not to love ourselves. If we say we hate ourselves then we are either lying to ourselves, or we are really hating the sin within us, but not realizing that it is sin. When we learn to recognize that sin and hate it, then we can begin to conform to Christ. Then we can love our spouses as we love our own bodies.

Christians and Slavery
Ephesians 6:5-9

"Slaves, be obedient to those who are your masters according to the flesh, with fear and trembling, in the sincerity of your heart, as to Christ."

One of the great lies presented by opponents of the Bible is that the Bible endorses slavery. Nevermind that the abolitionist movement was an explicitly evangelical Christian movement. Nevermind that slavery existed in every nation in human history until the Puritans first outlawed it in their colonies. Nevermind that the Apostle Paul was not the Caesar of Rome. Facts don't matter when you are trying to demonize the Bible. Nevertheless, it is true that many Christians have believed that slavery was acceptable and Paul is asking slaves to be obedient. The question is "why?"

As per usual, I will reserve my answer, simple as it may be, until the conclusion. First it is best to examine the historical and political context as well as the nation of Israel's view on slavery. The reader will see that contrary to the picture presented by hypocrites, the Bible was the central role in the abolition of slavery, but not via political revolution like Spartacus's ill fated attempt, but through the diffusion of the gospel and the sufferings of the church.

Israel and Slavery

Deuteronomy is usually the first book misquoted by Bible critics. President Obama even mocked Christians by implying that Deuteronomy was the basis for slavery in America, but what does Deuteronomy really say, and what was the law of Israel regarding slavery? After all, Paul was a Jew and an Israelite. So also was Jesus who explicitly said, "I have not come to abolish the law" (Matthew 5:17). Did that include slavery?

First, every school child should know that the Israelites were slaves under Egypt. Moses led the slaves to freedom. This is why the Jews were commanded six times in Deuteronomy to "remember that you were a slave in the land of Egypt" and act justly towards neighbors (Deuteronomy 5:15; 15:15; 16:12; 23:15; 24:18, 22).

Edward Poynter – Israel in Egypt – 1867

Second, while slavery existed in Israel, it existed in every nation, but only Israel placed severe restrictions upon slavery, even requiring that slaves be set free after six years of service (Exodus 21:2),[841] thereby being the first nation in human history to provide for abolition within its law.

174

Finally, Deuteronomy places numerous restrictions upon the slave holder and severely punishes the master who abuses his slaves. These restrictions made it impractical for most Israelites to own slaves at all, thereby ensuring that Israel always had fewer slaves than any surrounding nation and that the slaves who did exist had hope of freedom. Examples of the restrictive laws are as follows.

Exodus 21 lays out several laws punishing the master who injures his slave. In many cases the slave is to be set free (Exodus 21:26-27). Even if a slave is injured by accident while working for his master he can often be set free along with thirty shekels of silver (Exodus 21:32), which was a large sum in those days. More importantly, Deuteronomy (the very book misquoted by Bible critics) *forbids the return of escaped slaves* (Deuteronomy 23:15). Additionally, it was a crime punishable by death to obtain slaves by kidnapping (Exodus 21:16),[842] which eliminated the number one method of acquiring slaves for sale! The law reads in full, "he who kidnaps a man, whether he sells him or he is found in his possession, shall surely be put to death."

It is true that men like Heinrich Bullinger believed slavery was acceptable,[843] but any serious study of the laws of Israel and Deuteronomy make it clear that Israel was the only nation in antiquity which placed so many restrictions upon slave holders that slavery was largely unknown outside of its rich kings. Indeed, no serious scholar calls Israel a slave state. It was predominantly the kings of Israel who owned slaves, and many of those violated the laws of Moses. By the time of Paul few Jews outside of Herod owned slaves. The law of Israel had done its job in removing the stain of slavery from which the Jews had themselves escaped. This was not, however, the case with ancient Rome.

Historical Context

Rome was not Christian. Nero persecuted Christians. Christians had no say in the legality of slavery. It was a fact of Rome. Any statement by Paul must be understood in this context.

The fact is that "slavery was an established institution in Paul's day. At least half of the population were slaves."[844] By some estimates it "has been computed that in the Romans Empire there were 60,000,000 slaves."[845] William Barclay says that "even doctors and teachers were slaves."[846] Unlike the laws of Israel the Roman slave had no appeal to the law.[847] Men like Plato even said that it was better to let a slave die than pay money to heal them! Despite such cruel and barbaric conditions some have claimed that slavery was benevolent outside of America! In attempting to demonize the first abolitionist nation in history (and so the United States was so called by none other than Alexis deTocqueville),[848] they have actually trivialized the evil of slavery.

The fact is that slavery plagued Rome. The Spartacus revolt had not resulted in freedom for slaves but more harsh and brutal treatment. Rome responded to the revolt with severity in hopes that it would deter future revolts. Spartacus had thus resulted only in worse condition for slaves. As Barclay commented, "it is against that terrible background that Paul's advice to slaves has to be read."[849]

Political Context

The historical context set the stage for the political context. As aforementioned, the Spartacus revolt led to more strict laws. For example, an escaped slave was to be sentenced to death. This is why Paul was concerned with reconciling the escaped slave to his master in the epistle to Philemon. Paul feared for his life.

On a more practical level we must understand that Paul was not looking for political revolution. The "social gospel" may be an outgrowth of the gospel, but it cannot replace the gospel as many have done. Charles Findlay said that "to have proclaimed [slavery's] abolition would have meant universal anarchy."[850] It took two thousand years of the gospel to end slavery and even that ended in a bloody affair.

John Wesley, himself an abolitionist, commented that Paul's advice to slaves was "according to the present state of things; afterwards the servant is free from his master."[851] In other words, this world is not our own. Paul calls Satan the "god of this world" (2 Corinthians 4:4). To try to bring heaven to the earth through man's efforts is not only doomed to failure, but ultimately plays into the hands of the enemy. Some of the worst dictatorships in human history have been sold on the myths of a man-made Utopia. Communism is the best example. Its Utopian rhetoric only disguises the fact that it is a system that gives the government supreme powers above and beyond both family and religion. The result has been literally hundreds of millions of butchered dead and more poverty and inequality than any other political or economic system in history. Paul understood that government was not the answer; Jesus was. To that end, as R.C. Sproul said, "he is simply addressing those who happen to be in that particular situation."[852] This cannot be taken as an endorsement by any serious exegete.

Biblical Context

Several different approaches have been taken in examining Paul's comments here. One view is that "it cannot be demonstrated that the word here necessarily means *slaves*."[853] It is argued that as Paul is speaking of servants, rather than slaves, but the fact is that ancient Rome had few, if any, paid servants. They were slaves. There was no distinguishing between the two. It is also clear that Paul is not speaking allegorically. The word clearly refers to slaves.

The other approach is that of Charles Hodge who states that slavery "is neither enjoined nor forbidden."[854] Technically this is true of this passage. Paul is not discussing the evils or benefits of slavery at all. He is not discussing politics or abolitionism. Neither is he endorsing the institution, which has already been demonstrated was in violation of the Torah's law and regulations on slavery. Any attempt to argue that Paul's commands to slaves serves as an endorsement of slavery is dishonest. The entire context of Paul's remarks is to enjoin the believer to understand that we are not of this present evil world. We belong to a heavenly kingdom where "there is neither slave nor free man" (Galatians 3:28) but where we are all equals.

John MacArthur points out that the abolitionists were evangelical Christians.[855]   Indeed, from the earliest abolitionists to John Wesley, who founded the Methodist Church, Christianity was at the heart of abolitionism. Contrary to many people's understanding George Washington outlawed the African slave trade although it continued illegally for nearly a century until the Civil War. It is Christ who taught the equality of all men and, as one commentary states, "slavery must ultimately disappear where the gospel is proclaimed, with its implications of human equality, Christian brotherhood, and the lordship of Christ."[856] This is exactly what happened in America, the first true abolitionist country in human history.[857]

Francis Carpenter – The First Reading of the Emancipation Proclamation – 1864

Conclusion

Paul, who was executed by Rome, nevertheless told his followers to submit to Rome. He did not, however, ask us to deny Christ when Rome so ordered. We did not rebel or start a revolution, because this world is not our own. Submission does not mean obeying everything but it does mean not rebelling against anything. God must come first. Paul never obeyed Rome's demand to renounce Christ and sacrifice to Nero, but neither did he rebel and start an ill-fated war. This fact is essential to understanding *how* Christianity *overcame* Rome. It was not a war fought with bullets, but with the spirit.

Bear in mind that Paul wrote this epistle from prison. He was a slave to Rome in the absolute sense. Consequently, Paul's comments here are not about slavery as an institution, which Christianity necessarily condemns, but instructions on how to live as a Christian in an evil world hostile to our faith and freedoms. Slavery was abolished by evangelical Christians. No revisionist historian can deny it. Christ led to the formal abolition of slavery, but slavery still exist in various forms to this very day. Slavery will never truly end until Christ returns. We must learn how to survive with our innocence intact and understand that government is not the solution to our problems; Christ is.

Summary

Ephesians is one of Paul's first prison epistles. The church of Ephesus was one of the most prominent in Asia and close to Paul's heart. It would later serve as the church of John, and was one of the seven churches to whom John wrote in Revelation (2:1-7). The epistle here addresses various issues doctrinally and instructionally. In as much as Paul was unable to teach them in person he wrote the prison epistles to teach them via letter. Those epistles now serve to instruct all the churches of Christ to this very day.

6

Philippians

It is generally agreed that the church of Philippi was near and dear to Paul. It was certainly one of his favorites, and nothing negative is said about it by Paul. It is also one of only two churches in Revelation which has no critical remarks or warnings (Revelation 3:7-12). Although Paul does forewarn the Philippians of coming dangers and problems, the letter is not critical in tone at all. Most believe that Paul wrote the epistles as a thank you letter for their contribution (Philippians 4:18).[858]

It is no irony that Philippians is a name which is literally translated as "one who loves his brother." Of course the church simply took its name from the city, but the Philippians do appear to have been one of the most faithful and loyal churches. It is not surprising that Paul would have written to them during his long imprisonment, for when one is imprison it is encouraging to speak to those with whom you have a close affinity and bond. Philippians has thus been called one of Paul's most personal letters.

The Date and Occasion of the Epistle

As aforemention, the occasion of the epistle was Paul's desire to thank the Philippians for their gift to him (4:18) and to give instructions and teaching in his absence. That absence is explicitly said to be on account of his imprisonment (1:7, 13), but there is some debate as to which imprisonment Paul refers. Several different imprisonments have been suggested. The first two suggestions are the first and second imprisonments in Rome. A third argues that Paul was in Caesarea, but a fourth had gained prominence in recent years. That is the idea that Paul was writing from imprisonment in Ephesus (cf. Acts 19:22)[859] around 53-55 A.D.[860]

Evidence in favor of Ephesus is quite frankly meager and speculative. For example, arguments have been made that Paul's language and style changed slightly over the years and that Philippians is closer to Romans than to Ephesians. Nevertheless, as Merrill Tenney said, "language affinity is a very tenuous argument, since an author may change his style and vocabulary not only with the advance of his years but also with the needs of the situation for which he was writing."[861] He also notes that Philippi was more Roman in its culture than Ephesus.[862] Hence, the language would also likely be more Roman. However, the strongest evidence against Ephesus is Paul's mention of the praetorian guard (1:13) and of Caesar's household (4:22).

The mention of the praetorian guard (1:13) and Caesar's household (4:22) also indicates that he was most likely in Rome rather than Caesarea. The question is then whether or not this was Paul's first or second imprisonment in Rome (see *Apostles After Jesus* for a discussion of whether or not there was a second imprisonment in Rome).

Philippians 1:12-13 says, "my circumstances have turned out for the greater progress of the gospel, so that my imprisonment in *the cause of* Christ has become well known throughout the whole praetorian guard and to everyone else." This seems to imply that Paul had a certain amount of freedom to preach the gospel as was evident in his first imprisonment (Acts 28:30-31), but thus was not so in the second imprisonment. Thus it is likely that Philippians was written "toward the close of Paul's two years in Rome"[863] around 60 or 61 A.D.

Preaching from Impure Motives
Philippians 1:16-18

"The former proclaim Christ out of selfish ambition rather than from pure motives, thinking to cause me distress in my imprisonment. What then? Only that in every way, whether in pretense or in truth, Christ is proclaimed; and in this I rejoice. Yes, and I will rejoice."

We have all known preachers who are phony or insincere. Some have selfish motivations. Many are cult leaders seeking to elevate themselves. Here Paul is speaking out against some of his enemies and yet he makes a peculiar remark. He "rejoices" that the gospel is proclaimed! The question many have asked is whether or not the true gospel can be preached from false motives. Were these not cultish members who attacked Paul? Were they Judaizers? Who were they? More importantly, how is it that Paul says they preach the gospel if they attack the apostles?

The first question is who were these people? The overwhelming opinion has been that Paul is speaking of the Judaizers[864] who demanded converts to be circumcised and convert to Judaism before following Christ. This is an issue which Paul spent much of his life combating from the Council of Jerusalem to the epistle of Galatians. History also records that a number of the persecutors of early Christians were from sects such as there. For example, it is probably that the apostle Philip was martyred by the Ebionite Jewish-Christian sect which required the keeping of the Law.[865]

Other possibilities have also been offered. Some argue that these were "unconverted Jews"[866] but this makes little sense in the context of Paul's rejoicing at the gospel being preached, even if from impure motives. James Boice believed that these were "pugnacious Christians" but true Christians nevertheless.[867] Along this line of reasoning is Gordon Fee's allegation that they were in the practice of "sheep stealing,"[868] a term used for people who try to "steal" members of another church to add to their own congregation. The problem is that there is no evidence, internally or externally, to argue that Paul was speaking about fellow Christian church members. These were clearly the enemies of Paul who actively sought his imprisonment. When was Philippians written? When Paul was in prison. Who imprisoned him? He was originally imprisoned by the allegations of fellow Jews (Acts 23). So we must choose between the "unconverted Jews" and Judaizers among the Jewish-Christians. Contextually, it is clear that these could not have been unbelievers, but believers with false and impure motives (1:15). We must then agree with John Walvoord,[869] D. Martin Lloyd-Jones,[870] John Lightfoot,[871] Kenneth Wuest,[872] and countless others who believe that these were one the various Judaizer sects.

If they were, indeed, Judaizers then were they preaching the gospel at all? Many say "no," but Paul seems to imply otherwise. This hits on several important issues. The most obvious of which is whether or not you can teach false doctrine and still be preaching the gospel. Is it possible? Let us begin with those who say you cannot.

John Calvin believed that "this impurity was in the mind, and did not shew itself in doctrine."[873] He believed they taught pure doctrine. This is also the view of Richard Melick Jr. who says that "they clearly had a correct message."[874] So also the *Liberty Bible Commentary* says that "Paul could not and would not condone false teaching, but he graciously could and would tolerate wrong motives."[875] Certainly this is true on one level. Every epistle of Paul is filled with doctrinal instructions and a refutation of false doctrine. Doctrine was important to Paul because true doctrine is synoymous with truth. This should be accepted on its merits, but it does not stand alone. If these were Judaizers as many of these same people believe, then how can we say they had no doctrinal errors? Certainly Peter himself once stood with the Judaizers (cf. notes on Galatians 2:11-21). How can we resolve such a conflict in our minds? The resolution is one of degrees. Paul would never condone false teaching, but neither did he condemn all who had it. Instead, he corrected it. There is false teaching which denies Christ, and there is false teaching who distracts from Christ. The former is damnable. The latter opens the door to temptation and apostacy, but does not deny the gospel nor damn its proponents. So what then? Is false doctrine acceptable? Some say doctrine is not important.

If one extreme says their doctrine was pure, the other extreme is that which says that doctrine is relatively unimportant. I do not want to misquote these people, so I emphasize *relatively*. Lloyd Ogilvie, for example, believes that "the authentic tests of a man in Christ in his inclusiveness."[876] Apparently this would mean that inclusiveness extends to matters of false motives and even false doctrines! Karl Barth also emphasized unity above most all, but it is interesting that he contrast this with those who preached "another" gospel in Galatians 1:12, 2 Corinthians 11, Colossians 2, and Philippians 3.[877] I say interesting because Philippians 3 *may* actually be referring to the same people as here in chapter one!

Tertullian was not quite so inclusive as Ogilvie and Barth, but did believe that "it matters not" the motive as long as "one Christ alone was announced."[878] False doctrine could thus be tolerated as long as the one Christ alone was still the center of the picture. Does this mean that false doctrine is unimportant? This is the crux of the question and the controversy.

John Walvoord once said, "the greatest problem of the world then and now is not that the gospel is imperfectly preached, but that it is not preached at all."[879] Few accuse Walvoord of being soft on doctrine. Another commentator remarked that "even an imperfect gospel was to him precious in view of the nameless corruptions of pagan Rome."[880] I am reminded of a true anecdote about John Wesley and George Whitefield. Whitefield was a Calvinist and Wesley was an Armenian. In doctrine they were considered very different, although they both believe that Jesus was the Way, the Truth, and the Life, and that no one comes to Father except by Him (John 14:6). Once a man asked John Wesley point blank if he expected to see George Whitefield in heaven, to which Wesley replied that he did not because he expected Whitefield would be too close the throne of God for Wesley to spot him from the back![881]

Here then is the answer. There are two types of heresies in Christianity today. There are damnable heresies which deny Christ as God and Savior. These teachings cannot be equated with Christianity in any form for they preach another gospel. However, Paul also spent much time refuting naive heresies from people, including Peter. These were doctrines which distract from Christ without denying Him. By requiring circumcision the Judaizers were creating obstacles and moving the focus from God to the Law. They thought not in terms of right and wrong but in terms of the Law. This bred self righteousness, which in turn led to false motives and selfish ambitions. This is what Paul spent a great deal of time combating. We should never accept such false doctrines, but neither should we be so arrogant as to damn its practitioners.

I have been accused by some of being a "Catholic basher" for my strong stance against many of their doctrines. I question how many can be led to Jesus when so many obstacles are placed in their path, but I also know a number of Catholics who are true believers and have faith in Christ alone. Is that faith consistent with the church of which they profess? Maybe not, but humans are not consistent creatures either. I would never endorse or support an ecumenical movement with false teachings, but neither will be I condemn all its adherents. If we truly believe that salvation is by *grace* through faith, as we profess, then we cannot make it salvation by doctrinal purity as many have done. The difference is that I will instruct and educate those who are misguided, but I will never assume them to be lost unless they themselves deny the central doctrines of Jesus Christ Himself.

The chart which follows illustrates the issue. Those who are saved by grace are those who have Jesus at their center. Even though some are deceived, misled, and deluded, they are saved by God's grace as long as they believe in Jesus. Those false teachers who put obstacles in the way of Jesus will be judged, but as long as Jesus is taught, the gospel remains.

GOD THE FATHER

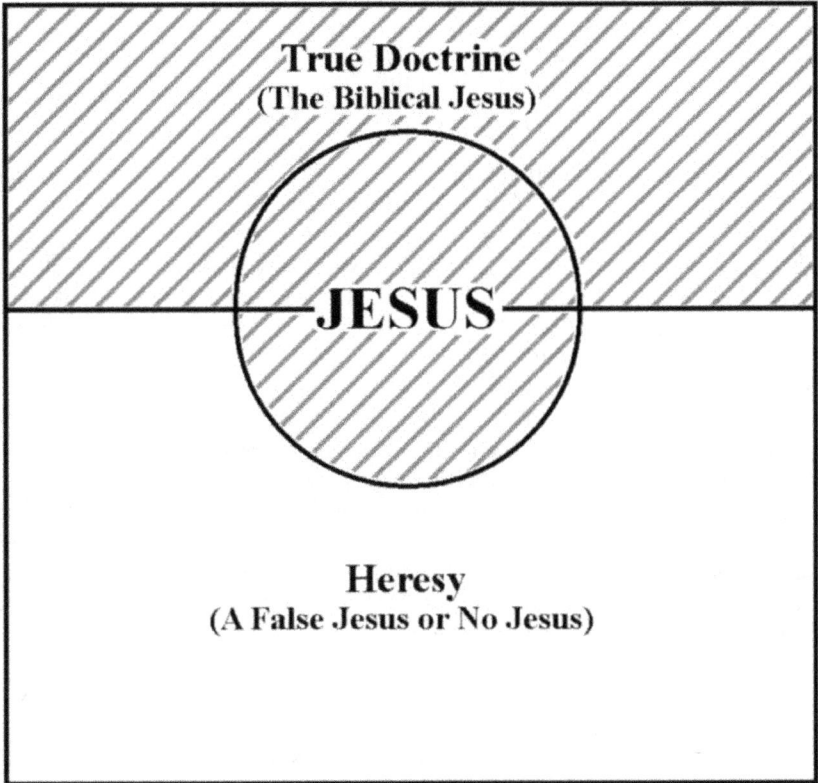

True Doctrine
(The Biblical Jesus)

JESUS

Heresy
(A False Jesus or No Jesus)

SATAN

Saved by Grace   The Lost

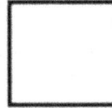

183

Godly Humility
Philippians 2:3-8

"Although He existed in the form of God, did not regard equality with
God a thing to be grasped, but emptied Himself, taking the form of a
bond-servant, *and* being made in the likeness of men. Being found in
appearance as a man, He humbled Himself by becoming obedient to the
point of death, even death on a cross."

Plato believed that humility was a vice.[882] He believed like the modern
generation that "self esteem" is a great virtue, but the Bible says the opposite.
Philippians 2:3 demands that "with humility of mind we ought to esteem others
more highly than ourselves." Self love is, by definition, selfish. We all love
ourselves. There is no exception, for the Bible says, "for no one ever hated his
own flesh" (Ephesians 5:29). Self-pity is a form of self love, not self hatred.
Humility is not related to any selfism. Someone once said that humility is not
thinking less of yourself, but thinking of yourself less. Is this true?

One of my pet peaves is seeing Hollywood movie stars or other
celebrities accept honors and awards and then say, "I am so humbled." Have we
really forgotten what the word humility means? Humility comes from the word
humiliate. Being beaten and left for dead in a ditch is humbling. Being honored
at an awards ceremony is the opposite of humbling, and yet this is the mindset
which our society has ingrained in our brains. Humility is being born in a
manager when you are the rightful king. It is being tortured to death for crimes
you did not commit by the very people who committed those crimes.

Christ Himself is the epitome of humility. He is the example that Paul
cites. It is Christ "who, although He existed in the form of God, did not regard
equality with God a thing to be grasped, but emptied Himself, taking the form of
a bond-servant, *and* being made in the likeness of men. Being found in
appearance as a man, He humbled Himself by becoming obedient to the point of
death, even death on a cross" (Philippians 2:6-8).

Many commentaries have debated the specifics of this. One
commentator remarked that "almost every word in these verses has been a
battlefield of contention."[883] The first battle of contention is over the question of
equality. John MacArthur believes this means that "before the Incarnation, from
all eternity past, Jesus pre-existed in the divine form of God."[884] John Walvoord
said, "the experssion 'being in the form of God' means not only that Christ is
God, but that He always was God and that He existed as God."[885] Another
commentator notes that "the word 'God' ... here used manifestly with a certain
distinctiveness of the Father."[886] Hence, the doctrine of the Trinity is drawn in
part from this very verse; the Son being equal to God the Father.

If Jesus is equal to God the Father, then the statement that He emptied
Himself takes on a far more profound meaning. It is not just that he "did not

regard equality with God a thing to be grasped" but that "although He existed in the form of God" He chose to "empty Himself, taking the form of a bond-servant, *and* being made in the likeness of men. Being found in appearance as a man, He humbled Himself by becoming obedient to the point of death, even death on a cross." John Calvin declared that Jesus "gave up his right."[887] In lowering Himself to human form Jesus is said to have surrendered His right. However, the *Liberty Commentary* is more clear on this meaning. It says that while "Christ was an equal with God, he laid aside His divine glory, but He did not and could not lay aside His divine nature ... He laid aside His rights as the Son and took His place as a Servant."[888] Jesus is still the true heir and rightful ruler of the earth, but He has not taken up that mantle in the worldly sense. He has allowed the "god of this world" (2 Corinthians 4:4), Satan, to continue exercising his claims in order that we might have a chance to repent, for if Jesus administered the justice which is our due, then none of us would have been saved. Someone must pay the price for the crimes of man. Jesus paid that price with His very blood. He now waits for the gospel to be dispensed into all the world, before returning to rule. Now this latter statement goes beyond what Paul is speaking of, for here Paul is speaking only of the depth and level of Jesus's humility, but by understanding how much He laid aside on our behalf, we can better understand the depths of His humility.

One final note should be rendered regarding the Greek. One commentary states that "γενομενος [becoming] is contrasted with 'υπαρχων [existed]. He entered into a new state."[889] In other words, the depth of Jesus's humility is when He left His heavenly estate and glorified Godly form to become human flesh (John 1:14). This carnal body is so far beneath the glory of the immortal God that it is hard to even grasp that the only possible comparison might be if we exhanged our bodies for that of a worm or cockroach. Would we do that for the one's we love?

Jesus said many times, "if anyone wishes to come after Me, he must deny himself, and take up his cross and follow Me" (Matthew 16:24; Mark 8:34; Luke 9:23). Self-sacrifice is what Jesus taught. Living for others, rather than for ourselves. Charles Spurgeon said that self-denial is fundamental aspect of the Christian life.[890] This is the meaning of true humility to which every Christian should strive.

"Work Out Your Own Salvation"?
Philippians 2:12

> "So then, my beloved, just as you have always obeyed, not as in my presence only, but now much more in my absence, work out your salvation with fear and trembling."

Few passages have been more of a bone of contention between Catholics and most Protestants. Perhaps only James 2:14-26 is more divisive between the two. This is because one of the primary reasons for the Reformation was the doctrine that salvation is solely by God's grace through faith in Jesus. No work can ever save us, nor can we contribute one *iota* to our salvation. Catholicism, however, has traditionally argued that faith and works are so intricately connected that they cannot be separated (see notes on James 2:14-26). This passage is thus one of the primary verses used to prove that salvation lies in some respects within our power. It was made possible by Christ, but allegedly lies within our power to achieve.

While this debate has largely between Catholics and Protestants over the centuries, it is by no means restricted to Catholics and Protestants. Indeed, many Protestants take the "Catholic" position. In addition, there are numerous other interpretations taken by various schools of thought. I have categorized essentially six different streams of thought. Some of these overlap another view and many of the authors quoted do not hold entirely to one view or another. Some are a conglomeration of views, so the reader should not assume that because I quote Erasmus, for example, under one view that this means that is the view to which he exclusively holds. He did, in fact, hold a moderated position in line which much Protestant thought even though he never left the Catholic Church. Let us examine these views.

The Calvinist Position

It is somewhat unfair to even refer to a "Calvinist position" at all, for John Calvin does not even mention this verse in his commentary on Philippians![891] Nevertheless, since Calvinists maintain the most rigid belief in Predestination and the rejection of free will, it is naturally problematic to have Paul referring to a "working out" of something which was determined before the creation of the world itself! To this Charles Spurgeon offers a succinct answer.

> "'Don't you believe in Predestination? What have we to do with looking to our own salvation? Is it not all fixed?' Thou fool, for I can scarce answer thee till I have given thee thy right title; was it not fixed whether thou shouldst get wet or not in coming to this place? Why then did you bring your umbrella?"[892]

To an extent he is evading the answer, but on one level he is absolutely correct. We do many things to prepare for that which we know are inevitable. Our salvation is assured, but that does not mean that we should not work for that. I will get a paycheck at the end of the week, but that does not mean that I should slack off and evade the work I am supposed to be getting paid for. Some people may do just that, but even though they will get a paycheck, they will never get a promotion. On this level Spurgeon is correct, but true as this may be, it is still an evasion of the Calvinist contradiction. Paul is clearly telling us to *do* something. He is referring to some human effort in some respect. The question then remains, "what is the role to which Paul is appealing?"

The Participation View
I have called this the "Participation view" because it is not solely a Catholic view and it would be unfair to call it the "Catholic view." A number of Protestants have also taken similar views, even if nuanced differences exist between them and the Catholic church. Since it is not my purpose here to debate the Reformation (which was sorely needed), I will quote only Protestant authors, with the exception of Saint Augustine.

The late Dean of Cambridge Dr. Farrar declared that "for man's salvation there must always be the union and *co-operation* of God's will and man's effort."[893] The esteemed Albert Barnes even went so far as to say that "*there is danger of losing the soul*"[894] (emphasis in original). So the Armenian believes that salvation can be lost. This stems in part from what has often been equated with Augustine. It is the idea that "without the exertion of [moral power] he would fall away again from the state of grace."[895] Grace can then be lost and found, like an coin. As with the Calvinist view, there is a grain of truth inasmuch as Paul is asking for our participation, but it is sheer heresy to claim that one can loose grace. Either we have grace or we do not.

Nevertheless, there are some within this view who take a more moderated position, saying "grace of itself engenders moral faculties and stimulates moral exertions. *Because* grace is given, man must work."[896] One thing which can be said in favor of this view is that Paul is using a "reflexive pronoun" indicating that "salvation was something essentially individual, something between each man and his God."[897] This is so, but if a personal individual relationship exist between me and the Lord, then there is mutual action. However, our actions will not and cannot "separate us from the love of Christ" (cf. Romans 8:35, 39) if indeed He is in us. So we must again search for a better answer.

The Lordship View
One evangelical option similar to the "Participation view" is the teaching of Lordship Salvation. Men such as John MacArthur argue that we must accept Jesus as Lord of our lives in order to be saved. Consequently, the "completion" of our salvation is an "active commitment and personal effort."[898] For MacArthur it is "perseverance, of faithful obedience to the end."[899]

This view differs slightly from the "Participation view" in that it denies you can actually lose salvation. However, it is possible under this view for a person to believe he is saved, when he is not. Certainly there are many false believers who believe they will be saved, but will be shocked on Judgment Day (Matthew 7:22). In this respect it is accurate.

Another aspect of this view is the idea that "working out" is synonymous with completion. Some translations actually paraphrase "work our your salvation" as "to bring to full and complete conclusion" (TEV). The New Living Translation renders this verse as "work hard to show the results of your salvation, obeying God with deep reverence and fear." Both show the idea of working to "complete your salvation."[900] Once again, this sounds good and bears a tinge of truth, but it is nevertheless, a sidestep. It is an evasion not unlike the Calvinist view. What does it mean to "complete" salvation? If we don't complete it do we still get it? If we don't get it, did we ever have it? Is this not just a nuanced evangelical version of the Catholic view which Protestants rebelled against?

The "Completion" View
A slight variant of the "Lordship view," and yet another evangelical variant of the "Participation view," is what I call the "Completion view." In Greek the word κατεργαζεσθε (*katergazesthe*) can be translated either as to "work out" or to "achieve."[901] Some argue that achievement here implies "completion." Erasmus stated that "it is your part to strive with all your might; it is God, however, who is working this in you, namely that, as far as your salvation is concerned, you both wish for and bring to completion what the mind's good purpose suggests to you."[902] The modern evangelical Harold Greenlee argued similarly that we must "work for the full realization of your salvation in this life."[903]

This theory then rejects the notion that we can loose salvation, but declares that our work is to complete that salvation. Perhaps a good analogy for this view would be when a prisoner is granted a pardon. He is free, but he must work to avoid being sent back to prison and obey the rules of his parole. This, however, is still heresy to many evangelicals since it implies at least the possibility of falling back into a state of fallen grace. Certainly neither Erasmus nor Greenlee would make that argument, but it does beg the question, what does "completion" mean? Did not Jesus say, "It is finished" on the cross (John 19:30)? The view reads too much into the word κατεργαζεσθε (*katergazesthe*) and does not sufficiently explain that it means to "complete" salvation.

The Positional Salvation View
One option is that Paul is not speaking about salvation in the larger sense of the word, but of "positional salvation." According to Robert Gromacki, while we cannot work to attain salvation "they can work out their spiritual position (Rom. 4:5; Eph. 2:8-10)."[904] In other words, this is alleged to refer to our standing and rewards on Judgment Day. They emphasize that none of us will be damned if we trust in Christ, but neither will we all have the same blessings and rewards in heaven; to each of us will be given according to our works. They argue that "it is each believer's own work in regard to his own salvation."[905]

Yet again here is a view which touches upon reality but fails to provide contextual proof within Philippians. It is true that we will not have the same rewards in heaven. I, for one, do not deserve the same rewards as the apostles or prophets who suffered and died for the truth. I will not be living in a mansion next to Peter's house in the New Jerusalem. Neither will I be living in a hubble

188

or shack as many of us do in this sinful world. Having said that, Paul does not appear to speak of rewards here at all. Neither does "with fear and trembling" sound like a working for rewards. It is highly suspect whether or not the word "salvation" ever refers to our positional outcome on Judgment Day. There may be truth to this, but contextually it is not what Paul is talking about here.

The Translation View

Another view is that "work out your salvation" is a misleading translation. Although the most literal translation of κατεργαζεσθε (*katergazesthe*) is indeed to "work out," "perform," or "achieve"[906] many scholars have noted that "the apostle does not speak of working *for* salvation, but of working *out.*"[907] H.A. Ironside once told an anecdote of a little girl who asked, "How can you work it out if you haven't got it in?"[908] So, to quote John Walvoord, "a person cannot work out salvation which he does not possess."[909]

How does this effect translation? Kenneth Wuest remarked that "the idea of working out an inworked salvation is merely a play upon the English words 'work out,' and has no support from the Greek ... the words 'work out' are the translation of a Greek word which means 'to carry out to the goal, to carry to its ultimate conclusion.'"[910] Gene Getz provides perhaps the best alternate translation, saying that it means we should "live out" our salvation with fear and trembling.[911] Karl Barth expressed a similar notion when he said, "it is a shortened expression for 'to *live* as a Christian.'"[912]

In some respects this view is best, although it overstates its case. "Work out" is the most literal translation. The proper interpretation may well lie within the idea of "living out" but this must be supplied by context.

Conclusion

Each of the views bears a grain of truth, but none of them sufficiently covers the context and full meaning of Paul. Obviously, the next verse provides much of the needed context. Paul concludes his remarks by saying, "for it is God who is at work in you, both to will and to work for *His* good pleasure" (2:13). So it is not truly *our* work, but God at work *in us*. Why then is there "fear and trembling?"

One commentary says that "salvation should be viewed in three tenses : past, justification; present, santification; and future, glorification."[913] We were saved at the Cross. All who have repented and turned to Christ have been justified by Christ. We are presently in sanctification which literally means "to be made holy." We are to transform ourselves to be like Christ. This is, however, what most Christians fail miserably at. "Working out" our salvation is not "working for" salvation. That is a thing of the past. Rather we are working to let Christ work within us; to transform us. The fear and trembling comes from an acknowledgement of our unworthiness.

Dwight Pentecost believed that Paul was commanding us to "translate what you know into action."[914] James Boice similarly said we are to "strive to

189

express this salvation in your conduct."[915] Salvation is a "gift which you now have"[916] but we will never be worthy of it. We must, therefore, strive to let Christ work within us to become more like Him. To show our gratitude with fear and trembling in the knowledge that we deserve only condemnation. This stems from humility which is the subject of this entire chapter. Paul was not randomly throwing together various theologies, but progressing point by point. Our humility should indicate our unworthiness, which in turn should magnify our gratitude. We should strive to show that gratitude by becoming more like Christ. In this we must work and strive daily, for our sin nature remains and our unworthiness should always leave us with "fear and trembling."

Summary

The Philippians were greatly loved by Paul. Where the Corinthians were like a spoiled child who needed discipling, the Philippians were a favorite child who obeys his father and is a delight to him. Paul expresses his love and gives fatherly advice to the Philippians during his imprisonment. So also we can take these words at apply them to our own lives, as beloved children of God, but only if we learn humility. This was the major theme of Paul's epistle. Humility is what draws us closer to Christ. Pride pulls us away from Christ. The two cannot co-exist.

7

Colossians

Many consider Colossians to be a companion piece with Ephesians. They are believed to have been written at the same time and delivered via the same messenger on a single journey.[917]   While some critics, as per their hobby, suspect the authenticity of Colossians, few, if any, serious scholars doubt it. It is quoted by many of the apostolic church fathers including Justin Martyr and Irenaeus, and was never questioned in the Canon.[918]   Even most secular critics claim Ephesians was a copy of Colossians, not vice versa.[919]

Despite the similarities between the two epistles, there are significant differences. The most obvious is that Colossians is much more explicit in its denunciation of the rising cult of gnosticism. Colossians refutes many gnostic heresies in a way not seen elsewhere. Certainly Paul refuted heresy and the dangerous rise of cults, but no other epistle deals so specifically deals with the doctrines of gnosticism as Colossians.

Central among the gnostic religion was the idea of the mystery cult. Mystery cults are those which claim that certain "enlightened" leaders have been revealed "mysteries" which can only be learned by initiation into higher levels of the cult. They use the idea of forbidden or mysterious knowledge as a lure and carefully screen all their members to insure loyalty. Modern day mystery cults range from the Klu Klux Klan to Masonic lodges. They may claim to be nominally Christian at the low entry level, but as initiates gain rank they are revealed "new mysteries" which are explicitly anti-Christian. The Klu Klux Klan, for example, was founded in part by alleged Luciferist Albert Pike whose bizarre writings reflect the mystery cults.[920]   In gnosticism, the mysteries were called γνωσις (*gnosis*) which literally means "knowledge," as in "secret knowledge. The gnostics derive their name from this very word.

Another tenant of gnosticism is the belief that God could not have created a world with evil in it.[921]   They believe that god-like entities, called "aeons," created each other, with each being inferior to its creator, until one "aeon," called "Wisdom," sought to create another "aeon" but then "aborted" its birth at the last moment, resulting in the earth.[922]   And so according to gnosticism, the earth is a mistake! Accordingly they believed that all matter is evil.[923] This in turn led a form of dualism.[924] By dubbing the physical world, including our bodies, "evil" and the spiritual realm as inherently "good" the gnostics developed a bizarre view of sin and redemption.   Some gnostics believed that "if the body were only temporary, its acts were inconsequential,"[925] and therefore adhered to a sensualistic libertinism.[926] These gnostics argued that "what we are to do is to leave the body to its own devices and let it follow the guidance of its own passions."[927]   Still other gnostics were strict ascetics, believing that we could not pollute our souls with even the most innocent of fleshy pleasures (such as good food).

One final aspect of gnosticism was the denial of the resurrection.[928] Since gnostics believe that all flesh is evil, they cannot believe that Jesus was ever flesh and blood. For the gnostics Christ was not physical, but a messenger without a real corporal body.[929] There could, therefore, be no resurrection. This may be why John, in his gospel, explicitly states that God "became flesh and dwelled among us" (John 1:14). It is certainly why Paul and the other disciples made clear many times that Jesus came in the flesh (Hebrews 5:7; 1 John 4:2; 2 John 1:7) and was resurrected from the dead! Here in Colossians Paul deals specifically with all three of these heresies; the myth of secret knowledge, the denial of God the Creator, and rejection of Jesus's physical resurrection from the dead.

The Deity of Christ
Colossians 1:15-19

> "He is the image of the invisible God, the firstborn of all creation. For by Him all things were created, *both* in the heavens and on earth, visible and invisible, whether thrones or dominions or rulers or authorities – all things have been created through Him and for Him."

Paul waste no time in attacking one of the most central teachings of gnosticism; the denial of Jesus as the physical incarnation of God, and creator of the Universe. Obviously, such a view is controversial even today. Many religious cults teach that Jesus was either just a man or an angel, but not God. These passages have thus been a major bone of contention. What exactly is Paul teaching?

Two major doctrines are found in these verses. The first is that Jesus is the "firstborn of all creation." To some this means that Jesus was, in fact, created. Others say the exact opposite. They argue that Jesus existed in eternity past. The second doctrine is that "by Him all things were created" (1:16). Did Jesus create the universe? Again, some argue that only God the Father creates, and that Jesus took no material part in creation. Others say this is proof that Jesus cannot be separated from the Father. The theological divisions split all lines. Catholics, Calvinists, evangelicals, and liberals are often divided even among themselves. Consequently, the two major doctrines must be examined individually before we bring them together.

The "Firstborn"
"He is the image of the invisible God, the firstborn of all creation." Few words have been more divisive than these. What does an image of an invisible God mean? Moreover, what does it mean to be "firstborn"?

The idea that Christ was the very "image" of God goes beyond mere physical imagery, for God is "invisible" according to verse fifteen. An image, like a mirror, reflects what it is the image of. Everything that makes God God is reflected in Jesus. He is not just an angel (see below) but the very image of God. More than that, He is the Creator of heaven and earth (see notes on verse 16 below). He is the second person of the Trinity.

This concept is hard for many to understand. How can an ant understand a man? How can a man understand the infinite God in the form of Jesus? To that end, some liberal theologians claim this is "meditation" allegory.[930] They reject any literal application to Jesus, preferring to see Him just as a good man. Eduard Schweizer even goes so far as to compare this "image" to Plato's "concept of the universe as a divine body"![931] However, John Lightfoot pointed out that the "*Logos*" of John is more of a parallel to Philo than to Plato, for Philo saw the Logos as the an image of God![932] So both Paul and John establish that Jesus was an image, a reflection, of God the Father. This is why Origen declared, 100 years before Constantine, that the Bible explicitly refers to "the persons of Father, Son and Holy Spirit."[933] Jesus is the Second Person of that Trinity; the "first-born" of God, but what does that mean?

Some argue that "first-born" proves that Christ was created. If he was born then He must have been created, or so the argument goes. Many others, however, have pointed out that the Greek is not not "'first-created' (*protoktistos*)" but first-born (*prototokos*).[934] The distinction is not trivial. Renowned Greek scholar Joseph Thayer, himself a Unitarian who denied the Trinity,[935] did not hesitate to admit that "this passsage does not with certainty prove that Paul reckoned the *logos*" in the number of created beings"[936] since the word is found in Hebrews 1:6 to refer to Christ as the "first-born among the dead."[937] In other words, "first-born" does not necessarily indicate birth *per se*. The word is used primarily of first-born children, but also used more generally to refer to "honor, favor, chosenness, uniqueness."[938] Specifically, it refers to the legal heir.[939] Says John MacArthur, "*prototokos* ... refers primarily to position."[940] Its application here to Christ is intended to prove that Christ is the true heir to all Creation and holds the prime position in heaven. The word is found as a "Messianic reference in Ps. lxxxix.28" and is accepted as such by Orthodox Rabbis.[941] So Paul is here using Messianic and legal language to indicate the primacy of Christ *over* Creation; not as a part of creation.

William Barclay pointed out that Israel is called "my first-born son" in Exodus 4:22.[942] This is further support for the idea of *prototokos* meaning an heir; one who is to inherit. So some believe that "this speaks of His pre-existence ... He was before all creation."[943] Neither is this a new theology, for Irenaeus, who pupiled under the disciple of John, declared that this verse proves Jesus had been "existing before all."[944] Tertullian also said that "He who ever spoke to Moses was the Son of God Himself; who, too, was always seen. For God the Father none ever saw, and lived."[945]

Further support for this is in the form of the Greek. Frederick Westcott noted that it is perfect passive tense which indicates not 'past' tense *per se* but continuing movement in the past.[946] Thus Christ is eternal. He did not simply come into being in the past, but had a continuous existence in the past, for all eternity. This is what Paul means in the next verse when he says, "He is before all things, and in Him all things hold together" (1:17). So "he existed before creation,"[947] but this leads to the next inevitable question. If Jesus was not a part of creation, then what is His role in creation. Certainly Christ could not be created if He is in fact the Creator! Let us then examine the net few verses.

The Creator of Heaven and Earth
"For by Him all things were created, *both* in the heavens and on earth, visible and invisible, whether thrones or dominions or rulers or authorities – all things have been created through Him and for Him" (1:16). Of these words, one commentator remarked, "there could not possibly be a more explicit declartion, that the universe was created by Christ, than this."[948] However, it is no surprise that others just as strenuously disagree. Even many Calvinists insist that Jesus had no active role in creation, since they believe only the Father can create.[949]

Let us look first at the Greek. The passage says two things of Christ's role in creation. The first part is "έν αυτω εκτισθη τα παντα" (*en auto ektisthe ta panta*), usually translated "by Him all things were created." The key words here are έν αυτῳ (*en auto*), "by Him." The second part of the passage says "τα παντα δι' αυτου και εις αυτον εκτισται" (*ta panta dia autou kaieis auton ektistai*), usually translated "all things have been created through Him and for Him." The key here is δι' αυτου και εις αυτον (*dia autou kai eis auton*), "through Him and for Him."

The first phrase, έν αυτῳ (*en auto*), is in what is called the dative case. The dative case, however, can convey a variety of meanings. One textbook notes that "a common function of dative nominals is to specify the means a person intentionally uses to achieve a particular end ... the dative of means can be translated into English as 'by,' 'with,' or 'by means of.'"[950] However, another use of the dative is what is called the "dative of advantage" which is translated "for."[951] So this phrase, in isolation, could be translated "by Him," "through Him," or "in Him." "By Him" is used in the KJV, NAS, NIV, Tyndale, Darby, ESV, and Geneva Bible. "Through Him" is preferred in the New Living Translation, while "in Him" is opted for by the RSV, ASV, Wycliffe's translation, and the Douay-Rheims.

The second phrase uses two more prepositions. The first, δια (*dia*), is genitive while εις (eis) is accusative. Now the normal meaning of δια (*dia*) in the genitive is "through," but it can also mean "one who is the author of the action."[952] In this case, it would be best translated as "by Him." Since "through Him" seems rather ambiguous in the context of Colossians, most translations have preferred "by Him" or "in Him."

194

The last phrase, εις (eis) in the accusative and can once again have various nuanced meanings. Here it is translated either "for Him" or "unto Him." It refers to something which has a "purpose or result."[953] In other words, creation was made for the purpose or result of Christ being heir to all creation. Was He, however, its Creator? Below is a list of all the major Bible translations and how they render these three prepositions.

Translation	ἐν αυτω	δι' αυτου	εις αυτον
KJV	"by Him"	"by Him"	"for Him"
MKJV	"in Him"	"through Him"	"for Him"
NKJV	"by Him"	"through Him"	"for Him"
NAS	"by Him"	"through Him"	"for Him"
NIV	"by Him"	"by Him"	"for Him"
RV	"in Him"	"through Him"	"unto Him"
RSV, NRSV	"in Him"	"through Him"	"for Him"
NLT	"through Him"	"through Him"	"for Him"
NAB	"in Him"	"through Him"	"for Him"
ASV	"in Him"	"through Him"	"unto Him"
ESV	"by Him"	"through Him"	"for Him"
Tyndale	"by Him"	"by Hym"	"in Him"
Webster	"by Him"	"by Him"	"for Him"
Wycliffe	"in Hym"	"bi Hym"	"in Hym"
Darby	"by Him"	"by Him"	"for Him"
Douay-Rheims	"in Him"	"by Him"	"in Him"

Notice that every translation contains at least one reference to either "by Him" or "through Him." All convey the idea that creation is made for Jesus as His inheritance. The debate then is between the idea of Creation being made "by Him" or "through Him." If it is "through Him" then is what is meant by this?

The hyper-Calvinist believes that only God the Father can create. Consequently, they take "through Him" to picture Christ as supervisor or architect, but not an actual creator. In this way they can maintain a rigid distinction between Father and Son, but it does not seem likely that Paul intended such a rigid distinction based on three simple prepositions. If Paul had intended to make such a sharp contrast, he would not have used such a beautifully simple sentence to convey Christ's role in creation. Paul meaning is as simple as his words. Everything was made by, through, and for Jesus!

One thing is certain. "This statement should of itself have ruled out any idea of Christ being included among created beings."[954] Once again, this is not a new teaching. The early church father Tatian, who lived in the early second century, declared that Christ was the creator,[955] and such was the orthodox view of the church throughout its history. Paul is emphasizing

195

"Christ's supreme role in creation"[956] to negate the gnostic heresy. He wants to be clear that Christ was both God *and* man; a teaching denied by the gnostics. In so doing Paul first establishes Christ as the Creator. Second, he insures that the reader is aware that this includes *all* creation, not just some. "For by Him *all* things were created, *both* in the heavens and on earth, visible and invisible, whether thrones or dominions or rulers or authorities – *all* things have been created through Him and for Him" (1:16).

Obviously, "all" means all. Nevertheless, some have quibbled over the exact meaning of "thrones" and "dominions." John Calvin, for example, believed that "thrones" refers to the "heavenly abode" and not angels.[957] Most argue that "thrones ... no doubt" refers to angels.[958] In either case, angels are a part of creation and if they are not included among the "thrones" (or those who sit on the thrones) then they are counted among the "authorities." Either way, angels were part of the creation of Jesus. He was *not* one of them as the Jehovah's Witnesses claim.

So by establishing that Christ Himself was Creator, Paul proves that Jesus was the very image of God, the Second Person of the Trinity; God incarnate. Few statements in the Bible can compare to this one in affirming the deity of Christ. He was not created, but Creator.

Conclusion

F.F. Bruce noted that Christ role in creation is emphasized in the "first main strophe" of the epistle.[959] This is necessary to stress that which follows. In disproving the heresy of gnosticism, Paul wants to insure that the Colossians understand that Christ was both God *and* man. Whereas verses 15-17 emphasize Christ the Creator existing eternally in the past, verses 18-20 references the resurrected Christ.

One author states, "some commentators regard 15-17 as descriptive of the Word before the Incarnation, the λογος ασαπκος; and 18-20 of the Incarnate Word, λογος ενσαρκος. But this is inconsistent with εστιν, 'is,' which shows that Paul is speaking of Christ in His present glorified state ... the exalted Christ is now and continues to be what He was in His own nature as the Word before He became incarnate."[960] In other words, the present glorified Christ is the same as the pre-incarnate Christ. He was and is the Second Person of the Trinity, the very "image of the invisible God" (1:15). As John Calvin said, "it is in Him alone that God, who is otherwise invisible, is manifested to us."[961]

Reconciliation of All Things
Colossians 1:20

> "It was the Father's good pleasure ... through Him to reconcile all things to Himself, having made peace through the blood of His cross; through Him, *I say*, whether things on earth or things in heaven."

For what purpose is this life? For what reason does this creation even exist? For what reason would an immortal invisible God become a weak mortal man in the flesh? These are the very questions that plague our very existence, and yet Paul simplifies the answer into this succinct passage. To be sure, the passage assumes a basic knowledge of the Bible and history, but within the proper context, this verse summarizes the whole of human history and the Cross. Its purpose to reconcile all things unto God!

Such a simple and sublime statement should not be controversial, but, of course, it is. If God is to reconcile "all things" then does this include demons? What of unbelievers? Does this means universal salvation?

To the first question, it is the rebellion of angels and the nature of sin that causes the earth to need reconciliation. Reconciliation does not necessitate that all are saved. According to Robert Gromacki, the word reconcile in Greek means "to change completely."[962] If we look at the root of the word, then it actually means to completely turn back. Ἀποκαταλλάξαι (*apokatallaxai*) is composed of three words. Ἀπο (*apo*) is a prefix generally meaning "from." Κατα (kata) is another prefix which usually indicates a joining or connection. Finally, αλλασσω (*allasso*) means to "change, alter, transform, or exchange."[963] Hence, αποκαταλλαξαι (*apokatallaxai*) literally means to change or transform from one thing back to another. This is the essense of reconciliation. It means that all things are put back in their proper place; not necessarily that all are saved. Certainly the two could be equal, but not necessarily.

Albert Barnes noted that "nothing is said of the inhabitants of hell."[964] He remarks that only heaven and earth are specifically mentioned, not hell. He says that there is to be a "harmony between heaven and earth [for] in heaven nothing is wrong."[965] Others believed that this reconciliation was limited to mankind alone,[966] and some, like Theodore Beza, apllied it only to the Church.[967] Each of these views seems to limit "all" to "some." This is natural given that the Bible, and specifically the apostle Paul, teaches against the doctrine of universal salvation, so can these doctrines be reconciled?

Notice that in reconciling these doctrines, I am not necessarily accepting both. If I am to reconcile universalism with universal reconciliation, I need not embrace them, but bring together the true elements, and reject the false ones. Reconcilation of a victim and a criminal does not necessarily free a prisoner from his responsibility. It means that he is reconciled to accept his sentence without further harm to his victim. Reconciliation therefore means that all things, which include demons and the inhabitants of hell, are no longer at war with God. It means that all things work as they were intended. It means that God is exercising his full authority and bringing peace to both heaven and earth. It also means that the inhabitants of hell are not free. Contrary to the teachings of heretics and Luficerists, the inhabitants of hell will not be free to rape and sin and commit their crimes in hell. It is a place of punishment; not freedom to sin. They will be reconciled to their fate and remain under God's restrictions.

Nevertheless, it is true that Paul is not speaking of hell. His point has nothing to do specifically with the inhabitants of hell or the unbeliever, but rather the reconciliation of heaven and earth and all the things therein contained. As Ironside pointed out, "the reconciliation of verse 20 carries us on to the new heaven and the new earth"[968] where "there will no longer be *any* death; there will no longer be *any* mourning, or crying, or pain" (Revelation 21:4). All this is made possible by Christ's sacrifice of atonement on the Cross. So in the most literal sense of the word, all things will be reconciled to God; not all things will be free. Paul's point is that the inheritance of Christ is purified of evil and brought into peace and harmony with heaven. "The entire universe has been reconciled with God through Christ."[969]

Hollow Philosophies
Colossians 2:3-8

"See to it that no one takes you captive through philosophy and empty deception, according to the tradition of men, according to the elementary principles of the world, rather than according to Christ."

I have previously stated that Paul's epistle to the Colossians is largely an attempt to refute gnostic heresy and teaching. Here he warns against the dangers of "philosophy and empty deception." It is ironic then that some today seek to restrict Paul's warnings to very specific philosophies, while opening the door to other man-made philosophies. The questions then are plentiful. Of what philosophies does Paul speak? Can we trust secular philosophy? Is "all truth God's truth"? Is "science" a philosophy?

Whose Philosophy?
The NIV translates this as "hollow and deceptive philosophies." Some consider this a reference to Hellenic philosophy. Others see it as an allusion to "heretical Judaism."[970] A few liberals, such as Eduard Schweizer, even restrict Paul's words only to those specifically mentioned in 2:16-23.[971] That this verse should not be restricted to any one philosophy, not even gnosticism, is evident by Paul's description of opinions which are "according to the tradition of men, according to the elementary principles of the world." In other words, world philosophies are not based on Christ, but feeble traditions, myths, and opinions of sinful men.

Having said this, Christians throughout the centuries have made excuse after excuse to excuse their own favorite philosophers. Origen, for example, is filled with double talk about Grecian philosophy. He said that "no man of sense, however, would say that those [words] of Celcus were 'according to the rudiments of the world'"[972] and that "there was a kind of greatness manifest in the words of the world's wisdom."[973] So while admitting that the world's philosophy is at odds with Christ, he then argues that some of "the words of the world's wisdom" are worthy to combine with Scripture.

I am reminded of a debate with a pastor over the legitimacy of integrating Christianity with popular psychology. He asked me if I believed that "all truth is God's truth." Dave Hunt once responded to that question by saying, "all lies are the devil's lies." When I tried to explain that psychology and psychiatry do not distinguish between etiology and physiology and, therefore, is not a legitimate science, it fell on deaf ears. He did not understand that they are pseudo-sciences based on the anti-Christian doctrine of naturalism. Naturalism is a *philosophy* which has erroneously been associated with "science" in the modern age, but it is no irony that "the Greeek word *philosophy* occurs only here in the New Testament."[974] Nor is it ironic that Paul describes many such philosophies as "science, falsely called" in 1 Timothy 6:20. Naturalism is the atheistic myth that the physical universe, nature, is all that exist. It argues, contrary to the laws of valid science, that the natural universe is self creating, self preserving, and self evolving. This myth itself stems from Platonic philosophy which views nature as the gods' body.[975]

Despite this some claim that "Paul is not condemning philosophy, Greek or Oriental, in general. His speech at Athens proves that he could recognize and appreciate and utilize elements of truth in current philosophy."[976] So we see the inherent desire of human nature to compromise and be accepted. Paul's speech in Athens does not prove that Paul saw great value in pagan philosophy (see my notes in *Controversies in the Acts of the Apostles*) but that he could use their own arguments against them. He was not embracing Plato but showing Plato's own insufficiency. Nature itself cries out that there is a God! Still, the history of Christian compromise has been a history of the church trying make Christianity fit with worldly philosophies. This is true whether it is Thomas Aquinas or the Protestant Reformer John Calvin, who declared that Paul was only attacking "corrupted" philosophy.[977] Aquinas reinterpreted the Scriptures to fit Platonic thought while Calvin interpreted much of the Scriptures in accordance with Aristotilean thought.

Most scholars agree that "Grecian philosophy"[978] was in Paul's mind when he wrote this, but also Jewish philosophy,[979] or even Jewish tradition. Warren Wiersbe believes that both Jewish and many "Christian" traditions fit the description of Paul in this passage.[980] To this Barnes adds, "perhaps also the Oriental or Gnostic philosophy."[981] Now while Paul admonishes us against all human philosophies, it is clear that gnosticism was what the Colossians were dealing with in particular. Paul spends much of this epistle specifically breaking down the heresies and lies of gnosticism. This teaching is not just a long dead cult, but one which has regained inordinate popularity in recent years, thanks in part to Hollywood.

One curiosity is the words Paul uses to describe these heretic's arguments. He speaks of φιλοσοφιας και κενης απατης (*philosophias kai kenes apates*) which is translated by the King James as "philosophy and vain deceit." The NAS translates it similarly as "philosophy and empty deception." However, the NIV takes the latter as descriptive of the former, saying, "hollow and deceptive philosophy." In this case, I like the NIV's translation. Although the KJV and NAS are more literal in their translation, the NIV carries the meaning more fully. Paul is connecting the two. John MacArthur calls it "persuasive rhetoric"[982] and F.F. Bruce prefers "empty illusion," but notes that "the 'philosophy' and the 'empty illusion' are identical."[983] They are not separate items.

Tertullian believed that Greek "philosophy would do violent injury to the truth."[984] John Wesley also warned that "philosophy blended with Christianity"[985] is a dangerous trend. Ironside is correct to remind us that, "from Plato to Kant, and from Kant to the last of the moderns, one system has overturned another, so that the history of philosophy is a story of contradicatory, discarded hypothesis."[986] To this day we think of ourselves as more enlightened and smarter than the generation which preceded us, but many generations had made the same blunder and the 20th Century proved to be the most savage in human history. The human race is not getting better or smarter, but more arrogant. We have put our philosophy above God's Word, or felt that God's Word needs to be amended, or that it is insufficient to live a Christ-like life. We feel we need psychotherapy and psychotropic drugs to make us happy, as if Christ is not enough. History doesn't change.

As Richard Melick Jr. pointed out "heretical arguments came in the appearance of deeper theology"[987] and they still do. "This is remarkable as the only passage in the New Testament in which the word 'philosophy' occurs"[988] and it occurs with a warning. How ironic that commentators throughout the ages have often found intriguing, even "vain and empty" arguments, to say that Paul was not referring to the philosophy to which the commentator subscribes.

The truth is that Paul is admonishing the Colossians to beware of *all* philosophies which rely upon man's wisdom. The universe is much bigger than we can imagine, and it takes a small mind to believe that man has the answers. Legitimate science is the study of God's *creation*. It is not naturalism, nor is it the power to play God. The more we humble ourselves the more we can learn. The more arrogant we are, the less we learn. This message is as true for us today as in Paul's day; perhaps even more so as pseudo-sciences not only abound in our modern society but are used to dehumanize and control the population. Darwinism, naturalism, psychology, abortionism, euthanasia, and a host of other philosophies (science, falsely so-called) are used for population control, not the betterment of mankind. How can mankind better himself if he distances himself from his Creator?

Marriage, Society, and Slavery
Colossians 3:18 – 14:1

"Whatever you do, do your work heartily, as for the Lord rather than for men."

I addressed in more detail the issues of submission and slavery under Ephesians 5:22-28 and Ephesians 6:5-9. Nevertheless, the issue appears here again, and is more easily misquoted by critics. However, the full quotation makes the critics quake because they interpret the Bible politically. It is true that it commands wives to submit to their husbands, children to obey their parents, and even slaves to obey their masters, but it actually says much much more, in context. Here is the full quotation:

> "Wives, be subject to your husbands, as is fitting in the Lord. Husbands, love your wives and do not be embittered against them. Children, be obedient to your parents in all things, for this is well-pleasing to the Lord. Fathers, do not exasperate your children, so that they will not lose heart. Slaves, in all things obey those who are your masters on earth, not with external service, as those who *merely* please men, but with sincerity of heart, fearing the Lord. Whatever you do, do your work heartily, as for the Lord rather than for men, knowing that from the Lord you will receive the reward of the inheritance. It is the Lord Christ whom you serve. For he who does wrong will receive the consequences of the wrong which he has done, and that without partiality. Masters, grant to your slaves justice and fairness, knowing that you too have a Master in heaven."

Once again, Paul is not declaring the institution of slavery right, nor making a political remark. He is ordering us, no matter what situation we may be in, to "do your work heartily, as for the Lord rather than for men." He commands masters to treat their slaves with justice and honor and not to abuse them. Erasmus stated that if an owner "commit any sin against a slave ... [he] will not go unpushied before God."[989] Paul's point is that our reward is in heaven. Whatever situation we have been placed in, even if it be an evil one, we must strive to do what is right knowing that God will reward us and punish the guilty.

While the critic is quick to misquote this passage, he neglects to mention Galatians 3:28, one of the main inspirations for the abolitionist movement, where Paul declares that in heaven there is "neither slave nor free man ... for you are all one in Christ Jesus."

Summary

Colossians is of Paul's prison epistles written during his first imprisonment in Rome. This letter was written to warn the Colossians of the dangerous heresies which were already spreading in the early church. He also wanted to comfort the Colossians and remind them that this is not our world. Slavery and persecution are just two evils which plagued Christians in the early church, but we were to endure them where necessary as examples of Christ. Colossians cannot be taken out of context to imply any political agendas. Paul's only agenda was to live this life in whatever circumstances we have as if living it for Christ alone.

8

1 & 2 Thessalonians

The epistles to the Thessalonians were among Paul's earliest epistles written early during his Second Missionary Journey. Thessalonica was the capital of Macedonia and Paul's first visit to Thessalonica is recorded in Acts 17. This probably took place around 50 A.D. From there he went to Athens, and then to Corinth (Acts 17:15-18:1) where most believe Paul wrote these epistles.[990] The main reason for believing this is a comparison of Acts 18:5 with 1 Thessalonians 3:1-6 where Timothy was sent to minister to the Thessalonians. Paul himself had been driven out of Thessalonica by his enemies as a result of the riot recorded in Acts 17:5. Consequently, he had not been able to finish teaching the doctrines of the faith completely. This, along with Timothy's report (cf. 1 Thessalonians 3:1-8), occasioned Paul's first epistle to the Thessalonians.

Merrill Tenney dates 1 and 2 Thessalonians to 51 A.D.,[991] Robert Thomas dates it to 52 A.D.,[992] and Merrill Unger places it as late as 53 A.D.[993] Either way, only Galatians was written before Thessalonians. Thus we have here two of the first three epistles of Paul.

With the exception of a handful of extreme Tübingen school theologians, no one doubts that these are authentic epistles of Paul. They are quoted by the earliest church fathers and were never questions for the canon. Even those Tübingen school critics who doubt Paul wrote the epistles concede that he "signed off" on it.[994] Burkitt, for example, argues that it was written by Silvanus (mentioned in 1:1) but Paul "signed off" on the epistle to give it more of an air of authority.[995] Burkitt makes this argument based solely upon what he calls the "changing eschatology" of Paul.[996] What "changing eschatology"? This is the most controversial aspect of Thessalonians. These epistles contain much concerning End Times, the anti-Christ, and the doctrine of the Rapture. Since "liberals" (and many others as well) reject the doctrine of the Rapture, they must find various ways of explaining away the theology which appears to contradict their own assumptions. Let us briefly look at the allegations independently.

Changing Eschatology?

One of the major themes of the Thessalonian epistles, particularly the second, is eschatology, meaning the study of end times. Paul discusses the signs of the end and the coming anti-Christ. Because some misunderstood what he wrote in 1 Thessalonians it was necessary to write 2 Thessalonians in which Paul clarified his position. Nonetheless, as is often the case, the Tübingen school of thought does not see things this way. They believe that First and

Second Thessalonians were written at vastly different times and reflect Paul's "changing eschatology."[997] This perspective is not restricted to the liberal Tübingen school of thought however. Even evangelicals such as David Wenham believed that Paul's "expectations about whether he would live until the Lord's return changed as he grew older."[998] They therefore see 2 Thessalonians and the rapture as a "new point of view"[999] which developed later in Paul's life.

The first thing to say about this argument is that it ignores the fact that First and Second Thessalonians were written very close to one another. Both were written years before 1 Corinthians, which also teaches the doctrine of the rapture without reference to time. So contrary to the belief of some that "the language proves beyond all doubt that when the Epistle was composed, St. Paul took it for granted that he would be alive at the second coming,"[1000] the doctrine of the rapture was not some "new point of view"[1001] invented to "unsatisfactorily"[1002] reconcile conflicting viewpoints of Paul, but was an integral part of Christian eschatology from the beginning. A closer look at First and Second Thessalonians should prove that there is no inconsistency in the teachings of the two epistles; only inconsistency in the interpretation of those who reject rapture.

The Rapture
1 Thessalonians 4:13-18

> "For this we say to you by the word of the Lord, that we who are alive and remain until the coming of the Lord, will not precede those who have fallen asleep ... Then we who are alive and remain will be caught up together with them in the clouds to meet the Lord in the air, and so we shall always be with the Lord."

These words rank among the most contentious in the Bible. The word "rapture," which critics claim does not exist in the Bible, actually comes from the Latin word for caught up, $'\alpha\rho\pi\alpha\zeta\omega$ (*harpazo*) in the Greek.[1003] The root word for "rapture" may also found in the old English translation by Wycliff : "schulen be rauyschid togidere with hem in cloudis." "Rauyschid" is the Old English word for "rapture."

So the doctrine of the "rapture" or being "caught up in the clouds" stems largely from the epistles of Thessalonians, as well as 1 Corinthians 15:50-54, sections of the Olivet Discourse, and possible allusions in other epistles. Some, for example, believe that the doctrine of "imminency" is an allusion to the rapture. What is the doctrine of "imminency"? It is the doctrine that Jesus could return at any time; not at a predictable time such as Armageddon. Rather imminency teaches that Jesus could return today, tomorrow, or a thousand years from now. This teaching, however, seems at odds with the idea that Jesus will return at Armageddon. How could Jesus return today if there are no armies at Armageddon? This seeming conflict lies at the heart of the doctrine of the rapture. Is the rapture synonymous with the Second Coming? If not, when does it happen? Can it really be separated from the Second Coming by a period of years as many believe?

In order to begin to answer these difficult questions we must answer many other questions first. It is, therefore, best to take this verse by verse.

Verse 13

> "We do not want you to be uninformed, brethren, about those who are asleep, so that you will not grieve as do the rest who have no hope."

These words introduce Paul's discussion of the rapture. All agree that sleep here is used to refer to those who have died. Jesus referred to death as "sleep" on several occasions (cf. Mark 5:35; John 11:11). The idea is that death is permanent, but sleep is temporary. Here too Paul indicates that the dead are but sleeping and will awake at the resurrection of the dead. This is the "hope" of Christians. We have hope in the resurrection of the death and eternal life.

One minor contention in this passage is the question of "soul sleep." Some believe that "the soul, during the period between death and resurrection, reposes in a state of unconsciousness."[1004] However, there is good cause to reject this interpretation. Jesus Himself spoke of the dead in a state of consciousness (Luke 16:20-31),[1005] and "death for Paul did not mean a state of unconscious repose, but a condition of being with Christ (Phil 1:23)."[1006] Said Oliver Greene, "the spirit of man will never cease to be conscious."[1007] For this reason the majority of evangelical and Protestant sects, along with most Catholics, believe with Thomas Constable that "this is not sleep of the soul, however, because Paul wrote elsewhere that a Christian who is absent from his body is present with the Lord (2 Cor. 5:8; cf. Phil 1:23; 1 Thes. 5:10)."[1008] The sleep refers only to the body, and not the soul.

Verses 14-15

> "For if we believe that Jesus died and rose again, even so God will bring with Him those who have fallen asleep in Jesus. For this we say to you by the word of the Lord, that we who are alive and remain until the coming of the Lord, will not precede those who have fallen asleep."

Here Paul indicates that those who have died "in Jesus" (i.e. believers) will return with Jesus at the Second Coming. At this stage some liberal Tübingen begin to see this resurrection as pure allegory, but most other Christians are still united. Matthew Henry declared that "the doctrine of the resurrection and the second coming of Christ is the great antidote against the fear of death and inordinate sorrow for the death of our Christian friends ... the death and resurrection of Christ are fundamental articles of the Christian religion, and give us hope of a joyful resurrection."[1009]

Perhaps the biggest debate in this verse is whether or not Paul is speaking of a general resurrection (meaning everyone will be resurrected) or a specific resurrection of those "in Christ." If the latter, then does this include the pre-Christian prophets and kings like David? Ultimately there are four views which come into play. First, there are those who believe this is a general resurrection of all who have died, regardless of their faith. Second, is the view that this refers to the resurrection of all saints both before and after Christ. Third, is the view that this speaks of the saints from the church age alone. Finally, some argue that this refers only to believers who have died during the Tribulation (the reign of the anti-Christ).

Hippolytus distinguishes between believers and unbelievers, but sees a general resurrection of believers.[1010] Curiously though, he quotes John 5:25 as "*many* shall hear my voice" and be resurrected. This is odd since the passage actually reads, "the dead shall hear my voice." If it is "many" of the dead, and not all of the dead, then it could not possibly be a general resurrection. This is parallel to Matthew 27:52 in which "many" (not all) "of the saints who had fallen asleep were raised."[1011] This took place at the resurrection of Christ. Consequently, while it is not proof of what will happen at the time of the end, it is emblematic of what may happen at the end. Of course, it may also indicate that some were already resurrected with Christ, hence this implies that these saints will not need to be resurrected at the second coming.

In fairness to Hippolytus, it appears that he considers this a general resurrection of believers, not a general resurrection of the dead collectively. Indeed, most agree with George Milligan that "the resurrection of *all* men does not here come into view."[1012] Paul is contrasting the hope of resurrection with the "hopelessness of the pagan world in the presence of death."[1013] So if only believers are intended then what are we to make of the term "in Jesus" ("in Christ" is the parallel found in verse seventeen)?

Gordon Fee believes that "in Christ" is used "solely to distinguish them from all others who have died" and argues that "one should not make too much of the pharsing 'the dead in Christ.'"[1014] Yet this begs the question. *How* does it distinguish them? Surely if Fee is admitting there is a distinction then we cannot disregard the distinction. Earnest Best attaches no significance to "in Christ"[1015] but then admits that "it implies that they were Christians."[1016] Obviously. The question is whether or not "Old Testament" Saints can be included as being "in Christ." Matthew 27:52 may answer that question.

In Matthew 27:52 it is said that "the tombs were opened, and many bodies of the saints who had fallen asleep were raised." This took place at the resurrection of Christ. Although no specifics are given, the fact that "many bodies of the saints" were resurrected along with Christ should indicate that "many" Old Testament Saints have already been resurrected and, therefore, cannot be included among those resurrected at rapture. This does, however, open the door as to whose bodies were not raised at this time. For that reason C.I. Scofield believed that the "dead in Christ" (v. 16) should be equated with "all the saints," but Lewis Sperry Chafer saw this as referring only to "saints of this dispensation."[1017] John Walvoord also this as saints from the church age.[1018]

Ultimately, whether or not we believe this refers only to believers from the church dispensation or all saints hinges not upon this verse but upon the plethora of other passages which speak of the resurrection of the just. It is clear in my mind that God does not make most of wait needlessly. Many were resurrected at the time of Jesus. Others will be resurrected at rapture. Many believe there will then be another resurrection at the Second Coming. Finally, there will be a general resurrection and judgment after the Millennial Kingdom (see notes on *Controversies in Revelation* for a defense of this view). At each stage the Lord will resurrect those believers who have not previously been resurrected. While there are legitimate questions about some of the saints and exactly when they are resurrected, it is apparent that most, if not all, will be resurrected at each stage. Here, however, Paul does not specify other to designate these as those who are "dead in Christ" (v. 16) or "asleep in Jesus."

Verse 16

> "For the Lord Himself will descend from heaven with a shout, with the voice of *the* archangel and with the trumpet of God, and the dead in Christ will rise first."

Here it is clear that the resurrection of the "dead in Christ" takes place in connection with the Lord's descent "from heaven with a shout, with voice of the archangel and with the trumpet of God." He also indicates that this resurrection takes place first, *before* the rapture described in the following verse.

This is the first indication of any specific time frame within Thessalonians as to the rapture. However, as we seen in 2 Thessalonians many within the church misinterpreted Paul's meaning. So also many are divided as to what time frame is indicated here. Some see this as proof that the rapture is synonymous with the Second Coming itself since Christ is descending from heaven. Others see the "trumpet of God" as synonymous with one of the seven Trumpets in the book of Revelation, *all* of which preceded the Second Coming. Still others believe that 2 Thessalonians 2 is written to clarify the time frame for these events.

What is obvious is that this event is closely connected to the Second Coming. Nevertheless, there are many "trumpets of God," and not all of them are found in the book of Revelation. In fact, the idea of a "voice of a trumpet" being descriptive of an angel's command is found throughout the Bible (Exodus 19:16, 19; 20:18; Psalms 47:7; Isaiah 27:13; Zechariah 9:14). So we cannot declare that this trumpet is the same as one in Revelation. We can, however, be sure that this trumpet is synonymous with that of Matthew 24:31 and 1 Corinthians 15:52, for both speak of the rapture and resurrection. It is for this reason that "posttribulationists" believe the rapture must be considered synonymous with the Second Coming and not separate from it. While this seems like a solid argument on the surface, there are problems with this view stemming from other passages including 2 Thessalonians 2 where Paul seeks to correct the misunderstanding of some Thessalonians. Since I am striving to take this exegesis one step at a time I will refer the reader to verse 17, 2 Thessalonians 2 and my appendix in *Controversies in Revelation* where I deal extensively with the theories of rapture. It is sufficient to say here that Paul is not giving a precise time line; only a general one.

Verse 17

> "Then we who are alive and remain will be caught up together with them in the clouds to meet the Lord in the air, and so we shall always be with the Lord."

These words describe the difference between the rapture and the resurrection. The resurrection of the dead apply to the dead, but "we who are alive and remain" will be transformed from mortal flesh into immortal without having experienced death. This is explained in 1 Corinthians 15:52-55. However, these words are Paul's first references to the rapture chronologically as this epistle was written many years before Corinthians. It is for this reason that the Thessalonians may have misunderstood Paul, even as many continue to misinterpret him. If we are to understand it, then there are two things in this passage which we should examine.

"We" Who are Alive

Obviously "we who are alive and remain" contrast those believers who have not died with those who have. However, liberal Tübingen scholars and their modern day disciples have argued that "the language proves beyond all doubt that when the Epistle was composed, St. Paul took it for granted that he would be alive at the second coming."[1019] Consequently, they believe that when Paul wrote 2 Thessalonians he had come up with a "new point of view"[1020] to explain away his previous expectations in a "rather unsatisfactory"[1021] manner!

The problems with this argument have already been addressed briefly. To reprise the main point. 2 Thessalonians was written probably with a year of 1 Thessalonians. Those who claim that Paul had written 2 Thessalonians many years later after becoming disappointed can offer no proof of a late date for the epistle other than their own assumptions about the "contradictory" nature of the epistle. However, since Paul explains his purpose is to clear up any misunderstanding caused by the first epistle, it is much more likely that Paul would not be writing many decades later.

Mal Couch interprets this in a radically different manner from the liberals. According to Couch this "supports the doctrine of the imminent return of Christ."[1022] This doctrine is defined as the belief that in regard to the rapture "Christ may return at any moment for His church, and no biblically predicted event must neccessarily precede it."[1023] This is in contrast to the Second Coming which must be preceded by numerous signs and events (see, for example, 2 Thessalonians 2) including the battle of Armageddon.

The doctrine of imminency stems from a comparison of many verses regarding the Second Coming and the rapture. Even when spoken of by the same author in the same book, there appear to be differences which cannot refer to the exact same event. For example, the Second Coming is Jesus coming *with* the Church, but the rapture is Jesus coming *for* His Church. Can they really be identical? No single passage can prove either the doctrine of imminency nor rejection of it. Most of those passages are discussed in my appendix of *Controversies in Revelation*. First and Second Thessalonians are among those, but in isolation one cannot prove one view over another. What is clear is that Paul believed he *could* be alive, not that he *would* be alive.

G.G. Findlay believed that "Paul did not count on a very near approach of the 2nd Advent (cf. II.ii.1f); but his language implies the possibility of the event taking place within his lifetime."[1024] Those, like F.F. Bruce, who argue that the "the writers rank themselves with those who will live to see the Parousia"[1025] must ignore the collective use of "we." They considered it a possibility, not a fact. The apostles certainly considered that Jesus could have come for them in their lifetime, but it is pure assumption to argue that they had a realistic expectation of that event. For this reason we must agree with Charles Ellicott who pronounced that this theory "must fairly be pronounced more than doubtful."[1026]

"Caught Up" in the Clouds
The second thing to remember about this verse is that our being "caught up together with them in the clouds to meet the Lord in the air" is the very definition of rapture. As Charles Ryrie noted, "the Latin translation of this verb ["caught up"] uses the word from which we get 'rapture' in English."[1027] So while "the term 'rapture' is never used in the Bible. The word means 'caught up' and is described in 1 Thess."[1028] It is also, however, found in Acts 8:39, 2 Corinthians 12:2-4, and Revelation 12:5.[1029] All three of these verses refer to a *miraculous* event. This event is further described in 1 Corinthians 15:52-55 as our transformation from mortal flesh to immortal resurrected bodies without having experienced physical death.

Without regard to timing, virtually all but the liberal theologians agree that this event is called rapture. It is cited by Saint Augustine and by John Calvin (both Amillennialists). Calvin declared that "those that survive ... would be exempted from death" and resurrected into a body and that this "sudden change will be like death."[1030] This event takes place in close proximity to the Second Coming and is a comfort to those of us who will be alive in the time of the coming anti-Christ.

Conclusion

The definition of the rapture is the translation of mortal living believers into immortal resurrected bodies without having experienced physical death. This "translation of all the changed saints is simultaneous."[1031] It has been compared to the translation of Elijah (2 Kings 2:11) and even Enoch (Hebrews 11:5).[1032]

The rapture and the Second Coming are closely connected. Of that we can be sure. Some have considered them so close that they are indistinguishable, but that mistake leads to certain misinterpretations which Paul sought to correct in his second epistle. Nevertheless, the existence of rapture in its basic definition is denied by few, if any, of the old and ancient theologians. Even Amillennialists such as Augustine[1033] and John Calvin[1034] saw a rapture, although they did not distinguish it from the Second Coming.

Among the pre-modern scholars, perhaps John Wesley best typifies the modern "posttribulationists." He argued that the rapture represents "the fewness of those who will be alive" after the Tribulation,[1035] hence effectively denying a rapture at all. In fact, he even saw the awakening as an awakening in the "spiritual sense."[1036] Thus Wesley allegorized the rapture, although he did hold to a literal Second Coming. This is not substantially different from modern posttribulationists like James Grant.[1037] However, this cannot be reconciled with the Bible.

H.A. Ironside summarizes the conflict, saying, "when the Lord Jesus Christ returns to establish His kingdom, He will come with all His saints. How can He do this if some are in heaven and some are on earth?"[1038] It is for this reason that Jesus's coming *for* the church must be distinguished from Jesus coming *with* the church.[1039] How much time elapses between these two events is not mentioned in this epistle and has become a major debate in recent years. Some dishonestly claim that the distinction is new and dates to the 1800s, but as early as the fourth century when Ephraem the Syrian explicitly defends a rapture three and a half years before the Second Coming (he saw the Tribulation as a three and a half year period rather than the seven generally accepted today).[1040] Additionally, many believe that the doctrine of imminency, which dates to the earliest of church fathers, is a reflection of their belief in a pretribulational rapture.

Without regard to the actual time frame, Paul clearly teaches rapture here in Thessalonians and 1 Corinthians. He says that we should "comfort one another with these words" (4:18). Therefore, let no one take away our comfort by denying the truth of these words. Nor should we be misguided in our interpretation as some of the Thessalonians were (see 2 Thessalonians 2). If we know and love the Lord then we should be comforted that God will call us to His bosom when the time is right, and none of us will be forgotten.

The Day of the Lord
1 Thessalonians 5:1-11

> "For you yourselves know full well that the day of the Lord will come just like a thief in the night. While they are saying, 'Peace and safety!' then destruction will come upon them suddenly like labor pains upon a woman with child, and they will not escape."

There are several names related to the time of the anti-Christ and the final days before Christ's return. Some of these names are technically distinct. They all relate to the same general time frame but are not necessarily the exact same. These names include the Tribulation (cf. Matthew 24:21, 29; Mark 13:19, 24), Last Days (cf. 2 Timothy 3:1; 2 Peter 3:2), End Times (cf. Ezekiel 35:5; Daniel 8:17, 19), Time of Jacob's Trouble (cf. Jeremiah 30:7), and the Day of the Lord. Among these the Day of the Lord is the most controversial. Some, like Marvin Rosenthal see the Day of the Lord as a specific time period within the Tribulation.[1041] Others see the Day of the Lord as synonymous with the Tribulation. Obviously this confusion is not new as Paul seeks to correct some misconceptions that the Thessalonians had about it in 2 Thessalonians, but here is Paul's introduction to the Day of the Lord.

He begins by saying that the Day of the Lord will come "like a thief in the night." This phrase is echoed in the Olivet Discourse (Matthew 24:43), 2 Peter 3:10, and Revelation (3:3; 16:15). This is then connected with the statement, "while they are saying, 'Peace and safety!' then destruction will come upon them suddenly." Because Revelation describes that destruction, some have argued that the "thief" reference in Revelation 16:15 could not possibly refer to the rapture, for destruction is already raging around them. Others say that it could not refer to the Day of the Lord for they are already in it. Still others believe it refers to nothing less than the Second Coming itself. Like pieces of a puzzle, we have clues here, but do not have the whole picture contained within these passages alone. Only by comparing the relevant passages can we hope to understand the full chronology, but that requires a belief in the inspiration of the Holy Scriptures, for Jesus, Peter, Paul, and John all wrote at different times and situation even though they all spoke of the same thing. Is there a contradiction? The skeptics say, "yes." The believer says, "no!" God Himself is the true author, so let us break down the three controversial issues and compare the relevant passages to one another.

A Primer on End Times
For the uninitiated, it is pertinent to define some basic terms and concepts before discussing End Times. Paul's audience had already been taught the basic

fundamentals of the Olivet Discourse and Old Testament prophecy, so Paul does not define those elements, but assumes his audience is familiar with them, as per his introductory words, "you have no need of anything to be written to you, for you yourselves known full well ..."

According to the Olivet Discourse and the Prophet Daniel there will be a time ruled by the anti-Christ before the (second) coming of the Messiah. He will be the last ruler of a united empire based on the Roman Empire. This time period is called the "Tribulation." Most believe that this is a seven year period whose beginning is marked by a seven year "peace treaty" brokered by the anti-Christ (cf. notes on Daniel 9 in *Controversies in the Prophets*). However, half way into this treaty, the anti-Christ will commit "the Abomination of Desolation" which will spark a world war and lead the Jewish people to repentance. During this final three and a half years many, if not all, of the plagues described in Revelation will be unleashed upon the earth, and the people of God will be severely persecuted. The "Day of the Lord" is connected in some way to this final three and a half years, sometimes called the "Great Tribulation."

There are the basics with which the Thessalonians were already familiar. Paul does not reprise this but begins with the "Day of the Lord." In 2 Thessalonians he then clarifies his opinions on the Abomination of Desolation and the anti-Christ.

"Day of the Lord"

1 Thessalonians 5:1-11 cannot be seriously understood without 2 Thessalonians 2:1-12, for there Paul elaborates on what he says here. Consequently, I will withhold debate until those passages below. Here it is merely necessary to highlight what Paul has already said. Namely, that the Day of the Lord will come "like a thief in the night" and when the people are deluded into believing that they have "peace and safety." These two points are crucial, as will be seen, in helping to establish a timeline within the Tribulation.

"Thief in the Night"

The image of the thief appears four times in the Bible outside of this verse. Three of those refer to a coming of Christ, and one of them refers to the "Day of the Lord." Here Paul relates it to the "Day of the Lord." Are they the same thing? Only by examining the context of each passage and then comparing it to Thessalonians can we have an honest answer.

The Olivet Discourse

The phrase is first heard by none other than the Lord Himself during the Olivet Discourse. The context of the passage is highly controversial because some believe that it is a reference to rapture while others believe that it is a reference to the Second Coming. Here is the full passage in context.

"For the coming of the Son of Man will be just like the days of Noah. For as in those days before the flood they were eating and drinking, marrying and giving in marriage, until the day that Noah entered the ark, and they did not understand until the flood came and took them all away; so will the coming of the Son of Man be. Then there will be two men in the field; one will be taken and one will be left. Two women *will be* grinding at the mill; one will be taken and one will be left. Therefore be on the alert, for you do not know which day your Lord is coming. But be sure of this, that if the head of the house had known at what time of the night the thief was coming, he would have been on the alert and would not have allowed his house to be broken into. For this reason you also must be ready; for the Son of Man is coming at an hour when you do not think *He will.*" (Matthew 24:37-44).

Some believe that this must be a reference to rapture. There are three reasons for this. First, "of that day and hour no one knows, not even the angels of heaven, nor the Son, but the Father alone" (Matthew 24:36). Surely this statement is hard to reconcile with the notion of Jesus's return at the battle of Armaggedon. Second, "for as in those days before the flood they were eating and drinking, marrying and giving in marriage, until the day that Noah entered the ark" (Matthew 24:37). As Dave Hunt noted, "they did eat, they drank, they married wives, they were given in marriage, they bought, they sold, they planted, they builded. That cannot be at the end of the Great Tribulation; the world is practically destroyed."[1042] Third, the image of one being taken and another left behind does not seem to fit Armageddon either, but rather the rapture.

Nevertheless, there are many who believe that this is a reference to theTribulation.[1043] Even greats like John Walvoord argued that this is not the rapture.[1044] Wierse believes that the reference here is not to Noah being "taken" but rather the wicked being taken in judgment.[1045] They declare that it is not rapture who takes the woman at the mill away but "the flood came and took them away."[1046] Nonetheless, this argument is flawed. First, a flood does not pick and choose its victims! The flood indiscriminately killed all who were not aboard the ark. Rather "the ark was the shelter for Noah and his family and it certainly lifted them up above the judgment ... The day he was taken out, here comes the judgment."[1047] This is exactly what Jesus said. Notice His words, "the day that Noah entered the ark" (24:38). The image is of Noah being taken away to be spared the flood.[1048] This is even admitted by at least one posttribulationist who says this "may suggest that just as Noah was saved by being taken away ... so believers" shall in the rapture.[1049]

Now I have said much more on this topic in *Controversies in the Gospels* under "The Last Days and the Days of Noah : Matthew 24:36-44 – Luke 17:22-37." I believe that the evidence favors rapture rather than Armageddon. As Oliver Greene reminds us, there are no signs preceding the rapture.[1050] There are many signs which precede the Second Coming. This is why posttribulationist James Grant's allegations that pretribulationists are akin to cult leaders like Charles Russell[1051] is dishonest. It is posttribulationists who predict dates for the Second Coming because the Bible list many signs before that coming, but there are no signs before the rapture. Rapture could happen at any time. For that reason, the imagery of a thief in the night best fits the rapture, and not the Second Coming. Nonetheless, even if we concede that the thief imagery refers to the Second Coming itself, it is apparent that this context of the thief here is different from that in Thessalonians. In the Olivet Discourse Jesus is speaking of His coming (either in rapture or the Second Coming) but here Paul is speaking of the "Day of the Lord" which is closely related, but not the same as we shall see.

2 Peter 3:10

Like Paul, Peter uses the thief imagery to refer specifically to the "Day of the Lord." He says, "the day of the Lord will come like a thief, in which the heavens will pass away with a roar and the elements will be destroyed with intense heat, and the earth and its works will be burned up." Notice that the "Day of the Lord" is accompanied by the destruction of the very elements (atoms), and "the earth and its works will be burned up." This is clearly a picture of the wrath of God and the destruction of the old world. Theoretically, it could refer to either the war of Armageddon or to the Last Battle found in Revelation 20:9 following the thousand year reign of Christ.

What is manifestly obvious is that the "Day of the Lord" is synonymous with a day of reconning and judgment. It is a day of wrath. The term is used throughout the Old Testament to refer to a time of judgment. Martin Luther said that "the prophets do not call only the final Day of Judgment 'the Day of the Lord.' They also give this name to any day of visitation."[1052] F.F. Bruce defines it as a "day when Yahweh would vindicate his righteous cause and execute impartial judgment."[1053] So technically the "Day of the Lord" can refer to any day of judgment,[1054] but contextually here, and elsewhere in the New Testament, it refers to the day of reconning in the Tribulation.

The Book of Revelation

There are two passages in Revelation which use the thief imagery. The first is in Revelation 3:3 when John warns the church of Sardis "if you do not wake up, I will come like a thief, and you will not know at what hour I will come to you" (Revelation 3:3). Could this possibly refer to the day of Armageddon? Will the church have fear this? This itself is another controversy (see notes on Revelation 3:3), but the point is that this seems to be a warning to the church to be awake and watch. Surely no Christian will be unaware of what the gathering of armies at Armageddon means? Surely this cannot be a reference to the final battle and the Second Coming? This passage is one used by pretribulationists to support the position that rapture takes place *before* the Day of the Lord, and not synonymous with or after it.

214

The second passage in Revelation is in 16:15 where Jesus declares, "Behold, I am coming like a thief. Blessed is the one who stays awake and keeps his clothes, so that he will not walk about naked and men will not see his shame" (Revelation 16:15). Unlike the first passage, this passage is amid a description of the gathering armies of Armageddon. Hence, it *appears* to be a reference to the Second Coming, rather than rapture.

Two possible explanations are given by pretribulationists. John Walvoord believes that "the underlying factor in all these [thief] passages is that the coming in view results in the loss for those who are not ready."[1055] Another explanation is that this is an aside, warning the reader in order that he might take heed and not have to experience that final battle. In fact, the NAS, RV, RSV, ASV, ESV, Geneva, and Darby translations all place this statement in brackets, indicating just that. This may be an aside, for it seems that the thief has already come and it is too late for those assembling at Armageddon. The passage is then an aside to warn us in advance before that day comes.

Summary of the Thief Analogy

"Jewish tradition was that the Messiah would come at midnight."[1056] To that end, some believe the thief analogy was first drawn, but it is clear that the context of the passages indicate that "a thief comes without giving any warning."[1057] The thief imagery is one of preparedness by believers and unpreparedness by unbelievers, but it is also more literally that of the thief ariving when no one is expecting.

To summarize what we have found, five passages in the New Testament allude to a "thief in the night." Of these two explicitly mention the Day of the Lord as coming like a thief. Three compare a coming of Jesus to a thief in the night. Of these three there is great debate as to whether it is the coming of Jesus for the church at rapture or the coming of Jesus with the church at Armageddon. This latter imagery does not seem to fit well, however. The imagery found in at least two, and probably four, of these passages is one where the thief appears when people least expect it. It is a time when the people are crying "Peace and safety." Such a condition is irreconcilable with the plagues, wars, and destruction described in the book of Revelation, and especially Armageddon. It is, therefore, our next step to examine this false peace and what it means.

"Peace and Safety"

According to the prophet Daniel, the anti-Christ will broker a seven year peace treaty between Israel and its enemies.[1058] In 2 Thessalonians 2 the apostle Paul makes it very clear that *this* is the "peace" to which he was referring in this passage. It is a false peace.

At least as far back as Irenaeus, the second generation disciple of John, it was believed that the Abomination of Desolation follows cries of "Peace and Safety."[1059] This is made abundantly clear in 2 Thessalonians 2, which is why I

215

will reserve most of my comments for the debate under 2 Thessalonians 2:1-3. At this point it is more important to point out that comparisons to the gospel of Luke,[1060] particularly in Luke 21, are no coincidence. The "words of Jesus ... are distinctly echoed"[1061] here, or are they? It would be more accurate to say that Luke's words are echoes of Paul, his teacher and friend. Ernest Best calls these parallels "Lukanisms"[1062] but forgets that the epistles of Thessalonians were actually written before the gospel of Luke. Luke wrote as a historian and interviewed the eyewitnesses of Jesus's life, death, and resurrection, but was not a witness himself. So the words of Paul here are no mere copies, but inspired revelation.

In short, before the Day of the Lord there will be a time of false peace when the world naively believes it is at peace. The utopian fervor which often accompanies some of the worst periods in human history will be repeated here, but "destruction will come upon them suddenly like labor pains upon a woman with child, and they will not escape" (5:3). As believers, however, "are not in darkness, that the day would overtake you like a thief" (5:4). We are to be prepared.

Conclusion

1 Thessalonians 5 is not about rapture. It is about the Day of the Lord. However, as John Walvoord remarked, "just as the translation of the church is the end of the day of grace it also marks the beginning of the Day of the Lord."[1063] It is for this reason that many, both then and now, are confused. James Frame said that "the day comes suddenly for both believers and unbelievers"[1064] but this is the problem. If believers are not to be in darkness, it should not overcome us suddenly as it does the unbeliever. Why then does Paul warn us? Obviously, some reject the doctrine of rapture and the Day of the Lord. We have then put ourselves in league with those who are living blindly.

Paul declared that "God has not destined us for wrath" (1 Thessalonians 5:9). This issue of wrath is a major issue in regard to the rapture debate. If we are not be the subject of wrath, and if the Tribulation is a time of God's wrath, then how can we be lifted out of wrath? Like the days of Noah God delievered the righteous from His wrath (cf. Matthew 24:36-44 and Luke 17:22-37). So also He will deliver us as well.

Those who reject the connection between rapture and the Day of the Lord invariably create contradictions in their theology. For example, one commentator rejects the idea that "peace and safety" refers to "international conditions" because he erroneously associates the Day of the Lord specifically with Armageddom.[1065] However, he never explains exactly what is meant by "peace and safety." How can he? If the world is engulfed in war and plagues, there can be no peace or safety! Walvoord believes that the Day of the Lord begins in Revelation 6.[1066] Others, like Robert van Kampen, connect it to the latter portion of the Tribulation.[1067] Still others believe that rapture may precede the Day of the Lord by a number of years. Hence the exactly timing of rapture is a legitimate debate, but the denial of rapture is not. What is certain is that rapture will precede the Day of the Lord, and that day will come suddenly upon an unbelieving world.

Trichotomy or Dichotomy?
1 Thessalonians 5:23 – Hebrew 4:12

"May your spirit and soul and body be preserved complete, without blame at the coming of our Lord Jesus Christ."

Here is a reference to our "spirit and soul and body." This three fold division is called the "trichotomy" of man. Many, however, deny that Paul is speaking of a trichotomy. They believe that man is a dichotomy (of two parts) with "spirit and soul" being equivalent to "heart and mind" or a similar phrase.[1068] Others, claim that the spirit is only a reference to the Holy Spirit and not a natural part of man.[1069] Still other opinions have surfaced over the year. One scholars even argues that man has more than three parts, accepting "heart, mind, conscience, and other parts."[1070] A total of a half dozen views have been presented upon the nature of the spirit and soul in this passage, but only five dominant views, four of which are outgrowths of the dichotomist view.

One author claims that "aside from 1 Thessalonians 5:23 [Paul] nowhere employs trichotomist language."[1071] This is, however, both misleading and irrelevant. Other passages speak of the spirit and soul as having a distinction, but even if this were the only passage in the whole of the Bible to make such an allusion we cannot so easily dismiss it if we believe in the inspiration of the Holy Spirit. Paul's words *meant* something. So while it may be true that Paul is not "analyzing" the various parts of man here[1072] and that "Paul is not here giving us a list of the separable parts of man,"[1073] it is equally true that Paul was not tossing around myths or wive's tales. He must have believed that the spirit and soul meant *something*. But what? The best way to answer this question is to begin with the use of "spirit" and "soul" in the New Testament itself.

Soul and Spirit in the New Testament
There are 47 instances of ψυχη (soul) in the New Testament and just over 350 uses of πνευμα (spirit). However, a half dozen or so of the references to "souls" simply refer to human beings (e.g. Acts 2:41). The use of "spirit" may also be distinguished for there are approximately 94 instances of the "Holy Spirit," another 152 instances which almost certainly refer to the Holy Spirit (some references, such as Matthew 4:1, may or may not refer to the Holy Spirit), and another 34 instances where "spirit" refers to angels or demons.

Thus in the context of these passages we have roughly 40 New Testament references to "soul" and approximately 65 references to the "spirit" of man. Below is a chart identifying each of these New Testament references to the ψυχη (Soul) and the πνευμα (Spirit).

ψυχη (Soul)	πνευμα (Spirit)	
Matthew 10:28	Matthew 5:3	Matthew 22:43 (?)
Matthew 11:29	Matthew 26:41	Matthew 27:50
Matthew 12:18	Mark 2:8	Mark 8:12
Matthew 16:26	Mark 14:38	Luke 1:17
Matthew 22:37	Luke 1:47	Luke 1:80
Matthew 26:38	Luke 8:55	Luke 9:55 (?)
Mark 8:36-37	Luke 23:46	John 3:6
Mark 12:30	John 4:23-24	John 6:63
Mark 14:34	John 11:33	John 13:21
Luke 1:46	John 19:30	Acts 7:59
Luke 2:35	Acts 17:16	Acts 18:25
Luke 10:27	Romans 1:9	Romans 8:10
Luke 12:19-20	Romans 8:15-16	Romans 12:11
John 12:27	1 Corinthians 2:11	1 Corinthians 4:21
Acts 2:27	1 Corinthians 5:3-5	1 Corinthians 7:34
Acts 14:22	1 Corinthians 14:2	1 Corinthians 14:14-16
Acts 15:24	1 Corinthians 15:45	1 Corinthians 16:18
Romans 2:9	2 Corinthians 2:13	2 Corinthians 4:13
1 Corinthians 15:45	2 Corinthians 7:1	2 Corinthians 7:13
2 Corinthians 1:23	2 Corinthians 12:18	Galatians 6:1
2 Corinthians 12:15	Galatians 6:18	Ephesians 1:17
1 Thessalonians 5:23	Ephesians 4:23	Philippians 1:27
Hebrews 4:12	Philippians 2:2	Philippians 2:20
Hebrews 6:19	Philippians 4:23	Colossians 2:5
Hebrews 10:38-39	1 Thessalonians 2:17	1 Thessalonians 5:23
Hebrews 13:17	2 Thessalonians 2:2	2 Timothy 1:7
James 1:21	2 Timothy 4:22	Philemon 1:25
James 5:20	Hebrews 4:12	James 2:26
1 Peter 1:9	1 Peter 3:4	1 Peter 3:8
1 Peter 1:22	1 Peter 3:18	1 Peter 4:6
1 Peter 2:11	1 John 4:6	
1 Peter 2:25		
1 Peter 4:19		
2 Peter 2:8		
2 Peter 2:14		
3 John 2		

Of all of these passages there are five which are of primary importance in understanding the difference between the spirit and soul, if there are any.

These passages are Matthew 12:18, John 3:6, 1 Corinthians 15:45, 1 Thessalonians 5:23, and Hebrews 4:12. The last two verses are, of course, what we are debating, so I will withhold judgment upon these verses for the time being.

Matthew 12:18 is a prophecy of the Messiah, Jesus. It says, "Behold, My Servant whom I have chosen, in whom my *soul* is well pleased, I will put My *Spirit* upon Him." Now the reference here is to God, so there can only be a limited application to man's spirit, but it is clear in this passage that God's *soul* is distinguished from His Spirit which He can, and does, bestow on others. No one could even comprehent what it might mean if God sent His "Holy Soul." This is because "soul" appears to have a singular personal context. Every passage in the Bible in which the "soul" is referenced has a clear connection with that being as an individual. Spirit, however, has a connection to God. Even *our* spirit appears in the Bible to have some higher connection beyond our selves.

The second verse of importance here is John 3:6 in which Jesus declares "that which is born of the flesh is flesh, and that which is born of the Spirit is spirit." This verse is a little more difficult from the perspective of determining what a spirit and soul entail. However, it is clear that the spirit is *born* of the Holy Spirit. Does that mean that an unbeliever has no spirit? No (cf. 1 Corinthians 2:11), but this is debated by some, so I will withhold debate until the section that follows. It does, however, mean that the spirit of man is at least dormant and effectively dead until it is born. Most importantly, all agree that *every* man has a soul. How then can the spirit be born of Spirit, but the soul exist in all men? Clearly there must be a difference between the two.

Excluding 1 Thessalonians 5:23 and Hebrews 4:12, which is the subject of this debate, there is one other critical passage which may help us. 1 Corinthians 15:45 quotes from Genesis 2:7 saying, "'The first man, Adam, became a living soul.' The last Adam became a life-giving spirit." Here the *soul* of Adam is contrasted with the *Spirit* of Christ. When we examine Genesis 2:7 we see that many Bible translations do not even use the word "soul" but simply "being" (NAS, NIV, NKJV), "person" (NLT, NIRV), or even "creature" (ESV). The soul is here connected to the person as an individual being whereas the spirit in this passage is once again connected to Jesus or God. The spirit thus is on a higher plane than the soul.

What of the final two passages? Technically, neither 1 Thessalonians 5:23 nor Hebrews 4:12 give us any specifics on the differences in the spirit and soul, but in both of these passages the two appear to be distinguished. Many different interpretations have arisen to explain this enigma. Let us, therefore, examine those interpretations before arriving at a conclusion.

The Five Primary Interpretations
Beyond the two views, trichotomy and dichotomy, there are five interpretations of these passages which fit into these two larger views. Four of these are attempts to fit the passages into a dichotomy. The fifth, of course, is a straightforward trichotomy.

1. The Accommodation Interpretation
I begin with the weakest view. This interpretation argues that Paul was "accomodating" the trichotomy view even though he was a dichotomist![1074] The theory argues that Paul was simply following popular opinion without regard for whether or not it was actually true. To this I will answer with the words of a dichotomist. He says that this argument evokes "questionable ... ethics."[1075] It essentially argues that Paul lied in order to appease his audience, but this is deception. I will never refer to the Freudian concept of "id, ego, and superego" as if it were true because I don't believe it. This would be to lend credibility to a theory which I find at odds with the Bible. So also it is disrespectful and dishonest to *assume* that Paul would do so. Whatever Paul's opinions were, it is obvious that Paul believed what he wrote!

2. The Rhetorical Interpretation
One of the most popular arguments is the rhetorical view. According to this view Paul is "not trying to distinguish between 'spirit' and 'soul'"[1076] but using a popular rhetorical device similar to "heart and soul."[1077] Advocates argue that this is just "rhetoric" for "the totality of human nature."[1078] Charles Masson said it could be paraphrased as "may your entire person, your soul and body."[1079] Yet this is the very problem, for Paul did not say "your entire person, your soul and body," but rather the entire person is of "your spirit *and* soul *and* body."

This is a slightly better, and more respectful, spin off of the first view, but it still has many problems. Although Charles Ryrie argues that if Paul were "analyzing man" he "would have to include 'heart' and 'mind'"[1080] he is assuming that heart and mind are unrelated to the soul, even though these same dichotomists believe they are! F.F. Bruce calls the distinction between spirit and soul "forced,"[1081] arguing that "few would care to distinguish sharply among the four elements 'heart' (καρδια), 'soul' (ψυχη), 'mind' (διανoυα), and 'strength' (ισχυς)."[1082] Yet it is here that the rhetorical argument falls apart, for they accept that these elements are all either synonymous or closely related, but then argue that they must be distinguished because Paul here distinguishes between spirit and soul. One dichotomist openly admits that the three parts are "within one and the same clause ... [and yet] the third of which is clearly of a totally different nature from the second."[1083] In other words, if spirit and soul are synonymous then why would they be coupled *in a single clause* with "body," with which it is obviously not synonymous. If this were Paul's intention then he would have separated "spirit and soul" in a separate clause from "body," such as saying, "may your spirit and soul, as well as your body." Instead all three are joined together in a single clause as *different* parts of man.

Consider the saying about "splitting hairs." Some might compare this to Hebrews 4:12, arguing that this proves they are the same,[1084] but splitting a single entity in two is not what Hebrews says. For "spirit and soul" are coupled with our "the thoughts and intentions of the heart." They clearly have a close relation to one another, but if they are the same, then this passage makes no sense. Would we ever say, "even able to divide between hair and folicle?" Of course not. We can *split* a hair, but we cannot divide between a hair and folicle. Why? Because splitting something involves cutting a single entity into two pieces, but division involves separating similar yet different groups. Jews and gentiles are different divisions. Although we are different, we can be united, but when a sect is split, it is irrevocably cut in half. So while spirit and soul are closely related, they cannot be the same. Or can they? Is there any Biblical evidence that these are synymous terms?

One argument made by dichotomists is the fact that Matthew 10:28 speak about body and soul but whereas 1 Corinthians 5:3 and 7:34 speak about the body and spirit.[1085] Some therefore conclude that the terms are interchangeable. Now while this seems a convincing argument at first, close examination of the passages make it suspect. While these passages contrast the spirit or soul against the body, this affinity between spirit and soul does not prove that they are identical. There is a close affinity between the heart and the lungs, but they are not the same. They are a part of the same body, but different organs. Here then is the question. Are the spirit and soul under the same umbrella? This is the view of the *Single Substance Interpretation* discussed below.

The failure of the rhetorical view is the fact that one of its own advocates refers to this as "a somewhat off-handed moment."[1086] Are we to believe that the apostle Paul, in the Holy Scriptures, had an "off-handed moment"?[1087] Are we to believe that rhetoric overtook Paul's careful and meticulous systematic approach to teaching? This view is the second weakest of the interpretations, leaving us only three viable options.

3. The Holy Spirit Interpretation

Three views remain. Each has some merit, and I have at least toyed with each view in my own mind at some time. According to this view the spirit to which Paul speaks is that of the Holy Spirit in us. Says James Frame, "the believer and unbeliever are so far alike that their individuality consist of an inner (ψυχη, νους, καρδια, 'ο εγω ανθροπος) and an outer part (σομα), but the believer differs from the unbeliever in that he has received from God the divine Spirit ... without the indwelling πνευμα, man at his best (ψυχικος) is mere man, unregenerate, σαρκικος."[1088] This was the view of John Wesley who saw in "natural man" only the body and soul.[1089] However, "of the three here mentioned, only the last two are natural, consistent parts of man. The first is adventitious and supernatural gift of God, to be found in Christians only."[1090]

On the surface this view seems sound as it explains the distinction between spirit and soul while accounting for those passages which seem to speak only of a body and soul (cf. Matthew 10:28). However, the view suffers from two fatal flaws. First, 1 Corinthians 2:11 seems to indicate that the "spirit of man" exist in all men, regardless of whether or not they know Christ (cf. Proverbs 20:27; Ezekiel 13:3; Daniel 2:1; Zechariah 12:1). If we interpret this as referring to the Holy Spirit, with which is appears to be *contrast*, then the passage would not make sense. Indeed, the following verse further seems to contrast the "Spirit of God" from the "spirit of this world" which appears to be parallel to the "spirit of man." The implication is that man's spirit is an extension of the self, but God's Spirit is an extension of Himself.

Another fatal flaw with this view is the fact that the passage would be implicating Holy Spirit in sin. How? Surely Paul "would not be expressing the wish that the Holy Spirit ... be kept sound and blameless ... [or] without flaw."[1091] This is the implication. If we are to keep ourselves free from blame then it follows that we could allow our "spirit and soul and body" to fall into blame! The passage is urging us to stay pure and free from sin. Surely Paul would have no need to urge us to keep the Holy Spirit blameless!

While far from being "absurd,"[1092] as one dichotomist uncharitably put it, this interpretation cannot sustain itself against the context of 1 Thessalonians 5:23 or other passages like 1 Corinthians 2:11. It should, therefore, be discarded with careful reservation.

4. The Single Substance Interpretation

We have now found ourselves down to two fundamentally different interpretations. The best dichotomist view is the substance interpretation. John Calvin describes this by saying that "the flesh as well as the Spirit belong to the soul."[1093] For Calvin the soul of man is his whole being. "The soul," he says, "has two principle faculties – the understanding and the will"[1094] but the spirit "denot[es] reason or intelligence."[1095] William Kelly explains that "'the soul' is the seat of personality, 'the spirit' is rather the expression of capacity."[1096] In short, they argue that there is but one substance which consist of smaller parts.

This view, alone among the dichotomist theories, can explain why spirit and soul sometimes appear synonymous while at other times appear to be distinguished. Like the heart and lungs are a part of the body, so it is argued that the spirit and body are a part of the soul. Now there are Bible verses which can be used to support this, but only in a limited way. Soul can sometimes be used to refer to the larger "being." Sometimes the soul or *psyche* (ψυχη) is translated merely as "person" or "being" (e.g. Acts 2:41). It is therefore used in a generic way to refer to the whole of man, but there are a great many other passages where it has a more specific meaning above and beyond the person as a whole.

"Soul" is often used to describe a person's emotional state (e.g. Mark 13:34), and in other instances it is set up in contrast to the body (Matthew 10:28). If the body is a part of the soul, as Calvin believes, then how is it that Jesus can say, "Do not fear those who kill the body but are unable to kill the soul; but rather fear Him who is able to destroy both soul and body"? Would not the destruction of the body be the destruction of at least part of the soul? If our heart stops beating would not our entire body die? If the body comprises part of the soul, would not its death cause the soul to die?

Additionally, the context of 1 Thessalonians 5:23 and Hebrews 4:12 do not match Calvin's thesis. Here Paul says to keep our "spirit and soul and body" pure. Hebrews 4:12 speaks of dividing spirit and soul. If the soul is the larger part, and the spirit is a smaller part of the whole, then 1 Thessalonians would not make logical sense. Like the rhetorical theory, Paul would be comprising a phrase here that defies logic. He would not say "may your spirit and soul and body be preserved" but "may your soul, both spirit and body, be preserved."

It appears that the substance interpretation is a simplification at best. It answers some questions, but ignores others. There is no doubt that there is a close relationship between spirit and soul, but they cannot be a part of the same thing. It is true that "soul" is sometimes used in a generic sense of the whole of man, but this is not always the case, nor is it possible to attach that definition here. A simple test would be to translate "soul" as "person" and see if the passage still makes sense. In many places we can do so, but try this in Matthew 10:28 ("do not fear those who kill the body but are unable to kill the person; but rather fear Him who is able to destroy both person and body in hell") or here in 1 Thessalonians 5:23 ("may your spirit and person and body be preserved complete"). It is apparent that this simply will not work.

5. The Trichotomy Interpretation

One dichotomist said that the trichotomy view "can be dismissed at once."[1097] He cites passages like Romans 8:10; 1 Corinthians 5:5, 7:34; 2 Corinthians 7:1; Ephesians 2:3; and Colossians 2:5 as proof that the trichotomy view cannot be true.[1098] However, arrogance often betrays ignorance, for these passages only show that the spirit is to be contrasted with the body, not that the spirit is synonymous with the soul. Without dealing with those passages where spirit and soul are distinguished the dichotomist does himself a disfavor by looking condescendingly upon those who look at all the passages equally. To that end, let us look at all the passages in question and determine Biblical how spirit and soul are used in the Bible. This is the only fair way to determine if the spirit and soul are distinct and, if they are, how they are distinguished.

Biblical Descriptions of the Spirit and Soul

It is true that trichotomists are somewhat divided as to what makes up the difference between the spirit and soul. There is general agreement on most

223

points, but not all. Some say that the soul is the seat of thought,[1099] while others allocate the mind to the spirit.[1100] Because of the affinity of the spirit and soul, it is perhaps natural that there will be confusion for few, whether dichotomists or trichotomists, have done an in depth word study on the spirit and soul. Here I shall endeavor to just that. Like a police detective, we must examine the evidence *before* reaching a conclusion.

How then is the word "soul" used in the Bible? How is "spirit" used in the Bible? Only when we examine this in detail can we determine if they are different, and what the relationship between the two may be. Let us, therefore, start with the soul.

1. The Role of the Soul

The word "soul" in the Bible is *psyche* (ψυχη) in the Greek and *nephesh* (נֶפֶשׁ) in Hebrew. The word is used in the Bible in one of several ways. The most common use of "soul" is synonymous with the self. In many cases it is even translated simply as "person" or "being." In these instances it is used in the larger sense of the *self*. It encompasses our entire being, as Calvin believed. However, the word also has a more specific use which is ignored by Calvin and others. Simply identifying the soul with the self is not sufficient to assign such a generic definition. Although the soul is connected to the self, it entails much more.

What does the Bible say about the soul? To begin with, the soul is immortal. Unlike the body, the soul cannot die. Matthew 10:28 makes this clear to the Christian, but even in the Old Testament, the belief in the immortality of the soul existed. Jesus said in Matthew 22:31-32 the use of the present tense to refer to Abraham, Isaac, and Jacob was itself proof of the resurrection of the dead. Other hints at immortality can be found in Genesis 35:18 where the soul is described as "departing" when the body dies. Job in particular speaks of immortality when he fears being abandoned to the pit (Job 33:18, 28, 30). For the Christian the immortality of the soul is unquestionable. So also, except for the Sadducees, the ancient Jews all accepted the immortality of the soul.

Next, this immortal soul is spoken of as possessing a great many emotions. A wide range of feelings and emotions are coupled with the "soul." The most prevalent are sorrow or despair (Leviticus 26:16; Deuteronomy 28:65; 1 Samuel 2:33; Job 24:12; Job 30:25; Psalm 7:2, 31:7, 9, 35:12, 42:5-6, 11, 43:5, 119:28; cf. Psalm 44:25, 57:4-6; Isaiah 53:11; Jeremiah 13:17; Matthew 26:38; Mark 14:34; John 12:27), distress (Genesis 42:21; 2 Kings 4:27; Jonah 4:8; Romans 2:9; cf. Psalm 88:3), desire (1 Samuel 3:21; Job 23:13; Proverbs 13:4, 9, 21:10; Ecclesiastes 6:2, 9; Isaiah 26:8; Micah 7:3), happiness or joy (Psalm 86:4, 94:19; Proverbs 29:17; Isaiah 42:1, 66:3; Ezekiel 24:21), bitterness (Job 3:20, 7:11, 10:1, 21:25, 27:2; Isaiah 38:15; Ezekiel 27:31), anger or hatred (Leviticus 26:15, 30, 43; Psalm 11:5, 107:18), and praise (Psalm 30:12, 35:9;

Isaiah 61:10; Luke 1:46). Other feelings include fear (Isaiah 19:10), dismay (Psalm 6:3), annoyance (Judges 16:16), satisfaction (Ecclesiastes 6:3), torment (2 Peter 2:8), pain (Lamentations 3:51), and an unsettling feeling (Acts 15:24). Additionally, the soul is spoken of as being "poured out" (1 Samuel 1:15; Job 30:16; Psalm 42:4), implying an evocation of feelings and sentiments. This is by no means an exhaustive list. Love, for example, is yet another attribute associated with the soul (Song of Solomon 1:7, 3:1-4), and the most important.

In 26 passages "heart" and "soul" are coupled together. This again implies a close relationship between the two. Since the heart is used of feelings and emotions, the connection to the soul is often interpreted to mean that "the soul is the seat of affections and emotions."[1101] The preceding list should serve as proof of this fact.

But this is not all. In addition to immortality and emotion, the soul is connected to several other important aspects. Most of these are negative, and begin with the simple fact that the soul is not self-sufficient. The soul "thirst" for something beyond itself (Psalm 42:1-2, 63:1, 107:9). The soul longs for and "yearns" for God (Psalm 84:2, 143:6, Isaiah 26:9). It is clear from the Bible that it is God who sustains and preserves the soul of man (Psalm 54:4, 97:10, Hebrews 10:39). He is said to restore the souls (cf. Lamentations 1:16) of those who wait upon the Lord (Psalm 130:5-6; cf. Psalm 119:81) and gives them rest (Matthew 11:29). There are many other verses that also hint upon the soul's insufficiency (cf. Psalm 33:20, 57:1, 62:1, 5, 63:8, 88:14, Isaiah 38:17). This also explains why even the pagan is drawn to religion. Every man needs something beyond himself. Every man knows in his heart that his soul is not self-sufficient. This also explains the next unpleasant aspect of the soul. Its need for salvation.

The soul is described in the Bible as proud (cf. Leviticus 16:29, 31, 23:27, 32; Psalm 35:13). Despite its lack of self sufficiency, it is proud and decieves itself (Psalm 24:4) into believing that it does not need anything else. To this end, the soul is capable of obedience or disobedience (Psalm 119:129, 167; cf. Proverbs 19:16; 1 Peter 1:22). Thus, sin is seated in the self; in the soul. This is why the soul is repeatedly spoken of as in need of atonement and salvation (Leviticus 17:11; Job 33:28; Psalm 34:22, 49:8, 15, 56:13, 69:18, 89:48, 116:8, 119:81; Proverbs 23:14; 2 Peter 1:9; cf. Psalm 6:4, 17:13, 19:7, 22:20, 23:3, 35:17, 55:18, 62:1, 5, 71:23, 86:13, Lamentations 3:58). Indeed, the very Law of Moses begins with this presumption, declaring that God desires "atonement for your souls" (Leviticus 17:11).

So we can see that at least 60% of the usages of "soul" in the Bible refer explicitly to the self.[1102] It is used of man as a being. It encompasses who he is as an individual divorced from those around him, but it is much more than this. It is the seat of our emotions, it is capable of love and obedience, but it is also proud despite not being self sufficient. Our soul needs God to complete us, and therefore it is our soul that needs salvation from its own sinfulness.

2. The Role of the Spirit

The word "spirit" in the Bible is *pneuma* (πνευμα) in the Greek and *ruach* (רוח) in Hebrew. These words are used many different ways. The majority of passages about spirit refer to God's spirit or the the spirits of angels and/or demons. Some use the term idiomatically to refer to a spirit of rebellion or sin among nations (cf. 2 Chron. 21:16, Isaiah 19:13, etc.), but even this term is etymologically borrowed from the idea that demonic spirits incite men to such rebellion.

In addition to these uses, there is no shortage of passages which speak about the spirit of man. A number of those passages do indeed parallel those of the soul, but many others utilize the spirit is used in a very different manner. I have found no fewer than nine aspects of the spirit found in the Bible. Let us look at these aspects before determining what connection the spirit has with the soul.

A) The Spirit Gives Life

In Genesis 2:7 the Bible declares that God "breathed into his nostrils the breath of life; and man became a living soul." The Hebrew word for "breathed" here is different from the Hebrew word for "spirit" but similar. "Spirit" in the Hebrew is *ruach* (רוח) which can also mean "breath" or "wind,"[1103] for both are unseen and yet vital parts of life. If one is not breathing, then he is not alive. So also the spirit is that which gives life. This is most apparent in Genesis 7:22 where there is a deliberate word play. In that passage it says, "all in whose nostrils was the breath of the spirit of life, died." Even in English it is apparent that the absence of spirit equals death, but the Hebrew "breath of the spirit of life" is "*nishmath-ruach* [נשמת-רוח]." *Nishamah* (נשמה) is another word which can alternately mean either "breath" or "spirit."[1104] However, *ruach* (רוח) is predominantly used of "spirit" whereas *nishamah* (נשמה) is predominantly used of "breath." Nevertheless, in Hebrew the two words form a sort of word play. It is thus clear that the spirit itself is the life of a man, "breathed" into man by God.

This is also apparent in Ecclesiastes 12:7 where the Teacher declares, "the dust will return to the earth as it was, and the spirit will return to God who gave it." So like the soul, the spirit is immortal, and as we see in John 19:30, whoever gives up his spirit dies (see also Acts 7:59), but this is not a New Testament teaching alone for Psalm 104:29 states that the Lord "takes away their spirit, they expire and return to their dust." Compare this with James 2:26 which says, "the body without the spirit is dead." Thus without the spirit our body dies because it is the spirit that gives us life. Nowhere is this more obvious and in Jesus's resurrection of Tabitha, for it is said, "her spirit returned, and she got up immediately" (Luke 8:55). Hence her resurrection is connected to the return of her spirit to her body.

This of course opens up a whole new debate about the difference between physical death and spiritual death. When Adam ate of the fruit of the forbidden tree it was said that he would die *on that very day* (Genesis 2:17). Did he? Yes, he did. His spirit died that very day, and his flesh would slowly die every day thereafter. It is for this very reason that God is said to "renew," "revive," and "preserve" our spirit (1 Sam 30:12; Job 10:12; Psalm 51:10; Ephesians 4:23). This may also be why Paul speaks of his spirit being as being "refreshed" (1 Corinthians 16:18; cf. 2 Corinthians 7:13) or "rested" (1 Corinthians 2:13). Although many take these latter references to be idiomatic, such idioms originate from somewhere. Our bodies must rest to revive its strength. So also the spirit of man must be renewed, but this touches upon the second debate. Do all men have spirits?

B) All Men Have a Spirit
As aforementioned, there are some who believe that the references to spirit always refer to the Holy Spirit.[1105] They deny that man has a spirit which may be distinguished from the soul or Holy Spirit. However, it is clear from both the Old and New Testaments that all men have a spirit; the *ruach* (רוּחַ) in Hebrew and pneuma (πνευμα) in Greek.

As far back as Moses, in Numbers 16:22 and 27:17 God is referred to as the "God of the spirits of *all* flesh." It is He who give us *all* a spirit. There is no indication here that only some flesh have spirits, but all flesh. The Holy Spirit is in addition to our spirit. It completes our spirit and renews it (among many other great things), but it cannot be synonymous with the "spirit of man" of which Job 32:8 speaks. Additionally, if all men do not have a spirit then how could Psalm 78:8 declare that some men's "spirit was not faithful to God." Surely the Holy Spirit is faithful to Himself! So also Ezekiel 13:3 rebukes false prophets who follow "their own spirit" instead of God's. A number of other Old Testament passages also speak of a "spirit of man" which cannot be confused with the Spirit of God in man (Deuteronomy 2:30; Proverbs 20:27; Daniel 2:1; Zechariah 12:1; Malachi 2:15-16).

The New Testament also seems to support the idea that unbelievers have spirits, for 1 Corinthians 2:11 indicates that the "spirit of man" exist in all men, regardless of whether or not they know Christ. Other passages speak of "your spirit" as opposed to God's spirit in us (cf. 2 Timothy 4:22; Philemon 25; and even Galatians 6:18). Moreover, if "the body without the spirit is dead" (James 2:26), as we affirmed in the first point, then all men must have a spirit or else they would not ever have lived!

C) The Spirit of Man Comes from God
If it is not clear already, then it must be stated here emphatically. The spirit of man, separate from the Holy Spirit, comes from God. Ecclesiastes 12:7 says that "the spirit will return to God who gave it" and Zechariah 12:1 states that the

Lord "forms the spirit of man within him." Thus the spirit of man, distinct from the Spirit of God, is connected to God who bestowed the spirit on all men. It is He who breathes the breath of life (*nishmath-ruach* [נִשְׁמַת-רוּחַ]) into man.

D) The Spirit Seeks God
This leads to the fourth, more controversial, fact regarding man's spirit. Not only did the spirit of man come from God, but *it* seeks God. Note that I said, "it seeks God," not "we" seek God. *Every* man seeks something beyond himself. *No* man's soul (as discussed above) is self-sufficient, but the soul can do nothing of itself. The spirit is that which seeks the God who gave us life. The soul, being proud, may reject the spirit's quest, and try to fill it with false gods or gold or some other substitute, or he may accept Christ, thereby filling the spirit of man with the Spirit of God to whom it is connected.

Consider Isaiah 26:9 wherein Isaiah says, "my spirit within me seeks You diligently." While it is true that Isaiah was a believer, it is significant that he speaks of *his* spirit seeking God. Paul also speaks of *his* own spirit praying to God (1 Corinthians 14:14). Origen made careful note that "he did not say, 'I pray with the soul,' but with the spirit.'"[1106] Once again, some will debate whether this can be used to distinguish between the spirit and soul, as well as whether or not Paul could be referring to the Holy Spirit, but by saying "my spirit" in a passage critical of those who believe praying in tongues makes them spiritually superior to others, it seems that Paul is not speaking of the Holy Spirit, for He could not make such an error as the Corinthians were making.

There is another reason to believe that the spirit God bestowed upon all men, believers and unbelievers alike, seeks God. The fact that it is the spirit from which our conscience arises. It is the spirit which convicts us of our sins. Whether we listen to our conscience or not does not deter from the fact that it exist within us all. This leads to the fifth vital point.

E) The Spirit Convicts Us
Where is the seat of the conscience? Do all men have a conscience? Romans 2:15 makes it clear that even the pagan has a conscience which condemns his sins. 1 Timothy 4:2 also affirms this by saying that the wicked man has seared his conscience. How can we sear what we do not have? Thus all men have a conscience which bears witness to their own sins.

Consider Proverbs 20:27. Solomon says, "the spirit of man is the lamp of the Lord, searching all the innermost parts of his being." It is the spirit which is therefore the seat of conscience, and thereby that which convicts us of sin when we listen to it.

F) Our Spirits are Under Our Control
A curious fact about the spirit is that the spirit is said to be under our control. This fact alone proves that the spirit and soul cannot be the same. It is the proud soul which controls the spirit within us. According to 1 Corinthians 14:32 even

"the spirits of prophets are subject to the prophets." Consider also Proverbs 16:32 which praises "he who rules his spirit." However, Proverbs appears to be using the term "spirit" in another sense, for Proverbs 25:28 compares a man who does not control his spirit to broken city wall. It speaks about "restraining" the spirit, which is a negative connotation. In this context, "spirit" appears to refer not to the spiritual part of man, but to the idiomatic use of a temperment or emotion. This use is common in the Old Testament. Examples include the "spirit of jealousy" (Num 5:14, 30), the "spirit of harlotry" (Hosea 5:4), "spirit of slavery" (Romans 8:15), and a "spirit of distortion" (Isaiah 19:14). Positive uses of this idiom include a "spirit of justice" (Isaiah 28:6) and a "spirit of gentleness" (Galatians 6:1). These are but a few examples (cf. Ephesians 1:17, 1 Timothy 5:21, 2 Timothy 1:7, Hebrews 12:23, 1 John 4:6).

Now if we ignore these idiomatic uses we are still left with the passage in 1 Corinthians which can in no way be idiomatic, for Paul is here stating a fact. He says "the spirits of prophets are subject to the prophets." Note that the word here is in the plural, "spirits." This cannot be the Holy Spirit, which is one, but the spirits of men who are prophets. The implication is that the soul is capable of ruling the spirit of man.

G) The Spirit has Emotions
Like the soul, the spirit is equated with many emotions. However, there is something unique about the descriptions of the spirit in this context. Joshua 5:1 and 1 Kings 10:5 both described fear as the *absence* of the spirit. This infers that the spirit is the source of spiritual strength, without which we fall prey to emotions like anguish (Job 7:11, 17:1; Psalm 34:18, 51:17; Proverbs 15:13, 17:22, 18:14; Isaiah 65:14), being troubled (Genesis 41:8; Lamentations 1:20, 2:11; Daniel 2:1, 7:15; John 13:21) and sorrow (1 Kings 21:5). It is even described as being faint (Psalm 77:3; Cf. Psalm 142:3). On the other hand, when the spirit is strong it is described as sober (1 Peter 4:7, 5:8), and/or gentle (Philippians 4:5; 1 Peter 3:4).

So while the spirit is occasionally described in terms of emotions, it may be that the emotions of the soul take root over the spirit when the spirit is weak. Since the soul controls the spirit, a weak spirit is succeptible and "stagnant" in faith (cf. Zephaniah 1:12). This is why the spirit can be either patient (Ecclesiastes 7:8) or anxious (Daniel 2:3). One might consider this a kind of war between the soul (self) and the spirit which is constantly being waged. The temptations of the flesh then contribute to the soul against the spirit.

H) The Spirit is Poluted by Sin
As we discovered earlier, the soul is connected to the self without God. It is inherently selfish, and therefore sinful. The spirit comes from God but has been cut off from its creator by sin. The spirit is therefore defiled by sin (cf. 2 Corinthians 7:1). It is occasionally associated with the sin of pride (Proverbs

16:18; Ecclesiastes 7:8; Daniel 5:20), but also with humility (Proverbs 16:19, 29:23; Isaiah 57:15, 66:2; Matthew 5:3; 1 Peter 3:8).

Because of the sin in the Garden of Eden spiritual death came to man. Our spirit died in its connection to God, but the spirit can be made alive again through Christ. Romans 8:10 says, "though the body is dead because of sin, yet the spirit is alive because of righteousness." This is not the Holy Spirit to which Paul refers, although the Holy Spirit is the primary agent in reviving the spirit of man to its state with God. Hence, the spirit of man has been poluted by sin and needs to be purified by the Lord Himself.

1) The Spirit has Has Wisdom and Understanding
Wisdom and understanding are never connected with the word "soul"; only the spirit (Exodus 28:3; Deuteronomy 34:9; Job 20:3; Isaiah 11:2). It alone is capable of searching out (Psalm 77:6) and reflecting upon the soul (Proverbs 20:27). This is why many consider the spirit, and not the soul, as the seat of intellect. John Walvoord believes that the spirit is the source of "our spiritual or intellectual life."[1107] Matthew Poole said, "by *spirit* we mean his superior faculties, as the mind, conscience, rational will."[1108] Another believes that "the spirit is the part of man that *knows.*"[1109]

3. The Distinction Between the Spirit and Soul
Having examined all the relevant passages regarding the spirit and soul, we should now look at the fundamental similarities and differences found therein. According to our study we can make the following conclusions.

ψυχη (Soul)	πνευμα (Spirit)
Immortal	Immortal
The Seat of Emotions	Gives Life
Selfish but not Self-sufficient	Connects us to Life Beyond Ourselves
Sinful and in Need of Atonement	The Seat of Conscience
Capable of Love and Obedience	Under Control of the Soul
	Poluted by Sin
	The Seat of Wisdom and Intelligence

So based on the uses of spirit and soul in the Bible, it appears that the soul is connected to the self. It is the seat of emotions, but those emotions can rule over the spirit when the spirit is weak. By itself the soul is not self-sufficient, and it is the spirit which convicts the soul of its sins. The spirit searches our heart and longs for God who made it. However, our spirit is hollow without the Holy Spirit to fill it, for in the Garden of Eden, spiritual death (as well as physical death which follows) came to man. The two are connected. Without the spirit the body dies. As our spirit dies, so also does our body. Because the soul is sinful and the soul has control over the spirit, the spirit is poluted by sin. Only through Jesus can our spirit be restored to the state in which it was made to be born. The spirit becomes born anew and our soul can finally grasp beyond the mere flesh to which it is bound in this life.

Conclusion

From the evidence we can conclude the following. First and foremost, the soul is connected to the self. The soul is what makes us who we are, as distinct from others. It is what makes us unique and different from others. The spirit, however, is connected to God. Even unbelievers have a spirit which is why they have an empty spot in their hearts. Without the spirit fulfilling its purpose, it is like a hollow shell and leaves the soul to its own devices. This leads to the second point.

The soul is not self-sufficient. Left to itself the soul is selfish. It knows nothing beyond itself. It cannot connect to anything outside of our physical bodies, which is why it is inherently selfish. As such, it is the spirit that provides our conscience and helps the soul to see beyond itself. The spirit is that part of us that allows the soul to see beyond the flesh and bones in which it is currently imprisoned. As one author stated that the "πνευμα [or spirit is] the higher of the two united immaterial parts ... ψυχη [or soul is] the sphere of the will and affections, and the centre of the personality."[1110] As Thomas Constable said, "the *spirit* is the highest and most unique part of man that enables him to commincate with God. The *soul* is the part of man that makes him conscious of himself; it is the seat of personality."[1111] The spirit thus allows the soul to communicate with God.

Origen, the church father, argued that 1 Corinthians 14:1-19 proves that it is the spirit, and not the soul, which communicates with God. "He did not say, 'I pray with the soul,' but with the spirit.'"[1112] Mal Couch also argued that it is not just God but others with which the spirit communicates. he said, "it is with the spirit that we communicate with each other ... (1 Cor. 2:11a) ... then, after Christ redeems us, it appears that the Spirit of God communicates with the child of God through His spirit."[1113] So also Oliver Greene believed that "through that spirit we can communicate with God when we believe His Word ... Job 32:8, Prov. 20:27, and Ps. 18:28."[1114]

Note that the spirit only only communicates with God when we allow it. "'Spirit' seems to be an esential element of man by nature, and not merely of man regenerate" (cf. 1 Corinthians 2:11).[1115] It cries out for the God for whom it is was made, but it exist in all men. It is not the soul which differentiates man from animal, but the spirit. Contrary to what some believe, animals are referred to as having souls in the Bible, but they are never mentioned in connection with the spirit. The spirit elevates us above beasts, so when man rejects his spirit and its desire for God, it is little wonder that man behaves like a beast.

So it appears that the soul oscillates between the body and the spirit. The soul is connected to the self. The spirit is connected to God. Even those who reject the Lord have a spirit, but it lies largely domant; seekings its connection to God and creating that vacant empty heart which every unbeliever has. Robert Thomas believed that "the spirit (*pneuma*) is the part that enables man to perceive the divine"[1116] and "the soul (*psyche*) is the sphere of man's will and emotions."[1117]

In summary, the body and the soul are separate. The soul is intimately connected to the individual, to the self. It is the spirit that connects us to those outside of ourselves, especially God. The spirit gives life to the body and soul, joining them together. The spirit also allows the soul to see beyond itself, and cries out for the God who gave this spirit. However, this spirit cannot be confused with the Holy Spirit, for all men have a spirit, and yet their spirit is incomplete with the Holy Spirit. As Oliver Greene once said, "when God created man, He said, 'Let us make man in our own image' ... God is a Trinity."[1118] So man, in the image of God, is a trichotomy; body, spirit, and soul.

The Authorship of 2 Thessalonians

Robert Thomas declared that "the external evidence for the Pauline authoriship of 2 Thessalonians is stronger than the 1 Thessalonians"[1119] which is doubted by no serious scholar. In fact, the first to question 2 Thessalonians was J.E.C. Schmidy in 1801 on the grounds of "contradictions" in eschatology.[1120] As aforementioned, this is based solely upon a rejection of the teaching of rapture and the belief in the inspiration of the Scriptures. The critic will never accept Biblical teaching on the Second Coming, and therefore attempts to claim that Biblical eschatology is a mixture of different opinions and changing theologies over time. He has no material evidence to support this. 2 Thessalonians is quoted by the three most ancient extra-Biblical authors, Polycarp (John's disciple), Ignatius (another of John's disciples), and the author of the *Didache*.[1121] All of these were within one generation of the apostles.

Has the Day of the Lord Come?
2 Thessalonians 2:1-2

> "[Do] not be quickly shaken from your composure or be disturbed either by a spirit or a message or a letter as if from us, to the effect that the day of the Lord has come."

One of the primary purposes for 2 Thessalonians was to correct some misconceptions the Thessalonians had regarding 1 Thessalonians and the Day of the Lord. He begins by saying that this letter is "with regard to the coming of our Lord Jesus Christ and our gathering together to Him" (1 Thessalonains 2:1). Note that there are two issues here. "The coming of our Lord Jesus Christ *and* our gathering together to Him." The gathering is separate from the coming. The gathering is the rapture. The coming is the Second Coming. In addition to this, a third issue is discussed: the Day of the Lord. Paul explicitly declares that the Thessalonians should "not be quickly shaken from your composure or be disturbed either by a spirit or a message or a letter as if from us, to the effect that the day of the Lord has come" (2:2). This epistle, therefore, sought to correct the heretical notion that the Day of the Lord had already passed.

Not only did some Thessalonians misinterpret Paul's previous epistle, but some were putting words in Paul's mouth and/or pretending to speak for him. Paul repudiates any and all who make such claims, telling the Thessalonians to reject any teaching "either by a spirit or a message or a letter as if from us" (2:2) which contradicts what he is writing to them now. Ironically, some liberal critics continue to maintain these very same teachings, claiming that Paul was now changing his theology to accomodate his false expectations!

2 Thessalonians 2 is best taken verse by verse because there is so much debate over practically every single verse within it! Here in verse two Paul is merely stating his premise that the Day of the Lord has *not* come. Not surpisingly, even the interpretation of this passage has been the subject of great contention. There are two particular areas in which this is the case. The first is the very meaning of what Paul means when he says "has come." Some translations read "at hand," which in turn is interpreted by some to mean that Paul rejected the doctrine of imminency. This doctrine, imminency, is then the second great debate, for many believe that Paul's statement only proves that rapture cannot happen *after* the Day of the Lord has begun, and that day *cannot* take place until the apostasy and anti-Christ are revealed! So it is argued that the Thessalonians thought they had missed the rapture!

"At Hand" or "Has Come"

The heresy which Paul was attempting to refute was the idea "that the day of the Lord has come" (2:2). However, the original King James, Webster, Geneva, ASV, and Douay-Rheims translations all say "at hand." The RV and Darby read "now present," while the other translations, including the New King James all read "has come." Although "at hand" does not necessarily change the meaning of the passage, it is more easily read to mean either that Paul is contradicting Jesus who used those very words, or that the Day of the Lord could not happen during their lifetimes, thereby negating the teaching of imminency. Consequently, before even beginning to debate imminency we must first determine the correct translation and meaning of ενεστηκεν (enesteken).

Now ενεστηκεν (enesteken) is the "perfect active indicative" of ενιστημι (enisthmi).[1122] In the future middle tense ενιστημι (enisthmi) means to "come upon," "impend," or be "close at hand."[1123] However, in the present is means "is present."[1124] But here we have the perfect active indicative case. According to one Greek textbook the "perfect" tense means "a present state resulting from a past action."[1125] Another text goes in further saying "contextually the perfect may refer to something past (Matt.19:8), present (Matth. 27:43), possibly future (Matt. 20:23; John 5:24; Jas. 5:2-3), omnitemporal (Rom. 7:2), or timeless (John 3:18)."[1126] Thus context is the key. Something which is impending in the perfect tense can be said to "have come." This is a definition listed by Greek dictionaries and lexicons.[1127] Therefore, we must examine the context to get the answer.

It has been pointed out that "at hand" cannot be the proper translation since Paul says elsewhere the day is "at hand" (Philippians 4:5; Romans 13:12).[1128] It is also the premise of Jesus's Olivet Discourse, warning believers to be on watch. How then can the liberal believer "hold [that] the doctrine that the Day of the Lord is at hand be treated by the apostles as an error?"[1129] Contrary to what critics claim 2 Thessalonians was written within a year of the first epistle. Paul is not contradicting himself, nor calling himself a heretic. Consequently, "the rendering 'at hand' cannot here be the correct translation."[1130]

That this would be a contradiction of the teachings of both Jesus and the apostles is admitted by John Calvin who says this "may seem ... at variance with many passages of scripture" but he gets around the problem by quoting the day is as a thousand years passage in Peter's epistle.[1131] Nevertheless, while Peter was talking about the expectations of many believers, there is a much more simple answer; it should be translated as "has come." Paul is not saying that these things will not happen but that they have not yet happened! Contextually, Paul is arguing against a past fulfillment, not against a future fulfillment; whether near or far. Yet this is the irony of the liberal critics. They claim that prophecy was fulfilled in 70 A.D. with the destruction of Jerusalem,[1132] but then argue that ενεστηκεν (enesteken) should be translated as "at any moment"[1133] in order to denounce the doctrine of imminency![1134] So in one breath they claim that Paul is denouncing imminency and supporting a "past" fulfillment (since they believe 2 Thessalonians was written after the destruction of Jerusalem), despite the fact that Paul is obviously deriding those who believed that the Day of the Lord had already begun.

If this seems confusing, it is because the critic does not understand, nor try to understand, prophecy. After all, the "rationalist" doesn't believe in prophecy. That is why they postdate the epistle to a time *after* the alleged fulfillment! They make Paul out to be prophesying about the past. In fact, the best translation is "has come." Even the New King James reads "had come." Contextually, the passage makes no sense any other way.

Finally, it should be pointed out that the word ενιστημι (enisthmi) is a compound word from εν (en) meaning "in or with" and ιστημι (histemi) meaning "to stand." So the most literal translation would be "standing it."[1135] Are we currently "standing in" or living in the Day of the Lord? Has the Day of the Lord already begun? This is what the Thessalonians believed, and this is

234

what Paul wanted to refute, not the doctrine of imminency. In fact, some believe that imminency is what Paul was teaching, but if so, what does it mean?

Day of the Lord or Rapture?

How could they have "missed" the Day of the Lord? This is the fundamental question to understanding Paul's epistle. The Thessalonians were clearly "shaken" and "disturbed" (2:2) by the notion that the Day of the Lord had already come, but how could they have believed that at all? Several theories have been raised to explain such a seemingly bizarre belief.

The most common argument is that the Thessalonians believed they were in the Tribulation.[1136] H.A. Ironside is among the supporters of this view, saying that they thought they were "entering the great tribulation era."[1137] Contextually this seems the most logical view, for Paul explained that this would not take place until after the apostasy and the revelation of the anti-Christ, but there is an intriguing minority opinion which should not be neglected.

Some believe that the Thessolonians were "disturbed" because they had been told that rapture had already occurred and they were left behind.[1138] This is also the line of reasoning used by partial rapturists like Joseph Seiss.[1139] Gordon Fee argues that these are all part of "the realm of speculation."[1140] What is not speculation is that all the ancients saw the Tribulation as future, not past. The *Sherpherd of Hermas*[1141] and works of Hippolytus are among the early church writings to maintain that the Day of the Lord was still to come.[1142] Charles Ryrie is correct to say that "it was the judgments at the beginning of that Day about which [the Thessalonians] were not clear."[1143]

John Walvoord said that "in order to understand the nature of the error Paul is correcting, it is necessary to define what is meany by the 'day of the Lord.'"[1144] To this end Paul states unequivacably that two things must occur before the Day of the Lord. These are the apostasy and the revelation of the anti-Christ.[1145] What then is the connection of the rapture to the Day of the Lord? Posttribulationists F.F. Bruce argues that "our gathering" cannot refer to a pretribulational rapture because, "it is difficult to suppose that the 'day of the Lord' in this section (v. 2) belongs to a different time from that in view in 1 Thess. 4:13-18 as is held by the Darbyite school of dispensationalism."[1146] However, this is misleading. Most agree, whether pretribulational or not, that rapture precedes the Day of the Lord. Therefore, it is not fair to say that there cannot be a short interim between the rapture and the Day of the Lord. After all, there is a gap of at least two thousand years between the first and second coming of Christ!

Ultimately, the argument for rapture is tied to the question of when the Day of the Lord begins, for rapture will occur before that. It seems best to assume that the Thessalonians believed that they were already in the Tribulation and feared that they would have to endure the wrath of God. However, to better answer this we must look at the apostasy and the revelation of the anti-Christ which all agree must precede the Day of the Lord.

Conclusion

The Thessalonians were being taught that the Day of the Lord had already begun. Misquoting from Paul's first epistle, many were claiming to speak for Paul himself. Various cult leaders and others purported to have spoken with Paul and perhaps even produced some false epistle to support this. Here Paul unquivacably rejects these teachers, as well as the modern critic who claims that Paul was "changing" his eschatology.[1147] Instead Paul makes perfectly clear that the Day of the Lord "will not come unless the apostasy comes first, and the man of lawlessness is revealed, the son of destruction" (2:3). We must then understand these two things before we can understand the Day of the Lord and any possible connection to the rapture which precedes it.

What is the Apostasy?
2 Thessalonians 2:3

"Let no one in any way deceive you, for *it will not come* unless the apostasy comes first."

What is the apostasy? The Greek word αποστασια (*apostasia*) literally means "rebellion,"[1148] but contextually it can refer to either a spiritual rebellion or a physical rebellion. It can be translated either as "falling away" (KJV, Webster, RV, ASV), "rebellion" (NIV, NLT, RSV, NRSV, ESV), "departing" (Tyndale, Cramner, Beza, Geneva), or "revolt" (Douay-Rheims). All are viable translations, but each can infer something different. Is it a spiritual rebellion? If so "falling away" may be a better translation. Is it "an agressive and positive revolt" as Charles Ryrie maintains?[1149] If so "revolt" may be the best translation.

The dominant view is that apostasy refers to spiritual defection. Apostasy is often used in modern vocabulary to refer to heretics who deviate from the Biblical faith, but the reader may be surprised to hear that this was not always the dominant view. In fact, the early church dominantly believed that "apostasy" was a title for none other than the anti-Christ himself. They saw it as a title; "the Rebel."[1150] Altogether there are four main views upon the apostasy. Each has merits, and each has weaknesses. Each should, therefore, be examined individually.

Four Theories

There are four dominant views throughout history regarding the apostasy. The most popular today is that of a spiritual defection or falling away from the faith. The second is an ancient view which saw this rebellion as a material rebellion against God; as war. More specifically, as the last war; the Tribulation. The most ancient view, however, appears to be the teaching that the apostasy is a title for the anti-Christ equating to "the Rebel." Lastly, there is the belief that the apostasy actually refers to the rapture itself. It is not a falling away from the faith but a "departure" from this world. *None* of these views should be dismissed summarily as the insecure will do. *All* deserve fair attention.

A Falling Away from the Faith

The most common belief is that there is a "spiritual defection"[1151] in the Last Days. The "falling away" is thus religious.[1152] Men like John Wesley believed that it was a falling away "from the pure faith of the gospel."[1153] It is also supported by such prominent dispensationalists as Charles Ryrie[1154] and Lewis Sperry Chafer.[1155]

This interpretation of the apostasy fits with passages like 2 Timothy 4:3-4 where Paul prophesies that "the time will come when they will not endure sound doctrine; but *wanting* to have their ears tickled, they will accumulate for themselves teachers in accordance to their own desires, and will turn away their ears from the truth and will turn aside to myths." Certainly religious apostasy is prophesied by Jesus, warning that "even the elect" would be deceived "if possible" (Matthew 24:11, 24; Mark 13:22). In fact, false prophets are mentioned just before the "Abomination of Desolation" in Matthew 24:11-15. It is also a major theme of both Peter and Paul (2 Peter 3:3; 2 Timothy 4:3-4). However, in Peter he is actually referring to a rejection of the belief in the Second Coming of Christ. It is not clear that he referring to Christians who have fallen away from the faith, or just mocking unbelievers. So also in 2 Timothy Paul speaks of much more than heresy. He says, "realize this, that in the last days difficult times will come. For men will be lovers of self, lovers of money, boastful, arrogant, revilers, disobedient to parents, ungrateful, unholy, unloving, irreconcilable, malicious gossips, without self-control, brutal, haters of good, treacherous, reckless, conceited, lovers of pleasure rather than lovers of God, holding to a form of godliness, although they have denied its power" (3:1-5). This certainly fits with the theme of a spiritual rebellion, but it not clear that this is necessarily the sign of which Paul was speaking, for elsewhere it is clear that there have always been false teachers and heretics (cf. Matthew 7:15; 1 John 4:1).

One problem which has been suggested with the theory is its seeming paradox. Does Paul expect that the church will apostasize? If not the church then "does he expect it of unbelievers?"[1156] The view generally refers to professing believers but not necessarily true believers, and yet since when have nominal believers ever truly been faithful to Christ? The Inquisition was run by false Christians, so we must assume that if this view is true it is speaking of a deception that will even lead believers astray (cf. Matthew 24:24; Mark 13:22). However, it is debateable whether or not a true believer can ever really apostatize. Consequently, the view is not without problems.

237

Spiritual rebellion is certain to happen in Last Days, but this does not necessitate that it is the sign to which Paul was referring. The idea of spiritual rebellion is a popular one, and a strong one, but it would be negligent to accept the view without first examining other possibilities.

War

If spiritual rebellion is on one end of the spectrum, then a real material war would be on the other end. Some describe the apostasy as "world-wide rebellion against God,"[1157] but not just a spiritual rebellion, but an active war. To this end some have believed that it refers to the Tribulation itself. The persecution of believers is certainly an act of rebellion against God, and one that has continued to take place throughout history.

Erasmus believed that the apostasy encompassed both spiritual and political rebellion against God. He said, "the Lord is not about to arrive unless a defection had preceded."[1158] So political, as well as spiritual, revolt against God is held to be a part of the apostasy. Indeed, the description given by the apostles of Last Days fits this prescription very well, but there are problems with this view.

Jesus said that there would be "wars and rumors of wars, but see that you are not frightened, for *those things* must take place, but *that* is not yet the end" (Matthew 24:6; Mark 13:7). How then can a war be a sign of the end? It is true that Jesus said these things would take place before the end, so in that context Paul's statement is somewhat parallel, but 2 Thessalonians seems to be talking about something specific. Not a war, but "the apostasy." The mere fact that preterist and others have tried to identify this war with something in the past, like the Jewish revolt of the first century, is further evidence that Paul was warning the Thessalonians *against* being "disturbed" by the claims.

A Title for the Anti-Christ

One of the earliest attested views is that the apostasy is a personal title for the anti-Christ. This was the position of Justin Martyr,[1159] Tertullian[1160] Chrysostom and even Augustine.[1161] Apostasy then becomes synonymous with "the Rebel."[1162] The argument is that an appositive use of the word αποστασια (*apostasia*), meaning that it is a description or adjective of the "man of sin" found in the same verse.[1163] While tempting, this view is the weakest for two reasons.

First, grammatically it is flawed. Apostasy cannot be viewed as modifying the "man of sin." Grammatically the Greek does not allow this. "Comes" modifies "apostasy" while "revealed" modifies "man of sin." Moreover, the και (*kai*), meaning "and," is a clear conjuction for two separate things. "Clearly [apostasy] is *not a person*."[1164]

Second, "'the falling away' is not the result of the appearance of the Man of Sin, but the *antecedent*."[1165] In other words, the apostasy either precedes the revelation of the "man of sin" or "the coming of the αποστασια and the revealing of the man of lawlessness are coincident."[1166] They are not, however, the same thing. Consequently, this view, popular as it may have been in the early church, is the weakest view.

Rapture
One of the lesser known views is also one of the most intriguing. While some summarily dismiss it, such dismissive attitudes reflect an insecurity. All views deserve a fair examination. None of the views are perfect, and neither are any of them feeble. This last view holds that the "apostasy" should be properly translated as "Departure" and refers to a physical departure from the earth; the rapture.

The first question which comes to mind when examining this verse is whether or not "it will not come" refers to the Day of the Lord or "our gathering together to Him." Contextually it appears to refer to the Day of the Lord, but Paul does not actually mention the "gathering together to Him" after verse one at all, unless it is synonymous with the Second Coming in verse eight. If so, why distinguish between the two at all? If not, then where does Paul speak of the "gathering"? If the Day of the Lord does not begin until after the revelation of the anti-Christ, and the rapture precedes the Day of the Lord, as most believe (including pretribulational, midtribulational, "pre-wrath," and even some posttribulational theologians), then might "apostasy" refer to the "gathering"? Four evidences are given to support this view.

1. Translation
As aforementioned, αποστασια (*apostasia*) has a relatively wide range of possible translations depending on the context. Advocates of this position note that most old English translations before the King James rendered the word as "departing." This includes the Tyndale in 1526, Coverdale in 1535, Cramner in 1539, Breeches in 1576, Beza in 1583, and the Geneva Bible of 1608. Additionally, Wycliffe's 1384 reads "dissencioun" which comes from the Latin word "discessio" meaning "departure."[1167]

If then "departure" is the correct translation, the question must be asked, "departure from what?" Departure is consistent with a departure from the faith, but it could also be consistent with a departure from the earth. According to H. Wayne House, *apostasia* (αποστασια) and its cognates are found 220 times in the Greek *Septuagint*.[1168] Sixty-six times it carries the meaning of physical departure and fifty-three times it carries the meaning of spiritual departure or a "falling away" from the faith.[1169] Additionally, John Sweigart has shown that the sister verb αφιστημι (*aphistemi*) usually refers to a physical departure,[1170] but this is only of limited use since the word here is *apostasia* (αποστασια), not αφιστημι (*aphistemi*).

So it would appear that αποστασια (*apostasia*) could refer to "the Departure" or "the rapture." However, it is fair to point out that there are other words for departure which would probably be used before αποστασια (*apostasia*). Even John Sweigart, who supports this view, list the meaning of αποστασια (*apostasia*) throughout Greek history. Accordingly, "revolt" or "rebellion" seems to have been the primary use in Classical Greek.[1171] Although it had come to take on a broader meaing by the time of the New Testament's *koine* Greek, the etymology of the word leaves us to wonder if Paul would not have chosen a more clear word to refer to rapture if this is the case. Nonetheless, "departure" is a viable translation which could be read either as "departure from the faith" or a "departure from the earth." If the latter, then this brings us to the question of "the gathering."

2. The Gathering
This discussion began with the statement, "with regard to the coming of our Lord Jesus Christ and our gathering together to Him." Note that the "coming of our Lord Jesus Christ" and "our gathering together to Him" are distinguished. As mentioned earlier scholars throughout the centuries have admitted that there is a techincal difference in the rapture and the Second Coming even if they do not distinguish between them in time. However, the Second Coming is not mentioned until verse eight, while the "gathering" does not *appear* to be mentioned at all. Logically, why would Paul distinguish between the Second Coming and the gathering in verse one and then fail to mention the gathering later? One possible answer is that the departure *is* the gathering.

While this may seem speculative it is arguably the strongest evidence in favor of the rapture. There is no doubt that Paul distinguishes between the rapture and Second Coming. No honest theologian, regardless of his position on the timing of the rapture, should deny this. If the gathering is syonymous with the Second Coming in verse eight, then why not in verse one? It is possible that the Thessalonians had already been taught about the αποστασια (*apostasia*) and needed no explanation of it. This may be why Paul asked, "Do you not remember that while I was still with you, I was telling you these things?" (2 Thessalonians 2:5). This is apparent since Paul nowhere expounds upon the αποστασια (*apostasia*) as he does the "man of sin."

The argument from the "gathering" is one that cannot be proven one way or another. Nevertheless, it is strong circumstantial evidence for the rapture. Surely if Paul is discussing the "gathering" with the Thessalonians then the gathering must be mentioned at some point in the epistle. If the αποστασια (*apostasia*) is not the gathering, then what is?

3. The Restrainer
Because I discuss the theories of the "restrainer" in verses six and seven below, I will not debate it here, but it is necessary to know that some have drawn a connection between the restrainer and either the church or the Holy Spirit which acts through the church. If, it is argued, the church has already been raptured then the "restrainer" would be gone. This fits the subject of verses six and seven

(see notes below), and could be further evidence that the rapture occurs in verse three shortly before the revelation of the anti-Christ.

4. The Definite Article

One final argument is in the use of the definite article. It has been argued that the definite article is used to make αποστασια (*apostasia*) a noun.[1172] Indeed, αποστασια (*apostasia*) is in the nominative Greek case, and therefore a noun. A similar argument is made among advocates of the "anti-Christ" title theory. In fact, the argument holds fairly well with most of the theories, since the "apostasy" is obviously used as a title for something with which the Thessalonians were already familiar. By itself this proves nothing, but as further circumstantial evidence it does bolster the case for rapture a little more.

Conclusion

The first and fourth theories are the best. The second is the weakest. Paul and Jesus both warned people not to be disheartened or disturbed by wars and rumors of wars, for these things must happen (cf. Matthew 24:6; Mark 13:7). The third theory, being that it is a title for the anti-Christ, has a strong tradition but Paul is distinguishing between the apostasy and the revelation of the anti-Christ so that they cannot be the same thing.

We must then choose between a departure from the faith or a departure from the earth. The truth is that we cannot infer one over the other based solely on vocabulary. "Falling away" and "departure" are both viable translations. The idea of a spacial departure cannot be rejected in light of Paul's allusion to the "gathering" which does not appear to be mentioned elsewhere in Thessalonians. Add to this the fact that almost all agree, regardless of whether they are pretribulational or posttribulational or other, that the rapture precedes the Day of the Lord. The question is then "when does the Day of the Lord begin." This passage seems to indicate that it begins after the revelation of the anti-Christ and the Abomination of Desolation (v. 4. cf. Matthew 24:15; Marl 13:14). As Donald Barnhouse said, "the anti-Christ will not be revealed until *after* the church will have been raptured."[1173] If so this fits either pretribulational or midtribulational rapture, and would fit with the apostasy being equal to the gathering. Nonetheless, this cannot be proven. Jesus predicted that deception and heresy would be so great in the Last Days that "if possible, even the elect" would be misled (Matthew 24:24; Mark 13:22). Moreover, the root word here is the same as that in 1 Timothy 4:1 "some will fall away from the faith." This would obviously fit the apostasy as a "falling away" from the faith.

I will leave to the reader to make his own decision. Traditionally I have favored the first view, but in recent years I have come to be attracted to the latter. Still I cannot come to fully embrace it only because the evidence is largely circumstantial, and 1 Timothy 4:1 appears to be speaking of the same thing. What is certain is that Paul nowhere explains what the apostasy means. It is evident that he had already taught the Thessalonians about the apostasy, but they were confused as to its timing and relationship to the Day of the Lord. They feared that the Day of the Lord may have already begun, so Paul reminded them that the Day of the Lord would not come until the apostasy comes *first*. Obviously, whatever the apostasy may be, it had not yet taken place, and that fact should have been obvious to them.

The Man of Lawlessness
2 Thessalonians 2:3-12

> "The man of lawlessness ... who opposes and exalts himself above every so-called god or object of worship, so that he takes his seat in the temple of God, displaying himself as being God."

"The Man of lawlessness" or "Man of Sin," as some translations read, is the title Paul uses for the anti-Christ. In fact, "anti-Christ" is a title which is only used of this man once in the Bible (1 John 2:18; but possibly in 4:3 as well). He is called by many names in the Bible. In addition to "man of sin" and "son of perdition" found here he is called "the lawless one" (2 Thessalonians 2:8), "the little horn" (Daniel 7:8), and "the prince" (Daniel 9:26). Additionally, some also believe that "the beast" (Revelation 11:7), "bloody and deceitful man" (Psalms 5:6), "the wicked one" (Psalms 10:2, 4), "man of the earth" (Psalms 10:8), "the mighty one" (Psalms 52:1), "the enemy" (Psalms 55:3), "the Adversary" (Psa. 74:8-10; Isaiah 59:19; Amos 3:11), "the violent man" (Psalms 140:1, 10-11), "the Assyrian" (Isaiah 10:5, 12), "son of the morning" (Isaiah 14:12), "the nail" (Isaiah 22:25), "the vile person" (Daniel 11:21), and "the wilful king" (Daniel 11:36) also refer to the anti-Christ, although this is debateable.[1174] John Wesley, like many of the early Reformers, believed "in many respects, the pope has an indisputable claim to those titles."[1175] At that time the Reformers tended to view the anti-Christ as a corporate title for the office of the papacy, thus extending over centuries, but it is clear in this passage that the anti-Christ is not an institution but a *man*; a "man of sin." It is also commonly believed that this man will be "a man ... in whom Satan dwells and operates."[1176] This is probably true, although I debate the issue in *Controversies in Revelation*.

By whatever name this man is called, he is central to the Tribulation of End Times, the Abomination of Desolation, and the persecution of the saints in Last Days. It is he who will institute the Mark of the Beast (Revelation 13) and of whom the prophet Daniel spoke. Because I have discussed the anti-Christ extensively in *Controversies in the Prophets*, *Controversies in the Gospels*, and *Controversies in Revelation*, I am hesitant to repeat too much of what I said there. However, I understand how distracting it can be to constantly refer the reader back to another book. Nevertheless, since this will be my biggest book I have decided to omit all but what is directly relevant to this passage. I will again repeat my "primer on End Times" for those unfamilar with the basic vocabulary and time frame. Then I will discuss the Abomination of Desolation as it relates to 2 Thessalonians and the question of the Temple. For all other topics related to the anti-Christ please consult my previous volumes.

A Primer on End Times (Repeated from 1 Thessalonians 5:11)
For the uninitiated, it is pertinent to define some basic terms and concepts before discussing End Times. Paul's audience had already been taught the basic fundamentals of the Olivet Discourse and Old Testament prophecy, so Paul does not define those elements, but assumes his audience is familiar with them, as per his introductory words, "you have no need of anything to be written to you, for you yourselves known full well ..."

According to the Olivet Discourse and the Prophet Daniel there will be a time ruled by the anti-Christ before the (second) coming of the Messiah. He will be the last ruler of a united empire based on the Roman Empire. This time period is called the "Tribulation." Most believe that this is a seven year period whose beginning is marked by a seven year "peace treaty" brokered by the anti-Christ (cf. notes on Daniel 9 in *Controversies in the Prophets*). However, half way into this treaty, the anti-Christ will commit "the abomination of desolation" which will spark a world war and lead the Jewish people to repentance. During this final three and a half years many, if not all, of the plagues described in Revelation will be unleashed upon the earth, and the people of God will be severely persecuted. The "Day of the Lord" is connected in some way to this final three and a half years, sometimes called the "Great Tribulation." Here in 2 Thessalonians 2 Paul describes the Abomination of Desolation in greater detail, which appears to inititate the Day of the Lord, or at least precedes it by a short time.

The Abomination of Desolation
An abomination of desolation is the term used for the desecration of the Holy Temple of Jerusalem. This first took place in 167 B.C., on December 16, when Antiochus Epiphanes erected an old image of Zeus (Jupiter) in the Holy Temple of Jerusalem and slaughtered a pig upon the altar.[1177] That blasphemous act of desecration spurred the great Maccabean revolt that is honored to this day among the Jews at *Hanukkah*. However, Jesus declared that there would be another abomination of desolation in the End Times which he said was the subject of Daniel's prophecy (Matthew 24:15; Mark 13:14; cf. Daniel 9:27). Here Paul refers to this prophesied abomination, stating that "he takes his seat in the temple of God, displaying himself as being God" (v. 4).

Some, called preterist, claim that this prophecy was fulfilled in the first century. These preterist all attempt to connect the prophecies with the fall of Jerusalem and the destruction of the Temple in 70 A.D. but they cannot seem to agree on exactly when this abomination of desolation took place. Caligula attempted to place a statue of himself in the Holy Temple in 40 A.D., but died before the order was carried out.[1178] Consequently, no desolation or desecration took place. This could not have been the prophesied event.

Other preterists have claimed that Nero, in some way not recorded in history, must have committed the abomination of desolation.[1179] In 66 A.D. the corrupt administration of Nero and the governor Florus had abused the citizens of Judea to the extent that rebellion broke out and the Jewish war began. Josephus considered the pillaging and mass slaughter at the Upper Market Place to be the final trigger which sparked the revolt.[1180] However, *wikipedia* eroneously claimed that the temple had been plundered and desecrated, despite the fact that Josephus records no such event![1181] [This is another reason to avoid *wikipedia*.] Moreover, even if such a plunder had taken place, this would not be an abomination of desolation for the temple had been plundered several times in history, from the Assyrians to the Babylonians, and none of those events were considered desolations. Only an act of sacriledge and blasphemy inside the Holy of Holies could be considered an abomination of desolation. No such thing ever took place under Nero, who never even visited the Holy Land!

Lastly, it is claimed by still other preterists that Titus committed the abomination of desolation when the temple was destroyed in 70 A.D.[1182] This too falls flat. First, Titus committed no religious act or desecration in the temple. A Roman standard in the temple could not be considered desecration or the destruction of Solomon's temple by Nebuchadnezzar would certainly have qualified, yet nowhere does Scripture record that event as an abomination of desolation, because no sacrifice nor sacriligious proclamations were made from the Holy of Holies. It was destroyed, not desecrated. The one is physical destruction. The other is religous sacriledge. They are not treated equally in the Bible. Second, the Prophet Daniel makes clear that the abomination of desolation is connected with the halting of sacrifices *in the middle* of the tribulation. Preterists cannot find these last three and a half years. They attempt to date the tribulation to the Jewish Revolt, but then blasphemously attribute the Second Coming prophecy to the coming of Roman armies to destroy Jerusalem![1183] Can any serious student of the Bible read the promises and *hope* of the Second Coming as a prophecy of death, rape, pillaging, and destruction? This view borders on blasphemy and cannot be taken seriously. The "man of sin" is commiting an act of desecration and blasphemy "so that he takes his seat in the temple of God, displaying himself as being God." This is not the destruction of the temple.

Now if the abomination of desolation did not take place in the past, and it is clear that it did not, then it must be future. It takes place by the anti-Christ in End Times in the middle of the Tribulation. However, this brings up the question of how an abomination of desolation can occur in a temple which no longer exist. The question is then whether or not the Holy Temple of Jerusalem will be rebuilt in the Last Days.

The Temple of Jerusalem

How can the Holy Temple be desolated if it does not exist? Paul said that when the anti-Christ come he will "take his seat in the temple of God." What is this temple? Will the Jews rebuilt the Holy Temple? Is it must a symbol for something else? If so, what and how will the anti-Christ desecrate it?

Five theories have developed over the years to explain this alleged problem.[1184] Some hold that the "temple" represents all religious places of worship. Thus he defiles all the religions of the world in some way. A second view holds that this is not *the* temple of God, but a sort of modern day pagan temple built explicitly for the anti-Christ. A variant on this view is that it represents some sort of Christian temple in the future. Yet another view argues that the temple of God must refer to the Church itself. The anti-Christ then desecrates the Church of God and persecutes His people. Finally, as early as the church fathers Irenaeus[1185] and Hippolytus,[1186] it has been believed that Israel would be restored in the Last days and rebuild the Holy Temple in Jerusalem. As usual, I will review each view individually.

View #1 – Representative of All Religious Buildings

One view is an extension of the belief that the anti-Christ will create a one-world religion. They see this "temple" as representative of all religious buildings. In other words, they take this merely as allegory for the fact that the anti-Christ will claim to be the god of all religions. Nevertheless, even if true it does not follow that Paul is using allegory here. Contextually nothing in 2 Thessalonians 2 is symbolic or allegorical language, so why would "taking his seat in the temple" be allegory? So-called "literalists" do not deny that the Bible uses symbolic language, but we do deny that words are arbitrarily used for allegory outside of a specific and clear context. Here there is no indication of an allegorical use. Most importantly, Paul's statement here is parallel to both Jesus and Daniel's prophecy of the abomination of desolation, and therefore should not be understood as allegory, for both Jesus and Daniel understood the abomination of desolation as a real literal event.

View #2 – A "Pagan" Temple

A slightly better view is that this is a literal temple, but not the Temple of Jerusalem. Some argue that the anti-Christ builds his own temple dedicated to himself and a new religion which they believe he will usher in. This is based on a somewhat suspect interpretation of the religion of the anti-Christ, but it is plausible that the anti-Christ will attempt to create his own religion. Building a temple to himself would be the height of arrogance, but it does not match what Jesus said about the abomination of desolation. For one thing, how can the anti-Christ desecrate his own temple? He can only desecrate a true temple "of God." Note that Paul call it just that; a "temple of God," not a temple of Satan or the anti-Christ. More importantly, Jesus warns his followers in *Judea* to flee before the abomination (Mark 13:14; Matthew 24:15-16). Luke makes it perfectly clear that the abomination takes place in Jerusalem. "But when you see Jerusalem surrounded by armies, then recognize that her desolation is near." (Luke 21:20). So the temple, whatever it is, must be located *in* Jerusalem. This does not fit with the idea of a pagan temple build specifically for the worship of the anti-Christ. Since the temple would take years to construct there is no way that Israelis would be ignorant of its intent. War would erupt long before the building would be finished. None of this fits the Biblical description of the peace treaty, the abomination of desolation, or the surrounding tribulation.

View #3 – A "Christian" Temple

A variant of this view, and slightly more popular, is that the temple represents a "Christian building corresponding to the Temple of the Jews."[1187] Based on the same principles and theories as the above, this view changes only that the temple is supposed to be used for "Christian" worship. Nonetheless, this view suffers from the same problems as the previous view. While it could be feasible to argue that this is the Vatican or similar church, the Bible explicitly places the abomination in Judea and specifically Jerusalem. In addition, I have defended the belief that the Vatican (or rather Rome) is destroyed by the anti-Christ in the middle of the tribulation (see *Controversies in Revelation*). While this does follow the abomination of desolation, there is no record in Daniel, Jesus, Paul, or Revelation of the destruction of the temple at this time; only its desecration. This theory too should be rejected.

View #4 – A Symbol of the Church

One of the most popular views, especially among Covenant theologians, is that the temple is merely a symbol for the "whole body of Christians on earth."[1188] They therefore see this as a symbol of the anti-Christ's persecution and contempt of believers. The problems with this, however, are greater than that of the third view. To begin with, if we call something a symbol that each thing within that context must have a specific representation. We cannot merely pick and choose. In this context what would be the meaning of, "takes his seat in the temple of God, displaying himself as being God" (v. 4). Let us substitute "believers" for "temple of God" and see if we can make sense of it : "He will take his seat among believers, displaying himself as being God." What then does that mean? The symbologist must explain the specific meaning before he can make such a claim, but this is the problem with many symbologists. They have a propensity to explain away difficult Bible passages or unpopular theology by claiming they are mere symbols, but when challenged to be specific on the meaning of the symbols they usually fall silent.

Another reason to reject the symbolic application is the fact that the parallel passages strongly suggest a literal temple, and Revelation speaks of the temple residing in the Holy City. If the temple is built in Jerusalem, then it appears to be speaking of a real temple, not the church (Revelation 11:2). So also Jesus's declarations in the Olivet Discourse appear to refer to a real army surrounding Jerusalem before the abomination of desolation (Luke 21:20). This does not support symbolism.

Another problem is the lack of support from the early church. While the church fathers were hardly right all the time, it seems odd that this view would be so neglected among the original followers of the apostles, and their disciples. Only Victorinus appears to see this passage symbolically.[1189] Most church fathers either saw the temple as the one destroyed by Titus or as a rebuilt temple in the future, but they all saw it as a real temple. This leads to the view; one supported from antiquity to the present.

View #5 – A Literal Temple

Irenaeus and Hipplytus were second and third generation disciples of the apostle John. Irenaeus lived a hundred years after the destruction of the temple in 70 A.D. He also believed that prophecy demanded that the one true and literal temple of God must be rebuilt so the anti-Christ can defile it.[1190] Hippolytus, not long after, declared that when the anti-Christ comes he "shall build the city of Jerusalem and restore the sanctuary."[1191] Other church fathers include Ephraem the Syrian and even in the Middle Ages Adso of Montier supported the idea of the Jews rebuilding a literal temple in Jerusalem.[1192] This is also the view of most modern dispensationalists like John Darby, Samuel Kellogg, Nathaniel West, Sir Robert Anderson, Walter Scott, Robert Govett, Joseph Seiss, G. H. Pember, H. A. Ironside, G. H. Lang, Arthur Bloomfield, Charles Ryrie, Henry Morris, Hal Lindsey, Robert Thomas, John Walvoord, and Tim LaHaye.[1193]

The strengths of the argument may be found not only in Thessalonians but also in the parallel passages. I have already concluded that the abomination of desolation cannot have taken place in ancient Rome. In fact, the book of Revelation was written long after the fall of Jerusalem. Consequently, some of the parallel passages were not even written before the temple's destruction. When we compare the parallel passages several facts become apparent.

Parallel Passages

Daniel 9:27	The Olivet Discourse (Matthew 24:15-31) (Mark 13:14-37) (Luke 21:20-28)	2 Thessalonians 2:1-8	Revelation 11:1-2

I discuss these passages in much greater detail in my other volumes, but most evangelicals would agree on the following. First, Daniel places the abomination three and a half years into the Tribulation. Revelation speaks of 42 months, which is also three and a half years. Second, the abomination of desolation spoken of by Jesus is the same as that of Daniel, to whom Jesus refers. That abomination is future. Third, Daniel, Jesus, and Revelation all appear to speak on a real literal temple in Jerusalem. While some may dispute this, the language of Jesus, if not Daniel and Revelation, make it apparent that this is no mere symbol. Consequently, if the temple is real in the parallel passages, then it must be real and literal here in 2 Thessalonians as well.

Throughout these passages Israel and the holy city of Jerusalem are spoken of as being trodden under and defiled by gentile armies. The symbolic use of these terms renders the entire prophesies as little more than vague ambiguous warnings about persecution, but Paul goes out his way to refute the idea that they were living in those times, despite being persecuted. Herein lies the paradox. To interpret all these passages as pure allegory is to argue that they are simply about persecution, but Paul calls it heresy to say that the "Day of the Lord" has already come. If then the "Day of the Lord" refers to a specific and literal time period before the Second Coming, then it follows that the temple and the abomination of desolation are also literal.

It should be noted that skeptics also rejected the belief of men like Joseph Mede who insisted that the Jews of Israel would be revived in the Last Days.[1194] Dispensationalists were repeatedly mocked for centuries until 1948 when Israel defied history and became a nation again; a nation which lays at the heart of the political climate of the world today! Israel was literally restored. So also shall its temple.

Conclusion

Paul had already taught the Thessalonians the basics of End Time eschatology (2:5). Here he is reminding them of the specifics, including the pivotal events of the apostasy and the abomination of desolation. Remember that the context is that the Day of the Lord cannot take place until these things occur first. Since the abomination of desolation requires a rebuilt temple in Jerusalem, the Day of the Lord cannot happen until it is rebuilt. The apostasy, however, may occur at any time before this.

The "man of sin" or "man of lawlessness" is none other than the anti-Christ himself. He is an actual individual of whom the prophets spoke and to whom Jesus alluded. In order to fully understand eschatology (the study of End Times) one must examine all the parallel passages including Revelation. Nonetheless, 2 Thessalonians is one of those pivotal passages which secures the time frame for several events and assures us that the Day of the Lord must follow the abomination of desolation while the apostasy can occur anytime before this. We should, therefore, take heed of Jesus's words so as to not be misled by false prophets or men who set dates for the Second Coming. While the Second Coming follows the battle of Armageddon, the rapture can occur at any time prior to the Day of the Lord.

The Restrainer
2 Thessalonians 2:6-7

"For the mystery of lawlessness is already at work; only he who now restrains *will do so* until he is taken out of the way."

The "man of lawlessness" is the future anti-Christ, but Paul says that "the mystery of lawlessness" is already at work. However, "what restrains him now" is at work to prevent his coming, but "in his time he will be revealed" after the restrainer is removed. So in two verses Paul speaks of "what restrains" and "he who now restrains." The question is, "what or who is this restrainer"? The answer is not so simply. A plethora of views have been presented over the centuries to explain who or what this "restrainer" may be. Many are variants of one another, so I will group those together for convenience sake. I will also present the views not in order of strengths or weaknesses, but progressively from one system of thought to another so that the reader can see how the various streams of thought have developed, and in hopes of leading us to better understanding.

Views # 1 through 3 : Governments of the World

There are three views which in one way or another attribute the retrainer to world governments or laws.[1195] The most popular and ancient of them is the idea that the Roman empire itself was the restrainer.[1196] This ancient theory argues that civil governments, no matter how evil, restrain anarchy and the complete unleashing of evil as would take place in an anarchist state.[1197] Romans 13:1-3 is often used as proof of this argument.[1198] According to these advocates then, this "realm" must then be taken out of the way for the unrestrained evil of the anti-Christ to take place.[1199]

Later variants of this view include the more generic idea that the restrainer simply refers to "gentile domination."[1200] Since Jesus speaks of the "times of the gentiles" (Luke 21:24) coming to a close in End Times, the argument has some appeal, particularly to those who hold that Israel has never relinquished its promises.

One final variants applies the restrainer not to the empires themselves, for they often create as much evil as they restrain, but rather to law in general.[1201] While governments often break their own laws, most laws are good and used to restrain crime and evil.

Now each of these views bear one thing in common. They all hold that governments, or their laws, exist to restrain evil. Certainly even the most corrupt and evil empires had laws to prevent anarchy. Nevertheless, these views cannot hold up against logic and the Bible. Consider the following.

First, anarchy cannot be what the anti-Christ brings for anarchy is the absence of government, and yet the anti-Christ is the head of the government!

He is the last emperor or ruler of the "Revived Roman Empire" as eschatologists have called it.[1202]

Second, it is fair to say that while even corrupt governments prevent anarchy, and thus restrain some evil, it is also fair to point out that the vast majority of evil in human history was committed by "lawful" governments. Whether Hitler's Germany or Stalin's Russia, or even ancient and more modern dictators, the governments of the world have slaughtered infinitely more people than criminals, rioters, and anarchists. Consequently, it does not seem adequate to ascribed the restrainer to the very governments that have practiced so much evil in history.

Finally, the Bible appears to call this "restrainer" a person. In Greek it is but a single word, κατεχων (*katachon*). This is a masculine participle which would normally be translated as a person. Said George Findlay, "it is better to render 'ο κατεχων 'he that restraineth,' rather than 'one that restraineth.'"[1203] However, in the previous voice the neuter form of the word is used, which can sometimes refer to a thing, hence "what restrains." Nevertheless, Thomas Constable believes this is inconsequential because "the neuter is sometimes used of the Holy Spirit (John 14:26; 15:26; 16-13-14)."[1204] If the Holy Spirit is sometimes called a person (masculine) and sometimes spoken of in the neuter, then this should not be a problem since verse seven is explicitly a masculine participle. Moreover, "το κατεχον is not a title *but the description.*"[1205] In other words, a neuter word can be used to describe a masculine person. In fact, one advocate of this position admits that because of "the masculine participle ... the power is regarded as a person,"[1206] but then turns around and says that it is "a reference to the principle of law and government"![1207]

The truth is that whomever the restrainer may be, the restrainer is a "he." The restrainer is a person. As a result, he cannot be a government. The anti-Christ himself will rule over a government, so the removal of a government is most likely not of what Paul speaks. This is especially true of the more popular Roman empire theory, for the Bible makes the anti-Christ out to be the empire's final ruler, not its successor. It is for this reason that it is called the "Revived Roman Empire." Historically, Rome is the only empire which was never defeated, conquered, or dissolved. It was merely divided into all the current nations of Europe, whose token emperors no longer exist ... until the rise of the anti-Christ. Rome, therefore, will not be taken out of the way until Christ crushes it at the Second Coming (Daniel 2:44; 7:27).

Views # 4 and 5 : Emperors and/or Popes

If the restrainer is not a thing, but a person, then it follows it might be the emperors of ancient Rome.[1208] John Wesley said that it is "the potentate who successively has Rome in his power; the emperors."[1209] This view is a logical variant of the Roman empire theory, and is equally as old as the empire theory. In recent years it has been taken up by preterists who attempt to attribute the restrainer to a specific individual. Some, for example, argue that the restrainer was Seneca,[1210] the Roman Senator and aide who ran the country in Nero's name until his forced retirement.

While this view is arguably stronger than its predecessors it is plagued with more problems than its predecessor. The preterists view in particular cannot agree on what individual the prophesy might have referred. This in itself is a strong indication that it has not been fulfilled; as well as the fact that Jesus has not yet returned. Moreover, why would one individual be considered a restrainer of the "mystery of lawlessness"? Especially since most of the emperors practiced lawlessness?

Matthew Poole sees this as the emperors collectively, saying "the idolatries and persecutions of the heathen emperors must be taken out of the way, to make way for those that arise under a Christian, rather antichristian state."[1211] This is better but still doesn't explain the connection to the "mystery of lawlessness." How do lawless emperors restrain the "mystery of lawlessness"?

One final variant of this view is that it is not the emperors but the papacy of which Paul speaks.[1212] This can be looked upon either positively or negatively. Are the popes restraining evil? Perhaps, like the emperors, they are just paving the way for the anti-Christ as many have believed? Neither can sufficiently suit the context. Certainly the popes were not all saints and the Inquisition is hardly well suited to the idea of restraint. Conversely, if a future pope were to be the anti-Christ as some allege then why would the papacy need to be taken away? If speaking of a specific individual then prophesy could suffer the same flaws as listed above. The prophesy would be meaningless; of course one ruler must fall for another to rise! What has this to do with the "mystery of lawlessness"?

These views attempt to improve upon the Roman empire/governments views, but ultimately fails to do so. By looking at the emperors collectively the view essentially becomes a clone of the Roman empire view, bringing nothing new to the table, and no individual ruler can be referenced here since Paul is speaking of a power and mystery beyond human control.

Views # 6 & 7 : Satan or the Anti-Christ

If the restrainer is neither an empire nor an emperor then perhaps the power is on a spiritual plane. After all, how could any earthly institution hold back the unrestrained power of evil? To this end some claim that Satan himself is the restrainer![1213] Thus the removal of the restrainer is the victory of Jesus, but this is not what Paul says. The anti-Christ comes when the restrainer is removed. It can be argued that because Satan knows of his ultimate defeat, he wants to delay that end as long as possible,[1214] but even if this argument is valid the fact remains that, in Charles Ryrie's words, "the restrainer must be more powerful than Satan who empowers the Man of Sin in order to hold back this evil one."[1215] How can Satan restrain himself?

A variant of this view is that the restrainer is the anti-Christ. John Calvin said, "I have no doubt that he refers to Antichrist."[1216] Another Calvinist, Zwingli, even went so far as to translate this passage as "until Antichrist is taken away"![1217] Once again, this makes no sense in context. If we forget that the Greek was "one who restrains" and accept Zwingli's erroneous translation, then it may make some sense, but it completely changes the logic of the passage. Let us look at his translation. "The mystery of lawlessness is already at work; and will be until the anti-Christ is taken out of the way." This translation makes a certain amount of sense isolated from context, but if this is a valid translation then verse six should be translated consistently. It says "you know what restrains him now, so that in his time he will be revealed." Now substitute anti-Christ for "what restrains him." It makes no logical sense. Paul's argument is that the anti-Christ has not yet come. That is the entire context of 2 Thessalonians. Paul is telling them that the anti-Christ will not be revealed until after the apostasy when he stands in the temple and makes himself equal to God. This is the entire gist of the epistle. By changing "restrainer" to Satan or anti-Christ, nevermind that the Greek word *is* "one who restrains," Paul's entire epistle becomes a contradiction. The anti-Christ will not be revealed until after the restrainer is removed. He cannot remove himself!

View # 8 : Angels

As poor as the Satan and anti-Christ views may be, they do have one strength. They acknowledge that only a spirit can restrain evil. No human force or institution can do this. For this reason some believe that the restrainer is an archangel of some kind. Ernest Best argued out that angels are shown binding Satan in the Bible.[1218] Revelation 9:14 depicts angels themselves as being bound, indicating that their actions were restrained until they are to be released. Consequently, it is believed that unrestrained evil is bound by an angel or archangel of God.

This is the first decent view but it has little evidence to prove its voracity over the latter views (see below). Would God assign a single angel to bind Satan's powers? While angels do have the power to bind demons, not even an archangels seems to have the power to bind this kind of evil by himself. It is possible, but there may be better options.

Views # 9 & 10 : God / The Holy Spirit

If an angel is not powerful enough to restrain Satan, then only one person can be. Charles Ryrie said "it is extremely difficult to see how the restrainer can be anyone other than God Himself."[1219] Indeed, only God is omnipotent. If He has the power to give an angel authority to restrain Satan, then He also has the power to restrain Satan Himself, but this does create one insurmountable problem. How can God "be taken out of the way"? He cannot. To that end it has been proposed that it is not God the Father, but God the Holy Spirit to whom the duty has been given.

The idea that the Holy Spirit is the restrainer is one of the most popular today. John Walvoord held to this position as well as a great many other evangelicals.[1220] H.A. Ironside remarked that "it is the Holy Spirit who restrain. This is exactly what we are told."[1221] Nevertheless, it does suffer from the same problem as the God view, albeit to a lesser extent. What does it mean to say that the Holy Spirit is taken out of the way? Critics say that the Holy Spirit can never "be taken out of the way" anymore than God can be taken out of the way.[1222] The response is usually one of two. The first is that the Holy Spirit will Himself remain but "His restraining activity will but cease."[1223] This answer may be sufficient, but one alternative has also been suggested; the church view listed below.

View # 11 : The Church

Now it seems that the Holy Spirit view is the best of those we have seen so far, but some have question *how* the Holy Spirit operates. Donald Barnhouse noted that the Holy Spirit dwells and operates through the church.[1224] The church is seen as a restraining influence upon the world due to the work of the Holy Spirit within and among us.[1225] Certainly this makes a certain amount of logical sense, but begs the question then, what does it mean to say when the church is taken out of the way? The answer is the ever controversial belief in rapture.[1226] To quote Thomas Constable:

> "When the church leaves the earth in the Rapture, the Holy Spirit will be taken out of the way in the sense that His unique lawlessness-restraining ministry through God's people will be removed (cf. Gen. 6:3). The removal of the Restariner at the time of the Rapture must obviously precede the day of the Lord."[1227]

If true then this fits perfectly with Paul's theme. From the beginning Paul has made it clear that the anti-Christ will not be revealed until after the apostasy when the restrainer power of the Holy Spirit has been removed. If the Holy Spirit's restraining work does operate through the church then "the very removal of both the church and the Spirit from the world will release the world to sin as it never has before."[1228] Furthermore, *if* the rapture theory of apostasy is correct, then Paul would be continuing with the exact same line of reasoning.

In many respects this is the best view, but it is not without its difficulties. The primary concern is that while the Holy Spirit operates through the church, His restraining work cannot be exclusively through the church for the gospel (and hence the church) never even reached many corners of the globe until recent times. Neither did the church did not exist before Christ. Even today countries like China persecute the tiny Christian population which gives the church no power to restrain the evil of its government. In short, the removal of the church will probably coincide with the removal of the restraining power of the Holy Spirit, but they are technically different and should not be confused.

Conclusion

What restrains the world from suicide? Who is it that holds back the coming of the anti-Christ? First, it is a person, not a thing. The empires and governments of the world traditionally have only contributed to evil and only restrain anarchy, but the anti-Christ will not be an anarchist. He will be a world leader. Only the Holy Spirit has the power to restrain evil on the earth. "It is plain that both the mystery of iniquity and the restraining agency are at work at the time of the writing of the epistle."[1229] Both have existed throughout history, but when the Holy Spirit ceases to restrain the mystery of iniquity, the anti-Christ will come and all the evil we have seen in history will be nothing by comparison.

Does the Holy Spirit operate through the church? Yes. Is this of what Paul speaks? The view is tempting, but there is not enough evidence to make it convincing over the Holy Spirit view. Technically both believe that the Holy Spirit is the active agency,[1230] and the Church view has the advantage of explaining how the restraining activity of the Holy Spirit could be removed without removing the Holy Spirit itself, and yet if the Holy Spirit's restraining power can be removed without the Spirit itself departing then there is no real need to distinguish, for there will be believers and converts in the tribulation.

There can be no doubt that the removal of the restraining power of the Holy Spirit and the church will coincide, but they are not the same thing. The Holy Spirit has been acting in its restraining power since Adam and Eve and operates in countries where Christianity barely exist. I therefore favor the restraining work of the Holy Spirit as distinct from the church, although the departure of the two will coincide.

<h2 style="text-align:center">A Deluding Spirit
2 Thessalonians 2:11</h2>

> "For this reason God will send upon them a deluding influence so that they will believe what is false."

Like the Restrainer, the deluding spirit is very controversial and hotly debated even among like minded invididuals. Two fundamental questions arise in regard to this issue. The first is the inevitable debate over free will and God's sovereign will. Is God deliberately deceiving people? If so, can God really be good? Why does the Bible say "God cannot lie"? Obviously the Calvinist, Armenians, and others battle over this verse, and I will not settle the ancient debate here, but it is an important issue which must be addressed.

The second issue is the question of the identity of the deluding spirit. Who or what is the deluding spirit? What is his purpose?

Free Will and God's Will

The very nature of this passage brings up heated and emotional debates. It is one I have debated elsewhere and would not repeat here at all save for the fact that it is God who is sending the deluding spirit. How does this fit with the declaration that "God cannot lie" (Titus 1:2)? I will not repeat what I have said concerning Calvinism (see Ephesians 1:1-12), but restrict myself to the issue of the delusion. It is my belief that God's sovereign will requires limited freedom, but that freedom has been restrained for our own good. As seen in the restrainer complete freedom does not make us better but allows sin to reign unbidden. In the End Times that restraint will be removed, and with it God will send a powerful delusion. That delusion, and God's role in that delusion, is the subject of this debate.

First we must define the issue before us. If we stick a gun to someone's head and say "believe me," then they will say "I believe you," but really won't. You cannot make someone believe what they choose not to. In the case of history the same is true. Men have chosen to rebel and reject God, but in their hearts they know the truth (cf. Romans 1:19-27). How then can they reject God? Because they choose to believe a lie in order to sooth their guilty consciences. Here in End Times the anti-Christ is the gun of history. He is the culmination of sin and evil in history. Men have chosen to reject God, but would they follow someone so evil knowing it will lead to their own destruction? No. So let us look at my analogy further.

When we reject God, despite knowing the truth in our hearts, we are commiting slow suicide, but if you hand someone a gun and tell them to shoot themselves most people will not do it. Neither would most people follow the anti-Christ knowing that he will lead the earth to ruin. This is why Donald Barnhouse believed that "'the lie' is another name for the Antichrist."[1231] So the issue is then why God sends a delusion to people to believe the lies of the anti-Christ. What is the purpose, and does that purpose fit with a loving God who never lies?

Matthew Henry said that "in righteousness [God] sometimes withdraws his grace from such sinners as are here mentioned; he gives them over to Satan, or leaves them to be deluded by his instruments."[1232] Matthew Poole declared that "they were first deluded, which was their sin; and God sends them strong delusion, and that is their punishment."[1233] Delusion then begins "at the moment of their rebellion,"[1234] but the delusion is initially one of the rebel's own choosing. He choses to reject the truth of his own eyes (Romans 1:22-23). Therefore, as John Wesley declared, God "judicially permits to come upon them"[1235] this delusion. As Robert Thomas remarked, "this is their only alternative because they have refused to love the truth (v. 10)."[1236]

In the context of End Times, the delusion allows Satan to wield ultimate control over those who have wilfully and knowingly rejected the truth. "God turns over to the baneful influence of Satan, the Prince of Lies, those who have of their own free will chosen not to listen to the truth but who by preference cleave to error."[1237]

In short, no man would reject God with his mouth if he knew the eternal outcome of that decision, but God judges by the heart, so rather than having a world of fakes, the Lord's judgment is to allow Satan to deceive their minds so that they will profess with their mouth what they believe in their hearts. They reject the truth for a lie, so they must live the lie. They can still turn away from that lie by repenting, but as long as they reject the Lord God, they will believe the unbelievable ... that there can be salvation without Christ! They will believe that a politician can be a savior!

What is the Deluding Spirit?

One author defined the delusion simply as "the loss of the power of perception, is the inevitable consequence of the refusal to attend to the offer of salvation."[1238] The Greek term is literally translated as "energy of deceit" which is a "Hebraism, meaning strong deceit."[1239] Many believe that the delusion is nothing less than the anti-Christ himself.[1240] Certainly the delusion is tied to the anti-Christ in some way for its purpose is to allow the culmination of all man's sins in the final war led by the anti-Christ. The delusion is to allow those who have wilfully rejected the truth to follow the anti-Christ to destruction.

It is not acceptable to apply the deluding spirit to the Holy Spirit as some have done. The Holy Spirit is the restrainer. Here God is turning men over to a deluding spirit in the same way that God unleashes demons in Revelation. They are bound so they cannot practice their full evil, but with the restrainer gone, the spirit of iniquity (2:7) is free to operate unchecked. The deluding spirit is connected in someway to the anti-Christ. This fits the theme of Romans 1:19-27. Think of it this way. When a man cheats on his wife he at first is careful not to get caught, but as sin and lust devour his conscience he begins to think he will always get away with it. He becomes less and less careful until he is caught in the act. Sinful men rarely think of the consequences of their acts. In Romans it is clear that delusion is a consequence of sin. Men become deluded and blind to the stupidity and consequences of rebellion against God. Here the delusion is greater than any in history. Everything is magnified in the tribulation; sin, evil, war, hatred, and deceit will reign supreme in those last days, proving that man is nothing without the God for whom he was created.

Conclusion

The delusion is parallel to the restrainer with a similar purpose. Sin and evil have always existed, but the restrainer has prevented unrelenting evil in history. That restraint will be removed in the tribulation so the full calamity of man's sin will be visible to all. Here the idea is similar. Delusion is the natural result of sin. We are blind to the consequences of our sins and the more we indulge sin, the more blind we become to its inevitable results. Like the alcoholic who knows his liver is going to give out. One of my uncles had been told point blank, if you drink any alcohol again, you will die. Sure enough, he did, and he died not long afterwards. Repentance frees us from the delusion which accompanies sin, but the delusion grows among those who rebel against God. Here the deluding spirit is released from its bonds. As the restrainer is removed, the deluding spirit is allowed by God to act unbridled. That spirit will lead those who continue to reject God to worship the anti-Christ and to be deceived until their ultimate destruction is assured.

Summary

2 Thessalonians is almost exclusively about the End Times. It is Paul's attempt to correct some misunderstandings which were being taught in the church. He both comforts and warns the Thessalonians. He assures them that the Day of the Lord will not begin until after the apostasy and the revelation of the anti-Christ. The revelation of the anti-Christ takes place three and a half years into the tribulation era mentioned by Daniel in chapter 9. It is the final week-year (seven year period) of the world before Christ returns to establish His kingdom. It is a time when the full culmination of sin, evil, and rebellion against God will lead men to blindly follow the anti-Christ and lead them to their destruction. It is also a time when God's wrath will accelerate man's choice between good and evil. He will either repent or bear the consequences of his own sin. So it is a period of mercy as well as wrath; for God could return and destroy all the wicked, but we would all have been lost. By showing what unrestrained evil truly is, men will be forced to make their choice quite literally between God and Satan.

Rembrandt – Paul at Writing Desk – 1627

9

1 & 2 Timothy

Timothy was like a son to Paul (1 Timothy 1:18; 2 Timothy 1:2). He accompanied Paul on his second and third missionary journeys and is listed in several of Paul's epistles as a co-author (in spirit – cf. 2 Corinthians 1:1; Philippians 1:1; Colossians 1:1; 1 Thessalonians 1:1; 2 Thessalonians 1:1). When Paul departed for Macedonia during his third missionary trip he asked Timothy to go to Ephesus and instruct the church (1 Timothy 1:3). Tradition claims that Timothy served as overseer at Ephesus for fifteen years,[1241] and it seems that Timothy also spent some time in prison for the faith (Hebrew 13:23), although it is uncertain when this took place. When Paul was awaiting execution at the end of his life, he asked Timothy to come visit him before his scheduled execution (2 Timothy 4:9).

Timothy was then Paul's nearest and dearest disciple. 2 Timothy was written during Paul's last imprisonment in Rome while he was awaiting execution, and 1 Timothy was written not too long before hand. Most all agree that Paul had already been imprisoned, but his last imprisonment probably didn't last very long, meaning that both epistles were written in close proximity. The first is generally dated to around 64 A.D. and the second in 65 A.D.[1242] This fits with my own conclusions that Paul died in 65 A.D.[1243] although I would probably date 1 Timothy the same year. Nonetheless, as usual, the liberal critics now doubt that Paul wrote the epistles at all.

Although literally no one doubted the authenticity of 1 and 2 Timothy for 1800 years, the Tübingen school immediately took up the cause citing four reasons to reject Pauline authorship. As usual they are frail subjective arguments used solely to cast doubt upon an otherwise unanimous tradition dating back to the first century.

Four "evidences" are presented to claim that the epistles (including Titus) were written by someone pretending to be Paul, and not the apostle. The first "evidence" is alleged historical innacuracies. It has been pointed out that Titus 1:5 mentions Paul leaving Titus at Crete and 1 Timothy 1:3 says that Paul left Timothy at Ephesus (cf. 2 Timothy 1:18; 4:12), but neither event is found in the book of Acts.[1244] They therefore conclude that Paul could not have written something that is filled with "historical errors." The frivolity of this claim is obvious by the mere fact that the book of Acts does not end with Paul's execution. Most scholars believe that Paul was released from prison after the close of Acts and traveled to Spain. The evidence for this is substantial (see *Controversies in the Acts of the Apostles*). He was later arrested following the fire in Rome and imprisoned a second time, during which time he wrote these epistles. Consequently, the events described therein took place after the book of

Acts ends. Moreover, A. Duane Litfin illustrates the brazen hypocrisy of the liberal critic who doubts the authenticity and accuracy of the book of Acts, but then uses the book of Acts to "disprove" events described in epistles written years after Acts![1245]

A second "proof" is the fact that Paul speaks of church offices such as deacons, elders (presbyters), and bishops, but those offices were allegedly not developed until a half century later.[1246] Once again, the critic assumes his own answers without proving them. In fact, Paul does not define these offices or their duties. To this very day Protestants and Catholics (as well as other sects) will argue over the Biblical meaning of bishops and their duties (see notes on Titus 1:7). The liberal critic simply attaches the Catholic hierarchical structure to Paul's epistles without proof and then declares that Paul would not have done such a thing![1247]

Next is the usual claim that the theology which Paul discusses was not developed until the second century. Specifically, they claim that gnosticism was not fully developed until the second century, and therefore Paul could not have refuted a doctrine which did not yet exist.[1248] Once again the critic assumes his own lies are true. Any serious scholar knows that Colossians (see notes there), as well as other Pauline epistles, was written in large part to refute gnosticism. The assumption that gnosticism is a second century theology stems from scholars who immediately dismiss evidence to the contrary, especially Biblical evidence. The fact is that many believe that Simon the Magician (Acts 8) was the inventor of gnosticism (see notes in *Controversies in the Acts of the Apostles*). While this is suspect, it is equally clear from extra-Biblical sources as well as Biblical sources that gnosticism developed very early and is refuted by Paul in many of his epistles. There is nothing new or different about Paul's emphasis upon "sound doctrine" found in the epistles to Timothy (1 Timothy 4:6; 2 Timothy 4:3; cf. Titus 1:9, 2:1). Paul's epistles are about that very thing!

Finally, they fall back on the silly subjective argument of "stylistic" and linguistic differences.[1249] They claim that Paul uses words 175 times in these epistles which do not appear elsewhere in his epistles.[1250] However, ignoring that they count the same word multiple times and that some of these words are driven by the subject matter, the fact remains that this is an inherently weak argument. To begin with there are 244 verses in these epistles[1251] which average roughly 20 words per verse. So out of approximately 4880 words 175 are not found in other Pauline epistles? That is less than 4% of the words! Considering that Paul's epistles are relatively short letters which cannot be used to prove his full extent of vocabulary and the topic driven nature of vocabulary, "such word-counting cannot support the weight of the critics' conclusions."[1252] The well respected Greek scholar Bruce Metzger even went on record saying that the statistical method is unsound.[1253]

So once again the closet atheists, otherwise known as nineteenth century German theologians, act more like defense lawyers relentlessly attacking the eyewitnesses to their clients' crimes because they cannot find any evidence to support their client. "The best defense is a good offense." This seems to be the logic of the Tübingen school of theology which continues to be taught in many of the more liberal (and even some "moderate") seminaries today. It is also the last vestige of the failed nihilistic philosophy of nineteenth century Germany that led to two world wars.

In short, these epistles were unequivacably written by Paul in the last year of his life as he awaited execution in Rome. Timothy was Paul's nearest and dearest disciple who taught at Ephesus for at least fifteen years. These epistles reflect Paul's thoughts and wishes upon his deathbed, as well as his love for Timothy and the church he was leaving behind.

Jesus and Prayer
1 Timothy 2:5

"For there is one God, and one mediator also between God and men, the man Christ Jesus."

This passage asserts two things. First, there is but one God. Monotheism is true. Second, that Jesus Christ alone is capable of bridging the gap between God and man. However, some Calvinists use this verse as proof that we should not pray to God the Father. They argue that if there is but one mediator then we must pray to Him alone, and not the Father. Nevertheless, when Jesus gave us an example of prayer in Matthew 6:9-15 it began with the words "our Father"! Martin Lloyd-Jones has said of this Calvinist teaching that it "is a terrible error and heresy."[1254]

Having said this, it is true that by declaring Jesus alone mediator between God and man, prayer to various saints or dead relatives is futile. They cannot mediate for us. Mary did not die for us. Only Jesus is the mediator between God and man. So when we pray we should pray either to Jesus or to God the Father in Jesus's name.

Modesty and the Christian
1 Timothy 2:9-10

"*I want* women to adorn themselves with proper clothing, modestly and discreetly, not with braided hair and gold or pearls or costly garments but rather by means of good works, as is proper for women making a claim to godliness."

Modesty in the church is a fading tradition. Modern feminism argues that modesty is somehow an attempt to tell women what they can do with their bodies. Such bizarre arguments only underline the problem with immodesty. The modern feminist wants to use her body as a means of power, but then finds that she doesn't really have as much control as she thinks. Modesty is not about control. Control is always a struggle. No one person truly has control, and those who think they are in control usually loose it. Immodesty is about bearing your body. Modesy is about bearing your soul.

In the modern era these simple truths are lost. Even some Bible commentaries now state that this passage should not be read "in a puritanical manner,"[1255] but I am reminded of C.S. Lewis's quote in the *Screwtape Letters* wherein the devil tells Screwtape, "'Puritanism' – may I remark in passing that the value we have given to that word is one of the really solid triumphs of the last hundred years."[1256] Indeed, it is doubtful if any in this generation are even aware of the fact that it is the Puritans who brought Democracy to the modern world! Let us then look at the issues of modesty in dress and adornments more closely.

Modest Dress

Donald Guthrie believes that "the word translated *apparel* (*katastole*) probably refers to demeanor as well as attire."[1257] While this could be true in principle it is equally true that "in large measure dress declares the character of a woman – and a man."[1258] The subject is modesty in dress.

Oliver Green tells us that "most men have respect for a lady who is her natural self than one who is made up."[1259] This is true. If woman wants to be appreciated for who she really is then she should emphasize her personality and character. "Simplicity of dress, at *all times*"[1260] creates less distraction from the natural soul of a woman. H.A. Ironside that it is "examples such as we have seen in our own mothers."[1261] How many of us can imagine our own mothers wearing string bikinis on the beach?

Still some see this as for "accepted civil virtues." Even John MacArthur argues that this is aimed primarily at dress in worship.[1262] Some argue it is a concession to society, but these authors forget that ancient Rome was hardly a virtuous one. Were this addressed to Israel alone then the subject would hardly have needed to be discussed. It is in societies where the temptation is to compete against the immodest competition wherein the issue arises.

John Calvin, in his usual uncharitable way, said that "a godly and honorable woman will undoubtedly dress differently from a prostitute."[1263] Another commentator stated that "immodesty in women helps to promote immorality."[1264] While these remarks are stark, there are not without merit. Contrary to what some people claim the purpose for provocative dress is not because tight and small clothing is more comfortable (it obviously is anything but). Rather its purpose is to attract attention, but the problem is that it attracts the wrong attention. If a man is looking at a woman's breasts, he is not looking at her soul. If he is looking at her butt, he is not looking at her heart. The same is true of men's attire. More and more men are wearing tight fitting pants and muscle shirts to attract women, oblivious to how superficial and imbecilic it makes them look.

Jewelry and Make-Up
A second issue here is that of jewelry and make-up. Most agree that jewelry and make-up are not forbidden, as some believe, but that "these are not to be understood as any further prohibited than that they are inconsistent ... it should be used in moderation."[1265] It is also of interest to note that "the Greek word [used here is that] from which we get the English word 'cosmetic.'"[1266] Beyond this, I address the subject more in 1 Peter 3:1-7. The point here is moderation and modesty. Let people admire your soul more than your beauty.

Conclusion
Immodesty is designed to garner attention, but it diverts what attention it receives from the soul to the body. Consequently, immoedesty gets the wrong attention. Modesty does not "prevent" rape or other crimes, but it is a safeguard when searching for a lifelong partner. The issue is not about "rights" but about right and wrong. A woman can dress how she chooses but if she wants to find a man who loves her for her soul, and will love her when she is old and of faded beauty, then she should display her soul over her body. The same is true of men. This is Paul's plea to Christians living in the decadence of ancient Rome, and it is a reminder to us living in the modern world as well.

Can Women Preach?
1 Timothy 2:11-12

"Do not allow a woman to teach or exercise authority over a man."

Allegations of sexism are constantly leveled at the Bible, despite the fact that Christianity elevated the role of women in society. Bible critics claims that Paul believed in the "general inferiority of the female sex"[1267] while the "evangelical feminist" believed that Paul was either expressing a non-binding opinion or that Paul was merely making a cultural concession. They have pointed out the names of many great women in the Bible whom they perceive to have violated this rule, but the crux of the issue is *how* one defines "equality" and status. It is also how one defines family; a word which has undergone serious, and dangerous, alterations in recent decades.

There are five issues before us. Is this a command or a concession? If it is a command then how can this be reconciled with strong women in the Bible? What role then are women to have, and is it inferior to men's? Most importantly, how does the structure and value of the family play into "gender roles"? What is it that God wants for us? Does He not know what is best and what will bring us true happiness and joy?

Who Does Not Permit?

Let us begin with the Bible itself. "Paul begins by saying *a women should learn* (2:11a)."[1268] Education is a fundamental part of Christian life. Women are not barred from being educated as in other religions and cultures, but required to learn. This is in contrast to the false stereotype of the Christian fundamentalist presented by Hollywood, but two examples of "radicals" is enough to disprove this. First, the Puritan, Quaker, and early Protestant settlers in America were far from the sexist pigs depicted in Hollywood. French deist and famed nineteenth century historian Louis deTocqueville said "the Americans are a very religious people [and so] they have tried to give arms to [woman's] reasoning powers" through education.[1269] He then immediately makes a disclaimer saying, "I know that such an education has its dangers."[1270] So the deist sees danger in education; not the Christian!

Another demonized politician is George Bush, and whatever we think of his politics or foreign affairs, the fact is that it is Bush who brought the right be educated, to vote, and to learn to women in the Middle East, which were largely lost and even reversed under Obama. The point is that it is not the secular liberal who has brought freedom and education to the modern world, but the "puritanical" Christians. It is Christianity which has elevated the education and status of women, but Christianity does distinguish between men and women.

Part of that distinguishment is the prohibition against women in a position of authority over men, but what does this mean? Are women barred from teaching in schools as they have done since the days of the Puritans? Paul says "I do not allow a woman to teach or exercise authority over a man" (v. 12). Some have argued that this is an opinion. Did Paul not say "*I do not,*" as if others might?

The common argument is that "Paul is here speaking as an apostle."[1271] It is no mere opinion but a command. John MacArthur says that "I want ... carries the force of a command."[1272] While not apparent in most English translations, this is apparent in the Greek because Greek states commands differently than English. In English, a command is rendered by dropping first or second personal pronoun in speech. "I do not permit" or "you do not permit" would become "do not permit" in order to be a command. Greek, however, cannot drop first, second, or third person because the person is incorporated into the word. In other words, the most basic form of a Greek word is not "to permit" as English would render it but "I permit." This is designated by the omega ending which is found on the end of *every single verb* in the Greek dictionary. While this may sound strange it is really no more strange then the way the Ten Commandments are presented. Rather than saying "Do not murder" it is rendered "you will not murder." "How do you know?" ask the psychopath. While the form sounds like a prophetic prediction it is the Hebrew manner for a command. In Greek the most basic form of the word, which is the

"I permit" form, *may* be used for a command. To express an opinion the author would either add a separate pronoun, which is not present here, or add what I call a disclaimer such as Paul used in 1 Corinthians 7:12 where he states "I say this (I, not the Lord)." The form of "I say" is the same form Paul uses when he makes a command. He therefore stopped in midsentence to clarify that this was his opinion; "I, not the Lord." This would be useless unless the "I say" form is construed as a command in Paul's usage. Indeed, this is exactly how Paul uses the form throughout the epistles and this is the same form that he uses in 1 Timothy 2:12.

When we add the inspiration of the Holy Spirit and the fact that Paul is offering instruction to an overseer and teacher, it is apparent that Paul is not expressing mere opinion, but a command. Thus Paul commands women to be educated, but not to teach. Teach what? That question will be answered, but first I would like to address the common argument that this command was made solely by way of concession, and not because of any Biblical precedent.

Cultural Concessions?
It is commonly argued that Paul is not stating a Biblical command but making a cultural concession much like polygamy, which was tolerated and even practiced by some of the Israelite Patriarchs and Kings, but never endorsed or supported by God or the Bible. Ignoring the fact that there are actually Biblical prohibitions against polygamy (cf. 1 Timothy 3:2, 12; 5:9; Titus 1:6), there are many reasons to reject this idea.

Greek and Roman Customs
William Barclay said that "it is written against a Greek background" and "the place of women in Greek religion was low."[1273] He then leaps to the conclusion that Paul is making concessions to the very society which he was preaching against. Consider that Timothy was a leader at the church of Ephesus where Paul's very life was threatened for offending the godess Artemis (Acts 19)? The Roman religion even employed temple prostitutes who were considered priestesses of a sort. Paul is not telling Timothy that he should compromise with the Ephesian religions. He is warning him against that temptation.

Some argue a different kind of cultural influence. George Montague says "some scholars think that Paul here has in view only the situation in Ephesus ... where some women were creating a disturbance (5:13)"[1274] but he notes that this cannot be the case for "the same principle is laid down in 1 Corinthians 14:33b-36"[1275] where no such disturbances were to be found.

It is simply invalid to claim that a Biblical *command* is simply a cultural restraint. We worship Jesus, not Roman culture. It is Jesus who changed the world, and He did not do so by yielding to pagan culture for safety sake. Nonetheless, there are those who believe it is not Greek or Roman culture which underlay this command, but a Jewish one.

Synagogue Customs

An alternative argument is that Paul was not addressing gentile culture, but Jewish culture. Donald Guthrie correctly points out that "Rabbinic prohibitions were much more severe than Christian."[1276] Women were required to sit separately and were not permitted to participate in certain activities. Even today women in Ultra-Orthodox familes must walk behind their husbands, and never beside them. In this respect, it is correct to show that Christianity was much more respectful and chivalrous than the culture in which they were living. Nevertheless, the fact remains that Paul was not one to bow to culture and compromise. He was scourged many times for disrespecting culture and eventually executed. This does not seem an appropriate answer.

Others have followed a similar line of reasoning, arguing that "speak" can he translated as "chatter."[1277] In other words, it is argued that Paul was simply telling women not to "chatter" and gossip during the service, but this cannot be for Paul adds "teach." What has teaching to do with gossip or chatter? It is clearly public speaking to which Paul refers (see below). In either case, it is clear that Paul prohibits public teaching in the church, and not by way of concession.

Wives or Women?

One final argument is semi-related to this cultural argument. It has been addressed more thoroughly under 1 Corinthians 11:3 and elsewhere. In this context it is said that Paul is ordering "wives" not to teach or hold authority over their husbands.[1278] Nevertheless, the context makes it perfectly clear that husbands and wives are not in any way addressed in this passage. It is about order within the church. Moreover, if we were to translate this as wives then it would make no sense. Wives cannot teach but single women can? Why? Wives cannot speak publicly in church but single women can? Why? This would be far more problematic than a universal prohibition for Paul is speaking about order in church, whereas this translation would make it about married women, as if they forfeit public rights by getting married. That would be unbiblical.

Conclusions

Compromise is not in Paul's vocabulary. Truth is truth. Right is right. Wrong is wrong. If the issue is not important then compromise might be an option, but if the issues is not important enough, then why does the modern critic scowl and cringe? Donald Guthrie argued that "there may have been local reasons for this prohibition of which we know nothing"[1279] but he has just admitted that there is no indication or evidence that Paul was bowing to tradition. Compromise was not in Paul's nature. Are we to believe that Paul ordered women to submit to something which he believed was wrong just to appease unbelievers? No good has ever come from compromising the truth. Compromise is for politicians, and they never want to do it! We are the ones who should never compromise, and we always do it! Compromise is not an option. We should therefore seek to understand what Paul was prohibiting and why rather than pretending that he did not say it.

Feminist in the Bible?
Before attempting to understand Paul's prohibition it is necessary to address one other argument made by many. Namely, if the Bible prohibits women from holding authority over men then why do women like Deborah, Esther, and Priscilla allegedly violate this law?

To each of these women there is a different answer. Esther, for example, never defied her husband or violated the rules of ettiquette as did Queen Vashti. Esther is a prime example of a how a woman can save a nation without violating the Biblical prohibitions. She is an example not of feminism, but of *femininity*. With a simple loving and submissive spirit she persuaded her unbelieving husband to save Israel. There is nothing inferior in being a woman, but much insecurity in women who feel they must act like men and occupy a man's position in society. Esther is not a violation of this prohibition but an example of a how women of godly virtues can influence the world without the need for title or manly authority. "Behind every great man is a woman." That was the saying from a more godly time. Today the feminist believes she must stand in front.

The case of Priscilla is also a misrepresentation of the facts. While "evangelical feminists" like to argue that Priscilla was the teacher and leader, Priscilla and Aquila are always mentioned together. Priscilla's name comes before his because she was a friend of Paul, not because she usurped his authority. They were a team who worked together. As Homer Kent said, "the case of Priscilla is no exception, for she was with her husband in the homes and both of them instructed Apollos (Acts 18:26)."[1280] She is once again an example of how a godly woman can impact the church without trying to supplant the authority of a man.

The last is more difficult. There is no doubt that Deborah acted as a judge and in so doing held power over men. However, her case too is misrepresented. Consider first that David was a child when he was anointed king of Israel. Was God suggesting that children should have the same rights as their parents or that they should have some say in the family affairs? Was God advocating "children's rights?" Of course not; God often used the fragile and the weak to mock the world. This included most of the apostles who were fishermen and plebeians. So also God used Deborah as a judge in Israel. This was something that Deborah recognized herself as she used her womanhood to mock the people of Israel for their own lack of faith. If the people would not give glory to God then God will give it to a woman (cf. Judges 4:9). Nothing in Deborah's story indicates that she was usurping a man's authority *per se*. A modern analogy might be Catholic nuns (and I use the Catholic hierarchy solely as an analogy, not an endorsement). Some nuns have had much more influence and impact that even Cardinals (e.g. Mother Teresa), but they did not have to usurp the Cardinal or call themselves Cardinals. They merely followed the path provided to them and did worked within that system to glorify their faith.

In short, appeals to strong Biblical women are to be encouraged when they are in context. To try to make strong Biblical women into something they were not is wrong and dangerous. None of these women would ever have made an impact upon the world had they tried to behave like men. This is one of the great lies of the modern feminist movement; that men and women are no different except in anatomical ways. The teaching promoted in colleges today is called "gender politics" wherein it is taught that it is society, and not nature, which teaches men to be strong and women to be gentle. They breed a society which has only harmed women and men; and particularly the family.

Nothing in these stories nullifies Paul's prohibition. The real question is, "what exactly is that prohibition?"

What Kind of Teaching?
On the subject of teaching there is much division even among like minded individuals. Does this prohibit school teacher? Does it apply only to the church? What about Sunday school?

Some argue that this applies only "in the meetings of the faithful."[1281] Others that is applies to "every form of *public* address."[1282] What all agree upon, however, is Calvin's assersion that "Paul is not saying that women should stop teaching their families at home, he is just excluding them from the office of teaching."[1283] Warren Wiersbe even believes that "there is nothing wrong with a godly woman instructing a man in private (Acts 18:24-28)."[1284] So perhaps it is best to start with what we can agree upon.

First, woman are to teach their children. The woman's role in the family is arguably the most important. It is she who nurtures, raises, and teaches the child in most aspects. Woman "was to build *the home*."[1285] Only the modern feminist would consider this inferior or degrading; after all, they abort their own children! Nevertheless, J.P. Greene once said that "man cannot do the woman's work, and he should not usurp her place; the same is true of the woman."[1286] Women teach future teachers in the home. This is in some ways more important that occupying the "official" office of teaching.

Second, woman can "teach the younger women and, indeed, they are urged to do so (Tit. 2:4)."[1287] The prohibition is against "teaching or holding authority of men." There is no prohibition against teaching other women or boys. At what age someone becomes a man has been defined culturally, but it is clear that young boys can be taught by women as has been the tradition in American schools from the days of our founders to the beginning of the twentieth century, as well as most other western cultures.

268

More debatable, but suspect, is whether or not women can teach secular studies to adult, but what is not debatable is that women are barred from teaching theology or holding positions of authority over men in the church. They can, and should, hold offices and duties in the church, but none that have authority over men. As Calvin believed, "to teach implies that the teacher has a superior authority and status over rulers."[1288] The reason why is debated under 1 Timothy 2:13-15 but there are two interesting theories as it relates to teaching. The more popular one is that "the man is more or less dominated by his head – if he has any head; whereas the woman is likely to be controlled by the heart."[1289] Since teaching is an intellectual endeavor then it is argued women should not teach. Now while there may be some truth to this, my experience has been that many men are just as emotional as women and some women are just as strong of thinkers as many men. Therefore, this argument has only limited application and is probably not the main reason for the prohibition.

A second unique argument is that of J.N.D. Kelly who says that Adam's sin "must have been all the greater since he sinned with his eyes open. His point is that since Eve was so gullible ... she clearly cannot be trusted to teach."[1290] In other words, while Adam allegedly had the "greater" sin, Eve's sin resulted from gullibility. This rationale is similar to the first and assumes that all the descendants of men and women respectively suffer from the same attributes. Once again it has only a limited application (but see notes on 1 Timothy 2:13-15).

Perhaps the real reason is that men and women have different, and equally important, duties for which they were made. The man is to lead the church and provide for the family while the woman is to teach her children and nuture them and raise a godly generation. No one duty is less important than the other. To that end we should look at the role of the woman in the family as ordained in the Bible.

Women in the Family
Somewhere along the way evangelical Christianity has forgotten *what* a family is, and how it works. We no longer understand *why* God created two sexes and how God ordained that they live for *His* greater glory.

While evangelicals extol the virtues of family they undercut it by accepting ideas which degrade it. Every day that women are at work or living "independent" and alone, is a day that could have been spend forming and nurturing the family and relationships; relationships that form the foundation for all other relationships, for the family life does not have to be a good one, it only need be a family, because the worse a family is, the more people must work at it to make it work, and the more they will be prepared to work and deal with others.

I have learned patience; because my father had no patience: I have learned self-control and even temperament; for my father had neither. My family life was not great, but because I did not abandon it, I learned from the structure that God established. If I can get along with certain relatives of mine, I can get along with most anyone. My family gave me my strength; even when it failed.

John MacArthur compares the subordination of the wife to our subordination to Christ and "Christ's relationship to the Father."[1291] He says that "subordination is not punishment, but privilege."[1292] The typical response is to give examples of poor husbands or abusive ones, but does not the law allow for divorce in such extreme examples? If such extreme examples are grounds for divorce then is this not just an excuse? In a sinful world there are no perfects wives or husbands, but family is the "tie that binds." There is an invisible bond that connects all families. Karl Marx believed that this invisible bond had to be broken for his utopian dream to come true.[1293] It is then little wonder than the role of the mother is demeaned. Whereas the Bible once said, "Can a woman forget her nursing child, and have no compassion on the son of her womb?" (Isaiah 49:15) we now see abortion hailed as a virtue and popular control is not so subtly introduced in "Obamacare." By destroying mothers, the entire family is destroyed.

Whereas it was once considered to be a blessing to be a mother we now see children are left in day-care centers all day while their mothers and fathers go off to pursue their careers. The curse which said "through painful toil eat of (the ground) all the days of your life (Genesis 3:17)" and "by the sweat of your brow you will eat your food (Genesis 3:19)" has been replaced with the career. Stress has replaces sweat. The curse of the woman, that her "desire will be for your husband and he will rule over you (Genesis 3:16)" has been replaced as well. The result are children growing up effectively orphans. As Allan Bloom once said amid cries of bigotry and intollerance, "children may be told over and over again ... that they will enjoy quality time instead of quantity time ... but children do not believe any of this ... to children, the voluntary separation of parents seems worse than their death precisely because it is voluntary."[1294] Teenage rebellion was not a common trait in history. It is a 20th century trait. "It is not the children who break away; it is the parents who abandon them."[1295]

In short, the deterioration of traditional mothers has led to a generation of children who know nothing of family or God. The woman is to teach in the home. The woman is to teach her children. In this way the woman is responsible for future generations even more so than the college professors. It is the man, however, who is to teach in the church and Bible college.

Conclusion

Church is not isolated from reality; nor is it counter-productive to the family. In fact, as the church has grown the family it has led to great social change. Its primary purpose has always been the promulgation of the gospel, but the side effects of the gospel include the growth of the family and social justice as a result. We should not go at these backwards as many have done, for social justice without the gospel is a myth. We are seeing that today as the family is being abandoned in the name of "social justice" and a falsely called "equality."

The prohibition on teaching does not negate the responsibility of the woman teaching her children, who will in turn be future teachers. It is the promotion of motherhood and family and a structure which is equally important in securing godly offspring. It is indeed ironic that the same modern feminist have drifted so far from the original "feminist" of the nineteenth century that they do not even realize how much "power" (and they obsessed with that word) they have surrendered by abandoning the family. This irony can be illustrated by Bollywood actress Rani Mukherji, who was promoting a film about "woman power," and wisely said "once you marry a man, you get a lot of power in the household ... there much power in the kitchen."[1296] Such refreshing comments illustrate that true women have much more power than imagine, but they do not understand it and do not use it here in the West.

Alexis deToqueville commented that "there have never been free societies without mores, and ... it is the woman who shapes these mores."[1297] She shapes these mores, however, in the home. Without a mother in the home, the home becomes nothing more than an orphanage. Paul's prohibition is not a prohibition against women, but a prohibition against the abandonment of God's structure within the church and family. Only when each part does its job can we see the fruits. One plants, another waters (cf. 1 Corinthians 3:7-8). When everyone wants to water, there is no one to plant. When everyone wants to plant, there is no one to water. In either case the plant dies and bears no fruit.

The Fall and Women
1 Timothy 2:13-15

"*It was* not Adam *who* was deceived, but the woman being deceived, fell into transgression."

Previously I stated that the primary reason for Paul's prohibition is the importance and structure of the family. However, I conceded that there is truth in the fact that there are others reasons as well. Here Paul argues that women cannot occupy positions of authority in the church because, as descendents of Eve, they are more easily deceived. This is a generalization, but as a principle it is considered just cause for the prohibition. Naturally, such seemingly harsh words bring about accusations of sexism and misogynism. One Bible commentary even goes so far as to claim that Paul believed in "general inferiority of the female sex"![1298] Such is the state of politics today.

It is best to start with verse 13 where Paul indicates the same principle he stated in 1 Corinthians 11:8-12. That passage reads:

"For man does not originate from woman, but woman from man; for indeed man was not created for the woman, but woman for the man ... [but] as the woman originates from the man, so also the man *has his birth* through the woman; and all things orignate from God."

Let us consider this. Woman was made to complete man. She was made from his side, but man is born from her womb. Men and women cannot exist apart from one another. The woman completes the man, who is incomplete with her. So also the man is the desire of every women (Genesis 3:16). All of this was a part of God's plan for the family structure from the very beginning, even before the Fall.

Now in verse fourteen Paul speaks about the Fall and how it reflects on the weaknesses of each sex. Both sinned. Both defied God. Both were guilty before God. Yet the reasons for their sins reflect upon the frailties of each sex. Paul makes clear that Eve believed Satan's lies whereas Adam was sinned in choosing Eve over God. Opinions on this have naturally varied somewhat. John Wesley said "she is more easily deceived, and more easily deceives."[1299] Another argued that "Eve was the more susceptible to deception."[1300] Still another that "women are susceptible to be 'led away.'"[1301] Satan then "approached Adam *through* Eve."[1302] He had not been deceived by the Serpent's lies, but, according to Ironside, "got into the transgression out of love for Eve."[1303] Dave Hunt said that Adam "didn't want to lose" Eve.[1304] He chose Eve over God.

J.A. Bengal said that "the Serpent deceived the woman; the woman did not deceive the man, but persuaded him."[1305] So "in her very persuasions [she became] the vehicle of the serpent's deceit."[1306] This is why John Calvin argued that "since the advice she gave proved fatal, it is right that she should have to depend on someone's power and will."[1307] Nevertheless, this assumes that the structure of the family is a post-Fall curse. This is not so. Verse thirteen indicates that God had planned the family structure from the very beginning. The Fall only proves the wisdom of God's plan. The man and woman need one another to complete one another. This was *always* God's plan.

Of course, some dispute this view of things. One author argues that it was "because of her greater trustfulness" that Eve was "more easily misled into false beliefs."[1308] James Montgomery Boice even goes so far as to say that Eve "fell with good will,"[1309] as if *anyone* sins with goodwill! Warren Wiersbe too denies women are more easily deceived.[1310] However, this does not help their cause for the temptation was to become a god. The lie which Eve believed was that she would become a kind of god. She wanted to usurp God, as Adam usurped God's authority by chosing Eve over Him. We cannot whitewash sin, but why was the brunt of the sin placed on Adam, we are asked?

One reason that Adam stands condemned for a sin that began with the woman is the very fact that man was to be the head of the family (cf. 1 Corinthians 11:3). The man is ultimately responsible for the actions of his family. John MacArthur argues that "when she stepped out from under the protection and leadership of Adam, she was highly vulnerable and fell."[1311] Part of the man's responsibility is to protect woman. This was from whence the code of chivarly developed in Charlemagne's day. We are protect women, but Adam failed to do so. He was therefore accountable for allowing her to be deceived.

This makes sense. If "the head of every woman is man" (1 Corinthians 11:3) then man must be accountable for his own household. Nevertheless, Paul declares also that "woman is the glory of man" (1 Corinthians 11:7). Woman is a part of man and she does not exist apart from him. The very name woman means "from man" because she was taken from man's side. The man and wife are one body and one flesh but the man is the head of the body. The body, is nevertheless, useless without hands, feet, and a heart (cf. 1 Corinthians 12). These were not roles created only after the fall. They were intended from the beginning. Genesis 2:20 states that Eve was formed because there was no suitable "helper" for man. In Genesis the word "helper" is modified by the word כְּנֶגְדּוֹ (cenegdo) which comes from the preposition "before" and usually carries the translation of "opposite."[1312] This may even be where the term "opposite sex" originated. The woman is a compliment to man, as man is to woman. We need to compliment one another. "Opposites attract" because we need to draw upon the strengths of one another. In this sense "equality" is misplaced. We may be created equal, but that does not mean that we were created for the same purpose and task. A father and mother serve different, and complimentary, purposes. A mother cannot be a father and a father cannot be a mother. Each must submit to his or her role in the family and not seek to usurp the other's role. Each serves a purpose when each obeys God. This is Paul's point. The fact that the woman was deceived is symptomatic, not causal.

Saved Through Childbearing?
1 Timothy 2:15

"*Women* will be preserved through the bearing of children if they continue in faith and love and sanctity with self-restraint."

The King James version reads, "saved in childbearing." In the modern world these words seem vastly offensive. Theologically, they can also be misunderstood. "Saved through childbearing"? What does it mean?

First, most all agree that salvation in the spiritual sense is never intended here. Gordon Fee said, "inconceivable that Paul [uses] saved in an absolute way."[1313] Two alternatives have been suggested. One medieval view is that the woman would be "saved from death in childbearing"[1314] but this odd view makes no sense contextually and seems derived from superstition. The other view is that "saved ... is used in its broader sense."[1315]

What then of childbearing? Here too there are two views. Some have believed that this refers to the birth of Christ.[1316] It is thus one child in particular, and hence salvation is used in the spiritual sense. While one critic calls this "far-fetched artificiality"[1317] it is an intriguing view, but probably not what Paul intended, for Christ is not mentioned by Paul again until 3:13. The more common view is that of motherhood.[1318]

The NEB translation is probably best. It reads, "saved through motherhood." The NAS, cited above, uses the word preserved rather than "saved." Each carries the idea that motherhood is the goal of a noble woman.

Throughout these past few passages I have emphasized the importance of family and motherhood. As one author said, "motherhood ... is their crown."[1319] The jewel in a woman's life should not be her career, or how much money she makes, but how great her children become. Most all of us have our fondest memories of our mother. It was her who cared for us when we were sick and it was her who fed us when we were hungry. Who can forget the words of Scripture speaking of a mother who will not leave her dying child's side (2 Kings 4:30), or the Psalms prophesying that "He makes the barren woman abide in the house; as a joyful mother of children" (113:9), Solomon instructing his children, "my son, observe the commandment of your father; do not forsake the teaching of your mother" (Proverbs 6:20), or Paul's analogy to the Thessalonians that "we proved to be gentle among you, as a nursing mother tenderly cares for her own children" (1 Thessalonians 2:7).

Unfortunately, "a woman who now wanted to be a woman in the old sense would find it very difficult to do so, even if she were to brave the hostile public opinion."[1320] A gentle and quiet spirit is not tolerated by the modern world. Like too many throughout history we have trusted in the world rather than in Christ's love. We like to pick and choose between what the world has to offer and what God has to offer. What is happening to the "evangelical church" today is the same thing that happened to the "liberals" of the eighteen hundreds. We have become like the tares that were thrown in among the thorns and the thorns grew up and choked them (Matthew 13:7). Evangelical publishers now print politically correct translations of the Bible "so that future generations will not have to grapple with the fact that God was once a sexist."[1321] As a result, like the world outside, the Christian community has become more and more unisexual.

Before the twentieth century, childbearing was considered a blessing, not a curse. For in times of old, there was no greater reward, nothing more sought by women, then to give birth to a human child. A mother was revered and honored as the forth commandment deeded. Rachel earnestly prayed for a child, considering it reproach that she bore none (Genesis 30). Leah rejoiced in her children. It was (and still is) the woman's job to nurture and raise the child. It was her duty to feed and care for him. "Woman is the glory of man" (1 Corinthians 11:7) and the child is the crown of woman.

1 Timothy 3:1 (Church Government) – See Titus 1:7

Can A Pastor Be Divorced?
1 Timothy 3:2, 12

"An overseer, then, must be above reproach, the husband of one wife."

Four times in the Bible church leaders are required to be "the husband of one wife" (1 Timothy 3:2, 12; 5:9; Titus 1:6). This is obviously a prohibition against polygamy, but many believe it is also a prohibition against divorced men serving in church leadership. Is this so?

As early as the second century this passage was interpreted to mean "married only once."[1322] This would not only prohibit divorcees, but also widowed men who marry a second time. Others have noted that the Greek is most literally translated as "one woman man."[1323] They then treat this more leniently, prohibitting only polygamy and promiscuity.

Curiously, this passage could also be interpreted to mean that an overseer *must* be married. Such a commandment would obviously negate the teaching of Catholic celibacy for the priesthood. Nevertheless, even Protestants agree that this "doth not oblige them" to marry,[1324] for Paul defends the right of celibacy elsewhere, as he does the right of marriage. Clearly, being married does not bar someone from serving in church leadership.

The real controversy is over divorcees. Matthew Henry, along with most early Protestants, believed that no divorcee could serve in leadership.[1325] Even if the divorce was for "just cause" or done before conversion to Christ, it marks a failure of the family and family leadership. How can one serve as a leader in God's family if he has failed as a leader in his own family? This is the traditional view among Christians throughout the ages, although by no means universal. Many believe that any divorce which took place before rebirth is a sin forgiven like any other. How can we judge a man for sins Christ has forgiven? How can a man be barred from leadership for sins done before he knew Jesus? If this were so would not Paul be barred as a man who once persecuted the church?

The arguments on both sides are good. Once a man has been born again, he begins a new life. His old life should not bar him from service to God anymore than Paul's barred him from being an apostle. However, it is evident that once a man is born of Christ he cannot continue in those sins and expect to serve in leadership. This is stated at the outset when says he "must be above reproach." Whatever the reasons for divorce, it is a failure of family leadership. If the prospective leader already knows Christ then he cannot plead ignorance. He must work to repair his own family, and may serve the Lord in many ways, but he may not serve in a leadership role of the church. Does Paul not say, "if a man does not know how to manage his own household, how will he take care of the church of God?" (1 Timothy 3:5). How indeed? This too takes us back to the previous passages where I discuss the importance of motherhood and family, but here we are discussing the importance of fatherhood and family. The man too has a duty to the family and if he fails in it, he will fail in leadership of the church. He is thus barred from service at that level.

In short, any sin committed before conversion to Christ Jesus is disposed of on the cross, but once someone has dedicted themselves to Christ they must display the leadership of the home before they can take leadership of the church. If they fail on the first, they will fail in the latter and are barred from being overseers, deacons, or any other church leadership position.

Apostasy
1 Timothy 4:1-3

"The Spirit explicitly says that in latter times some will fall away from the faith, paying attention to deceitful spirits and doctrines of demons."

2 Thessalonians 2:3 warned that the apostasy must take place before the anti-Christ is revealed. Although several theories as to the meaning of apostasy in that verse were debated, the word here is αποστησονται (*apostesontai*) which is a future tense verb of the word apostasy. Most believe that apostasy has always taken place to one degree or another, but here it is "*the* apostasy (from within) not '*a* falling away.'"[1326] This passage is thus the strongest evidence that the apostasy of 2 Thessalonians 2:3 is "a departure from the great doctrines which constitute the Christian faith."[1327] Nevertheless, this opens the door to many questions. The two primary questions are "when" and "what kind of doctrines"?

When is obviously "latter times," but some distinguish this from Last Days or End Times. Some argue that this "begun at Pentecost"[1328] and that "latter times refers to their present situation."[1329] This view is even held by many conservative and even dispensational authors. H.A. Ironside, for example, saied that "the 'latter times' are to be distinguished from 'the last days' described in 2 Timothy 3:1"[1330] and "is for us in the past."[1331] Guthrie argued that it "is a phrase which suggests a more imminent future than 'in the last days.'"[1332] Oliver Green said it could be translated "a little bit latter."[1333] In Greek "last days" is εσχαταις (*eschatais*) whereas here the word used is 'υστερois (*hysterois*). So there does appear to be distinguishing between "last days" and "latter times."

With such vast support from across the spectrum we are tempted to accept, for even as John Calvin stated, "just as the false teachers had once disturbed the people of Israel, so they will always upset Christ's church."[1334] The subject matter found in the ensuing verses appear to be aimed at the gnostic heresies plaguing the church at that time, so contextually it does support this view.[1335] Nevertheless, there is at least one reason to cast doubt upon this.

The majority of the parallel passages seem to refer to "last days," and not merely the near future (cf. Matthew 7:15; 24:11-15; Mark 13:22, 2 Thessalonians 2:3, 2 Timothy 3:1-4; 4:3-4; 2 Peter 3:3; 1 John 2:18-23). Now some of these passages also indicate that deceivers have already gone out into the world (1 John 2:18). Consequently, the idea here is not that the apostasy is something that will someday simply appear but that it grows and increases until the Last Days when "the" apostasy will have come. At least this is the general theory among those who see the apostasy of 2 Thessalonians 2:3 as a falling away from the faith (see notes there).

In either case, it is clear that false doctrines were already appearing and causing problems within the church. Tertullian applied this to pagan philosophy.[1336] The passages which follow appear to speak about gnosticism, the great heresy of the first three centuries of the church (glamorized by Hollywood today). Paul refers to this "deceitful spirits and doctrines of demons" (v. 1). It is thus "deceiving spirits, certainly not merely the false teachers themselves,"[1337] but what does doctrine of demons mean? Joseph Mede called this "demonolatry";[1338] a sort of idolatry of demons. However, it is clear that Paul is not making reference to any literal demon cult. Rather he is identifying the author of such teachings as demons. It is Satan and his demons who deceive and lead us astray. The doctrines of demons are intended to lead us away from Christ. A list follows of those teachings. Among them is the extreme asceticism found among gnostics, and practiced by some Christians sects to this day.

Celibacy of the Priesthood Condemned?
1 Timothy 4:3

"The hypocrisy of liars ... who forbid marriage."

Paul expressly condemns "the hypocrisy of liars ... who forbid marriage." The Protestant Reformers were firmly of the opinion that this was a scathing indictment of the Catholic Church's policy of celibacy for the priesthood.[1339] John Calvin said "this prophecy applies to Roman Catholics"[1340] and that "it is wrong for the Roman Catholic to put blame on some ancient heretics, as if Paul's teaching only applied to them."[1341] John Wesley said it referred to the practice of "forbidding priests, monks, and nuns to marry."[1342] The Catholic's response is that "the error of these false teachers is in making [them] a universal *law*"[1343] and argue that celibacy is "voluntary."

Now the application to the Catholic teaching is worthy of debate, and will be debated, but we must begin with the initial context. Paul is plainly attacking the doctrines of the gnostics[1344] to whom asceticism was sacred. This

277

stemmed from their belief in dualism was integral to their system.[1345] Since they believed that the flesh and spirit were diametically opposed to one another, some gnostics practiced an extreme asceticism to separate themselves from anything in the physical world, while others believed that the sins of the body could not effect the spirit since they were separate. The latter then indulged in all kinds of carnal sins. This irony is reflective of the heresy of such dualism. Nevertheless, here Paul is referring only to the former kind of gnostic dualism. These gnostics forbade marriage and the eating of certain foods.

This passage has been applied not only to gnostics but also to religious sects and practices since the time of the gnostics. One scholar even argued that it was an allusion to the "false asceticism"[1346] of the Essene sect of the Jews. Most, however, have tied this to the Catholic church, noting that traditionally Catholics are not supposed to eat meat on Friday.[1347]

One thing is certain. "Paul emphatically condemns the artificiality of unnatural asceticism."[1348] Jonathan Edwards called it an "injuction" against celibacy and "monastic life"[1349] while another notes that "marriage is natural and right."[1350] The Catholic church has maintained, however, that celibacy is voluntary.[1351] However, this argument reminds me of the military sergeant who "volunteers" his soldiers. "You don't *have* to be a priest" they say, but if you want to be a priest you must be celibate. That, they say, is voluntary. Nevertheless, that is the *same* argument the Obama administration tried to use at one point to defend their policy of attempting to *force* nuns to provide abortion pills to their orphans. They argued that it is not a violation of religious freedom because they don't *have* to run an independent orphanage. If you are placing restrictions upon someone's choice, then it is not truly voluntary. When you choose to join the military you *must* obey orders. Joining the military was voluntary. Obeying orders is not. When you choose to become a priest you *must* be celibate. Serving God was voluntary. Being celibate in that Catholic service *is not* voluntary.

The early church father Tertullian said that "the apostle sets a brand upon those who were want entirely to forbid marriage."[1352] He believed that monogomy was a requirement, but not celibacy.[1353] In fact, even the Catholic church did not require celibacy of the priesthood until pope Gregory VII in the eleventh century.[1354] So it is clear that Paul placed no prohibitions upon marriage of priests or nuns or any other church office, save that they be monogomous (cf. Titus 1:7). Paul did, however, condemn those who required celibacy and forbade the eating of certain foods. The ascetic lifestyle is not one practiced by the apostles, for they did not believe that we must physically remove ourselves from the material world, but that we must put our focus on spiritual matters without neglecting the world in which we live.

Christian Rebuke
1 Timothy 5:1-4

"Do not sharply rebuke an older man, but *rather* appeal to *him* as a
father, *to* the younger men as brothers, the older women as mothers, *and*
the younger women as sisters, in all purity."

In recent decades we are used to hearing one of two extremes. The one
side misquotes Matthew, saying "judge not lest thee be judged." The other side
acts like he thinks he is a prophet of God and hurls judgment and dire warnings.
Here Paul is explaining the natural order in rebuke.

Rebuke is both necessary and Biblical. It is false to say that we must
turn a blind eye to sin. If someone is attempting to commit suicide and we walk
away, or even worse buy him a rope, then we too are guilty, and yet this seems
to be the mindset of many today. Rebuke is scorned and neglected within the
church today, but as John Calvin said, correcting faults is always
unpalatable."[1355] It is also necessary.

How then are we to rebuke someone? First, we are to respect our
elders, and by elder it is meant "older person, [for that] is what elder here means
and not an official office."[1356] When we correct someone older than us we
should be particularly respectful and delicate. Second, we are rebuke those
younger than ourselves as if they were our own brothers or sisters. Rebuke is
not like the prophets of the Old Testament. The prophets were judging kings
and nations. That is not our job. Our job is to reflect Christ in all things. We
are speak the truth in love (Ephesians 4:15). This obviously implies two things;
truth *and* love.

Another thing which we must be acutely aware of is the fact that it is
Christ who changes us. The founder of the Salvation Army once said that
change without Christ still ends with death and hell.[1357] Therefore, when we
rebuke someone we must be willing to let Christ convict their heart. Any
change must be done out of love for Christ. I am reminded of an anecdote my
professor Mal Couch once told me. They had a recent convert who was the
epitamy of the "butch" woman. She dressed like a man, talked like a rough
man, and her head was shaven. They debated about whether to tell her that this
was not appropriate and decided to wait. Over time as she grew closer to the
Lord she change naturally. No one had to tell her. She naturally came to talk,
dress, and act like a Christian woman. It was Christ who changed her.

A similar analogy is in mission work. I saw a movie once where
Hollywood mocked Christian missionaries for bringing bras to women in a
South American tribe. The movie took great pains to pretend like Christians
were trying to force Indians do dress and act like European women, but in
reality modesty is natural. It is suppressed among pagan cultures, but when the
women came to know Christ they naturally wanted to cover up. No one taught
them; they did it naturally. If anything it was the men who did not want them

dressing modestly. This is what we must remember in rebuking someone. It is out job to warn and gently remind our brothers of the dangers of sin, but it is for Christ and Christ alone to change their heart to accept this.

1 Timothy 5:9 – See 1 Timothy 3:2, 12

Young Widows Encouraged to Marry
1 Timothy 5:14

"I want younger *widows* to get married, bear children, keep house, *and* give the enemy no occasion for reproach."

Some have argued that Paul opposed marriage, but here Paul encouraged young widows to marry. Some even argue that "I want ... carries the force of a command."[1358] This then opens the door to the misogynist attacks. Why must a woman marry? To this Calvin responded, "some silly people scoff at what Paul says here."[1359] As one commentator noted, "this is the design of the Creator."[1360] Marriage and family are sacred. To reject this "as some modern liberationists have done, is to cause women to question God's wisdom."[1361] In this case, two questions are asked.

The first question concerns an alleged contradiction with 1 Corinthians 7:39-40. There Paul says, "A wife is bound as long as her husband lives; but if her husband is dead, she is free to be married to whom she wishes, only in the Lord. But in my opinion she is happier if she remains as she is." So in Corinthians Paul appears to prefer that the widow "remain as she is," but here he seems to want them "to get married, bear children, keep house, *and* give the enemy no occasion for reproach." Is this a contradiction? No. In Corinth nothing said about the age of the widow, and most are presumeably older women. However, by the time 1 Timothy was written the persecutions of Nero had already begun and war was looming in the Roman empire. As a result there were a number of young widows who had not yet had children or families of their own.

This leads to the second question. Some see cultural constraints at work here. Ironside said that widows could not work[1362] and so some believe that "widows with no other means of support"[1363] should seek husbands to help alleviate the burden of the church. However, this seems too pragmatic and utilitarian. The gospel is not utilitarian. Marriage is not a means of financial support but the foundation of family. Others have said that idleness and the "danger of becoming restless"[1364] were motivation for Paul's advice, but this too wreaks of utilitarian reasoning. Certainly these things may contribute to the desire to bind a widow to a family, but family is the motivation. Family is the most basic structure after religion by which God made this current life liveable.

Contrary to the modern anti-family sentiment and the feminist stereotype of the woman's role in traditional families, the Bible elevates the woman's role in family, and particularly motherhood. As J.P. Greene said, "Ruling the household is an exalted calling. The home is the best place for every woman who is able to rule it."[1365] Consequently, if widow was young and had no children, Paul urged her to seek a husband and begin a new family, as all young men and women are urged to do. Family is sacred and we ought let no one degrade family, nor impugn Paul's love for the family.

Sharing Responsibility for Sin?
1 Timothy 5:22

> "Do not lay hands upon anyone *too* hastily and thereby share *responsibility for* the sins of others."

The King James, along with may other translations, reads "neither be partaker of other men's sins." The NAS, however, reads this passage in an entirely different manner reading, "share responsibility for the sins of others." Elsewhere I have stated that there are two extremes in Christian rebukes. The one believes we should never rebuke or "judge" another. Charles Spurgeon says of these men that we have made ourselves partakers of the sin "by not rebuking them for sinning."[1366] The other side acts like he thinks he is a prophet of God promising wrath upon the sinner. Here Paul is again rejecting both extremes, but what is he saying exactly? Is he urging us to avoid sharing in sin, or to share responsibility for sin?

The Greek is very simply μηδε κοινωνει ʽαμαρτιαις αλλοτριαις (*mede koinonei hamartias allotrias*). The two key words here are μηδε (*mede*) and κοινωνει (*koinonei*). The latter word literally means "fellowship, association, community, communion, joint participation, [or] intercourse."[1367] Μηδε (*mede*) is a simple particle usually meaning "nor"[1368] or "and not."[1369] So there are two ways to translate the clause. The first is as found in King James, NIV, RSV, ASV, ESV, and most older translations; "do not participate in the sins of others." The second way to translate the passage, as in the NAS, is to interpret μηδε (*mede*) as "and not sharing in the resposibility for sin" where "responsibility" is understood by context. Is this possible?

Let us look at the context. In the first clause Paul urges Timothy not to "lay hands upon anyone too hastily." Most of the church fathers, such as Tertullian, believed that "laying on of hands" was a reference to the ordination of elders or other church leaders. He therefore urged restraint upon baptism or ordination of those who ask.[1370] They believed that it was necessary to make sure they were making the right choice. If they did not then they would be partaking, or sharing, in the sins of the elder/convert.

Others see "lay hands upon anyone too hastily" as a warning against hastily judging someone for their sins. In this case, the second clause would be better reads as "sharing responsibility for sin." Notice how the interpretation of the first clause effects the second clause.

281

If the first view is taken then it is a clear prohibition suggesting that to ordain someone who is unworthy is to condone and share in their sins. The second takes a more generic view about judging others, and renders the second clause as a result of the first. Do not judge hastily or you will not be sharing responsibility. Honestly while the theology of the second interpretation is sound, its exegesis is suspect. First, when μηδε (*mede*) is used with an imperitive, such as κοινωνει (*koinonei*), it usually conveys a command.[1371] Second, the "laying on of hands" was probably not used in those days as a term of physical assault as today. While the idiom is ancient, it is more likely that to lay hands on someone did mean to ordain them as the church fathers understood. This historical support indicates that the modern idiom was probably not common at that time. Finally, the last clause is that we should "keep yourself free from sin." This fits better with not participating in the sins of others, rather than sharing resposibility.

Having said this, there is a valuable lesson here. We are far too quick to pass blame and not share in the responsibility for sin. Did we take a man who cannot hold his liquor to a place which serves liquor? Did we condone a sin by not speaking out or offering help when we could? Should we not share responsibility for sin and protect one another? Indeed we should. Nevertheless, Paul has been talking about rebuking elders in the previous verse. This context best fits the common translation.

The Yoke of Slavery
1 Timothy 6:1

"All who are under the yoke as slaves are to regard their own masters as worthy."

I have addressed slavery under Romans 13:1-5 and especially Ephesians 6:5-9. I will not repeat what I have said there except to answer those who point to this passage as an endorsement of slavery. It is clear that Paul is not addressing the morality of slavery but the victims who are forced to live under its "yoke"; the "yoke of slavery." The Greek word ζυγος (*zugon*) or "yoke" is used in the Bible as a "burden" or evil.[1372] Consider Jesus's repeated references to the "leaven" of the Pharisees (cf. Matthew 16:6). The word "leaven" is related to "yoke" and used in a similar way. Paul also uses "yoke" with negative connotations in Galatians 5:1 and Acts 15:10 also speaks of the "yoke" of legalism. As elsewhere Paul is not advocating slavery, which he here defines as a "yoke" or burden (even "evil" is an appropriate translation), but rather he is urging the believers who have to endure this "yoke" to try to bear it with goodwill, knowing that God will reward them in heaven. The Spartacus revolt failed. The apostles were not militant revolutionaries, they were missionaries. Here Paul says only that slavery is a "yoke" and an evil.

Sound Doctrine
1 Timothy 6:3

"If anyone advocates a different doctrine and does not agree with sound words, those of our Lord Jesus Christ, and with the doctrine conforming to godliness he is conceited *and* understands nothing."

It is common to hear people say that doctrine is divisive or ask "what difference does it make?" In so doing they show that they neither know what doctrine means nor understand that there is no such things a not having a doctrine. Everyone has a doctrine. Doctrine is the core fundamental beliefs of any person or system. In Christianity doctrine is to be synonymous with *truth*. Was it not Pilate who mockingly asked Jesus "what is truth" (John 18:38)? Like the modern sceptic he denied there was such a thing as truth, but in so doing he was admitting that he was wrong! If we are not true, then we are wrong.

There is a difference in saying that I know all truth and in saying that truth is unimportant. I cannot say that I am always right, but I can say that Jesus is always right. By trying to know Jesus better, I come closer to the truth. The closer I come to the truth, the better I become. Satan's job is the opposite. He wants to guide us away from truth. Sometimes he may tell us that truth is divisive (and it is). Other times he may tell us that there is no truth. Still other times he may tell us that truth is to be found in many different ways. In each case, his purpose is to lead us away from Jesus and make us look elsewhere for the truth.

This is what Paul meant when he said that the one who rejects truth in Christ "is conceited *and* understands nothing." If we look within for the truth then we will find only emptiness. If man were self sufficient we would not need God, nor would the world be filled with sinners. The world is evil because have sought truth within rather than seeking it from the Lord God Himself. Yet in His love He sent us Jesus who declared "I am the Way, the *Truth*, and the Life" (John 14:6). If Jesus is the truth then we can only know truth by seeking Him.

Has the Resurrection of the Dead Already Occurred?
2 Timothy 2:18

There are "*men* who have gone astray from the truth saying that the resurrection has already taken place, and they upset the faith of some."

What did Paul mean when he said that some teach "the resurrection has already taken place"? Obviously it is not a reference to the resurrection of Jesus which is past, but rather Paul is referring to our resurrection which takes place in the future. How then could anyone say *that* has already taken place? A plethora of views have developed to explain this statement. Some believe that it means that "a man lived on in his children"[1373] or that our "'dead selves' have risen to 'higher things.'"[1374]   Some simply say "we do not know"[1375] but the most common theory is one still heard today in liberal churches and seminaries around the world : the idea that the resurrection "is only the spiritual passing from death unto life."[1376]

St. Augustine supposed that they believed the resurrection was merely an allusion to the rebirth and denied a future bodily resurrection,[1377] as many churches do today.   Says the *Liberty Bible Commentary*, "they probably spiritualized the resurrection of the future as the gnostics of the day taught."[1378] So, like the liberal theologian, "death and resurrection were terms which had with these false teachers only a *spiritual* meaning."[1379] Such "spiritualizing" has been done throughout the centuries by cults ranging from the old Marcionites[1380] to the gnostics to the modern day Jehovah's Witnesses and many liberal theologians.   According to Walter Lock they believed "only a spiriutal Resurrection, which took place at Baptism."[1381] This is really just an extension of what John Calvin said in his day; "they invented some kind of allegorical resurrection, as has been attempted in our day."[1382]   The idea of "baptismal initiation"[1383] is one of many ways to allegorize the resurrection, and thus deny a literal resurrection which the wife of my pastor from youth mocked as "zombies rising up from the ground." It is no surprise that when my pastor was dying I came to realize that he wasn't sure there was even a heaven.[1384]

Patrick Fairbain believes this was due to Greek influence.[1385] So also we today tend to compromise in order to win favor with popular ideology. This was the case with the Tübingen liberal school of theology in nineteenth century Germany.   They believed that nature was all that existed and thus "demythologized" the Bible from all supernatural elements. The result was not new converts but the destruction of faith. Further results were two world wars, Marxism, and a decayed culture. As John MacArthur said, "by denying bodily resurrection, they were destroying the very foundation of the Christian faith."[1386] Without the resurrection we have no hope. The idea of disembodied spirits floating on clouds is really a sad dream. Can we not touch, hold, hug, and embrace our loved ones? If we can, then we *must* have some sort of resurrected body as Jesus did!

The resurrection of Jesus is the archetype for our resurrection. It is proof that God can and will resurrect us all. If resurrection is nothing more than "the soul's depature from the body"[1387] when we are no different from the religions of "spiritualism" seen in modern day horror films. There is no hope and no true salvation. The Christian religion becomes nothing more than another philosophy incapable of offering true hope or salvation. This is why the resurrection is the foundation for Christian hope. If Jesus was not resurrected from the dead, then he was just a mere mortal man and we can have no hope of resurrection.   If, however, the resurrection is real then we too shall be resurrected and be at home with our Lord for all eternity. The resurrection is the cornerstone of our hope, our salvation, and our faith.

Character in the Last Days
2 Timothy 3:1-5

"Realize this, that in the last days difficult times will come. For men will be lovers of self, lovers of money, boastful, arrogant, revilers, disobedient to parents, ungrateful, unholy, unloving, irreconcilable, malicious gossips, without self-control, brutal, haters of good, treacherous, reckless, conceited, lovers of pleasure rather than lovers of God, holding to a form of godliness, although they have denied its power."

The world has always been sinful. Wars, murder, rape, and hatred have always plagued the earth. However, in times past people still understood that selfishness was a bad thing. Today, it is considered a virtue under the guise of "self-esteem." Here, however, Paul gives stern warning against these last generations who shall be "lovers of themselves." William Barclay translates this passage as, "men will live a life that is centered in self."[1388] It is a generation when "the spirit of selfishness"[1389] shall reign supreme.

For centuries *self*ishness was considered a vice. The love of self was viewed as intrinsic. We must fight to think of others rather than just ourselves. All this changed in the 1960s. The "me generation" made selfishness a virtue by borrowing from atheistic psychologists. Today we are told by even the most conservative evangelical preachers, "love your neighbor as yourself means love yourself first"! This sad state of affairs reminds us of this prophecy that "men shall be eminently selfish – evidently under the garb of religion."[1390] It is not just selfishness but selfishness which "holds to a form of godliness." It is sin in the guise of righteousness.

The self-esteem movement swept throughout the evangelical church in the 1970s. Although some resisted it, most churches and seminaries not only accepted it, but created their own psychology departments (ignorant of the fact that psychology does not even recognize the foundation of causal science or the fact that its founders, to a man, created psychology as a *substitute* for religion). As Stam commented, "this humanistic attitude is *taught* as a philosophy of life in most of our colleges and universities."[1391] Not only that, it is taught in Seminaries under the guise of Christian psychology which introduced the Flower Child generation to the evangelical church, yet few have been willing to challenge this cult of self worship.

Now to the critic who will ask how it is good to hate one's self, I respond with Ephesians 5:29 which reads, "no one ever hated his own flesh, but nourishes and cherishes it." Self love is *intrinsic*. We only see the world through our own eyes because we are separated from God. This makes us, by definition, selfish. In another word, it makes us sinners. I can think of no one who has put the "self image" issue more in perspective than Dave Hunt and Tom McMahon when they say:

> "God made man in His own image. One thinks immediately of a mirror, which has *one purpose only*: to reflect a reality *other than its own*. It would be absurd for a mirror to try to develop a 'good self-image.' It is equally absurd and certainly unbiblical, for humans to attempt to do so. If there is something wrong with the image in the mirror, then the only solution is for the mirror to get back in a right relationship with the one whose image it was designed to reflect."[1392]

They also commented that "the person who says, 'I'm so ugly, I hate myself!' doesn't hate himself at all, or he would be *glad* that he was ugly. It is because he loves himself that he is upset with his appearance and the way people respond to him."[1393] Jesus is the solution to our problems, not selfishness.

The problem with "self esteem" is the same as the problems with pride. John Piper put it best when he said, "boasting is the voice of pride in the heart of the strong. Self-pity is the voice of pride in the heart of the weak. Boasting sounds self-sufficient. Self-pity sounds self-sacrificing."[1394] They are the flip side of the same problem; not self esteem but selfishness. Gordon Fee said of selfish love, "from such misdirected love all other vices flow."[1395] This "'lovers of self' the worldly self, [is] the first and worst sin."[1396] It is the opposite of what Christ called for when he declared, "if anyone wishes to come after Me, he must *deny himself*, and take up his cross and follow Me" (Matthew 16:24; Mark 8:34; Luke 9:23). This is also why the apostle Paul stated, "He died for all, so that they who live might *no longer live for themselves*, but for Him who died and rose again on their behalf" (2 Corinthians 5:15).

This is a prophecy of "people [who] put themselves on the throne of their lives and thus deny the very essence of Christianity, which is dying to one's self."[1397] Ironside noted that such "self-occupied"[1398] thoughts cannot be God focused and attributed verse six to the rise of modern feminism[1399] which tears down the nobility of the family and motherhood. Oliver Green noted that these are characteristics of dictators,[1400] but now they are the characteristics of a whole generation. According to John Wesley "the time of the Gospel dispensation, commencing at the time of the Lord's death"[1401] but would come to a close when the world had steeped into such selfish religion. We have always been sinners, and we have always been selfish, but in past generations selfishness was never considered a virture until the nineteenth century German philosophers and the rise of modern psychology. Even then the church rejected such heresy until the late twentieth century. Today few even dare to speak out against the "self-esteem" movement. The prophecy has already become past, for "in the last days difficult times will come. For men will be lovers of self, lovers of money, boastful, arrogant, revilers, disobedient to parents, ungrateful, unholy, unloving, irreconcilable, malicious gossips, without self-control, brutal, haters of good, treacherous, reckless, conceited, lovers of pleasure rather than lovers of God, *holding to a form of godliness*, although they have *denied its power.*"

Persecution
2 Timothy 3:12

"Indeed, all who desire to live godly in Christ Jesus will be persecuted."

Living in America I had not known persecution except in its mildest form until recent decades. Even now the impositions and obtrusions into our faith[1402] are mild compared to many countries where Christians risk their very lives by professing in Christ Jesus. Nonetheless, both Jesus and Paul both declared that *all* of us will suffer "persecution in some form or another."[1403] John Wesley clarified this, adding the words "more or less. There is no exception."[1404]

John Calvin asked, "should all people be martyrs? ... Satan has more than one way of persecuting Christ's servants."[1405] Indeed, we often associate persecution with martyrdom, and such is the apex of persecution, but it is not the sole definition. Albert Barnes said "persecution consist in subjecting a person to injury or disadvantage on account of his opinions."[1406] Such is the mild form of persecution to which Christians have been subject throughout history, and yet even in this form the degrees vary. Some countries impose sanctions or taxes upon the faithful, as was tried under the Obama administration in the United States. At other times, such as in my youth, it was merely the bullies, atheists, mockers, and scoffers who chided us and treated us as second class citizens. Throughout history this has always been our lot. At no time in history can anyone point to a time and place in which this was not done. While revisionist historians try to rewrite history, we all know full well that the Reformers were subject to the Inquisition, as were their forerunners; the Puritans fled to America to find freedom; and to this day many die for the faith around the world, such as Iraq where the terror group ISIS has been crucifying Christians including children.

One thing is certain. In the last days when the anti-Christ shall reign, all the true faithful will be subjected to brutal persecution and death. As we draw closer to the end, persecutions and discrimination shall increase. When Paul wrote this epistle the persecutions of Nero had already begun. Paul was reminding believers that if Jesus was persecuted, so shall we. As Jesus said, "If they persecuted Me, they will also persecute you" (John 15:20). We must remain faithful to the end and we shall receive the resurrection of the dead and eternal salvation as our reward.

Inerrancy
2 Timothy 3:16-17

"All Scripture is inspired by God and profitable for teaching, for reproof, for correction, for training in righteousness so that the man of God may be adequate, equipped for every good work."

One would not think that such a simple statement would be so controversial, and yet it is. Those who reject the inerrancy of the Scriptures even boldly proclaim that the Bible does not claim to be inerrant! Ignoring passages such as Proverbs 30:5, Psalms 12:6, 18:30 and elsewhere, the most obvious claim of inerrancy is here in this passage. For this very reason there are many who question its meaning and translation.

Three things are debated in this passage. The first is the very meaning of "inspiration." Does inspiration mean inerrancy? Can something be inspired and still be wrong, or at least only half right? Second, does the Bible really say *all* Scripture is inspired, or just part of Scripture? Finally, what is the profitability of the Scriptures? Are there limits upon its usefulness? Upon these three issues hinge the Biblical claim for inerrancy.

The Definition of Inspiration
Most Bibles translate the Greek word θεοπνευστος (*theopneustos*) as "inspired" (KJV, NKJV, RSV, NRSV, ASV, Douay-Rheims, etc.). However, some have chosen the more literal translation of "breathed out by God" or "God-breathed" (MKJV, NIV, ESV), Indeed, the Greek word θεοπνευστος is literally a compound of the words "God" (θεος) and "breath" or "spirit" (πνευστος). It is "God-breathed." Interestingly enough, the word of "breath" here can also mean "spirit" and thus indicates that "God's spirit" is infused into the Scriptures.

Walter Lock calls this "divinely breathed."[1407] The Scriptures came into being "with *its* breath given by God."[1408] The church father Ambrose chose a more literal translation himself, saying that "every Scripture breathes the divine grace of God."[1409] Donold Guthrie said that Timothy "is being reminded that the basis of its profitableness lies in its inspired character."[1410] The Scriptures are not mere opinion or semi-accurate histories, but the very Word of God breathed from His own spirit.

This leads to the second question. Is it truly every Scripture? Are the Old and New Testaments equally inspired? Was there even such a thing as the New Testament in Paul's day? Was Paul claiming inspiration for himself?

All Scripture, or Just Some?
Frederic Farrar, the Dean of Canterbury, represented the modern liberal viewpoint when he said, "not 'every Scripture *is* inspired' ... but 'every Scripture inspired by God is useful' ... not 'All Scripture.'"[1411] So according to some it is not "all Scripture" but "every scripture inspired of God" as seen in the RV and

ASV. They can then twist this translation to imply that "not 'every Scripture *is* inspired.'"[1412]

John MacArthur calls the RV and ASV bad translations which "leave open the possibility that *some* Scripture is *not* inspire."[1413] Indeed, the later Revised Versions (the RSV, NRSV) corrected the translation to "all scripture is inspired by God." Nonetheless, Origen is first to *allegedly* translate this as "every Scripture inspired by God"[1414] although we can see that this is really an interpretation of an interpretation. Even the translators of the RV and ASV never intended to imply that Paul was leaving open the option of rejecting some portions of Scriptures. It is clear that Paul believed that *all* Scripture, *every* one, was "God-breathed."

Still, it may be fairly asked, what did Paul regard as Scripture? Albert Barnes, for example, argued that "this properly refers to the Old Testament, and should not be applied to any part of the New Testament"![1415] After all, it is argued, the New Testament canon had not even been formed yet. This argument, however, is disingenuous on several levels. First, the canon was not determined by some church council or other human institution as often implied (see Appendix A). The Scriptures were the Scriptures from the day they were written, because they were written by the authority of God through prophets and apostles. Paul repeatedly affirms that he was an apostle, and Peter himself classified Paul's epistles as Scripture in 2 Peter 3:16. Peter also affirms that Scripture, such as Paul's writings, is given by God and God alone (2 Peter 1:19-21).[1416]

Despite this, some argue that the Greek word γραφη (*graphe*) should not be translated as "Scripture" at all, but "writings." This frivolous argument is but a distraction since Paul says it is "God-breathed" in either case. Moreover, "the perpetual meaning of γραφη in the New Testament" is Scripture.[1417] There is no separate word for Scripture, which itself means "sacred writings." Since Paul explicitly identified the "sacred writings" in 3:15, it is clear that he speaking of those *same* writings here. Moreover, since Paul declares they are "God-breathed" then these "writings" can refer to nothing else. So no matter how the so-called liberals try to translate the passage, it always comes back meaning that "every part of these inspired scriptures" is God-breathed.[1418] There is no way around it.

Samuel Ngewa provided the best answer to these critics. He says, "the strongest argument against [partial inspiration] is that Paul nowhere spends any time telling Timothy how to distinguish the specific Scriptures inspired by God from those that are not inspired by Him."[1419] All Scripture means all Scripture.

Profitability

Having established that all Scriptures are inspired by God, literally God-breathed, the Bible then says that all these Scriptures are "profitable for teaching, for reproof, for correction, for training in righteousness; so that the man of God may be adequate, equipped for every good work" (3:16-17). What does this then mean? Some limit the Bible's profitability. We are used to hearing that the Bible is not a "history textbook" or a "science textbook" as if to say that it errs in history and/or science when it speaks to the issue. Certainly the Bible does not exhaustively touch upon these subject, but when it does should we believe it is wrong? Throughout my *Controversies* series I have attempted to show that archaeology, history, and science in no way contradict that to which the Bible speaks. It may not speak to every issue, but where it speaks it is accurate, true, and faithful.

Notice that Paul does not stop by saying that "all Scripture being breathed by God" but adds that means all Scripture is profitbale, then listing "teaching, reproof, correction, training in righteousness; so that the man of God may be adequate, equipped for *every* good work" (3:16-17). Anecdotally, the Greek word ωφελιμος (*ophelimos*) is the last word found in the Biblical Greek lexicon and it means "profitibale," "helpful," or "useful."

William Barclay notes that there are four specific things listed here.[1420] The Scriptures are useful first and foremost for salvation. 2 Timothy 3:15 states, "the sacred writings are able to give you the wisdom that leads to salvation through faith which is in Christ Jesus." These are the Holy Scriptures to which Paul refers in the next verse. The Scriptures are useful to lead us to salvation through faith in Jesus.

Second, they are useful for teaching. Teaching implies knowledge. One cannot teach if they are ignorant. This then refutes those who limit in what the Bible is accurate and profitibale. It may not a "scientific textbook" but when it speaks to issues in science, such as Isaiah 40:22 (which says the world is a sphere), it is accurate and useful for teaching. In fact, a number of great scientist actually developed their principles of science *from* the Bible. Matthew Maury, for example, discovered ocean currents after reading about the "paths of the sea" in Psalms 8:8.[1421] Joseph Lister developed antiseptic surgery because he rejected the myth of spontaneous generation, central to Darwinism.[1422] A long list could ensure. It is sufficient to say that when the Bible speaks, in whatever matter it speaks, it speaks truly and accurately.

Third, the Bible is useful for correction, conviction, and reproof. Although Barclay list these as two separate items,[1423] they are really only one. By convicting us of our sins, correcting our errors and reproofing our mistakes, we learn the truth and grow closer to Jesus who alone can correct those sins, mistakes, and errors.

Finally, it is useful for *every* good work. It is not just "a" good work, but *every* good work. Without God even the most noble of intentions fails. "The road to hell is paved with good intention" was an old, if not entirely true, saying that means that the end does not justify the means. The Bible alone equips us for *all* good works. It is "for the good of a man's own soul."[1424]

Summary

Warren Wiersbe reminds us that the Word of God is what "Satan has attacked from the beginning ('Yea, Hath God said?' Gen. 3:1)."[1425] John Calvin affirmed that "the whole of Scripture ... are not teaching handed down at the whim of men"[1426] but by God Himself. To those who deny Paul's writings are a part of those Scriptures or that Paul even makes such a claim, it should be noted that "one reason why the Apostle declares that 'all Scripture' is God-breathed, is to emphasize the important fact that his writings too are thus inspired (cf. 1 Tim. 4:1; 2 Tim. 1:9-11; 1:13; Tit. 1:2,3)."[1427] Paul was an apostle, not a mere teacher.

I am reminded of a fellow Seminary student who once chided me when I disagreed with one of Albert Einstein's lesser known theories. What I found ironic is that Christians sometimes have more respect for the inerrancy of Einstein than of Jesus and the apostles! He would never think of disagreeing with Einstein on even unimportant issues, like the one I was discussing, but many of us are quick to doubt the Bible's inerrancy. If only we had as much respect for the Bible as we have for men!

Paul affirms clearly and definitively that all Scripture, *all* of the "holy writings" (3:15), are literally given by the very breath of God. They are useful for instructing, teaching, educating, training, and leading us to salvation. In short, all Scripture means all Scripture.

The Rejection of Sound Doctrine
2 Timothy 4:3-4

> "For the time will come when they will not endure sound doctrine; but *wanting* to have their ears tickled, they will accumulate for themselves teachers in accordance to their own desires and will turn away their ears from the truth and will turn aside to myths."

As in 1 Timothy 6:3 Paul again affirms the importance of truth; sound doctrine. Sound doctrine and truth are syonymous. They cannot be distinguished. Here Paul goes one step further. He prophesies of what could be described as our own generation wherein, to quote the NIV, men "will gather around them a great number of teachers to say what their itching ears want to hear." He also says that "we will turn aside to myths."

Irenaeus applied this prophecy to gnosticism,[1428] but it is clear that Paul is speaking of much more than cults and heresies which have plagued us throughout history. He is speaking about a time people will develop a theology that "pleases them"[1429] and their own selfish desire. I am reminded immediately of the "prosperity gospel" and those who teach that "abundant life" means material happiness and financial success. Indeed, some of the most famous and popular preachers and teachers believe that Jesus wanted us to be financially successful and prosperous in the material sense of the world. We gather preachers around us to tell us what we want to hear. Gone are the days when we went to hear what was not pleasing; that we are lost sinners unworthy of Jesus.

John Calvin believed that when Paul said "they will not endure sound doctrine" "he means not only that they will not like it and will despise it, but also that they will actually hate it."[1430] This too can adequately describe many people today. The gospel is too "divisive" we are told. We are further told that we must "bring people into the church" without a word spoken about the gospel. Megachurches thrive on being the biggest, as if that were the best. There is no more shepherding or nurturing; just cattle drives.

As to the myths, my mind instantly takes to images of people who believe that maggots and slugs are our distant cousins. Popular theories of the universe have replaced the Biblical worldview; usually in the name of "science falsely so-called" (cf. 1 Timothy 6:20). Pseudo-science, not true science, has become the playground of the world. The "philosophy" of the Greeks has been replaced with pseudo-sciences such as psychology, Darwinism, and the like.

This passage is parallel to many in the Pauline epistles. Although Paul does not explicitly refer to the Last Days in this passage, it is apparent that he believed this to be the case in the Last Days (cf. 2 Timothy 3:1-5). While such false preachers and worldly followers have always existed, they will magnify over time. Eventually, in the Last Days sound doctrine will be hated and despised as "divisive." We are told that preaching about sin and salvation drives people away from the gospel, as if counting heads were the same as winning a soul for Christ. Such is the time in which we live.

Summary

2 Timothy is most likely the last epistle Paul wrote before he was taken out to the Ostesian road and beheaded for his testimony of Jesus Christ.[1431] He left behind Timothy as his disciple and heir to his ministry. Timothy then served in Ephesus, probably with the assistance of John, until his own martyrdom many years later. With the passing of Paul, John, and Timothy the apostolic age passed into history, but not before Paul left us with these words to help guide us through the ages, even as they guided the young Timothy.

10
—
Titus & Philemon

The two shortest epistles of Paul are Titus and Philemon. Titus was written shortly after 1 Timothy, but before Paul's rearrest and imprisonment. It was written to encourage Titus in the face of opposition at Crete and is generally dated to around 64 A.D. although Merrill Unger places it as late as 65 A.D.[1432] However, since Paul was probably arrested early in 65 A.D. it is more likely that Titus was written the previous year.

Philemon is the more controversial of the two epistles; not because of any reason other than its frequently misquoted treatment of slavery. Onesimus was an escaped slave whom many believe had stolen from his master based on verse 18.[1433] Owing to the fact that Onesimus stood facing crucifixion for his crimes, Paul, having converted him, undertook to write Philemon to accept him back. Some take this as an advocation of slavery, but this is easily refuted (see below). Paul was in no position to change the laws of Rome. This is especially true since he was in prison at the time he wrote the epistle (vv. 1, 23). The question here is which imprisonment? Because of parallels to Timothy and Archippus in Colossians (Colossians 4:17-18; Philemon 1-2), it is assumed that Philemon was written about the same time. it is therefore dated to around 61 or 62 A.D.[1434]

Titus 1:6 – See 1 Timothy 3:2, 12

Church Offices in Biblical Times
Titus 1:7

"The overseer must be above reproach."

There has been much debate over the centuries as to church government and how it was intended to be formed. Catholics have an established hierarchy whereas most Protestants have a Presbyterian style of government, similar to modern democracies which sprang from these Protestants sects.[1435] Some sects even reject pastoral authority and have no pastor at all. They merely rotate church members to perform the duties of a pastor.

Traditionally there have been three forms of church government; episcopal, presbyterian, and congregational. However, some have what has been called a non-governmental system. Each claims to be based upon Biblical precedent, but none can truly prove it. An examination of each of the governmental styles is prudent for the Bible nowhere explicitly defines church government; a fact which in and of itself says a great deal.

293

Episcopal Government

The Greek word for bishop is επισκοπος (*episkopos*) from which we get the word "episcopal." Because the bishop has historically been associated with the episcopal government some translations have opted for more generic translation such as "overseer" (MKJV, NAS, ESV, Darby) or "elder" (NLV). What is most intriguing about this is that the Bible does not *anywhere* define the job or duty of the overseer or bishop. Because the word is singular it is assumed by many that he must be the head of the local church and not merely one of the supporting church authorities such as cardinals or elders.

In the episcopal system of church government there are three primary offices which form a hierarchy. The bishops are at the top, with the priests and deacons below them.[1436] In the Catholic church the Cardinals are a select group of bishops, and the pope is claimed to be the successor of the apostles; the supreme bishop. Some Protestants churches, like the Church of England, also have an episcopal form of government, although they have done away with the papacy, replacing it with an archbishop.

Biblical evidence for the episcopal style of church government is largely presumptive and based on passages involving the authority of the apostles. They then follow from this that the apostles have successors today, and all church members must submit to their authority. A system of hierarchy is then assumed. I addressed the issue of apostolic succession in *Controversies in the Acts of the Apostles*. Here I will merely state my conclusion. There were twelve apostles, and no more. One of the requirements of an apostle is that they had personally met Jesus and been chosen by Him (cf. Acts 1:21-22). Obviously no one living today can make that claim. Further, the lack of support from any direct Biblical quotations of a hierarchical structure is more than mere circumstantial evidence. If the apostles had intended such a hierarchy we might expect that Paul would have said something to establish this fact and highlight the exact duties of the bishops. It follows then by his silence Paul was not particularly concerned with defining the power of the bishops; only their godly credentials.

Presbyterian Government

The name presbyterian comes from the Greek word for elder, πρεσβυτερος (*presbyteros*). Like the office of the bishop or overseer the Bible says nothing about the duties of the presbyter or elder. The Bible is, once again, silent upon their job description. We only know that the plural is used in many cases indicating that there were more than one at local congregations.

On the other hand, while elders are not described in the New Testament, the Jewish synagogues had a well established government whose descriptions can be found in the Talmud and other Jewish writings. It is apparent that the early church, being primarily Jewish, took up the synagogue system in the early Judean churches. Nonetheless, there were differences.

294

In the Christian presbyterian style government, church members elect elders. This is taken from Acts 1:23-26 and 6:3 where elections were held to select Matthias and the seven deacons. Additionally, all elders are held to be of an equal level. Only the pastor, sometimes called a "teaching elder,"[1437] stands apart from the elders, but he is still accountable to them. From this democratic style of church government the early settlers in the northern American colonies developed.[1438] The problem, of course, is the question of whether or not the church should be a democracy. It is apparent, as we have seen in some liberal Protestant denominations, that as society moves away from God, church members often bow to the whims of society as well. For example, gay priests are now allowed in some denominations. Having said this, gay priests are also allowed in some episcopal style churches as well. Indeed, both the Presbyterian church and the Episcopal church have voted to allow gay clergy members so the problem cannot be blamed on a semi-democratic system.

Another strength of the presbyterian style government is the "deliberate coordinating of clergy and laity."[1439] Rather than laity being plebeians or peasants under the rule of a hierarchical clergy, the laity elect representatives among themselves who are qualified and meet the criteria required by the clergy. The two are then connected to one another.

Now some advocates of presbyterian church governments believe that the bishops (επισκοπος) and elders (πρεσβυτερος) are actually synonymous terms.[1440] Albert Barnes claimed that "these elders, or presbyters, were also called bishops."[1441] Since presbyterian governments usually have only elders, or presbyters, they fail to distinguish between the two. This is doubtless why the NLV translations επισκοπος as "elder." According to Mal Couch "in the early church, the bishop was one of the presbyters (elders)."[1442] Nevertheless, while the bishop or overseer may have been a presbyter or elder, the Bible uses two different words for them. Add to this the deacon (διακονος) and it is obvious that clergy were distinguished in one way or another. The question is how we understand those differences.

Congregational Government
A congregational government is similar to the presbyterian government except in two vital areas. First, it is more of a complete democracy, whereas the presbyterian government is closer to a Republic. In the presbyterian government the members elect qualified elders, but the elders run the church. In a congregational government the members vote on virtually all matters. Second, the congregational government is autonomous, meaning that each individual congregation is independent of all others.[1443]

In the first regard it is argued that the Bible does not show anyone, even the apostles, exercising some centralized authority over local congregations. "In Acts and the Epistles the primary focus is upon the local church."[1444] This is natural in at least one sense. How can a board, government, or clergy who do not live in the local community truly understand and deal with the local communities' problems? Local churches are best equipped to deal with the local community and its resources. "Each congregation calls it own paastor and determines its own budget. It purchases and owns property independently of any outside authorities."[1445]

Another supporting aspect of this system is that it honors the priesthood of all believers which has always been a fundamental cornerstone of Biblical Christianity. All church members are equal in the eyes of God (Galatians 3:28), and therefore all have a say in the local church. Conversely, Mal Couch commented that "this is equivalent to the sheep telling the shepherd what to do."[1446] Some believe that church is not and should not be a democracy. Such a view, we are told, leads to inevitable compromise and straying from the gospel, but I have illustrated above the fact that no church is exempt from such compromise. Both episcopal and presbyterian churches have begun to accept gay clergy, so it cannot be proven that congregational governments are any more susceptible to compromise than the other church governments.

In regard to the autonomy of the churches, the Independent Baptist churches are a prime example. The problem is that anyone who has attended Independent Baptist churches knows that no two Independent Baptist churches are alike. One may be a great solid Biblical church whereas the next could be a borderline cult. Because each is completely independent of one another there is no real way to tell what an individual church is going to be like. It is the "box of chocolates" analogy.

Non-Governmental Churches
Some church historians argue that there is actually a fourth church government; ironically called "nongovernmental."[1447] The best example is the old Quakers. They believed that the Holy Spirit was to be the only authority and therefore have no formal government *per se*. In terms of the function of the local church it is similar to the congregational government except that they do not have formal elections, nor a formal budget, nor formal structure. They are literally a group of Christian individuals who meet and hold Bible studies and choose to perform church functions and duties, but have no formal structure. Modern day examples might be the "home church" movement of the 70s which still exist to some extent today. These "home churches" are where local Christians meet together in homes to worship God, hold Bible studies, and act much like a local church without the formal structure of a building or official clergy. In terms of strengths and weaknesses, it is again very similar to the congregational government, but more pronounced in both its strengths and its weaknesses.

Summary and Conclusion
Before determining which church government is best, it is natural to try to understand which is Biblical. Unfortunately the Bible *nowhere* defines church government, not even the duties of the overseers (επισκοπος), elders

($\pi\rho\epsilon\sigma\beta\upsilon\tau\epsilon\rho\sigma$), and deacons ($\delta\iota\alpha\kappa\sigma\nu\sigma$). In fact, Sir Robert Anderson pointed out that ($\delta\iota\alpha\kappa\sigma\nu\sigma$) "is a generic word for servant. It was used both of household servants and of ministers of the gospel; and the Apostle Paul applied it to himself, and even to Christ."[1448]

One thing is certain. The most obvious reason that the Bible does not deliniate a church government is that the apostles simply took up the synagogue system they inherited from the Jews. Certainly some changes were made to accommodate Christian theology and the Lordship of Christ, but the basic structure appears to have been similar with the notable absence of the "priest." In the New Testament only Jesus Christ is called High Priest (throughout the book of Hebrews). Local church leaders are overseers or bishops ($\epsilon\pi\iota\sigma\kappa\sigma\pi\sigma$) only. The elders then occupy the other clergy and duties to be performed at the local church. Deacon ($\delta\iota\alpha\kappa\sigma\nu\sigma$) may well be a generic term for all clergy, just as government workers are supposed to be "public servants."

It would seem then that the presbyterian and congregational governments are closest to the Biblical times, but neither can claim superiority over the other. Perhaps one reason that the Bible does not define the duties of these church offices is because formal church structure was not important to the apostles; the gospel was. Paul corrected churches for their theology, not their government. He instructs members on the truth of the gospel, not on the validity of their leadership organization. What he does do is ensure that church clergy are qualified to lead, as we see below.

Qualifications for Overseers
Titus 1:7-10

"The overseer must be above reproach as God's steward, not self-willed, not quick-tempered, not addicted to wine, not pugnacious, not fond of sordid gain, but hospitable, loving what is good, sensible, just, devout, self-controlled, holding fast the faithful word which is in accordance with the teaching, so that he will be able both to exhort in sound doctrine and to refute those who contradict."

While Paul does not define the duties of the overseer, or elders, he does deliniate their qualification. These "qualifications are partly negative, partly positive."[1449] The first five are disqualifications; the last seven are qualifications. Of note are several things. First, "self-willed" is a disqualification. Contrary to the teachings of "self-esteem" and other modern philosophy, self-willed equals arrogance in the Bible.[1450] Calvin said we are to be "self-controlled. Not self-willed."[1451] This flies in the face of much of what is taught in some churches today. Consider these qualifications and weigh them against many of the mega-church leaders of todays.

Not only do many of today's leaders fall short, but so also do many priests throughout history. Consider another aspect. John Wesley argued that the requirement for one wife was "designed to leave the Romanists without excuse."[1452] Even the early church father Tertullian declared that bishops should be monogmous but not celibate.[1453] He said, "the apostle sets a brand upon those who were want entirely to forbid marriage."[1454]

The pastor is an "overseer of the flock"[1455] and as such must be like a godly father figure. Those who do not live up to these qualifications should be barred from the office. This was Paul's greatest concern. He was not concerned with the church government *per se*, nor with the exact manner of their election, for he discusses neither. What did concern Paul was that pastors be men of good character and intellect; faithful to the Word of the Lord.

Titus 2:13 – See Revelation 1:6-7

Pacifism and the Christian
Titus 3:1-2

> "Remind them to be subject to rulers, to authorities, to be obedient, to be ready for every good deed."

I have discussed this issue in some detail under Romans 13:1-5, as well as cursorily under Ephesians 6:5; Galatians 3:22; 1 Timothy 6:1, and elsewhere. It is again necessary to briefly address the issue here as it relates to the pacifism of the early church. Some believe that because the early church were pacifists, we too should be pacifists no matter what the situation.

As usual, the key to understanding anything is context. First, such pacifism and submission is not absolute. Tertullian said we must submit "so long as we keep ourselves separate from idolatry."[1456] When the government ordered us to sacrifice to idols, we refused even unto death. Still, we did not rebel or take up arms against the Romans. Such military revolts were not only doomed to failure but contrary to the idea that this is not our world. Government is not the solution to our problems; it is too often the cause of them. This is one fundamental aspect of socialism which is virulently anti-Christian for they see the government taking over the traditional roles of the church, and in so doing persecute the church. Polycarp, who was himself martyred, said to "give all due honor (which entails no injury upon ourselves) to the powers and authorities which are ordained by God."[1457]

Others have pointed to the political turmoil of Crete where Titus resided.[1458] "It is said that the Cretans were noted for their rebellious spirit."[1459] The "notoriously turbulent character of the Cretans, of which Polybius tell us"[1460] marks the backdrop of Paul's statement. It should be noted that Barnabas was almost certainly martyred in Crete some ten years earlier.[1461] Persecution then had already come to Crete and Christians were always in danger. Here Paul reminds them that to die a martyr is preferable than to die a rebel.

Submission to government is never absolute, but "to do away with this principal would lead to anarchy."[1462] Some argue that "this context includes the state acknowledging that it has a responsibility to God,"[1463] but Paul does not mention that here, and it is clear that Nero acknowledged only himself. Perhaps Gordon Fee best clarifies the early church's view of submission, saying that "when the state turns against the church ... believers still submit – unto death."[1464]

The Slave Returns
Philemon 15-16

"For perhaps he was for this reason separated *from you* for a while, that you would have him back forever, no longer as a slave, but more than a slave, a beloved brother, especially to me, but how much more to you, both in the flesh and in the Lord."

The Biblical view of slavery is addressed primarily under Ephesians 6:5-9, although I have also discussed aspects of slavery under Romans 13:1-5, Colossians 3:18 - 14:1, and Ephesians 5:22-28. However, Philemon 15-16 warrants special attention for the simple fact that this epistle was written to help secure the return of a slave to his former master. Naturally, this is taken completely out of context to infer Paul's approval of slavery, despite the fact that Paul explicitly says "have him back forever, *no longer as a slave*, but more than a slave, a beloved brother." Philemon then was not returned as a slave, but as a brother in Christ. Several historical and textual facts further strengthen the anti-slavery message of this short epistle.

First, as noted previously, escaped slaves were subject to crucifixion upon capture. Paul had nothing to do with Roman law and actually negotiating a peace which would save Onesimus's life. Second, "no longer as a slave" may indicate that "he needs to be manumitted and eventually set free."[1465] Still, this is a controversial opinion. On one side are those who argue that "it is not certain what kind of servant he was."[1466] In other words, they suggest that he was but a "servant" and not a slave at all. This should be refuted by Paul's own words, for he says Onesimus should "no longer [be] a slave" (vs. 16). Surely if he were a mere servant for hire, there would be no need to send him back at all, for he would have broken no laws and been under no obligation by Rome to return. No, he was certainly an escaped slave.

The other extreme argues that the translation should be softened to "no longer viewed as a mere slave"[1467] as if to imply that his slave status remained unchanged. They argue that he would remain a slave legally, but was now more than *just* a slave. This too is suspect, for Paul emphasizes that, in William Barclay's words, "he went away as a heathen slave; he comes back as a brother in Christ."[1468] Slavery was never accepted by any of the apostles, except slavery to Christ. Paul refers to himself as a slave of Jesus many times,[1469] but nowhere does the Bible endorse or advocate the laws of Rome which crucified Jesus and slew all but one of the apostles. We are strangers in this world and as a pacifist (see above) Paul did not seek another failed Spartacus revolt. He sought instead to return Onesimus "no longer as a slave but ... as a brother."

11

—

Hebrews

Hebrews is so called because it is believed to have been written to Jews and contains the most striking and strong Jewish characteristics of any epistle. Still, Hebrews is a highly controversial book on many levels. Some say it was not actually written to Hebrews, many debate the contents of Hebrews, and its greatest enigma is the fact that the authorship of Hebrews is one of the great mysteries of church history. Even though some Bibles bear the title "the Epistle of Paul to the Hebrews" this title is not actually found in the epistle itself. The title is given by the translators based on tradition, but nowhere does Hebrews identify its author. In addressing these issues alone I found myself running well beyond my allotted writing space, so I created a companion book entitled *Anonymous* which deals exclusively with the authorship of Hebrews and its composition. These issues I will address briefly below, before engaging in the debate over the content of the epistle itself.

The Date and Occasion of the Epistle

The date of the composition of Hebrews is important for several reasons. First, it gives a historical context to certain parts of Hebrews. Second, it helps to identify, or rule out, possible authors of Hebrews.

The wide range of date is between 55 A.D. and 90 A.D. at the latest since it is quoted by 1 Clement in 95 A.D. Several internal evidences help us narrow this down further.

First, it is clear from Hebrews 2:3 that the author of Hebrews "heard" the gospel second hand from the original followers of Christ. The passage indicates that both the readers and the author were second generation believers. Furthermore, the allusion to "former days" in 10:32 suggest that the days of Jesus and the early acts of the apostles were many years in the past. If the author is urging them to remember their "former days" and encouraging them not to abandon their zeal in the coming days of trials and tribulation, then we may logically conclude that *at least* a decade or two had passed. This is further supported by 13:7 where the author asked them to "remember those who led you." If they had to "remember" those who had "led" (past tense) them, then it is obvious that those leaders have either moved on, or more likely, passed on.

Second, despite a plethora of analogies and references to the Tabernacle, there is not a single mention of the destruction of the Temple which is one of the most significant events in Jewish history. To this very day Jews commemorate *Tisha B'Av* (the ninth day of the month of Av), and with good reason. The historical, prophetic, and theological significance of the destruction of the temple cannot be underestimated. Consequently, most agree that Hebrews was written sometime before 70 A.D. when the Temple was still standing.

Third, Hebrews appears to have been written during a time of persecution. Verses 10:32-36 urges the recipients to remain steadfast while 12:4 makes it clear that they may well have to shed their blood. The phrase "not yet" implies that martyrdom is a distinct possibility. This indicates that the epistle was written sometime after the persecutions of Nero, beginning in 64 A.D. and the co-inciding Great Revolt of Israel which began in 66 A.D. Logically it follows that the epistle must have been written no earlier than 65 or 66 A.D.

Fourth, Hebrews 13:23 states that "our brother Timothy has been released." Timothy, of course, was imprisoned by Nero during the infamous persecutions in which Peter and Paul met their martyrdom. It is likely that Timothy was not released from prison until after Nero's death in 68 A.D. This would then further fix the date for Hebrews sometime after 68 A.D.

Lastly, Hebrews 10:29-31 offers a strong indication that the Great Revolt of Israel, and perhaps even the siege of Jerusalem, had already begun.

> "How much severer punishment do you think he will deserve who has trampled under foot the Son of God, and has regarded as unclean the blood of the covenant by which he was sanctified, and has insulted the Spirit of grace? For we know Him who said, 'Vengeance is mine, I will repay.' And again, 'The LORD will judge His people.' It is a terrifying thing to fall into the hands of the living God" (10:29-31).

Such a sober warning of coming judgment fits well against the backdrop and context of the letter. Those Jews who followed Christ had been rejected as heretics and were cast out. Logically, the warnings and discussion of Levitical practices written to a Jewish audience make the most sense against the backdrop of this war which had begun in 66 A.D. This is further evidence that Hebrews should be dated after the rebellion began.

Based on these facts, it is apparent that Hebrews had to have been written after 66 A.D. and before 70 A.D. I believe the evidence favors a date much closer to 70 A.D., probably around 68 or 69 A.D. The occasion of the epistle then corresponds to this seige of Judah and the coming destruction of Jerusalem. The Jewish believers to whom Hebrews was written were being guided and instructed on how to follow Christ after this judgment has come and passed.

Who Were the Recipients?

The title "Hebrews" reflects an almost universal tradition that the epistle was indeed written to Hebrews: "Almost" but not quite. Some believe that gentiles were the recipients, but even among those who believe it was written to Jews, there is debate as to exactly where the epistle was directed. Was it Jerusalem or Jews outside of Judea? The answer is important primarily because it is often used as evidence as to the identity of the author of Hebews. Briefly I will summarize the different theories.

Some argue that the explanation of Jewish law would not have been necessary if the author was writing to Jews and the appearance of Jews in Hebrews does not negate a predominantly gentile audience.[1470] However, the author is not so much explaining Jewish law, as if the readers did not know it, but demonstrating how Jesus is the ultimate fulfillment of the law. If you wanted to present the gospel to your Hindu friend, which book would you use; Romans or Hebrews? The answer to this invalidates the theory that the recipients were gentile in any great number.

Others have argued that the recipients were not only Jews but priests. Ceslas Spicq believed that the Jews were priests formerly from the Qumran community.[1471] On the other hand J.V. Brown argued that they were actually the Jewish priests of Acts 6:7.[1472] Although the evidences are suspect, there seems little doubt that there were some priestly converts among the recipients. Moreover, if the date for the epistle of Hebrews, which I offered above, is correct is more than likely that Christian priests were driven out of Jerusalem shortly before the Roman siege. This would explain their concerns about ritual sacrifices, which would soon be halted. This may also be hinted at by Josephus who even considered the siege of Jerusalem to be God's punishment for the murder of James the Just![1473] Thus, he states that the siege began shortly after the apostle's martyrdom in Jerusalem. During this time the rebel leaders would have expelled Christians from Jerusalem, if they had not already been expelled after James's death. This then begs the question. Were the recipients actually in Jerusalem at the time Hebrews was written? If they had been driven out of Jerusalem, then where were they? Upon this there is no agreement. No fewer than nine different locations have been suggested over the years.

Some of the questionable suggestions have been offered over the years from Ephesus, Galatia, and Cyprus to Alexandria, Egypt and Rome. The latter two are intriguing if suspect, and I discuss these in *Anonymous* for those interested in the debate. My conclusion, however, is that Hebrews was written to Jewish Christian refuges somewhere in Palestine.

The belief that Hebrews was written to Jews in Jerusalem has been a long standing view of many scholars. The three primary evidences are the fact that the audience appears to have been predominantly Jewish; that Hebrews 13:12 appears to indicate a familiarity with the city's layout;[1474] and the belief that Hebrews 10:32-34 refers to persecution of Jews[1475] which would have occurred in Judea during the Great Revolt. However, some question why Hebrews was apparently written in Greek rather than Hebrew if it was written to Jerusalem. The strongest argument against Jerusalem is the date of the composition of Hebrews. If it was written in 68 or 69 A.D. then Hebrews

10:29-31 is probably an allusion to the Great Revolt and/or the siege of Jerusalem. If this is true then it is impossible that Jewish Christians were still living in the city. They would have been driven out by the rebels after the martyrdom of James the Just, described in Josephus.[1476]

If the recipients had left, or been driven out, of Jerusalem, then we might ponder to where they had fled. Antioch is one of the most popular choices. In the book of Acts it is listed as the relocated center of the apostles' ministry (cf. Acts 11, 14-15). Another suggestion has been Caesarea, but there seems little evidence to promote one city over another. It is likely that the Christians of Jerusalem did relocate to another city, but this relocation did not cease persecution as the author of Hebrews warned that they may soon face death (12:4). So it is most likely that Hebrews was written to Jews, including some priestly converts, who had been driven out of Jerusalem and were living somewhere inside Judea or Samaria.

Who Wrote Hebrews?

Tradition has often assigned Hebrews to Paul which is why some Bibles even erroneously entitle the book "the Epistle of Paul to the Hebrews." This title, however, is not found in the epistle and is not a part of the inspired Scriptures. It is a title given by the translators. It is also almost certainly incorrect. For one thing Hebrews appears to indicate that the author never met Jesus (2:3) whereas Paul often appealed to meeting Jesus on the road to Damascus to support his apostolic authority. Moreover, if Hebrews was written in the late 60s then Paul was already dead as he died in 65 A.D. under Nero's brutal persecution.[1477]

Now inasmuch as I wrote the 150 page companion piece *Anonymous* to debate the candidates for Hebrew's authorship I will here only summarize the qualifications, candidates, and my conclusions. As many as eighteen different names have been put forth as possible authors. Of these eighteen most are disqualified by virtue of seven different qualifications which I believe the author must have met based on Hebrews itself. Those criteria are as follows.

First, the author was almost certainly Jewish. He speaks with authority on matters of Judaism and several passages imply a Jewish author as well (cf. 2:16). Second, the author wrote shortly before the fall of Jerusalem as indicated in my timeline above. The author obviously must have been alive between 68 and 69 A.D. Third, although some doubt that Hebrews was originally written in Greek, the evidence is strong that it was at the very least translated into Greek by the original author (see notes in *Anonymous* for this defense). Consequently, the author must have been fluent in Greek as Hebrews displays some of the best Greek in the Bible. Fourth, the author never met Jesus. This appears to be the case based on Hebrews 2:3 and his identification of himself with second generation believers. Fifth, the author was well educated and eloquent in speech and discourse. Sixth, the author was and associate of Timothy based on Hebrews 13:23. Finally, the author spoke as one with authority to the Jewish community.

Based on these seven criteria the probability of the eighteen major candidates is as follows:

Candidate	Probability Factor
Clement of Rome	Possible
Mark	Possible
Apollos	Possible, but unknown
Luke	Possible, but not likely
Silas	Improbable, but possible
Aquila	Doubtful
Aquila and Priscilla	Doubtful
Paul	Doubtful, but possible
Barnabas	Highly doubtful
Jude	Unlikely, but possible
Timothy as co-author	Unlikely
Epaphras	Unlikely
Philip the Evangelist	Highly unlikely
Aristion	Highly unlikely
Titus	Extremely unlikely
Peter	Virtually impossible
Priscilla	Impossible
Timothy as sole author	Impossible

Notice that none of the candidates completely fits the bill. Only the top four are listed as "possible" and none of those candidates truly have any strong evidence in their favor. They have not been excluded on account of the criteria, but neither do they have strong evidence in their favor. Clement, for example, was probably not a Jew. Although it is possible, there is no real evidence to prove that Clement was a Jew with authority to speak to Judean refugees. Mark and Apollos are also possible candidates but there is no tradition of either in antiquity. This would be odd if one of them had indeed written Hebrews. Luke is also a surprisingly strong candidate but he was almost certainly a gentile based on Colossians 4:10-14. The other candidates all fall short on at least two of the seven criteria.

The truth is that we do not know who wrote Hebrews. It is an anonymously written epistle, but one with authority. The recipients knew who wrote it, but did not leave behind evidence of that knowledge. Whoever the author was will be given due glory by God in heaven. For us here on earth we can only say that it was written by the inspiration of the Holy Spirit. As to the rest, I can only quote Origen; "who wrote this epistle only God knows."[1478]

Was Christ More than an Angel?
Hebrews 1:5-13

"For to which of the angels did He ever say, 'You are My son, today I have begotten you'? And again, 'I will be a father to him and he shall be a son to me'?"

The author of Hebrews argues for the divinity of Christ using the Old Testament. He specifically argues that Jesus was much more than a mere angel; something which flies in the face of some cults such as the Jehovah's Witnesses who maintain that Jesus was an archangel. So was Jesus an archangel or much more than that?

John Brown commented that the author's point is that Jesus could not have been an angel of any kind. *"He* has a throne; *they* have a station before it. He is the ruler. They are but subjects. And His rule is not temporary, but perpetual : He reigns, and He shall reign for ever and ever."[1479]   There is more evidence in the quotation of Psalms 45:6, "Your throne, O God, is forever and ever, and the righteous scepter is the scepter of His kingdom" (Hebrews 1:8). It is Jesus who will sit upon this throne. Said Robert Govett, this Psalm "had no real fulfillment in Solomon's day; for it begins with the view of a warrior-king ... its describes the time of rejoicing which shall follow the Savior's victory in millennial days."[1480]

Such an interpretation is not strictly Christian at all. James Moffatt showed us that "Rabbinic traditions corroborate this interpretation."[1481]   The Jews themselves understood that it was a Messianic prophecy. So these quotations "are designed to show the Hebrew readers, from their own *Septugaint*, the superiority of Christ above the angels."[1482] He was not an angel, archangel or otherwise, but Messiah, God incarnate; superior to all other beings and sits upon the very throne of God (cf. Hebrews 1:8).

Angels
Hebrews 1:14 – 2:9

"Are they not all ministering spirits, sent out to render service for the sake of those who will inherit salvation?"

Hebrews is a favorite for the study of angelology. Although these passages are a continuation of the author's evidence that Jesus is more than an angel, they obviously give us a number of hints about the nature of angels and their purpose. This is a key passage, but no means the only passage in Hebrews which speaks of angels. A brief examination of the doctrine of angels is prudent.

What Are Angels?

Although science fiction has us pondering the existence of aliens from other planets, the Bible has only one breed of alien species; angels. These beings do not live on other planets or develop, strive, and grow like humans, for they have an entirely different purpose than man. They were created by God before man (Job 38:4, 7) and probably before the earth or even the physical universe as we know it. We do not know how long they existed, but we know that God already had a plan for mankind (cf. Colossians 1:15-20).[1483]

The word angel itself literally means "messenger." In ancient Hebrew the term "sons of God" was the proper name for angels.[1484] The first appearance of the word "angel" in the Bible is found in Genesis 16:7 where he is literally described as a "messenger of the Lord." The Hebrew word is מַלְאָךְ (*malak*) and the Greek word, found in the *Septuagint*, is αγγελος (*angelos*) from which we get the word "angel." Since angels are often messengers of the Lord, the term eventually became synonymous with the spirit "sons of God." Nevertheless, even then the Hebrew word מַלְאָךְ (*malak*) continued to be used of royal messengers as well as angelic ones.

Angels are actually found under many different names in the Bible. In addition to "sons of God" and "angels" the various titles which have been attached to one of more angels include "thrones, cherubim, seraphim, mights, dominions, powers, principalities, and archangels."[1485] They are sometimes classified into various groups, but these classifications often appear to overlap. For example, Michael is described as an archangel (Jude 9) but some then classify cherubim as a separate classification of angels.[1486] The problem is that it is by no means clear that an archangel cannot also be a cherubim or seraphim. Of course some argue that cherubim or seraphim "may be identical."[1487] This is rejected by C. I. Scofield who remarked that "the Cherubim or living creatures are not identical with the Seraphim of Isaiah 6:2-7. They appear to have to do with the holiness of God as outraged by sin; the Seraphim with uncleanness in the people of God."[1488]

A comparison of Ezekiel 1 and 10 with Isaiah 6:2-7 should dispel any doubt that they are the same, although the similiarities are obvious since "angels may be a part of the genus of spirits."[1489] So describing two different breeds of cats may vary widely, but they would still have basic similarities. The real question is whether or not such physical descriptions should be taken literally at all. In this I am reminded of the story of an explorer who returned home with fantastic tales that no one believed. In one case he described something like a living rock which swam in the water and whose nose was as large as its head, and whose mouth was like a giant cave. No one believed him, but it was eventually discovered that he was referring to a Hippopotamus. The natural appearance of angels is different from anything on this earth, so it is little wonder that Ezekiel and Isaiah's description sounds like fantasy, but such is not a valid argument to reject it as a literal physical description (see Revelation 4:6-8 and the photos there).[1490]

It is clear, however, that whatever their natural appearance may be they are spirits and are often invisible (cf. Colossians 1:16; Ephesians 6:12). Nevertheless, on many occasions they can look like mortal men (Hebrews 13:2; Genesis 16:7; Genesis 19:1-5; Mark 16:5; Luke 24:4; Acts 1:10; etc.).[1491]

In short, there are at least two different kinds of angels, cherubim and seraphim. Both of these are a part of the same species who have no compare on earth. They are spiritual beings who can take on physical forms but are often invisible. Their bodies may be compared to the resurrected bodies which we will have upon our glorification, physical appearances notwithstanding (Matthew 22:30).

Our Status

Having described angels, the immediate question which comes to mind is their relation to us. The differences between men and angels are pronounced in this life. Men can die; angels cannot. Men are bound by our physical bodies; angels can appear in physical bodies but are not bound by mortal flesh. Men grow old; angels stay the same forever. In all these ways, and many more, mankind was made "a little lower than the angels" (cf. Hebrews 2:7), and yet yet the Bible makes clear that we will be raised above angels, even judging the angels (1 Corinthians 6:3).

Perhaps nothing is more startling than the simple fact that Jesus died for the sins of man, but not for angels. Hebrews 2:16 declares that "He does not give help to angels, but He gives help to the descendant of Abraham." Why?

The very fact that man is currently lower than angels and are bound in "flesh and blood" (2:14) indicates that we must persevere. Hebrews says that men are "through fear of death subject to slavery all [our] lives" (2:15). These are things no angel ever had to endure or suffer; but they are things Jesus Himself suffered when He made Himself a mortal man and suffered unto death. So if we persevere and trust in Christ, then we will be lifted up and elevated above the angels. The Bible then makes clear that angels are "ministering spirits [which] indicates the servant status of angels."[1492] That brings us to the purpose for angels.

The Purpose of Angels

Why were angels created? Were they created solely to serve men, even though they are above us? James Montogomery Boice believes that there are three purposes for angels. The first is to worship God. The second is to serve God. The last, he says, is to "assist and defend God's people."[1493] Hebrews asks, "Are they not all ministering spirits, sent out to render service for the sake of those who will inherit salvation?" (1:14). Here "the interogative mode of expression, as it occurs in this verse, is not used to indicate any doubt or uncertainty on the part of the writer, but just the reverse."[1494] The answer is affirmative. It is a rhetorical question. Angels are "ministering spirits, sent out to render service for the sake of those who will inherit salvation."[1495]

The idea of guardian angels stems from this passage.[1495] Although it is not clear that every person has an individual guardian angel, it is apparent that the angels protect us in accordance with God's will. Bede said that "angels are frequently present, invisibly, at the side of the elect, in order to defend them from the snares of the cunning enemy."[1496]

Angels are also seen in Revelation and elsewhere holding back evil and restraining the works of demons. However, as Arthur Pink said, "the angels are *ministering* spirits,' they are not *governing* spirits."[1497] They serve as God's policemen; not his governors. They do only what they are permitted and allow what God allows. They may restrain evil on our behalf, or upon God's wrath unleash the evil they had formerly restrained. In every sense they are servants of God. This very fact leads to the final question.

Satan's Jealousy

Satan was a cherub (Ezekiel 28:14, 16).[1498] He was called the Morning Star (Isaiah 14:12). The name Lucifer comes from the Latin meaning "light bearer" or "morning star." He was among the greatest of the angels, but his pride was his downfall. He knew that man was to be the glory of God's creation. The angels are not omniscient, but neither are they ignorant. They knew from the start God's plan, and Satan knew that his glory would be humbled by man. This jealousy is what led to Satan's rebellion.

Revelation 12:4 says that a third of the stars were cast from heaven. This is universally held to refer to the rebellion of angels (Revelation 12:4-9). "The great dragon was thrown down, the serpent of old who is called the devil and Satan, who deceives the whole world; he was thrown down to the earth, and his angels were thrown down with him" (Revelation 12:9). So then a third of the angels followed Satan and became demons. Yet the Bible is also clear that when Jesus was to be born, the demons did not seek repentance, but sought vengeance upon the children of God. Jesus died for the sins of man, but not for angels. This fact is both humbling and revealing.

Demons do not repent. They never sought repentance. They seek only vengeance and wrath upon the children of God. Jesus gives mortal men a lifetime to repent and turn from our sins, but the demons either cannot or will not repent. This too adds to Satan's hatred of man. He is like the spoiled child who hates the new born son who takes attention away from him. He knows his eternal fate. Let the reader not doubt that Satan is no fool. He knew from the beginning that he was doomed to eternal punishment and it is for this very reason that his hatred and wrath are unparalleled (Revelation 12:12).

Summary

Jesus lowered Himself to our level. Consider whether we would ever choose to be a dog or a horse in order to serve the one we love; and yet God is so far above us, above even the angels, that His choice to dwell as a man is beyond humility. He degraded Himself not only in becoming a man, but a poor man born in a barn.

Because He suffered God glorified Him in His resurrection. He is raised far above the angels so that everything is under His feet (Hebrews 2:7-8). So also because of what we have endured, those of us who trust in Christ will also be elevated in the resurrection so that we will ourselves judge the angels (1 Corinthians 6:3). For this reason the Bible says that angels are "ministering spirits, sent out to render service for the sake of those who will inherit salvation" (1:14).

Jesus and Temptation
Hebrews 2:18

"For since He Himself was tempted in that which He has suffered, He is able to come to the aid of those who are tempted."

Can God be tempted? Does not James 1:13 state explicitly that "God cannot be tempted by evil"? How then can Jesus be said to have been tempted? This is a major controversy seized upon by religious cults, Bible critics, and sincere believers alike. How can Jesus be tempted? Answers have varied from heretical to frivolous, and yet the true answer is fundamental in understanding both Christ's compassion for us, His deity, and His sinless nature.

The Nature of His Temptation

Some believe that the Incarnation eliminates temptation.[1499] Since "God cannot be tempted by evil" (James 1:13) then they interpret temptation to mean merely to be tested. One author said, "the verb *peirastheis* ('tempted') sometimes means 'tested,' and here it might conceivably apply to the sufferings simply as trials to be endured."[1500] Such a view eliminates the problem with temptation, but also eliminates the empathy to which Jesus feels for us when we are tempted.

Various translations have been rendered, which reflect a particular interpretion. The Greek itself reads, πεπονθεν αυτος πειρασθεις (*peponthen autos peirastheis*) which is most literally translated "he having suffered he himself was tempted." Obviously this doesn't translate well into English. What is the relationship of suffering to temptation, or is there a direct relationship at all? Five different translations have appeared.[1501] Some translate this as "he himself hath suffered being tempted" (KJV, NKJV, RV, Webster, ASV, Darby). Some read that some read "he himself has suffered and been tempted" (RSV, NLV, Tyndale, Wycliff, Douay-Rheims, Geneva). Others that "He Himself was tempted in that which He has suffered" (NAS). Still others that "he himself was tested by what he suffered" (NRSV). Finally, some say, "he himself suffered when he was tempted" (NIV, ESV). Each of these translations conveys an interpretation. Let us look briefly at the ideas behind them.

The first is the most literal, but ambiguous of translation. This is perhaps best, for it leaves to the reader to gauge the context instead of deciding it for him. Of course, this also means that it does not give us an answer to the question, so we must continue our search for the answer.

The second translation interprets the temptation and suffering as separate; "he himself has suffered and been tempted." The problem is that there is a και (kai), meaning "and." The Greek makes it clear that there is a relationship between the temptation and suffering. The problem is in determining what that relationship may be, but there is definitely a relationship.

The third translation defines the relationship, arguing that His temptation was "in that which He suffered" (NAS). This is the view of Leon Morris cited in the first paragraph of this section. It is also supported by scholars like Franz Delitzsch.[1502] They, therefore, prefer the idea of "testing" rather than temptation. Albert Barnes said the word can mean "tried" or "put to the proof."[1503] This interpretation then suggest that Jesus was "tested" by way of suffering rather than being tempted by evil. So while this eliminates the problem with James 1:13 it, again, eliminates the empathy to which Jesus feels for us when we are tempted. The relationship between temptation and suffering must be explored more fully.

The fourth translation is similar to the second and conveys a similar idea. Thomas Aquinas believed that the temptation was "not in the flesh, but by the enemy."[1504] His suffering and temptation were connected in that Jesus could have chosen not to suffer. He could have taken the easy path and chosen not to suffer and die for us. This is theologically one of the strongest views, but it should be examined more closely as I will do in the next section.

The last translation is another version of the same idea found in the last two. It differs in that his temptation was "when" He was suffering. This conveys the idea that Jesus could have allowed His suffering to embitter Him. He did not have to forgive His persecutors from the Cross. Again, the theology is sound, but we must examine all the temptations of Christ to better understand what the author of Hebrews meant, for His temptation and suffering also allows Him to empathize with us. Does this translation take that into account?

As strange as it may seem, I prefer the ambiguous translation of the King James, Darby, and ASV. One of the last three translations may better convey the true meaning of the text, but I believe that whenever the meaning is unclear, it is best to translate as literally as possible, even if it is somewhat ambiguous. This compels the reader to study the context and reach his own conclusions rather than relying on the interpretation of the translator.

The Substance of His Temptation

The best way to understand the exact relationship between Jesus's temptation and suffering is to look at the temptation which Jesus faced. According to William Gouge, there were six periods of temptations Jesus faced in the gospels.[1505] By examining those we may better understand what the author of Hebrews meant by "temptations" and the empathy which resulted from them.

Temptation # 1 : Fasting in the Wilderness (Matthew 4:2-4; Luke 4:2-4)

Although the fasting in the wilderness is really related to the first temptation of Satan I will not quibble, for its nature is different from the other temptations Satan offered Jesus. Here the temptation was purely one of physical weakness and need. Our mortal bodies need nourishment. The purpose for fasting is to help us realize the fragility of our mortal frames, and turn to and appreciate God all the more. Fasting is a spiritual practice. The temptation was then to eat when he was extremely hungry.

How does this temptation relate to James 1:13? It does not, for the temptation here is not to do evil, but to put physical needs before spiritual needs. Yielding to such a temptation is not in itself evil, but can lead indirectly to evil by drawing us away from the spiritual. Is not "daily bread" one of the first requests found in the Lord's Prayer? Such physical sustenance is not evil in itself, but when it tempts us to place spiritual things afterwards, it is a danger. This was the temptation which Jesus rejected, and His very answer to Satan proved this. "Man shall not live on bread alone, but on every Word that proceeds out of the mouth of God" (Matthew 4:4; Deuteronomy 8:3). Bread sustains us physically, but it is God who gives us life.

Temptation # 2 : Satan's Temptations (Matthew 4:5-10; Luke 4:5-13)

Satan offered two more temptations. He tempted Jesus to prove He was who He said He was, and He tempted Him with the very kingdoms of the earth. Now I have discussed the question of whether or not the kingdoms are Satan's to give in *Controversies in the Gospels*. The point is only the nature of the temptation and whether or not it conflicts with James 1:13.

Here the temptation was to choose the easy way. As F.F. Bruce said, "time and again the temptations come to Him from many directions to choose some less costly way of fulfilling that calling than the way of suffering and death."[1506] Some will argue that since the temptation was to worship Satan, Jesus had to have been tempted by evil, but the temptation was not to worship Satan, but to reject the Way of the Cross. Satan was not the enticement, nor the reward, but the vehicle. If Jesus wanted to yield to the temptation to take the easy path, he would have to choose the vehicle of Satan. Evil was not the temptation, but the tempter. This is a fundamental difference. Most of us are tempted by evil itself. We are tempted to yield to sin. Jesus was not. Let me make an illustration to prove this point. Suppose a beautiful woman offers herself to us for nothing. She is the object of the temptation. Now suppose

Satan asks us to worship him with nothing in return. This is no temptation to any man. He demands worship as a condition to granting the temptation. The temptation he offered Jesus was a quick and easy path. Satan was not the temptation himself, and therefore Jesus could not be said to have been tempted by evil, although evil would have been the result.

Temptation # 3 : Temptations of Pharisees

Gouge believed that the Pharisees' grieving of Jesus was a temptation.[1507] While this could be disputed, there is some validity in it. The temptation was to give in to some desire but to stop caring; to give up hope. The temptation was to give up the Pharisees for lost. Once again, the temptation appears to have been choose the quick and easy path. It was not to yield to sin, but to give up.

Temptation # 4 : Peter's Temptation (Matthew 16:23; Mark 8:33)

Peter did what most of us would do. He swore to Jesus that he would let no harm come to Him. Jesus's response then shocked Peter and was as harsh as any: "Get behind me Satan!" Such strikingly harsh words illustrate how severe the temptation was at that point. His arrest was nearing and the time of Passion was approaching. The temptation to choose the easy path was growing ever increasingly strong.

Temptation # 5 : Gethesamane (Matthew 26:39; Mark 14:36; Luke 22:42)

Dr. Lenski once said that "all of the preliminary temptations ... were only preludes to the final one in Gethsemane."[1508] In the Garden Jesus prayed "take this cup from Me." The temptation to reject the Way of the Cross was at its peak, but Jesus overcame the temptation and prayed, "Your will be done." He prayed that God's plan prevail. In this was His triumph. As John Darby said, "the feelings of His soul, and the temptations of Satan, were before His actual death, in the garden of Gethsemane,"[1509] but in overcoming the temptation to reject the path of suffering, He became triumphant and proved Himself Messiah.

Temptation # 6 : His Sufferings

Finally, the sufferings of the Passion were themselves all part of the temptation. Time and time again a single word from Jesus could have saved His life during the trials. Time and time again Jesus remained silent. Of the few times He spoke, He enraged His enemies by declaring Himself king of the Jews (cf. Matthew 27:10). So also his enemies mocked Him saying, "if You are the Son of God, come down from the cross" (Matthew 27:40). This was no mere mocking, but a real temptation. Jesus could have done just that; but had He done that, we would all be damned and salvation would never have come to the world. "He suffered, never yielded."[1510]

The reader can see that almost every temptation Jesus faced was one of choosing the easy path. It was not a temptation to sin or to yield to evil, such as what James was speaking of, but a temptation to reject the Way of the Cross and leave us all without savlation.

Conclusion

The nature of temptation is to surrender. While the vast majority of temptations are a yielding to sin and evil, there is also temptations which are not evil in themselves, but which always lead us away from God and/or His intended path for our lives. Jesus was tempted many times to surrender to the quick and easy path, and yet He never yielded. So it is true that Jesus was not "tempted by evil" (cf. James 1:13). James does not say that "God cannot be tempted" but that "God cannot be tempted *by evil*" (James 1:13).

Consequently, while Jesus was never tempted by evil as we sometimes are, He understood temptation and the desire to surrender. Because He was tempted He is able to understand and empathize with our temptations. Even though the object of our temptations may be different, the desire to surrender remains the same. His temptation lie in taking the easy path and rejecting the path of suffering. His triumph was in that He did not yield to such temptations.

Hebrew 4:12 – See 1 Thessalonians 5:23

Can You Loose Salvation?
Hebrews 6:4-6 (See also Hebrews 10:26-27)

> "For in the case of those who have once been enlightened and have tasted of the heavenly gift and have been made partakers of the Holy Spirit, and have tasted the good word of God and the powers of the age to come, and *then* have fallen away, it is impossible to renew them again to repentance, since they again crucify to themselves the Son of God and put Him to open shame."

Hebrews 6:4-6 ranks as one of the most controversial passages in the whole of the New Testament; even the entire Bible. The fundamental question is whether or not one can "loose" their salvation. This question cuts to the core of the debate between Protestants and Catholics, as well as many other sects/cults. Nevertheless, not even Protestants and Catholics are united in their interpretations. By no means can this be considered solely a Reformation issue.

In researching this book I did not find a single evangelical Christian author who *claims* to believe that we can loose salvation. However, a number of evangelical authors parse their sentences very carefully, so that what they claim to say and what they *seem* to be saying are not consistent. William Newell is a prime example of the evangelical Protestant who denies it is possible to loose salvation, while at the same time appearing to say that we cannot know whether or not we are saved. In this respect, Newell agrees with Catholicism whether he is willing to admit it or not.

Robert Govett said of this that "the language of the passage is notoriously ambiguous."[1511] Perhaps, if so, this is why it is a passage often taken out of context. Nowhere is this more evident than in the Novatian schism of the third century. During the brutal persecutions which arose in the first two and a half centuries of the church, some renounced Christ and sacrificed to Caesar in order to save their lives. When the persecutions were over many of these men and women repented and asked to be rebaptized into the church. Novatian cited this passage as proof that they were forever damned and could never repent again, but is this really of what the author of Hebrews was speaking?

Edwin Long – Diana or Christ – 1881

The *Liberty Bible Commentary* suggest that there are essentially four different interpretations upon eternal security in this passage,[1512] but I have found nine. Of course it is possible to parse the views, for several of them are similar and even overlapping. Depending on how we parse the interpretations it is possible to have even more than nine. Nevertheless, I prefer overparsing to generalizing too much.

View # 1 : Apostasy of True Believers
The first interpretation is obviously the one which creates the controversy. If we can loose our salvation then is it truly possible for us sinners to be saved at all? If we must work to keep our salvation then is it salvation by faith, or salvation by works? Can the grace of God be lost, and if it can, is it really grace at all?

In favor of this view is the fact that the author "is not intending to raise obstruse questions in philosophy or in theology. This warning ... is a practical exhortation ... as it points out the absolute hopelessness of apostasy."[1513] It is a warning. It is an exhortation. The epistle was almost certainly written in times of persecution[1514] and was a warning against denying Christ simply to escape persecution, but that alone does not answer the question, for it could imply that "people who deliberately abandon their Christian confession of faith are beyond recovery"[1515] and it was this very interpretation that led to the Novatian schism of the third century (see notes on View #5).

The key to interpretation hinges in part upon the meaning of "impossible." Some prefer to translate this as "difficult" rather than impossible,[1516] thereby leaving the door open for repentance. One scholars said, "with men it is impossible ... but with God all things are possible."[1517] The Greek word is αδυνατος (adunatos).[1518] This word is the anti-thesis of δυναμαι (dunamai) meaning power or ability. Thus αδυνατος (adunatos) means powerless or unable. There is no way to get around this. If we accept this interpretation then must accept that "the impossibility here spoken of is a real one. Spiritual death is supposed to have come upon the apostate."[1519] We must close the door to any hope, if this view is correct.

So the next key hinge is whether or not this does refer to true believers. Albert Barnes seemed to think so when he said, "it seems to me that it refers to true Christians; and that the subject is to keep them from apostasy, and that it teaches that if you should apostatize, it would be impossible to renew them again to save them."[1520] Milligan also believed that these were "truly converted" individuals whose "hearts have been so hardened by sin, that no power consistent with the will and government of God can soften them."[1521]

In order to soften the blow which such a position strikes against the grace of God men like William Newell argue that it applies to those who "willfully cast away known revealed truth"[1522] and "it is not a falling into sin that is meant, but a falling away from God, from Christ, from salvation."[1523] He argues that the "the gift of God" in verse four "is eternal life"[1524] and thus if one has had the gift and reject it, they cannot be saved, but this is the logical problem. If the gift of God is eternal life and we had it, how can we loose it? If you don't have eternal life, you never had it. *You can't loose something which is eternal!*

John Wesley argued that "of these wilful, total apostates, it is impossible to renew them again to repentance (though they were renewed once)"[1525] and Newell compares their apparent possession of the Holy Spirit (cf. v. 4) with King Saul.[1526] He then laments the "present day trend of false security"[1527] but elsewhere he says "we are not at all questioning the blessed doctrine of the security of Christ's sheep ... [but] ... there is then a 'choosing' by Christ, and an association with Him, which may not mean eternally abiding in Him."[1528] Such double talk is the problem. How can we have eternal security if you can loose it? If you hire a security agency which promises you will never be robbed, and you are robbed, then the agency did not speak the truth. If Jesus promised us eternal security, which Newell admits, then it must be eternal security. This cannot be the case.

Despite the support of authors such as Robert Gromacki[1529] and Franz Delitzsch[1530] this view is not consistent with the teachings of the Scripture. Indeed, the words of one advocate demonstrate this, for Lenski declared that "one may go so far that even God's grace can no longer reach him."[1531] He is thus limitting God's grace! The biblical Jesus requires only one thing : to trust in Him. If we repent and turn to Jesus, we will be saved. If we do so, sin again, but cannot turn back, then God's grace is no longer grace. This was the very doctrine that led many away from the medieval church, and yet it is the view now accepted by many of the same. Surely there is a better answer.

View # 2 : Apostasy of Nominal Believers

If the warning does not apply to true believers, then might it apply to nominal believers? John Nelson Darby believed that "the nominal church of God is just in this state."[1532] David Allen argues that the shift in language from "you" to "they" hints at unbelievers.[1533] When the author is addressing the recipients of the epistle he refers to them personally as "you." Here, however, it is "they" indicating some group outside of the church to whom the author was writing.

To further support this view, William Kelly states that "it is observable that we read here of enlightment, not of the new birth or eternal life."[1534] The problem is that "'heavenly gift' is a euphemism for salvation,"[1535] but H.A. Ironside commented that "they had tasted ... does not in itself imply that they had eaten of the Living Bread."[1536] So these scholars parse the verse carefully to demonstrate that "tasting of the heavenly gift and having been made partakers of the Holy Spirit" (v. 4) does not necessarily indicate that they had received the Holy Spirit or heavenly gift. They had but sipped of the Water of Life.

While a tempting view, the trouble with this position should be obvious. Consider John MacArthur's words; "Christians are not being addressed, and it is the opportunity for *receiving* salvation, not salvation itself, that can be lost."[1537] This finely parsed sentence mixes the Calvinist view (see below) with the Nominal Christian theory. They avoid the problem of loosing salvation by saying they never could even *receive* it. This, however, spins back on itself for it remains evident that whomever these people are they "once tasted" and now can never taste again. If they had sipped the Water of Life they clearly at least had the opportunity to drink of it (to *receive* it). This leads to the third position, which is an offshoot of this view.

View # 3 : The Withered Seeds

In the Parable of the Sower (Matthew 13:3-23) Jesus likened the gospel to someone who plants seeds. Of these planted seeds some wither and die because they had no root in the ground (Matthew 13:20-21). He said:

"The one on whom seed was sown on the rocky places, this is the man who hears the word and immediately receives it with joy; yet he has no *firm* root in himself, but is *only* temporary, and when affliction or persecution arises because of the word, immediately he falls away."

Note that Jesus even mentioned persecution, which is generally believed to be the backdrop of this epistle. These individuals fall away out of fear of persecution because they had no firm root. So then the Word of God was not truly sown in their hearts, even though they tasted of it. Ironside believed that "it was not that the Holy Spirit as a divine Person ever indwelled them, but they had participated in the blessings that the Holy Spirit had given."[1538]

F.B. Meyer argued that the gift is "the life of God in the soul; it is Christ himself, and he is willing to be in us"[1539] but "some are content not to receive it; only to taste it."[1540] So these men argue "it is not said that they had been converted, regenerate, or filled by the Holy Ghost,"[1541] but only that they had tasted it, like the seed sown on rocky places.

The similarities between this view and the previous one are obvious, and so are its drawbacks. "It is impossible to renew them again to repentance" (v. 6) does indicate that they had repented and been "renewed." This obvious indicates that they had been "renewed" which seems to be synonymous with the rebirth. So while William Kelly denies that the new birth is spoken of in these passages,[1542] the "renewal" may be just that. This view is thus tenable, but suspect. Let us see what alternatives exist before deciding.

View # 4 : Loss of Sanctification

One unique, and rare, view is that of Dwight Pentecost. Like others he is quick to indicate that "this 'falling away' is not accidental. It is deliberate,"[1543] but unlike others he argues that "the 'falling away' is a believer's failure to progess to maturity,"[1544] not their loss of salvation. In other words, he attributes this to sanctification rather than salvation.

Another author who reflects a similar perspective is Brooke Westcott who speaks of the "the necessity of progress."[1545] One might compare Samson to these individuals. Was he saved? Yes. He was even a mighty man of faith according to Hebrews (Hebrews 11), but he was also a very immature man who did not follow the path of righteousness very well. The result was his own humiliation, torture, and death. Could this be what Hebrew is speaking about? In a word; no.

While this view sound theologically, it is weak exegetically. It is not talking about spiritual backsliding, and if it were then it would be "impossible to renew them again to repentance" afterwards! There is simply no way to get around the fact that the author is speaking of the impossibility of these individuals, whomever they may be, turning back to Christ. They "tasted" the gifts but rejected them. We must, therefore, understand what it is they tasted, before we can truly understand who these individuals were.

View # 5 : Novatianism and Rebaptism
The Novatian view is not so much an exegetical position as a political one. Novatian was a bishop of Rome who was not concerned so much about whether or not these "lapsed sinners" were true believers as what the church was to do with them. The Novatian schism was about whether or not these "lapsed" Christians should be allowed to return to the church after recanting the faith. The backdrop to this was one of the brutal persecutions of the Roman emperor Decius. Decius gave each Christian an opportunity to renounce our faith and offer sacrifices to the Roman gods. Some Christians, in order to save their lives or families, did just that, but when the persecutions were over they sought readmittance into the church.[1546] Novatian denied them readmittance using this passage as proof that they could not be redeemed a second time.

The Novatian schism led to a great debate over this passage and its meaning. Theodoret of Cyr argued that this was re-baptism, not readmittance. "The followers of Novatian use the words to contest the truth, failing to understand that the divine apostle, far from prohibiting the remedies of repentance set the limit for divine baptism."[1547] In other words, he said they should not be baptized again, but denied that they had ever lost their position with God. This was also the view of Ephraem the Syrian[1548] and Chrysostom[1549] whereas Photius denied repentance for the fallen.[1550]

Thomas Aquinas took a moderated position of sorts, arguing that "they had in the present a spiritual regeneration" (by which he means baptismal regeneration)[1551] but then refutes Novatian.[1552] So believes that regeneration occured at baptism and supposed readmittance to the church.

One thing is certain. Hebrews was written at a time of persecution.[1553] The author was indeed warning the Hebrews against so easily recanting the faith. Nonetheless, this is not the debate. The debate is over who these individuals are that have become beyond redemption. Novatianism commits the heretical sin of becoming Judge in place of God. I think most all Christians will agree that whomever these individuals are, only God knows their hearts and therefore only He has the right to determine who is beyond redemption. The question then remains.

View # 6 : The Calvinistic View / Perseverance Without Knowledge
Many Christians assume that the Calvinistic teaching of the perseverance of the saints is the same as the assurance of salvation and eternal security, but in reality this is not so. One has to only read the Calvinist teachings upon this verse to understand that Calvinism really teaches that we cannot truly know whether or not we are truly saved until Judgment Day.

In regard to Hebrews 6:4-6 Calvinists quite frankly engage in doublespeak. F.F. Bruce said that the author "is not questioning the perseverance of the saints ... rather he is insisting that those who persevere are true saints."[1554] This is the classic Calvinist answer, and technically, it is true. Those who are saved will be saved and those who are damned will be damned. Such an obvious answer, however, ignores the topic; why is Hebrews making this warning? He is not just issuing double talk. There is a point to the passage.

One Calvinist said that the purpose was to serve as a warning not to continue sinning "in case we sin."[1555] Yet again, this evades the central question.

John Calvin himself said, "the knot of the question is in the word, *fall away*. Whoever then understands it meaning, can easily extricate himself from every difficulty."[1556] He then goes on to describe his own view on the perseverance of the saints, but this view is not synonymous with the assurance of salvation. Reformed theologians usually deny the assurance of salvation.[1557] Their favorite saying is that acceptance of Christ it is not a railway ticket or bank note assuring us.[1558] So ironically, the Calvinists who attack Armenianism so greatly really believe the same thing, with a slightly different spin. It is no wonder that Armenius was a disciple of Calvin.[1559] Armenius simply discarded the facade of predestination, but the theology is the same. Both Calvinism and Armenianism deny that we can ever truly know if we are saved.

View # 7 : As Israel

Another unique view is to attribute this to a prophecy about Israel as a nation. Perhaps, it is argued, that the author is speaking of the imminent fall of Jerusalem. Steven Ger, for example, argues that this is a reference to the nation of Israel.[1560] Robert Gromacki is another who believes that there is at least an alluson to Israel's falling away,[1561] as well as the famous C.I. Scofield.[1562]

This view is tempting inasmuch as it fits the historical context of the War of the Jews and the imminent fall of Jerusalem, as well as deflecting the problem of loosing one's salvation. It also has the advantage of the fact that Hebrews was written to Jews about matters of the Jewish faith and religion. Nevertheless, it has seriously flaws which cannot be overlooked. The biggest obstacle is the fact that it speaks of returning "again unto repentance" and of "crucifying the Son of God a second time." How can either of these apply to a nation? Did Israel accept Christ, only to reject Him later? What of crucifying Christ again? Christ atoned for our sins "once for all" (Hebrews 10:10). Once we have accepted that atonement, there is no other. The point is that we cannot turn to Christ, leave Him, return again, and leave Him again as it suits our needs. None of this fits the context of prophetic history. Moreover, Steven Ger himself is well aware that Israel will be redeemed in the Last Days, so if this passage applied to Israel as a nation then there could be no redemption as it is about the "impossibility" of "renewing against to repentance." In short, the view is tempting, but has too many flaws and is not good exegesis.

320

View # 8 : Rhetorical

Perhaps the most popular view among evangelicals has been the rhetorical or hypothetical view. This is based on many translations which follow the King James reading, "it is impossible ... *if* they shall fall away, to renew them again unto repentance." Steven Ger argues that the "if" is not conditional, but rather "the original text provides no such modications, indicating ... [that if] is not hypothetical in nature."[1563] Warren Wiersbe also remarks that "in verse four the writer changed the pronouns from 'we' and 'us' to 'those.' This change also suggests that he had a hypotheical case in mind."[1564]

This argument hinges upon the meaning of the particle παραπεσοντας (*parapesontas*). This is the word translated as "those who have fallen away." Now David Allen asks us whether it is a substantival or adverbial participle.[1565] In other words, how does this particle relate to the previous sentence. This is the key. Since the author of Hebrews is speaking of the impossibility of "renewing again" then "those who have fallen away" obviously refers to the same, but in English the connection is often conveyed by means of "if." Often, but not always. Let us consider the translations.

The Tyndale, King James, New King James, Webster, NIV, and RSV all translate this with "if." "It is impossible ... if they shall fall away." However, the often forgotten Modern King James (MKJ) does not follow this translation choice. It reads, along with Wycliff, NAS, NLT, RV, NRSV, ASV, Darby, Douay-Rheims, and ESV, "it is impossible for those ... who have fallen away." The problem with the "if" translation is quite simply that the word "if" is not there. There are two words for "if" in Greek. The conditional "if" to which Steven Ger alluded is αν (*an*). Ger is correct to indicate that no such conditional "if" is to be found here, but neither is the more hypothetical εαν (*ean*). There is only the particle παραπεσοντας (*parapesontas*), "those who have fallen away."

Ultimately, this view hinges upon a suspect translation. It is popular view because it negates the possibility of loosing one's salvation, but it also negates the entire point of the argument. What is the point of hypothesizing something which cannot happen? This theory was once my favorite, but the more I study it the less it appears well grounded. It is a theological interpretation, not an exegetical one.

View # 9 : Millennial Exclusionism

There is a final view that I discuss in much more detail under Hebrews 10:26-31. It has been called the "Protestant purgatory"[1566] and teaches that disobedient believers will be punished in *Gehenna* for a thousand years.[1567] Some, like G.H. Lang, believe that the parable of Lazarus and the rich man in Luke 16 is reference to this.[1568] Its problem, of course, is not much different from the first view. While they deny that Christians can loose our salvation, they assign us to a purgatory like state for a thousand years. This cuts at the heart of the gospel. Did not Jesus pay the price for our sins? Why must we then be purged by fire? If Jesus died for our sins, then how is it that we must still pay for them. Is it really atonement if we must make atonement for our own sins in *Gehenna*?

This view "solves" the problem with the address apparently being directed toward Christians, but its solution is little different from saying that we can loose salvation. They nuance their position to say that we are loosing rewards (which is certainly possible), but a loss of rewards is not the same thing as dwelling in *Gehenna* for a thousand years. That is purgatory and belittles, if not denies, the atonement once for all (Romans 6:10; Hebrews 7:27; 10:10 1 Peter 3:18).

Conclusion

Few passages in the entire Bible are as controversial as this one. So controversial is it that I have noticed at least one foreign language translation of the Bible omits these passages![1569] These verses exist in every ancient and medieval manscript ever found so there is no reason to omit the passages except because of their controversial nature.

No fewer than nine views exist to explain this controversial passage. The chart on the following page I have comprised to briefly show the strengths and weaknesses of each view. We can break down these views by their strengths and weaknesses. In so doing we can eliminate the fourth, fifth, and seventh views. The view of sanctification is theological sound, but exegetically weak. The passage is obvious speaking of more than sanctification. The Novatian view is a political interpretation which makes a bishop judge instead of God. Novatian was a schismatic pope rejected even by the Catholic church today, and so he should be. We too should reject his interpretation. Finally, the theory on Israel sounds good, but only as an analogy for the passage is obviously speaking about individuals and we cannot apply this as a prophecy about Israel, especially when prophecy is clear that Israel will repent.

The next best views are the Rhetorical and Calvinistic interpretations. The Rhetorical view is another theological interpretation which sounds good but ultimately negates the entire point of the passage. It is a warning. Why warn against apostasy if true apostasy can't happen? Why issue a warning against something which cannot take place? Tempting as this view may be, it is poor exegetically.

The Calvinist view too should be rejected for similar reasons. It sounds good to say that the saved will persevere and the unsaved will be lost, but this is not the author's point. That is like saying up is up and down is down. It is self evident. The Calvinist teaching on the perserverance of the Saints is actually a denial of the assurance of salvation. It says we cannot know if we are saved. Jesus said "if anyone enters in Me, he *will* be saved" (John 10:9). This is not theoretical; it is the Word of God. We *will* be saved. Thus the Calvinist view must also be rejected.

Chart on Hebrews 6:4-6

View	Description	Strengths	Weaknesses
True Believers	Believes that true believers can lose salvation.	Appears the most straightforward interpretation.	It conflicts with the doctrine of salvation by grace through faith alone.
Nominal Believer	Believes these are nominal Christians.	This view negates the problem with believers loosing salvation.	The verse implies more than just nominalism since it mentions "tasting" the Holy Spirit.
Withered Seeds	Believes these people experiment with Christ, but ultimate reject Him.	Best moderates between the two above views, and comes from the Parable of the Sower.	"Tasting" the Holy Spirit may imply more than exper-imenting with the faith.
Sanctification	Believes this refers to a loss of sanctification, not salvation.	Elimnates the problem with loosing one's salvation.	The passage seems to refer to a conversion exper-ience, not san-ctification.
Novatianism	Believes that Christians who renounce Jesus in persecution cannot be readmitted to the church and are lost.	Best fits the context of apostasy amid persecution.	This makes the church judge instead of Christ. There is nothing political in the passage.
Calvinistic	Believes we cannot know whether or not we are truly saved.	Technically, it is a true in a philosophical kind of way. The saved are saved, the lost are lost.	Jesus gives us assurance so we can know. Why search our hearts (2 Cor-inthians 13:5) if we cannot know.
Israel	Argues this refers to Israel as a nation.	Works as an analogy and fits the context of an epistle about Hebrews.	Ignores the context and is prophetically incorrect as Israel *will* repent in the Last Days.
Rhetorical	Argues this is a purely hypothetical argument.	It eliminates the theological prob-lems with the passage.	There is no "if" in Greek. A hypothet-ical argument negates the whole point.
Millennial Exclusionism	Argues this refers to believers, but salvation is not questioned. They replace loss of salvation with a purgatory like punishment.	It solves the difficulty with reconciling believ-ers and a loss of salvation.	It is essentially a protestant version of purgatory based on assumption and suspect exegesis.

323

This leaves us with four views. The first one is the controversial one. If it is true then it suggest that it is possible to loose that which Jesus said we already have; salvation. This cast doubt upon the doctrine of the security of the believer. Can we be saved, and then not saved? The very question is paradoxical! The ninth view solves this only by creating a sort of protestant purgatory which cuts away at the doctrine of atonement. Did not Jesus pay the price for our sins? Why must we then be purged by fire?

What about nominal believers? Could they be the ones to whom the author was speaking? This is not likely for two primary reasons. First, "having once been enlightened and have tasted of the heavenly gift and have been made partakers of the Holy Spirit, and have tasted the good word of God and the powers of the age to come" (6:4-6) indicates much more than mere lip service. Second, if it speaks of "renewing them again to repentance" (v. 6) then it implies that there was a first repentance and renewal. Nominal Christians have never truly been converted in the first place or they would not be nominal. This leads us to the third view.

The best analogy might be the story of Larry Flynt. The world famous pornographer claimed to have become a "born again Christian" in the 1970s, but a year later he was still publishing his magazine and eventually came to call himself an atheist. He had "tasted" or experimented with the "heavenly gift" which is salvation, but he rejected it. Now it is true that "having been made partakers of the Holy Spirit" (v. 4) and "renewing again to repentance" may imply more than mere experimentation, but "partaking" does not necessarily mean "possessing." The Greek word μετοχους (*metochous*) means "sharing in."[1570] This is not the same thing as possessing the Holy Spirit. Likewise, "renewing again to repentance" may not necessarily mean that they were truly born again; only that they had professed to be "born again" even as Larry Flynt once claimed.

I have come to believe that the parable of the Sower best fits this passage and its warning. Because Larry Flynt's had no root in his heart he left the faith. This analogy fits what the author of Hebrews was warning us about. He seemed to be stating that Christianity is not a drug to take when we feel bad, but a life long commitment to the Lord Jesus. He was then urging those who professed to know Christ not to easily abandon Him in times of persecution. He offers no indication that the lapsed may not return to the church or that Christians may not "backslide" and fall into sin; but he does warn that following Christ is not to be taken lightly. He is warning us about bad seeds who appear on the surface to be true believers, and much more than mere nominal ones, but have no true root. They turn away from the faith in hard times and will never return. These seeds must be distinguished from the seeds which are choked and do not grow to maturity (see notes on Matthew 13:3:-23 in *Controversies in the Gospels*). Those seeds are saved, but never sanctified.

Is the Law Useless?
Hebrews 7:18-19

> "For, on the one hand, there is a setting aside of a former commandment
> because of its weakness and uselessness (for the Law made nothing
> perfect), and on the other hand there is a bringing in of a better hope,
> through which we draw near to God."

Is the law useless? On one side, there are those who use this passage to
discard the whole of the Old Testament. Another side uses this passage to imply
that Scripture contradicts itself and that Paul's assertion that "all Scripture is
profitibale" (2 Timothy 3:16) is irreconcilable with this assertion.

The answer to both these misconceptions is the same. It is found in
context and in Romans 2–5 which I have discussed previously. The law is
useful for convicting us of sin, but it is useless for salvation. This is the context
and is clear. The author of Hebrews states clearly that there is "a better hope,
through which we draw near to God." That hope is Jesus. The law condemns.
Jesus gives life (cf. 2 Corinthians 3:6). Hebrews does not say that the Law was
useless in regard to its purpose but that it is useless in bringing us closer to God.
Whereas the law condemns us, Jesus pardons us. This is why Theodoret of Cyr
said "the law ceases to have effect."[1571]

Now it is not my habit to quote books I have not thoroughly read, but
inasmuch as some Islamic websites misquote this passage to imply that the
Christian Bible contradicts itself, I will quote from the Quran where it says
virtually the same thing. According to Sura 3:49-50, Jesus said "I have come to
to make halal what was haram," which can be translated as "I have come to
affirm the Law which was before me and to make lawful what was before
forbidden." If anything, this seems more of a contradiction than Hebrew's
statement, for the law was never intended to bring about salvation; it was only
intended to prove to us the need for salvation.

"Errors" in Hebrews?
Hebrews 7:27; 9:1-4; 10:11

> "Behind the second veil there was a tabernacle which is called the Holy
> of Holies, having a golden altar of incense and the ark of the covenant
> covered on all sides with gold, in which was a golden jar holding the
> manna, and Aaron's rod which budded, and the tables of the covenant."

Many critics, Jewish, secular, and "Christian," have accused the author
of Hebrews of being ignorant of the Temple and its ritual. They have attributed
three "errors" to Hebrews which even a number of evangelicals have found
convincing. Nevertheless, an examination of the facts and context make these
"errors" suspect given their proper context. These three "errors" are as follows.

Daily Sacrifices?

Twice the book of Hebrews implies that daily sacrifices were offered by the high priest. Critics have attacked this one two grounds. Some split hairs, arguing that if the high priest offered sacrifices for his own sins (7:27) then Jesus would have to have sacrificed for Himself as well and since Jesus never sinned, this would blasphemy. Obviously this is frivolous for the comparison is not whether or not Jesus sinned, but that Jesus is our high priest who made a sacrifice for us all!

The second criticism is also a technicality. They claim that the high priest did not offer daily sacrifices as the author of Hebrews states, and was thus ignorant of Temple laws and rituals, but these claims are fallacious on several levels.

First, as F.F. Bruce commented, "there is indeed no explicit command for a daily sin-offering ... but inadvertent sinning, of the kind provided for in Lev. 4:1ff, could well have been a daily hazard."[1572] Robert Milligan said, "he was not required by any law of statute to offer the daily sacrifice in person, but as the head of the priesthood, he was of course chiefly responsible."[1573] In other words, while the high priest was not required to participate in daily sin-offerings, he was free to do so, and as high priest, would probably choose to do so as an example to his priests and the people. We therefore cannot say that high priests did not offer daily sacrifices; only that they did not have to.

Second, if the critic wishes to be technical then another technicality could be pointed out. Namely, the fact that Leviticus 6:20 required that "the high priest had indeed to offer a cereal offering morning and eveing."[1574] Josephus himself stated that "the [high] priest also, of his own charges, offered a sacrifice, and that twice every day." [1575] The criticism that it "was not a sin-offering, only an offering of cereals"[1576] is again an attempt to split hairs.

Finally, it is a fact that the "high-priest took part in the daily sacrifices on special occasions."[1577] It is debateable whether or not the author of Hebrews ever intended to imply that the priests offered sacrifices 360 days a year.[1578] Hebrews 10:11 states that "every priest stands daily ministering and offering time after time the same sacrifices." It is noteworthy that the NIV translates this as "day after day" (as does Darby). Arthur Pink said, "they were obliged to offer 'daily' from time to time, 'day by day.'"[1579] In other words, while they were not required to offer sin-offerings 360 days a year there were times when they were required to offer sacrifices every day during a particular feast. So the critic is again trying to be hyper-technical, but if we are being techinal then it is equally true that "they were obliged to offer 'daily' from time to time."[1580]

What Rest in the Ark?

Two more attacks center on verse 9:4. I will begin with the lesser of the two controversies; that being the statement that within the Ark of the Covenant "was a golden jar holding the manna, and Aaron's rod which budded, and the tables of the covenant." Critics point out that 1 Kings 8:9 says, "there was nothing in the ark except the two tablets of stone which Moses put there at Horeb." They then suggest that Hebrews is wrong and the author mistaken and/or ignorant.

The fundamental problem with this argument is that assumes that 1 Kings 8:9 is the standard and ignores the likely implications of Exodus 16:33-34 and Numbers 17:10. There it is stated that "Moses said to Aaron, 'take a jar and put an omerful of manna in it, and place it before the LORD to be kept throughout your generations.' As the LORD commanded Moses, so Aaron placed it before the Testimony, to be kept." In Numbers 17:10 it is again affirmed that Aaron returned to rod after using it. Now three things must be said of these passages.

First, while the Hebrew "does not say what the jar was made of, the LXXX says it was golden,"[1581] so Hebrews is correct in this regard. Second, while Exodus does not explicitly say that the pot and rod were placed in the Ark, as opposed to near it, this is the logical deduction for they were probably not placed out in the open uncovered. If they were to placed "before the LORD" then they would be in the Holy of Holies and that would mean the Ark was the only storage in which to place them! Finally, 1 Kings 8:9 referred to Solomon's temple but "the author [of Hebrews] is not concerned with the temple [of Solomon]. He is writing about the tabernacle, and it is possible that a different arrangement held there."[1582] Thus the critic shifts the burden of proof. He assumes that because the Ark held only the tablets when Solomon's temple was opened, the Ark could never have held the pot or rod either before or after that! This is assumption; not proof.

The Location of the Altar of Incense
Another problem with Hebrews 9:4 is the statement that the altar of incense was found in the Holy of Holies. Some fervently deny this, and yet this is not the only debate, for some quesion whether or not the Greek word here is properly alter or censer. Some believe that it was the Golden censer of Leviticus 16:12 while others insist it is the Golden Altar of Exodus 30:7-8.[1583] So we must first identify which one Hebrews is speaking of and then determine whether or not it was ever found in the Holy of Holies as the author states.

The Greek word θυμιατηριον (*thymiaterion*) comes from the root word for incense, but it can be used either of the censer or the altar upon which the incense is burned.[1584] Josephus uses this word interchangeably for both the altar of incense and censer.[1585] Philo uses the word for the incense-altar,[1586] as do Symmachus and Theodotion.[1587] However, Martin Luther, J.A. Bengal, and others believe it refers to the Golden censer of Leviticus 16:12.[1588]

Translators are also divided. Golden censer is found in the KJV, NKJV, RV, Tyndale, Webster, Wycliff, Darby, Douay-Rheims, and the Geneva Bible. The Golden altar of incense found in Exodus 30 is preferred by the NAS, NIV, MKJV, NLV, RSV, NRSV, ASV, and the ESV.

Most believe that "the symbolism of the passage is in favor of the sense 'Altar of incense.'"[1589] This is probably true, but it is equally true that whether it speaks of the censer or the altar on which it was burned simply doesn't matter. The question is whether or not Hebrews describes its location behind the veil accurately. Some critics quote 1 Kings 6:22 in which the altar was said to be "by the inner sanctuary." Thus they say it was not inside, but next to it. Obviously if "golden censer" is the appropriate translation then this might help alleviate the apparent problem. Conversely, the altar does seem to make more sense contextually. The censer itself would obviously be taken to the altar for burning anyway, so the real question is whether or not the altar was "behind the second veil" is Hebrews 9:3 states or "by the inner sanctuary" as 1 Kings 6:22 states.

Before continuing it is necessary to explain the layout of the tabernacle and temple. The tabernacle itself was a sort of mobile temporary temple. The structures were similar in design except that the tabernacle had to be constructed so that it could be disassembled and moved as the Israelites wondered the desert. The temple was, of course, permanent and made of stone and gold and cedar. In both cases there was an inner and outer curtain which separated the holy places. The Holy of Holies was the most sacred where the Ark of the Covenant was kept. It was the most sacred part of the temple where only the priests could enter. Most of the other sacred elements were kept behind the first veil, but not behind the second veil which covered the Holy of Holies. This is the controversy. Hebrews appears to describe the golden altar of incense as sitting beside the Ark of the Covenant inside the Holy of Holies.

Lenski believes that the problem can be solved simply. He argues that the Greek word μετα (*meta*) can be alternately translated as either "behind" or "after." So rather than "behind the second veil" he suggest it should be "after the second veil."[1590] He then further argues that εχουσα (*echousa*) "can include both 'an altar of incense' *in front* of the veil and 'the ark of the testament' *behind* the veil."[1591] This explanation, however, seems a stretch. In essense he is arguing that instead of the altar being "behind the second veil" as one enters the tabernacle it is "after the second veil" as one exits the Holy of Holies. This seems tenuous at best.

Another explanation is the curious fact that the apocryphal "Apocalypse of Baruch" places the altar inside the Holy of Holies.[1592] This, it is argued, proves that the altar may have been placed inside the Holy of Holies at certain periods in history even if it was not kept in the Holy of Holies in the time of Moses and Solomon. While possible, there is a better explanation which fits the context of Hebrews much better.

The entire context of Hebrews is about atonement, and Leviticus 16:12 explicitly states that on the Day of Atonement the altar of incense was to be moved inside the Holy of Holies! It says, "[The high priest] shall take a firepan full of coals of fire from upon the altar before the LORD and two handfuls of finely ground sweet incense, and *bring it inside the veil*. He shall put the incense on the fire before the LORD, that the cloud of incense may cover the mercy seat that is on *the ark of* the testimony, otherwise he will die" (Leviticus 16:12-13).

So Arthur Pink pointed out that while the altar was outside the veil "359 day a year," it was inside the veil on the Day of Atonement.[1593] On this day the Ark and altar were "conjoined"[1594] for the ceremony. Since the entire subject of Hebrews concerns the Sacrifice of Atonement by Jesus Christ, our High Priest, then it makes perfect sense that the author of Hebrews was speaking of the Day of Atonement. Consequently, the statement of Hebrews 9:4 is 100% accurate.

Conclusion
It is significant that the author of Hebrews "describes only the Tabernacle, not the Temple of Solomon, of Ezra, of Herod, least of all that of Leontopolis."[1595] He goes back to Moses, not because the temple had already fallen, but because he was quoting from the Law of Moses and the Torah which was written before the temple was built. It is the critic, and not Hebrew's author, who mistakenly take arrangements in Solomon's day and project them back to Moses's day. They take a single descriptive passage of Solomon's newly built temple, infer something from it, and disregard the explicit laws of Moses in the Torah. No one can reasonably say that the statements of Hebrews 9:4 were not written by a Levite intimately familiar with the Jewish ordinances.

Willful Sins
Hebrews 10:26-31

> "For if we go on sinning willfully after receiving the knowledge of the truth, there no longer remains a sacrifice for sins."

This is another passage used to imply that a believer can loose his salvation. Some argue that Christians cannot sin. Others that we will never stop being sinners in this life. The two extremes; legalism and libertarianism, again come to blows here. This passage is, therefore, closely connected to the controversy of Hebrew 6:4-6, but is the passage connected to it?

Three issues are involved in this dilema. First, to whom is this addressed? Is it the same as in Hebrews 6:4-6? Are the subjects believers or unbelievers? Second, what is the nature of these "willful" sins? Can a believer still sin? What constitutes "willful" sins? Finally, what is the nature of the judgment? Can we loose our salvation? Does this refer to hell, earthly punishment, purgatory, or something else?

To Whom Is This Addressed?
Many believe that this passage is addressed to the same people of whom the author speaks in Hebrews 6:4-6. Others believe that they are a different

audience. Evidence for this is to be found in the simple fact that Hebrews 6:4-6 speaks of "they" whereas here the author speaks of "us."

Some have tried to argue for an "editorial 'we'" but Robert Govett is among those who says "this addresses itself to believers."[1596] Arthur Pink also noted that the author "did not say, 'if *ye* sin willingly,' but 'if *we*,' thus including himself."[1597]

Many are not convinced. They insist that, like Hebrews 6:4-6, this cannot refer to believers.[1598] John MacArthur argues that this too refers to apostasy, saying "an apostate has seen and heard the truth – he knows it well – but he willfully rejects it."[1599] One might compare such a man to Balaam who knew the word of the Lord but fought against (Numbers 22-24; 31:8). John Calvin also said that "the apostle here refers only to apostates."[1600] The strongest evidence in this favor is the statement, "after receiving the knowledge of the truth." It is obvious that "receiving the knowledge of the truth" and being born again are not the same thing. If Hebrews was speaking of believers, we would have chosen a more clear phrase than merely expressing "knowledge of the truth."

Contextually it appears that "the author uses 'we' to include himself with his readers,"[1601] but if so then this would again leave us with the problem of losing our salvation. Moreover, "knowledge of the truth" and conversion to Christ are not the same thing. Hebrews 10:26-27 does not mention rebirth; only knowledge. Additionally, the argument seems similar to that in Hebrew 6:4-6. Having said this, it is hard to ignore the author's apparent inclusion of himself. Consequently, it is impossible to affirmatively decide to whom the author is speaking until we understand exactly what he is saying. That requires us to examine the nature of the sins in question and the nature of the punishment.

The Nature of the Sin
"No sinning in ignorance or in weakness is referred to; but the deliberate voluntary sinning."[1602] John Nelson Darby said it is "not failure or disobedience but apostasy"[1603] to which the author refers. The key word here is "willful." It is not "sinning" but "sinning willfully."

It is worth noting that in Greek word order is often used for emphasis. Unlike English, a Greek sentence can be constructed with relatively loose word order. Here in this sentence, the first word is εκουσιως (*ekousios*) meaning "willfully" or "deliberately." It speaks of "a state of deliberate and voluntary defiance to the will of God."[1604]

Opinions have differed as to what constitute these deliberate sins. Not surprisingly the opinions depend a great deal upon whether or not the commentator believes the passage speaks to believers or unbelievers and whether or not they believe in a purgatory or similar punishment bestowed on unfaithful believers. Ironside, for example, believed that "the willful sin in this passage is the definite rejection of His atoning sacrifice."[1605] In other words, he said that rejecting Christ is the "willful sin," but why does the author appear to include himself by saying "we"? Moreover, does not "sinning" imply multiple sins?

Perhaps the most popular view is that Hebrews is talking about "total apostasy from God,"[1606] as John Wesley believed. Franz Delitzsch said "the sin meant is that of apostasy; unfaithfulness to God, and to His manifestation in Christ, being the ground and foundation of all other sin."[1607] William Kelly even commented upon the fact that "forsaking the assembly" is mentioned "in such proximinty to apostasy,"[1608] but this again brings up the question of whether or not the apostate has lost his salvation or whether he ever had it to start with. To that end Arthur Pink emphasizes the "if" aspect again.[1609] He takes this as another hypothetical argument warning us not to forsake Christ.[1610] He said, "salvation is a supernatural thing, which changes the heart, renews the will, transforms the life"[1611] and so he denied that anyone can ever truly apostatize if they know Christ.

Once again, Pink's argument is sound theology but bad exegesis because once again the word "if" is not there. Once again the word is a participle. The Wycliff and Darby translations are the closest to the original Greek, which is best translated literally as "when we deliberately continue sinning." Robert Gromacki reminds us that this is a present active participle meaning the "constant repetition of sin."[1612] Milligan calls it "sin of *habit*"[1613] and another, "the deliberate continuity of such sins as a self-chosen law of life."[1614]

As such many believe that believers are in mind. Theodore of Mapsuesta, for example, said that "such an individual abolishes repentance ... and ... inable to assent to repentance."[1615] He believed that such men loose their salvation. He is not alone. Some believe that "if, after we are converted and become true Christians, we should apostatize, it would be impossible to be recovered again."[1616] Like Clement of Alexandria, they believe that "continual and repeated repentence for sins is no different from those who have once and for all turned away from the faith ... to repeat an action repented is a deliberate" sin.[1617]

Now there is another option. Robert Govett is among those who believe that this passage does indeed speak of believers, but he does not believe that it speaks of loosing salvation. He argued that there are two "classes" of sins. The first is occasional sins or sins of ignorance and error. The second sins, which he considered "willful" are those of abiding or deliberation.[1618] However, he considers "spontaneous" sins to be a part of the latter![1619] He then takes this as a warning against the second class of sins, but the result of these sins is not damnation or the loss of salvation, but punishment via Millennial Exclusion.[1620] What does this mean? This is our final debate; what is the punishment of which Hebrews speaks?

The Nature of the Punishment

How we perceive the punishment spoken of in verses twenty-seven to thirty-one determines in part whether or not we think believers are the ones to whom the passage is addressed. Essentially there are only three views upon this.

The first is obviously that the author of Hebrews is speaking hell itself. The "fury of a fire which will consume the adversaries" is actually a paraphrase of Isaiah 26:11 which refers to the destruction of God's enemies. It is also reminiscent of the fire of hell which Jesus describes in many places (cf. Matthew 13:42, 50; Luke 16:23-24, etc.). Moreover, verse twenty-nine reads,

> "How much severer punishment do you think he will deserve who has trampled under foot the Son of God, and has regarded as unclean the blood of the covenant by which he was sanctified, and has insulted the Spirit of grace?"

These words hardly seem to suit any punishment less than the fires of which verse twenty-seven spoke. Finally, verse thirty-one ends by stating, that "it is a terrifying thing to fall into the hands of the living God." All of this seems to speak of a literal hell, but not all agree. Tertullian, for example, say this more analogically, saying that the man "who after baptism renews his sins" is destined to punishment, but he does not seem to have believed that the fire was literal *per se.*[1621] This is the second view.

Chrysostom also took the cause of grace by arguing that "he did not say that no more is there repentance or no more is there remission, but 'no longer' is there a 'sacrifice'; that is, there is no need for a second cross."[1622] So Chrysostom denies that a believer can loose salvation and, in turn, makes the punishment an earthly punishment, and yet this begs the question. If we are destined to punishment despite the Cross of Jesus, then what is the true nature of that punishment? The passages describe "fire" and "terrifying" consequences. Can this describe our earthly torments? Would this not be more in line with eastern karma than the teachings of Jesus? To that end one last view is adopted in different forms.

Catholics believe in purgatory. This is a doctrine outright rejected by protestants, and yet some protestants teach a view very similar to it. Sir Robert Anderson even called the view a "Protestant purgatory."[1623] It is better known as Millennial Exclusionism which was popular for a time in the late 1800s only to fade away until recent times when it has resurfaced. According to this doctrine saints who willfully sin face *"severe consequences."*[1624] This consequence is said to be the "temporary death of the body and *the soul!"*[1625] J.D. Faust even goes so far as to argue that the "second death," which he admits refers to eternal hell in the unbeliever, also refers to a temporary state for the disobedient Christian![1626] Others, like Chuck Missler take a slightly more moderated view, arguing that the disobedient Christian cannot enter "the rest" which God promised.[1627]   Of course, that means that they will still have to endure the punishments left for those without God.

G.H. Lang called these Christians "dives." He believed that the parable of Lazarus and the rich man in Gehenna (Luke 16) referred not to an unbeliever but to a "dive."[1628]   In that story the rich man was so tormented by the fires of *Gehenna* (translated *Hades*) that he begged Abraham, "send Lazarus so that he may dip the tip of his finger in water and cool off my tongue, for I am in agony in this flame."   Hence this is the fate to which Millennial Exclusionists allocate the carnal Christian!

A similar view is taught by partial rapturists who believe that sinful believers will have to suffer the torments of the Tribulation in the End Times.[1629] This is certainly preferable to those who see *Hades* as a fate for some Christians, but it cast serious doubt upon the grace of God and places too much emphasis upon the works of man.   Now there is much in the teachings of the Millennial Exclusionists which is correct, but there is equally as much which is false, even heretical.   The fires of which Hebrews speaks clearly refers to hell, as such is inadvertently admitted even by the Millennial Exclusionists, but Jesus promised to deliver us from such wrath.   1 Corinthians 3:15 is a passage often spoken of in this regard.   There Paul warns that "if any man's work is burned up, he will suffer loss; but he himself will be saved, yet so as through fire."   Notice, however, that it is his works that is burned up, not the man.   He will not receive his reward (3:14) but neither will he be punished in hell, temporarily or eternally, if He has received Christ.

Conclusion

As Warren Wiersbe points out it is of interest to note that, "under the Old Covenant, there were no sacrifices for deliberate and willful sin (Ex. 21:12-14; Num. 15:27-31)."[1630]   Sinning "with a high hand" was never accomodated in Hebrew sacrificial law.[1631]   Numbers 15:30 says, "the person who does *anything* defiantly, whether he is native or an alien, that one is blaspheming the LORD; and that person shall be cut off from among his people."

Of course, such people have rejected the Lord.   They are not believers. This is the crux of the issue.   If Hebrews is speaking to believers then it would appear that we could loose our salvation.   Worse, it would be saying that Jesus died only for past sins and no future sin can be forgiven.   In response to that Chrysostom offers an apt answer; "He did not say that no more is there repentance or no more is there remission, but 'no longer' is there a 'sacrifice'; that is, there is no need for a second cross."[1632]

Nevertheless, the better answer is that Hebrews 10:26-31 is a parallel argument to Hebrews 6:4-6.   He is not speaking of true believers, but of those who know the truth and have rejected it.   Like Balaam there are those who understand intellectually the gospel, but reject it in their hearts.   These are like the withered seeds (Matthew 13:20-21).

Why then does the author include these among us? Why does he say "we" instead of "they" as he does in Hebrews 6:4-6? The answer may be that the withered seeds live among us. Not everyone who goes to church or calls himself a believer is truly a believer. Matthew 7:22-23 may even be describing the same thing as Hebrews does here. There on Judgment Day stand the phony believers who protest that they prophesied in Jesus's name and even cast out demons in His name, but the Lord responds to them, "I never knew you," and cast them out. These are the ones to whom Hebrews refers. These are the ones who live among us and profess to be one of us, but in their hearts they have only their own interest in mind. They do not love the Lord, nor turn from their sins. For these there is a terrible justice that awaits.

Definition of Faith
Hebrews 11:1

"Now faith is the assurance of *things* hoped for, the conviction of things not seen."

Atheists and liberals have long created a false dichotomy on faith and reason. Faith, they argue, is "blind." Misquoting this passage they equate faith with ignorance, and yet the same ones who make this argument insist that maggots are our distant cousins. It is the atheist who has blind faith, not the Christian. Nevertheless, Hebrews does say that faith is "the conviction of things not seen." What does this mean? What is faith in the Biblical sense? Who is the one with and without faith?

As surprising as it may seem, there are many who believe that faith is not defined here. John Calvin said, "greatly mistaken are they who think that an exact definition of faith is given here."[1633] Another author said that faith "is nowhere defined in Scripture, nor is it defined here, for the writer rather describes in its effects than in its essence."[1634] These individuals believe that "the principle of faith ... is under discussion here,"[1635] not faith itself. Even J. Dwight Pentecost commented that "since the word *faith* is used without the article, it refers to faith as a principle."[1636]

Many disagree. Robert Govett believed that "the writer of Hebrews begins his example list with a two-part definition of faith."[1637] Nonetheless, many theologians ask what kind of faith is the author speaking? John Wesley said that all faith must be "justifying faith" and must be in Christ.[1638] This is perhaps going to far. I have found that atheists have more faith than me; just not in the same thing. They have faith that the universe is a mere accident, that slugs are of the same ancestry as man, and that life is meaningless. I do not have that kind of faith. I have a different kind of faith.

Warren Wiersbe believes that "three words in Hebrews 11:1-3 summarize what true faith is : *substance, evidence,* and *witness.*"[1639] Another author divides faith into a different three fold division. He lists a promise,

334

believing in the promise, and assurance of the promise.[1640] One thing is certain. *"hoping* for something is not yet *faith."*[1641]

Personally, I define faith more simply as trust. Do we trust God? Do we believe in His Word? Do we truly have faith in His promises to us? In short, do we trust that God is not a liar? Some forget that the author doesn't just define faith, but gives examples. The famous "faith list" is made up of individuals who were not ignorant men, but men who trusted in the Lord. Some were weak and sinful, but they trusted God (see notes in Hebrews 11:31-32). None were perfect, but they were perfected by the Lord. It is our faith in God that sanctifies us, for by trusting in Him and His promises, God perfects us.

Does Hebrews Err?
Hebrews 11:21 – Genesis 47:31

> "By faith Jacob, as he was dying, blessed each of the sons of Joseph, and worshiped, *leaning* on the top of his staff."

In yet another attempt by critics to cast doubt upon the credibility of the Bible, it is said that this passage is irreconcilable with Genesis which reads, "Israel [Jacob] bowed himself at the head of the bed." Was he "leaning on the top of his staff" or did he "bow himself at the head of the bed"?

It is worth noting that the Greek *Septugaint* reads "staff" or rod. So we are told that "our author follows the *Septuagint*."[1642] John Calvin even went so far as to say that "the apostles were not so scrupulous ... as not to accomodate themselves to the unlearned."[1643] In other words, Calvin seems to think that the author deliberately mistranslated the passage even knowing it was wrong! Such a remark is neither helpful, nor accurate for the student of Hebrew knows that the word for "bed" and "staff" are homonyms in paleo-Hebrew. Because ancient Hebrew did not have written vowels, homonyms were more common even though the words may have been pronounced slightly different.

In Hebrew מִטָּה (*mittah*) is a head of a bed, but מַטֶּה (*matteh*) is a staff or rod.[1644] Without the vowel points, which did not exist when Genesis was written, they were spelled exactly the same, מטה (*m-tt-h*). Now the translators of the Greek *Septuagint* were themselves Jews, so it is highly probable that it is the modern translators and the later Massorettes who were mistaken, and not the author of Hebrews. In short, both Genesis and Hebrews are correct.[1645] In fact, the NIV even chooses to translate "staff" in Genesis 47:31. There is good reason for this.

"The Massoretic text describes an act of adoration, and not simply a sinking back into exhaustion."[1646] This better fits "staff" than "bed." Moreover, some see the staff as an allusion to rod of Christ.[1647] Since Jacob was blessing his children, a staff would have been the appropriate symbol for blessings. The church fathers said that the use of a staff was for "showing the obeisance"[1648] to the rod of the promised Messiah.[1649] This fits the context of both Genesis and Hebrews.

In short, the ancient Hebrew text read "staff," just as does Hebrews. The staff was a symbol of leadership and power in times of old. It is also reminiscent of the rod which was prophesied to the Messiah. Hebrews is speaking of Jacob's faith, not his age or infirmity. Consequently, the NIV is correct to translate Genesis 47:31 as "staff" even as the Hebrew author of Hebrews did so here.

James Tissot – Samson Slays the Lion – 1902

Questionable Men of Faith
Hebrews 11:31-32

"And what more shall I say? For time will fail me if I tell of Gideon,
Barak, Samson, Jephthah, of David and Samuel and the prophets."

Some have questioned a "faith list" that includes a prostitute, someone
who solicits prostitutes, a murderer, and even someone who is believed to have
murdered his own daughter. Are these really men to emulate?

We have a tendancy to idolize our heroes, but the Bible does not cover
for the sins of its saints. Only Jesus was without sin. Moses murdered a guard,
King David committed adultery and murdered her husband to cover the sin, and
Solomon reverted to idolatry for love of his thousand wives. Even Peter could
be said to have drifted into a cult had not Paul chastized him (Acts 15:13-29;
Galatians 2:12-14). The point of Hebrews is not to idolize god-like heroes, but
to show real flesh and blood men and women who placed their faith in God.

Let us, like the author of Hebrews, look at some of the more
controversial figures here, but unlike Hebrews I will look at their sins and how
God transformed them into the examples given here. Rahab, for example, is the
only woman mentioned in the list, and the author does not fail to mention that
she was a harlot, but he does mention that she "did not perish along with those
who were disobedient." Instead "she had welcomed the spies in peace" and
protected them. She did not wage battle for the Israelites, nor betray her king
except to keep silent. She only trusted that something better was awaiting the
land of Canaan than human sacrifice and the very harlotry she had submitted to
for so many years. Her faith was not "great" in the sense of Moses or Elijah.
She performed no miracles, nor was she a great prophetess. She merely trusted
that God had a better way than she had.

Samson is another example of an imperfect man. He consorted with
prostitutes, had a bad temper, and many consider his last act to have been
"self-murder," i.e. suicide.[1650] However, E.W. Bullinger said that "His morals
are not to be judged by the standards of the modern views of 'holiness.' All that
is written is 'for our learning,' not for our criticism."[1651] John MacArthur
commented that "we are inclined to judge Samson by his weakness. But God
commends him for his faith."[1652] This is the point. We are all sinners (Romans
3:23). If our salvation depends on our righteousness then we are all doomed.
What God cares about is that we repent and trust in Him.[1653] It is our faith in
Him that makes us strong; not our weaknesses.

Jephthah is the final controversial figure and there is more here to
grapple with than I wish do in this volume. I discuss the debate over Jephthah's
sin in detail in *Controversies in the Scriptures Vol. II*. In summary, Jephthah
was raised in a land where human sacrifice had been common. Israel put a stop
to such sacrifices but the Canaanites had not yet been driven completely from
the land and such practices continued illegally for centuries. When Jephthah

made a hasty and rash vow, he believed it was a worse sin to break his vow to God than to commit the atrocity he had unwittingly promised. Bullinger, like many, denied that he sacrified his daughter,[1654] but whatever his sin, it was no small sin. The land mourned and wept for her and the Israelites commemorated the event for years as a travesty. His sin was not a minor one, but his faith is what Hebrews commends him for. Our sins condemn us. Our faith leads us to repentance and to God's caring arms.

Edwin Long – Jephthah's Vow - The Martyr – 1885

Now Farrar believed that "these latter verses [33-40] are obvious allusions to the sufferings of the *chasideas* ('the Pious') in the days of the priest Matthathias, and the Maccabees."[1655] If so we are again left with examples who were far from perfect, but who trusted in God and had faith that He would redeem Israel.

"The apostle does not commend *all* that they did."[1656] He commends their faith. John Calvin sums this up well when he said, "in all the saints, something reprehensible is ever to be found, yet faith, though halting and inperfect, is still approved by God."[1657]

Does God Change?
Hebrews 13:8

"Jesus Christ *is* the same yesterday and today and forever."

Here is a controversial doctrine. Does God change? Here it is stated plainly that "Jesus Christ is immutable."[1658] This is parallel to Malachi 3:6 in which it is said, "I, the LORD, do not change." This is considered by many another passage proving that Jesus is "the incarnate God,"[1659] but the dissension is not over the divinity of Christ so much as it is over whether or not the God depicted in the Old Testament is the same as the New.

Even the *Liberty Bible Commentary* says that "Christ had not changed since the early days of the New Covenant,"[1660] but this implies that He did change before the New Covenant! Hebrews states emphatically that He is the same "yesterday, today, and forever." Malachi 3:6 declares that God the Father does not change. The "God of the Old Testament" (as some refer to the Father) is the same as the "God of the New Testament." In fact, to use these terms to describe God is dishonest for implies that the "God of the New Testament" is somehow different from the Old, but is He?

God may operate differently at different times, but His purpose has always been the same. This is part of the point of chapter eleven. If the "God of the Old Testament" were different from the New then would he have redeemed sinners like Samson, Rahab, and Jephthah? Could King David, who murdered a man to steal his wife, ever have been called "a man after God's own heart"? People who call the "God of the Old Testament" different from the New understand neither one. "Time changes us" but not Him.[1661] This is important to understand. When dealing with terrorist, for example, they see mercy as weakness. We see mercy as righteousness, because God has changed us. God dealt with Israel harshly because He wanted to make a "nation of priests" (Exodus 19:6) which stood out from the rest of the world in order that He might bring the Messiah Jesus to redeem us all.

God is the same. Charles Spurgeon declared that He "is always the same in his doctrine"[1662] as well. Even the doctrine and teachings of the Old Testament are not different from the New. They have a different *context* and they are not *complete*, but they are the same. They are a *part* of the complete picture; not the whole. Some people do not understand the Old Testament because they have been taught that Christ came to deliver a new law. People think that the standards by which we judge ancient Israel are new, and yet this is the great irony, for without ancient Israel those standards would never have existed. Without the Ten Commandments we could not be appalled at the murders commited in Israel. Without destoying the Canaanites, barbaric as it may seem today, human sacrifice would never have ceased. So we judge ancient Israel by the very standards that they helped to create!

No, God does not change. It is we who have changed, and if we let Him, God can continue to change us, and make us more like Him.

Summary

Hebrews is arguably the most unique of all the epistles. It stands out the most because it is the most Jewish. It is probable that Hebrews was written to a Jewish community which included former priests from the temple, and that this community had been expelled from Jerusalem shortly before its seige by Rome. The terrible events which were to follow would shake the beliefs of the Jewish faithful for millennia, but the author of Hebrews assured the community that Jesus was the true high priest and that no more temple sacrifices were necessary. Life without a temple is a harsh thing for the Jewish faithful, but for those who trust in the Messiah, Jesus we have all that we need.

12

—

James

James is in some respects the most controversial of all the epistles. Martin Luther infamously called it an "epistle of straw" and while he *did* include it in his translation of the Bible (contrary to the claims of some) he did not write a commentary upon it since he believed it should never have been included among the canon.

Most of the controversies all revolve around a single thing; the doctrine of works. Luther had a vehement reaction against any teaching in regard to works because he had been taught his whole life that a thousand years or more of purgatory awaited those who did not have good works. Upon learning of the grace of Christ, he rejected anything to do with works. This overreaction was a result of his Catholic upbringing more than Biblical exegesis, and as the reader will see, James is perfectly consistent with the teachings of Paul and Christ.

Who Wrote James?

Some have also questioned who wrote James. There is no question that it was written by one of the Jameses mentioned in the Bible, but there is much confusion among historians and theologians as to whether or not James the Greater, James the Lesser, or James the Just wrote the epistle. A few have even suggested that James, the father of Judas Iscariot, wrote the epistle![1663]

Most agree that it could not have been written by James the Greater for he was executed in 44 A.D.[1664] While many believe that James was the earliest of the epistles, anytime before 44 A.D. seems far to early. Moreover, the diaspora mentioned in James 1:1 implies that this was probably written after the persecution which dispersed the Jewish followers of Christ (Acts 11:19).

This leaves two serious candidates; James the Less and James the Just. Now under Galatians 1:19 I debated the centuries old dispute over whether or not James the Less and James the Just are actually the same person. I will not repeat that here except in brief. A comparison of Matthew 27:55-56; Mark 15:40; Luke 23:10; and John 19:25 proves that James the Less is the same James who was at the foot of the cross. John 19:25 also proves that there were at least three Mary's at the foot of the cross, one of whom was married to a Clopas or Cleophas, which Calvinist John Gill believed was the Greek transliteration for Alphæus in the Hebrew.[1665] When we further examine Matthew 13:55-56 and Mark 6:3 it becomes apparent that James the Less was a part of Jesus's extended family who all lived together in Nazareth, but he was the son of Mary of Alphæus (Cleophas), and not Mary the mother of Jesus. While Jesus did have half-brothers, James the Less was not one of them. James the Less and James the Just, bishop (or overseer) of Jerusalem, were one and the same person.

That James the Just wrote the epistle may be inferred from the heavily Jewish nature addressed to the "diaspora" but it is also affirmed by ancient tradition ranging from Origen, Eusebius, and Jerome[1666] to Cyril, Athanasius, and Augustine.[1667] A handful of Tübingen school scholars claim that James was merely a "pseudonym" by an anonymous author[1668] but few take them seriously since they have no evidence.

To quote Merrill Tenney, "in any case, James was brought up in the same environment as Jesus and was in close touch with him throughout the years that led up to his ministry."[1669] James the Just was the overseer of Jerusalem and a close family member of Jesus.[1670] He was at the foot of the cross and is called a "pillar of the church" by the apostle Paul (Galatians 2:9). There seems little doubt that it is he who penned this epistle.

The Date and Occasion of the Epistle

A better question is to whom was it addressed and when was it written. James the Just was martyred approximately 62 A.D.[1671] Therefore the broad range is between 45 A.D. and 62 A.D. Narrowing it down further is not hard.

James 1:1 proves this was written to the Jewish-Christian diaspora. It also strongly implies that this was probably written after the persecution which dispersed the Jewish followers of Christ (Acts 11:19). However, it was almost certainly not written after 49 A.D. because the council of Jerusalem is never mentioned, nor alluded to.[1672] Furthermore, several facts indicate an earlier date.

First, the term "synagogue" (James 2:2 in the Greek) is used to refer to the Christian assembly.[1673] Second, in addition to the failure to mention the council of Jerusalem there is also no mention of the circumcision debate or Judaizers,[1674] both of which were major issues in the early church. Some have also commented upon the evidence for a "simple" church made up only of teachers and elders.[1675] Such a structure further implies an early date before churches were largely independent of their synagogual roots. Finally, the heavy "Jewish orientation"[1676] and illustrations from the Old Testament[1677] all suggest that the gentiles had not yet come into the church in any great numbres.

Nevertheless, there are those who argue that this is inconclusive and "a limitation of the address to Jewish Christians and the strongly Jewish outlook of James himself can account for" these evidences.[1678] Despite such protest, the evidence heavily indicates that James was written sometime between 45 and 49 A.D., but probably closer to 45 or 46 A.D. before the issues with circumcision came to the forefront.

If circumcision was not the occasion for the epistle, then why was it written? The best answer seems to be found in James 1:1, Acts 11:19, and subject matter of the epistle. After the Jewish believers were driven away from

Jerusalem, they were outcast. To the Jewish mind this was significant. Jerusalem is the Holy City. Is the center of Jewish worship and James was the overseer or bishop of the church in Jerusalem. To have fled Jerusalem was to be part of the diaspora to which James speaks (1:1). It is perhaps significant that James only addresses the letter to the believers who were scattered abroad and not to those who remained in Judah. The synagogues of Christ, and such they still were, needed guidance and James wrote to them as Jews in Christ. There is no reference to gentiles because gentiles had not yet come into the church in any significant number. In fact, even the Jews of Samaria had only just begun to come to the church (Acts 8-9).

Consequently, James, along with Hebrews, constitutes the most "Jewish" epistle in the New Testament. It reflects Judaism and the early church. Any controversy in James should also be weighed against this fact, for the Jews are, and remain, God's chosen people. Gentiles are brought into communion through Christ, but the special purpose for Israel has not ceased. The Jews of Israel did not reject their religion to become Christians, but affirmed Jesus's own statement; "I did not come to abolish the law, but to fulfill it" (Matthew 5:17).

Does God Tempt?
James 1:13

"Let no one say when he is tempted, 'I am being tempted by God'; for God cannot be tempted by evil, and He Himself does not tempt anyone."

Under Hebrews 2:18 I addressed the question of whether or not Jesus could be tempted by evil. Here I will restrict myself to the question of whether or not God tempts us.

The question is more philosophical than many wish to admit. It involves the very questions; What is evil? Was evil created? If God created everything and everything was good (Genesis 1:31), then how did evil come into being? Like most philosophical questions, sometimes people look too deeply for answers which may be floating on the surface.

Allegedly when posed with this very question a famous man of science said that just as darkness is merely the absence of light, so also evil "is the absence of love, faith and true belief in God."[1679] Evil is not a thing created but it is the absence of good. In ancient Jewish theology man is said to have two natures; the *yetser Hatob* and *yetser Hara* which are good and evil natures, not unlike the original non-Freudian Jekyll and Hyde novel.[1680] To be more precise, however, it is not two natures, but rather the absence of God in men's lives. All men were created good, but we are born without God. We are therefore devoid of the potential for good which is in us. Evil is the inevitable result of when we reject God. While there is still good within us, as dictated by our conscience,

343

our rejection of God also sears our conscience (1 Timothy 4:2) and leaves us with evil. So when men say, "I am good, I deserve to go to heaven," we should be reminded that true goodness is found only in God. While men are still capable of good as dictated by conscience, no man who rejects the Lord can ever be truly good. He has rejected good, and therefore evil reigns in his heart, for evil is the absence of God. This then leads to the question of temptation. What is temptation?

The Nature of Temptation
Theologians have tried various methods of resolving the problem of temptation with the sovereignty of God. If God is good and God is really in charge of everything which happens, then how can temptation happen at all? As the reader can see, the question is directly related to the question of evil resolved above. Still, scholars dispute how this relates to temptation. To that end three resolutions are offered.

View # 1 : God's Permissive Will
Tertullian paraphrased this passage as "suffer us not to be led into it, by him (of course) who temps."[1681] He thus asserted that God allows Satan to tempt us but never does so Himself. This view is erroneously associated with Armenianism because it allows for the active role of Satan, but it is actually consistent with the doctrine of the permissive will of God taught by even the most hardened Calvinist.[1682] The problem is that is can be seen as a cop-out of sorts. Is God's allowing Satan to tempt us really any different from God tempting us? Charles Swindoll believes it is not and argues that "God isn't even *indirectly* involved in temptation."[1683]

View # 2 : Temptation as Testing
Another common understanding is that temptation refers not to true temptation or incitement to sin, but testing or trials such as Job endured.[1684] Zane Hodges notes that "Job *endured* his trials and *resisted* the temptation."[1685] There is a difference.

The Venerable Bede declared that "there is a two fold kind of temptation, one which deceives, the other which tests."[1686] John Darby believed that "temptations springing from the inner man"[1687] and Andreas the church father said "any testing which comes from God is for good ... it is quite otherwise with the devil. He tempts in order to kill."[1688]

Certainly, like the first view, there is an element of truth to this, for James clearly demarks a difference between testing and temptation, but some argue that a "trial of any kind [which may] induce us to sin"[1689] is still a temptation. In other words, failure of a test leads to sin, and this leads to the third view.

View # 3 : The Calvinistic Answer

John Calvin said that "it is abundantly evident that the external temptations, hitherto mentioned, are send to us by God."[1690] He then argued that "inward temptations ... [are the result of] inordinate desires which entice to sin."[1691] In other words, "if a test becomes a temptation, it is sinful human nature that makes it so."[1692] Hence failure leads to temptation.[1693] This is the view taken by men such as John MacArthur who said "if a believer responds in faithful obedience to God's Word, he successfully endures a trial; it he succumbs to it in the flesh ... he is tempted."[1694]

The problem with this view is similar to the others. It skirts around the issue by deflecting God's role in temptation, but if God is sovereign then it is insufficient to say that our failure in a test is not the same thing as a temptation to sin. It is an attempt to split hairs. In some ways Calvinism makes God more involved than the previous views.

Evaluation and Conclusion

The answer may be more simple than we think, but to understand it, we must look at the translation of the passage, for some argue that it holds the key. The word "temptation" occurs five times in James 1:13-14.

> "Let no one say when he is *tempted*, 'I am being *tempted* by God'; for God cannot be *tempted* by evil, and He Himself does not *tempt* anyone. But each one is *tempted* when he is carried away and enticed by his own lust." (James 1:13-14).

Because the word can be translated either "test" or "temptation" some have argued that it can be translated variously. In other words, there are three alleged translations possible. The first is that it should be rendered "test." This, however, looses continuity for it would be saying that God does not "test" when God does test, even as He tested Abraham (Genesis 22:1).

The second is to split the translation with the first instance being translated as "test" and the latter as "tempt. It would read in effect, "no one, when *tested*, should say, 'I am being *tempted* by God.'"[1695] This too must be rejected.[1696] It is not proper exegesis to translate the same word two different ways in the *same* sentence. That is interpretation, not translation.

The final translation is the correct one taken by all translators; render all readings as to "tempt." This is the subject of the passage; temptation. Consequently, the answer is not to be found in the Greek and anyone who makes such a claim is being disingenuous to himself.

The answer lies in not one of the three views stated above, but all of them. However, to understand the connection it is necessary to understand evil. That is why I began with the entire concept of evil. Evil is the absence of God. God cannot be absent from Himself. He, therefore, cannot succumb or be tempted by evil. Man, however, succumbs to temptation and evil during times of testing, because he must ultimately choose whether or not to trust God. Testing involves faith. The absence of faith leads to a rejection of God's will, and that in turn opens the door to the devil and temptation to evil, which is the absence of God to one degree or another. So when we are faced with testing or temptation, we should remember that it is our choice to reject God that leads to the temptation itself. As long as we follow the Lord we will pass every test and every temptation. When we fail it is because we have chosen our own path over that of the Lord God.

The Lawbreaker
James 2:10

"For whoever keeps the whole law and yet stumbles in one *point,* he has become guilty of all. "

The argument of James here is important in understanding the debates which follow. It is also parallel to much of what Paul said in Romans. We cannot be saved by obeying the law or by good works, for if we have sinned in anything, we have broken the law, but some question whether or not this is moral equivalency. If using the Lord's name is vain is the same as murder, then why is it punished more severely? Should not all crime be treated the same? If we are all guilty of breaking the whole law, then why not commit murder, ask the cynic?

Saint Augustine said that "a man is guilty of every crime"[1697] and yet this leads to the moral equivalency question. To answer it we must understand the argument properly. First, Jesus stated that if a man is angry in his heart, then he is guilty of murder in the eyes of the Lord (Matthew 19:18) for the Lord judges by the heart. Does this mean that it would have been better if he had actually commited the murder? Of course not! Such absurdities miss the entire point. A society cannot function without laws, but God judges by the heart. Hatred leads to murder, and hatred is sin. We cannot plead innocent before God when our hearts testify against us. This is the first point James is making. Nor is this new to the New Testament. Leviticus 5:4-5 is an example of where a man must offer a sacrifice even for things he has thought or may not have been aware of at the time.

Second, if we are caught speeding in traffic and get a ticket, we may choose to contest the ticket in court. If we go to court and tell the judge, "but I have obeyed the law thousands of times before and never transgressed the limit before," the court will not care. The judge is not interested in how many times we obeyed the law, but how many times we have broken the law. Says Zane Hodges, the point is that we are all "lawbreakers."[1698] When we break the law, we are guilty and become criminals.

So the point of James's remark is not moral equivalency, but moral accountability. We are *all* guilty before the Law. We are *all* criminals. We are *all* lawbreakers. We *all* need atonement for our sins. Understanding this is important in understanding the following passages, which are among the most controversial in the Bible.

Works and Faith
James 2:14-26

"What use is it, my brethren, if someone says he has faith but he has no works? Can that faith save him?"

Martin Luther so despised the words found in these verses that he rejected the book of James in its entirety. Although he included it in his translation of the Bible, he wrote no commentary upon it and ignored it wholly, for Luther had been raised as a Catholic priest in the Middle Ages. He was taught that good works alone could secure the grace of God. So intertwined was faith and works in the medieval mind set that after finding the grace of God Martin Luther could never accept any works into the equation. To this day both Catholics and Protestants read these passages with biased eye glasses. Neither one wanting to admit they are wrong. To Luther's mind James taught salvation by works. To the Catholic mind, God's grace is obtained through works. Both are sorely mistaken.

The irony is that most Catholic commentators are not significantly different from Protestant commentaries. The primary difference seems to be the nuances, and it is in those nuances that such strong emotions are carried. This is why it is important to remember that just four verses before this one, James said we are all guilty of breaking the whole law. Logically, "the results, guilty of all, contradicts salvation by works."[1699] James is not speaking of salvation by works, and even Catholics do not *claim* to teach such, but he is saying that faith produces works. The controversy is primarily over James's statements, "faith, if it has no works, is dead" (2:17) and "faith without works is useless" (2:20). How are faith and works connected? If we are saved by grace through faith alone, then what has works to do with it?

Perhaps it is best to trace the history of the doctrine. Augustine is sometimes called the father of the Middle Ages. His teachings provided the impetus for medieval theology and the church as it came to be known. He also asserted that Christ said "if you want to enter into eternal life, keep the commandments"[1700] (cf. Matthew 19:17). Notice how Augustine's interpretation of that passage shifts "keeping the commandments" from being the result of faith, to the cause of "entering into eternal life." Nevertheless, not even all of the great medieval theologians agreed with Augustine on this point. Leo the Great declared that "faith provides the basis for works"[1701] while Hilary of Arles went even further in the other direction, stating that "works give life to faith," not *vice versa!*[1702] This is the crux of the debate. Protestant William Barclay said, "the fact is that no man can be saved by works; but equally no man

347

can be saved without producing works."[1703] Faith and works are related to one another, but how?

Some argue that works are related only to sanctification, and not to salvation. Jonathan Edwards, for example, said that too many do "not distinguish between the first and second justification. The first justification, which is at conversion, is a man's becoming righteous, his coming to have a righteousness belonging to him, or imputed to him. This is by faith alone. The second is at judgment, which is that by which a man is proved and declared righteous. This is by works, and not by faith alone."[1704] So he believed that salvation was "by faith alone" but sanctification, or justification, is "not by faith alone." Such words are considered near blasphemy to some, because many consider justification synonymous with salvation. Edwards refers to "two" justifications. Is this true?

James 2:24 states that "a man is justified by works and not by faith alone." He then goes on to say that "Rahab the harlot [was] also justified by works when she received the messengers and sent them out by another way" (2:25). In fact, this section of James is parallel to the Hebrews faith list, with one exception. Hebrews speaks of Rahab's faith while James speaks of Rahab's works. Once again, the two are connected. Hebrews emphasizes the faith which created the works which James emphasizes. Once again we are left with the same question; what is the exact relationship between the two. Nevertheless, this does beg a second question which too few even examine. What is "justification"?

Salvation, Sanctification, and Justification

Some see a direct contradiction between Paul's assertion that Abraham was not justified by works (Romans 4:2-5) and James's assertion that Abraham was justified by works (James 2:21-24). Certainly it is easy to see why some react so vehemently against James, for the words appear at odds, and yet when we read the context they are actually very closely parallel to one another. Nonetheless, the key to understanding the relationship may be in understanding the differences, if any, between salvation, justification, and sanctification.

Salvation, of course, means being saved. We are saved from sin and death, but especially from the second death (Revelation 20:6, 14). Salvation is spoken of by name no fewer than 140 times in the New Testament and is a major theme of the gospels and epistles. It is *the* reason that Jesus died on the cross. How then are we saved? This is the very question at issue. Protestants believe that salvation is grace through faith alone (Ephesians 2:8). Catholics believe that salvation is by grace, but according to the *Catechism of the Catholic Church* "God's salvation, accomplished once for all through Christ Jesus and the Holy Spirit, is made present in the sacred actions of the Church's liturgy."[1705] In other words, that grace is only manifested through the works of the sacraments.

Was James then saying that salvation itself is only accessible through good works? No. Salvation is only mentioned once in this section, and that is discussed in connection with faith (see below). James is talking about justification, not salvation.

Before addressing justification it is necessary to define sanctification. This word comes from the Greek word meaning to be made holy. This is a process by which we are made more and more like Christ. The apostle Paul speaks of sanctification many times, but the word and its cognates does not appear even once in James. Instead he speaks of justification.

Unlike salvation and sanctification there is a wide variety of opinions as to exactly what justification entails and what it means. In Greek it is δικαιοω (*dikaio*) which literally means to "render righteous."[1706] Sometimes it is used in a more negative sense, as in "declared guiltless" or "acquited of a crime."[1707] The first definition is closer to sanctification while the second definition is closer to salvation. Merrill Unger defined justification almost solely in relation to salvation, saying, "justification is a divine act whereby an infinitely Holy God judicially declares a believing sinner to be righteous and acceptable before Him because Christ has borne the sinner's sin on the cross."[1708] Likewise, James Montgomery Boice connects justification directly to propitiation and redemption. He says that because of Christ's propitiation "we, who initate nothing, receive both justification and redemption."[1709] This is the traditional Protestant view that connects justification solely to God and the cross.

The criticism of this view is that if we restrict justification to the acquital of our sins at the cross then we have problems reconciling James 2:21, 24-25 where James states explicitly that we are "justified by works." Now many of us try to skirt around this problem. One author argues that James is speaking not of "justification that is by faith alone" but justification "in the eyes of other people."[1710] However, since when has God ever cared what other people think of Him? Since when is being a Christian transcendent upon other's opinions of us? True, we must live like Christians and not be hyprocrites, but is that not a work? Is that obedience to the Law? No matter how we dodge the issue, it is clear that justification is used beyond the acquital usage.

So Protestants generally see justification as related to salvation wherein "man is passive and God is active ... [but in] sanctification, here man is active."[1711] Nevertheless, James clearly uses justification in an active, not passive, sense of the word. We must, therefore, either conclude that salvation is by works as the heretics claim or that justification is used in connection with sanctification *as well as* salvation.

In short, justification begins at the Cross where we are acquited of our sins through no action of our own, despite our blood guilt. However, justification is not synonymous with salvation. It is a result of salvation, but it is also related in some way to sanctification. The question is how?

James and Paul on Justification

Justification is a major theme in both Romans and James, and they *appear* to have different views of justification. Edited and left in isolation without context, Romans 4:2 and James 2:21 appear in direct contradiction to one another, but when we understand justification and the context of each, the parallels are undeniable.

When we read Romans 4:2+ and James 2:21+ we see amazing parallels. Notice now that both Paul and James use the term "justification" in the same manner. Paul emphasizes that it was Abraham's faith that justified him, but James emphasizes the works that sprang from that faith. However, James goes further, saying "that faith was working with his works, and as a result of the works, faith was perfected" (James 2:22). Hence, James also begins with faith, which produces works, which in turn perfects his faith. How so? Like the author of Hebrews, it begins with faith alone. Then our actions display that the faith is real. Next the results of those actions prove that our faith was not in vain. In this illustration Abraham believed and had faith when he had nothing but God's promise (Romans 4:2). God reconned it to him as righteousness. His faith then displayed itself by his taking Isaac to the mountain and preparing the sacrifice (James 2:22). Next, God kept His promise, showing that Abraham's faith was not misplaced. The result was a more perfect faith (James 2:22).

Paul and James essentially say the same thing except that Paul was speaking as to children. He was writing to gentile converts who knew very little of the Bible or the faith. James was writing to Jewish believers who understood full well the doctrines of grace. James wanted to insure that the church was doing its duty. Paul wanted to teach the church the fundamentals of the faith. The same teachings, but different emphasis for different audiences.

Paul begins with faith and ends with faith. James begins with faith, moves to justification, and ends with perfected faith. There is no difference except in emphasis and audience.

Still this does not settle the issue for many because of centuries of abuse by legalists and libertarians. The Protestants cannot accept works even cursorily involved in salvation (and with good reason) whereas the Catholics will never accept what they see as a libertarian view of salvation (do anything and get a free ticket to heaven). Protestants generally love Paul and ignore James. Catholics generally love James and ignore Paul. Neither will admit to this. Both are wrong. In order to resolve this we must again examine James's comments on "faith that saves" and "dead faith."

Faith That Saves

James says, "What use is it, my brethren, if someone says he has faith but he has no works? Can that faith save him?" (James 2:14). Later he states that "faith, if it has no works, is dead, *being* by itself" (James 2:17). Can that faith save him? Is faith without works dead? These are the two central passages that theologians argue about with fervor and emotion, for how James intended them to be understood ultimately dictates how this entire section on justification is to be understood.

In regard to the first passage, "James does not state that the hypothetical person 'has' faith, but merely a man says he has faith. It distinguishes the one who 'possess' from the one who 'professes.'"[1712] Indeed, James is refuting his alleged faith. It is noteworthy that the Greek contains a definite article before the word faith. This distinguishes his faith from true faith.[1713] It is not, as some Bible have, "can faith save him" (KJV, NKJV, Doauy-Rheims, Darby, Websters), but rather "can *that* faith save him" (NAS, NIV, NLT, RSV, ASV, ESV, Geneva). This is further supported by James's statement, "You believe that God is one. You do well; the demons also believe, and shudder" (James 2:19). Hence, intellectual belief is not true faith.

Some, like Zane Hodges, reject this view, however. He says that "the introduction of words like 'that' or 'such' as qualifiers for 'faith' is really an evasion of the text."[1714] He insist that James is talking about true faith without works, but then evades the text himself by arguing that "save" is not used in the eternal sense, but as saved from "outcome of sin."[1715] Of course the outcome of sin is "death" according to Paul (Romans 6:23), so we cannot get around the fact that James is speaking of salvation.

This leads to the second verse in question. Is faith without works dead? This statement is repeated three times in James. It is found in verses seventeen, twenty, and twenty-six, but some have made careful note of the fact that the Greek word for "dead" in verse twenty is different from the word found in seventeen and twenty-six.[1716] In twenty the word is properly translated as "useless," not dead. If true then this implies that James was not speaking of spiritual death, but of the uselessness of that faith. Still, the King James Bible and many others have "dead" in all three passages. Why? Because the ancient texts are not themselves in agreement.

The majority text or *textus receptus* reads "dead" in all three passages. That reading is also supported in the ancient Codices Sinaiticus (א) and Alexandrinus (A). The word "useless" is found in ancient Codex Vaticanus (B) as well as some other important manuscripts. The Codex Ephraemi (C) is divided with some copies reading "dead" and others "useless." Additionally, the papyrus 74 ($\mathfrak{P}^{74}$) contains the word "empty," which is a synonym for "useless." Obviously some scholars believe that the Sinaiticus (א) and Alexandrinus (A) inadvertently used "dead" because it is found in the parallel passages, but the appearance of "useless" in equally ancient manuscripts may well be the correct one. This is particularly so since the Greek phrase would actually be a play on words, εργων αργη (*ergon arge*).[1717]

The word "dead" in verse twenty is found in the KJV, Tyndale, Webster, Darby, Doauy-Rheims, and Geneva. "Useless" or "barren" or a similar translation is found in the NAS, NIV, NLT, Wycliff, RSV, RV, ASV, and ESV. In either case, the substance is the same. Verses seventeen and twenty-six all contain the word "dead." Once again, that James is referring to false faith, and not true faith, may be inferred from James 2:19, "You believe that God is one. You do well; the demons also believe, and shudder." So it seems that demons have the same faith as the hypothetical man to whom James refers.

Summary and Conclusion

Charles Spurgeon suggests that true faith produces four works. These are work of repentance, works of secret piety, works of obedience, and separating works.[1718] Like most Calvinists Spurgeon believed that perseverance of the saints is not the same thing as the security of the beliver. Calvinists argue that Paul is attacking a "false sense of security"[1719] among the flock. For the Calvinists we cannot know whether or not we are truly saved.[1720] This is ironically very similar to the teaching of the Catholic church where our faith is only "revealed" through the sacraments and our works.

Many Protestants differ from these views, taking the other extreme. One commentator says that "some display this passage to support the notion that genuine faith *inevitably* produces good works."[1721] It is noteworthy, however, that he italicizes "inevitably" and adds a few more addendums to insure that the reader is not left with the impression that faith does not produce good works; only that our salvation does not depend upon it.

It is not difficult to see that these views are as much reactions against heretical extremes as they are exegetical interpretation; perhaps more so. When we examine James and compare it to Romans there is actually a very close parallel save in the use of the term "justification." Paul refers to justification as the direct result of Jesus's sacrifice. James, however, uses the term more in accordance with sanctification. If we understand that we were justified at the cross, but that this justification takes us to and through the process of sanctification then the discrepancies between Paul and James is eliminated. Both begin with faith, and both end with faith, but James is speaking to Jewish believers and emphasizing the sanctifying process which perfects our faith (cf. James 2:22).

John Wesley said that James "refutes not the doctrine of St. Paul, but the error of those who abused it."[1722] John Calvin asked, "Can faith be separated from love?"[1723] Can we claim to love God and hate our brother? As John MacArthur said, "what we do reveals who we are,"[1724] and John Darby said, "the principle of love has to be shewn, not in words but in deeds."[1725] So also Bede commented that "he truly believes who carries out in deed what he believes."[1726]

It is not our works that save us, but rather it is our faith that produces good works. "The very definition of true faith includes the necessity that it will exhibit itself by works."[1727] As Chuck Swindoll asked, "what good is it to carry around a driver's license if you can't actually drive?"[1728] More important than these interpreters or their opinions are the words of Jesus Christ. He declared that a tree is known by the fruit it bears (cf. Matthew 12:33). The real problem is that God alone is the one who sees and taste of the fruits. It is not for us to judge the fruits, but we think it is. We look at our own fruits, or the fruits of others and make judgments about them, but God is the judge. "By their fruits the principles held by men are known."[1729]

One author compares James to an instruction book on skydiving. It closes by explaining that it is not enough to say you are going to pull the ripcord. You have to actually do it.[1730] It is true that some, as Ironside said, "ignor[e] the need of that inner change which Savior described as a new birth."[1731] This is the problem. It is not James which is the problem, nor is it works which is the problem. Nor yet it is the belief in the security of the believer or salvation by grace through faith. The problem is with men who want to sit in the place of God. Whether it is us looking to our own works for comfort and self-righteousness, or looking to others works, it is wrong for man to put the focus on himself.

That James did not believe salvation could be attained by works is clear from James 2:10 where he affirms that we are all guilty before God. "The results, guilty of all, contradicts salvation by works."[1732] James, like Jesus (cf. Matthew 19:17), believed that faith produces works, but works does not produce faith. Works will not save you. Grace saves us through faith, which in turn produces works. The two cannot be confused.

The Greater Judgment
James 3:1

"Let not many *of you* become teachers, my brethren, knowing that as such we will incur a stricter judgment."

In the world of politics we all know that the greater the power one has, the less accountability he has. We also know that the less accountability a politician has, the more corrupt they become. In God's eyes the opposite is true. The more with which we are entrusted, the greater the judgment. Preachers, teachers, and leaders will be held to a higher standard. That is why Jesus said, "to whom much is given, much is expected" (Luke 12:48).

John Wesley believed that James "includes himself"[1733] among these teachers. Indeed, "it was a solemn responsibility to assume the role of a teacher."[1734] Each generation ultimately becomes what the teachers teach them to be, but many seek teaching positions for prestige and honor,[1735] rather than out of pure motives. This is also one reason that Hollywood and the entertainment culture have caused so much harm. They have become the new teachers for the younger generation. With the takeover of public education by secularists, marxists, and other anti-Christian groups, our new generations are increasingly becoming antagonistic against Christ Jesus.

Some believe that more is meant that just teaching. They believe that this is tied more directly to speech.[1736] John Darby noted that "humility in the heart makes a man slow to speak."[1737] This fits the context which follows, for there James speaks about keeping a tight reign on our tongues, saying that the "tongue is a fire" (3:6) and "no one can tame the tongue; *it is* a restless evil *and* full of deadly poison" (3:8). Although James was speaking of teachers, he was also indicating that what we say to one another is a form of teaching as well. We all teach our children, and our actions and words teach the world about who we really are.

Necessity of Humility
James 4:6-10

> "He gives a greater grace. Therefore *it* says, 'God is opposed to the proud, but gives grace to the humble.'"

We have heard churches today teach the Flower Child "Me generation" doctrine of "self-esteem" and "self-worth." We hear teachers like James Dobson telling us to "brag on ourselves"[1738] but the Bible tells us "God is opposed to the proud, but gives grace to the humble." Humility is the key to living like Christ.

Isaiah 57:15 says, "I dwell *on* a high and holy place, And *also* with the contrite and lowly of spirit. In order to revive the spirit of the lowly and to revive the heart of the contrite." No one can approach the throne of God who is proud. Pride was the sin that cast Satan from heaven, for he did not wish to serve man.

John MacArthur believes that this humility is tied to salvation.[1739] He denies that James is speaking to believers, but to unbelievers. Charles Spurgeon said that God demands "unconditional surrender."[1740] Humility is thus a prerequisite to repentance. Certainly the proud have no need of God, for they believe they are self-sufficient. Only a humble man needs help. Douglas Moo argued that "God's gift of sustaining grace is enjoyed only by those willing to admit their need and accept the gift."[1741] Now I will not engage in a debate upon Lordship salvation, for I have debated that before; but I do agree that pride and Christianity have no place together. The proud man cannot repent and turn to God. Only the humble man who admits his unworthiness before God will ever even admit to needing God.

Humility is the lost virtue of the church. The modern church has echoed the secular world and its lie of self-sufficiency and self-gratification. Jesus called for self denial. "If anyone wishes to come after Me, he must deny himself, and take up his cross and follow Me" (Matthew 16:24; Mark 8:34; Luke 9:23).

354

Summary

James is a controversial book because few understand its background. James was writing to early Jewish Christians. They were dispersed among the gentiles and felt cut off from their own people. The context of James is Jewish. Many have noted similarities between James and the Sermon on the Mount.[1742] Indeed, many of the same controversies exist in both.

James was close to Jesus and a follower in the days of Jesus's ministry. He heard Jesus and was taught by Jesus. His audience was Jesus's audience. Paul spoke to new gentile converts. James spoke to lifelong Jews. Paul spoke to spiritual infants. James spoke to those to whom the word had been entrusted. The content of their teachings is the same, but the recipients were different, so the emphasis and flavor differ.

James was also the first epistle written. It reflects the early church even before the controversy over circumcision erupted. As such it is an important book which cannot and should not be neglected, discarded, or dismissed. Too much time has been spent trying to "reconcile" James to the teachings of a particular sect. It needs no such reconciliation. The Word of God stands on its own, and needs no help from man. James was neither Catholic, nor Calvinist, nor any other sect. He was an apostle.

Rembrandt – The Apostle Peter Kneeling – 1631

13

—

1 & 2 Peter

James was the first epistle written, but First and Second Peter are among the last epistles written, just before Peter was martyred. All but the Tübingen school of thought agree that the first epistle of Peter generally dates to around 63 or 64 A.D. while the second one was written most likely from prison in 65 A.D. shortly before his death, but, as expected, the Tübingen school does not agree. In fact, 2 Peter is among the most disputed epistles in the Bible.

The Date and Occasion of 1 Peter

1 Peter was written against the "ominous shadow of persecution,"[1743] as one historian put it. However, there is some question as to the exact date for some question if there was already an "imperial ban" since he still speaks of government as protector (2:13-17),[1744] but this is not a good argument. Peter is telling Christians not to rebel against Rome. We are submit in whatever manner does not require us to disobey God. This is the history of the early church. We could have rebelled. We could have risen up and been slaughtered as revolutionaries, but instead we quietly and passively walked into the lion's den. Moreover, while revisionist historians claim that the persecution of Nero was restricted to Rome, this is not true. For one thing, there was no such thing as a regional imperial edict. Secondly, why would Christians not just leave Rome if that is the case? It is true that the persecution was less severe outside of Rome, but that explain Peter's warnings. The persecutions had probably already begun in Rome, or were about to begin. Peter's warnings thus meet an immediate need.

Nonetheless, critics reject a date for Nero altogether, and hence Petrine authorship. They claim that an imperial ban better fits Domitian or the Trajan persecution of 98-117 A.D.[1745] They also claim that 1 Peter is "dependent" upon New Testament writings[1746] and "deutero-Pauline epistles."[1747] Since they claim that the New Testament was not canonized until much later than the first century, they question a first century author. Of course this is disengenous for Peter would certainly have been familiar with the writings of his fellow apostles! Additionally, calling Paul's epistles "deutero-Pauline" is dishonest for it assumes the Pauline epistles are not genuine. Since Peter acknowledges them, then they argue Peter cannot be genuine either. Such double talk is not scholarly.

Another reason for attempting to late date 1 Peter are the similarities between 1 Peter and the epistle of Barnabas and Clement of Rome.[1748] Of course this is even less sincere for it is just as likely that the epistle of Barnabas and Clement borrowed from Peter! This would then support a first century author.

Next, some critics say that Peter was "unschooled" and therefore question the polished Greek of 1 Peter.[1749] This argument seems to based on a modern western mindset which says that no one can write or speak multiple languages unless they have a college degree, but Jews were all home schooled. It was a part of Judaism to teach children at home. This is why the Jews became the bankers of medieval Europe. They were the only ones educated enough to do so! Moreover, Peter grew up near the Greek Decapolis which almost certainly meant that he would have learned to speak, read, and write Greek.[1750]

Finally, critics hurl the typical "style arguments"[1751] which says that the "style" is not Peter's. Of course, if Peter didn't write 1 and 2 Peter then we would have no writings of Peter, so one what basis does the critic say that these epistles are not his "style"? They show differences between 1 and 2 Peter (see below) but considering the brevity of the letters and the different subject matter the judgment of "style" is necessarily subjective.

In fact, the style is actually very close to what we do know about Pter. There are, for example, close parallels between this and Peter's sermons in Acts. Compare 1 Peter 1:20 with Acts 2:23 or 1 Peter 4:5 with Acts 10:42. Even 1 Peter 2:7-8 bears similarities to Acts 4:10-11.[1752]

The fact is that Petrine authorship and a Neronian dating were accepted by Polycarp (John's disciple), Clement (mentioned in Philippians 4:3), and Irenaeus.[1753] Such strong and very early testimonial support cannot be discarded by superficial and subjective theories. Peter wrote this epistle probably in 64 A.D. not long after the fires in Rome were blamed on Christians. The letter was distributed to warn Christians about the coming persecution and to urge us not to rise up in rebellion but to prove our good citizenship and innocence.

The Date and Occasion of 2 Peter

Unlike 1 Peter, which is disputed only by Bible critics, 2 Peter is among the most disputed books of the New Testament. It is one of only seven epistles whose place in the canon was questioned during the second century and it is not identified by name in any *extant* writing until Origen at the beginning of the third century.[1754] Nevertheless, this is not really problematic. For one thing, the fact that it does not appear to be quoted exactly in any extant first or second century document does not mean that it was not quoted. Indeed, Origen admits to its existence in the second century. Moreover, it is acknowledged that there are very close similiarities to the epistles of Barnabas and Clement[1755] as well as the late first and early second century writings, *Shepherd of Hermas* and the *Didache*.[1756] All these early writings may well have been paraphrasing Peter, since none quote the Scriptures by name. Additionally, the early papyrus 72 ($\mathfrak{P}^{72}$) "shows acceptance of 2 Peter as canonical."[1757]

Aside from the fact that it was not widely distributed in the second century, is there really any reason to reject Petrine authorship? The best arguments in favor of Peter are the general weakness of the arguments against it. Eleven arguments have been leveled against 2 Peter.[1758] None of them is particularly strong.

The first argument is the one already mentioned. There is no long line of Petrine tradition can be traced back to the first century. However, "because of the letter's brevity, governmental persecutions of the early churches, and communication problems in the ancient world, the lack of a long tradition for 2 Peter is hardly surprising."[1759] Moreover, extant writings from the first and second century are very limited. The fact that 2 Peter even exist today is very strong evidence of such a tradition. Its preservation in papyrus 72 ($\mathfrak{P}^{72}$) and every early Codex strongly supports its antiquity.

The second argument is that its "style" is too different from 1 Peter to have been written by the same author. Some have answered this by saying that the differences may due to a different amanuensis (secretary)[1760] but this is not likely since Peter, and not his secretary, was the true author. The fact is that stylistic arguments are inherently the most subjective. Considering the brevity of these two (and only two) letters attributed to Peter it is impractical to argue that you can ascertain someone's "style" based on two short letters. Style is effected by many things, including subject matter. Moreover, some will argue the opposite. For example, similarities to 1 Peter include the fact that "of the 686 *hapax legomena* in the New Testament, 1 Peter contains 62 and 2 Peter has 54."[1761] A *hapax legomena* is a word found only in the New Testament, indicating unique vocubulary choices. Additionally, similar idioms are used in both epistles. Compare 1 Peter 1:2 with 2 Peter 1:2; 1 Peter 2:9 with 2 Peter 1:3; 1 Peter 3:31 with 2 Peter 1:14; and 1 Peter 1:19 with 2 Peter 2:13, 3:14.[1762] The similarities are more obvious in the Greek! So also, 1 and 2 Peter feature unique vocabulary shared only with Peter's sermons in Acts (compare Acts 4:21 with 2 Peter 2:9; Acts 33:12 with 2 Peter 1:3; and Acts 1:18 with 2 Peter 2:13, 15).[1763] The argument from style is subjective and can go either way.

Third, critics note that the gnostics created many pseudo-Petrine works, but this is frivolous for all those fake gospels and epistles have *always* been recognized for what they were ... frauds. Using this phony reasoning one could argue that the gospels are fakes simply because gnostics created fake heretical gospels in the second century (such as the "Gospel of Thomas"). This is intellectual dishonesty *at best*.

Another argument is that knowledge of 2 Peter was "geographically limited." This argument is similar to the first, but acknowledges that 2 Peter was indeed known, so in a way this argument actually contradicts the first. More importantly, "persecution, the brevity of 2 Peter, or its remote destination resulted in it not being widely circulated"[1764] in the first century. Since it was written in the mid-60s, it is hardly surprising that its distribution would be limited amid these circumstances for 35 years, and into the second century.

Another argument for a late date of 2 Peter, and therefore a rejection of Petrine authorship, is its alleged dependence on Jude. While similarities between 1 and 2 Peter are ignored or dismissed, similarities between Jude and 2 Peter are used to argue that 2 Peter must have "borrowed" from Jude, and therefore date after Jude's writing. Of course, this is flawed for two major reasons. First, it assumes a late date for Jude, and second, it assumes that Jude could not have "borrowed" from 2 Peter. Since the alleged relationship between the two is tentative, there is no evidence that 2 Peter "borrowed" from Jude and it is equally possible that Jude "borrowed" from 2 Peter. This argument is frivolous since depends on unproven assumptions.

Like the argument against 1 Peter, it is alleged that the "conceptual and rhetorical language is too Hellenistic for a Galilean fisherman."[1765] In other words they again attack the Biblical Peter as an "unschooled" fisherman,[1766] just as Jesus was criticized (cf. Matthew 13:54-56). The rebuttal is that Peter lived about five miles from the Greek Decapolis![1767] He would certainly have known Greek. It is not uncommon even today for poor and "uneducated" people to speak multiple languages, depending on the part of the world you live in. Since Jews were known for home schooling their children, it is highly likely that Peter was fluent in Greek, Hebrew, and Aramaic. Some have also suggested that his amanuensis (secretary) translated for him.[1768] Either way, it is a poor argument to say that someone cannot write because they are from a poor background.[1769]

A seventh argument is that the "delay" of the second coming (2 Peter 3:8) is a "second century teaching" which did not exist in the first century. This is yet another assumption which not only cannot be proven, but can, in fact, be easily refuted within the Bible itself. Consider passages like John 21:20-23 and 2 Thessalonians 2:1-4, as well as possible allusions in Matthew 25:1-13 and Acts 1:6-11. The critic again makes an assumption without proof and uses that assumption to invalidate evidence that he is wrong!

Eighth, it is alleged that Peter's acceptance of Pauline epistles as scripture (2 Peter 3:16) dates to second century since they believe Paul's epistles could not have been canonized before them. Nevertheless, Peter was not relying on any church council, but the Word of God. "That Luke or Timothy were traveling companions of Paul makes them likely collectors of his writings."[1770] Both were also known to Peter so there is no question that Peter knew of and read all of Paul's epistles. His testimony that they are Scripture is based on his authority as an apostle, and not some later church council!

A ninth argument is essentially a repetition of the first and fourth arguments, designed to make it look like they have more evidence than they really do. Why, they asks, is 2 Peter not quoted by any second century author? The rebuttal is the same as in points one and four. "Much of the literature of the early church has not survived"[1771] and what has survived may at least allude to

2 Peter even if they don't quote him verbatin (see notes on the first and fourth arguments above).

Next, it is argued that the epistle resembles "early Catholicism" rather than first century Christianity. Obviously this relies on "questionable assumptions"[1772] and is highly debateable regardless of whether or not you are a Catholic or Protestant. Indeed, one might asked why Peter never asserts his authority as "pope" if this is a late forgery representative of "early Catholicism."

Finally, they asks why, if Peter really wrote this, was there ever any doubt as to its authenticity. Notice how the same argument is used four times (see arguments one, four, and nine). They think that somehow saying the same thing four different times makes their list of "proofs" sound stronger, but the weakness of all of these arguments is further strength of its authority.

The fact is that Petrine authorship is strongly supported from within the epistle itself. Not only does it bear striking similarities to the sermons of Peter in Acts, but "the letter gives no hint of a second-century environment or of problems such as the monarchical bishop, developed gnosticism, or Montanism."[1773] The epistle also mentions 1 Peter in 2 Peter 3:1.[1774] It is found in early Biblical collections such as papyrus 72 ($\mathfrak{P}^{72}$) and every early Codex. Despite its recognition by every church father and council since the early third century, some deny Petrine authourship but still accept it as canonicity![1775] This absurdity would make one of the Biblical authors a liar!

The best evidence supports that this was Peter's last epistle written on his deathbed. He most likely wrote the epistle from prison while awaiting his execution. As I discuss under 1 Peter 5:13 it is likely that Peter was held in prison while Nero attempted to extract a "confession" for the fire in Rome. As a leader of the church he was a prize who was held for execution on a day of bread and circuses when thousands of Christians, including Peter and Paul (for a defense of this see my debate in *The Apostles After Jesus*) were executed across Rome. Like 2 Timothy for Paul, this was Peter's farewell epistle.

Pre-existence of Christ
1 Peter 1:20

"For He was foreknown before the foundation of the world, but has appeared in these last times for the sake of you."

Predestination has been discussed before (see Ephesians 1:1-12) but the question of the pre-existence of Christ has only been alluded to in such passages. His pre-existence is evident in passages like Colossians 1:15-19 but here another allusion.

Some have questioned this. They say that the "foreknowledge of God does not necessarily imply pre-existence."[1776] While technically true, it is apparent that Christ is pre-existent and eternal. The obvious reference is in Colossians 1:15-19 where it is apparent that Christ was not made. He was the

Creator; God incarnate. Here Peter only alludes to the fact that Christ was foreknown or foreordained. Some Bible translate this is "chosen." Now "'foreordained' in the Greek text means 'to designate before hand.'"[1777] History was always intended to revolve around Christ. As discussed in Ephesians 1:1-12 and elsewhere, history is no accident. History is a chance for us all to see the folly of Satan and his angels. We cannot live without God. We cannot love without God. Only through Christ Jesus can we truly know God.

Lenski said that "all such references to eternity ... are beyond human comprehension."[1778] How can a temporal creature even comprehend what eternity past means? For us there always a beginning and an end. It is that end that drives man in either his fear or in his love.

The ancient *Shepherd of Hermas* says that "He became manifest in the last days of the dispensation."[1779] It was by "prior determination on the part of the Father, to send the Son"[1780] in order that we might be reconciled to him. Here in this short sentence Peter parallels Ephesians 1:1-12 and Colossians 1:15-19, showing that all history is, and has ever been, about is our Lord Jesus Christ.

Family, Women, and Modesty
1 Peter 3:1-7

> "Your adornment must not be *merely* external – braiding the hair, and wearing gold jewelry, or putting on dressesbut *let it be* the hidden person of the heart, with the imperishable quality of a gentle and quiet spirit, which is precious in the sight of God."

The issue of women, family, and modesty was addressed under 1 Timothy 2:9-10. Here again Peter affirms what Paul teaches. Here again, the Bible is erroneously accused of "sexism" and "misogynism" for love of family and modesty. Of particular offense is the use of the term "weaker" in verse seven and the reference to Sarah calling her husband "Lord" (see notes below on 1 Peter 3:6).

As to the term "weaker sex" it has been argued that this refers to "physical strength"[1781] but whether that is true or not, it is the duty of every Christian man to protect the weak. The "weaker sex" is not an insult to revile women, but a reminder that a woman is to be protected and loved. Jonathan Edwards said "a weaker vessel must be taken more care of, and more tenderly used than another. The stronger must give honor to the weaker in respect of service; the weaker has the greater need of being served, needs to have more done for it."[1782] This was the code of chivalry in a nutshell, now demonized by a culture which thinks that unisexuality is "equality." We are told, erroneously, that "under Jewish law a woman was a thing,"[1783] and yet such an outrageously false statement, uttered by a Christian theologian no less, only serves to degrade the Biblical reverence for motherhood and family. The human race was made

362

with two sexes for a reason. It was not to be unisexual, nor to for the two to hate one another, but for the two to complement one another's strengths and weaknesses, and to raise godly children. For that reason, the question of submission once again arises.

Some "liberal" theologians argue that "Peter is not legitimizing a patriarchal familial regime ... Peter simply deals with the household regime that exist in his time."[1784] Notice how he uses the word "regime" to define family. Traditional families where mothers are revered and worshipped by their children are now "patriarchal familial regimes"![1785] We expect that children are to be raised by nannies or day care centers, and if someone objects we hear a lecture on bad fathers. Such is the world in which we live.

In the Bible submission has nothing to do with inferiority. Christians are even expected to submit to the very government which fed us to lions. Submission is about a principle of love. R.C. Sproul said that "a submissive spirit might bear witness to the truth of the gospel."[1786] More than this, it is a witness. St. Augustine famously praised his mother Monica for winning his pagan father to Christ "through her conduct."[1787] She obeyed 1 Peter 3:1-4 and showed him what a Christian woman was like. Martin Luther thought that "it is the wife's duty to be submissive to her husband, even though he is a heathen or unbeliever."[1788] This was the case with Queen Esther, who is revered by men and women alike, but when we read the story of Esther we see a woman who won her husband over and saved a nation by behaving like a woman, and by acting submissive rather than domineering. This is why H.A. Ironside believed that "dominating women will drive her husband further from God"[1789] but a loving submissive wife will show her husband God's love. It is about "the silent preaching of a lovely life."[1790]

A great analogy is the one whereby "divine revelation has often been compared to the sun."[1791] By it we see, and we can feel its warmth, but it does not need to beat us or burn us. It is a soft ray of light that shows us what we see. Through love we show the world that our words are not empty and vain. This is also to be shown in our conduct and our dress.

The purpose for provocative clothes is to get attention, but it is usually the wrong kind of attention. This is why the apostle tells us that a woman's "beauty should not come from outward adornment, such as braided hair and the wearing of gold jewelry and fine clothes. Instead, it should be that of your inner self, the unfading beauty of a gentle and quiet spirit, which is of great worth in God's sight. It was in this way long ago that holy women who trusted in God used to adorn themselves by accepting the authority of their husbands."

Allan Bloom has noted that "central to the feminist project is the suppression of modesty ... modesty in the old dispensation was *the* female virtue."[1792] Since feminism is about power, sex becomes a means to an end, and yet in "liberating" women from their virtues "men have also become liberated from their old constraints."[1793] The feminist has created her own worst enemy.

If she can use her body for her own means, then the man too is more than eager to use her body for his own means. The result is anything but equality. Such problems have always existed, but modesty forces men to look at woman's heart and soul. It also makes the woman use her heart and soul.

Does wearing jewelry make a woman decadent? Of course not, but "conspicuous, extravagant, intricate artificiality"[1794] does make a woman look artificial. As MacArthur said, "the text does not prohibit wives from styling their hair, wearing jewelry or lovely clothing, which is why the translation added 'merely'"[1795] but such jewelry, hair design, and make-up should be kept to a minimum. As a man I can testify that relying too much on make-up and jewelry does not really enhance a woman's beauty at all. It only makes her look fake. Here then Peter is again pleading with us to let our spirit and soul show through our lives. There is nothing wrong with a woman trying to look attractive, but her attraction should be more than mere physical beauty, but the beauty of soul which never fades or grows old.

Did Sarah Call Abraham "Lord"?
1 Peter 3:6

"Just as Sarah obeyed Abraham, calling him lord."

Here Peter paints a picture of Sarah's submission by noting that she called him "lord." Such a statement is not only controversial from the perspective of modern feminism, but many say that there is no such passage in the Bible. In fact, the latter statement is incorrect. While there is no explicit verse stating that she called him "master," the word Hebrew word בעל (Ba'al) means "lord" or "master" and is the *same* word as is sometimes used for "husband."[1796] The root of this word means "to have dominion over" or "to possess."[1797]

So in the Bible the husband is the "master of the house." This is probably where the phrase originated. Consequently, the idea once again revolves around the family, not slavery or superiority. It is not about control or domination, but an orderly structure for family. The family is the basic premise by which these principles are based. "Men must love and be loyal to their family and their peoples in order to preserve them,"[1798] and yet this is the very reason that Karl Marx believed the family had to be abolished. He stated in the *Communist Manifesto* that Communism seeks "abolition of the family."[1799] In order for his mythical utopia to exist, "society," as defined by the state, must supercede family. Families preserve one another at all cost. Governments sacrifice people for the "good of society." Consequently, the two are often at odds. This is why the family structure has been under attack since the publication of the *Communist Manifesto*. This is why we are told that motherhood is somehow akin to slavery. God, however, made the mother the most important thing in a child's life. The man is the "master of the house" but the mother is the life of a child. Why?

Perhaps one reason that most mothers love their children even more than their husbands is because the child sprouted forth from their own womb, but more than that, the mother goes through excrutiating pain when she gives birth to a child. That pain actually strengthens her attachment to the baby. Perhaps this is also why natural childbirth is more healthy for both the baby and the mother.

Preaching to the Dead
1 Peter 3:18-22

"For Christ also died for sins once for all, *the* just for *the* unjust, so that He might bring us to God, having been put to death in the flesh, but made alive in the spirit in which also He went and made proclamation to the spirits *now* in prison."

Here is one of the most controversial and divisive passages in the New Testament. Of this passage Martin Luther once said, "this is a strange text and certainly a more obscure passage than any other passages in the New Testament. I still do not know for sure what the apostle means."[1800]

It is parallel to Ephesians 4:9, but even more explicit and clear that that passage. That passage reads, "Now this *expression,* 'He ascended,' what does it mean except that He also had descended into the lower parts of the earth?" (Ephesians 4:9). There were four major interpretations of those words. The first was that it refers only to the incarnation, but that obviously cannot be to what Peter refers. The second was that Ephesians refers to the physical death of Jesus, but again Peter is speaking of making a "proclamation to the spirits in prison." The third and fourth views are divided between *Sheol* or *Hades,* and Hell itself. It would seem that Peter is referring to one of these two options (but even this is in dispute). Nonetheless, the division is not only over what is meant by preaching to the spirits in prison, but what this means theologically. Is there a chance to repent after death? What was Jesus proclaiming? What is the "quickening" of which verse eighteen speaks? Each of these is debated and has been debated throughout the ages.

The Quickening
After His death Jesus was "made alive in the spirit." This phrase, "made alive," is in the Old English "quickening." The question posed by some is whether he was quickened "*in* the Spirit" or "*by* the Spirit." This subtle difference ultimately is a question of two things. Was He resurrected by the Holy Spirit as Matthew Poole believed,[1801] or it is a contrast between his physical body and His own spirit as held by many others?[1802] If this refers to the former, then it may be a reference to the resurrection. If this be so then the "preaching" of Jesus to the

"spirits in prison" would have to have taken place *after* the resurrection and not during the time *before* His resurrection. This obviously factors into one's interpretation of the "the spirits in prison."

One problem with this from an exegetical standpoint is the fact that the Greek is ambiguous. Virtually every text simply reads "spirit" without a preposition. The word "spirits" is in the dative case in Greek which, depending on the context, can be translated either "in" or "by" so that the Greek is not particularly helpful.[1803] This could be why the ancient papyrus 72 ($\mathfrak{P}^{72}$) adds the word "in," but no other extant manuscript contains this word. It thus represents an ancient interpretation.

The critcicism of "in the spirit" is that it "might suggest that the spiritual aspect of Christ (His divine soul) died" along with His body.[1804] This would, of course, be blasphemy, but it is also not the logical interpretation. The parallelism of flesh and spirit, body and soul, strongly suggest that this is the analogy Peter was making. Moreover, if we argue that this is a veiled reference to the resurrection then the problem with the "spirits in prison" is not solved as some believe. It may, in fact, be amplified.

"By the Spirit" may be found in the KJV, NIV, NKJV, Webster, and Geneva, but "in the Spirit" is prefered by the NAS, MKJV, NLT, RV, RSV, NRSV, Tyndale, Wycliff, ASV, Darby, Douay-Rheims, and ESV translations. It is also supported in the ancient papyrus 72 ($\mathfrak{P}^{72}$).

It would seem that "in the Spirit" is the most natural understanding. If Peter referred to the Holy Spirit he would almost certainly have added the adjective "Holy" which is lacking here. More over, the parallelism to His physical body would be lost, for was not Jesus's *body* resurrected? It was not His Spirit that was raised from the dead, as the gnostic heretics claimed, but His body. Our souls never die, but our temporal bodies inevitably will. In either case, the Spirit of Christ is contrasted with His body. He had died, but His Spirit lived. Peter is thus speaking of what happened after Jesus's death on the cross, not what happened after His resurrection.

What is the Prison?

Jesus preached to "the spirits in prison" after his death. This is the subject, and this is the controversy. Martin Luther called this a "strange" and "obscure"[1805] passage and there are no ends to the debates over its meaning. Five basic views have dominated over the centuries, although some are more prominent than others.

"Those Who are Now Dead"

Some have taken this to mean that "the dead could mean that they were dead when Peter writes, but were alive when the gospel was preached to them."[1806] They thus make this out to be a reference to those to whom Jesus preached when He was alive, and who have since passed away unto death. This view, however, cannot stand. First, it is explicitly clear *that after* Jesus's death

"He went and made proclamation to the spirits *now* in prison." If we remove the passage about Jesus being made alive in the Spirit, the full sentence reads, "having been put to death in the flesh ... He went and made proclamation to the spirits *now* in prison." The addition of the word "now" in the NAS is interpretive for the word is not to be found in the Greek nor in any other translation. Logically and exegetically Peter is speaking of a sequence of events, and this proclamation made to the spirits was clearly made after His death, not during His lifetime.

Literal Prisoners in this World

A similar argument is that after His resurrection Jesus preached to literal prisoners.[1807] A few may argue that He did so during his imprisonment and trial, but this would again fail the exegesis test in regard to Peter's sequence of events. As to preaching after His resurrection, there is no indication that Jesus preached to prisoners anywhere in Acts, the Gospels, or anywhere else. Some have further commented that if Jesus had been preaching to living people, Peter would have used the word "souls" rather than "spirits."

According to this allegorical view, held by men like Bede,[1808] these prisoners are "slaves and captives of Satan."[1809] The passage is thus not taken as literal spirits but men. Nevertheless, this fails to explain the context of the "days of Noah" and the "disobedient" ones who were judged. What is the connection? To take this as some analogy is not sufficient unless we can explain the logical connection to Noah and the fact that "angels and authorities and powers had been subjected to Him" (3:22). Surely these are not unrelated.

Preaching in the Days of Noah

Verse twenty connects these spirits in prison to those "who once were disobedient, when the patience of God kept waiting in the days of Noah." Consequently, some have devised an extravagant interpretation whereby Peter is referring to a preincarnate Christ who had preached the gospel to the wicked generation of Noah.[1810] Gleason Archer combines this view with the first view suggesting that it was to the spirits of those who died in the days of Noah that Jesus preached.[1811]

This view is the only one thus far that addresses the "days of Noah" but it does so in a way that again looses all continuity with the previous passage. It is after Jesus's death that he preaches to the spirits; not millennia before He was born incarnate.

Hell

It has been established that Peter is speaking about what happened *after* Jesus's death. It seems equally apparent that this happened before His resurrection. Therefore a common argument is that the "spirits in prison" refers to demons, or the dead who have been sent to hell. This is the view held by some charismatics who believe that the Passion included not only the cross but

367

also a visit to hell before His resurrection.[1812] Obviously, this has theological problems as well as reading too much into the context.

Interestingly enough, there are some variants of this view which avoid the necessity of Jesus being in hell. Calvin believed that this was a spiritual presense and not a "real presense"[1813] while Linski argued that Jesus went directly to heaven upon His death,[1814] but then says at resurrection "in that instant, but timelessly, Christ in his human body and spirit descended to hell and did what Peter relates."[1815]

As the reader can see, the view seems the most straightforward on the surface, but has many problems and assumptions. How can we reconcile Christ preaching in hell without Him being there, and if He was in hell then the words of Jesus in Luke 23:43 would be a lie, for there Jesus told the repentant thief on the cross, "Truly I say to you, today you shall be with Me in Paradise." Obviously Paradise is not hell.

Sheol

One view remains. Some have wrongly confused it with the doctrine of purgatory but, in fact, the Fourth Council of Toledo in 633 does not teach that purgatory is referenced here.[1816] They instead appear to agree with most evangelicals, that Peter is referring to Paradise (Luke 23:43; 2 Corinthians 12:4) or "Abraham's Bosom" (Luke 16:22). According to this, the abode to where all the dead descend is called *Sheol* (sometimes called *Hades* from the Greek). This place is divided into two halves; one where the wicked await judgment and hell and the other where the righteous await the resurrection and heaven. The wicked are placed in a place often called *Hades* (although not all make this distinction) whereas the righteous rest in Paradise (Luke 23:43; 2 Corinthians 12:4) or "Abraham's Bosom" (Luke 16:22).

The doctrine of *Sheol* is found throughout the Bible and Jewish literature (see notes on Ephesians 4:9). It may be referenced in Acts 2:27 as well.[1817] "The Syriac here is 'in Sheol,' referring to the abode of the dead,"[1818] and thus showing ancient support for this interpretation. If true, it solves most of the problems above. "If Jesus descended into *Hades* [or Paradise], then Jesus Christ really and truly died ... if ... then it means that the triumph of Christ is literally universal ... and if He ... preached there, then there is no corner of the universe into which the message of grace has not come."[1819]

This view is accepted by a vast diversity of scholars throughout the ages from Irenaeus[1820] down to Charles Swindoll.[1821] It is found in the Creed of Sirmiun (circa 359 A.D.)[1822] and the Apostle's Creed. It is the most straightforward understanding of the passage and solves the problems with chronology, exegesis, and even the preaching to the dead, although there is dispute as to exactly whom Jesus was preaching, and what the message He was preaching may have been.

What Was Preached and To Whom?

Obviously one's interpretation of the prison is directly tied to the belief in whom Jesus was preaching. Even then the message of what Jesus is questioned. One could break the interpretations down into as many as a half dozen or more view, but some are so similar that they can be classified together into one of four different categories. Let us again look at these individual theories and interpretations.

View # 1 : Preaching the Gospel to Those in Hades

One of the most popular views is that Christ extends the offer of salvation to the lost who have died.[1823] Clement of Alexandria believed that Jesus preached to those who had never heard the gospel.[1824] Some go even one step further, saying "if ever hereafter they accept the Gospel" they might be saved.[1825] Now this latter remark may be rejected for the entire point of this life is that we will choose to either harden our hearts or repent. Faced with the fires of hell who wouldn't *pretend* to repent?[1826] Clement of Alexandria's thesis is better, but unnecessary. If God judges by the heart then it is fair enough to say that He knows who would have accepted the gospel (if any) had they heard it.

The strongest support for this view comes from the parallel passage in 1 Peter 4:6. There it is said that "the gospel has for this purpose been preached even to those who are dead." This seems strong support, but the context around that verse can also favor the other views listed below. For that reason I will withhold comment here.

This view is favored by those who feel that it gives hope to the lost. Said William Barclay, "the doctrine of the descent into *Hades* conserves the precious truth that no man who ever lived is left without a sight of Christ, and without the offer of the salvation of God."[1827] Such was even the view of the great church father Justin Martyr,[1828] but it is nevertheless suspect.

Sir Robert Anderson noted, "there is nothing in our text about 'preaching the gospel.' The word the Apostle uses means 'to proclaim as a herald' or 'as a conqueror.'"[1829] However, this is the exact same word used in reference to preaching the gospel. Consequently, the answer is not to be found in the Greek. However, the answer may be found in verse twenty for it offers no hint of repentance. On the contrary, verse twenty indicates that these spirits in prison rejected the preaching of Noah. There is therefore nothing in 1 Peter that indicates these "spirits in prison" can or will repent. It appears that Jesus is not preaching repentance, for everyone had that chance in life.[1830] Rather He is proclaiming something else.

View # 2 : Proclaiming Victory to the Saved

A second view is that Jesus was proclaiming his victory over sin and death to those who will inherit salvation.[1831] According to this view Jesus was preaching to the saints in Paradise.[1832] This view is probably as ancient as the

369

first view. It is also the official position of the Fourth Council of Toledo[1833] and is held by scholars of all different persuasions.

The most obvious problem with this view is that Peter speaks of the "spirits in prison." A prison hardly conjures up the image of Paradise. Despite this William Kelly argues that even Abraham's Bosom can be called a prison.[1834] He maintains that all of *Sheol* is a prison for the dead. Having said, this is not likely. Peter would hardly call Paradise a "prison." Moreover, the imagery of the unrepentant in the days of Noah again cast doubt upon this thesis. Any view we take must take into account the connection with the days of Noah.

View # 3 : Proclaiming Judgment to the Damned

A similar view is that Jesus was indeed proclaiming victory, but not to the saints. Rather He was proclaiming condemnation and judgment against the damned such as those of Noah's generation.[1835] John Wesley held that Jesus was preaching the sentence for their crimes.[1836]

William Kelly said that "the word 'preached' or 'proclaimed', by no means necessarily infers that He preached either faith or repentance."[1837] The first view held that repentance was preached. The second that faith was preached. This third view holds that judgment is preached.

This seems to be the strongest view thus far, but it still leaves some questions unanswered. Surely Noah's generation are the not the only ones awaiting judgment in *Sheol*. Why are they called "spirits" rather than "souls"? What is the connection to Noah's generation?

View # 4 : Proclaiming Victory to the Demons

Before solidifying the answer, we must understand the context of Peter's remarks about Noah. What is the relationship of Noah's generation to the proclamation to "spirits in prison." Remember that Peter was speaking to Jews. He did not have to explain the context because every Jewish child had been raised on the traditions of Noah, as well as the Biblical account. A brief recollection of what was all but universally accepted in Peter's time may help us understand the mindset of the people to whom Peter was speaking.

In the Biblical account the depravity of man was exemplified by the fact that the "sons of God" married the "daughters of men" and gave birth to Nephilim, called in the King James "Giants." This is one of the most controversial passages in the whole of the Bible. It is therefore no surprise that the controversy carries over into 1 Peter, for the connection is not accidental. According to the Greek *Septuagint*, Josephus, the apocryphal Book of Enoch and probably Jude 1:6, these "sons of God" were fallen angels, or demons. I have debated this in depth in *Controversies in the Pentateuch*. One thing is certain. This was the view passed down and accepted almost universally by the Jews at the time of the apostles. When Peter speaks of those who were "disobedient" the Jewish reader would instantly have thought of fallen angels. R.A. Torrey believed that Jude 1:6 and Genesis 6:2 both speak of demons in connection to Noah's generation.[1838] It is likely that Peter's readers would also have pictured this image in their mind.

Another clue is the use of the words "spirits in prison." John MacArthur argues that "spirits" cannot refer to humans or Peter would have used the word "souls" instead. Angels and demons, however, are spoken of as spirits very often.[1839] He therefore believes that this can only refer to demons.

Further evidence of this is in the Biblical use of "spirits in prison" found outside of 1 Peter. Revelation, for example, speaks of "a dwelling place of demons and a prison of every unclean spirit" (Revelation 18:2). It also refers to hell as a "prison" for Satan (Revelation 20:7). Finally, in Revelation 9:14 demons are spoken of as being "bound" to a specific place as if by chains. The parallels to Revelation may also indicate that demons are intended.

Conclusion
The first view is a "happy" view, but ignores the entire purpose for our life on earth. By the time we die we have either hardened our hearts to God or repented. As to those who have never heard the gospel, God knows who would and would not have accepted the gospel had they heard it, so that the idea of hearing the gospel in hell is both unnecessary and self defeating (see notes on Roman 2:11-16). Hell is reserved for those who have willingly rejected the Lord in their hardened hearts. 1 Peter 4:6 is the best support for this view, but I discuss that passage below.

The next two views can be rejected because they do not fully account for the context of Noah and his generation. The best argument seems to be that Jesus proclaimed victory and judgment to "disobedient spirits."[1840] This alone appears to answer all the questions and the only argument against it appears to be the instinctive gut reaction against demons being pictured in Genesis 6:2. The evidence, however, is overwhelming. Whatever controversy there may be in that passage, it is clear that the sin was no mere act of polygamy or intermarriage, but had something to do with demons (see notes in *Controversies in the Pentateuch*). This was the view of Peter's day, and is the allusion drawn both here and in Jude 1:6.

Salvation for the Dead?
1 Peter 4:6

> "For the gospel has for this purpose been preached even to those who are dead, that though they are judged in the flesh as men, they may live in the spirit according to *the will of* God."

We have already discussed 1 Peter 3:18-22. Many believe that there is a direct relationship between that passage and this one, but others argue that "the vocaubulary of the text and its context differ."[1841] Indeed, the passage begins with the words "for this reason," indicating a direct cause and effect relationship with the previous verse. So it is best to examine the views in context.

Although there is a close parallel with the previous debate, the parallel interpretations are not as close as we might assume. There are three different dominant interpretations, but they do not necessarily correspond to those of 1 Peter 3:18-22, and the interpretation taken in those passages does not necessarily indicate which interpretation will be taken here. This is because even though the subject matter is similar, and *may* allude to the same thing, the context is obviously quite different.

The Context

The context of 1 Peter 3:18-22 was what transpired between the crucifixion and resurrection, as well the allusion to the generation of Noah. Here, however, Peter is speaking in a different context. The verse begins with "for this reason." What reason?

> "For the time already past is sufficient *for you* to have carried out the desire of the Gentiles, having pursued a course of sensuality, lusts, drunkenness, carousing, drinking parties and abominable idolatries. In *all* this, they are surprised that you do not run with *them* into the same excesses of dissipation, and they malign *you;* but they will give account to Him who is ready to judge the living and the dead."

There is no hint of repentance or salvation here. These wicked men "malign" us because we do not engage in the "sensuality, lusts, drunkenness, carousing, drinking parties and abominable idolatries" but "they will give an account to Him who is ready to judge the living and the dead." It is *"for this reason"* that the gospel has been preached unto "those who are dead." The context appears to be that of judgment (vs. 5), not salvation which they had *already* been offered and had rejected.[1842]

The Interpretations

Although it is possible to subdivide the views into more than three, there are only three primary views. Some see this as an allegory referring to the spiritually dead. Others see this in one way or another connected to believers who have passed on. Still others view this as some kind of preaching, or proclamation, to the dead in *Sheol.*

View # 1 : The Spiritually Dead

Undoubtedly the most popular view since the Middle Ages and up to the present is the allegorical view. This interpretation argues that it is the "spiritually dead"[1843] of whom Peter is speaking. This was the dominant view of the Middle ages from Andreas[1844] to Hilary of Arles,[1845] from Cyril and Augustine[1846] to Bede,[1847] and into the Reformation where men like Martin

Luther[1848] and Erasmus saw this as "dead in tresspasses and sin."[1849] It is also the view of Whitby and a great many others.[1850]

Of course popularity does not make a correct view. The problem with this interpretation is that it answers none of the questions. "For this reason" the gospel is preached "*even* to those who are dead." It is a point of emphasis. This is not a mere offering of the gospel to the lost, for that would be redundant. Of course the gospel is preached to the lost! We were all lost once. No, Peter's point is that the gospel has been proclaimed "*even* to those who are dead." It has been proclaimed even to those who have *already* died. This leaves two possibilities.

View # 2 : Believers Who Have Passed On

Some believe that this refers only to the saved who died before Christ.[1851] Others, like Ironside, say that it is "those who had preceded them in the path of faith"[1852] (i.e. believers before the time of Christ). R.C. Sproul[1853] and John MacArthur count themselves among the former in this group.[1854] MacArthur says it is "those who had heard and believed the gospel but had died by the time he wrote."[1855]

This is a literal interpretation, but it ignores the context of verse five. We cannot disregard "for this reason." Verse five speaks of condemnation of the wicked. It does not speak of the saved. Consequently, if verse six is directly tied to verse five, and it is, then this cannot refer to believers, before or after Christ. This leaves only one other view.

View # 3 : The Wicked

John Calvin,[1856] Lenski[1857] and many others believe that it is to the dead in *Sheol* to whom the gospel has been preached. Even in the Middle Ages some held to this position such as Oecumenius.[1858] However, there is a difference of opinion as to whether or not these dead are being given a third chance (not a second) for repentance or whether judgment is being preached.

The view taken in 1 Peter 3:18-22 obviously reflects the opinion take here and while the explicit mention of the gospel does lend credibility to the idea of repentance, the context of verse five rules this out. The gospel is good news for those who receive it, but it is also proof that the wicked deserve their fate. The direct connection to verse five indicates the latter.

Conclusion

"For this reason the gospel was preached also to those who are dead" (NKJV). This should not be taken as mere allegory, but literally. Referring back to 1 Peter 3:18-22 it is clear that Jesus preached when He was in Paradise before the Resurrection. The question is what kind of preaching was it? If the gospel was preached "for this reason," then we must asks, "what reason?" Why? For the reason cited in verse five; to prove that these men deserve their fate. These are people who had never accepted the gospel and would never have accepted the gospel had they known it. This is Peter's point. He is issuing a somber warning amid the backdrop of imminent persecution. He is talking about the just fate of the wicked. There are two edges of the gospel sword. One sets us free from sin. The other condemns those who reject it and deserve their fate.

Babylon or Rome?
1 Peter 5:13

"She who is in Babylon, chosen together with you, sends you greetings, and *so does* my son, Mark."

For centuries "Babylon" was interpreted as an idiom for Rome. Much like we speak of Sodom or "Sin City" in Las Vegas, "Babylon" had become a byword among the Jews for any oppressors of Israel. Recently, however, some Protestants have interpreted this as literal Babylon. They believe that Peter was never even in Rome! This is a topic I addressed fully in *The Apostles After Jesus*, and much of what I reproduce below is extracted from those pages.[1859] Nonetheless, I will again deviate from my usual practice and begin with my conclusions.

A few Protestants react against the teaching that Peter was pope by denying that Peter was ever in Rome. They argue that Babylon in Iraq is the literal interpretation and should be accepted at face value. However, this is untenable for eight reasons I debated in *The Apostles After Jesus*. I will summarize those reasons below.

First, it is clear that 1 and 2 Peter were written against the backdrop of persecution in the days of Nero. However, if Peter was in Babylon then he was in Parthia outside the realm of the Roman Empire. The persecutions of Nero could have no effect upon Peter who died in those persecutions. In fact Parthia and Rome were at enmity with one another. For a missionary to freely pass back and forth between the nations is unthinkable and travel in those days was hardly quick, expeditious, or cheap. When the apostles went to a foreign country, they spent their lives there and rarely, if ever, returned.

Another reason to reject Babylon is the simple fact that the fall of ancient Babylon had long preceded Peter's time. While some argue that Babylon will rise again there is no question that the ancient city was rubble in Peter's day. Historian Georges Roux speaks about a "half-ruined city"[1860] in the time of the Greeks, noting that "it was already partly deserted, a great number of its inhabitants having been transferred to Seleucia."[1861] In the wars that would ensue between the Parthians and the Greeks, and later the Parthians and Romans, Babylon would again trade hands many times. In 126 B.C. the Parthians took control of Babylon[1862] but they would also have trouble keeping the city. Crassus of Rome was the first to threaten the Parthians in Babylon, and under Roman conquests Babylon would again change hands several times.

If the city existed at all in Peter's time then was an insignificant city which lay largely deserted and had no significant population or presumably Jewish community. There is no reason to believe that it would be of any missionary significance to Peter.

Moreover, no history, tradition, or even legend of Peter having gone to the east exist. It is unthinkable to believe that the most famous apostle traveled to Parthia left not a single solitary tradition, record, or even legend of his travels behind!

There are several other reasons to reject Babylon as well, but the strongest is the Bible itself. In fact, the strongest reason to reject Babylon of Parthia here is 1 Peter 5:13! Why? Because he says that Mark sends his greetings form Babylon, but Mark was in Rome (2 Timothy 4:11)! Yes, according to Paul in 2 Timothy, which dates to within a year of 1 Peter, Mark was in Ephesus and came to Rome immediately thereafter. If Mark was in Babylon it is beyond comprehension that he could have traveled from Bablon to Ephesus and thence to Rome within a year in countries which were at war with one another.

The simple fact is that Mark was in Rome in 65 A.D. when 2 Timothy and 2 Peter were written. 1 Peter was probably written a year before this at the earliest. While Mark may have traveled to Ephesus in the interim it is not credible to have Mark traveling all the way to Parthia and back. The simple fact is that Peter died in Rome under the Great Persecution of Nero, and 1 Peter was probably written not more than a year before that day.

False Prophets
2 Peter 2:1

"But false prophets also arose among the people, just as there will also be false teachers among you, who will secretly introduce destructive heresies, even denying the Master who bought them, bringing swift destruction upon themselves."

Jesus and Paul had spoken many times of warnings about false prophets and teachers (cf. Matthew 24:24; Mark 13:22; 2 Timothy 4:3-4 to name a few). Here Peter too warns about heretics and liars who come like wolves in sheep's clothing (Matthew 7:15).

D.M. Lloyd-Jones prepared a list of ways of how *not* to tell if someone is a false teacher.[1863] First, is it new? This is irrelevant. In fact, "newer" is not better. Often it is heretics who come claiming some "new" revelation or interpretation. This leads to the second false test. Is it old? In other words, has it been accepted in the church over the centuries. While it is important, this is the antethesis of the first test, and just as dangerous for there are many false teachings that are very old and have been taught by one ancient church or another for centuries. Third, Lloyd-Jones says is "the fallacy of always assuming that if the teaching is popular it must be right."[1864] Popularity is not always right, and is in fact often quite wrong. Matthew 7:13 makes it clear that the wide gate is not the right gate. The path to destruction is wide and popular. So none of these are good guides for determining the truth.

How then can one tell a false teacher from a true teacher? How can one tell a false prophet from a true prophet of God? There is only one way. It is the Bible.[1865] This is why knowledge of the Bible is so critical. It is also why false teachers have always done one of four things. They either restrict access to the Bible as was done in the Middle Ages. Or they might add to the Bible as done by Mohammad, Joseph Smith, and many others. This could also include "prophecies" or "knowledge" provided by a "prophet" or "apostle." It is not restricted to a book or writing. Others will subtract from the Bible, rejecting the Old Testament or the Pauline epistles or some other portions of the Bible. If all of these fail then they may claim that the layman cannot understand the Bible without their aid and assistance. They trivialize the perspicuity of the Scriptures to imply that it is too complicated for anyone but the "learned" to properly understand. In all cases, the false prophet or teachers inserts himself into the equation, and reduces the authority of the Bible in our individual lives.

Our faith is, and should always be, in Jesus Christ and Jesus Christ alone. No "prophet," modern day "apostle," or teacher should take away from the Bible or add to it (cf. Revelation 22:18-19). This is why the knowledge of the Bible is so critical to having a strong faith and to protecting us from false teachers.

The Sin of the Angels
2 Peter 2:4

> "God did not spare angels when they sinned, but cast them into hell and committed them to pits of darkness, reserved for judgment."

Demon are fallen angels who rebelled against God out of jealousy, envy, and pride. At first glance this appears to be the obvious reference by Peter, but some argue that "Peter is propbably not referring here to the angels who originally fell, since they were not immediately incarcerated in hell."[1866] Moreover, the very next sentence speaks again of Noah's generation which conjures up the images of Jude 6 and the angels "whose sin was that of fornication."[1867] Is this so?

While I have argued that Peter does refer to the sin of the demons in Genesis 6:2, this is not certain in this passage. Some have tried to connect this to the Book of Enoch[1868] and R.C. Sproul even goes so far as to say that "Peter borrows an image from the Greek poet,"[1869] but Peter is not borrowing from some extra-Biblical source. The passage also speaks of Sodom and Gomorrah (v.6) so there is no necessity of drawing a direct connection to Noah save that each was a severe judgment by God for man's unrepentant sins.

The best argument is that of John MacArthur who noted that the angels were not immediately damned to angel when they rebelled against God.[1870] Nevertheless, there is no proof that the demons of Genesis 6:2 were immediately sent to hell either. God's judgment has already been passed upon them, and they cannot act unrestrained (see notes on 2 Thessalonians 2:6-7). Consequently, there may an allusion to the demons of Genesis 6:2 but that is not clear. Peter is merely referring to all the judgments of God upon the wicked and unrepentant.

The Bondage of Sin
2 Peter 2:4-22

"For if God did not spare angels when they sinned, but cast them into hell and committed them to pits of darkness, reserved for judgment ... It has happened to them according to the true proverb, 'a dog returns to its own vomit,' and, 'a sow, after washing, *returns* to wallowing in the mire.'"

The doctrine of the bondage of sin is one found in both Catholic and Protestant theology and goes far beyond the pages of this book. Nonetheless, Peter here makes clear that such a bondage exist in some form. "As a dog returns to its own vomit" (Proverbs 26:11) man inevitably returns to his crimes and sin unless Jesus sets him free from that bondage.

Charles Spurgeon once said that "whoever we may be, we may never reckon that, on account of our position or condition, we shall be free from the assaults of sin."[1871] Peter is again speaking about judgment and comparing our sin nature to dog's eating their own vomit and sows wallowing in the mud. This is what sin does to our souls. It is soiled and poluted and can only be washed clean by the blood of Christ.

Denying the Second Coming
2 Peter 3:3-4

"Know this first of all, that in the last days mockers will come with *their* mocking, following after their own lusts and saying, 'Where is the promise of His coming? For *ever* since the fathers fell asleep, all continues just as it was from the beginning of creation.'"

Evangelicals have often been mocked for our belief in the Second Coming of Jesus, but none more so than those who deny rapture. The irony is that Peter is prophesying here that "the Parousia itself shall come after these mockers have appeared."[1872] One commentator noted that "the appearance of scoffers who mock the reliability of prophecy is itself a fulfillment of prophecy."[1873] They are thus helping to fulfill this very prophecy!

Now it is true that such scoffers have always existed in one form or another. Theophlylact applied these scoffers to the gnostics[1874] and John Calvin saw them as the persecutors of Christianity,[1875] but he also believed that such scoffers would increase in the time before the Second Coming.[1876] Martin Luther believed that this prophesied the rise of atheism "before the Last Day."[1877] Finally, Charles Swindoll is not the first to associate this with the doctrine of uniformitarianism in modern science.[1878] Indeed, according to that theory "all continues just as it was from the beginning." This is eroneously applied to evolutionary geology even though it is patently false.

Certainly these are all true, but there is something more specific in what Peter is saying. He seems to be speaking of a time when not only unbelievers will mock us, but believers as well. Many Christian churches today see the Second Coming as allegory. Some preterists argue it refers to Jesus coming to destroy the Temple in Jerusalem! Some liberals apply the Second Coming to Pentecost, never mind that Peter wrote these words long after Pentecost. Others believe that it is the prophecy of the rapture which will be mocked. Indeed, Warren Wiersbe has pointed out that much of the mocking of rapture comes from within the church itself.[1879] They see rapture theorists as an embarrasment. Because the world laughs and mocks us, they think that they can appease the skeptics by mocking us as well. They are more concerned with what the world thinks than what the Bible says. Peter rejects one and all as fools who will be overtaken by the judgment to come, even as the mockers of Noah's day were caught completely unaware (vs. 6).

Apocalypse Foretold
2 Peter 3:6-7

"But by His word the present heavens and earth are being reserved for fire, kept for the day of judgment and destruction of ungodly men."

The book of Revelation speaks of these events in details. Peter says that the "earth is being reserved for fire." Some believe that this refers to the apocalypse itself (Revelation 8:7). Others that it refers to the end of the Millennium when God will create a new heaven and a new earth (Revelation 21:1).[1880] In fact, it is probably a general all encompassing statement which can refer to both.

That the earth would be destroyed by fire is not new to Peter. Jewish tradition records in Josephus that Adam prophesied "that the world was to be destroyed at one time by the force of fire, and at another time by the violence and quantity of water."[1881] Here Peter alludes to both.

Some have seen this purely as "metaphorical"[1882] while others believe the fire could be connected to atomic power.[1883] Still others believe that the fire comes directly from God as part of His wrath. All of this is debated in detail in *Controversies in Revelation*. One thing is certain, however. The earth will not continue on its present state forever. Judgment will come. Jesus will return. And this present earth will be consumed by fire.

"A Day is as a Thousand Years"
2 Peter 3:8-9

"With the Lord one day is like a thousand years, and a thousand years like one day."

For centuries this passage was almost universally interpreted according to its context. The most controversial aspect of it was whether or not this could be applied to the dispensations of the earth. The so-called *Epistle of Barnabas*, for example, cited this as proof that Christ would return in the 6000th year of the earth.[1884] A similar argument was taught by Theophilis to Autolycus[1885] Athanasius and Augustine.[1886] John Wesley believed that the would "conclude at the seventh age of the world."[1887]

Of course the context was merely about the fact that "the Lord is not slow about His promise" for many had wished the Lord to return in their lifetimes. Peter is telling them that it may be a thousand years (or two thousand).

Today a new interpretation has arisen having absolutely nothing to do with Peter's context about the Second Coming. That theory is one that attempts to apply this to Genesis in order to accomodate the alleged evidence for a 4.5 billion year old earth.[1888] The "Day-Age" theory speculates that if a day is a thousand years then the "days" of Genesis could be, they say, be millions of years. Of course this theory is no better scientifically than exegetically, since (to name one of many problems) plants cannot exist with animals for thousands of years, nor could life exist without the sun for thousands of years. Nevertheless, the attempt to wed 2 Peter to Genesis is ill conceived. Even Lenski, no literalist in regard to Genesis, admits that this is misplaced, saying "Peter does not say : 'A single day *is* a thousand, and a thousand years *are* a single day.'"[1889]

The passage is parallel to Psalms 90:4 which says, "for a thousand years in Your sight Are like yesterday when it passes by, or *as* a watch in the night." The point is about the eternal God and temporal man. We measure time by our short lives, but God is eternal and timelessness.[1890] God "does not experience time as such," said Kenneth Wuest, "and the passing of a thousand years is no different to Him than the passing of a day."[1891] When Jesus said "I am coming soon" (Revelation 22:7, 12) He did not mean that He would necessarily return in their lifetime, but that in the eyes of an eternal God He would return "quickly." It may be today, tomorrow, or a thousand years from now. Peter was assuring them that the mockers who question the return of Christ (3:3-4) are liars, and Jesus will keep His promise, even if it is not in our lifetimes.

Salvation, Damnation, and Universalism
2 Peter 3:9

"The Lord ... is patient toward you, not wishing for any to perish but for all to come to repentance."

In context Peter is still talking about the Second Coming and coming judgment upon the earth, but he is saying that God is patient and will wait until the gospel has disseminated around the world. The gospel must be presented to all men, for God does not wish "for any to perish but for *all* to come to repentance." Here is the controversy and it is yet another Calvinist/Armenian debate. Does "all" mean "all"? If God wants all men to repent, then why won't they? Is God not sovereign? These are the question asked by Calvinists and Armenians, because they see an irreconcilable conflict between free will and God's sovereignty (see notes on Ephesians 1:9).

Naturally, the Calvinist and the Armenian hold to two different extremes. The Calvinist says that "'all' does not mean 'all.'"[1892] One of my Calvinist friends said it is "all the elect," although the word "elect" is not to be found here. Had it been, it would be redundant. Is Peter saying that God wants the saved to saved? Really?

The Armenians take the other extreme, saying that all men *will* be saved. This is the doctrine of Universalism. Note that both are based on the assumption that God's will and His sovereignty cannot be reconciled with man's free will, even in a limited way. They effectively negate the idea that God's will may *include* giving men choices. This has always been at the core of the Calvinist/Armenian debate. Here it is no different.

Arthur Pink resolves this problem by simply saying that "'all' does not mean 'all.'"[1893] It is surprising then that John Calvin did not take this stance. Calvin himself merely dismissed the problem by saying that "no mention is here made of the hidden purpose of God."[1894] In other words, he acknowledged that God wants all men to be saved, but he desires something else even more. What else? Calvin does not say, for that might make him question his own views on limited free will.

Many Armenians (although not Arminius himself) also distort this text. They ignore the many passages about hell and judgment, arguing that if God wants all men to be saved then all men will be saved. I had a pastor when I was young who even insisted that Hitler would be forgiven (never mind that Hitler never asked for forgiveness).

So the hyper-Calvinist and many Armenians both reach false conclusions based on the *same* assumption. They both assume that they understand God's will. The Calvinist assumes that God does not want *all* men to be saved and many Armenians assume that this is God's *only* will, and so all men must be saved. In fact, Peter is not even debating the question of freedom of the will. God wants us to be saved, but He equally wants us to choose Him.

This, of course, opens a can of worms in regard to how much freedom we have as well as the question of the bondage of sin, but those issues are beyond the scope of this passage. Perhaps a simple analogy is best, even if it is flawed.

We love our pets. Most people love dogs and cats, but dogs and cats have a will of their own (particularly cats). They do not always obey. Why do we love them so much? Would not a machine or toy be better? No. Why? Because when they choose to love us, it makes that love all the more special. We love our pets, even though they may sometimes disobey us, or even bite us. Am I less than my dog? Is my will subject to my dog's will? Has my dog become my master? How absurd would such a claim be? How much more is God's love of us than ours for a dog? How much more freedom and forgiveness has God given to us, than we give to our dogs? Should I compare myself to a dog in God's eyes? Yes, for I am not even worthy of being called a dog, and yet my Lord loves me.

Proverbs 16:9 states that "the mind of man plans his way, but the LORD directs his steps." This simple passage best explains the relationship between God's will and man's. The Lord will prevail in all things, but part of that will is that we be free to call out to the Lord for help.

A Thief in the Night
2 Peter 3:10a

"But the day of the Lord will come like a thief."

The "thief in the night" analogy is found seven times in the Bible. It is first used by Jesus Himself in Matthew 24:43 and Luke 12:39. The apostle Paul also uses the analogy in 1 Thessalonians 5:2-4 (which I discussed previously). Finally, John uses the reference two in Revelation (3:3 and 16:15). The point is obviously that we do not know when Jesus is coming, but in Revelation it would seem we do know ... He comes at Armageddon! Here then is the debate. How are we to take the analogy? Is the prophecy about the Second Coming or rapture as some believe? Is it addressed to us, to unbeliever, or to both?

The first question is actually misleading. This is where we make our first mistake. Because Jesus compared His coming to a thief in the night (Matthew 24:43; Luke 12:39) many have followed in the assumption that Peter is either referring to the rapture or the Second Coming. However, a careful comparison of the passages shows that Peter and Paul both specifically tied this to the "Day of the Lord." There is obviously a close connection between rapture, the Day of the Lord, and the Second Coming so that the three can, depending on the context, be used interchangeably. Nevertheless, they are different and it is important to understand the differences, so what we can understand the context of each of these "thief" passages.

I have debated the exact meaning of the Day of the Lord in *Controversies in Revelation*. I believe that the Day of the Lord usually refers to the last three and a half years of the Tribulation, also called the Great Tribulation (Matthew 24:21). Rapture occurs sometime before this, and the Second Coming follows at the end of the Great Tribulation. So chronologically there is rapture, followed shortly thereafter by the Day of the Lord and the Second Coming. Now let us look at the passages in question.

Matthew 24:43 and Luke 12:39 speak of the same thing. There is great controversy over whether or not it refers to the rapture or to the Day of the Lord (see notes in *Controversies in the Gospels*), but in this case it does not matter, for the context fits with Peter. Peter is definitely referring to the Day of the Lord and Jesus (although probably referring to the rapture) also speaks of the Great Tribulation which follows this event. So whether the thief imagery refers to the rapture or the Great Tribulation, it is clear that the events, which trigger one another, occur when the world is not expecting it. Thus Matthew 24:43 and Luke 12:39 do not refer to the Second Coming, but either to rapture or the Day of the Lord.

1 Thessalonians 5:2-4 is another critical passage (see notes there), and like Peter he is specifically referring to the Day of the Lord.[1895] As Ironside said, "the Day of the Lord is not to be confounded with the day of Christ."[1896] So both Peter and Paul are saying that "the Day of the Lord will come suddenly and unawares as a thief will be the second half of the seven-year" tribulation.[1897] They are in perfect agreement.

Finally, Revelation has two passages which refer to the thief imagery. These are more difficult for the Great Tribulation has already been described when Jesus says, "I am coming like a thief" (16:15). Revelation 3:3 also contains a reference to Jesus coming like a thief in judgment. Both of these passages have a different context and are more difficult. It is of interest to note that Revelation 16:15 is an aside. In fact, the NAS, RV, RSV, NRSV, ASV, Darby, Geneva, and ESV all place these words in brackets to indicate such. Consequently, the address is to the reader to take warning, and not to those who are already in the midst of the Day of the Lord. Likewise Revelation 3:3 is a warning. It provides no specific clues as to what Jesus is referring to other than judgment. This would again fit the idea of the Day of the Lord which is associated with wrath.[1898]

As we can see all the thief imagery refers to a time of judgment. All of them connect either directly or indirectly with the Day of the Lord. I am of the opinion that Matthew and Luke speak of the rapture, but even then the context is warning of the judgment which follows those who are left behind. So each and every passage correlates to coming judgment and the Day of the Lord. "A thief comes and aims to come when no one expects him."[1899] So also the final world war and the plagues of Revelation will erupt at a time when no one is expecting it. Bear in mind that Peter is speaking of a panorama of the End Times, so his statement is valid, even if there is a year or two between certain events which take place. The point is that the end began at a time when the world was crying "peace and safety" (1 Thessalonians 5:2-4).

Is the Earth Eternal?
2 Peter 3:10b

"The heavens will pass away with a roar and the elements will be destroyed with intense heat, and the earth and its works will be burned up."

Most everyone is familiar with the doxology prayer, which is also found in the King James (Ephesians 3:21), ending with "world without end, amen." Ecclesiastes 1:4 also says that "a generation goes and a generation comes, but the earth remains forever" (Ecclesiastes 1:4). Some also believe that Genesis 8:21 negates the idea of the earth being completely destroyed for God promised Noah, "I will never again destroy every living thing." So many have believed that the world is without end, but here in Peter he states that the very "elements will be destroyed." Can these two views be reconciled? If not, which was is in error.

The answer is not as difficult as some have made it. The Venerable Bede, for example, attempted to look at it from the mind set of a medieval scientist. There were four known basic elements; earth, air, fire, and water. Bede said, "fire will lay waste all these. But yet it will not consume them that they will completely cease to exist, but it will consume two entirely, two in fact it will restore to a better apprearance."[1900] In other words, fire cannot destroy fire, and it cannot destroy water, but it would cleanse the earth and air.

Henry Morris offered a more modern scientific explanation, saying, "second Peter 3:10 prophesies that ... all the atomic structure of the earth [is] permitted to disintegrate instantly into other forms of energy – sound, heat, and fire."[1901] He believed that these elements would, however, be formed into the new earth of Revelation 21. He calls that new earth a "renewal" of the old:

"'All these things' had to be 'dissolved,' with the elements melting in fervent heat (2 Peter 3:10-12). By the principle of mass/energy conservation, however, nothing had been really lost, except the effects and evidences of sin. After terrestrial matter had been converted either into the vapor state or, more probably, into pure energy, God had once again exercised His mighty powers of creation and integration, and the new heavens and new earth had appreared out of the ashes, so to speak, of the old."[1902]

So both Bede and Henry Morris provide scientific explanations, and both seem valid, but there may be a more simple answer. Joseph Seiss says that "in those passages which speak of the *passing away* of the earth and heavens (see Matt. 5:18, 24, 34, 35; Mark 13:30, 31; Luke 16:17, 21, 33; 2 Pet. 3:10, Rev. 21:1), the original word is never one which signifies termination of existence, but παρερχομαι, which is a verb of very wide general meaning, such as *to go* or *come* to a person ... as a ship through a sea; to pass from one place or condition to another."[1903] Indeed, in Revelation the "new heaven and new earth" use the word καινος (*kainos*). Now "καινος is new over against old. Heavens and earth are to be new in this sense and not in the sense of νεος, just called into existence."[1904] It is a re"new"al of the old earth, which has been cleansed by fire and made anew.

Summary

Peter's epistles are both short letters written during the closing days of his life and at a time when the persecutions of Nero were imminent and active. They are filled with promises of the Second Coming, but also warnings of judgment. The End Times is likened to the days of Noah when God's patience was exhausted and the earth had to be cleansed from its evil. Nevertheless, Peter made clear that God is patient and so these events might not transpire for a thousand years, or two. His epistles are thus as important today as when he wrote them.

14

—

1, 2, & 3 John

Few if any doubt that John wrote these epistles. They bear the strong mark of Johannine theology as well as this simple but eloquent vocabulary and writing style so that even the critics cannot deny their authenticity. To further stiffle any question of their legimacy is their acceptance by every early church fathers, some of whom tutored under John.

The question of when these epistles were written is much more difficult and few, if any, agree. Most are in agreement that the epistles were written after his Gospel,[1905] but there is no solid evidence how long afterwards they were written. Zane Hodges believes that "there is no particular reason why 1 John may not be assigned to the same period" as the gospel.[1906] So he believes that the gospels and epistles were all written in the 60s, but many disagree with his dating of the gospel. I argued that it was probably written in the 90s.[1907] Glenn Barker argues for the 70s as the date for both the gospel and the epistles[1908] based on the belief that the Johannine community in Asia Minor arose after the fall of Jerusalem.[1909] Yet another view is that of Merrill Unger who also dates the epistles around the same time as the gospel, but like myself, places the gospel in the 90s.[1910]

One question which might be asked is why John wrote these epistles at all. He was writing to refute gnostic heresy, and of that all agree, but why not teach in person? John was well known and respected leader of the church in Asia Minor and the last of the apostles. By the 90s all the other apostles had died leaving John to shepherd the churches of Asia Minor. He travelled among the churches teaching and shepherding them, but we also know that in the persecutions of Domitian he was exiled where he wrote the book of Revelation (see notes there). Obviously John could not visit any churches while in exile. It is possible that John wrote these epistles because he was unable to visit the churches himself. A date in the 90s is thus likely. If so then all of John's writings took place in the 90s, possibly while he was in exile on Patmos.

Does the Christian Sin?
1 John 1:8-10; 3:6-9; 5:18

"If we say that we have no sin, we are deceiving ourselves and the truth is not in us ... If we say that we have not sinned, we make Him a liar and His word is not in us."	"No one who is born of God practices sin, because His seed abides in him; and he cannot sin, because he is born of God."	"We know that no one who is born of God sins; but He who was born of God keeps him, and the evil one does not touch him."

385

Here are three passages which are misunderstood, misquoted, and misreprented by many. When misinterpreted, they also may be made to appear to be saying two different things, for John clearly declares we have, and do, sin, but later states that the Christian does not abide in sin. Those who misquote the latter to imply that they cannot sin are ironically the very ones to whom John was condemning.

The early gnostic cult maintained that because the body and spirit were seperate, the spirit was untainted by carnal sins.[1911] For many gnostics "sin was a slight matter."[1912] So "John again combats the gnostics heresy which held that we do not have any principle of sin within us."[1913] Now it is important to understand that the gnostic dualism had two aspects to it which John refutes. One, that we "have no sin in us" (1:8) and two, that "we have not sinned" (1:10). John makes clear that "if we say that we have no sin, we are deceiving ourselves and the truth is not in us" (1:8) but also that "if we say that we have not sinned, we make Him a liar and His word is not in us" (1:10).

Now later John says that "no one who is born of God practices sin" (3:9) and even that "no one who is born of God sins" (5:18). Some see this as a contradiction of his first thesis in 1:8-10. Nevertheless, John uses syllogism, a form of logical argument, throughout his writings. A consistent and fair interpretation assures us that John is, at least in his own mind, consistent. We should, therefore, examine his line of reasoning before concluding that he is wrong, mistaken, or in contradiction of himself.

Let us look at the three critical passages in isolation before we put them together. This way the individual context of each is more clear. Only then can we see how they relate to one another.

We Are Sinners : 1 John 1:8-10

John begins with the fundamental Christian doctrine that we are *all* sinners. James Boice stated that the gnostics denied that they "do not have sin now" but also that that "he has never sinned."[1914] In refuting these John affirms that we have sinned in the past, and continue now to sin.

Liberty Bible Commentary states that verse ten "is different from saying that we have no sin in verse 8. In verse 8 it is a matter of recognizing what can be classed as sin in our lives; in verse 10 it is a mater of denying that we have ever" sinned.[1915] Robert Lightner says that we "still possess the capacity and tendency to sin ... sin nature."[1916]

So Charles Spurgeon saw these as one in the same but in two stages of deceit : lying to yourself, and then calling God a liar.[1917] John has thus established that we not only were sinners, but that sin remains a constant struggle in our lives. The gnostic denies both, thereby deceiving him and calling God a liar.

Abiding Sin : 1 John 3:6-9

Having established that we *are* sinners, and not just *were* sinners, John now states not only that "born of God practices sin" but even more, that "because [God's] seed abides in him; he cannot sin." John Calvin believed that "the word *sin* here is meant not only corrupt and vicious inclination, but the fault or sinful act" itself.[1918] If so, then does this not contradict 1:8? Not necessarily.

First, "in both cases the verb *to sin* is in the *present* tense."[1919] Kenneth Wuest believes that "the present tense in Greek ... speaks of continuous, habitual action."[1920] So most believe that John is saying only that we "do not sin habitually or characteristically."[1921] John MacArthur says that we "cannot live in an unbroken pattern of sin."[1922] To better carry this meaning into English H. A. Ironside believes that it should be translated as "doth not practice sin."[1923] This idea is found in the NAS, NIV, NLT, and the ESV, but many older translations (KJV, NKJV, RV, RSV, NRSV, ASV, Duoay-Rheims, and Geneva) retain the more strict "does not commit sin."

The latter would indeed contradict 1 John 1:8. The former is consistent with it. As a result, many Christians see this as a part of the sanctification process.[1924] A correlation is made with 1 John 3:6 and the "abide" comment. In other words, it is not that Christians cannot sin (1 John 1:8 disagrees) but that the one who abides in Christ cannot sin. Even John Calvin believed that God does not "wholly regenerates us at once" but slowly piece by piece.[1925] The Quakers had a saying; "sin is not in the sanctified, but in the unsanctified."[1926] Note that these last two are by no means "free grace" theologies. Calvinists and Quakers lean heavily towards legalism and strict observances. The fact that these men acknowledge that Christian can and do sin is a testament to the fact that no believer can or should deny this, even as 1 John 1:8 states.

Nor is this a new view. Maximus the Confessor related this passage to to sanctification we have not yet acheived.[1927] When we "abide in Him" (3:6) we cannot sin, but abiding in the Lord is a process. It is a part of sanctification. No man has acheived that perfect abiding except Jesus Christ Himself. Even Peter denied Christ when Jesus needed Him the most.

So 1 John 3:6-9 indicates that sanctified perfection with God makes us free from sin, but that perfection will never be acheived in his lifetime. We are, even now, sinners (1 John 1:8). We do not abide perfectly in Christ as we should. We are still imperfect, but when we are born of God we have received new life and the Holy Spirit, and that Spirit cannot sin. If the Spirit is in us, how can we then sin? Let us look at the final passage.

Born of the Spirit : 1 John 5:18

"No one who is born of God sins; but He who was born of God keeps him." Once again there *appears* to be a contradiction with 1 John 1:8. How can John say that we even now have sin and then say that "no one who is born of God sins"?

Some translations again read "practices sin" although the NAS, which reads "practices sin" in 3:9 here simply reads "sins." Although the Greek form is slightly different, there is no grammatical reason for rendering the translations differently. So we are again left with the same problem.

As a result some Christians have chosen to interpret 1:8 solely in terms of sin nature, saying that while "sin as a root" is still in us[1928] we can no longer sin. Oliver Greene, for example, emphasizes no less than seven times inability sin![1929] This normally solid expositor has thus committed the sin of 1:8 and is "deceiving himself." Others, like Tertullian, acknowledge the power of sin, but leans toward legalism saying that sin may "never to be returned to after repentance."[1930] In this respect it is argued that John "excludes the possibility of his committing sin as an expression of his true character, though actual sins may, and do, occur."[1931] Because sin is "in the present tense [it is] to imply a life characterized by sin, rather than an isolated act of sin."[1932] So also Jonathan Edwards taught that "what we are to understand by it is that he that is born of God makes doing righteous his practice, and not the commission of sin."[1933] Although this is true, it once again fits the translation of "practices sin" which is probably not justified in this particular passage. However, there is an addendum to this which makes sense of the passage.

It has been argued that "who *is* born of God" in the first clause cannot be the same as he "who *was* born of God."[1934] Indeed, the full passage reads, "no one who is born of God sins; but He who was born of God keeps him" So "He" keeps "him"? Who are "He" and "him"? The second pronoun in the second clause clearly refers back to the first clause; the one who is born of God is kept, or protected. By whom? There is a debate as to whether or not "He" refers specifically to Christ or to the Holy Spirit in us. In either case, the image shifts. John Darby believed that this passage was saying that "the divine nature cannot sin."[1935] We have in us two natures. The sin nature is still inherent within us, but the Spirit of God is also in us and He cannot sin. So "the new nature sinneth not. If he sins at all, therefore, it must be because he is acting the flesh."[1936] The point is not that a Christian cannot sin, as some argue, but that God cannot sin, and if we obey the Holy Spirit we will not sin. One cannot constantly disobey the Spirit of God if he truly has the Spirit of God. Nevertheless, we will fall, we will sin, and we will never be completely sanctified until we meet the Lord in heaven.

Conclusion

John's purpose in these passages was not to instill a new legalism, nor to support the heretical libertinism of some gnostics. He wanted believers to understand that we are still susceptible to our sin nature, and we will sin, but the Holy Spirit in us "cleanses from the guilt of sin"[1937] and leads us toward a sinless life. The Holy Spirit cannot sin, and when we are obedient we will not sin. As was once said, "a saint is not a man who never falls; he is a man who gets up and goes on every time he falls."[1938]

Propitiation or Expiation?
1 John 2:2

> "He Himself is the propitiation for our sins; and not for ours only, but also for *those of* the whole world."

Two major issues arise in this passage. The first is over the word "propitiation." The word conjures up images of wrathful and vengeful pagan gods who toyed with men and whose anger had to be appeased. This imagery offends many Christians and so the translation and meaning of the first clause is hotly debated.

The second issue is what John means when he says "not for ours only, but also for those of the whole world"? Does this teach universalism? Did He died for the pagan as well as the Christian? If He died for the whole world, will not the whole world be saved?

Propitiation or Expiation?

Was Jesus the propitiation for our sins or the expiation of our sins? This may seem a strange question, for many do not even understand the difference. Indeed, according to Webster's English dictionary "propitiate" means "to in the good favor of; appease or conciliate [sacrifices made to *propitiate* the gods]."[1939] "Expiate" means "to make amends," "to make a satisfaction or atonement," or "to pay the penalty of."[1940] Note that there is very little difference in the two. The main problem is that "propitiate" is the word used of pagan sacrifices to vengeful and wrathful gods. The idea behind propitiation is appeasing a god's anger and wrath. Expiation seems a little less angry so to speak.

Now the Greek word ἱλασμος (*hilasmos*) is defined in Thayer's Greek Lexicon as "an appeasing, propitiation."[1941] The root word it says means "relating to appeasing or expiating."[1942] So it seems that the Greek word can refer to either a propitiation or an expiation. Translations are divided as to its best rendering. Even older versions are split. For example, Tyndale's version read, "he it is that obteyneth grace for oure synnes" and Wycliff's said, "he is the foryyuenes for oure synnes." So once again, what is the division?

Propitiation "denotes the price which must be paid to avoid the divine punishment upon sin."[1943] John Wesley said it was the "atoning sacrifice, by which the wrath of God is appeased."[1944] John MacArthur insists that "propiation is necessary because of sins."[1945] Is this not what the Bible teaches? This it the controversy. Propitiation "in pagan usage it mean 'to appease, to conciliate to one's self, to make a god propitious to one.'"[1946] James Boice said that it means the "placation or mollification" found "extensively in ancient pagan writings."[1947] This is why so many Christians reject propitiation. They believe it makes God look like some vengeful vindictive god, but ἱλασμος (*hilasmos*) was also used in Jewish culture.[1948] Nevertheless, it is "not used in precisely the same way."[1949] Consequently, some argue that it is "not so much to pacify and to placate God, as to disinfect man from the taint of sin."[1950] They therefore prefer the word "expiate."

H.A. Ironside is one who prefers *atonement* or *expiation*.[1951] Somewhat surprisingly, so does John Calvin[1952] and, of course, Martin Luther used "expiation."[1953] The best argument for this seems to be from 1 John 4:10 where the same word is used,[1954] but in the context that "He loved us and sent His Son *to be* the propitiation for our sins." Nevermind that the word there is translated "propitiation," it indicates not vengeful wrath, but love that motivated God to send Jesus. Brooke Westcott noted that Christ was the *propitiation*, not the propitiator.[1955]

In all honesty I have always found this debate ironic. It is like the critic who chastizes ancient Israel using moral standards that grew out of Israel. So also those who object to "propitiation" as pagan imagery forget that God used that same imagery for a reason. Jesus came and died in a way that the world could understand not only God's love, but also the need for that love. It is important to understand the depths of sin and how unrighteous it makes us. The word ἱλασμος (*hilasmos*) is the same word used of pagan sacrifices so when John used the word he fully understood its meaning. He intended to use that same word. Sin is an ugly thing so that propitiation is needed, but "the object of propitiation in Jewish through, as shown in their Scriptures, is not God, as in Greek thought, but man who estranged himself from God."[1956] It is God Himself who provided the sacrifice He did not require of Abraham (Genesis 22:8).

The Whole World?
The second issue is found in the simple words, "not for our [sins] only, but also for *those of* the whole world." Such words once again strike at the core of the Calvinist/Armenian debate. John Calvin naturally suggested that the whole world referred to the whole church scattered over the world![1957] As usual, he adds words to the text and takes away words from the text. John does not say church, he says "world" which is expressly set up *against* "our sins" which can only refer to believers!

Now Calvin was not the only one to make this argument. It was a common view of the medieval church. Hilary of Arles, for example, saw the "whole world" as representing the "whole church."[1958] Likewise, Bede argued that it was "for the whole Church which is spread ... throughout ... the world."[1959] Notice how each adds words not found in the text? This is the only way that one can interpret the passage to mean for the elect only.[1960] Nevertheless, Charles Dodd was correct to say that "the world is in this epistle as a rule an expression for the hostile pagan order."[1961] This is why the "world" is set up on apposition to us ("our sins only"). "The world of the elect," said Robert Govett, cannot be the case for "the elect are chosen *out* of the world; they are *not* of the world."[1962]

What then does John mean? Does this mean universalism as some Armenians hold? Perhaps it is "potentially" the whole world?[1963] No. Neither is correct. How then can Jesus die for the whole pagan world if they are not saved? Would this not nullify the cross? Of course not! When Ronald Reagan offered amnesty to illegal aliens in the 1980s, those who were in the United States illegally still had to step forward and present themselves to the courts as illegal aliens in order to receive the amnesty offered. Those who didn't trust the government and thought it was some sort of trick did not step forward and remained illegal aliens. They never received amnesty because they did not step forward and admit to being in the country illegally. So Jesus died for the sins of the "whole world" in order that *any* who step forward, confess our sins, and turn to Jesus *will* be saved and receive the blessings which resulted from His propiating sacrifice.

Conclusion

John's words are clear, but too many hold assumptions that want to muffle the sound of those words. God is not a barbaric pagan god, but sin is a terrible thing. It is God who sent Jesus as a propitiating sacrifice. The imagery is intentional. Because it is God who sent Jesus as the sacrifice no honest man can imply that God is vengeful or hateful, but neither can they deny the awfulness of sin and how greatly it divides us from Him.

So God sent Jesus as a propitiating sacrifice out of His love (1 John 4:10) for the "whole world" so that *anyone* from this world may repent and accepts the benefits of that sacrifice. All they need do is step forward, confess our sins, and trust in the Lord Jesus. This is love. Let no one take away from this, nor add to it.

Anti-Christs
1 John 2:18-19

> "Children, it is the last hour; and just as you heard that antichrist is coming, even now many antichrists have appeared; from this we know that it is the last hour."

The term "antichrist" is found only in 1 and 2 John. He is called elsewhere the "man of sin" (2 Thesslonians 2:3), the "son of perdition" (2 Thessalonians 2:3), "the lawless one" (2 Thessalonians 2:8), "the little horn" (Daniel 7:8), "the prince" (Daniel 9:26), "the beast" (Revelation 11:7), and many other names. However, John states here that "the" anti-Christ is just the epitome of the "many antichrists" who have already appeared.

Robert Lightner has asked whether or not "anti-Christ" should be taken as "either substitution or opposition" for Christ.[1964] In the former anti-Christ denotes a false Christ. In the latter, it denotes someone opposed to Christ. The former replaces Jesus. The latter could be an atheist or pagan. Lightner favors the latter in this particular context.[1965] Tertullian, however, believed that all heretics were anti-Christs,[1966] hence favoring substitution. The same was said by Bede,[1967] but in reality there is very little distinction.

Kenneth Wuest believes that "the distinction between a false Christ (pseudochristos) and an antichrist (antichristos) is that the former is a pretender to the Messianic office, whereas the latter is against Christ."[1968] In reality they both eliminate the Biblical Christ. Whether replacing Him with a false Messiah or rejecting Him, the outcome is the same. They are two different tactics by the same master; Satan. Consequently, the anti-Christ who comes in the Last Hour could theoretically be either one of these, or even a combination of the two. Andreas believed that "Anti-christ will come at the end of the world, and the heresies have already announced his coming."[1969]

This is John's warning. It is a warning against false doctrine. While some say that "doctrine is not important," doctrine is synonymous with truth. All doctrine is not salvific, but all is important and false doctrine leads us away from Christ. John warns us against such teachers who are in the world even in his day but will multiply the closer we come to the End Times, so that the appearance of false Christ is a sign of End Times (Matthew 24:24; Mark 13:22).

1 John 3:6-9 – See 1 John 1:8-10 ; 3:6-9 ; 5:18

Testing the Spirit
1 John 4:1

"Beloved, do not believe every spirit, but test the spirits to see whether they are from God."

John warns believers not to "believe every spirit." Some have compared this to the "charismatic gifts"[1970] and similar spirits, but others say that "it is not certain that the apostle refers here to any such supernatural power."[1971] John Calvin defined this narrowly to "mean someone who boasts that he is endowed with the gift of the Spirit to perform his office as a prophet,"[1972] but John Wesley is correct to say that "we are to try all spirits by the written word."[1973] To restrict these tests to any specific "spirit" is a mistake.

One thing is certain. In verse two John specifically refers to the gnostic cult which denied the physical incarnation of Jesus as God in the flesh.[1974] In that passage he says "by this you know the Spirit of God: every spirit that confesses that Jesus Christ has come in the flesh is from God." Now it is debateable whether or not John intended to say that this is the only test, for there are certainly cults which accept Jesus as flesh, but they invariably deny that

Jesus was the one and only God made flesh and that He alone is the Way, the Truth, and the Life (John 14:6). To this end Jonathan Edwards suggested that there are actually three tests. There are 1) Confessing that Jesus was born in flesh. 2) That the spirit abides by foundations of the Christian faith, and 3) That it has the Spirit of love.[1975] Martin Luther added 1 Timothy 1:15 as a standard test as well.[1976] Were these men adding to the words of the Bible? No, for John is here dealing specifically with the gnostic heretics. He is not denying that other cults and heresies have also existed. Consider that Islam accepts that Jesus came in the flesh, but they deny that He was the Son of God. They hold that Jesus was merely a prophet, and an inferior prophet to their own.

Didymus the Blind compares this passage and its concerns to ancient Israel when false prophets abounded, claiming to speak for God.[1977] William Barclay believed that the first century was unique to such spirits, calling it "a Spirit-filled world."[1978] In fact, angels and demons are no less active today, although they may not appear to men as often today. Satan's greatest trick, so it is said, is to convince men that he does not exist. So these tests remain today and forever. The point is that we should not believe every spirit. This is applies whether we are in a "spirit-filled" church, in the secular world, reading a theology book, or performing missions in foreign countries, for even "Satan disguises himself as an angel of light" (2 Corinthians 11:14).

Three That Testify
1 John 5:7-8

"For there are three that testify: the Spirit and the water and the blood; and the three are in agreement."

In regard to the authenticity (not interpretation) there are, despite the disengenuous claims of Bible critics, really only three legitimately debateable passages in the entire New Testament. The first is Mark 16:9-20. The second is John 8:1-11 (both are addressed in *Controversies in the Gospels*). Here is the third.

The King James Bible follows the third edition of the *textus receptus*, but *not* the Majority text,[1979] which reads:

"For there are three that bear record in heaven, the Father, the Word, and the Holy Ghost: and these three are one. And there are three that bear witness in earth, the Spirit, and the water, and the blood: and these three agree in one" (1 John 5:7-8).

The first part of the passage, called the *Comma Johanneum*,[1980] appear in most older English translations from the 19th century or earlier, as well as the Douay-Rheims, but all other modern translations either place it in brackets, footnote it, or omit it altogether, reading only:

"For there are three that testify: the Spirit and the water and the blood; and the three are in agreement" (1 John 5:7-8).

Now some theologians have accused modern translations of trying to omit the Trinity while atheists and cults use (or abuse) this passage to imply that the Trinity was an invention of later theologians. Both are absurd. The answer is both simple and ironic, as we shall see.

The Evidence

The history of the *Comma Johanneum* is unique. It is not found in any Greek manuscript before the twelfth century (and that is a later marginal note), it is not quoted by a single solitary church father,[1981] nor is it found in any ancient Syriac, Coptic, Armenian, Ethiopic, Arabic, or Slavonic translations, not to mention the Old Latin and early Vulgate copies.[1982]

Its first appearance is as a marginial note in a fourth century Latin text.[1983] Even the Latin Vulgate does not contain the passage until around 800 A.D.[1984] When Desiderius Erasmus prepared the famous *textus receptus*[1985] he actually omitted the passage from the first two editions on the grounds that it could not be found in any Greek manuscript. When he was challenged by some priests he promised to include the passage if anyone could produce a single solitary Greek manuscript which contained it.[1986] One was then discovered, some say "made to order," in codex Montfortianus (ms. 61) which is dated to around 1520.[1987] Erasmus kept his promise and added the passage but wrote a lengthy footnote on the suspect passage.[1988] It was then removed again from subsequent editions.[1989]

In addition to these there are only six other Greek manuscripts which contain the passage. The codex Regius of Naples (Greg. 88) dates to the twelfth,[1990] or possibly fourteenth, century[1991] and is a marginal correction written by another hand added unknown years later.[1992] Likewise ms. 221, a tenth century manuscript, contains this passage as another marginal correction dating to a later period.[1993] The same is true of ms. 429 and 636 which both date to the sixteenth century.[1994] Additionally it is found in the Tisch. ω 110, Greg. 629,[1995] ms. 918, and ms. 2318 which were all composed after the sixteenth century.[1996]

To summarize the evidence, it is not found in an any Greek text before the twelfth century. Of the thousands of manuscripts in existence, it is found in less than a dozen Greek manuscripts and most of those are marginal "corrections." It is also missing from early Latin manuscripts as well as all ancient translations. It does not appear even in the Latin Vulgate until around 800 A.D. Most importantly, it is never quoted by any of the church fathers. This is critically important, as we shall see, for even during the great Trinitarian debate at the Council of Nicaea, no church father appeals to this passage.[1997] This is ample proof that the passage did not exist in antiquity. Its first appearance is in the margins of a Latin text, and was probably intended as a marginal commentary which was never meant to be a part of the Bible.

Theological Signifance

Even the New King James Bible places a footnote to indicate that the passage does not exist in antiquity. Virtually all scholars concede that it is a late addition which arose and was erroneously added to later Latin Vulgate texts. The real question is then what impact this has upon the doctrines of the inerrancy and the Trinity.

Impact Upon the Doctrine of the Trinity

One of the strongest evidences against the authenticity of this verse is the fact that it is not quoted by any church father even during the the Trinitarian debate at the Council of Nicaea.[1998] This is also the strongest evidence that the doctrine of the Trinity does not derive from a single passage or misreading of a single verse. Rather it is proof that the church "derived the doctrine of the Trinity not from a particular verse but from the whole of Scripture."[1999]

Of the countless verses quoted to support the Trinity 1 John 5:7-8 was never used as evidence. John 1 and a plethora of other passages were cited, but not this one. The impact upon the doctrine of the Trinity is thus nonexistent. It had no impact because it did not exist. The Trinity is not based on this passage and Christians would do well to avoid quoting as proof of the Trinity when debating Unitarians or other anti-Trinitarians. Passages like Matthew 28:19 and even 2 Corinthians 13:14 are more useful, not to mention the entire first chapter of John's gospel.

Impact Upon the Doctrine of the Inerrancy

One of the fundamental principles of the inerrancy is that the original manuscripts are free from error and the pure unadulterated Word of God.[2000] The question asked here is how can we know what is and is not a part of the original manuscript and if errors such as this can creep into the King James Bible, then what else can be trusted?

Textual criticism is the science whereby we can determine what the original manuscripts said by comparing, evaluating, and studying ancient transmission of texts as well as the ancient texts themselves. This is how we know that the *Comma Johanneum* was not a part of the original manuscript. Nevertheless, it is true that copiest can make mistakes and some, like religious cults, can deliberately distort the text as translations like those done by the Jehovah's Witnesses. One famous Bible, called the "Adulterer's Bible," even infamously omitted, by accident, the word "not" from one of the Ten Commandments so that it read, "Thou shalt commit adultery"! Obviously, this was a mistake easily caught and retracted, but some mistakes, such as the *Comma Johanneum* have crept into *some* translations. How then can the reader feel "safe"?

Two points that are relevant here. First, the passage is in no way harmful or heretical and thus whether it is authentic or not bears no impact upon our understanding of the gospel. The inerrancy exist in such a way as to allow God to transmit His word without interfering in human will, including occasional errors or even intentional distortions, but such errors are always either unimportant, trivial, or easily caught and exposed by the serious student of the Bible, so that anyone who sincerely studies the Scriptures will be fooled into believing some distortion.

Second, because this passage is not central to the belief in the Trinity its authenticity (or lack thereof) is of no importance to any central doctrine. The Trinity is based on many other passages, not this one. Consequently, it bears no impact upon our study of the Bible or the Word of God. The inerrancy requires that the Word of God itself remains intact as originally written for our instruction. Trivial errors of no consequence may occur but do not effect the sincere student's study of the Word.

So the appearance of the *Comma Johanneum* in a handful of translations is of no consequence or harm to the inerrancy. In fact, it is far less harmful than some poor translations that subtly distort God's word to fit current cultural beliefs (such as politically correct translations of the Bible).

Conclusion

The famous *Comma Johanneum* is only controversial because of its unique history and the fact that Bible critics use it to cast doubt upon the whole of Scriptures. The doctrine of the Trinity is based on countless verses, but not this one. It is never even mentioned at the Council of Nicaea, and therefore its authenticity (or lack thereof) has no bearing upon the Trinity.

Sin Unto Death
1 John 5:16-17

> "There is a sin *leading* to death; I do not say that he should make request for this. All unrighteousness is sin, and there is a sin not *leading* to death."

Much debate has occured in regard to this sin. What sin could lead to death, and why not pray over it? Does this refer to a sin that leads to damnation? Is it an unforgiveable sin? Traditionally, this has been the belief which is why so many pages have been spent trying to understand what the sin might be. Others reject this entirely, saying that all sin leads to death, but this would seem to conflict with verse seventeen. What could John be saying? Let us look at the entire passage.

> "If anyone sees his brother committing a sin not *leading* to death, he shall ask and *God* will for him give life to those who commit sin not

leading to death. There is a sin *leading* to death; I do not say that he should make request for this. All unrighteousness is sin, and there is a sin not *leading* to death."

There are three issues related to this subject; all of which will help us to understand the answers to these questions. First, who is the brother? Second, why not pray? Why does John say that there is no reason to pray for this sin? Finally, of course, is the question of the sin itself and the nature of the sins to which John refers.

The Brother
The word "brother" in the Bible has multiple meanings. It can refer to a biological member of the family, to close relatives, to close friends, or to fellow Christians. Contextually it is obvious that John is either referring to a Christian brother, or more generically to all friends and loved ones, believer or not.

Robert Lightner, like most, believes that this refers to Christian brothers in the faith.[2001] The New Living Translation even paraphrases this as "Christian brother" rather than the more literal, if ambiguous, generic "brother." However, one problem with identifying this brother with fellow Christians is the fact that John speaks of the "sin leading to death" which is not worth praying over! Obviously, whether or not this is a Christian brother or an unbelievering brother depends in large part upon what the "sin leading to death" is and what is meant by not needing to make a request (prayer) for them. This leads to the second question.

The Prayer
The Greek word literally means "request," but as it is a request to God it is synonymous with prayer. The question is the nature of the prayer. In the first part of the passage John says that we "shall ask and *God* will for him give life." This, however, applies only to those sins (or the sin – see below) which does not lead to death. For those sins (or sin) leading to death John says, "I do not say that he should make request for this."

Here is the confusion. We are to pray for sins not leading to death and God grants life. Is this eternal life? Is it physical life as Robert Lightner believes?[2002] If the latter then is this taken as physical illness or capital punishment for some crime? This is connected to the theories listed below so I will reserve comment for now. What is clear is that we are to pray for our "brothers" when we see them sin. Note that it is not the sinner who is praying, but the friend praying for a brother. If the sin leading to death applies to Christian brother for whom prayer is useless, then many issues crop up, so once again, before we can answer either of the first two questions, it seems we must understand the sin or sins in mind.

The Sin (and Its Interpetations)

The sin (or sins) leading to death remains among the most controversial of passages in the Bible. What is meant by this? The answer effects our understanding of the rest of the passage. Are we praying for Christian brothers? If so, can he loose salvation? Is it physical death or spiritual death?

One of the dominant questions is whether or not John is referring to a single "unpardonable sin"[2003] or to many sins. It is said by some that the word is singular even though there is no indefinite article in Greek.[2004] The lack of a definite article, "*the* sin," therefore leads some to believe that it is a not a single "unpardonable sin"[2005] but one of many. Before examining the dominant interpretations, it is best to look at the full text of the passage, including specifics on the word "sin."

> "If anyone sees his brother committing a sin [singular] not *leading* to death, he shall ask and *God* will for him give life to those who commit sin [plural] not *leading* to death. There is a sin [singular] *leading* to death; I do not say that he should make request for this. All unrighteousness is sin [singular-collective], and there is a sin [singular-collective] not *leading* to death."

Note that only the second use of sin is plural. The rest are singular, but *at least* two of them are used in the collective sense of the word. The lack of a definite article, "the," probably does not indicate that there is but a single sin to which John refers. Consequently, sin is probably used here in a collective sense.

As expected there are a great many theories passed down over the centuries, but only five dominant ones have found themselves repeated over time. Each deserves careful consideration.

View # 1 : Capital Crimes

One of the most popular views over the centuries has been that John is speaking of physical life and death.[2006] While some consider physical illness and the like a punishment by God (cf. 2 Kings 2:1-6; 2 Chronicles 32:24), most have viewed this as "sins which are *punishable* by death"[2007] in the civil order. It has variously been viewed as God's punishment, civil punishment in the form of the death penalty, or even excommunications in the Middle Ages.[2008]

H.A. Ironside subscribed to this view but was careful to point out that he did not believe that this was eternal death or damnation.[2009] Physical death has always been the result of God's curse on sin since the Garden of Eden. Matthew Henry stated that "all sin, as to the merit and legal sentence of it, is unto death."[2010] This is also the view of men like Charles Hodges.[2011]

Obviously the view's strengths speak for themselves and can be supported by passages like 2 Kings 2:1-6 and 2 Chronicles 32:24 where King Hezekiah was granted fifteen more years of life because of his righteous prayer. Nonetheless, its weaknesses are equally strong.

398

First, if we distinguish between civil death penalty and God's wrath, then we can easily dismiss the civil interpretation. If a crime is punishable by death there may indeed be no point in praying for his physical life, but if he commits a crime which is not punishable by death then what is the use of praying for his life at all? After all, he is in no danger of death anyway!

The idea that John is speaking of a situation similar to Hezekiah's is stronger, but still suspect. First, while all death is the result of God's curse for sin, we know that the righteous suffer and die young in this world while the wicked prosper. Of course some have linked this with Ananias and Sapphira in Acts five[2012] so it is clear that God still chastises those whom He loves, although even if we accept this, the question would still remain what is the sin that leads to death. What sins (or sin) would lead God to cast such a punishment upon a believer? Consequently, this view is good at examining the context but poor in regard to actually defining what sin (or sins) in mind. It simply doesn't fully answer the question.

View # 2 : Seven Deadly Sins

A popular view in the Middle Ages was that John was referring to one of the seven death sins.[2013] This is arguably the weakest of all the view for the simple fact that even in Catholic theology the seven deadly sins are at the root of *all* sins. They break sins into one of seven basic categories from which all other sins stem. If true then every sin would be one of the seven deadly sins. The idea of connecting a "sin leading unto death" with a "deadly sin" is fitting, but not logical, for all sins fall under the umbrella of the seven deadly sins.

View # 3 : Sins Persisted Until Death

Another popular view is that it refers to "sin persisted in *till* death."[2014] The Venerable Bede took "the sin to death"[2015] quite literally, saying, "the sin to death can properly be understood as the sin persisted in up to the time of death."[2016] Support for this view is the fact that "'sinneth' is present tense, continuous action."[2017] It is not a "past" verb, but present. It is something which is continuing to take place. As such, the Greek strongly supports such an interpretation. Having said that, the context strongly rejects this view.

Consider that the context is about praying for the life of a brother who sins. John then says there is no need to pray for the one who "sins unto death," but this would make no sense if John was speaking of "sin persisted until death." How do we know whether or when a man will repent. Did not the thief crucified with Jesus repent on his deathbed (Luke 23:42-43)? Logically, a "sin unto death" must be something recognizable to us and not to God alone. Since no man can judge my heart but God this view cannot account for John's conceding the futility of praying for such sins.

View # 4 : Blasphemy

Some view the sin as apostasy[2018] or the "unpardonable sin" to which Jesus alludes in Matthew 12:31-32.[2019] What is that sin? Jesus said:

> "Therefore I say to you, any sin and blasphemy shall be forgiven people, but blasphemy against the Spirit shall not be forgiven. Whoever speaks a word against the Son of Man, it shall be forgiven him; but whoever speaks against the Holy Spirit, it shall not be forgiven him, either in this age or in the *age* to come."

Now considering that the "blasphemy against the Holy Spirit" is as controversial as this passage, the connection is not particularly helpful as far as determining what this sin may be, but it is generally viewed as blasphemy. What kind of blasphemy? What blasphemy is unpardonable? Kenneth Wuest noted that some have argued the sin unto death is a "denial of the Incarnation" of Christ,[2020] but this again leads us back to the same fundamental problem as was inherent in some of the previous views. If John is speaking to believers about brothers in Christ, then how could a believer commit the unpardonable sin? Can a believer loose his salvation (see notes on Hebrews 6:4-6 and Hebrews 10:26-27)?

Once again we are faced with the choice of rejection this view, accepting that Christians can loose their salvation, or understanding that John was speaking of prayer for unbelievers. Before examining that last possibility, let us look at the fifth dominant interpretation.

View # 5 : Rejecting Christ

Arguably the most popular view among evangelicals is that the sin (singular) leading unto death is the rejection of Christ.[2021] Martin Luther likened this sin unto death to that of Judas and Saul, a kind of outright defiance of God.[2022]

While the view has many great supporters because of its theological implications, the fact that it is a theological interpretation, rather than an exegetical one, is part of the problem. Moreover, even theologically it is not *technically* accurate. No, salvation and damnation are not the same thing, as so many often seem to assume. What I mean is that they are not flip sides of the same coin. Biblically speaking damnation is always for our sins; not for our beliefs. Technically, we are not damned for rejecting Christ, but for our sins. We are *saved* through Christ, but we are damned for our sins, and for no other reason. This is important to understand because it underlines the justice of God.

Think about it. Virtually every religion believes in some way or form that they will work their way into heaven by merit. To the man who says he will be weighed on the scales of justice, God will do just that very thing, and he will be found wanting. To the man who says he is righteous, every unrighteous deed will be laid before him. No man will escape justice. Jesus, however, has the power to pardon our sins, and whosoever accepts the pardon and turns from his sins will be saved. Thus *salvation* is of Christ, but damnation is of sin.

So theologically the view is not even technically correct. Moreover, James Boice noted that Peter did not die physically or spiritually when he denied Christ.[2023] The second death (Revelation 20:6, 14) has no power over believers. So once again we are left with the same problem as in previous views. How could John be speaking of praying for those who commit the "sin unto death" if the "sin unto death" is rejecting Christ? That would mean we are never to pray for unbelievers, or it would mean that believers can loose their salvation! Both options are heretical and there is no third option.

As we can see none of the five dominant views is particularly strong overall. They either fail to consider the context of prayer for a "brother" or they read theology into the text, neglecting proper exegesis. Although several of them have merit (the first, third, and fourth) they fail to explain properly the overall context of John's remarks. The correct interpretation must account for all three; exegesis, context, and Johannine theology.

Conclusion

John urges us to pray for a brother's life. Several facts are apparent from the context.

1) John cannot be talking about eternal life, for if it is a Christian brother then he cannot loose eternal life and if it is an unbeliever he cannot have eternal life bestowed on him by any other than Christ.

2) John is probably not talking about physical life, for *all* sin leads to physical death as a result of the curse in Eden.

Now since sin leads to spiritual death as well, we appear at an impass, or do we? Not necessarily for our spiritual life is connected to our walk with Christ and sin separates us from that life we have within us. To speak of spiritual life is not necessarily to speak of eternal life, although we cannot have eternal life without it. Consequently, John is probably speaking of praying for those who need their spiritual life and walk with Christ restored.

The only problem with my thesis is the same as with other views. How could John tell us not to bother with prayer for "sins unto death"? This where the second issue comes into play. I am inclined to believe that John is speaking of brothers generically, not only believers (although we are certainly included), but also unbelieving brothers. We are to pray for them as well, but in Jewish law sins of ignorance or similar sins were viewed differently from sins of wilfulness (see notes on Hebrews 10:26-27).[2024] This was also true in the Qumran community where they "distinguished betweeen sins requiring expulsion and those requiring penance."[2025]

With this in mind, it is probable that John was referring generically to all brothers (Christian or not) but noted that praying for those who defy God and live for murder and rape is not required. This is not to say that they can never come to repentance, but that the church is not, and never has, been in the habit of praying for evil. When we pray for unbelievers in church, we never said a pray for Bin Laden's repentance or for Hitler's eventual salvation. True, it is possible even for the most wicked men to repent as did King Nebuchadnezzar (Daniel 4), but the church does not need to expend its prayer on such crimes as those commited by these men, for few are they who will repent.

Now I concede that my solution is not settled. If this passage were easy to understand it is likely that there would not be so much controversy over it. Nevertheless, I believe we must consider that the prayer is life, and that the life must be spiritual, but not necessarily eternal in nature. Second, we must account for the fact that John enjoins us to pray for some brother's sins, but not all. Brother is therefore probably generic in nature, as we pray for our leaders (most of whom are not believers) in church. Finally, "sin" is used in a collective sense throughout most of the passage so it is probable, but not certain, that John is not speaking of any "blasphemy against the Holy Spirit" (Matthew 12:31-32), but of serious sins by men who have scorned and rejected the Lord. Although their salvation may still be possible, the church need not expend energy on prayers for such men.

1 John 5:18 – See 1 John 1:8-10 ; 3:6-9 ; 5:18

Summary

John's writings bear the stamp of beauty and simplicity with love being their major theme. John did not, however, believe in libertarianism. Love was not an excuse to do wrong, but a motive for doing what was right and obeying the Lord. John's writings reflect a strong Jewish mindset whereby the spirit and the law are but two different sides of the same coin. He did not see the spirit as emnity with the law, but its spiritual father. Those who live under the law bear the weight of sin, but the Spirit lifts us from that sin into life. We then do what the law requires without even considering that there is such a law, for if we love one another, we will do what is right, and if we truly do what is right we will do not wrong. This was the constant theme of John; neither libertarianism nor legalism, but perfect love.

15

—

Jude

Jude is a very short epistle filled with allusions to Biblical and extra-Biblical accounts. Most of the debates revolve around Jude's use of these extra-Biblical "apocalyptic" literature. In addition, questions have arisen in regard to the relationship between Jude and 2 Peter, an epistle which bears resemblances to Jude, as well as the identity of "Jude, a bond-servant of Jesus Christ, and brother of James."

Regarding similarities between 2 Peter and Jude some argue 2 Peter and Jude both paraphrased some extra-Biblical source.[2026] No such evidence exist for this assumption and the critics who make this claim are the usual suspects who accuse the Biblical authors of plagerism with no proof. While it is apparent that Jude quotes extra-Biblical sources, I have quoted over a thousand people in this work. That does not make my work any less my own. There is no hint that either Peter or Jude "borrowed" from an unknown source. If they borrowed from anyone, His name was Jesus Christ.

Others have argued that 2 Peter borrowed from Jude or that Jude borrowed from Peter.[2027] Even this seems a simplistic way of looking at the similarities, for both authors were followers of Jesus and dealing with a similar problem. Nevertheless, Jude 17-18 does appear to be a direct quote of 2 Peter. It says, "you, beloved, ought to remember the words that were spoken beforehand by the apostles of our Lord Jesus Christ, that they were saying to you, 'In the last time there will be mockers, following after their own ungodly lusts.'" Notice, however, two things. First, Jude gives due credit to his source, referring to "the apostles of our Lord Jesus Christ." It is a quotation of the apostles. Was he actually quoting 2 Peter, as many believe, or were 2 Peter 3:3 and Jude 17-18 both quotes of some other apostle, or even Jesus? It really doesn't matter, but it does indicate that Jude had read the works of the apostles, to whom he gives full credit. This then leads to the question of when Jude wrote.

Dates for the epistle of Jude have ranged from 40 and 80 A.D.[2028] but most place it in the 60s, either before or after 2 Peter, depending on whom they believe wrote first. Nonetheless, the word "beforehand" in verse seventeen seems to indicate that some time had passed. If verse eighteen is a quote from Jesus, then the late 60s makes sense, but if it is a quote of 2 Peter, as many believe, then Jude would have to have been written much closer to 80 A.D. some years after Peter's epistle had circulated, and long enough for Jude to refer to its writing as "beforehand."

Yet another quarrel has been over the identify of Jude. He refers to himself as "brother of James," but there were many Jameses in the Bible.

Whichever James he refer to apparently needed no further clarification for the readers were fully aware of James and Jude.

Now Jude is short for Judah or Judas (which the Greek rendition). It was a very common name in Biblical times. Two of the apostles were named Judah (Judas Iscariot and Judas Thaddæus) as well as a half-brother or cousin of Jesus (Matthew 13:55; Mark 6:3). Which of these, if any, is the Jude of this epistle?

A few facts are apparent. First, Jude does not count himself among the apostles (v. 17). This eliminates the belief of some that this is the apostle Judas Thaddæus who is introduced as "Judas of James" in Acts 1:13. Moreover, "Judas of James" most probably means "son of James," not the brother of James.

Second, Jude introduces himself as the "brother of James," *not* the "brother of our Lord." This is significant for most Protestants believe that Jude was the half-brother of Jesus apparently mentioned in Matthew 13:55 and Mark 6:3. However, a close examination of these passages reveals that this is not the case. Consider that Merrill Unger acknowledges James the Less is the apostle,[2029] but forgets that Mark 15:40 identifies James the Less as the same James found in Matthew 13:55 and Mark 6:1-3.[2030] I have debated this in detail in *Apostles After Jesus*, but it is sufficient to say that Matthew 13:55 and Mark 6:1-3 refer to the extended family of Jesus. I do not deny that Jesus had half-brothers and sisters, but James the Less and Jude, his brother, were not among those. They were both cousins who were a part of the extended family of Jesus, Joseph, and Mary who all lived together in Nazareth.

Additional support for this may be found in history, and the relationship of James the Less, also called James the Just, to the church of Jerusalem. When Jude was writting to Jews he needed no other introduction than "brother of James" for he was the overseer or bishop of Jerusalem. However, as indicated above, this was probably written after the destruction of Jerusalem (see *Apostles After Jesus* for more on this probability). Consequently, Jude was probably writing to Christian Jews expelled from Jerusalem before the seige. He was well know among the former members of the church of Jerusalem, and quite possibly the only surviving member of Jesus's extended family.

Jude's Use of Apocalyptic Literature

"Apocalyptic literature" is term given by theologians to literature which deals with "End Times" or "Last Days." It is a modern label which erroneously attempts to read certain assumptions into the literature; namely that it is somehow to be treated differently from other prophecy. It is the myth that prophecy about End Times should not be taken as literally as prophecy about the coming of Christ. I have elsewhere refuted the false assumptions behind this label (see notes in *Controversies in Revelation*). The reader only need know that Jude quotes from several extra-Biblical sources which deal with End Times and which in some cases claim to be prophetic in nature. This is the controversy. Can an inspired Biblical author quote an uninspired work which appeals to prophecy? For example, if the *Book of Enoch* claims to be written by a prophet and was not, would Jude not be endorsing the works of a false prophet?

Such questions are fair on one level, but only one level. It is not logical to argue that an inspired book can never quote from an unispired one. I have quoted hundreds of authors with whom I not only disagree, but often opposed. I have also quoted many authors with whom I agree, even though I may believe they err in certain points. Now I do not claim inspiration for myself, but the comparison is valid. There is no sin in quoting literature, whether that literature is good or bad. Indeed, Seneca once said, "I will not hesitate to quote a bad author if the line is good." Why can the same not be said for Jude?

Now I said that the complaint is fair on one level. By that I mean that if the *Book of Enoch* and the *Assumption of Moses,* both of which *appear* to be quoted by Jude, claim to be written by prophets and were not, then Jude might be perceived as endorsing false prophets even though his epistle is actually a warning against false prophets! On this level, it is fair to question Jude's use of these works, but only if it can be proven that the *Book of Enoch* and the *Assumption of Moses* make claim to inspiration and that Jude accepted such a claim.

In regard to the *Book of Enoch* no real inspiration is claimed by its author. It should be compared to a work of historical fiction not unlike a Biblical epic such as *Ben-Hur* or the *Robe*. In fact, the book is acknowledged by all to have been written thousands of years after Enoch. The prophetic elements of the book are based on Jewish tradition. Consequently, it is debateable whether or not Jude is even quoting from the *Book of Enoch* as opposed to the Jewish tradition upon which the *Book of Enoch* was based. "Both Jude and the author [of Enoch] may have quoted a common tradition."[2031] It cannot be proven one way or another, so it is not valid to assume that Jude was not only quoting the *Book of Enoch* but also viewed it as inspired.

Now some argue "he spoke of [these works] in the same way in which he ... [spoke of] any other fact of history."[2032] In other words, the *Book of Enoch* and the *Assumption of Moses* are works of historical fiction, and Jude was quoting the historical aspects, not the fictional ones. To that end, Albert Barnes denies that Jude was quoting the *Assumption of Moses*.[2033] He could be correct, for the only allusions Jude makes to either of these apocryphal works may also be found in Jewish tradition. Was Jude quoting apocrypha or tradition? Ultimately it doesn't matter because Jude was not citing the traditions as Scripture, but alluding to history. So while some argue that Jude was not saying the stories were true[2034] it is apparent that Jude does believe the tradition behind the stories. He does not quote word for word from either apocrypha, but quotes only those aspects of those stories which are historical and found in other Jewish literature. Let us look more at the specific examples.

Jude 6 – See 2 Peter 2:4 and Jude 14-15

The Body of Moses
Jude 9

> "Michael the archangel, when he disputed with the devil and argued about the body of Moses, did not dare pronounce against him a railing judgment, but said, 'The Lord rebuke you!'"

Jude 9 contains the first allusion to extra-Biblical Jewish tradition. In it he mentions a dispute of the body of Moses. In the Bible it is only said that Moses was buried in the valley of the land of Moab "but no man knows his burial place to this day" (Deuteronomy 34:6). The secret burial of Moses is generally believed to have been to prevent future generations from turning his grave into an idol or worshipping over it. Nothing is said of Satan in this passage, but some believe that Jude is quoting Zechariah. This was the position of both Bede[2035] and John Calvin[2036] for Zechariah 3:2 says that Satan was rebuked with these very words! The problem is that the context is entirely different and Moses is not mentioned at all in Zechariah 3, and neither is Michael.

Most believe that Jude is alluding to the apocryphal *Assumption of Moses*, but both Albert Barnes[2037] and Robert Lightner[2038] deny this with good reason, for in all surviving copes of the *Assumption of Moses* these words are not to be found therein, neither is the dispute with Michael! Nevertheless, Origen and Gelasius both make mention of such a story in a work called the *Ascension of Moses*.[2039] Scholars have assumed that this is the "lost" complete copy of the *Assumption of Moses* but no proof has yet surfaced to back up this claim. The so-called *Ascension of Moses* could well post-date Jude and be completely unrelated to the *Assumption of Moses*.

Even if the *Assumption of Moses* did contain such a story, the more likely scenario is that Jude was referring to a Jewish tradition from which both were derived. As Ironside said, Jude's source "is not given"[2040] so speculation is idle. Jonathan Edwards noted that inspired men "do mention particulars not recorded in those histories."[2041] They do not need to. Jude was quoting an event from history. Some call it a mere "illustration"[2042] but Jude's quotation gives every indication that he believed the story to be a hundred percent true and accurate.

In my opinion it is most likely that Jude was quoting from tradition. Indeed, there were many traditions revolving around the death of Moses. Clement of Alexandria believed that Moses was taken to heaven like Elijah.[2043] This he doubtless received from a tradition found in Josephus which says that "a cloud stood over [Moses] all of the sudden, and he disappeared in a certain valley, although he wrote in the holy books that he died, which was done out fear, lest they should venture to say that, because of his extraordinary virtue, he went to God."[2044] Such a legend is interesting, but untrue. Jude does not refer to this tradition, for the Bible clearly states that Moses died and was buried (Deuteronomy 34:6) and the Scriptures do not lie.

Theologians are sometimes too much like critics. They speculate rather then exegete. One theory, for example, argues that the "body of Moses" is mere allegory for Israel.[2045] Such interpretations and speculations go far beyond the scope of Scripture. Jude is citing historical events in Israel's history to show the struggle is not between men, but a spiritual battle. To make such words allegory or fictional "illustrations" is to deny the entire point of Jude's words. The point is to show from *history* that our war is a spiritual one. The dispute between Michael and Satan is not to be found in the Bible, nor in any existing copy of the *Assumption of Moses*. It is a historical event which Jude mentions and needs no citation.

Enoch's Prophecy
Jude 14-15

> "*It was* also about these men *that* Enoch, *in* the seventh *generation* from Adam, prophesied, saying, 'Behold, the Lord came with many thousands of His holy ones, to execute judgment upon all, and to convict all the ungodly of all their ungodly deeds which they have done in an ungodly way, and of all the harsh things which ungodly sinners have spoken against Him.'"

In addition to the *Assumption of Moses,* Jude is accused of borrowing from the *Book of Enoch,* another great apocalyptic writing from about the third century before Christ. While it is possible, and even probable, that Jude had seen and read the *Book of Enoch,* it remains to be seen if he is actually quoting from the *Book of Enoch,* quoting from countless Jewish traditions, or some historical event not specifically mentioned in the Bible.

The Angels Rebellion
The allusion in Jude 6 was discussed briefly in 2 Peter 2:4. Many interpreters believe that it could be a reference to the idea that demons intermarried with mortals in Genesis 6. Since a number of theologians do not believe that this ever happened they argue that Jude must have been "borrowing" from the apocryphal *Book of Enoch* which recounts the ancient tradition. However, there are many reasons to suspect this assumption.

First, the story of fallen angels intermarrying with mortal women is found in many places outside of the *Book of Enoch.* It is found in the Greek *Septuagint* translation of Genesis 6, among the Talmudic interpreters and

Targum, Josephus, and is the most ancient interpretation of Genesis 6 by both Jews and Christians. So regardless of our own personal interpretation of Genesis 6, it cannot be said that Jude was borrowing from the *Book of Enoch*.

Second, Jude does not refer to this as some legend or myth, but as history. Consequently, if he is referring to Genesis 6 then it is because Genesis 6 teaches that demons intermarried with women; not that he was "borrowing" from some myth or fictional literature.

Third, it may be that the passage refers to Satan's rebellion in heaven. The application to Genesis 6 is possible given that it is historically placed before the events of Sodom and Gomorrah, but this is not sufficient to prove the case.

Jude's point here, once again, is to prove from Hebrew history that "our struggle is not against flesh and blood, but against the rulers, against the powers, against the world forces of this darkness, against the spiritual *forces* of wickedness in the heavenly *places*" (Ephesians 6:12).

The Prophecy of Enoch

Enoch is found only in Genesis 5:21-24 and Hebrews 11:5. Hebrews, like Jude, alludes to extra-Biblical history concering Enoch who was a prophet of God in the days before Noah. Jewish tradition is rich with the stories of Enoch and his prophecies. The best known tradition survives to this day in extant copies of the apocryphal *Book of Enoch*, which Jude 14-15 *may* quote. In that passage Jude refers to a prophecy of Enoch which said:

> "Behold, the Lord came with many thousands of His holy ones, to execute judgment upon all, and to convict all the ungodly of all their ungodly deeds which they have done in an ungodly way, and of all the harsh things which ungodly sinners have spoken against Him."

Now a parallel is to be found in a few copies of the *Book of Enoch*, in Enoch 1:9. It reads:

> "Look! He cometh with the myriads of His holy ones to execute judgment upon all, and to destroy all the wicked: and to convict all humanity for all the wicked deed they have done, and the proud and hard words that wicked sinners have spoke against Him."[2046]

Notice that the citations are very close. William Barclay believes that Jude was quoting the *Book of Enoch* verbatim and sees no problem with this.[2047] Others deny this. Two possibilities are offered in its stead. The first of the possibilities is that both Jude and the *Book of Enoch* are quoting some historical source no longer in existence. The second possibility is that later copies of the *Book of Enoch* actually emulated Jude. This is actually a viable theory because all the ancient copies known to exist *do not* contain Enoch 1:9. The only copies known to exist with contain this passage are Ethiopean translations which date to the Christian era.[2048] So it is argued that Enoch 1:9 was actually added to later Christian copies of 1 Enoch. While possible, this is pure speculation as there is not enough evidence to prove one theory over another.

Gerard Hoet – Enoch Ascends to Heaven – 1728

409

My own personal inclination is that both Jude and the *Book of Enoch* quote a commonly accepted historical tradition of Enoch's prophecy, but Jude was probably not quoting directly from the *Book of Enoch*. Nevertheless, many believe that he was doing just that, so if this is true, how does this impact the inspiration of Jude?

Tertullian seemed to have accepted the entire *Book of Enoch* as Scripture.[2049] He said "since Enoch in the same Scripture has preached likewise concering the Lord, nothing at all must be rejected by us which pertains to us; and we read that 'every Scripture suitable for edification is divinely inspired.'"[2050] On the other hand Bede believed that the *Book of Enoch* was "tainted" but did contain some historical truths[2051] while Augustine taught that the entire *Book of Enoch* was a forgery.[2052] The latter are more accurate. As aforementioned, a great many traditions have been passed down over the centuries by the Jews. The prophecies of Enoch were not invented by the *Book of Enoch*, but rather it was a piece of historical-fiction written thousands of years after the Biblical Enoch. It contains some historical quotations, including that which is also quoted by Jude. The relationship between *Book of Enoch* and Jude is cursory only. Jude is the inspired Word of God and his quotations are all historical and accurate. There is no fictional illustration or borrowing of ideas. There is only the historical prophecy of Enoch.

Conclusion
John Wesley summarized Jude's point. "The First coming of Christ was revealed to Adam; his second glorious coming to Enoch; and the seventh from Adam foretold things which will conclude the seventh age of the world."[2053] These facts may not be elaborated upon in Scripture, but they are historical, and when Jude cites them, he is citing history, not fiction, nor any extra-Biblical "Scripture." We should be no more concerned with Jude's citations than we would be if he made a historical reference to Judas Maccabeus.

Summary

Jude is one of the shortest epistles in the Bible. His work is intended to warn Jewish believers, probably dispersed after the fall of Jerusalem, of the influx of heretics and false doctrine. He illustrates from the history of the Jews that our war is a spiritual war. His epistle could be seen as an illustration of Paul's words in Ephesians 6:12, "our struggle is not against flesh and blood, but against the rulers, against the powers, against the world forces of this darkness, against the spiritual *forces* of wickedness in the heavenly *places*."

16

Revelation 1-5

The last book in my Controversies series was actually the first one I wrote. *Controversies in Revelation* is over 200,000 words in length, but I still felt that I could not address every controversy, so I had made the conscious decision to omit the first five chapters of Revelation from that book. I wanted to concentrate upon the actual prophecies of the Tribulation itself and the events which transpire. *Controversies in Revelation* thus began with Revelation 6:1 and continued on to the end of the book.

As I wrote *Controversies in the Epistles* I decided to correct this. After all, the first three chapters of Revelation are themselves short epistles written to seven churches in Asia. Therefore, I include here Revelation 1-5, but unlike *Controversies in Revelation* I will continue the pattern of my other Controversies books inasmuch as I will not address every passage; only those passages which are of controversy.

Authorship of Revelation

Oddly enough, I neglected the debate of the authorship of Revelation in *Controversies in Revelation*. At that time I wanted to focus solely upon the prophecies of Revelation and the various interpretations throughout the ages. I focused on exegesis of each and every passage from Revelation 6:1 onward, but in so doing I neglected debates over the authorship and composition of John's Revelation.

The author specifically identifies himself as "John" (1:4, 9) and states that he was writing from exile on Patmos (1:9). Most scholars traditionally agreed that this is the apostle John. Not until Dionysius of the late third century, did anyone doubt this, and Dionysius rejected the inspiration of Revelation because he rejected a Millennial hopes![2054] Therefore, he had to reject apostolic authority of its author. In recent years some modern scholars have also come to reject the apostolic authority, arguing that it was written by another John. Many of these believe that it was a "John the Elder" referred to by Papias.

It was Eusebius who first suggested that "John the Elder" (also called "John the Presbyter") wrote Revelation.[2055] He quoted, or misquoted, Papias, the apostolic father, as saying that there were "two men in Asia [that] had the same name that that there are two tombs at Ephesus, each called John's."[2056] He then speculated that it was John the Elder who wrote Revelation, and not John the Apostle.[2057] The truth is that neither of these assersions are correct.

To begin with the actual quotation of Papias does not refer to two separate John's at all. Rather it refers to two classes of men. Let us look at the actual quote. It reads:

> "Whenever anyone came who had been a follower of the elders, I asked about their words: what Andrew or Peter had said, or Philip or Thomas or James or John or Matthew or any other of the Lord's disciples, and what Aristion and the presbyter John, disciples of the Lord, were still saying. For I did not think that information from books would help me as much as the word of a living, surviving voice."[2058]

Eusebius believed that Papias was citing two different classes of men; the apostles and a secondary group including Aristion and John the Elder (for "presbyter" means "elder"). However, a number of interpreters believed that Eusebius had a certain agenda that made him misunderstand Papias's words,[2059] for a careful reading of the above quote proves the opposite. To begin with, Papias refers to the apostles as elders ("presbyter" in the Greek) in the first sentence. Moreover, the second classification of people are also called "disciples of the Lord," even as the first group was called. Furthermore, the second group are those whom Papias says were "surviving voices" who were "still saying" what they had seen. In other words, the second group are those who had seen Jesus with their own eyes and were still alive in the early days of the second century. John was one of these. That is affirmed by Papias himself in a later quote (for Euebius is selective in his quotation of Papias). Elsewhere Papias states clearly that the Apostle John wrote five books, not four, and that he was himself a pupil of John![2060] Eusebius tries to claim that Papias was a pupil of this "second" John but ignores that Papias attributes all five books (the gospel of John, the three epistles of John, and Revelation) to this same person! In other words, John the Elder and John the Apostle were one and the same. That Papias uses "elder" and "disciple" interchangeably is obvious from Eusebius's own quotation.

Another argument against John the Apostle being the author is the claim that the vocabulary and style of the Greek is radically different from the works of John's gospel and epistles.[2061] Now while it is true that the vocabulary is different, this is because the subject matter is so different. Obviously vocabulary is going to be topic driven to a large extent. As to the style, I completely object to claims that it is different. When I first learned Greek we were always told that John's writings are the best to begin reading because he uses a very simple and beautiful writing style that is easy for beginning Greek students to read. I chose Revelation. Its Greek is very similar to John in terms of style, simplicity, and grammer. It is only the vocabulary which differs.

The best evidence that John wrote Revelation is in the fact that every church father and historian records that the Apostle John was exiled to Patmos, and the author of Revelation himself states that he wrote from Patmos and that

412

his name was John (Revelation 1:9). Moreover, his own pupil, whom he personally taught, was a certain Papias who identifies John the Apostle as the author of five books, including Revelation. The identity of John as the author of Revelation is as certain as any New Testament book.

Pedro Orrente – John on Patmos – 1620

The Date of Revelation's Composition

Literally for almost two thousand years no one doubted that Revelation was written during John's exile on Patmos under the reign of Domitian. Hippolytus, who was a pupil of John's students,[2062] said that "John, again, in Asia, was banished by Domitian the king to the isle of Patmos, in which also he wrote his Gospel and saw the apocalyptic vision."[2063] Such as the universal view until the rise of a theological interpretation known as preterism.

Preterism is an interpretation of Revelation which holds that all the prophecies of Revelation relate to Nero or some other early Roman emperor.[2064] Consequently, the book must be dated earlier than Nero in order for the theory to work. The problem, of course, is that the Bible explicitly states that John "was on the island called Patmos because of the word of God and the testimony of Jesus" (Revelation 1:9). If John was exiled by Domitian, then there is no way that the book can be a prophecy about a man who had died almost thirty years before!

In an attempt to support their theologial agenda, some try desperately to shift the Patmos exile from Domitian to Nero. Bernard Ruffin implies that Tertullian and Jerome place John's exile under Nero,[2065] but in fact they say nothing of the sort. They do not give the name of the emperor in question, but others do. Each and *every* church father who mentions the time or emperor places his exile under Domitian's reign in the mid 90s. *No* church father names Nero.[2066] Tertullian's quotation is simply that Rome is "where the Apostle John was first plunged, unhurt, into boiling oil, and thence remitted to his island exile."[2067] He says nothing more. It is the other church fathers who identify the emperor as Domitian. Moreover, the church fathers also state that he returned from exile under Nerva, or some say Trajan (for Nerva rule was very short). Can we really expect that he was in exile for over thirty years and multiple emperors?

The fact is that there is not a single *iota* of historical evidence, tradition, or even legend that places the Patmos exile under Nero. Those who make this claim are one and all preterists who have a theological agenda. Proper interpretation, historical research, and scholarship should not be agenda driven but based on proper exegesis, research, and knowledge.

In short, it was the universal view of history that John was exiled to Patmos by Domitian in the 90s when John was very old. Some believe that all his works were written in island exile. Others that only Revelation was written during this time. While the date for the gospel and the epistles is open to legitimate debate, the date for Revelation is fixed by John's own words in Revelation 1:9; "I, John, your brother and fellow partaker in the tribulation and kingdom and perseverance *which are* in Jesus, was on the island called Patmos because of the word of God and the testimony of Jesus."

Revelation 1:4 – See Revelation 4:5

The Trinity
Revelation 1:6-7 – Titus 2:13

"He has made us *to be* a kingdom, priests to His God and Father."

"The glory of our great God and Savior, Christ Jesus.'"

414

Some might ask what these two passages have to do with one another. The question is technical, but highly significant for two reasons. The first is the question of the doctrine of the Trinity. The second is over the debate with those who believe that the King James should be the only English version used, and that all other versions are false and heretical.

The technical question is over how Greek joins synonyms. Since *koine* Greek is a dead language there was no universal agreement on the question, but in the eighteenth century "Sharp's rule" gained acceptance. It states that "if two substantives are connected by και and both have the article they refer to different persons or things; if the first has an article and the second does not, the second refers to the same person or thing as the first."[2068] The King James Bible was written before this rule became commonly accepted, so it differs on passages where this might apply. Let us compare the two relevant passages, beginning with Revelation 1:6.

NAS	KJV
"He has made us *to be* a kingdom, priests to His God and Father."	"Hath made us kings and priests unto God and his Father."

Notice that in the King James version it appears that God has a Father! This would be a Trinitarian reference, indicating that "God" is a reference to Jesus and not God the Father, who is joined with Him by the και ("and"). Naturally when King James only advocates see the New American Standard's translation they claim that the translators deliberately removed a reference tot he Trinity, but when we look at Titus 2:13 we see the exact opposite.

NAS	KJV
"The appearing of the glory of our great God and Savior, Christ Jesus."	"The glorious appearing of the great God and our Saviour Jesus Christ."

Consider that it is now the NAS which is clearly Trinitarian whereas the King James considers "great God" and "our Savior" to be two distinct individuals. In the NAS, however, it is specifically Jesus Christ who is called "our great God"! In this case, the modern translation is more Trinitarian the the King James.

John Wesley, who did not have a modern translation, saw Titus as a Trinitarian passage,[2069] but not Revelation 1:6.[2070] Translators have thus been divided over the technical issue for centuries as modern Greek differs from *koine* Greek. Nevertheless, the significance should not be underestimated for God does not leave us to ponder or wonder based on a single passage. For every passage where the King James only advocate argues the modern translator has removed an important rendering, I can show a passage where the exact opposite is the case. The truth is that Titus 2:13 is more strongly Trinitarian than the King James reading of Revelation 1:6. The Trinity is not based on a single passage but a plethora of passages, and the reader is never left to wonder about the truth because his translation is somehow inferior to another. I can even show a Jehovah's Witness the Trinity in their own dishonest translation of the Bible, for even they could not competely remove what God has put in.

Testing the Apostles
Revelation 2:2

> "I know your deeds and your toil and perseverance, and that you cannot tolerate evil men, and you put to the test those who call themselves apostles, and they are not, and you found them *to be* false."

It is common to hear people call themselves apostles. Too many churches are filled with people calling themselves the "apostle Bob" or some other title. It was no different in the early second century when all among the apostles had died but John.

Scholars are divided as to whether or not these men "claim[ed] to have been of the number of apostles selected by the savior" or whether "they had claimed to be the *successors* of the apostles."[2071] The latter is more likely, and has continued to be the case throughout the centuries, but here the church of Ephesus is commended for testing such men and refusing to accept their claims.

I have argued in *Controversies in Acts of the Apostles* that there are but twelve apostles. While the term "apostle" is occasionally used of missionaries, the word, when used as a title, applies only to the twelve (of whom Paul was a member). Even if the term "apostle" is used of others, as many believe, the fact is that it comes with a voice of authority. It refers to one who has been commissioned by the Lord. Consequently, these false teachers and heretics always attempt to apply apostolic authority to their heresies. John, however, had taught them to test these "apostles" and to reject false doctrines. Warnings against false doctrines can be found by apostolic writings in one or more of their epistles. It is a common danger, and a tactic of Satan. If he cannot keep us from truth, then he will pervert the truth to keep us from bearing fruit and to deceive us.

Also note that Revelation does not say "some of them have been found to be false" but that they were all found to be false. This caters to my assersion that there are no true "successors" of the apostles. God still sends men to do His work, but they do not have the authority of the apostles. The Ephesians were then careful not to accept anyone who did not meet the test of Biblical authority. What was that test? Revelation does not say, but John hints at the test in his first epistle (1 John 4:1). The Ephesians obviously took that test seriously, although they probably applied other tests as well.

Heretics in the Early Church
Revelation 2:15 & 20

"So you also have some who in the same way hold the teaching of the Nicolaitans."

Heretics are mentioned in several of the seven churches, but the heresies that were creeping into the churches of Pergamum and Thyatira remain largely a mystery. Revelation 2:15 mentions the "teachings of the Nicolaitans" and Revelation 2:20 mentions a false prophetess named Jezebel, but little is known of either of these sects. Who were they, and what did they teach?

Nicolaitans

The Ephesians had rejected the teachings of the Nicolaitans (2:6) but some in the church of Pergamum accepted their teachings. What were those teachings? Who were the Nicolaitans?

The simple truth is that the Bible says nothing about the Nicolaitans or who they were. The early church fathers, however, have much to say about the sect. They claim to have been the followers of Nicolas, one of the seven the deacons found in Acts 6:5.[2072] This is denied by both Ignatius[2073] and Clement of Alexandria who argue that they took Nicolas's name in vain and perverted his words for their own purposes.[2074] Others believe that Nicolas did indeed apostasize from the faith. To this end many strange legends about Nicolas arose. Nevertheless, whether or not the Nicolaitans were truly founded by Nicolas or not, Ignatius, the apostolic father, calls them a licentious and hedonstic sect.[2075] Irenaeus also claims that they engaged in "unrestrained indulgence."[2076]

Later scholars have tried to define the cult more specifically. Some claim that they held to the "doctrine of Balaam."[2077] This stems from Revelation 2:14, but it seems that the two heresies are not related for verse fifteen is in addition to fourteen, not a definition of it. Despite this, elaborate methods have been devised to try to connect the name "Nicolaitan" with "Balaam."[2078] Others have tried equally hard to connect the name to a system of hierarchy, arguing that the heresy of the Nicolaitans was an early form of Catholic hierarcy.[2079]

The truth is that we know nothing of them except what the apostolic and church fathers said. According to them the Nicolaitans were a licentious sect claiming to be followers of Nicolas the Deacon of Acts 6:5. From the brief descriptions given by the apostolic fathers, it appears that they were an early form of gnostic cult which taught that physical sins could not effect the spirit. This heresy is discussed under the Introduction of Colossians as well as under

417

my discussion of 1 John 1:8-10; 3:6-9; 5:18. The Nicolaitans were almost certainly among those sect of gnostic teachers.

Jezebel

Another mystery is the identity of the false prophetess Jezebel in Revelation 2:20. We know more about her teachings, for it states that "she teaches and leads My bond-servants astray so that they commit *acts of* immorality and eat things sacrificed to idols."

In the first part of the description Jezebel appears to be yet another member of the licentious gnostic sect that encouraged sexual immorality among its flock. However, she differed from the Nicolaitans in that she also required her followers to eat food sacrificed to idols.

The question of eating food sacrificed to idols is discussed by Paul in 1 Corinthians 8:1-13 and 10:25-32 (see notes there). Interestingly enough, Paul seems to take a somewhat moderated position on this, saying that there is no sin in eating food sacrificed to idols *per se*, but then urges believers not to knowingly do so, as it leads the weak in faith astray and can be seen as an affront to Jesus. It is thus apparent that when Paul was concerned about leading those of weaker faith astray, he was referring to people like Jezebel. One analogy may be those who insist that Jewish converts eat pork. While we agree that there is no sin in eating pork, it is a matter of conscience. When a sect requires Jews to eat pork, they are setting a litness test which is not only wrong, but can cause Jews to sin against their conscience! This appears to be what Jezebel was doing. She was *requiring* people to eat food sacrificed to idols, which is in direct opposition to Paul's command.

Many believe that Jezebel actually went further than merely eating food sacrificed to idols and that she actually engaged in idol worship. Some have argued that Jezebel was not a person but a label or moniker[2080] which is a reference to Romanism and its idolatry.[2081] Still others see Jezebel merely as a "symbolic" reference to the Old Testament Queen who led Israel astray to worship idols.[2082] One thing is certain. John refers to this Jezebel as a real person and a false prophetess. He chastizes Thyarita because they "tolerate the woman Jezebel, who calls herself a prophetess." This is no mere symbolism but an actual woman who calls herself a prophetess. Was Jezebel her real name? We cannot say, although it appears that she was commonly known by that name. There is no attempt to further identify her, so the Thyatirans must have known instantly to whom John was referring. This indicates that if Jezebel was not her true name, she was already known by that moniker before John wrote his epistle.

Conclusion

Heresy and religious cults have existed from the very beginning. If Satan cannot keep us from truth, then he will try to send up thorns and thistles to keep us from bearing fruit (cf. Matthew 13:7, 22). Were the followers of these cults saved? Perhaps some were, but many were not. They have been described as wolves in sheep's clothing (Matthew 7:15) and they continue down to this very day. Indeed, false teachers and heresies is actually one of the signs of End Times (cf. Matthew 7:15; 24:11-15; Mark 13:22, 2 Thessalonians 2:3, 2 Timothy 3:1-4; 4:3-4; 2 Peter 3:3; 1 John 2:18-23), so we must be weary and put these men to the test, even as the Ephesians did (Revelation 2:2).

Will Christians Miss the Rapture?
Revelation 3:10

"Because you have kept the word of My perseverance, I also will keep you from the hour of testing, that *hour* which is about to come upon the whole world, to test those who dwell on the earth."

Most of this section is lifted from my Appendix on Rapture in *Controversies in Revelation*.

There are few things in the Bible more controversial than the rapture, but there are few rapture passages, or alleged rapture passages, more controversial that this one. I say alleged for many believe that the rapture is in no way to be found in this passage, and that is a sentiment held even by many dispensational pretribulational premillennialists.

The passage itself is directed to the church of Philadelphia during the reign of Domitian so it has been argued by some critics that this is a promise made only to the church of Philadelphia to be protected during Domitian's persecutions. While that may have been a possibility, the problem with this argument is that the persecutions of Domitian had already begun since John was exiled to Patmos by Domitian during that persecution. Moreover, the phrase "those who dwell upon the earth" is used many times in Revelation and always refers to the tribulation, as does the phrase "about to come upon the whole world." Furthermore, "'those who live on the earth' is repeated in Revelation a number of times and refers not to believers, but to unbelievers who are the object of God's wrath; i.e., the 'beast-worshipers' (Revelation 6:10, 8:13, 11:10, 12:12, 13:8, 12, 14)."[2083] That the passage at the very least has a double prophetic meaning referring to the last days is acknowledged even by George Ladd, a posttribulationist, who denies that the "hour of testing" refers to deliverance by means of rapture.[2084] However, he believes that God will protect believers from wrath without rapture.

This is a favorite passage among "partial rapturists." Partial rapturism is a minority interpretation which argues that some believers, but not all, will be raptured at various times throughout the tribulation. They believe rapture is a reward for Christians who have achieved a certain level of sanctification, but other believers will be left behind.

The key to the verse for partial rapturists is "because you have kept the word of My perseverance." It has been confessed that this verse "refers to the condition under which the promise is valid."[2085] However, it is important to note that the passage does not say "*if* you keep the word of My perseverance, I also will keep you from the hour of testing," but "*because you have* kept the word of My perseverance, I also will keep you from the hour of testing." If this is a rapture passage, as many believe, then it is promised to all. Although partial rapturists cling to the idea that it is only promised to those who "have kept the word," it is interesting that Joseph Seiss, a partial rapturists, makes no mention of 3:10 in his excellent commentary on Revelation. Perhaps this fact, in itself, stands as an indictment against partial rapturists' interpretation of the passage. Revelation 3:10 is certainly consistent with partial rapturism but is by no means a convincing passage for proof of partial rapture. Partial rapture must be read into the passage, but does not naturally flow out of the verse. On the contrary, the conditional promises found in the epistles to the seven churches contain some variation of warning usually following the pattern, "I know your deed ... I have this against you ... therefore, repent ... or else." Revelation 3:10 makes clear that the promise *will* be carried out. There is no warning issued and no "if" found in the passage. By itself, Revelation 3:10 cannot prove partial rapture theory.

The better question is whether or not this is a rapture passage at all! The application to Domitian is logical, but not particularly convincing for the persecution of Domitian was already in process. By the time the letter reached the church of Philadelphia the persecution would have been in full swing, if it had not already. Now it could be that they were already protected and Jesus was assuring them that His protection would continue, but if Christians, including the righteous apostles (such as John), were persecuted and never protected from such testing, then why would the church of Philadelphia. The phrases "those who dwell upon the earth" and "about to come upon the whole world" are used repeatedly in Revelation, and clearly refer to the tribulation. For this reason, many believe that this is a rapture passage which at the very least has a dual application to the Last Days. While I am reluctant to count this as a rapture passage, it is highly possible that there is at least an allusion to rapture.

Hot and Cold
Revelation 3:16

"So because you are lukewarm, and neither hot nor cold, I will spit you out of My mouth."

This famous passage has historically been interpreted as saying that the Laodicean church had "neither burning zeal for His Word, nor yet absolute repudiation of Christ."[2086] "Hot and cold" are likened to "warm zeal and fervor"[2087] and to "the coldness of hostility to the gospel."[2088] However, some in recent years have objected to this analogy saying that "the application of 'hot' and 'cold' to spiritual temperature, though familiar to us, would have been completely foreign to first-century Christians."[2089] More important is the concern that the passage might be saying that rejection of the gospel is preferable to their "condition of indifference."[2090]

To this latter remark it may be said that they may be reading too much into the analogy. As Walter Scott remarked, it speaks of "'hot' and 'cold,' not 'dead' and 'alive'" so salvation is not in mind.[2091] The point is not that hostility to the gospel is preferable to "gross indifference"[2092] nor is it that "a church of dead orthodoxy is better than one of prosperous but neutral evangelicalism"[2093] but that a church which is indifferent, does not evangelize, and lacks the love and zeal of God is useless and guilty of defying God's love.

Consider the proper analogy. It has been said that "people in the ancient world customarily drank what was either hot or cold – never lukewarm."[2094] Hot water came from the "hot springs of nearby Hierapolis"[2095] and cold water always taste good, but lukewarm water is something that no one wants to drink. God's analogy is just this. We should not take this analogy beyond its scope as if to imply that the Laodiceans are to be damned, nor that it is better to reject Christ, but we should take that there is a greater sin in knowing of God's love and refusing to put it in action than there is in a pagan rejecting the love of a God he does not know! The Laodiceans know Jesus, yet show indifference. The pagan does not know Jesus. He has the excuse of not knowing. The Laodicean does not. The analogy is thus graphic and valid. The issue is not salvation, but sanctification and judgment. Believers will be judged (see notes in *Controversies in Revelation*) but will not be damned. Our judgment involves rewards and positioning, and the Laodiceans risk being called "the least in the kingdom of heaven" (cf. Matthew 5:19).

Twenty-Four Elders
Revelation 4:4

"Around the throne *were* twenty-four thrones; and upon the thrones *I saw* twenty-four elders sitting, clothed in white garments, and golden crowns on their heads."

Who are these elders? The Bible does not say, but that has never stopped speculation. Some see the elders as angels.[2096] William Newell[2097] and George Eldon Ladd are among them.[2098] Ladd tries to prove this by comparing them with the angels who were surrounding the throne in 7:9-11,[2099] but those angels appear to be distinguished from the elders both there and in 5:11.[2100] They have thus destroyed their own argument.

Most agree that the description is not in any way inapplicable to humans. In fact, Henry Morris pointed out that "the term 'elder' is always used elsewhere in the Bible only of men."[2101] Elders are found in Israel, in the Church, and even in the pagan court of Egypt (Genesis 50:7). They are always a governing body of men. Nowhere is the term used of angels, so the question is not so much whether these are men or angels but who are these men?

421

The traditional view is that they are twelve Old Testament Patriarchs and the twelve apostles.[2102] In this way the council of elders represents both Old and New Testament saints, but there are problems with this assumption. The most obvious is the fact that John was still living at the time, so how could John be seeing himself sitting on a throne? The answer would be that he is obviously looking at the future, but would he not note that he was among those on the throne? Again it could be argued that humility prevented him from speaking, but it is likely that the elders are a separate body from the apostles. The elders of Israel were not the prophets, nor were the priests prophets. So should the apostles be identified with an office different from their own. Each office is unique, and therefore should not be easily mixed or confused.

E.W. Bullinger even goes so far as to say that "they were not, and cannot be, the church of God" because they *already* received their crowns,[2103] whereas the Church would not receive its blessings until after the tribulation. Bullinger thus represents the ultra-dispensational view, making all of the elders Old Testament Jews. This is not, however, simply an ultra-dispensational theory for John Wesley also believed "very probably that the twenty-four elders represent the Jewish church,"[2104] by which he meant Old Testament believers. He went on to say that they are "the most holy of all former ages (Isa. xxiv.23, Heb. xii.1) representing the whole body of the saints,"[2105] apparently from before the time of Jesus.

Another view is that of Joseph Seiss who notes that these elders sang a song in Revelation 5:9 which he believes was about their own conversion. In that song Jesus redeemed "from every tribe and tongue and people and nation," hence he believed they were not Jews or apostles but a mix of all nations.[2106]

A final question related to the elders is "why twenty-four?" Various theories have been presented from the belief that it is twelve patriarch and twelve apostles[2107] to the more likely scenario that it can be equated with the twenty-four orders of priesthood (cf. 1 Chronicles 24:7-19).[2108] Some Bible critics have even made the ridiculous argument that the number twenty-four is borrowed from the alleged twenty-four star-gods of the Babylon pantheon![2109] Of course, this is a disingenuous accusation. Historian C. Leonard Woolley said that ancient Babylon's "gods were innumerbale."[2110] Assyriologist Georges Roux traces the Babylonian pantheon from its early stages to its latter development. He states that there were "at first hundreds [of gods] but later less numerous owing to an internal syncretism."[2111] In other words the gods became classified according to a sort of hierarchy of gods, but Roux admits that "to classify them is not an easy task."[2112] The atheist thus has created his own classification, identifying twenty-four "star-gods" but one is want to find such a classification among the Babylonians themselves. It is an artificial designation which is not recognized by anyone but the Bible critics themselves.

We can no more know the reason that twenty-four elders were selected than we can know exactly why our forefathers chose two senators from each state instead of one, or three. The most likely answer is that it is from the twenty-four orders of priesthood (cf. 1 Chronicles 24:7-19), but we simply cannot know exactly. As to the identity of the elders, we can only say that they are men, not angels. They were chosen because of their righteousness. Were they Jews, the church, or a combination thereof? We cannot say, although I favor that they are from all the people of God throughout history.

The Seven Spirits of God
Revelation 4:5

"*There were* seven lamps of fire burning before the throne, which are the seven Spirits of God."

The seven spirits of God are first mentioned in Revelation 1:4 and appear again in 3:1, 4:5, and 5:6. The identification of the seven spirits has been a highly contested one. Some see the spirits as angels.[2113] E.W. Bullinger believed that they were the guardian angels of the seven churches to whom John wrote.[2114] However, this cannot be. First, angels appear to be distinguished from the "living beings" (see below) and the elders in 5:11. While these could be different angels, verse 5:6 eliminates this possibility by connecting the seven spirits of God directly to the Lamb, which is Christ.

If the seven spirits of God are connected to the Lamb of God, which is Christ, then how? Most believe that the Holy Spirit is envisioned in some way. George Ladd claimed that "the preceding phrase refers to God the Father and the following phrase to God the Son, [thus] it is certain that John included a reference to the Holy Spirit."[2115] Nonetheless, how is the Holy Spirit a sevenfold spirit? No conclusive answer has ever been given, but the most popular are defined below.

The Seven Spirits

Having established that the seven spirits are in some way connected to the Holy Spirit and to the Lamb of God which is Jesus Christ, we may now seek to understand *how* the Holy Spirit is sevenfold. This is not an easy task. Literalism does not, and never has, negated symbolism; it merely rejects high allegory and holds that the Bible speaks of literal historical (and future historical) people, places, and events. It teaches that symbols, where they occur, have literal and real meanings which should not be interpreted as ambiguous allegory or mystical jargon with subjective meanings. Bearing this in mind, let us look at the best theories offered over the centuries.

Zechariah

There is a close parallel between the lamps of 4:5 and Zechariah 4:1-10.[2116] Logically, when symbolism does occur in the Bible, it is not ambiguous and has a practical application found elsewhere in the Bible. A dove, for example, can represent the Holy Spirit or, given proper context, peace. Examples of this can be found throughout representative literature. It is not ambiguous. Consequently, if the lamps and spirits of God are symbols (and some deny that they are) then they should have a parallel elsewhere in the Bible. Zechariah is the best place to begin our search.

Zechariah 4:2 mentions a lampstand with seven lamps or candles. The parallel is close, but not exact. In fact, the parallel is actually closer to Revelation 11 (see notes in *Controversies in the Prophets* and *Controversies in Revelation*). John Darby makes a clear comparison of Zechariah 4 to Revelation 11[2117] but expressly denies that they are the same thing.[2118] Tertullian disageed, arguing that they are one and the same,[2119] but logically this cannot the case. The are similar imagery, but different subjects. In the case of Zechariah, the lamps are fed by oil. The light is fed by oil, so the lamps represent something such as the Word of God that is fed by something else (generally viewed as the church – or *vice versa*). Here, however, the lamps are specifically said to be the "seven spirits of God" (see notes below). So the imagery is similar, but the context is different. Consequently, although Zechariah is relevant in regard to Revelation 11:2, it is not of as much help here as we might have hoped.

"Complete"

Seven is a holy number. Of that all agree. Our weeks are seven days because God created the earth in six days and rested upon the seventh. Seven is thus repeatedly used in the Bible as a holy number. Consequently, some argue that seven represents "completeness."[2120] Others that "'seven' is the number of dispensational fulness."[2121]

Now it is true that seven has a symbolic value in regard to the fulness or completeness of something Holy, but this does not really answer the question. This is a distraction, for even if seven has a holy significance, it does not answer what the "seven spirits" represent. This cannot in itself be an answer.

Seven Attributes

One of the best arguments is based on a comparison with Isaiah 11:2. Henry Morris said that "the Holy Spirit is sevenfold in His gracious character and imputation of spiritual attributes."[2122] This is also the view of Charles Ryrie,[2123] but it is not without difficulty. Isaiah says that the Spirit of the Lord has "the spirit of wisdom and understanding, the spirit of counsel and strength, the spirit of knowledge and the fear of the LORD." This, however, is only six, not seven. Joseph Seiess makes the seventh in verse three where it says "He will delight in the fear of the LORD."[2124] This refers to the Messiah, Jesus Christ. So the application seems solid except that "delight in the fear of the Lord" does not properly seem to join with the six attributes stated in the previous verse. Rather it is Jesus's delight in the fear of the Lord (which is the sixth attribute). Can we consider "delight" a seventh attribute?

Seven Horns and Eyes

Perhaps the answer is within Revelation itself. Verse 5:6 explicitly states that the "seven horns and seven eyes [of the Lamb], are the seven Spirits of God." What then are the seven horns and seven eyes? This is actually an easier answer, for horns always represent power and authority in prophecy (see notes in *Controversies in the Prophets* and *Controversies in Revelation*). Eyes obviously indicate sight and vision. God sees all things, including our hearts. Aphrahat declared that these "seven eyes are the sevenfold Spirit of God."[2125] If the seven spirits of God are identified with Jesus's power and vision, then it is obviously a reference to the Holy Spirit. We have only to decipher the exact meaning of "seven" beyond the identification of "completeness."

As the reader can see, the imagery is clear on one level, but difficult on a higher level. The seven spirits of God represent the Holy Spirit in both the power and sight of Jesus. A more specific understanding of the sevenfold nature should go beyond "completeness" and the answer is probably to be found in Isaiah 11:2 as the seven attributes of the Holy Spirit; widsom, understanding, counsel, strength, knowledge, fear of the Lord, and possibly delight or appreciation of the Lord. This is, however, said with reservation and I will leave to the reader to reach his own conclusions.

The Lamps
One last issue is the identification of the seven lamps. John Lightfoot identified the seven candlesticks as the church,[2126] but Revelation 4:5 states that the "seven lamps of fire burning before the throne, are the seven Spirits of God." So the "seven lamps of fire depict the seven spirits of God"[2127] or do they? Arthur Bloomfield said that "the seven torches are not symbols of the Holy Spirit ... but a manifestation of the Holy Spirit."[2128] He saw the lamps in the most literal fashion possible.

One thing is certain. Lamps give off light. Jesus the light of men (John 1:4). If the lamps are the seven spirits of God, which is a seven fold manifestation of the Holy Spirit, then the Light of Jesus shines through the Holy Spirit and His attributes.

Conclusion
Revelation is a book intended for believers. The nature of its prophecies is that it is intended for those who believe to understand while those who do not will reject it and mock it. This is similar to the nature of parables, save that prophecy is literal future history. In Matthew 13:10-15 Jesus explained why He spoke in parables, saying "while seeing they do not see, and while hearing they do not

hear, nor do they understand." He also quoted from Isaiah who said "you will keep on hearing, but will not understand; you will keep on seeing, but will not perceive." So also "mockers will come with *their* mocking, following after their own lusts, and saying, 'Where is the promise of His coming? For *ever* since the fathers fell asleep, all continues just as it was from the beginning of creation'" (2 Peter 3:3-4). Revelation is then written is such a way that the unbeliever will read it but never understand it, and the believer will read and understand, but we will be mocked for it until He comes.

The Four Living Beings
Revelation 4:6-8

"In the center and around the throne, four living creatures full of eyes in front and behind. The first creature *was* like a lion, and the second creature like a calf, and the third creature had a face like that of a man, and the fourth creature *was* like a flying eagle."

In addition to these elders, there are four "living creatures." The King James calls them "beasts" from the Greek word ζωα (*zoa*) from which we get the word "zoo." Modern translations have generally preferred "living beings" since these are obviously not dumb animals. Exactly what they are, however, is not agreed upon.

Some see these simply as "symbolic beings"[2129] but then fail to come to any concensus as to what they symbolize. Some argue that the living beings are symbolic of the very same elders,[2130] but they are obviously distinguished from them. Another said "very probably that the twenty-four elders represent the Jewish church ... if so, the living creatures may represent the Chrsitain church."[2131] Among the most disrepectful theories is that of Bible critics who claim that the faces of the Living Beings are actually borrowed from four signs of zodiac (Taurus, Leo, Scorpio, and Aquarius). Nevertheless, they have never explained exactly how Aquarius became eagle![2132]

The truth is that the symbolic views are more fanciful and wild than the literal view. They offer no Biblical support or parallel passages to justify any of their allegorical presuppositions and cannot explain how said symbol fits the context. This is not to say that there are no parallel passages, for there are, but those passages, one and all, describe angels.

It is unknown how many species of angels God created, but the Bible describes two kinds : the Seraphim and the Cherubim. Although similar, there are differences. According to Isaiah 6:2 Seraphim "each having six wings: with two he covered his face, and with two he covered his feet, and with two he flew." Ezekiel 1:5-26 and 10:8-17 contains a much longer and more descriptive narrative, which critics say is fantastic and unreal.

According to Ezekiel 1:5-26 Cherubim have only four wings. They are human like in form except for their wings and faces. According to Ezekiel they had four faces and all sides of their head. One face was similar to a man's, another closer to a lion, one like a bull (also called a cherub's face in 10:14), and the other like an eagle (1:10). They are also described as being full of many eyes (10:12), perhaps like a fly's eyes.

Here Revelation describes "living beings" whose description is parallel to the Cherubim of Ezekiel with the exception being that these have six wings rather than four. Based on the description of the faces, they would appear to be Cherubim,[2133] but the wings match that of Seraphim.[2134] Cherubim is favored by men like E.W. Bullinger[2135] and Charles Ryrie[2136] while Seraphim is favored by Edward Hindson.[2137] Tertullian called them simply "angels"[2138] choosing not to define them further. Since Isaiah does not describe the faces of the Seraphim it is not illogical that they are similar to that of the Cherubim. Since these angels have six wings rather than just four, it is probable that they are Seraphim. This could also explain the minor differences in description, although those could also be attributed to the fact that they are trying to describe something unseen by human eyes in human terms!

It is noteworthy that Ezekiel uses the word חיות (chayoth) to describe the angels. That word is usually translated as "living beings," the same translation attributed to the ζωα (zoa) here in Revelation 4:6-8. These are not "symbols"[2139] but angels whose natural appearance has never been seen by most mortal eyes. This is why the descriptions sound so strange. Because of such an incredible description scholars and interpreters have tried fruitlessly to find symbolic value in the description, but why? Consider that before the age of photography, television, and the internet, most people had never seen animals that are not native to our environment. People used to laugh at descriptions of kangaroos, and I remember reading a story about a missionary who returned to tell a seemingly fantastic tale of an animal he had seen. I do not remember the exact description, but he was describing something like a giant floating rock which swam in the water, had a mouth as big as its head, and nostrils as big as a baseball. People refused to be believe him. He was, of course, talking about a hippopotamus. Now consider the following rare animals (see pictures on the following page) which few have seen even in the modern age of television and consider what words you would use to describe these real life creatures![2140]

In describing the Venezuelan Poodle Moth I would describe it as like the Abominable Snowman except that it walks on six legs, has wings, two giant antenae which look much like a second pair of wings, the nose of a baby elephant, and eyes like a fly. How many readers would have believed me if you could not look at the picture with your own eyes?

It is human nature to disbelieve what we have not seen. Marco Polo was imprisoned for his fantastic tales of the orient, but history proved him to be telling the truth. Upon his deathbed, when asked to recant of his stories, he replied that he had told only half of what he saw.[2141] Let us then carefully learn the lessons of history and be slow to reject what Isaiah, Ezekiel, and John all gave a descriptive narrative of the angels. I do not deny that there are symbols given in a specific context within the Bible, but I reject those who would attempt to allegorize everything that they do not understand, dislike, or have never seen with their own eyes.

Top Left : A Venezuelan Poodle Moth ||| Top Right : A "living fossil" of a Goblin Shark
Bottom left : Saiga ||| Bottom Middle : Glaucus Atlanticus SeaSlug ||| Bottom Right : "Thorny Dragon"

Revelation 5:6 – See Revelation 4:5

Summary

Revelation is one of the most fascinating and important books in the Bible. It is the culmination of everything in the Bible. It is the consummation of history. It is for this reason that I wrote a single volume upon every single verse from Revelation 6:1 onward. That volume, *Controversies in Revelation*, is the last in this series, but was the first one I wrote. It was due to the overwhelmingly positive response I received from people that undertook to write the rest of this series. I hope the reader will have been enlightened by my works and better able to respond to the increasing tide of critics, atheists, and individuals antagonistic towards God's word. My desire was to enable the reader to better understand and defend the Word of God in an increasingly hostile world which is headed quickly for the events describes in the final seventeen chapters of Revelation.

428

—

The Authenticity of the New Testament

This appendix is an almost exact reproduction of an appendix found in the last two volumes, *Controversies in the Gospels* and *Controversies in the Acts of the Apostles*. I have reproduced it here for convenience sake.

The Canon of the New Testament

The internet and books like *The DaVinci Code* have served to promote some absurd myths about the Bible and Christianity. One of those myths is the idea that the Bible somehow relates to the time of Constantine the Great. In fact, nothing could be further from the truth. The Bible had long been established, accepted, and canonized before Constantine was ever born. In fact, "the Council of Nicea did not address the issue of canonicity"[2142] for that issue had long been settled.

The "canon" is a term used to represent those books which have been recognized as the authoritative Word of God. Other books, while they may be instructive, useful, or historical, are not considered canon. Only those books in the canon are considered to be the infallible Word of God. So the question is, how did the canon come to be? As aforementioned, the Council of Nicea had *nothing* to do with the canon, because it was accepted centuries earlier. Let us look at the debate and the facts.

The Acceptance of the Canon

The primary questions concerning the canon are "when" and "how." We will begin with "when." As already mentioned, some attempt to argue that the canon was never settled until the time of Constantine. Even some evangelical publishers have blindly published books by "scholars" who argue for a late canon date based on suspect arguments. Lee Martin McDonald, for example, sites ancient authors who may have rejected part of the canon (even as some do today) or perhaps even accepted other books (even as the Mormons and others do today).[2143] Furthermore, if a church father quoted from an apocryphal book (see below) he *assumes* that the church father accepted it as canon.[2144] He nowhere proves this assumption. Others argue that it was the Council of Laodicea in 363 A.D. which settled the canon.[2145]

Now some might wonder how this is a controversy at all. Either the books are in the Bible or they are not! Right? Wrong. "Books" was we know them today did not exist in antiquity. They used scrolls which were kept separate. A scroll could obviously be only so large. No one denies that all twenty-seven books of the New Testament existed in the early church, but so did many other books. Since "books," in the traditional sense of the word, did not exist until Constantine's time, it is easy for some to dishonestly argue that the canon did not exist until Constantine's time. However, the facts invalidates these claims.

As early as the second century we have a list of the canonical books. The discovery of the Muratorian canon in the nineteenth century demonstrated that the canon had most likely been accepted by the time of its composition, circa 170 A.D.[2146] Nevertheless, there are some problems with the Muratorian canon. For one thing the manuscript is damaged and so the first two books of the canon are not visible. However, the gospel of Luke is explicitly said to be the third gospel, indicating that Matthew and Mark were the first two gospels.[2147] Additionally, Hebrews, James, 1 and 2 Peter, and 3 John appear to be omitted.[2148] Still, some believe that they may have been in the document; its fragmentary nature being evidence that the books *could* have been listed.[2149] Alternately, the Muratorian canon includes the Wisdom of Solomon (an apocryphal Old Testament book) as among the canon of the New Testament.[2150] Consequently, some critics use these discrepancies as evidence that the canon was not settled.

The irony of the critics is their inate ability to contradict themselves. Consider that one author admits that there was "wide agreement"[2151] on the Scriptures under Diocletian's persecutions, but then goes on to claim that the canon dates to the time of Eusebius[2152] (a contemporary of Constantine). Of course, how could he deny that the Scriptures were not already "widely" agreed upon, for the emperor Diocletian not only persecuted Christians but actively sought to find and destroy "all copies of the Bible."[2153] To this end Christians were tortured until they revealed where their copies were hidden. Obviously, one cannot search out and destroy copies of the Scriptures if there was no Biblical canon!

The fact is that from earliest time the church fathers refer to the "Scripture"[2154] of New Testament authors. All twenty-seven books of the New Testament are cited *as* Scritpure by one or more of the fathers. The following chart shows all the major Uncials (complete "books" of the Bible, as opposed to individual scrolls popular in the early days of Christianity), apostolic fathers, and ante-Nicean church fathers (those who preceded Constantine and the Council of Nicea) who quote a specific book *as* Scripture. It is noteworthy that just because a church father did not quote a book does not mean that the book was not a part of Scripture. I, for example, did not quote from Titus in this book, and yet it is a part of Scripture. Nevertheless, the citations should prove that there was uniformity upon the canon from the earliest of times. I have also included those apocryphal books which are not a part of Scripture, but appear to be quoted as such from a few fathers (this will be explained in a section below). A more detailed explanation of the chart and its implications will follow.

Biblical Book	Primary Uncials	Apostolic Fathers	Ante-Nicean Church Fathers
Matthew	ℵ / A / B / C / D	Cl / Ba / Δ / Ig P / Ir / CA / M	J / Hp / Cy / N / M / T / L Mu
Mark	ℵ / A / B / C / D	Cl / Δ / Ig / P / Ir CA / M	J / Hp / Cy / N / M / T / L Mu
Luke	ℵ / A / B / C / D	Cl / Δ / Ig / P / Ir CA / M	J / Hp / Cy / N / M / T / L Mu
John	ℵ / A / B / C / D	Cl / Ba / H / Ig Ir / CA / M	J / Hp / Cy / N / M / T / L Mu
Acts	ℵ / A / B / C / D	Cl / Δ / H / Ig / P Ir / CA / M	J / Hp / Cy / N / M / T / L Mu
Romans	ℵ / A / B / C / D	Ba / Δ / Ig / P/ Ir / CA / O / M	J / Hp / Cy / N / M / T / L Mu
1 Corinthians	ℵ / A / B / C / D	Di / Δ / H / Ig P / Ir / CA / O / M	J / Hp / Cy / N / M / T / L Mu
2 Corinthians	ℵ / A / B / C / D	Di / P / Ir / CA O / M	Hp / Cy / N / M / T / L Mu
Galatians	ℵ / A / B / C / D	Ig / P / Ir / CA O / M	J / Hp / Cy / N / M / T / L Mu
Ephesians	ℵ / A / B / C / D	Di / Ig / P / Ir CA / O / M	Hp / Cy / N / M / T / L Mu
Philippians	ℵ / A / B / C	Di / H / P / Ir CA / O / M	Hp / Cy / N / M / T / L Mu
Colossians	ℵ / A / B / C / D	Ig / Ir / CA / O / M	Hp / Cy / N / M / T / L Mu
1 Thessalonians	ℵ / A / B / C	P / Ir / CA / O / M	Hp / Cy / M / T / L / Mu
2 Thessalonians	ℵ / A / B / C	P / Ir / CA / O / M	J / Hp / Cy / M / T / L Mu
1 Timothy	ℵ / A / C / D	Di / P / Ir / CA O / M	Hp / Cy / N / M / T / L Mu
2 Timothy	ℵ / A / C / D	P / Ir / CA / O / M	Hp / Cy / T / L
Titus	ℵ / A / C / D	Di / Ir / CA / O / M	Hp / Cy / N / M / T / L Mu
Philemon	ℵ / A / C / D	Ir / O / M	L
Hebrews	ℵ / A / B / C / D	Δ / Ir / CA / O	J / Hp / Cy / M / T / L
James	ℵ / A / B / C / D	Ig / Ir / CA / M	J / Hp / Cy / M / T / L
1 Peter	ℵ / A / B / C / D	H / Ig / P / Ir CA / O	J / Hp / Cy / M / T / L Mu
2 Peter	ℵ / A / B / C / D	P / Ir / CA / O	J / Hp / Cy / M / T / L Mu
1 John	ℵ / A / B / C / D	Δ / H / P / Ir / CA O / M	J / Hp / Cy / M / T / L Mu
2 John	ℵ / A / B / C / D	Ir / O / M	Cy / T / Mu
3 John	ℵ / A / B / C / D	O	T
Jude	ℵ / A / B / C / D	Δ / CA / O / M	Hp / Cy / M / T / Mu
Revelation	ℵ / A / C / D	H / Pa / Ir / CA / O / M	J / Hp / Cy / M / T / L Mu

Table

Primary Uncials

ℵ = Sinaticus / A = Alexandrinus / B = Vaticanus / C = Ephraemi / D = Claromontanus (Bezae)

Table cont.

Apostolic Fathers

Cl = Clement of Rome / Ba = Epistle of Barnabas / P = Polycarp / Ig = Ignatius / Δ = Didache / Ir = Irenaeus / Pa = Papias / H = Shepherd of Hermas / CA = Clement of Alexandria / Di = Diognetus / O = Origen / M = Muratorian canon

Ante-Nicean Church Fathers

J = Justin Martyr / Hp = Hippolytus / Cy = Cyril / N = Novatian / M = Methodius / T = Tertullian / L = Lactantius / Mu = Muraturian fragment

431

Apocryphal Book	Primary Uncials	Apostpolic Fathers	Ante-Nicean Church Fathers
Hermas	ℵ / D	Ir	-
Barnabas	ℵ / D	Cl	-
Apoc. Peter	D	Cl	-
Acts of Paul	D	-	-
1 Clement	A	-	-
2 Clement	A	-	-
Didache	-	Cl	-

Looking at the preceding charts, several things should be apparent. First, every book in the New Testament was accepted as Scripture by one or more of the earliest church fathers. Second, the books which have the fewest citations are the smallest books, indicating that the lack of citations is not because they were not accepted was Scripture but because there was not as much material to quote (even as I have not quoted from 3 John in this book). Third, of the five earliest Uncials no book from the New Testament is found in fewer than four of them. Also note that some of these Uncials are damaged meaning that the missing books could have been there, although we cannot prove it. Four, no apocryphal book from the New Testament has more than three major sources! Five, the "Gospel is Thomas," which the "Jesus Seminar" placed alongside the four true gospels, is not cited by a single author, father, or Uncial! *No one* believed the "Gospel of Thomas" to be anything but a forgery.[2155]

Another intriguing proof that the canon had been settled long before Constantine is the fact that critics appeal to the heretic Marcion who compiled a canon of Scripture which omits some of the current twenty-seven books of the Bible, but neglect to mention that "Marcion formed his Bible in declared opposition to the holy scriptures of the church from which he had separated."[2156] In other words, Marcion's canon demonstrates only that he was in opposition to the canon which already existed!

In short, there can be no doubt that the twenty-seven books which comprise the New Testament were accepted as canon from the earliest of times. By at least the second century, the majority of Christians agreed upon the sacred scriptures, and some books were accepted from the time of their writing (cf. 2 Peter 3:16). Attempts to date the canon to Constantine's time or later are naive at best, and dishonest are worst. Modern day "books" date to that era, but the scrolls which comprise the Bible were accepted as Scripture from the time of the apostles and their disciples.

How Was the Canon Formed?

A fair question is "how was the canon formed?" The fact that this is not an easy question to answer should in itself refute those who claim that some church

432

council formed the canon. Were this true the evidence would be undeniable. The problem is that before Constantine's time there was no unified church government throughout the land. This fact alone demonstrates that the acceptance of the canon (as shown above) was not the work of some council or church authority, but the work of the Holy Spirit.

It has been argued that the writings of the apostles were accepted from the very beginning as they were written.[2157] This is partially true, but not entirely. It is possible that Paul wrote more letters than have become a part of the Bible, and it is certain that some writings of the apostles, notably John's *Revelation*, were debated for some time before becoming accepted. The early church was not naive and were cautious to insure that no false or heretical forgery made it into the canon. Because there were no chuch councils or popes to rule on these issues, there was occasional division as evidenced by the church father's writings. This, however, only further substantiates that the guiding force was the Holy Spirit, for it seems certain that at least twenty-five of the twenty-seven New Testament books were accepted as canon by the end of the second century, and probably much earlier.

Entire books have been written upon the question of "how." Consequently, I will refer to reader to Randall Price's *Searching for the Original Bible* or similar work. For the purposes of this appendix I will merely summarize my conclusions. First, apostlic authority was the primary requirement for canonization, and no book which could not be demonstrated to have been either written by an apostle, or by a close associate of an apostle, would be accepted. Second, the book had to be inspired and instructive. As Paul stated, "All Scripture is inspired by God and profitable for teaching, for reproof, for correction, for training in righteousness" (1 Timothy 3:16). Finally, the church was careful to insure that nothing contrary to the teachings of Jesus (as indicated by those gospels accepted *from the beginning*) would enter into the canon. As a result, some books were held to be instructive and useful but *not* Scripture (see below). In other words, the Holy Spirit guided the early church and insured that only those works inspired by the Holy Spirit and by witnesses and disciples of the apostles would enter into the canon.

Apocryphal Books
The term "lost books of the Bible" is a term floated around by people with suspect motives and agendas. Some, like the sham "Jesus Seminar", count the fraudulent "Gospel of Thomas" as one of "five gospels" in order to cast doubt on the four authentic gospels, but none tell you that *no one* other than the gnostic cults has ever accepted the Gospel of Thomas. Nevertheless, books entitled "the Lost Books of the Bible" imply that there are indeed "lost books" which did not make into the Bible. Why? What are these books?

Many books are written today. It was no different in the days of the early church, but what comprised a Biblical book and a non-Biblical book? As discussed above, the first criteria is whether or not it was written by a disciple of Christ or someone connected to the apostles who had first hand knowledge of either Jesus or His apostles. *No* book could be accepted to the canon which did not meet this criteria, no matter how good a book it might be.

It is true that religious cults have always existed, and to that end there were cults which attempted to create their own Scriptures and their own "gospels." Nevertheless, *none* of these books were ever accepted by mainstream churches. Despite what the critics imply, there are only six books excluded from the canon which were ever truly considered for the canon. No other book, especially those of the gnostics, were ever even debated in the mainstream church. What of those seven books?

Of all the so-called "lost books" only six appear in any early Uncials, and only four are quoted among the apostlic fathers. These are the *Shepherd of Hermas, the Epistle of Barnabas, the Apocalypse of Peter, the Acts of Paul*, the epistles *1 & 2 Clement*, and the *Didache* or *"Teachings of the Apostles."*

The Shepherd of Hermas

The *Shepherd of Hermas* is essentially a long parable. It uses allegory to tell moral Christian messages and to represent the church. It is certainly of early Christian origin although probably not from the first century. Those few who did accept it as authoritative argue that the author was the Hermas mentioned in Romans 16:14, thus connecting the author to the apostle Paul.[2158] However, most of the church fathers believe it was written by the brother of the bishop of Rome, Pius I, in the second century.[2159] This fact alone would exclude it from the canon although it did engender respect from many. Athantasius, for example, considered *Hermas* to be "a most profitable book"[2160] but most definitely "not belonging to the canon."[2161] This widespread respect has often been used to imply its controversy, but in fact only Irenaeus quotes *Hermas* as "scripture." The book can be found in the Codex Sinaiticas and the Codex Bezae, but nowhere else is placed alongside Scripture. Considering how widespread the church had become by the time of Irenaeus it is apparent that very few accepted *Hermas* as scripture. Since there are those, to this very day, who differ on the Biblical canon (religious cults and "liberal" theologians, for example), the fact that Irenaeus seems to stand alone is a testament to the uniformity of the early church fathers.

The Epistle of Barnabas

After the *Shepherd of Hermas*, only the *Epistle of Barnabas* comes close to eliciting real controversy. The epistle is supposed by many to be the writing of the apostle Paul's long time companion, but the epistle nowhere makes this claim for itself.[2162] Most believe that the epistle was written sometime between 70 A.D. at the earliest and 132 A.D. at the latest.[2163] This makes the epistle among the earliest non-Biblical books, and explains why it is so popular, but like the *Shepherd of Hermas*, respect for its antiquity and content does not lend support to any claim for canonicity. It is found in both the Codex Sinaiticas and the Codex Bezae alongside *Hermas* but quoted only by Clement

434

of Rome as possible scripture. Again, considering how widespread the church and the scriptures were at this time, this is meager support to argue against an established canon. The *Epistle of Barnabas* is a book indicative of early Christian thought, but not a part of scripture, nor does its author even make this assertion.

The Apocalypse of Peter

The *Apocalypse of Peter* was not written by Peter, but is acknowledged to be a forgery written in the second century. Nonetheless, because of its proximity to the early church it was popular among some in the early church. It obviously draws its inspiration from the book of Revelation, but differs from it in numerous ways. A great deal of *Peter's Apocalypse* is a vision of hell and a description of the punishments bestowed on people for various sins. Those punishments often correspond to their crimes. For example, unrepentant mothers of abortion must wade in the blood and corpses of dead children. This book is found only in the Codex Bezae and quoted as scripture only by Clement of Rome. No other church father calls its scripture, nor is there any real support for its inclusion in the canon.

The Acts of Paul

First mentioned by Tertullian in the second century, but not as a canonical work, the *Acts of Paul* is a collection of traditions about Paul as well as containing the "third epistle" to the Corinthians (see below). The traditions include the story of Peter being crucified upside down. The Acts is dated to the middle of the second century and is nowhere cited as scripture by any church father. Nevertheless, it is found in the Codex Bezae. It has never been accepted as a part of the canon.

The 1st and 2nd Epistles of Clement

Clement is generally believed to be Clement of Rome. Various traditions make him either the second of fourth bishop of Rome.[2164] Some church fathers believe that this Clement was Flavius Clemens, the emperor Domitian's cousin and former consul, who was martyred by the emperor around 96 A.D.[2165] Others argue that he was the Clement mentioned in Philippians 4:3, but this is less likely.[2166] If it were the Clement of Paul's epistle then he would be from Philippi, not Rome. It also seems unlikely that this Clement was Clemens who died in 96 A.D. since tradition, if it to be accepted, makes Clement the pope from 91 A.D. to 101 A.D.[2167] In any case, his proximity to the apostles and the tradition that he learned from the apostles themselves have made the epistles very popular among the early church, but despite this fact, they are nowhere cited as scripture, nor do the epistles make claim to spiritual authority.[2168] Of the texts cited above, they are found only in the Codex Alexandria. It is also worth noting that some church fathers rejected 2 Clement as genuine.

The Didache or "Teachings of the Apostles"

The *Didache* has been described as "a church-manual of primitive Christianity."[2169] It is divided into two sections. The first is considered a "moral treatise" while the second "gives directions affecting church rites" such as baptism, prayer, and fasting.[2170] The author is unknown and the *Didache* is nowhere called canonical by the early church except via Clement of Rome's extensive quotations from it.

One may have noticed that Clement of Rome factors into five of these seven "lost books." Clement, of course, was not an apostle, but allegedly tutored under one of the apostles. Two of the seven were his epistles (actually the second may not have been his at all) and it is in those epistles that he alone refers to three other books as Scripture. If we reject Clement's opinions then only the *Shepherd of Hermas* is cited by any apostolic father as scripture. No other apocryphal book is quoted as anything more than "a profitable" but non-canonical book.[2171]

Other books which have been presented as "lost books" include the *Third Epistle of Paul to the Corinthians*, the *Epistle of Paul to the Laodiceans*, the *Gospel of Thomas*, and even the *Gospel of Judas*!

The Third Epistle of Paul to the Corinthians

The *Third Epistle of Paul to the Corinthians* is an extract taken out of the *Acts of Paul* (see notes above). It is suggested that it may be a letter referred to in 1 Corinthians 5:9 or even 2 Corinthians 7:8. Certainly it is an indication that not everything written by Paul was made a part of Scripture. This is not troublesome since only those books inspired by the Holy Spirit are to be considered canon. *If* this epistle is genuine, and many doubt it, it is a useful epistle and instructive, but not inerrant or inspired, and therefore is not a part of the canon.

The Epistle of Paul to the Laodiceans

Colossians 4:6 says, "When this letter is read among you, have it also read in the church of the Laodiceans; and you, for your part read my letter *that is coming* from Laodicea." Like the missing letter to the Corinthians, it is clear that not everything Paul wrote became a part of Scripture, nor should they have. The epistle here is alleged to be one of those missing letters, although most all agree that this letter is a forgery. Not only is it not accepted by any mainstream church father but they actively oppose it. This is because the letter is believed to be a forgery used to promote false and heretical doctrines. This is also why it is listed as Scripture by a few early gnostic cults and by the heretic Marcion. The Muratorian canon explicitly rejects the epistle as a forgery.[2172]

The Gospel of Thomas

The gnostics were one of the earliest Christian cults in Christendom. This "gospel" was attacked as a gnostic forgery and as heretical by Hippolytus and other church fathers, even including the "liberal" allegorist Origen.[2173] It has never been included in any list of canons discovered. There is no question as to its late gnostic origin. Depite this it has been hailed as a "lost gospel" by modern Bible critics and cults, even being the basis for some of the conspiracies

436

in books and movies like the *DaVinci Code*. In fact, no serious scholar believes this "gospel" was written by Thomas or even that it dates to the first century as some critics claim.[2174] The irony is that the same critics who will date Thomas to the first century without a shred of evidence, reject the true gospels as dating to the first century. Such dishonesty would not even be worthy of mention were it not for the rise of gnosticism popularized by secular Hollywood.

The Gospel of Judas

Another gnostic "gospel," this forgery dates to the late second century or possibly much later. Containing a dialoque between Jesus and Judas, who betrayed Christ, it is apparent that the "gospel" is used to promote heresies about Jesus, and sympathizes with the traitor of Jesus. No one has ever accepted it as authentic or canonical. Once again, it would not be worth mentioning at all were it not for the National Geographic channel airing gnostic propaganda disguised as new.[2175]

Conclusion

The Biblical canon was closed and complete by sometime in the second century. Although there were dissenters and hold-outs who did not agree completely on the canonitical books, all twenty-seven books of the New Testament were accepted by most mainstream churches, and long before Constantine the Bible was as it is now so that when the emperor Diocletian sought to eradicate the Bible, he knew exactly what books to look for. The uniformity of the Biblical canon from early church is itself a testament to the fact that it was the Holy Spirit, and not some church council, that moved men to accept the inspired works of the New Testament.

The Authenticity and Transmission of Text

Critics claim that the Bible has been substantially altered since it was originally written, and even deny that the Bible was written in the early dates to which it is credited. In short, they claim that the Bible cannot be trusted in what it says. They ask, without wanting an answer, "how can we know what is authentic and what is not?" Many of these critics subscribe to what is called "higher criticism," but contrary to their claims it is the "higher critics" who disregard facts for unsubstantiated theories. *Textual criticism* is the *science* or study of the transmission of ancient texts. Textual criticism relies on *facts* such as the findings of the Dead Sea scrolls and witnesses to ancient scribal practices. Textual criticism is the science by which we can say with confidence that the Bible is authoritative in that it faithfully transmits the original authors words in all substantive and important matters, as the reader will see.

Having said this, it is true that all scholars, whether liberal or conservative, agree that scribes make occasional mistakes in the transmission and copying of texts. The issue is not whether or not any errors can be found in the texts, but whether or not we can determine what errors exist and whether or not these errors have become incorporated into our modern text.

It is easy for the skeptic to mislead people into believing that we are left to ponder what the original texts said with phony numbers, dishonest representations, and lies about antiquity, but by studying the facts it becomes easily and readily apparent that with very few exceptions, scribal errors are not only easy to detect but the original remains faithfully recorded elsewhere, for there were many scribes and many texts made. We do not rely on a single scribe or a single document but the works of many men from different places in different times. Moreover, the scribes were not the only people to see or read the texts, thus the work of the scribes would be exposed to outside examination and scrutiny. While the critic portrays the scribes as dishonest and unethical men, history shows to the contrary. The scribes believed that what they were doing was sacred, and hence they tried faithfully, with fear and trembling, to reproduce copies without error. The proof of this follows.

Surviving Texts

Critics will make a point of saying that we do not have any of the original manuscripts the apostles wrote. They deliberately ignore that we do not have the original manuscripts from *any* book in antiquity, nor could you prove it if we did. Can anyone reading this tell me what the apostle Paul's handwriting looks like? If not, then you could not prove we had the original even if we did! Moreover, even after the invention of the printing press one could easily asks, "do we have the original plates?" The answer would probably be "no."

How then can we know what was originally written. Obviously, as copies are spread out across the world, it becomes harder and harder to "forge" or alter the original without making it vastly different from other copies distributed elsewhere. Even a vast conspiracy would not be able to co-ordinate alterations of copies across the east and west, across multiple countries and continents, or across different language translations. Consequently, the more copies one has, the easier it is to determine if mistakes or alterations were made, and how series these alterations may have been made. It may even be possible to determine which is the original and which is the alteration by comparing the different texts (see next section).

In regard to the New Testament there has been what some have called "an embarrasment of riches"[2176] and an "abundance of textual evidence"[2177] unparralleled in antiquity. The riches are composed of two parts. First is the sheer number of ancient manuscripts from all over the various parts of the known world and in many different languages and translation. Second is the antiquity of the manuscripts. In fact, while we cannot honestly claim to have any "original autographs" we can say with fair certainty that we have at least one manuscript (probably two or three) which date to a time when apostle John, and probably John Mark, were still living!

The oldest manuscripts known to exist are papyri 32 ($\mathfrak{P}^{32}$), 45 ($\mathfrak{P}^{45}$), 46 ($\mathfrak{P}^{46}$), 52 ($\mathfrak{P}^{52}$), 64 ($\mathfrak{P}^{64}$), 66 ($\mathfrak{P}^{66}$), and 75 ($\mathfrak{P}^{75}$).[2178] All of these manuscripts are dated to before 200 A.D. However, scholars are reluctant to date most of these before then because of the difficulty in proving such a date. Nonetheless, there is good evidence to date at least three to the early second century, or even before then.

Papyrus 46 ($\mathfrak{P}^{46}$) is formally dated to around 200 A.D.[2179] as are most all papyri which are suspected to be second century, but which cannot be proven with certainty. Nevertheless, paleographer Young Kyu Kim argued that based on the style of Greek lettering (which changes over time, just the modern letter "s" used to be written as "ſ") it should be dated to "Later First Century."[2180] The only arguments used against this dating is that "$\mathfrak{P}^{46}$ is a perfectly ordinary copy"[2181] and that "it must have taken some time for the nine Epistles that are preserved in $\mathfrak{P}^{46}$ to have been collected."[2182] On this basis Metzger rejects a date of 80 A.D. for the manuscript, but nowhere does he provide evidence for dating it later than the first part of second century. If we then accept Metzger's silent admission that Kim's thesis is sound save the time needed for preservation, and we acknowledge that such collections are found in the early second century, then we would have no reason to reject $\mathfrak{P}^{46}$ as dating somewhere between 100 and 115 A.D.

Papyrus 52 ($\mathfrak{P}^{52}$) is among "the oldest copy of any portion of the New Testament known to be in existence today."[2183] It dates to at least 125 A.D. if not before.[2184] Additionally, Papyri 66 ($\mathfrak{P}^{66}$) is yet another second century document which Herbert Hunger, director of the papyrological collections at the National Library in Vienna, dates to the early second century.[2185]

Now if tradition is to be believed the apostle John died in the time of emperor Trajan at age one hundred.[2186] Traditional also makes John a teenager at the time of Jesus' ministry. Since Trajan ruled from 98 to 117 A.D. and because Jesus died in 33 A.D. we may conclude that John was no more than twenty at this time. Eighty years later would be around 113 A.D. Of course one tradition or another have both John and John Mark dying in 106 A.D.[2187] Although I do not suppose that John wrote $\mathfrak{P}^{46}$, $\mathfrak{P}^{52}$, or $\mathfrak{P}^{66}$ is apparent that the New Testament can make a closer claim to the autographs than any other writing of antiquity in history. It is of interest to note, however, that both $\mathfrak{P}^{52}$ and $\mathfrak{P}^{66}$ are papyri of John's gospel. It is inconceivable that forged and/or altered copies of John's gospel would be circulating at a time when John still lived without his raising a hand in objection! Surely, the manuscripts we have lend credibility to the fact that we have authentic replicas.

The chart below compares the Biblical texts with all other major works of antiquity (none of which the critics doubt to be authentic).[2188]

Author/Book	Oringally Written	Earliest Existing Copy	Difference	# of Copies
Homer's *Iliad*	900 B.C.	400 A.D.	500	643
Euripedes	5th Cent. B.C.	Circa 1000 A.D.	1500	9
Herodotus	5th Cent. B.C.	1st Cent. A.D.	400	75
Sophocles	5th Cent. B.C.	Circa 1000 A.D.	1400	100+
Thucydides	5th Cent. B.C.	900 A.D.	1300	20
Aristotle	4th Cent. B.C.	Circa 1000 A.D.	1400	5
Demostenes	4th Cent. B.C.	900 A.D.	1300	200
Plato	4th Cent. B.C.	900 A.D.	1200	7
Julius Caesar	1st Cent. B.C.	900 A.D.	1000	10
Lucretius	60 B.C.	1550 A.D.	1600	2
Livy	59 B.C.-17 A.D	350 A.D.	400	27
Tacitus	Circa 120 A.D.	1100 A.D.	1000	20
Suetonius	Circa 140 A.D.	950 A.D.	800	200+
The New Testament	40-95 A.D.	100-150 A.D.	25-50	5700+

Obviously the wealth of textual data belongs to the Bible before any other book of antiquity. Ironically this has become a double edged sword for critics will count the number "errors" by scribes at around 200,000 while neglecting to mention that of 5700 manuscripts and the 7958 verses (averaging very roughly 25 words per verse) in the New Testament (totalling over one billion words in all) these "errors" not only represent a tiny percentage of the New Testament, but, as we shall see, only around 40 verses are truly in doubt, and less than a dozen make any real difference to the texts, two of which are here in the gospels which I have addressed (see notes on Mark 16:9-20 and John 8:2-11).

Analysing the Scribal Errors

How can I say that 40 of the 7958 verses in the New Testament are in doubt? Actually, I believe the number is far fewer, but not all scholars are as conservative as I am, so in fairness it is worth examining how we arrive at these conclusions. It has already been demonstrated that there is a wealth of information about the New Testament from various countries, languages, and people very early in Christian history. Copies do not get disseminated quickly or easily in antiquity. *If* the Bible were altered then we would expect to find one of several things. First, we might expect a passing of centuries before copies are discovered such as implied in the *DaVinci Code* and other anti-Christian conspiracies. Since this is not the case, and far from it, we can discount this. A second thing we might look for would be substantial differences in various copies of a certain country or region as opposed to those of another (the same might be true of translations into other languages). In this case, it is argued that there are differences, but as we shall see the differences are linguistic, minor, and easy to distinguish.

The four major textual designations are the Byzantine textual tradition, the Alexandrian textual tradition, the Western textual tradition, and the Caesarean textual tradition.[2189] Nonetheless, contrary to the what the critic wishes, these textual "traditions" are extremely close. The greatest differences between these arise from linguistic and educational differences. For example, the Alexandrian tradition has a tendancy to alter quotation of the Old Testament from the author's translation to conform to the famed Greek *Septuagint* translation so well known in Alexandria.[2190] The modern day equivalent would be if an author quoted the New American Standard Bible translation, but a copy distributed in England changed the quotations to all be from the King James Bible. Another example of alterations made by one of these "traditions" is the use of synonyms for outdated words.[2191] For example, a famous verbal spar erupted once in Eusebius' time over a priest who substituted the then modern word for "bed" or "pallet" for the antiquated Biblical word found in John 5:8.[2192] Such fights, however, only show how great was the desire to be faithful to the original text. Moreover, an examination of the types of errors and mistakes found in these manuscripts also serves to demonstrate how easy it is to spot the errors from the original text!

Errors of Sight
There are various kinds of errors of sight, all of which are easy to catch. For example, the Greek letters Λ and the Δ look very similar. Sometimes a scribe may mistake one letter for another as in Acts 15:40 where the Greek word ΕΠΙΛΕΞΑΜΕΝΟΣ (*epilaxamenos*) meaning "having chosen" is mistakenly taken for ΕΠΙΔΕΞΑΜΕΝΟΣ (*epidaxamenos*) meaning "having received" in the Codex Bezae.[2193] Other examples are when a scribe sees the same word in close succession and accidentally skips over the first appearance of the word. In these instances a short sentence or clause may have been omitted, but it is, once again, easy to catch the mistake in the manuscript.

Errors of Writing
These errors could be summarized simply as ancient *typos*. Misspelled words or poor penmanship which might then be mistaken for something else typify these types of errors. Obviously there are the easiest to spot and of no significance.

Errors of Hearing
Sometimes scribes would have a copy read to them rather than reading it themselves. On occasion there will be words which sound very similar or have similar endings. Various diphthongs, for example, may be confused for one another. Again, these are usually pretty obvious and easy to catch. One example is from papyrus 46 (𝔓[46]) in which νεικος (*neikos*) meaning "conflict" is mistaken for νικος (*nikos*) meaning "victory."[2194]

Errors of Memory

A common error is when a reader looks at the text and then begins to write the copy from his mind he may forget trivial things like word order (particularly if he is tired). A common error found is the fact that some texts often read "Jesus Christ" while others read "Christ Jesus." Most of these errors make no difference in the meaning or translation of a text, and are easy to recognize.

Misunderstanding

Misunderstandings can fit in with some of the errors listed above but can also include things such as misunderstanding common abbreviations which were often used by scribes. For example, θεος (*theos*) meaning "God" is sometimes abbreviated simply as θς (*ths*), which can easily be mistaken for ος (*os*) which is a relative pronoun.[2195] Thus "God" is mistakenly replaced with the pronoun "He."[2196] Such instances are again obvious and insignificant.

Grammatical Changes

Another common change is the substitution of words or grammar for more modern (for the time of the writing) ones. The use of synonyms to replace words was common. As mentioned above, John 5:8 is an example of where a later Greek word for "bed" or "pallet" was substituted for the more antiquated one used by Jesus.[2197] A modern day parallel is the updating of English grammar in newer translations. Since no one uses "ye" or "thou" anymore, "you" is used to replace those words. The same thing took place with Greek copies. Nevertheless, by looking at textual traditions and using a basic knowledge of *Koine* Greek, these instances are also quite easily recognizable and insignificant.

Intentional Changes

All of the changes or errors listed above are either accidental errors or minor changes in grammar and vocabulary. Here, however, we come to those changes which are of importance for these would be deliberate changes to the text. Note that of all the "errors" and "changes" to which the critic appeals, these actually represent the tiniest of percentage of the discrepancies. Moreover, these alterations are often even easier to spot because of the plethora of diverse manuscripts, textual traditions, and translations available. Any serious alterations to the original apostles' manuscripts would have to have been done while the apostles were still living, and they would surely have objected! Indeed, as aforementioned, we have at last two manuscripts which date to the time when two of the gospel authors were still alive![2198] Consequently, this tiny percentage of alterations among the hundreds of thousands of verses known to exist in ancient manuscripts is insignifact; particularly in light of the fact that no doctrine of the Christian faith rest upon a single passage, but many passages!

So it should be obvious that the claims that we cannot know what the original texts of the apostles contained are frivolous. Only forty verses are seriously contested by any but the most atheistic or liberal of critics. Of these forty only four are of any real significance; two of which are here in the gospels (see notes on Mark 16:9-20 and John 8:2-11).

Summary

The wealth of textual copies available of the New Testament is unparalleled in history. No book in antiquity compares to the "embarassment of riches"[2199] available for the New Testament. It is for this very reason that critics attempt to exploit textual variants ("errors") found in these texts while neglecting to mention that the sheer volume of information available to us makes it easy to detect well over 99% of these mistakes, and no information leads us to believe that the Bible handed down to us today was intentionally altered. Let us compare the Biblical debate to that of other works of antiquity.

Homer's *Iliad* is among the most famous works of antiquity. No scholar denies that we have is a faithful copy of what he wrote. However, of the 15,600 lines that make up Homer's classic, 764 lines are in question[2200] whereas "of the approximately 20,000 lines that make up the entire New Testament, only 40 lines are in question. These 40 lines represent one quarter of one percent of the entire text and do not in any way affect the teaching and doctrine of the New Testament."[2201] Consider that "these 764 lines [in Homer's *Iliad*] represent over 5% of the entire text, and yet nobody seems to question the general integrity of that ancient work."[2202] The 40 lines of the New Testament represents less than on half of one percent of all the verses in the New Testament or .005%. No serious person can deny that we have faithful reproductions of what the apostles wrote.

Conclusions

There has been much talk about the "historical Jesus" among so-called "liberal scholars" but how can we discover the true "historical Jesus" if we reject the historical documents written by those who actually knew and lived and worked with Jesus? These "scholars" claim to want to know the "real" Jesus by rejecting the writings of those who did know the real Jesus. They attempt to replace true history with their own imagination. They make Jesus into their image without any witnesses, while scorning the witnesses and testimony of the apostles left to us in the New Testament.

Former Chief Inspector for Scotland Yard, Sir Robert Anderson, said of the "higher critics" who reject the gospels, "if the case could be brought before any serious judicial tribunal it would be 'laughed out of court.'"[2203] He noted that, "as usual with experts, the critics look only at one side of the question."[2204] When examining the Bible from a legitimate critical viewpoint Anderson said, "I am not assuming that the Evangelists were *inspired*, but merely that they were competent and trustworthy witnesses."[2205] He did believe that the Bible was inspired, but his *faith* in the inspiration of the Bible was not based on ignorance, but knowledge.

Sir Anderson said that "our belief in God tends to a belief in the existence of a written revelation."[2206] The Bible is that written revelation. History proves this. What we have are what the disciples wrote. What we read is what Jesus taught to His followers. What we *know* about the Bible is why we have *faith* in what it says. No man's beliefs are 100% fact nor 100% faith. This is the great lie that insecure agnostics and critics present. They *assume* miracles cannot happen and declare this to be a fact. They then reject all facts that do not fit this assumption. They operate on faith but claim to operate on facts. The honest Christian knows that his faith is a question of trust. Every man has a different level of trust. Certainly God will reward those who have a higher level of trust in Him, but this does not make our faith in Him contrary to the facts, but in accordance with them.

A man has *faith* that his wife is not cheating on him. He does not *know* this, but his faith is based on what he does know about his wife. If his wife slept around a lot before their marriage, his faith might be misplaced, but if his wife was a virgin on their wedding night he has good cause to believe in her faithfulness. Fidelity before marriage is a good indicator of faithfulness after marriage. Yes, we can sometimes misplace our faith, but that faith is not based on ignorance. Because we know the Bible is true and accurate in all that can be examined, we have faith that it is true and accurate when it speaks of what cannot be examined. I *know* that Moses led the Jews out of Egypt (a fact even admitted by the pagan Egyptian priest Manetho).[2207] I have *faith* that Moses parted the Red Sea. I *know* that Jesus was crucified, dead, and buried under Pontius Pilate and that His body disappeared on the third day. I have *faith* that He was resurrected from the dead. Faith is what pleases God, ignorance displeases God. The two are at odds with one another. Our faith is based on God's faithfulness and the truth of His word, for "without faith it is impossible please God" (Hebrews 11:6).

ENDNOTES

1 Sir Robert Anderson, *The Critics Criticized* Pickering & Inglis (London, England) 1904 pg. 153

2 Sir Robert Anderson, *The Bible and Modern Criticism* Pickering & Inglis (London, England) 1907 pg. 222

3 Ibid. pg. 130

4 Ibid. pp. 142-143

5 Merrill Tenney calls it "didactic" in nature. Merrill Tenney, *New Testament Survey* William B. Eerdmans (Grand Rapids, Mich.) 1985 pg. 305

6 Cf. Robert Gundry, *A Survey of the New Testament* Zondervan Publishing (Grand Rapids, Mich.) 1994 pg. 377

7 Ibid.

8 Ibid.

9 Tenney, op. cit. pg. 303

10 Merrill Unger, *Unger's Bible Dictionary* Moody Press (Chicago, Ill.) 1957 pg. 933

11 Everett Harrison, "Romans," *The Expositor's Bible Commentary Vol. 10* Frank Gaebelein, ed., Zondervan Publishers (Grand Rapids, Mich.) 1976 pg. 4

12 Unger, op. cit. pg. 836

13 David Criswell, *Controversies in the Acts of the Apostles* Fortress Adonai Press (Dallas, TX) 2013 pg. 180

14 Irenaeus, "Against Heresies," 3:2, *Ante-Nicene Fathers Vol. 1* Alexander Roberts & James Donaldson, eds., Charles Scribner (New York, NY) 1886 pg. 415

15 Laurence Browne, *Indian Church Commentaries - Acts of the Apostles* Diocesan Press (London, England) 1925 pg. 323

16 R.C.H. Lenski, *The Interpretation of the Acts of the Apostles* Warburg Press (Columbus, OH) 1944 pp. 799-800

17 Peter Abelard, *Fathers of the Church – Medieval Vol. 12 – Commentary on Romans* Steven Cartwright, trans., Catholic University Press of America (Washington, D.C.) 2011 pg. 111

18 Albert Barnes, *Barnes' Notes on the New Testament One Volume ed.* Kregel (Grand Rapids, Mich.) 1962 pg. 549

19 Ibid.

20 Donald Barnhouse, *Romans Vol. 1* Wm. B. Eerdmans (Grands Rapids, Mich.) 1952 pg. 177

21 James Montgomery Boice, *Romans Vol. 1* Baker Books (Grand Rapids, Mich.) 1991 ed. pg. 55

22 Charles Hodge, *Commentary on the Epistle to the Romans* Wm. B. Eerdmans (Grand Rapids, Mich.) 1886 (1950 ed.) pg. 29

23 Martin Luther, *Commentary on the Epistle to the Romans* Kregel Publishers (Grand Rapids, Mich.) 1954 pg. 40

24 Jerry Falwell & Ed Hindson, eds., *Liberty Commentary on the New Testament* Liberty Press (Lynchburg, Virginia) 1978

25 Desiderius Erasmus, *Collected Works of Erasmus, Vol. 42 – Paraphrase on Romans & Galatians* University of Toronto Press (Toronto, Canada) 1984 pg. 17

26 Desiderius Erasmus, *Collected Works of Erasmus, Vol. 56 – Annotations on Romans* University of Toronto Press (Toronto, Canada) 1994 pg. 42

27 Leon Morris, *The Epistle to the Romans* Wm. B. Eerdmans (Grands Rapids, Mich.) 1994 pg. 68

28 D.M. Lloyd-Jones, *Romans : An Exposition in Chapter 1* Zondervan Publishers (Grands Rapids, Mich.) 1985 pg. 292

29 Ambrosiaster, *Ancient Christian Commentary on Scripture Vol. XI Romans* Gerald Bray, ed., Intervarsity Press (Downers Grove, Ill.) 1988 pg. 29

30 Frederick Louis Godet, *Commentary of Romans* Kregel Publishers (Grand Rapids, Mich.) 1977 pg. 92

31 Ibid.

32 R.C.H. Lenski, *The Interpretation of St. Paul's Epistle to the Romans* Wartburg Press (Columbus, Ohio) 1945 pg. 76

33 Ibid.

34 Cf. Ibid. pg. 163
35 Lloyd-Jones, *Romans : Chapter 1* op. cit. pg. 292
36 John Calvin, *Commentary on the Epistle of Paul to the Romans* Wm. B. Eerdmans (Grand Rapids, Mich.) 1947 pg. 96
37 F.W. Farrar, *Texts Explained* F.M. Barton (Cleveland, Oh.) 1899 pg. 240
38 Heinrich Meyer, *Critical and Exegetical Commentary on the New Testament Romans Vol. 1* T & T Clark (Edinburgh, Scotland) 1873 pg. 160
39 Henry Cook, *The Epistle to the Romans* Carey Press (London, England) 1930 pg. 36
40 Leon Morris, *The Epistle to the Romans* Wm. B. Eerdmans (Grands Rapids, Mich.) 1994 pg. 125
41 Tertullian, *Ante-Nicene Fathers Vol. III*, Alexander Roberts & James Donaldson, eds., Charles Scribner (New York, NY) 1886 pg. 96
42 Erasmus, *Collected Works of Erasmus, Vol. 56* op. cit. pg. 81
43 Erasmus, *Collected Works of Erasmus, Vol. 42* op. cit. pg. 20
44 Abelard, *Fathers of the Church – Medieval Vol. 12* op. cit. pg. 135
45 Farrar, op. cit. pg. 240
46 Constantius, *Ancient Christian Commentary on Scripture Vol. XI Romans* Gerald Bray, ed., Intervarsity Press (Downers Grove, Ill.) 1988 pg. 65
47 Augustine, *Ancient Christian Commentary on Scripture Vol. XI Romans* op. cit. pg. 65
48 John MacArthur, *Romans 1-8* Moody Press (Chicago, Ill.) 1991
49 Pelagius, *Ancient Christian Commentary on Scripture Vol. XI Romans* op. cit. pg. 66
50 Karl Barth, *Epistle to the Romans* Oxford (London, England) 1950 ed. pp. 67-69
51 Woodrow Kroll, *The Book of Romans* AMG Publishers (Chattanooga, TN) 2002 pg. 32
52 R.C. Sproul, *The Gospel of God : Romans* Christian Focus Publishers (Ross-shire, Great Britain) 1994 pg. 52
53 Robert Govett, *Govett on Romans* Conley & Schoettle (Miama Springs, FL) 1981 pg. 46
54 Clement of Alexandria, *Ancient Christian Commentary on Scripture Vol. XI* op. cit. pg. 95
55 Karl Barth, *Epistle to the Romans* Oxford (London, England) 1950 ed. pg. 90
56 Farrar, op. cit. pg. 571
57 Warren Wiersbe, *Be Right* Victor Books (Wheaton, Ill.) 1984 pg. 32
58 Godet, *Romans* op. cit. pg. 144
59 Ibid.
60 Lenski, *Romans* op. cit. pg. 244
61 Hodge, *Romans* op. cit. pg. 81
62 Rene Lopez, *Roman Unlocked* 21st Century Press (Springfield, MO) 2009 pg. 60
63 Heinrich Meyer, *Critical and Exegetical Commentary on the New Testament Romans Vol. 1* T & T Clark (Edinburgh, Scotland) 1873 pg. 161
64 Abelard, *Fathers of the Church – Medieval Vol. 12* op. cit. pg. 161
65 Donald Barnhouse, *Romans Vol. 2* Wm. B. Eerdmans (Grands Rapids, Mich.) 1952 pg. 275
66 Erasmus, *Collected Works of Erasmus, Vol. 56* op. cit. pp. 163-164
67 MacArthur, *Romans 1-8* op. cit. pg. 299
68 Barnes, *Notes - One Volume ed.* op. cit. pg. 585
69 Farrar, op. cit. pg. 243
70 Lenski, *Romans* op. cit. pg. 364
71 Wesley, op. cit. pg. 387
72 *Ancient Christian Commentary on Scripture Vol. XI* op. cit. pp. 139-140
73 Abelard, *Fathers of the Church – Medieval Vol. 12* op. cit. pg. 209
74 Erasmus, *Collected Works of Erasmus, Vol. 42* op. cit. pg. 34
75 Robert Govett, *Govett on Romans* Conley & Schoettle (Miama Springs, FL) 1981 pg. 140
76 Erasmus, *Collected Works of Erasmus, Vol. 56* op. cit. pp. 163-164
77 William Newell, *Lessons on the Epistle of Paul to the Romans* J.I.C. Wilcox, (Toronto, Canada) 1925 pg. 75

78 Martin Luther, *Commentary on the Epistle to the Romans* Kregel Publishers (Grand Rapids, Mich.) 1954 pg. 96

79 Douglas Moo, *Romans – NIV Application Commentary* Zondervan Publ. (Grand Rapids, Mich.) 2000 pg. 182

80 Hodge, *Romans* op. cit. pg. 159

81 David Criswell, "Etiology and Physiology," *Journal Of Biblical Ethics in Medicine*

82 Warren Wiersbe, *Be Right* Victor Books (Wheaton, Ill.) 1984 pg. 54

83 Heinrich Meyer, *Critical and Exegetical Commentary on the New Testament Romans Vol. 1* T & T Clark (Edinburgh, Scotland) 1873 pg. 261

84 Frederick Louis Godet, *Commentary of Romans* Kregel Publishers (Grand Rapids, Mich.) 1977 pg. 210

85 Woodrow Kroll, *The Book of Romans* AMG Publishers (Chattanooga, TN) 2002 pg. 79

86 F.F. Bruce, *The Letter of Paul to the Romans* Wm. B. Eerdmans (Grand Rapids, Mich.) 1985 pg. 123

87 Kroll, op. cit. pg. 79

88 D.M. Lloyd-Jones, *Romans : An Exposition in Chapter 5* Zondervan Publishers (Grands Rapids, Mich.) 1985 pg. 206

89 R.C. Sproul, *The Gospel of God : Romans* Christian Focus Publishers (Ross-shire, Great Britain) 1994 pg. 104

90 Donald Barnhouse, *Romans Vol. 5* Wm. B. Eerdmans (Grands Rapids, Mich.) 1952 pg. 47

91 James Montgomery Boice, *Romans Vol. 2* Baker Books (Grand Rapids, Mich.) 1991 ed. pp. 756-760

92 Ibid. pg. 756

93 MacArthur, *Romans 1-8* op. cit. pg. 386

94 Barnes, *Notes - One Volume ed.* op. cit. pg. 600

95 Boice, *Romans Vol. 2* op. cit.. pg. 757

96 J.I. Packer, *Keep in Step with the Spirit* Fleming Revell (Old Tappan, NJ) 1984 pg. 144

97 Boice, *Romans Vol. 2* op. cit. ed. pg. 757

98 Donald Barnhouse, *Romans Vol. 6* Wm. B. Eerdmans (Grands Rapids, Mich.) 1952 pg. 238

99 Boice, *Romans Vol. 2* op.c it. pg. 759

100 Godet, *Romans* op. cit. pg. 285

101 John Brown, *Analytical Exposition of the Epistle of Paul to the Romans* William Oliphant (Edinburgh, Scotland) 1857 pg. 75

102 Boice, *Romans Vol. 2* op. cit. pg. 758

103 MacArthur, *Romans 1-8* op. cit. pg. 386

104 Ibid.

105 Erasmus, *Collected Works, Vol. 42* op. cit. pg. 44

106 Aquinas, *Romans* op. cit. pg. 6

107 *Ancient Christian Commentary on Scripture Vol. XI* op. cit. pp. 193-194

108 Sproul, *Romans* op. cit pg. 126

109 John Witmer, "Romans," *Bible Knowledge Commentary : New Testament* John Walvoord & Roy Zuck, eds., Victor Books (Wheaton, Ill.) 1986 pg. 467

110 Boice, *Romans Vol. 2* op. cit. pg. 760

111 Packer, *Keep in Step* op. cit. pg. 129

112 Leon Morris, *The Epistle to the Romans* Wm. B. Eerdmans (Grands Rapids, Mich.) 1994 pg. 294

113 Karl Barth, *Epistle to the Romans* Oxford (London, England) 1950 ed. pg. 263

114 John Calvin, *Commentary on the Epistle of Paul to the Romans* Wm. B. Eerdmans (Grand Rapids, Mich.) 1947 pg. 267

115 H.A. Ironside, *Lectures on the Epistle to the Romans* Loizeaux Brothers (New York, NY) 1927 pg. 90

116 Lenski, *Romans* op. cit. pg. 481

117 Robert Govett, *Govett on Romans* Conley & Schoettle (Miama Springs, FL) 1981 pp. 271-272

118 Lopez, op. cit. pg. 154
119 Ibid.
120 Robert Govett, *Govett on Romans* Conley & Schoettle (Miama Springs, FL) 1981 pg. 271
121 Kroll, op. cit. pg. 117
122 Charles Spurgeon, *Treasury of the New Testament Volume Three* Zondervan Publishers (Grand Rapids, Mich) 1950 pg. 57
123 Charles Hodge, *Commentary on the Epistle to the Romans* Wm. B. Eerdmans (Grand Rapids, Mich.) 1886 (1950 ed.) pg. 230
124 *Liberty Commentary* op. cit. pp. 328-329
125 Cf. James Montgomery Boice, *Ephesians* Baker Books (Grand Rapids, Mich.) 1988 pp. 15-16
126 Lewis Sperry Chafer, *The Ephesian Letter* Dunham Publications (Findlay, Ohio) 1953 pg. 37
127 Ibid. pp. 37-38
128 Robert Alden, "Malachi," *The Expositor's Bible Commentary* Vol. 7 Frank Gaebelein, ed., Zondervan Publishers (Grand Rapids, Mich.) 1986 pg. 709
129 John Walvoord, *Every Prophecy of the Bible* Chariot Victor Publishing (Colorado Springs, Co.) 1999 pg. 335
130 Robert Govett, *Govett on Romans* Conley & Schoettle (Miama Springs, FL) 1981 pg. 451
131 Barnes, *Notes - One Volume ed.* op. cit. pg. 627
132 Wiersbe, *Be Right* op. cit pg. 121
133 Leon Morris, *The Epistle to the Romans* Wm. B. Eerdmans (Grands Rapids, Mich.) 1994 pg. 394
134 William Genenius, *Gesenius' Hebrew and Cahaldee Lexicon to the Old Tesament* Samuel Tregelles, trans., Baker Books (Grand Rapids, Mich.) 1847 (1984 ed.) pg. 735
135 Joseph Thayer, *Thayer's Greek-English Lexicon* Baker Book House (Grand Rapids, Mich.) 1977 pg. 482
136 Genenius, op. cit. pg. 735
137 Martin Luther, *Commentary on the Epistle to the Romans* Kregel Publishers (Grand Rapids, Mich.) 1954 pg. 152
138 John MacArthur, *Romans 9-16* Moody Press (Chicago, Ill.) 1991 pg. 90
139 Martin Luther, *Commentary on the Epistle to the Romans* Kregel Publishers (Grand Rapids, Mich.) 1954 pg. 152
140 Ambrosiaster, *Ancient Christian Commentary on Scripture Vol. XI* op. cit. pg. 282
141 Peter Abelard, *Fathers of the Church – Medieval Vol. 12 – Commentary on Romans* Steven Cartwright, trans., Catholic University Press of America (Washington, D.C.) 2011 pg. 313
142 Heinrich Meyer, *Critical and Exegetical Commentary on the New Testament Romans Vol. 2* T & T Clark (Edinburgh, Scotland) 1873 pg. 222
143 Calvin, *Romans* op. cit. pg. 428
144 Lopez, op. cit.
145 Ibid.
146 Barth, *Romans* op. cit. pg. 409
147 Wiersbe, *Be Right* op. cit. pg. 129
148 Hodge, *Romans* op. cit. pg. 368
149 Sproul, *Romans* op. cit. pg. 189
150 Douglas Moo, *Romans – NIV Application Commentary* Zondervan Publ. (Grand Rapids, Mich.) 2000 pg. 371
151 Barnes, *Notes - One Volume ed.* op. cit. pg. 634
152 *Liberty Commentary* op. cit. pg. 348
153 Donald Barnhouse, *Romans Vol. 8* Wm. B. Eerdmans (Grands Rapids, Mich.) 1952 pg. 136
154 Leon Morris, *The Epistle to the Romans* Wm. B. Eerdmans (Grands Rapids, Mich.) 1994 pg. 413
155 Erasmus, *Collected Works of Erasmus, Vol. 56* op. cit. pg. 306
156 Abelard, op. cit. pg. 322
157 Irenaeus, *Ante-Nicene Fathers Vol. I* op. cit. pg. 536

158 Heinrich Meyer, *Critical and Exegetical Commentary on the New Testament Romans Vol. 2* T & T Clark (Edinburgh, Scotland) 1873 pg. 224

159 Barclay M. Newman, Jr., ed., *A Concise Greek-English Dictionary of the New Testament* United Bible Society (Stuttgart, Germany) 1971 pg. 55

160 Lopez, op. cit.

161 F.F. Bruce, *The Letter of Paul to the Romans* Wm. B. Eerdmans (Grand Rapids, Mich.) 1985 pg. 206

162 Charles Swindoll, *Insights in Romans* Zondervan Publishers (Grands Rapids, Mich.) 2010 pg. 230

163 Lopez, op. cit.

164 John Nelson Darby, *The Collected Writings of J.N. Darby Prophetic No. 1 Vol. 2* Bible Truth Publishers (Addison, IL) n.d. pp. 320-321

165 Theodoret of Cyr, *Ancient Christian Commentary on Scripture Vol. XI* op. cit. pg. 299

166 Origen, *Ancient Christian Commentary on Scripture Vol. XI* op. cit. pg. 298

167 Cyril of Alexandria, *Ancient Christian Commentary on Scripture Vol. XI* op. cit. pp. 298-299

168 Martin Luther, *Commentary on the Epistle to the Romans* Kregel Publishers (Grand Rapids, Mich.) 1954 pg. 161

169 Irenaeus, *Ante-Nicene Fathers Vol. I* op. cit. pg. 465

170 Cited in Martin Luther, *Commentary on the Epistle to the Romans* Kregel Publishers (Grand Rapids, Mich.) 1954 pp. 162-163

171 Augustine, *Ancient Christian Commentary on Scripture Vol. XI* op. cit. pg. 298

172 Aquinas, *Romans* op. cit. pg. 111

173 Abelard, op. cit. pg. 323

174 Martin Luther, *Commentary on the Epistle to the Romans* Kregel Publishers (Grand Rapids, Mich.) 1954 pp. 162-163

175 Calvin, *Romans* op. cit. pg. 437

176 Erasmus, *Collected Works of Erasmus, Vol. 42* op. cit. pg. 67

177 F.F. Bruce, *The Letter of Paul to the Romans* Wm. B. Eerdmans (Grand Rapids, Mich.) 1985 pg. 209

178 Barth, *Romans* op. cit. pg. 416

179 Jonathan Edwards, *"The Blank Bible" Part 2* Stephen Stein, ed., Yale University Press (New Haven, CT) 2006 pg. 1028

180 H.A. Ironside, *Lectures on the Epistle to the Romans* Loizeaux Brothers (New York, NY) 1927 pg. 143

181 Kroll, op. cit. pg. 183

182 Lenski, *Romans* op. cit.

183 Sir Robert Anderson, *Forgotten Truths* [online version may be found at www.newble.co.uk/anderson/truths/app5_notes.html]

184 Barnes, *Notes - One Volume ed.* op. cit. pg. 635

185 Hodge, *Romans* op. cit. pg. 374

186 *Liberty Commentary* op. cit. pg. 348

187 Sproul, *Romans* op. cit. pg. 191

188 Barnhouse, *Romans Vol. 8* op. cit. pg. 150

189 James Montgomery Boice, *Romans Vol. 3* Baker Books (Grand Rapids, Mich.) 1991 ed. pp. 1375-1376

190 Thomas Chalmers, *Lectures on the Epistle of Paul the Apostle to the Romans* Robert Carter & Bro. (New York, NY) 1855 pg. 431

191 Lopez, op. cit. pg. 234

192 John MacArthur, *Romans 9-16* Moody Press (Chicago, Ill.) 1991 pg. 128

193 Wiersbe, *Be Right* op. cit. pg. 132

194 Chalmers, *Romans* op. cit. pg. 432

195 Hodge, *Romans* op. cit. pg. 405

196 Govett, *Romans* op. cit. pg. 490

197 Tertullian, *Ante-Nicene Fathers Vol. III* op. cit. pg. 648
198 William Newell, *Lessons on the Epistle of Paul to the Romans* J.I.C. Wilcox, (Toronto, Canada) 1925 pg. 258
199 Jonathan Edwards, *"The Blank Bible" Part 2* Stephen Stein, ed., Yale University Press (New Haven, CT) 2006 pg. 1031
200 Wesley, op. cit. pg. 348
201 Sproul, *Romans* op. cit. pp. 212-213
202 Polycarp, *Ante-Nicene Fathers Vol. I* op. cit. pg. 41
203 Irenaeus, *Ante-Nicene Fathers Vol. I* op. cit. pg. 552 & 310
204 Theodoret of Cyr, *Ancient Christian Commentary on Scripture Vol. XI* op. cit. pg. 325
205 Cf. Criswell, *Rise and Fall of the Holy Roman Empire*, op. cit.
206 Ibid.
207 Ibid.
208 Augustine, *Ancient Christian Commentary on Scripture Vol. XI* op. cit. pg. 325
209 Erasmus, *Collected Works of Erasmus, Vol. 42* op. cit. pg. 75
210 John MacArthur, *Romans 9-16* Moody Press (Chicago, Ill.) 1991 pg. 208
211 Barnes, *Notes - One Volume ed.* op. cit. pg. 648
212 Ibid.
213 Chalmers, *Romans* op. cit. pg. 468
214 *Liberty Commentary* op. cit. pg. 355
215 H.A. Ironside, *Lectures on the Epistle to the Romans* Loizeaux Brothers (New York, NY) 1927 pg. 155
216 Heinrich Meyer, *Critical and Exegetical Commentary on the New Testament Romans Vol. 2* T & T Clark (Edinburgh, Scotland) 1873 pg. 275
217 James Montgomery Boice, *Romans Vol. 4* Baker Books (Grand Rapids, Mich.) 1991 ed. pg. 1640
218 Paraphrased from F.F. Bruce, *The Letter of Paul to the Romans* Wm. B. Eerdmans (Grand Rapids, Mich.) 1985 pg. 221
219 D.M. Lloyd-Jones, *Romans : An Exposition in Chapter 13* Zondervan Publishers (Grands Rapids, Mich.) 1985 pg. 7
220 Leon Morris, *The Epistle to the Romans* Wm. B. Eerdmans (Grands Rapids, Mich.) 1994 pg. 458
221 Spurgeon, *Treasury Vol. 3* op. cit. pg. 123
222 Calvin, *Romans* op. cit. pg. 494
223 Barnes, *Notes - One Volume ed.* op. cit. pg. 653
224 Erasmus, *Collected Works of Erasmus, Vol. 56* op. cit. pg. 366
225 Abelard, op. cit. pg. 355
226 Chalmers, *Romans* op. cit. pg. 484
227 Govett, *Romans* op. cit. pg. 498
228 R.C.H. Lenski, *The Interpretation of St. Paul's Epistle to the Romans* Wartburg Press (Columbus, Ohio) 1945 pg. 812
229 Hodge, *Romans* op. cit. pg. 417
230 James Montgomery Boice, *Romans Vol. 4* Baker Books (Grand Rapids, Mich.) 1991 ed. pg. 1733
231 Constantius, *Ancient Christian Commentary on Scripture Vol. XI* op. cit. pg. 337
232 William Newell, *Lessons on the Epistle of Paul to the Romans* J.I.C. Wilcox, (Toronto, Canada) 1925 pg. 273
233 Erasmus, *Collected Works of Erasmus, Vol. 42* op. cit. pg. 80
234 Farrar, op. cit. pg. 251
235 Douglas Moo, *Romans – NIV Application Commentary* Zondervan Publ. (Grand Rapids, Mich.) 2000 pg. 447
236 Leon Morris, *The Epistle to the Romans* Wm. B. Eerdmans (Grands Rapids, Mich.) 1994 pg. 478

237 Barclay Newman, Jr., *A Concise Greek-English Dictionary* United Bible Societies (Stuttgart, Germany) 1971 pg. 42

238 Matthew Henry, "Romans," *Commentary on the Whole Bible Vol. 6* Hendrickson Publishers (Peabody, Mass.) 1998 ed. pg. 401

239 John Witmer, "Romans," *The Bible Knowledge Commentary : New Testament* John F. Walvoord & Roy Zuck, eds., Victor Books (Wheaton, Ill.) 1986 pg. 499

240 Ibid.

241 Everett Harrison, "Romans," *The Expositor's Bible Commentary Vol. 10* Frank Gaebelein, ed., Zondervan Publishers (Grand Rapids, Mich.) 1976 pg. 161

242 Witmer, *Bible Knowledge* op. cit. pg. 499

243 Gleason Archer, *Encyclopedia of Bible Difficulties* Zondervan Publishers (Grand Rapids, Mich.) 1982 pg. 397

244 *Liberty Commentary* op. cit. pg. ??

245 Barnes, *Notes - One Volume ed.* op. cit. pg. 702

246 R.C.H. Lenski, *The Interpretation of St. Paul's First and Second Epistles to the Corinthians* Wartburg Press (Columbus, Ohio) 1937 pg. 175

247 Frederic Godet, *Commentary on First Corintians* Kregel Press (Grand Rapids, Mich.) 1977 ed. (1889) pg. 217

248 George Montague, *Catholic Commentary on Sacred Scripture : First Corinthians* Baker Academics (Grand Rapids, Mich.) 2011 pg. 85

249 Gordon Fee, *The First Epistle to the Corinthians* Wm. B. Eerdmans (Grand Rapids, Mich.) 1987 pg. 168

250 Charles Hodge, *Commentary on 1 & 2 Corinthians* Banner of Truth (Carlisle, PA) 1857 pg. 70

251 Cf. Albert Barnes, *Notes on First Epistle of Paul to the Corinthians* Harpers Brothers (New York, NY) 1854 pg. 85

252 Gordon Fee, *The First Epistle to the Corinthians* Wm. B. Eerdmans (Grand Rapids, Mich.) 1987 pg. 167

253 Ibid. pg. 168

254 H.A. Ironside, *Addresses on the First Epistle to the Corinthians* Loizeaux Brothers (New York, NY) 1938 pg. 152

255 Lenski, *Corinthians* op. cit. pg. 175

256 Godet, *First Corintians* op. cit. pg. 217

257 F.F. Bruce, *1 & 2 Corinthians* Oliphants (London, England) 1971 pg. 48

258 Kenneth Chafin, *The Communicator's Commentary 1, 2 Corinthians* Lloyd Ogilvie, ed, Word Pblishers (Wavo, TX) 1985 pg. 68

259 Dan Mitchell, *The Book of First Corinthians* AMG Publishers (Chattanooga, TN) 2004 pg. 77

260 John Calvin, *Commentary on the Epistle of Paul the Apostle to the Corinthians Vol. 1* Wm. B. Eerdmans (Grand Rapids, Mich.) 1948 pg. 179

261 John MacArthur, *1 Corinthians* Moody Press (Chicago, Ill.) 1984 pg. 122

262 F.F. Bruce, *1 & 2 Corinthians* Oliphants (London, England) 1971 pg. 55

263 Pastor of Hermas, *Ante-Nicene Fathers Vol. II* Alexander Roberts & James Donaldson, eds., Charles Scribner (New York, NY) 1885 pg. ??

264 Montague, *First Corinthians* op. cit. pg. 93

265 John N. Darby, *Notes on the Epistles to the Corinthians* G. Morrish (London, England) n.d. pg. 30

266 Ibid.

267 Erasmus, *Collected Works of Erasmus Vol. 43 Paraphrases on the Epistles to the Corinthians, Ephesians, Philippians, Colossians, and Thessalonians* University of Toronto Press (Toronto, Canada) 2009 pg. 71

268 Warren Wiersbe, *Be Wise* Victor Books (Wheaton, Ill.) 1984 pg. 65

269 Thayer, op. cit. pg. 387

270 Ibid.

271 Ibid. pg. 75

272 Ibid.
273 Ibid.
274 Dwight Wright, "Homosexuals or Prostitutes," *Vigiliae Christianae* No. 38 (1984) pg. 125
275 Ibid. pg. 126
276 Ibid. pg. 141
277 *Diagnostic and Statistical Manual of Mental Disorders* (DSM-III) American Psychiatric Association (Washington, D.S.) 1987 pg. 292
278 Montague, *First Corinthians* op. cit. pg. 114
279 Godet, *First Corintians* op. cit. pg. 322
280 Lenski, *Corinthians* op. cit. pg. 108
281 Cf. Godet, *First Corintians* op. cit. pg. 319
282 John Calvin, *Commentary on the Epistle of Paul the Apostle to the Corinthians Vol. 1* Wm. B. Eerdmans (Grand Rapids, Mich.) 1948 pg. 222
283 Hodge, *1 & 2 Corinthians* op. cit.
284 Warren Wiersbe, *Be Wise* Victor Books (Wheaton, Ill.) 1984 pg. 76
285 John MacArthur, *1 Corinthians* Moody Press (Chicago, Ill.) 1984 pg. 155
286 Godet, *First Corintians* op. cit. pg. 319
287 Montague, *First Corinthians* op. cit. pg. 115
288 Roy Harrisville, *Augsburg Commentary on N.W. 1 Corinthians* Augsburg Publishers (Minneapolis, MN) 1987 pg. 106
289 Severian, *Ancient Christian Commentary on Scripture Vol. VII 1-2 Corinthians* Gerald Bray, ed., InterVarsity Press (Downers Grove, Ill.) 1999 pg. 59
290 Pelagius, *Ancient Christian Commentary on Scripture Vol. VII 1-2 Corinthians* op. cit. pg. 60
291 Irenaeus, *Ante-Nicene Fathers Vol. I* op. cit. pg. 480
292 Archibald Roberston & Alfred Plummer, *A Critical & Exegetical Commentary on First & Second Corinthians* T. & T. Clark (Edinburgh, Scotland) 1911 pg. 132
293 Mitchell, op. cit. pg. 109
294 Bruce, *1 & 2 Corinthians* op. cit. pg. 66
295 Kenneth Chafin, *The Communicator's Commentary 1, 2 Corinthians* Lloyd Ogilvie, ed, Word Pblishers (Wavo, TX) 1985 pg. 88
296 Chrystostom, *Ancient Christian Commentary on Scripture Vol. VII 1-2 Corinthians* Gerald Bray, ed., InterVarsity Press (Downers Grove, Ill.) 1999 pg. 60
297 Montague, *First Corinthians* op. cit. pg. 114
298 Tertullian, *Ante-Nicene Fathers Vol. III* op. cit. pg. 443
299 Barnes, *Notes - One Volume ed.* op. cit. pg. 717
300 Wesley, op. cit. pg. 435
301 Ironside, *First Corinthians* op. cit. pg. 202
302 Cf. David Criswell, *Apostles After Jesus* Fortress Adonai Press (Dallas, TX) 2013
303 John Calvin, *Commentary on the Epistle of Paul the Apostle to the Corinthians Vol. 1* Wm. B. Eerdmans (Grand Rapids, Mich.) 1948 pg. 252
304 http://biblicaldiscipleship.org/content/relationships-and-bible
305 Erasmus, *Collected Works of Erasmus Vol. 43 Paraphrases on the Epistles to the Corinthians, Ephesians, Philippians, Colossians, and Thessalonians* University of Toronto Press (Toronto, Canada) 2009 pg. 92
306 Wesley, op. cit. pg. 434
307 Tertullian, *Ante-Nicene Fathers Vol. IV* Alexander Roberts & James Donaldson, eds., William B. Eerdmans Publishers (Grand Rapids, Mich.) 1885 pg. 44
308 Ibid. pp. 44-47
309 Ibid. pg. 47
310 Farrar, op. cit. pg. 190
311 Fee, *First Corinthians* op. cit. pg. 300
312 Bruce, *Romans* op. cit. pg. 235
313 Tertullian, *Ante-Nicene Fathers Vol. IV* op. cit. pg. 103

314 Albert Barnes, *Notes on First Epistle of Paul to the Corinthians* Harpers Brothers (New York, NY) 1854 pg. 153
315 Wiersbe, *Be Wise* op. cit. pg. 87
316 Bruce, *1 & 2 Corinthians* op. cit. pg. 78
317 Lenski, *Corinthians* op. cit. pg. 333
318 Godet, *First Corintians* op. cit. pg. 401
319 MacArthur, *1 Corinthians* op. cit. pg. 188
320 Godet, *First Corintians* op. cit. pg. 403
321 Erasmus, *Collected Works Vol. 43* op. cit. pg. 110
322 Hodge *1 & 2 Corinthians* op. cit. pg. 156
323 Archibald Roberston & Alfred Plummer, *A Critical & Exegetical Commentary on First & Second Corinthians* T. & T. Clark (Edinburgh, Scotland) 1911 pg. 181
324 Tertullian, *Ante-Nicene Fathers Vol. IV* op. cit. pg. 65
325 Ibid. pg. 69
326 Augustine, *Ancient Christian Commentary Vol. VII* op. cit. pp. 80-81
327 Clement of Alexandria, *Ancient Christian Commentary Vol. VII* op. cit. pg. 80
328 Eusebius, *The Church History*, 3:36, Paul Meier, trans. Kregel Publishers (Grand Rapids, Mich.) 1999 pg. 123
329 Archibald Roberston & Alfred Plummer, *A Critical & Exegetical Commentary on First & Second Corinthians* T. & T. Clark (Edinburgh, Scotland) 1911 pg. 181
330 MacArthur, *1 Corinthians* op. cit. pg. 201
331 Clement of Alexandria, "Miscellanies," 7.11.63-64 *Ante-Nicene Fathers Vol. 2* op. cit. pg. 541
332 Clement of Alexandria, "Miscellanies," 3.6.52 *Ante-Nicene Fathers Vol. 2* op. cit. pg. 390
333 Clement of Alexandria, "Miscellanies," 7.11.63-64 *Ante-Nicene Fathers Vol. 2* op. cit. pg. 541
334 Lenski, *First and Second Epistles to the Corinthians* op. cit. pg. 356
335 Wesley, op. cit. pg. 438
336 Wiersbe, *Be Wise* op. cit. pg. 99
337 Erasmus, *Collected Works Vol. 43* op. cit. pg. 121
338 Tertullian, *Ante-Nicene Fathers Vol. IV* op. cit. pg. 69
339 Godet, *First Corintians* op. cit. pg. 436
340 Barnes, *Notes - One Volume ed.* op. cit. pg. 735
341 Matthew Poole, *A Commentary on the Holy Bible : Vol. III Matthew-Revelation* Hendrickson Publishers (Peabody, Mass.) n.d pg. 573
342 W. Harold Mare, "1 Corinthians," *The Expositor's Bible Commentary Vol. 10* op. cit. pg. 249
343 David K. Lowery, "1 Corinthians," *Bible Knowledge Commentary : New Testament* op. cit. pg. 527
344 Archer, op. cit. pg. 401
345 Barnes, *First Epistle of Paul to the Corinthians* op. cit. pg. 219
346 Barnes, *Notes - One Volume ed.* op. cit. pg. 753
347 *Liberty Commentary* op. cit. pg. 409
348 Montague, op. cit. pg. 185
349 Fee, *First Corinthians* op. cit. pp. 493-494
350 Cf. Bruce, *1 & 2 Corinthians* op. cit. pg. 103
351 Lenski, *First and Second Epistles to the Corinthians* op. cit. pg. 433
352 MacArthur, *1 Corinthians* op. cit. pg. 253
353 Cyril of Jerusalem, *Ancient Christian Commentary Vol. VII* op. cit. pg. 104
354 Wiersbe, *Be Wise* op. cit. pg. 111
355 Ironside, *First Corinthians* op. cit. pg. 330
356 Calvin, *Corinthians Vol. 1* op. cit. pg. 354
357 This is what a Salvation Army spokesperson told me years ago when I applied for a job as a janitor.

358 John N. Darby, *Notes on the Epistles to the Corinthians* G. Morrish (London, England) n.d. pg. 85

359 I am not here attempting to justify or debate the validity of the Catholic church or its officers. The point is to illustrate that women can achieve greatness without violating God's order.

360 D.A. Carson, *Showing the Spirit* Baker Book (Grand Rapids, Mich.) 1987 pg. 33

361 Lenski, *First and Second Epistles to the Corinthians* op. cit. pg. 499

362 Fee, *First Corinthians* op. cit. pp. 590-591

363 Wesley, op. cit. pg. 447

364 *Liberty Commentary* op. cit. pg. 414

365 Godet, *First Corintians* op. cit. pg. 623

366 Erasmus, *Collected Works Vol. 43* op. cit. pp. 151-152

367 Montague, op. cit. pg. 208

368 MacArthur, *1 Corinthians* op. cit. pg. 298

369 I emphasize "true" mother for today our generation is so wicked that some mothers often slay their own children while they are yet in the womb.

370 Gesenius, op. cit. pg. 277

371 This is common among certain television evangelist who stop in mid-sentence, saying, "I am receiving a word of knowledge." They then speak in gerenal terms about some "revelation" they are receiving from the Lord.

372 Cf. Dave Hunt & T.A. McMahon, *The Seduction of Christianity* Harvest House (Eugene, OR) 1984

373 Mitchell, op. cit. pg. 179

374 Carson, op. cit. pg. 38

375 Mare, op. cit. pg. 262

376 Wesley, op. cit. pg. 447

377 *Liberty Commentary* op. cit. pg. 414

378 Godet, *First Corintians* op. cit. pg. 623

379 Ibid.

380 Erasmus, *Collected Works Vol. 43* op. cit. pg. 164

381 Ibid. pp. 151-152

382 MacArthur, *1 Corinthians* op. cit. pg. 298

383 Fee, *First Corinthians* op. cit. pg. 593

384 Barnes, *Notes - One Volume ed.* op. cit. pg. 764

385 Montague, op. cit. pg. 209

386 Carson, op. cit. pg. 38

387 MacArthur, *1 Corinthians* op. cit. pg. 299

388 Wesley, op. cit. pg. 447

389 Ibid.

390 Henry Morris, *Men of Science, Men of God* Master Books (El Cajon, CA) 1982 pp. 60-62; 66-67

391 Cf. Mitchell, op. cit. pg. 179 who takes this word for word from the *Liberty Bible Commentary.*

392 Godet, *First Corintians* op. cit. pg. 625

393 *Liberty Commentary* op. cit. pg. 414

394 MacArthur, *1 Corinthians* op. cit. pg. 300

395 Carson, op. cit. pg. 40

396 Cf. D.A. Carson, "Matthew," *Expositors Bible Commentary Vol. 8* Frank Gaebelein, ed., Zondervan Publishers (Grand Rapids, Mich.) 1986 pg. 294

397 MacArthur, *1 Corinthians* op. cit. pg. 301

398 Tertullian, *Ante-Nicene Fathers Vol. III* op. cit. pg. 322

399 Montague, op. cit. pg. 210

400 *Liberty Commentary* op. cit. pg. 414

401 Darby, *Corinthians* op. cit. pg. 131

402 Ibid.

403 Hodge, *1 & 2 Corinthians* op. cit. pg. 247

404 Roberston & Plummer, op. cit. pg. 266

405 MacArthur, *1 Corinthians* op. cit. pg. 303

406 Godet, *First Corintians* op. cit. pg. 626

407 Erasmus, *Collected Works Vol. 43* op. cit. pp. 151-152

408 Cf. Calvin, *Corinthians Vol. 1* op. cit. pg. 403

409 Cf. Darby, *Corinthians* op. cit. pg. 131

410 David Lowery, "1 Corinthians," *The Bible Knowledge Commentary : New Testament* John F. Walvoord & Roy Zuck, eds., Victor Books (Wheaton, Ill.) 1986 pg. 533

411 Carson, op. cit. pg. 40

412 Mitchell, op. cit. pp. 179-180

413 *Liberty Commentary* op. cit. pg. 414

414 Barnes, *Notes - One Volume ed.* op. cit. pg. 765

415 Barnes, *First Corinthians* op. cit. pp. 247-250

416 Wesley, op. cit. pg. 449

417 Calvin, *Corinthians Vol. 1* op. cit. pg. 403

418 Cf. Thayer, op. cit. pg. 50

419 Cf. Newman, op. cit. pg. 107

420 Thayer, op. cit. pg. 50

421 Newman, op. cit. pg. 16

422 Thayer, op. cit. pg. 50

423 Newman, op. cit. pg. 104

424 Barnes, *First Corinthians* op. cit. pg. 246

425 Godet, *First Corintians* op. cit. pg. 619

426 Ibid.

427 Richard Young, *Intermediate New Testament Greek* Broadman & Holman (Nashville, TN) 1994 pg. 224

428 Origen, the church father, considered in order of importance, words of wisdom, knowldege, faith, miracles, and then healing with tongues apparently last (Origen, *Ante-Nicene Fathers Vol. IV* op. cit. pg. 483)

429 D.A. Carson adds, "for a prooftext." (Carson, op. cit. pg. 51)

430 MacArthur, *1 Corinthians* op. cit. pg. 359

431 Ibid.

432 This is not Carson's opinion. He is merely summarizing the cessationist view (Carson, op. cit. pg. 66)

433 Lenski, *Corinthians* op. cit. pg. 563

434 Ronald Baxter, *Charistmatic Gfits of Tongues* Kregel Publications (Grand Rapids, Mich.) 1981 pg. 61

435 Godet, *First Corintians* op. cit. pg. 679

436 Carson, op. cit. pg. 66

437 Ibid. pg. 67

438 Origen, *Ancient Christian Commentary Vol. VII* op. cit. pg. 134

439 Ronald Baxter, *Gifts of the Spirit* Kregel Publications (Grand Rapids, Mich.) 1983 pg. 161

440 Ibid.

441 *Liberty Commentary* op. cit. pg. 417

442 Wiersbe, *Be Wise* op. cit. pg. 124

443 Baxter, *Gifts of the Spirit* op. cit. pg. 161

444 Lowery, op. cit. pg. 536

445 Mitchell, op. cit. pg. 190

446 Ibid. pg. 191

447 Barnes, *First Corinthians* op. cit. pg. 271

448 Barnes, *Notes - One Volume ed.* op. cit. pg. 773

449 Matthew Henry, *Commentary on the Whole Bible Vol. 6* Hendrickson Publishers (Peabody, Mass) 1988 464

450 Hodge, *1 & 2 Corinthians* op. cit. pg. 272

451 Roberston & Plummer, op. cit. pg. 297

452 Cited by M.M.B. Turner, "Spiritual Gifts Then and Now," *Vox Evangelica* No. 15 (1985) pg. 39

453 Cf. Jack Nakashima, www.facebook.com/groups/scripturally.speaking/

454 Ironside, *First Corinthians* op. cit. pg.

455 Ibid.

456 Cf. www.facebook.com/groups/scripturally.speaking/

457 Tertullian, *Ante-Nicene Fathers Vol. III* Alexander Roberts & James Donaldson, eds., Charles Scribner (New York, NY) 1886 pg. 443

458 Ibid. pg. 188

459 Irenaeus, *Ante-Nicene Fathers Vol. I* op. cit. pg. 401

460 Ironside, *First Corinthians* op. cit. pg. ??

461 Godet, *First Corintians* op. cit. pg. 626

462 *Liberty Commentary* op. cit. pg. 414

463 www.facebook.com/groups/scripturally.speaking/

464 Carson, op. cit. pg. 58

465 Ronald Baxter, *Charistmatic Gift of Tongues* Kregel Publishers (Grand Rapids, Mich.) 1981 pg. 86

466 Wesley, op. cit. pg. 550

467 Mitchell, op. cit. pg. 190

468 Cf. Carson, op. cit. pg. 58

469 Henry, *Vol. 6* op. cit. pg. 461

470 Poole, *Vol. III* op. cit. pg. 585

471 Erasmus, *Collected Works Vol. 43* op. cit. pp. 165-166

472 Godet, *First Corintians* op. cit. pp. 627-628

473 Roberston & Plummer, op. cit. pg. 306

474 Ibid.

475 Laurence Browne, *Indian Church Commentaries - Acts of the Apostles* Diocesan Press (London, England) 1925 pg. 34

476 Bruce, *1 & 2 Corinthians* op. cit. pg. 133

477 *Liberty Commentary* op. cit. pg. 421

478 Lenski, *Corinthians* op. cit. pg. 600

479 MacArthur, *1 Corinthians* op. cit. pg. 381

480 Ibid.

481 *Liberty Commentary* op. cit. pg. 417

482 Baxter, *Tongues* op. cit. pg. 67

483 *Liberty Commentary* op. cit. pg. 222

484 MacArthur, *1 Corinthians* op. cit. pg. 381

485 Roy Harrisville, *Augsburg Commentary on N.W. 1 Corinthians* Augsburg Publishers (Minneapolis, MN) 1987 pg. 239

486 Ibid.

487 Montague, op. cit. pg. 248

488 I say "generally" for the commandment is often interpreted that way, but rarely enforced. For one thing, no one can say the prophecy is false until the time has passed. Second, the true prophets were usually the ones accused of false prophecy and heresy. Third, the passage itself says "speaking what I did not command." This requires knowledge of God's command, making the passing of a guilty verdict difficult.

489 Barnes, *Notes - One Volume ed.* op. cit. pg. 765

490 Ibid. pg. 776

491 Calvin, *Corinthians Vol. 1* op. cit. pg. 403

492 Godet, *First Corintians* op. cit. pg. 692
493 Montague, op. cit. pg. 258
494 Barnes, *Notes - One Volume ed.* op. cit. pg. 782
495 Bruce, *1 & 2 Corinthians* op. cit. pg. 135
496 MacArthur, *1 Corinthians* op. cit. pg. 393
497 Barnes, *First Corinthians* op. cit. pg. 294
498 Roberston & Plummer, op. cit. pg. 325
499 Tertullian, *Ante-Nicene Fathers Vol. III* op. cit. pg. 446
500 Ibid. pg. 677
501 Erasmus, *Collected Works Vol. 43* op. cit. pg. 172
502 Lenski, *Corinthians* op. cit. pg. 616
503 Origen, *Ancient Christian Commentary Vol. VII* op. cit. pg. 146
504 Godet, *First Corintians* op. cit. pg. 741
505 Wesley, op. cit. pg. 454
506 Godet, *First Corintians* op. cit. pg. 739
507 Hodge, *1 & 2 Corinthians* op. cit. pg. 305
508 Ironside, *First Corinthians* op. cit. pg. 454
509 *Liberty Commentary* op. cit. pg. 421
510 Tacitus, *Histories* 5.9.2
511 Josephus, "Antiquities" XVII.x.6 *The Complete Works of Flavius Josephus* Kregel Publishers (Grand Rapids, Mich.) 1981 pg. 371   Also compare with Josephus, "War" II.iv.2 *Complete Works* op. cit. pg. 473
512 www.haaretz.com/weekend/week-s-end/in-three-days-you-shall-live-1.218552
513 Calvin, *Corinthians Vol. 2* op. cit. pg. 10
514 MacArthur, *1 Corinthians* op. cit. pg. 402
515 Ironside, *First Corinthians* op. cit. pg. 462
516 Thayer, op. cit. pg. 456
517 Hodge, *1 & 2 Corinthians* op. cit. pg. 313
518 Cyprian, *Ante-Nicene Fathers Vol. V* Alexander Roberts & James Donaldson, eds., Charles Scribner (New York, NY) 1886 pg. 525
519 Lactantius, *Ante-Nicene Fathers Vol. VII* Alexander Roberts & James Donaldson, eds., Charles Scribner (New York, NY) 1886 pp. 122, 241
520 Henry, *Vol. 4* op. cit. pg. 905
521 Montague, op. cit. pg. 264
522 www.haaretz.com/weekend/week-s-end/in-three-days-you-shall-live-1.218552
523 Ironside, *First Corinthians* op. cit. pg. 494
524 Godet, *First Corintians* op. cit. pg. 811
525 Barnes, *First Corinthians* op. cit. pp. 322-323
526 Ironside, *First Corinthians* op. cit. pp. 491-492
527 Edwards, *"The Blank Bible" Part 2* op. cit. pg. 1062
528 Ironside, *First Corinthians* op. cit. pg. 497
529 Godet, *First Corintians* op. cit. pg. 814
530 Ibid. pg. 817
531 Ibid. pg. 815
532 Ibid. 817
533 Archer, op. cit. pg. 401
534 Ibid. pg. 402
535 Ibid.
536 Lenski, *Corinthians* op. cit. pg. 689
537 Montague, op. cit. pg. 275
538 Calvin, *Corinthians Vol. 2* op. cit. pg. 36
539 Ibid.
540 Ironside, *First Corinthians* op. cit. pg. 497

541 Barnes, *First Corinthians* op. cit. pp. 322-323
542 MacArthur, *1 Corinthians* op. cit. pg. 425
543 Ibid,
544 Ibid.
545 Calvin, *Corinthians Vol. 2* op. cit. pg. 36
546 *Liberty Commentary* op. cit. pg. 425
547 MacArthur, *1 Corinthians* op. cit. pp. 424-425
548 Roy Harrisville, *Augsburg Commentary on N.W. 1 Corinthians* Augsburg Publishers (Minneapolis, MN) 1987 pg. 270
549 Hodge, *1 & 2 Corinthians* op. cit. pg. 337
550 Cf. Tertullian, *Against Marcion* v.10 & *De. Ress Carn* 48
551 Godet, *First Corintians* op. cit. pg. 812
552 Didymus the Blind, *Ancient Christian Commentary Vol. VII* op. cit. pg. 166
553 Bruce, *1 & 2 Corinthians* op. cit. pg. 148
554 Farrar, op. cit. pg. 204
555 Wiersbe, *Be Wise* op. cit. pg. 153
556 MacArthur, *1 Corinthians* op. cit. pg. 424
557 Godet, *First Corintians* op. cit. pg. 811
558 Ibid. pg. 815
559 Tertullian, *Ante-Nicene Fathers Vol. III* op. cit. pg. 449
560 Ibid. pg. 582
561 Points borrowed in part from Hodge, *1 & 2 Corinthians* op. cit. pg. 337
562 *Liberty Commentary* op. cit. pg. 425
563 Calvin, *Corinthians Vol. 2* op. cit. pg. 57
564 Tertullian, *Ante-Nicene Fathers Vol. III* op. cit. pg. 452
565 Wesley, op. cit. pg. 459
566 Hippolytus, *Ante-Nicene Fathers Vol. V* Alexander Roberts & James Donaldson, eds., Charles Scribner (New York, NY) 1885 pg. 458
567 Darby, *Corinthians* op. cit. pg. ??
568 Bruce, *1 & 2 Corinthians* op. cit. pg. ??
569 Calvin, *Corinthians Vol. 2* op. cit. pg. 59
570 Hodge, *1 & 2 Corinthians* op. cit. pg. 356
571 Ambrosiaster, *Ancient Christian Commentary Vol. VII* op. cit. pg. 180
572 Barnes, *Notes - One Volume ed.* op. cit. pg. 800
573 David Wenham, "Unity and Diversity in the New Testament," *A Theology of the New Testament by George Eldon Ladd* Wm. B. Eerdmans (Grand Rapids, Mich.) 1974 pg. 698
574 Lenski, *Corinthians* op. cit. pg. 737
575 Cf. David Criswell, *Controversies in the Acts of the Apostles* Fortress Adonai (Dallas, TX) 2013 pg. 183
576 Cf. Murray Harris, "2 Corinthians," *Expositor's Bible Commentary Vol. 10* op. cit. pg. 302
577 Edwards, *"The Blank Bible" Part 2* op. cit. pg. 1069
578 William Kelly, *Notes on the 2nd Epistle to the Corinthians* G. Morrish (London, England) 1882 pg. 49
579 Origen, *Ante-Nicene Fathers Vol. IV* Alexander Roberts & James Donaldson, eds., Charles Scribner (New York, NY) 1886 pg. 242
580 Darby, *Corinthians* op. cit. pg. 189
581 Wesley, op. cit. pg. 467
582 Barnes, *Notes - One Volume ed.* op. cit. pg. 830
583 Dan Mitchell, *Second Corinthians* AMG Publishing (Chattanooga, TN) 2008 pg. 70
584 Erasmus, *Collected Works Vol. 43* op. cit. pg. 219
585 Warren Wiersbe, *Be Encouraged* Victor Books (Wheaton, Ill.) 1988 pg. 42
586 Hodge, *1 & 2 Corinthians* op. cit. pg. 448

587 H.A. Ironside, *Addresses on the Second Epistle to the Corinthians* Loizeaux Brothers (New York, NY) 1938 pg. 90

588 Calvin, *Corinthians Vol. 2* op. cit. pg. 182

589 Calvin, *Corinthians Vol. 2* op. cit. pg. 183

590 Albert Barnes, *Notes on Second Epistle of Paul to the Corinthians and Galatians* Harpers Brothers (New York, NY) 1853 pg. 62

591 Frederick Danker, Augsburg Commentary on the N.T. II Corinthians Augsburg Press (Minneapolis, MN) 1989 pg. 57

592 Cf. Gundry, op. cit. pg. 370; Tenney, op. cit. pg. 300

593 Poole, *Vol. III* op. cit. pg. 620

594 Cf. Gundry, op. cit. pg. 370; Tenney, op. cit. pg. 300

595 Gundry, op. cit. pg. 370

596 Henry, *Vol. 6* op. cit. pg. 492

597 Gundry, op. cit. pg. 372

598 Ibid. pg. 371

599 Murray Harris, "2 Corinthians," *Expositor's Bible Commentary Vol. 10* op. cit. pg. 305

600 Ibid.

601 Gundry, op. cit. pg. 372

602 See my notes in *Controversies in the Pentateuch*, *Controversies in the Old Testament Vol. 2*, and *Controversies in the Prophets* for a refutation of these idle speculations.

603 Cf. Gundry, op. cit. pg. 370; Tenney, op. cit. pg. 300

604 David Lowery, "2 Corinthians," *Bible Knowledge Commentary : New Testament* op. cit. pg. 552

605 Ibid.

606 Ibid.

607 Paul Feinberg, "The Meaning of Inerrancy," *Inerrancy* Norman Geisler, ed., Academic Books (Grand Rapids, Mich.) 1980 pg. 303

608 Thomas Stegman, *Second Corinthians* Baker Academic (Grand Rapids, Mich.) 2009 pg. 293

609 Rudolf Bultmann, *The Second Letter to the Corinthians* Augsburg Publishers (Minneapolis, MN) 1985 ed. pp. 244-245

610 Hodge, *1 & 2 Corinthians* op. cit. pg. 681

611 Ibid.

612 Frederick Danker, Augsburg Commentary on the N.T. II Corinthians Augsburg Press (Minneapolis, MN) 1989 pg. 210

613 Dan Mitchell, *Second Corinthians* AMG Publishing (Chattanooga, TN) 2008 pg. 70

614 Lenski, *Corinthians* op. cit. pg. 1332

615 Darby, *Corinthians* op. cit. pg. 254

616 Barnes, *Notes - One Volume ed.* op. cit. pg. 910

617 Hodge, *1 & 2 Corinthians* op. cit. pg. 681

618 James Montgomery Boice, "Galatians," *Expositor's Bible Commentary Vol. 10* op. cit. pg. 420

619 Donald Campbell, "Galatians," *Bible Knowledge Commentary : New Testament* op. cit. pg. 588

620 Ibid.

621 See *Apostles After Jesus* for a chronology of the Council of Jerusalem.

622 Cf. Gundry, op. cit. pp. 312-313; Tenney, op. cit. pg. 270

623 John Gill, "Commentary on the New Testament," John 19:25 E-Sword Software Commentary Series

624 Calvin, *Galatians* op. cit. pg. 34

625 John Calvin, *The Epistle of Paul the Apostle to the Galatian, Ephesians, Philippians, and Colossians* Wm. B. Eerdmans (Grand Rapids, Mich.) 1965. pg. 34

626 Robert Govett, *Govett on Galatians* Conley & Schoettle Pub. (Miami Springs, FL) 1981 ed. (1872) pg. 35

627 C.I. Scofield, *The Epistle to the Galatians* The Gospel Hour (Greenville, SC) 1903 pg. 10

628 Charles Elliot, *A Critical and Grammatical Commentary on St. Paul's Epistle to the Galatians* Warren Draper (Andover, CN) 1896 pg. 52

629 Albert Barnes, *Notes on Second Epistle of Paul to the Corinthians and Galatians* Harpers Brothers (New York, NY) 1854 pg. 312

630 Barnes, *Notes - One Volume ed.* op. cit. pg. 929

631 Farrar, op. cit. pg. 225

632 *Liberty Commentary* op. cit. pg. 478

633 John MacArthur, *Liberated for Life* Bible Comm. For Laymn (Glendale, CA) 1976 pg. 39

634 Ibid.

635 Warren Wiersbe, *Be Free* Victor Books (Wheaton, Ill.) 1976 pg. ??

636 Cf. Henry Morris, *Men of Science, Men of God* Master Books (El Cajon, CA) 19??

637 William Kelly, *Lectures on the Epistle of Paul to the Galatians* G. Morrish (London, England) n.d. pp. 69-70

638 Martin Luther, *A Commentary on St. Paul's Epistle to Galatians* Theodore Graebner, trans., Zondervan Publishers (Grand Rapids, Mich.) 1900 pg. 131

639 Martin Luther, as cited by Barnes, *Notes One Vol. Ed.* op. cit. pg. 335

640 Herman Riddarbas, *The Epistle of Paul to the Churches of Galatia* Wm. B. Eerdmans (Grand Rapids, Mich.) 1953 pg. 127

641 Heinrich Meyer, *Critical and Exegetical Commentary on the New Testament Vol. VII Galatians* T & T Clark (Edinburgh, Scotland) 1884 pg. 154

642 Edwards, *"The Blank Bible" Part 2* op. cit. pg. 1080

643 J.B. Lightfoot, *The Epistle of St. Paul to the Galatians* Zondervan Publishers (Grand Rapids, Mich.) 1865 (1957 ed.) pg. 140

644 F.F. Bruce, *Epistle to the Galatians – A Commentary on the Greek Text* Wm. B. Eerdmans (Grand Rapids, Mich.) 1982 pg. 165

645 John Calvin, *The Epistles of Paul the Apostle to the Galatians, Ephesians, Philippians, and Colossians* Wm. B. Eerdmans (Grand Rapids, Mich.) 1965 pg. 55

646 Ernest De Witt Burton, *A Critical and Exegetical Commentary on the Epistle to the Galatians* T & T Clark (Edinburgh, Scotland) 1921 pg. 172

647 Ibid. pg. 173

648 H.A. Ironside, *Galatians* Loizeaux Brothers (Neptune, NJ) 1941 pg. 110

649 John Nelson Darby, *Notes on the Epistle to the Galatians* G. Morrish (London, England) n.d. pg. 63

650 Wesley, op. cit. pg. 494

651 Darby, *Galatians* op. cit. pg. 63

652 Ironside, *Galatians* op. cit. pg. 110

653 Luther, *Galatians* op. cit. pg. 13o

654 Justin Martyr, *Ante-Nicene Fathers Vol. I* op. cit. pg. 247

655 Tertullian, *Ante-Nicene Fathers Vol. III* op. cit. pg. 164

656 Donald Guthrie, ed., *Galatians* The Attic Press (Greenwood, SC) 1969 pg. 103

657 F.F. Bruce, *Epistle to the Galatians – A Commentary on the Greek Text* Wm. B. Eerdmans (Grand Rapids, Mich.) 1982 pg. 274

658 Lightfoot, *Galatians* op. cit. pg. 225

659 Meyer, *Galatians* op. cit. pg. 350

660 Calvin, *Galatians, Ephesians, Philippians, and Colossians* op. cit. pg. 118

661 Warren Wiersbe, *Be Free* Victor Books (Wheaton, Ill.) 1976 pg. 157

662 Barnes, *Notes One Vol. Ed.* op. cit. pg. 397

663 Barnes, *Notes - One Volume ed.* op. cit. pg. 961

664 Riddarbas, *Galatia* op. cit. pg. 227

665 Robert Govett, *Govett on Galatians* Conley & Schoettle Pub. (Miami Springs, FL) 1981 ed. (1872) pg. 235

666   Charles Ellicott, *A Critical and Grammatical Commentary on St. Paul's Epistle to the Galatians* Warren Draper (Andover, Mass.) 1896 pg. 154

667   Edwards, *"The Blank Bible" Part 2* op. cit. pg. 1091

668   Ibid.

669   *Liberty Commentary* op. cit. pg. 500

670   Victorinus, *Marius Victorinus' Commentary on Galatians* Stephen Cooper, trans. Wm. B. Eerdmans (Grand Rapids, Mich.) 2005 pg. 345

671   Meyer, *Galatians* op. cit. pg. 350

672   John MacArthur, *Liberated for Life* Bible Comm. For Laymn (Glendale, CA) 1976 pg. 138

673   William Kelly, *Lectures on the Epistle of Paul to the Galatians* G. Morrish (London, England) n.d. pg. 197

674   Guthrie, *Galatians* op. cit. pg. 162

675   Ernest De Witt Burton, *A Critical and Exegetical Commentary on the Epistle to the Galatians* T & T Clark (Edinburgh, Scotland) 1921 pg. 358

676   William Kelly, *Lectures on Galatians* G. Morrish (London, England) n.d. pg. 196

677   Tenney, op. cit. pg. 321

678   Gundry, op. cit. pg. 397

679   Harold Hoehner, "Ephesians," *Bible Knowledge Commentary : New Testament* op. cit. pg. 614

680   Ibid.

681   Criswell, *Apostles After Jesus* op. cit. pp. 162-164

682   A. Skevington Wood, "Ephesians," *The Expositor's Bible Commentary* Vol. 11 Frank Gaebelein, ed., Zondervan Publishers (Grand Rapids, Mich.) 1986 pg. 5

683   Ibid. pg. 6

684   Cited in Ibid.

685   Summarized in Ibid. pg. 7

686   Ibid.

687   Hoehner, *Bible Knowledge Commentary : New Testament* op. cit. pg. 613

688   Young Kyu Kim, "Paleographical Dating of $\mathfrak{P}^{46}$ to the Later First Century," *Biblica*, lxix (1988) pp. 248-257

689   Wood, *Expositor's Bible Commentary* Vol. 11 op. cit. pg. 7

690   R. C. Sproul, Jr., *Almighty Over All* Baker Books (Grand Rapids, MI) 1999 pg. 54

691   www.gty.org/Resources/Articles/A189

692   thegospelcoalition.org/blogs/justintaylor/2012/02/13/is-god-the-author-of-sin-jonathan-edwards-answer/

693   James Montgomery Boice, *Ephesians* Baker Books (Grand Rapids, Mich.) 1988 pp. 15-16

694   J. I. Packer, *Evangelism and the Sovereignty of God* InterVarsity Press (Downer's Grove, IL) 1961 pg. 212

695   Charles Spurgeon, *Exposition of the Doctrine of Grace* Pilgrim Publications (Pasadena TX) n.d. pg. 298

696   Aristotle, *De Interpretatione* 19a23–5

697   Heinrich Bullinger, *Reformation Commentary on Scripture* Vol. X Galatians & Ephesians Gerard Bray, ed., IVP (Downers Grove, Ill.) 2011 pg. 240

698   John H. Gerstner, *A Primer on Free Will* Presbyterian and Reformed Publishing Co., (Phillipsburg, NJ) 1982 pg. 10

699   John MacArthur, *Ephesians* Moody Press (Chicago, Ill.) 1986 pg. 11

700   Ibid.

701   Arthur W. Pink, *The Sovereignty of God* Baker Books (Grand Rapids, Mich.) 1986 pg. 218

702   Bullinger, *Galatians & Ephesians* op. cit. pg. 240

703   *Liberty Commentary* op. cit. pg. 505

704   D.M. Lloyd-Jones, *Christian Unity Ephesians 4:1-16* Baker Books (Grand Rapids, Mich.) 1980 pg. 149

705   Dave Hunt, *What Love is This?* Loyal Publishing (Sisters, OR) 2002 pp. 75-78

706 F.F. Bruce, *The Epistle to the Ephesians* Pickering & Inglis (London, England) 1961 pg. 29
707 Marcus Barth, *The Broken Wall* Judson Press (Valley Forge, VA) 1959 pg. 17
708 R.C. Sproul, *The Purpose of God* Christan Focus Publications (Fearn, Scotland) 1994 pg. 23
709 G.G. Findlay, *Expositor's Bible – Ephesians* Armstrong & Sons (New York, NY) 1898 pg. 29
710 John MacArthur, *Ephesians* Moody Press (Chicago, Ill.) 1986 pg. 11
711 James Montgomery Boice, *Foundations of the Christian Faith* InterVarsity Press (Downers Grove, Ill.) 1986 pg. 476
712 H.A. Ironside, *In the Heavenlies* Loizeaux Brothers (New York, NY) 1937 pg. 26
713 Lewis Sperry Chafer, *The Ephesian Letter* Dunham Publications (Findlay, Ohio) 1953 pg. 37
714 Ibid. pp. 37-38
715 Warren Wiersbe, *Be Rich* Victor Books (Wheaton, Ill.) 1977 pg. 19
716 Arno Gaebelein, *God's Masterpiece* Our Hope (New York, NY) 1913 pg. 26
717 Gene Getz, *Looking Up When You Feel Down* Regal Books (Ventura, CA) 1985 pg. 33
718 H.A. Ironside, *In the Heavenlies* Loizeaux Brothers (New York, NY) 1937 pg. 29
719 Albert Barnes, *Barnes Notes on Ephesians, Philippians, & Colossians* Harper & Row (New York, NY) 1854 pg. 22
720 James Montgomery Boice, *Ephesians* Baker Books (Grand Rapids, Mich.) 1988 pp. 15-16
721 Charles Talbert, *Paedeia : Ephesians and Colossians* Baker Books (Grand Rapids, Mich.) 2007 pg. 45
722 John Calvin, *Reformation Commentary on Scripture Vol. X Galatians & Ephesians* Gerard Bray, ed., IVP (Downers Grove, Ill.) 2011 pg. 337
723 James Montgomery Boice, *Ephesians* Baker Books (Grand Rapids, Mich.) 1988 pg. 134
724 T.K. Abbott, *Critical & Exegetical Commentary – Epistles to the Ephesians* T & T Clark (Edinburgh, Scotland) 1897 pg. 112
725 Peter Williamson, *Catholic Commentary on Scripture : Ephesians* Baker Academics (Grand Rapids, Mich.) 2009 pg. 115
726 Three are mentioned by Charles Hodge, *Ephesians* Crossway Books (Wheaton, Ill.) 1994 pp. 131-133
727 Albert Barnes, *Barnes Notes on Ephesians, Philippians, & Colossians* Harper & Row (New York, NY) 1854 pg. 86
728 Barnes, *Notes - One Volume ed.* op. cit. pg. 993
729 Farrar, op. cit. pg. 280
730 John MacArthur, *Ephesians* Moody Press (Chicago, Ill.) 1986 pg. 137
731 Talbert, op. cit. pg. 110
732 Barnes, *Ephesians, Philippians, & Colossians* op. cit. pg. 87
733 Ironside, *In the Heavenlies* op. cit. pg. 183
734 Robert Govett, *Govett on Ephesians* Conley & Schoettle Publ. (Miami Springs, FL) 1981 ed. (1889) pg. 202
735 William Barclay, *The Letters to the Galatians and Ephesians* Westminister Press (Philadelphia, PN) 1954 pg. 160
736 Charles Hodge, *Ephesians* Crossway Books (Wheaton, Ill.) 1994 pg. 130
737 Walter Lock, *The Epistle to the Ephesians* Westminister Methuen & Co. (London, England) 1929 pg. 47
738 Barnes, *Ephesians, Philippians, & Colossians* op. cit. pg. 86
739 Archer, op. cit. pg. 404
740 Barnes, *Ephesians, Philippians, & Colossians* op. cit. pg. 88
741 Barnes, *2 Corinthians and Galatians* op. cit. pg. 993
742 Hodge, *Ephesians* op. cit. pg. 134
743 Wesley, op. cit. pg. 512
744 Ibid.
745 David Petersen & Kent Richards, *Interpreting Hebrew Poetry* Fortress Press (Minneapolis, MN) 1992 pg. 21
746 Abbott, op. cit. pg. 115

747 Charles Elliott, *Ephesians* Logmans Green (London, England) 1884 pg. 85
748 Ibid.
749 Barnes, *2 Corinthians and Galatians* op. cit. pg. 993
750 R.C. Sproul, *The Purpose of God* Christan Focus Publications (Fearn, Scotland) 1994 pg. 101
751 Govett, *Ephesians* op. cit. pg. 212
752 Ibid. pg. 211
753 F.F. Bruce, *The Epistle to the Ephesians* Pickering & Inglis (London, England) 1961 pg. 83
754 Chafer, *Ephesian Letter* op. cit. pg. 129
755 Edwards, *"The Blank Bible" Part 2* op. cit. pg. 1102
756 Dave Hunt, *In Defense of the Faith* Harvest House (Eugene, OR) 1996 pg. 332
757 Farrar, op. cit. pg. 280
758 Talbert, op. cit. pg. 111
759 E.g. Irenaeus, "Against Heresies," 4:27:2 *Ante-Nicene Fathers Vol. I* op. cit. pg. 499
760 *Ante-Nicene Fathers Vol. I* op. cit. pg. 309
761 Irenaeus, "Against Heresies," 5:31:1 *Ante-Nicene Fathers Vol. I* op. cit. pg. 560
762 Tertullian, "A Treatise on the Soul," 55 *Ante-Nicene Fathers Vol. III* op. cit. pg. 231
763 MacArthur, *Ephesians* op. cit. pg. 140
764 Cf. notes in D.M. Lloyd-Jones, *Christian Unity Ephesians 4:1-16* Baker Books (Grand Rapids, Mich.) 1980 pg. 157
765 John Calvin, *The Epistles of Paul the Apostle to the Galatians, Ephesians, Philippians, and Colossians* Wm. B. Eerdmans (Grand Rapids, Mich.) 1965 pg. 176
766 D.P. Simpson, ed., *Cassell's Latin Dictionary* MacMillan Press (New York, NY) 1959 pg. 304
767 Talbert, op. cit. pg. 111
768 Walter Lock, *The Epistle to the Ephesians* Westminister Methuen & Co. (London, England) 1929 pg. 48
769 Thomas Abbott, *A Critical and Exegetical Commentary on the Epistles to the Ephesians and to the Colossians* T & T Clark (Edinburgh, Scottland) 1897 pg. ??
770 John Calvin, *The Epistles of Paul the Apostle to the Galatians, Ephesians, Philippians, and Colossians* Wm. B. Eerdmans (Grand Rapids, Mich.) 1965 pg. 179
771 Although this is technically not true, it is arguable based on the use of the pronoun which is not required with Greek verbs. D.M. Lloyd-Jones, *Christian Unity Ephesians 4:1-16* Baker Books (Grand Rapids, Mich.) 1980 pg. 171
772 Cf. William Barclay, *The Letters to the Galatians and Ephesians* Westminister Press (Philadelphia, PN) 1954 pp. 171-172 & Abbott, *Ephesians* op. cit. pg. 117
773 *Liberty Commentary* op. cit. pg. 516
774 Boice, *Ephesians* op. cit. pg. 136
775 Abbott, *Ephesians* op. cit. pg. 118
776 Lock, *Ephesians* op. cit. pg. 48
777 Ironside, *In the Heavenlies* op. cit. pg. 187
778 MacArthur, *Ephesians* op. cit. pg. 142
779 Wiersbe, *Be Rich* op. cit. pp. 101-102
780 R.C. Sproul, *The Purpose of God* Christan Focus Publications (Fearn, Scotland) 1994 pg. 102
781 My point is that prophets cannot be restricted to the formation of the Bible or End Times prophecies. The term is often used in a wider sense.
782 Charles Elliott, *Ephesians* Logmans Green (London, England) 1884 pg. 87
783 Peter Williamson, *Catholic Commentary on Scripture : Ephesians* Baker Academics (Grand Rapids, Mich.) 2009 pg. 177
784 Hodge, *Ephesians* Crossway Books (Wheaton, Ill.) 1994 pg. 135
785 Farrar, op. cit. pp. 280-281
786 Ibid. pg. 281
787 Lock, *Ephesians* op. cit. pg. 48
788 Calvin, *Galatians, Ephesians, Philippians, and Colossians* op. cit. pg. 179
789 F.F. Bruce, *The Epistle to the Ephesians* Pickering & Inglis (London, England) 1961 pg. 96

790 Barnes, *Ephesians, Philippians, & Colossians* op. cit. pg. 100

791 Chafer, *Ephesian* op. cit. pg. 141

792 Calvin, *Galatians, Ephesians, Philippians, and Colossians* op. cit. pg. 192

793 Hodge, *Ephesians* op. cit. pg. 160

794 Ironside, *In the Heavenlies* op. cit. pg. 225

795 *Liberty Commentary* op. cit. pg. 519

796 Erasmus, *Collected Works Vol. 43* op. cit. pg. 336

797 Tertullian, *Ante-Nicene Fathers Vol. III* op. cit. pg. 685

798 Williamson, op. cit. pg. 132

799 Abbott, *Ephesians* op. cit. pg. 140

800 R.C. Sproul, *The Purpose of God* Christan Focus Publications (Fearn, Scotland) 1994 pg. 114

801 Abbott, *Ephesians* op. cit. pg. 140

802 Wesley, op. cit. pg. 514

803 MacArthur, *Ephesians* op. cit. pg. 185

804 Lock, *Ephesians* op. cit pg. 54

805 *Liberty Commentary* op. cit. pg. 519

806 Govett, *Ephesians* op. cit. pg. 230

807 Shepherd of Hermas, *Ante-Nicene Fathers Vol. II* Alexander Roberts & James Donaldson, eds., Charles Scribner (New York, NY) 1886 pg. 28

808 Karl Marx and Frederick Engels, *The Communist Manifesto* Article II, Progress Publishers (Moscow, Russia) 1848

809 Robert Gromacki, *Stand Perfect in Wisdom* Baker Books (Grand Rapids, Mich.) 1981 pg. 147

810 MacArthur, *Ephesians* op. cit. pg. 280

811 Ibid.

812 Wesley, op. cit.

813 Warren Wiersbe, *Be Complete* Victor Books (Wheaton, Ill.) 1983 pg. 124

814 Melick, Jr., *Philpipians, Colossians, and Philemon* op. cit. pg. 312

815 Erasmus Sarcerius, *Reformation Commentary Vol. X* op. cit. pg. 383

816 Erasmus, *Collected Works Vol. 43* op. cit. pg. 346

817 John Calvin, *The Epistles of Paul the Apostle to the Galatians, Ephesians, Philippians, and Colossians* Wm. B. Eerdmans (Grand Rapids, Mich.) 1965 pg. 205

818 Findlay, *Ephesians* op. cit. pg. 356

819 Farrar, op. cit. pg. 284

820 Wesley, op. cit. pg. 516

821 Ignatius, *Ante-Nicene Fathers Vol. I* op. cit. pg. 81

822 Ibid. pg. 95

823 Findlay, *Ephesians* op. cit. pg. 356

824 Hodge, *Ephesians* op. cit. pg. 183

825 Warren Wiersbe, *Be Rich* Victor Books (Wheaton, Ill.) 1977 pg. 141

826 Barnes, *Notes - One Volume ed.* op. cit. pg. 1010

827 R.C. Sproul, *The Purpose of God* Christan Focus Publications (Fearn, Scotland) 1994 pg. 131

828 *Liberty Commentary* op. cit. pg. 524

829 Govett, *Ephesians* op. cit. pg. 248

830 Newman, op. cit. pg. 7

831 Young, op. cit. pg. 181

832 Ignatius, *Ante-Nicene Fathers Vol. I* op. cit. pg. 95

833 David Dickson, *Reformation Commentary Vol. X* op. cit. pg. 384

834 *Reformation Commentary Vol. X* op. cit. pp. 383-387

835 F.F. Bruce, *The Epistles to the Colossians, to Philemon, and to Ephesians* Wm. B. Eerdmans (Grand Rapids, Mich.) 1984 pg. 164

836 I choose the word "modern feminist" to distinguish it from the original "suffragettes" who were largely Christians and pro-life. The famed "feminist" Susan B. Anthony, for example, believed that abortion was one of the worst crimes imaginable and even opposed abortion in cases of rape.

837 Ogilvie, *Loved and Forgiven* op. cit. pg. 128

838 Dave Hunt and T.A. McMahon, *The Seduction of Christianity* Harvest House (Eugene, OR) 1985 pg. 200

839 Ibid. pg. 195

840 I do not know where this quote originated exactly, but it is too good not to quote and all sources seem to attribute it to John Piper.

841 See my notes on Edoxus 21:2 in Controversies in the Pentateuch for a discussion of whether or not this applied only to Hebrew slaves (as some translations imply) or to all slaves.

842 This law is quoted by John MacArthur, *Ephesians* Moody Press (Chicago, Ill.) 1986 pg. 323

843 Bullinger, *Reformation Commentary Vol. X* op. cit. pg. 395

844 Wiersbe, *Be Complete* op. cit. pg. 130

845 Barclay, *Galatians and Ephesians* op. cit. pg. 212

846 Ibid.

847 Barnes, *Notes - One Volume ed.* op. cit. pg. 1076

848 Alexis de Tocqueville, *Democracy in America* Harper & Row (New York, NY) 1969 ed. (original 1800s) pp. 349-363

849 Barclay, *Galatians and Ephesians* op. cit. pg. 214

850 Findlay, *Ephesians* op. cit. pg. 388

851 Wesley, op. cit. pg. 518

852 R.C. Sproul, *The Purpose of God* Christan Focus Publications (Fearn, Scotland) 1994 pg. 141

853 Barnes, *Notes - One Volume ed.* op. cit. pg. 1010

854 Hodge, *Ephesians* op. cit. pg. 205

855 John MacArthur, *Colossians and Philemon* Moody Press (Chicago, Ill.) 1992 pp. 165-166

856 *Liberty Commentary* op. cit. pg. 526

857 See French deist Alexis de Tocqueville's notes in a day when slavery was still legal. De Tocqueville, *Democracy in America* op. cit. pp. 349-363

858 Robert Lightner, "Philippians," *Bible Knowledge Commentary : New Testament* op. cit. pg. 648

859 Gundy, op. cit. pg. 403

860 Homer Kent, "Philippians," *Expositor's Bible Commentary Vol. 11* op. cit. pg. 97

861 Tenney, op. cit. pg. 325

862 Ibid.

863 Ibid.

864 Charles Ellicott, *A Critical and Grammatical Commentary on Philippians, Colossians, and Philemon* Warren Draper (Boston, MS) 1876 pg. 32

865 Criswell, *Apostles After Jesus* op. cit. pg. 161

866 Gene Getz, *The Measure of a Christian* Regal Books (Venture, CA) 1983 pg. 49

867 James Montgomery Boice, *Philippians* Zondervan Publishers (Grand Rapids, Mich.) 1971 pg. 67

868 Gordon Fee, *Paul's Letter to the Philippians* Wm. B. Eerdmans (Grand Rapids, Mich.) 1995 pg. 123

869 John Walvoord, *Triumph in Christ* Moody Press (Chicago, Ill.) 1991 pg. 38

870 D. Martin Lloyd-Jones, *The Life of Joy* Baker Books (Grand Rapids, Mich.) 1989 pg. 61

871 J.B. Lightfoot, *St. Paul's Epistle to the Philippians* MacMillan (London, England) 1868 pg. 88

872 Kenneth Wuest, *Philippians* Wm. B. Eerdmans (Grand Rapids, Mich.) 1942 pg. 42

873 John Calvin, *Commentary on Philippians, Colossians, and Thessalonians* Wm. B. Eerdmans (Grand Rapids, Mich.) 1948 ed. pg. 37

874 Richard Melick, Jr., *New American Commentary Vol. 32 Philpipians, Colossians, and Philemon* Broadman Press (Nashville, TN) 1991 pg. 77

875 *Liberty Commentary* op. cit. pg. 536

876 Lloyd John Ogilvie, *Let God Love You* Word Books (Waco, TX) 1974 pg. 37

877 Karl Barth, *The Epislte to the Philippians* John Know Press (Louisville, KT) 2002 ed. pg. 31

878 Tertullian, *Ante-Nicene Fathers Vol. III* op. cit. pg. 472

879 John Walvoord, *Triumph in Christ* Moody Press (Chicago, Ill.) 1991 pg. 40

880 John Hutchinson, *Exposition of Paul's Epistle to the Philippians* Klock & Klock (Minneapolis, MN) 1887 (1985 ed.) pg. 52

881 Warren Wiersbe, *Be Joyful* Victor Books (Wheaton, Ill.) 1974 pg. 43

882 Farrar, op. cit. pg. 256

883 Hutchinson, *Philippians* op. cit.

884 John MacArthur, *Philippians* Moody Press (Chicago, Ill.) 2001 pg. 122

885 John Walvoord, *To Live is Christ* Dunham Publishers (Findlay, Ohio) 1961 pg. 42

886 H.C.G. Moule, *Studies in Philippians* Kregel Publishers (Grand Rapids, Mich.) 1893 (1977 ed.)

887 John Calvin, *Commentary on Philippians, Colossians, and Thessalonians* Wm. B. Eerdmans (Grand Rapids, Mich.) 1948 ed.

888 *Liberty Commentary* op. cit.

889 Martin Vincent, *A Critical and Exegetical Commentary on the Epistles to the Philippians and to Philemon* T & T Clark (Edinburgh, Scotland) 1897 pg. 59

890 Spurgeon, *Treasury Vol. 3* op. cit. pg. 473

891 Cf. Calvin, *Galatians, Ephesians, Philippians, and Colossians* op. cit. pg. 64

892 Spurgeon, *Treasury Vol. 3* op. cit. pg. 483

893 Farrar, op. cit. pg. 258

894 Barnes, *Notes - One Volume ed.* op. cit. pg. 1033

895 Heinrich Meyer, *Critical and Exegeticl Handbook to the Epistles to Philippians and Colossians* T & T Clark (Edinburgh, Scotland) 1898 pg. 110

896 Martin Vincent, *A Critical and Exegetical Commentary on the Epistles to the Philippians and to Philemon* T & T Clark (Edinburgh, Scotland) 1897 pg. 65

897 Charles Ellicott, *A Critical and Grammatical Commentary on Philippians, Colossians, and Philemon* Warren Draper (Boston, MS) 1876 pg. 63

898 MacArthur, *Philippians* op. cit. pg. 161

899 Ibid. pg. 162

900 Lloyd John Ogilvie, *Let God Love You* Word Books (Waco, TX) 1974 pg. 75

901 Thayer, op. cit. pg. 339

902 Erasmus, *Collected Works Vol. 43* op. cit. pg. 373

903 J. Harold Greenlee, *An Exegetical Summary of Philippians* SIL International (Dallas, TX) 1992 pg. 115

904 Robert Gromacki, *Philippians and Colossians* AMG Press (Chattanooga, TN) 2003 pg. 62

905 Hutchinson, *Philippians* op. cit. pg. 114

906 Thayer, op. cit. pg. 339

907 H.A. Ironside, *Notes on Philippians* Loizeaux Brothers (New York, NY) 1946 pg. 49

908 Ibid.

909 Walvoord, *Triumph in Christ* op. cit. pg. 63

910 Wuest, *Philippians* op. cit. pg. 73

911 Gene Getz, *The Measure of a Christian* Regal Books (Venture, CA) 1983 pg. 99

912 Barth, *Philippians* op. cit. pg. 72

913 *Liberty Commentary* op. cit. pg. ??

914 J. Dwight Pentecost, *The Joy of Living* Zondervan Publishers (Grand Rapids, Mich.) 1973 pg. 87

915 James Montgomery Boice, *Philippians* Zondervan Publishers (Grand Rapids, Mich.) 1971 pg. 162

916 D. Martin Lloyd-Jones, *The Life of Joy* Baker Books (Grand Rapids, Mich.) 1989 pg. 163

917 Cf. Norman Geisler, "Colossians," *Bible Knowledge Commentary : New Testament* op. cit. pg. 667

918 Curtis Vaughan, "Colossians," *Expositor's Bible Commentary : Vol. 11* op. cit. pg. 164

919 Tenney, op. cit. pg. 361

920 Cf. Albert Pike, *Morals and Dogmas* Freemason Society (Charleston, SC) 1871

921 Merrill Tenney, *New Testament Survey* Wm. B. Eerdmans (Grand Rapids, Mich.)1985 pg. 73
922 Justo Gonzalez, *The Story of Christianity Vol. 1* HarperCollins (San Francisco, CA) 1984 pg. 59
923 Ibid.
924 Kenneth Scott Latourette, *A History of Christianity Vol. 1* Harper & Row (New York, NY) 1953 pg. 123
925 Tenney, *New Testament Survey* op. cit. pg. 74
926 Gundry, *A Survey of the New Testament* op. cit. pg. 60
927 Gonzalez, *The Story of Christianity Vol. 1* op. cit. pg. 60
928 Gundry, *A Survey of the New Testament* op. cit. pg. 61
929 Gonzalez, *The Story of Christianity Vol. 1* op. cit. pg. 59
930 Cf. C.F.D. Moule, *The Epistles of Paul the Apostle to Colossians and to Philemon* Cambridge University (Cambridge, England) 1968 pg. 59-62
931 Eduard Schweizer, *The Letter to the Colossians* Augsburg (Minneapolis, MN) 1976 pg. 58
932 J.B. Lightfoot, *St. Paul's Epistles to the Colossans and to Philemon* MacMillan (London, England) 1875 pg. 210
933 Origen, *Ante-Nicene Fathers Vol. IV* op. cit. pg. 262
934 Robert Gromacki, *Stand Perfect in Wisdom* Baker Books (Grand Rapids, Mich.) 1981 pg. 63
935 Thayer, op. cit. pg. vii
936 Ibid. pg. 555
937 Ibid. pg. 556
938 Lloyd John Ogilvie, *Loved and Forgiven* G/L Publications (Glendale, CA) 1977 pg. 28
939 Robert Gromacki, *Philippians and Colossians* AMG Press (Chattanooga, TN) 2003 pg. 147
940 MacArthur, *Colossians and Philemon* op. cit. pg. 46
941 J.B. Lightfoot, *St. Paul's Epistles to the Colossans and to Philemon* MacMillan (London, England) 1875 pg. 212
942 William Barclay, *The All-Sufficient Christ* Westminster Press (Philadelphia, PN) 1963 pg. 58
943 *Liberty Commentary* op. cit. Colossians 1:15
944 Irenaeus, *Ante-Nicene Fathers Vol. I* op. cit. pg. 391
945 Tertullian, *Ante-Nicene Fathers Vol. III* op. cit. pg. 163
946 Frederick Westcott, *A Letter to Asia* MacMillan (London, England) 1914 pg. 51
947 Warren Wiersbe, *Be Complete* Victor Books (Wheaton, Ill.) 1983 pg. 48
948 Barnes, *Notes - One Volume ed.* op. cit. pg. 1062
949 This was the position of my college Calvinist Professor, John Pretlove.
950 Richard A. Young, *Intermediate New Testament Greek* Broadman & Holman (Nashville, TN) 1994 pg. 49
951 James Brooks & Carlton Winbery, *Syntax of New Testament Greek* University Press of America (Lanham, MD) 1979 pg. 33
952 Thayer, op. cit. pg. 133
953 Logos Bible Software (Greek notes in Colossians 1:16)
954 Lewis Radford, *The Epistle to the Colossians and the Epistle to Philemon* Methuen & Co. (London, England) 1931 pg. 168
955 Tatian, *Ante-Nicene Fathers Vol. II* op. cit. pg. 73
956 Douglas Moo, *The Letters to the Colossians and to Philemon* Wm. B. Eerdmans (Grand Rapids, Mich.) 2008 pg. 120
957 Calvin, *Galatians, Ephesians, Philippians, and Colossians* op. cit. pg. 309
958 Barnes, *Ephesians, Philippians, & Colossians* op. cit. pg. 285
959 F.F. Bruce, *The Epistles to the Colossians, to Philemon, and to Ephesians* Wm. B. Eerdmans (Grand Rapids, Mich.) 1984 pg. 57
960 Abbott, op. cit. pg. 210
961 Calvin, *Philippians, Colossians, and Thessalonians* op. cit. pg. 149
962 Robert Gromacki, *Philippians and Colossians* AMG Press (Chattanooga, TN) 2003 pg. 154
963 Newman, op. cit. pg. 8

964 Barnes, *Ephesians, Philippians, & Colossians* op. cit. pg. 288
965 Barnes, *Notes - One Volume ed.* op. cit. pg. 1064
966 Abbott, op. cit. pg. 220
967 Ibid.
968 H.A. Ironside, *Lectures on the Epistles to the Colossians* Loizeaux Brothers (New York, NY) 1928 pg. 50
969 Meyer, *Philippians and Colossians* op. cit. pg. 301
970 Charles Ellicott, *A Critical and Grammatical Commentary on Philippians, Colossians, and Philemon* Warren Draper (Boston, MS) 1876 pg. 163
971 Schweizer, *Colossians* op. cit. pg. 127
972 Origen, *Ante-Nicene Fathers Vol. III* op. cit. pg. 396
973 Ibid.
974 Lewis Radford, *The Epistle to the Colossians and the Epistle to Philemon* Methuen & Co. (London, England) 1931 pg. 223
975 Cf. Schweizer, op. cit. pg. 58
976 Radford, *Colossians and Philemon* op. cit. pg. 223
977 Calvin, *Galatians, Ephesians, Philippians, and Colossians* op. cit. pp. 329-330
978 Barnes, *Ephesians, Philippians, & Colossians* op. cit. pg. 301
979 Frederick Westcott, *A Letter to Asia* MacMillan (London, England) 1914 pg. 100
980 Warren Wiersbe, *Be Complete* Victor Books (Wheaton, Ill.) 1983 pg. 76
981 Barnes, *Notes - One Volume ed.* op. cit. pg. 1068
982 John MacArthur, *Colossians and Philemon* Moody Press (Chicago, Ill.) 1992 pg. 91
983 F.F. Bruce, *The Epistles to the Colossians, to Philemon, and to Ephesians* Wm. B. Eerdmans (Grand Rapids, Mich.) 1984 pg. 98
984 Tertullian, *Ante-Nicene Fathers Vol. III* op. cit. pg. 183
985 Wesley, op. cit.
986 H.A. Ironside, *Lectures on the Epistles to the Colossians* Loizeaux Brothers (New York, NY) 1928 pp. 71-72
987 Richard Melick, Jr., *New American Commentary Vol. 32 Philpipians, Colossians, and Philemon* Broadman Press (Nashville, TN) 1991 pg. 246
988 Farrar, op. cit. pg. 264
989 Erasmus, *Collected Works Vol. 43* op. cit. pg. 424
990 Gundry, op. cit. pg. 354
991 Tenney, op. cut. pg. 282
992 Robert Thomas, "1 Thessalonians," *Expositor's Bible Commentary Vol. 11* op. cit. pg. 232
993 Unger, op. cit. pg. 1088
994 A.R. Buckland, *St. Paul's 2nd Epistle to the Thessalonians* Union Press (Philadelphia, PN) 1909 pg. xxxiv
995 Ibid. pg. xxxiv
996 Ibid.
997 Cf. Ibid.
998 David Wenham, "Unity and Diversity in the New Testament," *A Theology of the New Testament by George Eldon Ladd* Wm. B. Eerdmans (Grand Rapids, Mich.) 1974 pg. 698
999 Buckland, *2nd Thessalonians* op. cit. pg. 46
1000 Ibid. pg. 45
1001 Ibid. pg. 46
1002 James Dunn, *Unity and Diversity in the New Testament* SCM Press (Canterbury, England) 2006 pg. 350
1003 *Liberty Commentary* op. cit. pg. 587
1004 Millard Erickson, *Christian Theology* Baker Book House (Grand Rapids, Mich.) 1983 pg. 1176
1005 Note that Abraham is also conscious.
1006 Thomas, "1 Thessalonians," *Expositor's Bible Commentary Vol. 11* op. cit. pg. 276

1007   Oliver Greene, *The Epistles of Paul the Apostle to the Thessalonians*   Gospel Hour (Greenville, SC) 1964 pg. 135

1008   Thomas Constable, "1 Thessalonians," *Bible Knowledge Commentary : New Testament*   op. cit. pg. 703

1009   Henry, op. cit. pg. 632

1010   Hippolytus, *Ante-Nicene Fathers Vol. V* op. cit. pg. 251

1011   Ibid. pg. 290

1012   George Milligan, *St. Paul's Epistles to the Thessalonians*   Fleming Revell (Old Tappan, NJ) 1982 pg. 60

1013   Ibid. pg. 56

1014   Gordon Fee, *The 1st and 2nd Letters to the Thessalonians*   Wm. B. Eerdmans (Grand Rapids, Mich.) 2009 pg. 178

1015   Ernest Best, *A Commentary on the 1st and 2nd Epistles to the Thessalonians*   Hendrickson Publishers (Peabody, Mass.) 1988 pg. 194

1016   Ibid. pg. 197

1017   John Walvoord, *The Thessalonian Epistles*   Dunham Publishing (Findlay, Ohio) 1955 pg. 72

1018   Ibid.

1019   Buckland, *2nd Thessalonians* op. cit. pg. 45

1020   Ibid. pg. 46

1021   Dunn, op. cit. pg. 350

1022   Mal Couch, *The Hope of Christ's Return*   AMG Publishers (Chattanooga, TN) 2001 pg. 123

1023   Tim LaHaye, Ed Hindson, eds., *The Popular Encyclopedia of Bible Prophecy*   Harvest House (Eugene, OR) 2004 pg. 144

1024   G.G. Findlay, *The Epistle of Paul the Apostle to the Thessalonians*   Cambridge University (Cambridge, England) 1904 pg. 98

1025   F.F. Bruce, *World Biblical Commentary Vol. 45   1 & 2 Thessalonians*   Word Books (Waco, TX) 1982 pg. 99

1026   Charles Ellicott, *Commentary on the Epistle of St. Paul to the Thessalonians*   Zondervan Publishers (Grand Rapids, Mich.) 1861 (1957 ed.)   pg. 62

1027   Charles Ryrie, *1st and 2nd Thessalonians*   Moody Press (Chicago, Ill.) 1959 pg. 66

1028   Gene Getz, *Standing Firm*   Regal Books (Venture, CA) 1986 pg. 136

1029   William Hendrickson, *New Testament Commentary Exposition of I & II Thessalonians*   Baker Books (Grand Rapids, Mich.) 1955 pg. 118

1030   Calvin, *Philippians, Colossians, and Thessalonians* op. cit. pg. 283

1031   William Kelly, *The Epistle of Paul the Apostle to the Thessalonians*   F.E. Race (London, England) 1912 pg. 51

1032   Buckland, *2nd Thessalonians* op. cit. pg. 46

1033   Cited in Poole, *Commentary   Vol. 3* op. cit. pg. 746

1034   Calvin, *Philippians, Colossians, and Thessalonians* op. cit. pg. 283

1035   Wesley, op. cit. pg. 547

1036   Ibid.

1037   James Grant, *1 & 2 Thessalonians*   Crossway Books (Wheaton, Ill.) 2011 pp. 124-128

1038   H.A. Ironside, *Addresses on the 1st and 2nd Epistles of Thessalonians*   Loizeaux Brothers (New York, NY) 1947 pg. 48

1039   Larry Crutchfield, "The Blessed Hope and the Tribulation in the Apostolic Fathers," *When the Trumpet Sounds*   Thomas Ice & Timothy Demy ed., Harvest House (Eugene, OR) 1995 pp. 85-103

1040   Ephraem the Syrian, *When the Trumpet Sounds*   Thomas Ice & Timothy Demy ed., Harvest House (Eugene, OR) 1995 pg. 113

1041   Marvin Rosenthal, *The Pre-Wrath Rapture of the Church*   Thomas Nelson Publishers (Nashville, Tn.) 1990 pg. 137

1042   http://www.thebereancall.org/node/1220

1043   Cf. John MacArthur, *The MacArthur New Testament Commentary Matthew 24-28*   Moody Bible Institute (Chicago, Ill.) 1985 pp. 71-75

1044 John Walvoord, *Thy Kingdom Come : Matthew* Moody Press (Chicago, Ill.) 1974 pg. 193

1045 Warren Wiersbe, *Be Loyal* Victor Books (Wheaton, Ill.) 1987 pg. 178

1046 Leon Morris, *The Gospel According to Matthew* Wm. Eerdmaans (Grand Rapids, Mich.) 1992 pg. 614

1047 www.thebereancall.org/node/1220

1048 Oliver Greene, *The Epistles of Paul the Apostle to the Thessalonians* Gospel Hour (Greenville, SC) 1964 pg. 153

1049 Douglas Moo, Paul Feinberg, *The Rapture : Pre- Mid- or Posttribulational?* Zondervan (Grand Rapids, Mich.) 1984 pg. 196

1050 Greene, *Thessalonians* op. cit. pg. 155

1051 James Grant, *1 & 2 Thessalonians* Crossway Books (Wheaton, Ill.) 2011 pg. 173

1052 Martin Luther, *Luther's Works Vol. 18* Concordia House Publishing (St. Louis, MS) 1958 pg. 90

1053 F.F. Bruce, *World Biblical Commentary Vol. 45 1 & 2 Thessalonians* Word Books (Waco, TX) 1982 pg. 109

1054 Ellicott, *Thessalonians* op. cit. pg. 68

1055 John Walvoord, *The Revelation of Jesus Christ* Moody Press (Chicago, Ill.) 1966 pg. 238

1056 Farrar, op. cit. pg. 174

1057 Barnes, *Notes - One Volume ed.* op. cit. pg. 1101

1058 See my extensive notes in *Controversies in the Prophets* and *Controversies in Revelation.*

1059 Irenaeus, *Ante-Nicene Fathers Vol. I* op. cit. pg. 559

1060 Leon Morris, *The Epistle of Paul to the Thessalonians* Wm. B. Eerdmans (Grand Rapids, Mich.) 1958 pp. 91-92

1061 Findlay, *Thessalonians* op. cit. pg. 110

1062 Ernest Best, *A Commentary on the 1st and 2nd Epistles to the Thessalonians* Hendrickson Publishers (Peabody, Mass.) 1988 pg. 207

1063 John Walvoord, *The Thessalonian Epistles* Dunham Publishing (Findlay, Ohio) 1955 pg. 81

1064 James Everett Frame, *A Critical and Exegetical Commentary on the Epistle of St. Paul to the Thessalonians* T & T Clark (Edinburgh, Scotland) 1912 pg. 180

1065 C.F. Hogg & W.E. Vine, *The Epistles of Paul the Apostle to the Thessalonians* Pickering & Inglis (London, England) 1929 pg. 155

1066 Walvoord, *Thessalonian Epistles* op. cit. pg. 80

1067 Robert van Kampen, *The Sign* Crossway Books (Wheaton, Ill.) 1992

1068 Cf. Charles Ryrie, *1st and 2nd Thessalonians* Moody Press (Chicago, Ill.) 1959 pg. 83

1069 Wesley, op. cit. pg. 549

1070 Thomas Constable, "1 Thessalonians," *The Bible Knowledge Commentary New Testament* Victor Books (Wheaton, Ill.) 1986 pg. 710

1071 William Hendrickson, *New Testament Commentary Exposition of I & II Thessalonians* Baker Books (Grand Rapids, Mich.) 1955 pg. 147

1072 Charles Ryrie, *1st and 2nd Thessalonians* Moody Press (Chicago, Ill.) 1959 pg. 83

1073 *Liberty Commentary* op. cit. ?

1074 William Hendrickson, *New Testament Commentary Exposition of I & II Thessalonians* Baker Books (Grand Rapids, Mich.) 1955 pg. 146

1075 Ibid. pg. 147

1076 Fee, *Thessalonians* op. cit. pp. 227-228

1077 Hendrickson, *I & II Thessalonians* op. cit. pg. 146

1078 E.J. Bicknell, *The 1st and 2nd Epistles to the Thessalonians* Methuen & Co. (London, England) 1932 pg. 64

1079 Hendrickson, *I & II Thessalonians* op. cit. pg. 148

1080 Charles Ryrie, *1st and 2nd Thessalonians* Moody Press (Chicago, Ill.) 1959 pg. 83

1081 F.F. Bruce, *World Biblical Commentary Vol. 45 1 & 2 Thessalonians* Word Books (Waco, TX) 1982 pg. 130

1082 Ibid. pg. 130

1083 Hendrickson, *I & II Thessalonians* op. cit. pg. 147
1084 Leon Morris, "Hebrews," *The Expositor's Bible Commentary Vol. 12* Zondervan Publishers (Grand Rapids, Mich.) 1978 pg. 44
1085 Ellicott, *Thessalonians* op. cit. pg. 84
1086 Fee, *Thessalonians* op. cit. pp. 227-228
1087 Ibid.
1088 Frame, *Thessalonians* op. cit. pp. 211-212
1089 Wesley, op. cit. pg. 549
1090 Ibid.
1091 Hendrickson, *I & II Thessalonians* op. cit. pg. 147
1092 E.J. Bicknell, *The 1st and 2nd Epistles to the Thessalonians* Methuen & Co. (London, England) 1932 pg. 64
1093 Calvin, *Romans* op. cit. pg. 267
1094 Calvin, *Philippians, Colossians, and Thessalonians* op. cit. pg. 304
1095 Ibid.
1096 William Kelly, *The Epistle of Paul the Apostle to the Thessalonians* F.E. Race (London, England) 1912 pg. 73
1097 Hendrickson, *I & II Thessalonians* op. cit. pg. 146
1098 Ibid.
1099 G.H. Lang, *The Epistle to the Hebrews* Schoettle Publishing (Hayesville, NC) 2008 pg. 82
1100 Poole, op. cit. pg. 752
1101 Greene, *Thessalonians* op. cit. pg. 196
1102 This is my own number for the interpreter may disagree, but the true percentage may actually be higher. As a rule of thumb I substitute "person" for "soul" in a given passage and see if it still makes sense. If it does, then "being" or "self" is probably, but not necessarily, the intended meaning.
1103 Friedrich Gesenius, *Gesenius' Hebrew and Chaldee Lexicon* Baker Books (Grand Rapids, Mich.) 1979 pg. 760
1104 Gesenius, op. cit. pg. 571
1105 Wesley, op. cit. pg. 549
1106 Origen, *Ante-Nicene Fathers Vol. IV* op. cit. pg. 579
1107 Walvoord, *Thessalonian Epistles* op. cit. pg. 99
1108 Poole, op. cit. pg. 752
1109 Greene, *Thessalonians* op. cit. pg. 196
1110 Ellicott, *Thessalonians* op. cit. pg. 84
1111 Thomas Constable, "1 Thessalonians," *The Bible Knowledge Commentary New Testament* Victor Books (Wheaton, Ill.) 1986 pg. 710
1112 Origen, *Ante-Nicene Fathers Vol. IV* op. cit. pg. 579
1113 Mal Couch, *The Hope of Christ's Return* AMG (Chattanooga, TN) 2001 pg. 156
1114 Greene, *Thessalonians* op. cit. pg. 197
1115 C.F. Hogg & W.E. Vine, *The Epistles of Paul the Apostle to the Thessalonians* Pickering & Inglis (London, England) 1929 pg. 205
1116 Robert Thomas, "1 Thessalonians," *The Expositor's Bible Commentary Vol. 11* Zondervan Publishers (Grand Rapids, Mich.) 1978 pg. 295
1117 Ibid.
1118 Greene, *Thessalonians* op. cit. pg. 194
1119 Robert Thomas, "2 Thessalonians," *The Expositor's Bible Commentary Vol. 11* Zondervan Publishers (Grand Rapids, Mich.) 1978 pg. 302
1120 Frame, *Thessalonians* op. cit. pg. 40
1121 Thomas, "2 Thessalonians," *Expositor's* op. cit. pg. 302
1122 Wesley Perschbacher, *Refresh Your Greek* Moody Press (Chicago, Ill.) 1989 pg. 795
1123 Cf. Thayer, op. cit. pg. 216
1124 Ibid.

1125 Brooks & Winbery, op. cit. pg. 104

1126 Young, op. cit. pg. 126

1127 Cf. Newman, op. cit. pg. 61

1128 Leon Morris, *The Epistle of Paul to the Thessalonians* Wm. B. Eerdmans (Grand Rapids, Mich.) 1958 pg. 125

1129 John Eaide, *A Commentary on the Greek Text of the Epistles of Paul to the Thessalonians* James & Klock (Minneapolis, MN) 1877 pg. 261

1130 Ibid.

1131 John Calvin, *Commentary on Philippians, Colossians, and Thessalonians* Wm. B. Eerdmans (Grand Rapids, Mich.) 1948 ed. pg. 324

1132 Bicknell, *Thessalonians* op. cit. pg. 73

1133 Frame, *Thessalonians* op. cit. pg. 248

1134 Cf. Bicknell, *Thessalonians* op. cit. pg. 74

1135 Couch, op. cit. pg. 205

1136 Donald Barnhouse, *Thessalonians* Zondervan Publishers (Grand Rapids, Mich.) 1977 pg. 96

1137 H.A. Ironside, *Addresses on the 1st and 2nd Epistles of Thessalonians* Loizeaux Brothers (New York, NY) 1947 pg. 90

1138 Cf. personal notes from Dave Hunt lecture.

1139 Seiss, op. cit. pg. 315

1140 Fee, *Thessalonians* op. cit. pg. 273

1141 Shepherd of Hermas, *Ante-Nicene Fathers Vol. II* op. cit. pg. 11

1142 Hippolytus, *Ante-Nicene Fathers Vol. V* op. cit. pg. 218

1143 Charles Ryrie, *1st and 2nd Thessalonians* Moody Press (Chicago, Ill.) 1959 pg. 100

1144 Walvoord, *Thessalonian Epistles* op. cit. pg. 117

1145 Ibid. pg. 118-120

1146 Bruce, *1 & 2 Thessalonians* op. cit. pg. 163

1147 Cf. Buckland, op. cit. pg. xxxiv

1148 Morris, *Thessalonians* op. cit. pg. 126

1149 Charles Ryrie, *1st and 2nd Thessalonians* Moody Press (Chicago, Ill.) 1959 pg. 103

1150 Fee, *Thessalonians* op. cit. pg. 282

1151 John Eaide, *A Commentary on the Greek Text of the Epistles of Paul to the Thessalonians* James & Klock (Minneapolis, MN) 1877 pg. 265

1152 Ellicott, *Thessalonians* op. cit. pg. 108

1153 Wesley, op. cit. pg. 551

1154 Charles Ryrie, *Dispensationalism Today* Moddy Pres (Chicago, Ill.) 1965 pg. 151

1155 Lewis Sperry Chafer, *Systematic Theology Vol. IV* Dallas Seminary Press (Dallas, TX) 1948 pg. 353

1156 Best, op. cit. pg. 282

1157 Bicknell, *Thessalonians* op. cit. pg. 74

1158 Erasmus, *Collected Works Vol. 43* op. cit. pg. 465

1159 Justin Martyr, *Ante-Nicene Fathers Vol. I* op. cit. pg. 253

1160 Tertullian, *Ante-Nicene Fathers Vol. III* op. cit. pg. 464

1161 Eaide, *Thessalonians* op. cit. pg. 266

1162 Fee, *Thessalonians* op. cit. pg. 282

1163 John Sweigart, "Is There a Departure in 2 Thessalonians 2:3?" *Conservative Theological Journal* Vol. 1 No. 15 August 2001 pg. 188

1164 Buckland, *Thessalonians* op. cit. pg. 89

1165 Eaide, *Thessalonians* op. cit. pg. 266

1166 Bruce, *Thessalonians* op. cit. pg. 167

1167 Wayne House, "Apostasia in 2 Thessalonians 2:3 : Apostasy or Rapture?" *When Trumpet Sounds* Harvest House (Eugene, OR) 1995 pg. 270

1168 Ibid. pg. 280

1169 Ibid.

1170 Sweigart, op. cit. pp. 197-199
1171 Ibid. pp. 193-197
1172 Ibid. pp. 191-193
1173 Donald Barnhouse, *Thessalonians* Zondervan Publishers (Grand Rapids, Mich.) 1977 pg. 99
1174 Arthur Pink, *The Antichrist* Bible Truth Publishers (Swengel, PA.) 1917
1175 Wesley, op. cit. pg. 551
1176 Frame, *Thessalonians* op. cit. pg. 253
1177 Stephen R. Miller, *Daniel : New American Commentary Vol. 18* Broadman & Holman (Nashville, TN.) 1994 pp. 301-302
1178 Emil Schurer, *A History of the Jewish People First Div. Vol. II* Hendrickson Publishers (Peabody, Mass.) 1890 (2009 ed.) pg. 99
1179 Clement of Alexandria, *Ante-Nicene Fathers Vol. II* op. cit. pg. 329
1180 Josephus, "War of the Jews," II .iv. 9. Comp*lete Works* op. cit. pg. 485
1181 en.wikipedia.org/wiki /First_Jewish–Roman_War
1182 Jonathan Edwards, *The Works of Jonathan Edwards Vol. 15 Notes on Scriptures* Yale University Press (New Haven, Conn.) 1998 pg. 420
1183 Farrar, op. cit. pg. 125
1184 Four of them are listed in C.F. Hogg & W.E. Vine, *The Epistles of Paul the Apostle to the Thessalonians* Pickering & Inglis (London, England) 1929 pp. 250-251
1185 Irenaeus, "Against Heresies," *Ante-Nicene Fathers Vol. 1* pg. 553
1186 Hippolytus, *Ante-Nicene Fathers Vol. V* op. cit. pg. 184
1187 Hogg & Vine, *Thessalonians* op. cit. pp. 250-251
1188 Ibid.
1189 David Criswell, *Controversies in Revelation* Fortress Adonai (Dallas, TX) 2007 pg. 107
1190 Irenaeus, "Against Heresies," *Ante-Nicene Fathers Vol. 1* pg. 553
1191 Hippolytus, *Ante-Nicene Fathers Vol. V* op. cit. pg. 184
1192 See Criswell, *Controversies in Revelation* op. cit. for extensive footnotes and citations of these authors.
1193 Ibid.
1194 Joseph Mede, *The Apostasy of the Latter Times* Macintosh Printer (London, England) 1865 ed. pg. 211
1195 Cf. Bicknell, *Thessalonians* op. cit. pg. 76
1196 Farrar, op. cit. pg. 179
1197 Cf. Barnes, *Notes - One Volume ed.* op. cit. pg. 1115
1198 George Milligan, *St. Paul's Epistles to the Thessalonians* Fleming Revell (Old Tappan, NJ) 1982 pg. 101
1199 Erasmus, *Collected Works Vol. 43* op. cit. pg. 467
1200 Hogg & Vine, *Thessalonians* op. cit. pg. 259
1201 Hendrickson, *I & II Thessalonians* op. cit. pg. 181
1202 See Criswell, *Controversies in Revelation* op. cit.
1203 Findlay, *Thessalonians* op. cit. pg. 177
1204 Constable, "2 Thessalonians," *Bible Knowledge* op. cit. pg. 719
1205 Frame, *Thessalonians* op. cit. pg. 262
1206 Leon Morris, *The Epistle of Paul to the Thessalonians* Wm. B. Eerdmans (Grand Rapids, Mich.) 1958 pg. 129
1207 Ibid.
1208 Henry, *Vol. 6* op. cit. pg. 643
1209 Wesley, op. cit. pg. 552
1210 Walvoord, *Thessalonian Epistles* op. cit. pg. 122
1211 Poole, *Vol. 3* op. cit. pg. 761
1212 Barnes, *Notes - One Volume ed.* op. cit. pg. 1115
1213 Ryrie, *Thessalonians* op. cit. pg. 110
1214 Cf. Frame, *Thessalonians* op. cit. pg. 262

1215 Ryrie, *Thessalonians* op. cit. pg. 109
1216 Calvin, *Philippians, Colossians, and Thessalonians* op. cit. pg. 334
1217 Eaide, *Thessalonians* op. cit. pg. 279
1218 Best, *Thessalonians* op. cit. pp. 296-297
1219 Ryrie, *Thessalonians* op. cit. pg. 111
1220 Walvoord, *Thessalonian Epistles* op. cit. pg. 124
1221 H.A. Ironside, *Addresses on the 1ˢᵗ and 2ⁿᵈ Epistles of Thessalonians* Loizeaux Brothers (New York, NY) 1947 pg. 97
1222 George Milligan, *St. Paul's Epistles to the Thessalonians* Fleming Revell (Old Tappan, NJ) 1982 pg. 101
1223 Couch, op. cit. pg. 220
1224 Donald Barnhouse, *Thessalonians* Zondervan Publishers (Grand Rapids, Mich.) 1977 pg. 100
1225 Greene, *Thessalonians* op. cit. pg. 267
1226 Ironside, *Thessalonians* op. cit. pp. 97-98
1227 Constable, op. cit. pg. 719
1228 Walvoord, *Thessalonian Epistles* op. cit. pg. 126
1229 Bruce, *1 & 2 Thessalonians* op. cit. pg. 171
1230 Greene, *Thessalonians* op. cit. pg. 267
1231 Barnhouse, *Thessalonians* op. cit. pg. 101
1232 Henry, *Vol. 6* op. cit. pg. 644
1233 Poole, *Vol. 3* op. cit. pg. 763
1234 Constable, op. cit. pg. 720
1235 Wesley, op. cit. pg. 552
1236 Robert Thomas, op. cit. pg. 328
1237 Archer, op. cit. pg. 410
1238 Bicknell, *Thessalonians* op. cit. pg. 79
1239 Barnes, *Notes - One Volume ed.* op. cit. pg. 1116
1240 Barnhouse, *Thessalonians* op. cit. pg. 101
1241 Thieleman J. van Braght, *Martyrs' Mirror* Herald Press (Scottdale, PN) 1950 ed. (1660 orig.) pg. 98
1242 Tenney, op. cit. pg. 335
1243 Criswell, *Apostles After Jesus* op. cit. pg. 156
1244 Ralph Earle, "1 Timothy," *Expositors Vol. 11* op. cit. pg. 341
1245 A. Duane Litfin, "1 Timothy," *Bible Knowledge* op. cit. pg. 727
1246 Earle, "1 Timothy," *Expositors Vol. 11* op. cit. pg. 341
1247 Litfin, "1 Timothy," *Bible Knowledge* op. cit. pg. 728
1248 Earle, "1 Timothy," *Expositors Vol. 11* op. cit. pg. 341
1249 Litfin, "1 Timothy," *Bible Knowledge* op. cit. pg. 728
1250 Earle, "1 Timothy," *Expositors Vol. 11* op. cit. pg. 341
1251 This counts Titus as the critics include that in their number counting [Tim LaHaye, Gen. Ed., *Tim LaHaye Prophecy Study Bible* AMG Publishers (Chattanooga, TN) 2001]
1252 A. Duane Litfin, "1 Timothy," *Bible Knowledge* op. cit. pg. 728
1253 Cited by Earle, "1 Timothy," *Expositors Vol. 11* op. cit. pg. pg. 343
1254 D. Martin Lloyd-Jones, *Love So Amazing* Baker Books (Grand Rapids, Mich.) 1995 pg. 229
1255 Risto Saarinen, *The Pastoral Epistles with Philemon and Jude* Brazos Press (Grand Rapids, Mich.) 2008 pg. 55
1256 C.S. Lewis, *The Screwtape Letters* Collier (New York, NY) 1961 pg. 47
1257 Donald Guthrie, *The Pastoral Epistles* Wm. B. Eerdmans (Grand Rapids, Mich.) 1957 pg. 74
1258 J.P. Greene, *The Pastoral Epistles* S.B.C. (Nashville, TN) 1915 pg. 36
1259 Oliver Green, *The Epistles of Paul the Apostle to Timothy and Titus* Gospel Hour (Greenville, SC) 1964 pg. 91
1260 Charles Ellicott, *A Critical and Grammatical Commentary on the Pastoral Epistles* Warren Draper (Philadelphia, PN) 1884 pg. 50

1261 H.A. Ironside, *Addresses on the 1st and 2nd Epistles of Timothy, Titus, and Philemon* Loizeaux Brothers (New York, NY) 1947 pg. 65

1262 John MacArthur, *1 Timothy* Moody (Chicago, Ill.) 1995 pg. 79

1263 John Calvin, *1, 2 Timothy & Titus* Crossway Books (Wheaton, Ill.) 1998 pg. 47

1264 Cornelius Stam, *Commentary on the Pastoral Epistles of Paul the Apostle* Berean Bible Society (Chicago, Ill.) 1983 pg. 64

1265 Patrick Fairbairn, *Commentary on the Pastarol Epistles* Zondervan Publishers (Grand Rapids, Mich.) 1874 (1956 ed.) pg. 125

1266 Warren Wiersbe, *Be Faithful* Victor Books (Wheaton, Ill.) 1987 pg. 35

1267 Risto Saarinen, *The Pastoral Epistles with Philemon and Jude* Brazos Press (Grand Rapids, Mich.) 2008 pg. 57

1268 Samuel Ngewa, *1 & 2 Timothy and Titus* Zondervan Publishers (Grand Rapids, Mich.) 2009 pg. 51

1269 Louis deToqueville, *Democracy in America Vol. 2* Perrenial Library (New York, NY) 1966 ed. pg. 591

1270 Ibid. pg. 592

1271 Ngewa, op. cit. pg. 52

1272 MacArthur, *1 Timothy* op. cit. pg. 212

1273 William Barclay, *The Letters to Timothy, Titus, and Philemon* Westminister Press (Philadephia, PN) 1956 pg. 77

1274 George Montague, *First Second Timothy, Titus* Baker Books (Grand Rapids, Mich.) 2008 pg. 64

1275 Ibid.

1276 Guthrie, *The Pastoral Epistles* op. cit. pg. 76

1277 Green, *Timothy and Titus* op. cit. pg. 96

1278 Charles Erdman, *The Pastoral Epistles of Paul* Westminister Press (Philadephia, PN) 1923 pg. 35

1279 Guthrie, *The Pastoral Epistles* op. cit. pg. 76

1280 Homer Kent, *The Pastoral Epistles* Moody (Chicago, Ill.) 1958 pg. 113

1281 Fairbairn, *Pastarol Epistles* op. cit. pg. 127

1282 Ellicott, *Pastoral Epistles* op. cit. pg. 52

1283 John Calvin, *1, 2 Timothy & Titus* Crossway Books (Wheaton, Ill.) 1998 pg. 47

1284 Warren Wiersbe, *Be Faithful* Victor Books (Wheaton, Ill.) 1987 pg. 37

1285 J.P. Greene, *The Pastoral Epistles* S.B.C. (Nashville, TN) 1915 pg. 38

1286 Ibid. pg. 37

1287 Cornelius Stam, *Commentary on the Pastoral Epistles of Paul the Apostle* Berean Bible Society (Chicago, Ill.) 1983 pg. 66

1288 Calvin, *1, 2 Timothy & Titus* op. cit. pg. 48

1289 Ironside, *Timothy, Titus, and Philemon* op. cit. pg. 70

1290 J.N.D. Kelly, *A Commentary on the Pastoral Epistles* Adam and Charles Black (London, England) 1963 pg. 68

1291 John MacArthur, *1 Timothy* Moody (Chicago, Ill.) 1995 pg. 86

1292 Ibid. pg. 87

1293 Marx and Engels, *Communist Manifesto* Article II, op. cit.

1294 Allan Bloom, *The Closing of the American Mind* Simon and Schuster (New York, NY) 1987 pg. 119

1295 Ibid. pg. 115

1296 www.rediff.com/movies/report/slide-show-1-rani-when-i-admit-my-children-to-school-i-will-change-my-name/20140625.htm.

1297 Louis deToqueville, *Democracy in America Vol. 2* Perrenial Library (New York, NY) 1966 ed. pg. 590

1298 Saarinen, op. cit. pg. 57

1299 Wesley, op. cit. pg. 559

1300 Cornelius Stam, *Commentary on the Pastoral Epistles of Paul the Apostle* Berean Bible Society (Chicago, Ill.) 1983 pg. 66
1301 *Liberty Commentary* op. cit. pg. 609
1302 Green, *Timothy and Titus* op. cit. pg. 97
1303 Ironside, *Timothy, Titus, and Philemon* op. cit. pg. 71
1304 Dave Hunt, *The Cult Explosion* Harvest House (Eugene, OR) 1983 pg. 115
1305 Guthrie, *The Pastoral Epistles* op. cit. pg. 77
1306 Ellicott, *Pastoral Epistles* op. cit. pg. 53
1307 Calvin, *Timothy & Titus* op. cit. pg. 48
1308 Charles Erdman, *The Pastoral Epistles of Paul* Westminister Press (Philadelphia, PN) 1923 pg. 36
1309 James Montgomery Boice, *The Foundations of the Christian Faith* InterVarsity Press (Downers Grove, Ill) 1986, revised, pg 195
1310 Warren Wiersbe, *Be Faithful* Victor Books (Wheaton, Ill.) 1987 pg. 38
1311 John MacArthur, *1 Timothy* Moody (Chicago, Ill.) 1995 pg. 88
[1312] Cf. Benjamin Davidson, *The Analytical Hebrew and Chaldee Lexicon* Zondervan House (Grand Rapids, Mich.) 1848 pg. 532
1313 Gordon Fee, *1 & 2 Timothy, Titus* Harper & Row (San Francisco, CA) 1984 pg. 38
1314 Stam, *Pastoral Epistles* op. cit. pg. 67
1315 Ibid. pg. 68
1316 Walter Lock, *A Critical and Exegetical Commentary on the Pastoral Epistles* T & T Clark (London, England) 1924 pg. 33
1317 Farrar, op. cit. pg. 291
1318 Lock, *Pastoral Epistles* op. cit. pg. 32
1319 William Barclay, *The Letters to Timothy, Titus, and Philemon* Westminister Press (Philadephia, PN) 1956 pg. 79
1320 Bloom, op. cit., pg 128
1321 Ibid. pp. 65-66
1322 Earle, *Expositors Vol. 11* op. cit. pg. 364
1323 Litfin, *Bible Knowledge* op. cit. pg. 736
1324 Poole, op. cit. pg. 779
1325 Henry, op. cit. pg. 656
1326 Farrar, op. cit. pg. 178
1327 Barnes, *Notes - One Volume ed.* op. cit. pg. 1145
1328 Stam, *Pastoral Epistles* op. cit.
1329 Gordon Fee, *1 & 2 Timothy, Titus* Harper & Row (San Francisco, CA) 1984 pg. 60
1330 Ironside, *Timothy, Titus, and Philemon* op. cit. pg. 93
1331 Ibid.
1332 Guthrie, *The Pastoral Epistles* op. cit. pg. 91
1333 Green, *Timothy and Titus* op. cit. pg. 144
1334 Calvin, *Timothy & Titus* op. cit. pg. 66
1335 Litfin, *Bible Knowledge* op. cit. pg. 739
1336 Tertullian, *Ante-Nicene Fathers Vol. III* op. cit. pg. 246
1337 Ellicott, *Pastoral Epistles* op. cit. pg. 69
1338 Fairbairn, *Pastarol Epistles* op. cit. pg. 159
1339 Barnes, *Notes - One Volume ed.* op. cit. pg. 1147
1340 Calvin, *Timothy & Titus* op. cit. pg. 69
1341 Ibid.
1342 Wesley, op. cit. pg. 561
1343 George Montague, *First Second Timothy, Titus* Baker Books (Grand Rapids, Mich.) 2008 pg. 93
1344 Lock, *Pastoral Epistles* op. cit. pg. 47

1345 J.N.D. Kelly, *A Commentary on the Pastoral Epistles* Adam and Charles Black (London, England) 1963 pg. 95

1346 Ellicott, *Pastoral Epistles* op. cit. pg. 70

1347 Green, *Timothy and Titus* op. cit. pg. 151

1348 Farrar, op. cit. pg. 292

1349 Edwards, *"The Blank Bible" Part 2* op. cit. pg. 1128

1350 Greene, *The Pastoral Epistles* op. cit. pg. 58

1351 George Montague, *First Second Timothy, Titus* Baker Books (Grand Rapids, Mich.) 2008 pg. 93

1352 Tertullian, *Ante-Nicene Fathers Vol. IV* op. cit. pg. 71

1353 Ibid. pg. 69

1354 David Criswell, *Rise and Fall of the Holy Roman Empire* Publish America (Baltimore, MD) 2005 pp. 137-138

1355 Calvin, *Timothy & Titus* op. cit. pg. 79

1356 *Liberty Commentary* op. cit. pg. 614

1357 Ironside, *Timothy, Titus, and Philemon* op. cit. pp. 113-114

1358 John MacArthur, *1 Timothy* Moody (Chicago, Ill.) 1995 pg. 212

1359 Calvin, *Timothy & Titus* op. cit. pg. 88

1360 *Liberty Commentary* op. cit. pg. 615

1361 Ibid.

1362 Ironside, *Timothy, Titus, and Philemon* op. cit. pg. 119

1363 Guthrie, *The Pastoral Epistles* op. cit. pg. 100

1364 William Barclay, *The Letters to Timothy, Titus, and Philemon* Westminister Press (Philadephia, PN) 1956 pg. 132

1365 Greene, *The Pastoral Epistles* op. cit. pg. 71

1366 Spurgeon, *Treasury Vol. 3* op. cit. pg. 811

1367 Thayer, op. cit. pg. 352

1368 Ibid. pg. 411

1369 Young, op. cit. pg. 201

1370 Tertullian, *Ante-Nicene Fathers Vol. III* op. cit. pg. 677

1371 Young, op. cit. pg. 143

1372 Thayer, op. cit. pg. 272

1373 Barclay, *Timothy, Titus, and Philemon* op. cit. pg. 200

1374 Charles Erdman, *The Pastoral Epistles of Paul* Westminister Press (Philadephia, PN) 1923 pg. 108

1375 Greene, *The Pastoral Epistles* op. cit. pg. 121

1376 Wesley, op. cit. pg. 571 (This is not Wesley's personal view. He accepted a literal resurrection in the future).

1377 Barnes, *Notes - One Volume ed.* op. cit. pg. 1175

1378 *Liberty Commentary* op. cit. pg. 624

1379 Ellicott, *Pastoral Epistles* op. cit. pg. 144

1380 Fairbairn, *Pastarol Epistles* op. cit. pg. 347

1381 Lock, *Pastoral Epistles* op. cit. pg. 99

1382 Calvin, *Timothy & Titus* op. cit. pg. 139

1383 Kelly, *Pastoral Epistles* op. cit. pg. 185

1384 How could he? If there is no bodily resurrection then there is really no need for heaven at all. We would just be spirits wandering lost like a Hollywood horror film.

1385 Fairbairn, *Pastarol Epistles* op. cit. pg. 347

1386 John MacArthur, *2 Timothy* Moody (Chicago, Ill.) 1995 pg. 80

1387 Fairbairn, *Pastarol Epistles* op. cit. pg. 347

1388 Barclay, *Timothy, Titus, and Philemon* op. cit. pg. 211

1389 Fairbairn, *Pastarol Epistles* op. cit. pg. 365

1390 Barnes, *Notes - One Volume ed.* op. cit. pg. 1176

1391 Stam, *Pastoral Epistles* op. cit. pg. 193

1392 Dave Hunt and T.A. McMahon, *The Seduction of Christianity* Harvest House (Eugene, OR) 1985 pg. 195

1393 Ibid. pg. 200

1394 I do not know where this quote originated exactly, but it is too good not to quote and all sources seem to attribute it to John Piper.

1395 Gordon Fee, *1 & 2 Timothy, Titus* Harper & Row (San Francisco, CA) 1984 pg. 220

1396 Greene, *The Pastoral Epistles* op. cit. pg. 131

1397 Ngewa, op. cit. pg. 259

1398 Ironside, *Timothy, Titus, and Philemon* op. cit. pg. 213

1399 Ibid. pg. 218

1400 Green, *Timothy and Titus* op. cit. pp. 329-332

1401 Wesley, op. cit. pg. 572

1402 So called "Obamacare" imposed $1000 a day fines to even the smallest of Christian businesses for refusing to violate our faith and pass out abortion pills to our students, orphans, and/or employees. The Obama Administration even threatened a group of nuns who ran an orphanage with fines which would have run into the millions. Since the average Christian businessman only makes around $50,000 a year, it is not hard to see how the law was used to deny us the right to run a business and technically could have resulted in our arrest for "failure to pay taxes" had the Supreme Court not narrowly overturned the Abortion Mandate. Even then Obama and his minions began a campaign to demonize us and accuse us of waging a "war on women" for refusing to pay for their abortions. At least one Holocaust survivor has compared this to 1930s Germany when Hitler was stirring up antagonism against the Jews.

1403 Fairbairn, *Pastorol Epistles* op. cit. pg. 374

1404 Wesley, op. cit. pg. 572

1405 Calvin, *Timothy & Titus* op. cit. pg. 198

1406 Barnes, *Notes - One Volume ed.* op. cit. pg. 1179

1407 Lock, *Pastoral Epistles* op. cit. pg. 227

1408 Ibid. pg. 110

1409 Saarinen, op. cit. pg. 156

1410 Guthrie, *The Pastoral Epistles* op. cit. pg. 164

1411 Farrar, op. cit. pg. 301

1412 Ibid.

1413 MacArthur, *2 Timothy* op. cit. pg. 142

1414 Ellicott, *Pastoral Epistles* op. cit. pg. 162

1415 Barnes, *Notes - One Volume ed.* op. cit. pg. 1180

1416 Green, *Timothy and Titus* op. cit. pg. 356

1417 Ellicott, *Pastoral Epistles* op. cit. pg. 164

1418 Charles Erdman, *The Pastoral Epistles of Paul* Westminister Press (Philadephia, PN) 1923 pg. 116

1419 Ngewa, op. cit. pg. 287

1420 Barclay, *Timothy, Titus, and Philemon* op. cit. pp. 229-232

1421 Henry Morris, *Men of Science, Men of God* Master Books (El Cajon, CA) 1982 pg. 49

1422 Ibid. pp. 66-67

1423 Barclay, *Timothy, Titus, and Philemon* op. cit. pp. 229-232

1424 Ibid.

1425 Wiersbe, *Be Faithful* op. cit. pg. 160

1426 Calvin, *Timothy & Titus* op. cit. pg. 155

1427 Stam, *Pastoral Epistles* op. cit. pg. 207

1428 Irenaeus, *Ante-Nicene Fathers Vol. I* op. cit. pg. 389

1429 Greene, *The Pastoral Epistles* op. cit. pg. 151

1430 Calvin, *Timothy & Titus* op. cit. pg. 159

1431 "The Acts of the Holy Apostles Peter and Paul," *Ante-Nicene Fathers* Vol. 8 Alexander Roberts & James Donaldson, eds., Charles Scribner (New York, NY) 1886 pg. 486
1432 Unger, op. cit. pg. 1104
1433 Ibid. pg. 856
1434 Ibid.
1435 Cf. DeToqueville, op. cit.
1436 Mal Couch, *A Biblical Theology of the Church* Kregel (Grand Rapids, Mich.) 1999 pg. 157
1437 Millard Erickson, *Christian Theology* Baker House (Grand Rapids, Mich.) 1983 pg. 1076
1438 See Samuel Elliot Morison, *The Oxford History of the American People* Oxford Press (New York, NY) 1965
1439 Erickson, op. cit. pg. 1077
1440 Ibid. pg. 1075
1441 Barnes, *Notes - One Volume ed.* op. cit. pg. 1192
1442 Couch, *Biblical Theology* op. cit. pg. 158
1443 Erickson, op. cit. pg. 1078
1444 Ibid. pg. 1079
1445 Ibid.
1446 Couch, *Biblical Theology* op. cit. pg. 158
1447 Erickson, op. cit. pg. 1082
1448 Sir Robert Anderson, "Misunderstood Texts of the Bible," *The Collected Works of Sir Robert Anderson* David Criswell, ed., Fortress Adonai (Dallas, TX) 2010 pg. 318
1449 Lock, *Pastoral Epistles* op. cit. pg. 130
1450 Green, *Timothy and Titus* op. cit. pg. 415
1451 Calvin, *Timothy & Titus* op. cit. pg. 183
1452 Wesley, op. cit. pg. 577
1453 Tertullian, *Ante-Nicene Fathers Vol. IV* op. cit. pg. 69
1454 Ibid. pg. 71
1455 Fairbairn, *Pastarol Epistles* op. cit. pg. 261
1456 Tertullian, *Ante-Nicene Fathers Vol. III* op. cit. pg. 71
1457 Polycarp, *Ante-Nicene Fathers Vol. I* op. cit. pg. 41
1458 Ironside, *Timothy, Titus, and Philemon* op. cit. pg. 270
1459 Greene, *The Pastoral Epistles* op. cit. pg. 199
1460 Kelly, *Pastoral Epistles* op. cit. pg. 249
1461 Criswell, *Apostles After Jesus* op. cit. pg. 164
1462 *Liberty Commentary* op. cit. pg. 636
1463 Ngewa, op. cit. pg. 394
1464 Fee, *1 & 2 Timothy, Titus* op. cit. pg. 154
1465 Saarinen, op. cit. pg. 207
1466 Barnes, *Notes - One Volume ed.* op. cit. pg. 1208
1467 Murray Harris, *Colossians & Philemon* William B. Eerdmans (Grand Rapids, Mich.) 1991 pg. 267
1468 Barclay, *Timothy, Titus, and Philemon* op. cit. pg. 322
1469 Paul introductory "servant of Christ" found in most of his epistles is actually the word used here and is usually translated as "slave."
1470 Alexander Nairne, *The Epistle to the Hebrews* Cambridge University Press (Cambridge, MS) 1917 pg. lvii
1471 George Guthrie, "The Case for Apollos as the Author of Hebrews," *Faith and Mission Vol. 18 No. 2 Spring 2001*
1472 David Allen, *Lukan Authorship of Hebrews* B&H Academic (Nashville, TN) 2010 pg. 355
1473 Josephus, "Antiquities of the Jews," XX.ix.1 op. cit. pg. 423
1474 Warwick Aiken, Jr., "The Authorship of the Epistle to the Hebrew," *A Thesis for Dallas Theological Seminary* July 1946 pg. 34
1475 Ibid.

1476 Josephus, "Antiquities of the Jews," XX.ix.1 op. cit. pg. 423

1477 Criswell, *Apostles After Jesus* op. cit. pg. 156

1478 Eusebius, *Eusebius : The Church History* VI.25 Paul Meier, ed., Kregel Publications (Grand Rapids, Mich.) 1999 pg. 227

1479 John Brown, *An Exposition on the Epistles of the Apostle Paul to the Hebrews Vol. 1* William Oliphant (Edinburgh, Scotland) 1862 pg. 56

1480 Robert Govett, *Govett on Hebrews* Conley & Schoettle (Miama Springs, FL) 1981 pg. 22

1481 James Moffatt, *A Critical and Exegetical Commentary on the Epistle to the Hebrews* Charles Scribners (New York, NY) 1924 pg. 12

1482 *Liberty Commentary* op. cit. pg. 649

1483 If Christ was to reconcile all things even before all things were made, then it is apparent that God predestined history as Ephesians 1:5 states. Man was planned from the very beginning, even before angels were created.

1484 For a defense of this see, David Criswell, *Controversies in the Pentateuch* Fortress Adonai (Dallas, TX) 2010 pp. 83-84

1485 Erickson, op. cit. pg. 435

1486 James Montgomery Boice, *Foundations of the Christian Faith* InterVarsity Press (Downers Grove, Ill.) 1986 pg. 168

1487 Ibid. pg. 169

1488 Scofield, *First Scofield Reference Bible* op. cit. ref. Ezekiel 1:5

1489 Erickson, op. cit. pg. 438

1490 For a defense of this see, David Criswell, *Controversies in the Prophets* Fortress Adonai (Dallas, TX) 208 pp. 117, 128

1491 Steven Waterhouse, *Not By Bread Alone* Westcliff Press (Amarillo, TX) 2007 pg. 35

1492 *Liberty Commentary* op. cit. pg. 650

1493 Boice, *Foundations of the Christian Faith* op. cit. pg. 170

1494 R. Milligan, *Epistle to the Hebrews* Chase and Hall Publishers (Cincinatti, Oh.) 1876 pg. 73

1495 Robert Gromacki, *Stand Bold in Grace* Baker Books (Grand Rapids, Mich.) 1984 pg. ??

1496 Bede, *Ancient Christian Commentary on Scripture Vol. X* Erik Heen, Philip Krey, eds., Intervarsity Press (Downers Grove, Ill.) 2005 pg. 30

1497 Arthur Pink, *An Exposition of Hebrews* Baker Books (Grand Rapids, Mich.) 1954 pg. ??

1498 Steven Waterhouse, *Not By Bread Alone* Westcliff Press (Amarillo, TX) 2007 pg. 35

1499 David Allen, *Hebrews* B&H Publishers (Nashville, TN) 2010 pp. 226-235

1500 Leon Morris, "Hebrews," *The Expositor's Bible Commentary Vol. 12* Frank Gaebelein, ed., Zondervan Publishers (Grand Rapids, Mich.) 1986 pg. 30

1501 Allen, *Hebrews* op. cit. pg. 225

1502 Franz Delitzsch, *Commentary on the Epistle to the Hebrews Vol. 1* Wm. B. Eerdmans (Grand Rapids, Mich.) 1952 pg. 150

1503 Barnes, *Notes - One Volume ed.* op. cit. pg. 1243

1504 Thomas Aquinas, 2:4:154, *Commentary on the Epistle to the Hebrews* St. Augustine Press (South Bend, ON) 2006 pg. 74

1505 William Gouge, *Commentary on Hebrews* Kregel Publishers (Grand Rapids, Mich.) 1640s (1980 ed.) pg. 190

1506 F.F. Bruce, *The Epistle to the Hebrews* Wm. B. Eerdmans (Grand Rapids, Mich.) 1964 pg. 53

1507 Gouge, op. cit. pg. 190

1508 R.C.H. Lenski, *The Interpretation of the Epistle to the Hebrews and Epistle of James* Lutheran Books (Columbus, Oh.) 1938 pg. 97

1509 John Nelson Darby, *Notes from Lectures on the Epistle to the Hebrews* G. Morrish (London, England) n.d. pg. 14

1510 John Darby as cited by Arthur Pink, *An Exposition of Hebrews* Baker Books (Grand Rapids, Mich.) 1954 pg. 150

1511 Robert Govett, *Govett on Hebrews* Conley & Schoettle (Miama Springs, FL) 1981 pg. 223

1512 *Liberty Commentary* op. cit. pg. 655
1513 Charles Erdman, *The Epistle to the Hebrews* Westminister Press (Philadelphia, PN) 1934 pg. 69
1514 William Barclay, *The Letter to the Hebrews* Westminister John Knox Press (Loeisville, KY) 1955 (2002 ed.) pg. 69
1515 James Moffatt, *A Critical and Exegetical Commentary on the Epistle to the Hebrews* Charles Scribners (New York, NY) 1924 pg. 77
1516 John MacArthur, *Hebrews* Moody Press (Chicago, Ill.) 1983 pg. 127
1517 Farrar, op. cit. pg. 339
1518 Thayer, op. cit. pg. 12
1519 Robert Govett, *Govett on Hebrews* Conley & Schoettle (Miama Springs, FL) 1981 pg. 152
1520 Barnes, *Notes - One Volume ed.* op. cit. pg. 1165
1521 R. Milligan, *Epistle to the Hebrews* Chase and Hall Publishers (Cincinatti, Oh.) 1876 pg. 174
1522 William Newell, *Hebrew : Verse by Verse* Moody Press (Chicago, Ill.) 1947 pg. 185
1523 Ibid. pg. 192
1524 Ibid. pg. 186
1525 Wesley, op. cit. pg. 597
1526 Newell, *Hebrew* op. cit. pg. 188
1527 Ibid. pg. 193
1528 Ibid. pg. 355
1529 Gromacki, *Stand Bold in Grace* op. cit. pg. 110
1530 Delitzsch, op. cit. pg. 287 as cited by Allen, *Hebrews* op. cit. pg. 254
1531 Lenski, *Hebrews and James* op. cit. pg. 180
1532 Darby, *Hebrews* op. cit. pg. 54
1533 Allen, *Hebrews* op. cit. pg. 350
1534 William Kelly, *An Exposition of the Epistle to the Hebrews* T. Weston (London, England) 1905 pg. 106
1535 Allen, *Hebrews* op. cit. pg. 349
1536 H.A. Ironside, *Studies in the Epistle to the Hebrews and Epistle to Titus* Loizeaux Brothers (New York, NY) 1932 pg. 79
1537 John MacArthur, *Hebrews* Moody Press (Chicago, Ill.) 1983 pg. 126
1538 Ironside, *Hebrews and Titus* op. cit. pg. 79
1539 F.B. Meyer, *The Way Into The Holiest* Fleming Revell (New York, NY) 1893 pg. 112
1540 Ibid. pg. 113
1541 Ibid.
1542 Kelly, *Hebrews* op. cit. pg. 106
1543 J. Dwight Pentecost, *A Faith That Endures* Discovery House (Grand Rapids, Mich.) 1992 pg. 109
1544 Ibid. pg. 107
1545 Brooke Westcott, *The Epistle to the Hebrews* Wm. B. Eerdmans (Grand Rapids, Mich.) 1970 pg. 147
1546 C.f. Gonzalez, op. cit.
1547 Theodoret of Cyr, *Ancient Christian Commentary on Scripture Vol. X* Erik Heen, Philip Krey, eds., Intervarsity Press (Downers Grove, Ill.) 2005 pg. 84
1548 Ephraem the Syrian, *Ancient Christian Commentary Vol. X* op. cit. pg. 85
1549 Chrysostom, *Ancient Christian Commentary Vol. X* op. cit pp. 86-87
1550 Photius, *Ancient Christian Commentary Vol. X* op. cit pg. 84
1551 Thomas Aquinas, 6:1:289, *Commentary on the Epistle to the Hebrews* St. Augustine Press (South Bend, ON) 2006 pg. 126
1552 Aquinas, 6:1:291, Ibid. pg. 127
1553 William Barclay, *The Letter to the Hebrews* Westminster John Knox Press (Loeisville, KY) 1955 (2002 ed.) pg. 69
1554 Bruce, *Hebrews* op. cit. pg. 118

1555 Gouge, *Hebrews* op. cit. pg. 723
1556 John Calvin, *Commentary on the Epistle to the Hebrews* Wm. B. Eerdmans (Grand Rapids, Mich.) 1949 pg. 136
1557 Richard Phillips, *Hebrew* Presbyterian & Reformed (Philipsburg, NJ) 2006 pg. 195
1558 Ibid.
1559 Dave Hunt, *What Love is This?* Loyal Publishing (Sisters, OR) 2002 pp. 75-78
1560 Steven Ger, *The Book of Hebrews : Christ is Greater* AMG (Chattanooga, TN) 2009 pg. 102
1561 Gromacki, *Stand Bold in Grace* op. cit. pg. 110
1562   C.I Scofield Reference Bible Online /www.biblestudytools.com/commentaries/scofield-reference-notes/hebrews/hebrews-6.html
1563 Steven Ger, *The Book of Hebrews : Christ is Greater* AMG (Chattanooga, TN) 2009 pg. 102
1564 Warren Wiersbe, *Be Confident* Victor Books (Wheaton, Ill.) 1982 pg. 66
1565 Allen, *Hebrews* op. cit. pg. 346
1566 I thought I had first coined the term myself, only to find that many others have seen this same thing, even using the same term. Cf. Sir Robert Anderson, *Forgotten Truth* Pickering (London, England) 1914 pg. 131
1567 G.H. Lang, *Hebrews* Schoettle Publishing (Hayesville, NC) 1951 (2008 ed.) pg. 184
1568 Ibid.
1569 One Hindi translation I saw omits these verses altogether.
1570 Newman, op. cit. pg. 115
1571 Theodoret of Cyr, *Ancient Commentary Vol. X* op. cit. pg. 116
1572 Bruce, *Hebrews* op. cit. pg. 157
1573 R. Milligan, *Epistle to the Hebrews* Chase and Hall Publishers (Cincinatti, Oh.) 1876 pg. 215
1574 James Moffatt, *A Critical and Exegetical Commentary on the Epistle to the Hebrews* Charles Scribners (New York, NY) 1924 pg. 102
1575 Josephus, "Antiquities of the Jews," iii.X.7 *Complete Works* op. cit. pg. 80
1576 James Moffatt, *A Critical and Exegetical Commentary on the Epistle to the Hebrews* Charles Scribners (New York, NY) 1924 pg. 102
1577 Brooke Westcott, *The Epistle to the Hebrews* Wm. B. Eerdmans (Grand Rapids, Mich.) 1970 pg. 196
1578 The old Hebrew calendar was a 360 day lunar calendar with an extra month added every few years to adjust for the solar year.
1579 Arthur Pink, *An Exposition of Hebrews* Baker Books (Grand Rapids, Mich.) 1954 pg. 423
1580 Ibid.
1581 Morris, "Hebrews," *Expositor's Vol. 12* op. cit. pg. 82
1582 Ibid.
1583 Milligan, *Hebrews* op. cit. pg. 245
1584 Morris, "Hebrews," *Expositor's Vol. 12* op. cit. pg. 81
1585 Cf. Josephus, Antiquities 4.ii.IV; 3.vi.VIII; and 3.viii.III
1586 Bruce, *Hebrews* op. cit. pg. 185
1587 Morris, "Hebrews," *Expositor's Vol. 12* op. cit. pg. 81
1588 Milligan, *Hebrews* op. cit. pg. 245
1589 Westcott, *Hebrews* op. cit. pg. 247
1590 C.f. Lenski, *Hebrews and James* op. cit. pg. 279
1591 Ibid. pg. 281
1592 James Moffatt, *A Critical and Exegetical Commentary on the Epistle to the Hebrews* Charles Scribners (New York, NY) 1924 pg. 114
1593 Pink, *Hebrews* op. cit. pg. 468
1594 Allen, *Hebrews* op. cit. pg. 431
1595 Lenski, *Hebrews and James* op. cit. pg. 276
1596 Govett, *Hebrews* op. cit. pg. 354
1597 Pink, *Hebrews* op. cit. pg. 610
1598 *Liberty Commentary* op. cit. pg. 662

1599 John MacArthur, *Hebrews* Moody Press (Chicago, Ill.) 1983 pg. 233

1600 Calvin, *Hebrews* op. cit. pg. 243

1601 Allen, *Hebrews* op. cit. pg. 520

1602 Lenski, *Hebrews and James* op. cit. pg. 362

1603 Darby, *Hebrews* op. cit. pg. 101

1604 Farrar, op. cit. pg. 342

1605 Ironside, *Hebrews and Titus* op. cit. pg. 123

1606 Wesley, op. cit. pg. 608

1607 Franz Delitzsch, *Commentary on the Epistle to the Hebrews Vol. 2* Wm. B. Eerdmans (Grand Rapids, Mich.) 1952 pg. 184

1608 Kelly, *Hebrews* op. cit. pg. 192

1609 Pink, *Hebrews* op. cit. pg. 612

1610 Ibid. pg. 607

1611 Ibid. pg. 605

1612 Gromacki, *Stand Bold in Grace* op. cit. pg. 173

1613 Milligan, *Hebrews* op. cit. pg. 285

1614 F.W. Farrar, *The Epistle of Paul the Apostle to the Hebrews* Cambridge (Cambridge, England) 1896 pg. 155

1615 Theodore of Mapsuesta, *Ancient Commentary Vol. X* op. cit. pg. 166

1616 Barnes, *Notes - One Volume ed.* op. cit. pg. 1309

1617 Clement of Alexandria, *Ancient Commentary Vol. X* op. cit. pg. 165

1618 Govett, *Hebrews* op. cit. pg. 355

1619 Ibid.

1620 Ibid. pg. 354

1621 Tertullian, *Ante-Nicene Fathers Vol. III* op. cit. pg. 673

1622 Chrysostom, *Ancient Commentary Vol. X* op. cit. pg. 166

1623 I thought I had first coined the term myself, only to find that many others have seen this same thing, even using the same term. Cf. Sir Robert Anderson, *Forgotten Truth* Pickering (London, England) 1914 pg. 131

1624 J.D. Faust, *The Rod* Schoettle Publishing (Hayesville, NC) 2003 pg. 139

1625 Ibid. pg. 141

1626 Ibid. pp. 143-153

1627 Chuck and Nancy Missler, *The Kingdom, Power, and Glory* King's Highway Ministries (Coeur d'Alene, ID) 2007 pg. 263

1628 G.H. Lang, *Hebrews* Schoettle Publishing (Hayesville, NC) 1951 (2008 ed.) pg. 184

1629 Cf. Erdman, *Hebrews* op. cit. pp. 107-110

1630 Wiersbe, *Be Confident* op. cit. pg. 116

1631 Bruce, *Hebrews* op. cit. pg. 258

1632 Chrysostom, *Ancient Commentary Vol. X* op. cit. pg. 166

1633 Calvin, *Hebrews* op. cit. pp. 260-261

1634 Farrar, *Hebrews* op. cit. pg. 161

1635 Gromacki, *Stand Bold in Grace* op. cit. pg. 182

1636 J. Dwight Pentecost, *A Faith That Endures* Discovery House (Grand Rapids, Mich.) 1992 pg. 185

1637 Govett, *Hebrews* op. cit. pg. 374

1638 Wesley, op. cit. pg. 609

1639 Wiersbe, *Be Confident* op. cit. pg. 121

1640 F.B. Meyer, *The Way Into The Holiest* Fleming Revell (New York, NY) 1893 pg. 198

1641 Newell, *Hebrews* op. cit. pg. 372

1642 Delitzsch, *Hebrews Vol. 2* op. cit. pg. 256

1643 Calvin, *Hebrews* op. cit. pg. 291

1644 Barnes, *Notes - One Volume ed.* op. cit. pg. 1323

1645 Milligan, *Hebrews* op. cit. pg. 317

1646 Westcott, *Hebrews* op. cit. pg. 369
1647 Govett, *Hebrews* op. cit. pg. 405
1648 Photius, *Ancient Commentary Vol. X* op. cit. pg. 195
1649 Chrysostom, *Ancient Commentary Vol. X* op. cit. pg. 196
1650 Gouge, *Hebrews* op. cit. pp. 869-870
1651 E.W. Bullinger, *The Great Cloud of Witnesses* Lamp Press (London, England) 1956 pg. 322
1652 MacArthur, *Hebrews* op. cit. pg. 312
1653 Gouge, *Hebrews* op. cit. pg. 869
1654 Bullinger, *The Great Cloud of Witnesses* op. cit. pg. 329
1655 Farrar, op. cit. pg. 343
1656 Barnes, *Notes - One Volume ed.* op. cit. pg. 1327
1657 Calvin, *Hebrews* op. cit. pg. 303
1658 Gromacki, *Stand Bold in Grace* op. cit. pg. 218
1659 Delitzsch, *Hebrews Vol. 2* op. cit. pg. 380
1660 *Liberty Commentary* op. cit. pg. 667
1661 F.B. Meyer, *The Way Into The Holiest* Fleming Revell (New York, NY) 1893 pg. 255
1662 Charles Spurgeon, *Treasury of the New Testament Volume Four* Zondervan Publishers (Grand Rapids, Mich.) 1950 pp. 251
1663 J. Ronald Blue, "James," *Bible Knowledge Commentary* op. cit. pg. 815
1664 James Ussher, *Annals of the World* Master Books (Green Forest, AR) 2003 pg. 843
1665 John Gill, "Commentary on the New Testament," John 19:25 E-Sword Software Commentary Series
1666 Donald W. Burdick, "James," *Expositor's Vol. 12* op. cit. pg. 161
1667 J. Ronald Blue, "James," *Bible Knowledge Commentary* op. cit. pg. 816
1668 Donald W. Burdick, "James," *Expositor's Vol. 12* op. cit. pg. 161
1669 Tenney, *New Testament* op. cit. pg. 265
1670 Criswell, *Apostles After Jesus* op. cit. pp. 104-105
1671 Josephus, "Antiquities of the Jews," XX.ix.1 op. cit. pg. 423
1672 J. Ronald Blue, "James," *Bible Knowledge Commentary* op. cit. pg. 816
1673 Burdick, "James," *Expositor's Vol. 12* op. cit. pg. 162
1674 Ibid.
1675 Ibid.
1676 Ibid.
1677 Tenney, *New Testament* op. cit. pg. 264
1678 Gundry, *Survey New Testament* op. cit. pg. 434
1679 The story is often attributed to Albert Einstein although there is no independent verification of the story.
1680 Cf. William Barclay, *The Letters of James and Peter* Westminister Press (Philadelphia, PN) 1958 pg. 59
1681 Tertullian, *Ante-Nicene Fathers Vol. III* op. cit. pg. 684
1682 James Montgomery Boice, *Foundations of the Christian Faith* InterVarsity Press (Downers Grove, Ill.) 1986 pg. 476
1683 Charles Swindoll, *Insights on James and 1 & 2 Peter* Zondervan Publishers (Grand Rapids, Mich.) 2010 pg. 35
1684 H.A. Ironside, *Notes on the Epistle of James* Loizeaux Brothers (Neptune, NJ) 1947 pg. 17
1685 Zane Hodges, *The Epistle of James* Grace Evangelical Seminary (Irving, TX) 1994 pg. 27
1686 Bede the Venerable, *The Commentary on the Seven Catholic Epistles* Cistercian Publishers (Kalamazoo, Mich.) 1985 pg. 14
1687 John Nelson Darby, *Exposition of the Epistle of James* G. Morrish (London, England) n.d. pg. 1
1688 Andreas, *Ancient Christian Commentary on Scripture Vol. XI* Gerald Bray, ed., InterVarsity Press (Downers Grove, Ill.) 2000 pg. 11
1689 Barnes, *Notes - One Volume ed.* op. cit. pg. 1358

1690   John Calvin, *Commentaries on the Catholic Epistles*   Wm. B. Eerdmans (Grand Rapids, Mich.) 1948 pg. 288
1691   John Calvin, *Commentaries on the Catholic Epistles*   Wm. B. Eerdmans (Grand Rapids, Mich.) 1948 pg. 288
1692   Daniel Dorian, *James : Reformed Expositary Commentary* (Phillipsburg, NJ) 2007 pg. 35
1693   Daniel Dorian, *James : Reformed Expositary Commentary* (Phillipsburg, NJ) 2007 pg. 35
1694   John MacArthur, *James* Moody Press (Chicago, Ill.) 1998 pp. 45-46
1695   Scot McKnight, *The Letter of James* Wm. B. Eerdmans (Grand Rapids, Mich.) 2011 pg. 115
1696   Cf. Douglas Moo, *The Letter of James* Apollos (Leicester, England) 2000 pg. 72
1697   Augustine, *Ancient Christian Commentary on Scripture*   Vol. XI   Gerald Bray, ed., InterVarsity Press (Downers Grove, Ill.) 2000 pg. 24
1698   Zane Hodges, *The Epistle of James* Grace Evangelical Seminary (Irving, TX) 1994 pg. 54
1699   *Liberty Commentary* op. cit. pg. 674
1700   Augustine, *Ancient Christian Commentary on Scripture*   Vol. XI   Gerald Bray, ed., InterVarsity Press (Downers Grove, Ill.) 2000 pg. 29
1701   Leo the Great, *Ancient Christian Commentary on Scripture*   Vol. XI   Gerald Bray, ed., InterVarsity Press (Downers Grove, Ill.) 2000 pg. 29
1702   Hilary of Arles, *Ancient Christian Commentary on Scripture*   Vol. XI   Gerald Bray, ed., InterVarsity Press (Downers Grove, Ill.) 2000 pg. 29
1703   William Barclay, *The Letters of James and Peter* Westminister Press (Philadelphia, PN) 1958 pg. 87
1704   Edwards, *"The Blank Bible" Part 2* op. cit. pg. 1171
1705   *Catechism of the Catholic Church* Para. 115; www.vatican.va/archive/ENG0015/__P5.HTM
1706   Thayer, op. cit. pg. 150
1707   Ibid.
1708   Unger, op. cit. pg. 624
1709   Boice, *Foundations* op. cit. pg. 323
1710   George Meisinger, "Salvation by Faith Alone," *The Fundamentals for the Twenty-First Century* Mal Couch, ed., Kregel Publishers (Grand Rapids, Mich.) 2000 pg. 280
1711   Erickson, op. cit. pg. 903
1712   *Liberty Commentary* op. cit. pg. 674
1713   *Liberty Commentary* op. cit. pg. 674
1714   Zane Hodges, *The Epistle of James* Grace Evangelical Seminary (Irving, TX) 1994 pg. 60
1715   Zane Hodges, *The Epistle of James* Grace Evangelical Seminary (Irving, TX) 1994 pg. 61
1716   George Meisinger, "Salvation by Faith Alone," *The Fundamentals for the Twenty-First Century* Mal Couch, ed., Kregel Publishers (Grand Rapids, Mich.) 2000 pg. 279
1717   Bruce Metzger, *A Textual Commentary on the Greek New Testament* United Bible Society (Stuttgart, German) 1994 ed. pg. 610
1718   Spurgeon, *Treasury Vol. 4* op. cit. pg. 306
1719   Daniel Dorian, *James : Reformed Expositary Commentary* (Phillipsburg, NJ) 2007 pg. 81
1720   Richard Phillips, *Hebrew* Presbyterian & Reformed (Philipsburg, NJ) 2006 pg. 195
1721   George Meisinger, "Salvation by Faith Alone," *The Fundamentals for the Twenty-First Century* Mal Couch, ed., Kregel Publishers (Grand Rapids, Mich.) 2000 pg. 278
1722   Wesley, op. cit. pg. 624-625
1723   John Calvin, *Commentaries on the Catholic Epistles*   Wm. B. Eerdmans (Grand Rapids, Mich.) 1948 pg. 309
1724   John MacArthur, *James* Moody Press (Chicago, Ill.) 1998 pg. 119
1725   John Nelson Darby, *Exposition of the Epistle of James* G. Morrish (London, England) n.d. pg. 32
1726   Bede the Venerable, *The Commentary on the Seven Catholic Epistles* Cistercian Publishers (Kalamazoo, Mich.) 1985 pg. 28
1727   Farrar, op. cit. pg. 312

1728 Charles Swindoll, *Insights on James and 1 & 2 Peter* Zondervan Publishers (Grand Rapids, Mich.) 2010 pg. 58
1729 Barnes, *Notes - One Volume ed.* op. cit. pg. 1367
1730 https://www.facebook.com/groups/scripturally.speaking/?hc_location=stream
1731 H.A. Ironside, *Notes on the Epistle of James* Loizeaux Brothers (Neptune, NJ) 1947 pg. 29
1732 *Liberty Commentary* op. cit. pg. 674
1733 Wesley, op. cit. pg. 626
1734 Zane Hodges, *The Epistle of James* Grace Evangelical Seminary (Irving, TX) 1994 pg. 78
1735 Gene Getz, *Doing Your Part* Regal Books (Venture, CA) 1984 pg. 38
1736 John MacArthur, *James* Moody Press (Chicago, Ill.) 1998 pg. 144
1737 John Nelson Darby, *Exposition of the Epistle of James* G. Morrish (London, England) n.d. pg. 41
1738 James Dobson, *Hide and Seek* Revell (Ada, MI) 1974 pg. 84
1739 John MacArthur, *James* Moody Press (Chicago, Ill.) 1998 pp. 201-203
1740 Spurgeon, *Treasury Vol. 4* op. cit. pg. 320
1741 Douglas Moo, *The Letter of James* Apollos (Leicester, England) 2000 pg. 191
1742 James Burdick, "James," *Expositor's Vol. 12* op. cit. pg. 164
1743 Tenney, op. cit. pg. 347
1744 Gundry, op. cit. pg. 437
1745 Edwin Blum, "1 Peter," *Expositor's Vol. 12* op. cit. pg. 211
1746 Ibid.
1747 Ibid.
1748 Ibid.
1749 Roger Raymer, "1 Peter," *Bible Knowledge* op. cit. pg. 837
1750 Edwin Blum, "2 Peter," *Expositor's Vol. 12* op. cit. pg. 259
1751 Raymer, "1 Peter," *Bible Knowledge* op. cit. pg. 837
1752 Ibid.
1753 Ibid.
1754 Blum, "2 Peter," *Expositor's Vol. 12* op. cit. pg. 257
1755 Ibid.
1756 Tenney, op. cit. pg. 366
1757 Blum, "2 Peter," *Expositor's Vol. 12* op. cit. pg. 257
1758 Ibid.. pg. 258
1759 Ibid.
1760 Ibid.
1761 Kenneth Gangel, "2 Peter," *Bible Knowledge* op. cit. pg. 860
1762 Ibid.
1763 Ibid.. pg. 861
1764 Blum, "2 Peter," *Expositor's Vol. 12* op. cit. pg. 259
1765 Ibid.. pg. 258
1766 Raymer, "1 Peter," *Bible Knowledge* op. cit. pg. 837
1767 Blum, "2 Peter," *Expositor's Vol. 12* op. cit. pg. 259
1768 Ibid.
1769 I am reminded of the amusing conspiracy theory about William Shakespeare. Since he was not a noble, they insist he could never have written such profound works of art!
1770 Edwin Blum, "2 Peter," *Expositor's Vol. 12* op. cit. pg. 259
1771 Ibid.
1772 Ibid.. pg. 260
1773 Ibid.. pg. 261
1774 Archer, op. cit. pg. 425
1775 J.N.D. Kelly, *A Commentary on the Epistles of Peter and of Jude* Harper and Row (New York, NY) 1969 pg. 225

1776 Charles Bigg, *A Critical and Exegetical Commentary Epistles of St. Peter and St. Jude* T & T Clark (Edinburgh, Scotland) 1978 pg. 120

1777 Kenneth Wuest, *First Peter in the Greek New Testament* Wm. B. Eerdmans (Grand Rapids, Mich.) 1948 pg. 43

1778 R.C.H. Lenski, *Interpretation of the Epistles of St. Peter, St. John, and st. Jude* Wartburg Press (Columbus, OH) 1945 pg. 67

1779 Shepherd of Hermas, *Ante-Nicene Fathers Vol. II* op. cit. pg. 47

1780 *Liberty Commentary* op. cit. pg. 691

1781 Ibid. pg. 697

1782 Edwards, *"The Blank Bible" Part 2* op. cit. pg. 1179

1783 William Barclay, *The Letters of James and Peter* Westminister Press (Philadelphia, PN) 1958 pg. 258

1784 Douglas Harink, *1 & 2 Peter* Brazos Press (Grand Rapids, Mich.) 2009 pg. 86

1785 Ibid.

1786 R.C. Sproul, *1-2 Peter* Crossway Books (Wheaton, Ill.) 2011 pg. 93

1787 Dan Keating, *First and Second Peter, Jude* Baker Academic (Grand Rapids, Mich.) 2011 pg. 73

1788 Martin Luther, *Complete Works Vol. 30 The Catholic Epistles* Concordia Publishing (St. Louis, MO) 1967 pg. 87

1789 H.A. Ironside, *Notes on the Epistles of Peter* Loizeaux Brothers (Neptune, NJ) 1947 pg. 39

1790 William Barclay, *The Letters of James and Peter* Westminister Press (Philadelphia, PN) 1958 pg. 260

1791 John Brown, *Expository Discourses on the First Epistle of the Apostle Peter* Robert Carter & Bro. (New York, NY) 1855 pg. 363

1792 Bloom, op. cit. pg 101

1793 Ibid.. pg 114

1794 Kenneth Wuest, *First Peter in the Greek New Testament* Wm. B. Eerdmans (Grand Rapids, Mich.) 1948 pg. 75

1795 John MacArthur, *1 Peter* Moody Press (Chicago, Illl.) 2004 pg. 179

1796 Gesenius, op. cit. pg 130

1797 Ibid.

1798 Bloom, op. cit. pg 37

1799 Karl Marx and Frederick Engels, *The Communist Manifesto* Article II, Progress Publishers (Moscow, Russia) 1848

1800 Martin Luther, *Complete Works Vol. 30 The Catholic Epistles* Concordia Publishing (St. Louis, MO) 1967 pg. 113

1801 Poole, op. cit. pg. 910

1802 Raymer, "1 Peter," op. cit. pg. 851

1803 Young, op. cit. pg. 47

1804 Ibid.

1805 Martin Luther, *Complete Works Vol. 30 The Catholic Epistles* Concordia Publishing (St. Louis, MO) 1967 pg. 113

1806 *Liberty Commentary* op. cit. pg. 700

1807 Cf. John Calvin, *Commentaries on the Catholic Epistles* Wm. B. Eerdmans (Grand Rapids, Mich.) 1948 pg. 113

1808 Bede the Venerable, *The Commentary on the Seven Catholic Epistles* Cistercian Publishers (Kalamazoo, Mich.) 1985 pg. 102

1809 Brown, *Peter* op. cit. pg. 515

1810 Blum, "1 Peter," op. cit. pg. 241

1811 Archer, op. cit. pg. 423

1812 Cf. notes in D.M. Lloyd-Jones, *Christian Unity Ephesians 4:1-16* Baker Books (Grand Rapids, Mich.) 1980 pg. 157

1813 Calvin, *Catholic Epistles* op. cit. pg. 113

1814 Lenski, *Peter, St. John, and st. Jude* op. cit. pg. 161
1815 Ibid.
1816 Dan Keating, *First and Second Peter, Jude* Baker Academic (Grand Rapids, Mich.) 2011 pg. 91
1817 William Barclay, *The Letters of James and Peter* Westminister Press (Philadelphia, PN) 1958 pg. 280
1818 Barnes, *Notes - One Volume ed.* op. cit. pg. 1424
1819 Barclay, *James and Peter* op. cit. pp. 286-287
1820 E.g. Irenaeus, "Against Heresies," 4:27:2 *Ante-Nicene Fathers Vol. I* op. cit. pg. 499
1821 Charles Swindoll, *Insights on James and 1 & 2 Peter* Zondervan Publishers (Grand Rapids, Mich.) 2010 pg. 204
1822 Talbert, op. cit. pg. 111
1823 Blum, "1 Peter," op. cit. pg. 241
1824 Charles Bigg, *A Critical and Exegetical Commentary Epistles of St. Peter and St. Jude* T & T Clark (Edinburgh, Scotland) 1978 pg. 162
1825 Farrar, op. cit. pg. 328
1826 Some have argued that these are people who "repented in the hours of their death," but why would they need the gospel proclaimed in *Hades* if they had already repented before death? (cf. Bigg, *Peter and St. Jude* op. cit. pg. 162)
1827 Barclay, *James and Peter* op. cit. pg. 287
1828 Ibid.
1829 Anderson, "Misunderstood Texts of the Bible," *Collected Works* op. cit. pg. 328
1830 In regard to those who never heard the gospel I frequently say that God knows who would and would not have accepted the gospel. Whether you believe that any of them would is irrelevant. God knows and will judge to each of us accordingly.
1831 Blum, "1 Peter," op. cit. pg. 241
1832 Barclay, *James and Peter* op. cit. pg. 285
1833 Keating, *First and Second Peter, Jude* op. cit. pg. 91
1834 William Kelly, *The Preaching to the Spirits in Prison* Bible Truth Publishers (Oak Park, Ill.) 1970 pg. 33
1835 Blum, "1 Peter," op. cit. pg. 241
1836 Wesley, op. cit. pg. 640
1837 Kelly, *Spirits in Prison* op. cit. pg. 15
1838 R.A. Torrey, *Difficulties in the Bible* Whitaker House (New Kensington, PA) 2003 ed. pg. 201
1839 John MacArthur, *1 Peter* Moody Press (Chicago, Illl.) 2004 pg. 209
1840 Blum, "1 Peter," op. cit. pg. 242
1841 Ibid. pg. 245
1842 In regard to those who have not heard the gospel I have previous discussed in Roman 2:11-16 and briefly touched upon in 1 Peter 3:18-22.
1843 Barnes, *Notes - One Volume ed.* op. cit. pg. 1429
1844 Andreas, *Ancient Christian Commentary on Scripture Vol. XI* Gerald Bray, ed., InterVarsity Press (Downers Grove, Ill.) 2000 pg. 113
1845 Hilary of Arles, *Ancient Christian Commentary on Scripture Vol. XI* Gerald Bray, ed., InterVarsity Press (Downers Grove, Ill.) 2000 pg. 113
1846 Bigg, *Peter and St. Jude* op. cit. pg. 171
1847 Bede the Venerable, *The Commentary on the Seven Catholic Epistles* Cistercian Publishers (Kalamazoo, Mich.) 1985 pg. 109
1848 Luther, *Complete Works Vol. 30* op. cit. pg. 121
1849 Bigg, *Peter and St. Jude* op. cit. pg. 171
1850 Barnes, *Notes - One Volume ed.* op. cit. pg. 1429
1851 Cf. Calvin, *Catholic Epistles* op. cit. pg. 126
1852 H.A. Ironside, *Notes on the Epistles of Peter* Loizeaux Brothers (Neptune, NJ) 1947 pg. 48

1853 R.C. Sproul, *1-2 Peter* Crossway Books (Wheaton, Ill.) 2011 pg. 144
1854 MacArthur, *1 Peter* op. cit. pg. 231
1855 Ibid.
1856 Cf. Calvin, *Catholic Epistles* op. cit. pg. 126
1857 Lenski, *Peter, St. John, and st. Jude* op. cit. pg. 148
1858 Oecumenius, *Ancient Christian Commentary on Scripture Vol. XI* Gerald Bray, ed., InterVarsity Press (Downers Grove, Ill.) 2000 pg. 114
1859 Criswell, Apostles After Jesus op. cit. pp. 20-24
1860 Georges Roux, *Ancient Iraq* Penguin Books (New York, NY) 1992 ed. pg. 416
1861 Ibid.
1862 Ibid. pg. 414
1863 D. M. Lloyd-Jones, *Expository Sermons on 2 Peter* Banner of Truth (Carlisle, PN) 1983 pp. 126-129
1864 Ibid. pg. 127
1865 Ibid. pg. 129
1866 John MacArthur, *2 Peter and Jude* Moody Press (Chicago, Illl.) 2005 pg. 85
1867 Kenneth Wuest, *In These Last Days* Wm. B. Eerdmans (Grand Rapids, Mich.) 1954 pg. 49
1868 Bigg, *Peter and St. Jude* op. cit. pg. 275
1869 R.C. Sproul, *1-2 Peter* Crossway Books (Wheaton, Ill.) 2011 pg. 249
1870 John MacArthur, *2 Peter and Jude* Moody Press (Chicago, Illl.) 2005 pg. 85
1871 Spurgeon, *Treasury Vol. 4* op. cit. pg. 448
1872 Lenski, *Peter, St. John, and st. Jude* op. cit. pg. 338
1873 Keating, *First and Second Peter, Jude* op. cit. pg. 175
1874 Theophlylact, *Ancient Christian Commentary on Scripture Vol. XI* Gerald Bray, ed., InterVarsity Press (Downers Grove, Ill.) 2000 pg. 156
1875 Calvin, *Catholic Epistles* op. cit. pg. 414
1876 Ibid. pg. 420
1877 Luther, *Works Vol. 30* op. cit. pg. 192
1878 Charles Swindoll, *Insights on James and 1 & 2 Peter* Zondervan Publishers (Grand Rapids, Mich.) 2010 pg. 313
1879 Warren Wiersbe, *Be Alert* Victor Books (Wheaton, Ill.) 1987 pp. 78-79
1880 Cf. Arthur Bloomfield, *The Key to Understanding Revelation* Bethany House (Bloomington, MN) 2002 reprint pg. 300
1881 Josephus, "Antiquities," I.ii.3 *Complete* op. cit. pg. 27
1882 Robert Harvey & Philip Towner, *2 Peter and Jude* InterVarsity Press (Downers Grove, Ill.) 2009 pg. 123
1883 Wiersbe, *Be Alert* op. cit. pp. 82-83
1884 Epistle of Barnabas, *Ante-Nicene Fathers Vol. I* op. cit. pg. 146
1885 Theophilus of Autolycus, *Ante-Nicene Fathers Vol. II* op. cit. pg. 120
1886 Cf. *Ancient Commentary Vol. XI* op. cit. pg. 158
1887 Wesley, op. cit. pg. 675
1888 Cf. Keating, *First and Second Peter, Jude* op. cit. pp. 176-180
1889 Lenski, *Peter, St. John, and st. Jude* op. cit. pg. 345
1890 Bede the Venerable, *Catholic Epistles* op. cit. pg. 148
1891 Kenneth Wuest, *In These Last Days* Wm. B. Eerdmans (Grand Rapids, Mich.) 1954 pg. 70
1892 Arthur Pink, *Exposition of the Gospel of John Vol 2.* I.C. Herendeen (Cleveland, OH) 1924 pg. 80
1893 Ibid.
1894 Calvin, *Catholic Epistles* op. cit. pg. 419
1895 Wiersbe, *Be Alert* op. cit. pg. 86
1896 H.A. Ironside, *Notes on the Epistles of Peter* Loizeaux Brothers (Neptune, NJ) 1947 pg. 98
1897 Kenneth Wuest, *In These Last Days* Wm. B. Eerdmans (Grand Rapids, Mich.) 1954 pg. 72
1898 MacArthur, *2 Peter and Jude* op. cit. pg. 124

1899 Lenski, *Peter, St. John, and St. Jude* op. cit. pg. 347
1900 Bede the Venerable, *Catholic Epistles* op. cit. pg. 151
1901 Henry Morris, *The Biblical Basis for Modern Science* Baker Book House (Grand Rapids, Mich.) 1984 pg. 226
1902 Henry Morris, *The Revelation Record* Tyndale House (Wheaton, Ill.) 1983 pg. 436
1903 Joseph A. Seiss, *The Apocalypse* Kregel Publications (Grand Rapids, Mich.) 2001 reprint pg. 484
1904 Lenski, *Peter, St. John, and st. Jude* op. cit. pg. 350
1905 Zane Hodges, "1 John," *Bible Knowledge* op. cit. pg. 882
1906 Ibid.
1907 David Criswell, *Controversies in the Gospels* Fortress Adonai Press (Dallas, TX) 2012 pg. 292
1908 Glenn Barker, "1 John," *Expositor's Vol. 12* op. cit. pg. 301
1909 Ibid.
1910 Unger, op. cit. pg. 599
1911 Irenaeus 1:6:28; R.C.H. Lenski, *Interpretation of the Epistles of St. Peter, St. John, and st. Jude* Wartburg Press (Columbus, OH) 1945 pg. 390
1912 William Kelly, *An Exposition of the Epistle of John the Apostle* T. Weston (London, England) 1905 pg. 390
1913 Kenneth Wuest, *In These Last Days* Wm. B. Eerdmans (Grand Rapids, Mich.) 1954 pg. 103
1914 James Montgomery Boice, *The Epistles of John* Zondervan Publishers (Grand Rapids, Mich.) 1978 pp. 39-41
1915 *Liberty Commentary* op. cit. pg. 720
1916 Robert Lightner, *First, Second, and Third John and Jude* AMG (Chattanooga, TN) 2003 pg. 19
1917 Spurgeon, *Treasury Vol. 4* op. cit. pg. 491
1918 John Calvin, *1 John* Crossway Classics (Wheaton, Ill.) 1998 pg. 23
1919 William Barclay, *The Letters of John and Jude* Westminister Press (Philadelphia, PN) 1958 pg. 96
1920 He actually mistakenly states that this is in the present infinitive, but it is actually present active indicative. [Kenneth Wuest, *In These Last Days* Wm. B. Eerdmans (Grand Rapids, Mich.) 1954 pg. 150]
1921 Barnes, *Notes - One Volume ed.* op. cit. pg. 1482 & 1496
1922 John MacArthur, *1-3 John* Moody Press (Chicago, Ill.) 2007 pg. 206
1923 H.A. Ironside, *Addresses on the Epistles of John and an Exposition of the Epistle of Jude* Loizeaux Brothers (Neptune, NJ) 1931 pg. 221
1924 Robert Govett, *Govett on 1 John* Conley & Schoettle (Miami Springs, FL) 1985 pp. 23-25
1925 John Calvin, *1 John* Crossway Classics (Wheaton, Ill.) 1998 pg. 58
1926 Govett, *1 John* op. cit. pg. 24
1927 Maximus the Confessor, *Ancient Christian Commentary on Scripture Vol. XI* Gerald Bray, ed., InterVarsity Press (Downers Grove, Ill.) 2000 pg. 200
1928 Oliver Greene, *Epistles of John* Gospel Hour (Greenville, SC) 1966 pg. 35
1929 Ibid. pp. 129-133
1930 Tertullian, *Ante-Nicene Fathers Vol. III* op. cit. pg. 660
1931 A.E. Brooke, *A Critical and Exegetical Commentary on Johannine Epistles* T&T Clark Edinburgh, Scotland) 1912 pg. 89
1932 *Liberty Commentary* op. cit. pg. 728
1933 Edwards, *"The Blank Bible" Part 2* op. cit. pg. 1194
1934 Robert Lightner, *First, Second, and Third John and Jude* AMG (Chattanooga, TN) 2003 pg. 81
1935 J. N. Darby, *Notes on the Epistles of John* G. Morrish (London, England) n.d. pg. 48
1936 Ibid. pp. 82-83

1937 H.A. Ironside, *Addresses on the Epistles of John and an Exposition of the Epistle of Jude* Loizeaux Brothers (Neptune, NJ) 1931 pg. 30

1938 William Barclay, *The Letters of John and Jude* Westminister Press (Philadelphia, PN) 1958 pg. 145

1939 *Webster's New World College Dictionary* Wiley Publishing (New York, NY) 2004 pg. 1150

1940 Ibid. pg. 500

1941 Thayer, op. cit. pg. 301

1942 Ibid.

1943 *Liberty Commentary* op. cit. pg. 720

1944 Wesley, op. cit. pg. 657

1945 John MacArthur, *1-3 John* Moody Press (Chicago, Ill.) 2007 pg. 47

1946 Kenneth Wuest, *In These Last Days* Wm. B. Eerdmans (Grand Rapids, Mich.) 1954 pg. 110

1947 James Montgomery Boice, *The Epistles of John* Zondervan Publishers (Grand Rapids, Mich.) 1978 pg. 48

1948 Barclay, *John and Jude* op. cit. pg. 46

1949 Boice, *John* op. cit. pg. 49

1950 Barclay, *John and Jude* op. cit. pg. 47

1951 H.A. Ironside, *Addresses on the Epistles of John and an Exposition of the Epistle of Jude* Loizeaux Brothers (Neptune, NJ) 1931 pg. 44

1952 Calvin, *Catholic Epistles* op. cit. pg. 173

1953 Luther, *Works Vol. 30* op. cit. pg. 237

1954 R.C.H. Lenski, *Interpretation of the Epistles of St. Peter, St. John, and st. Jude* Wartburg Press (Columbus, OH) 1945 pg. 400

1955 Brooke Westcott, *The Epistles of St. John* MacMillian (London, England) 1886 pg. 44

1956 A.E. Brooke, *A Critical and Exegetical Commentary on Johannine Epistles* T&T Clark Edinburgh, Scotland) 1912 pg. 28

1957 Calvin, *Catholic Epistles* op. cit. pg. 173

1958 Hilary of Arles, *Ancient Christian Commentary on Scripture* Vol. XI Gerald Bray, ed., InterVarsity Press (Downers Grove, Ill.) 2000 pg. 177

1959 Bede the Venerable, *The Commentary on the Seven Catholic Epistles* Cistercian Publishers (Kalamazoo, Mich.) 1985 pg. 167

1960 John Calvin, *1 John* Crossway Classics (Wheaton, Ill.) 1998 pg. 30

1961 C.H. Dodd, *The Johannine Epistles* Hodler & Stoughtor (London, England) 1946 pg. 27

1962 Robert Govett, *Govett on 1 John* Conley & Schoettle (Miami Springs, FL) 1985 pg. 31

1963 Ibid.

1964 Robert Lightner, *First, Second, and Third John and Jude* AMG (Chattanooga, TN) 2003 pg. 36

1965 Ibid.

1966 Tertullian, *Ante-Nicene Fathers Vol. IV* op. cit. pg. 110

1967 Bede the Venerable, *The Commentary on the Seven Catholic Epistles* Cistercian Publishers (Kalamazoo, Mich.) 1985 pg. 175

1968 Kenneth Wuest, *In These Last Days* Wm. B. Eerdmans (Grand Rapids, Mich.) 1954 pg. 129

1969 Andreas, *Ancient Christian Commentary on Scripture Vol. XI* Gerald Bray, ed., InterVarsity Press (Downers Grove, Ill.) 2000 pg. 187

1970 Boice, *John* op. cit. pg. 131

1971 Barnes, *Notes - One Volume ed.* op. cit. pg. 1486

1972 John Calvin, *1 John* Crossway Classics (Wheaton, Ill.) 1998 pg. 72

1973 Wesley, op. cit. pg. 663

1974 Robert Lightner, *First, Second, and Third John and Jude* AMG (Chattanooga, TN) 2003 pg. 60

1975 Edwards, *"The Blank Bible" Part 2* op. cit. pg. 1195

1976 Luther, *Works Vol. 30* op. cit. pg. 285

1977 Didymus the Blind, *Ancient Christian Commentary on Scripture Vol. XI* Gerald Bray, ed., InterVarsity Press (Downers Grove, Ill.) 2000 pg. 208

1978 William Barclay, *The Letters of John and Jude* Westminister Press (Philadelphia, PN) 1958 pg. 108

1979 Here I distinguish between the *textus receptus* and the Majority text, for although they are the same 99.9% of the time, it would be misleading to say they are the same here for *no* text, including those normally counted among the Majority texts, contains these words before the 15th century.

1980 Bruce Metzger, *The Text of the New Testament* Oxford University (Oxford, England) 1992 pg. 101

1981 Bruce Metzger, *A Textual Commentary on the Greek New Testament* United Bible Society (Stuttgart, Germany) 1994 pg. 648

1982 Ibid.

1983 Ibid. pg. 102

1984 Ibid.

1985 Randall Price, *Searching for the Original Bible* Harvest House (Eugene, OR) 2007 pg. 221

1986 J. Harold Greenlee, *Introduction to New Testament Textual Criticism* Hendrickson Publishers (Peabody, MS) 1995 pg. 64

1987 Metzger, *Text of the New Testament* op. cit. pg. 101

1988 Ibid.

1989 Greenlee, *New Testament Textual Criticism* op. cit. pg. 64

1990 *Nestle-Aland NovumTestamentum Graece* United Bible Society (Stuttgart, Germany) 1898 pg. 703

1991 Metzger, *A Textual Commentary* op. cit. pg. 647

1992 Metzger, *The Text of the New Testament* op. cit. pg. 101

1993 Metzger, *A Textual Commentary* op. cit. pg. 647

1994 Ibid. pp. 647-648

1995 Metzger, *The Text of the New Testament* op. cit. pg. 101

1996 Metzger, *A Textual Commentary* op. cit. pp. 647-648

1997 Ibid. pg. 648

1998 Ibid.

1999 Dan McCartney & Charles Clayton, *Let The Reader Understand* BridgePoint Book (Wheaton Ill.) 1994 pg. 48

2000 Cf. Norman Geisler, ed., *Inerrancy* Academie Books (Grand Rapids, Mich.) 1980

2001 Robert Lightner, *First, Second, and Third John and Jude* AMG (Chattanooga, TN) 2003 pg. 80

2002 Ibid.

2003 W.A. Criswell, ed., *Criswell Study Bible* Thomas Nelson (Nashville, TN) 1979 pg. 1468

2004 Robert Lightner, *First, Second, and Third John and Jude* AMG (Chattanooga, TN) 2003 pg. 79

2005 Criswell, *Criswell Study Bible* op. cit. pg. 1468

2006 Robert Lightner, *First, Second, and Third John and Jude* AMG (Chattanooga, TN) 2003 pg. 80

2007 Barclay, *John and Jude* op. cit. pg. 140

2008 Ibid.

2009 Ironside, *John and Jude* op. cit. pp. 220-221

2010 Henry, *Vol. 6* op. cit. pg. 883

2011 Hodges, "1 John," *Bible Knowledge* op. cit. pg. 902

2012 John MacArthur, *1-3 John* Moody Press (Chicago, Ill.) 2007 pg. 205

2013 George Findlay, *Fellowship in the Life Eternal* Wm. B. Eerdmans (Grand Rapids, Mich.) 1955 pp. 405-406

2014 Ibid. pp. 406

2015 Bede the Venerable, *The Commentary on the Seven Catholic Epistles* Cistercian Publishers (Kalamazoo, Mich.) 1985 pg. 225

2016 Ibid.

2017 Wuest, *In These Last Days* op. cit. pg. 182

2018 Poole, *Vol. 3* op. cit. pg. 941

2019 W.A. Criswell, ed., *Criswell Study Bible* Thomas Nelson (Nashville, TN) 1979 pg. 1468

2020 Wuest, *In These Last Days* op. cit. pg. 181

2021 John MacArthur, *1-3 John* Moody Press (Chicago, Ill.) 2007 pg. 205

2022 Luther, *Works Vol. 30* op. cit. pg. 325

2023 Boice, *John* op. cit. pp. 175-176

2024 Barker, *Expositor's Vol. 12* op. cit. pg. 355

2025 Ibid. pg. 358

2026 Tenney, op. cit. pg. 370

2027 Ibid. pp. 370-371

2028 Edwin Blum, "Jude," *Expositor's Vol. 12* op. cit. pg. 383

2029 Unger, op. cit. pg. 552

2030 Unger, op. cit. pg. 616

2031 Barnes, *Notes - One Volume ed.* op. cit. pp. 1518-1519

2032 Ibid. pg. 1516

2033 Ibid. pg. 1516

2034 Ibid. pg. 1516

2035 Bede the Venerable, *Catholic Epistles* op. cit. pg. 245

2036 Calvin, *Catholic Epistles* op. cit. pg. 439

2037 Barnes, *Notes - One Volume ed.* op. cit. pg. 1516

2038 Lightner, *First, Second, and Third John and Jude* op. cit. pg. 150

2039 www.earlyjewishwritings.com/testmoses.html

2040 Ironside, *John and Jude* op. cit. pg. 44

2041 Edwards, *"The Blank Bible" Part 2* op. cit. pg. 1202

2042 Lightner, *First, Second, and Third John and Jude* op. cit. pg. 150

2043 Clement of Alexandria, *Ancient Christian Commentary on Scripture Vol. XI* Gerald Bray, ed., InterVarsity Press (Downers Grove, Ill.) 2000 pg. 252

2044 Josephus, "Antiquities," IV.viii.48, *Complete Works* op. cit. pg. 103

2045 *Ancient Christian Commentary on Scripture Vol. XI* Gerald Bray, ed., InterVarsity Press (Downers Grove, Ill.) 2000 pg. 252

2046 George Nickelsburg & James VanderKam, trans., *1 Enoch* Fortress Press (Minneapolis, MN) 2004 pg. 20

2047 Barclay, *John and Jude* op. cit. pg. 220

2048 http://lavistachurchofchrist.org/LVanswers/2011/04-12b.html

2049 Tertullian, *Ancient Christian Commentary on Scripture Vol. XI* Gerald Bray, ed., InterVarsity Press (Downers Grove, Ill.) 2000 pg. 254

2050 Tertullian, *Ante-Nicene Fathers Vol. IV* op. cit. pg. 16

2051 Bede the Venerable, *Catholic Epistles* op. cit. pg. 250

2052 Augustine, *Ancient Christian Commentary on Scripture Vol. XI* Gerald Bray, ed., InterVarsity Press (Downers Grove, Ill.) 2000 pg. 255

2053 Wesley, op. cit. pg. 675

2054 Alan Johnson, "Revelation," *Expositor's Vol. 12* op. cit. pg. 404

2055 Eusebius, *Church History* III.39 op. cit. pg. 127

2056 Ibid.

2057 Ibid.

2058 Ibid.

2059 Steve Waterhouse, *Who Wrote Revelation & John's Gospel?* Westcliff Press (Amarillo, TX) 2012 pg. 23

2060 Papaias, quoted in Irenaeus, "Against Heresies" 5:33, *Ante-Nicene Fathers* op. cit.

2061 Justo Gonzalez, *Story of Christianity Vol. 1* Harper Collins (New York, NY) 2010 pg. 36

2062 He was a pupil of Irenaeus who was taught by Polycarp, the disciple of John.

2063 Hippolytus, "On the Twelve Apostles," *Ante-Nicene Fathers Vol. VIII* Alexander Roberts & James Donaldson, eds., Charles Scribner (New York, NY) 1886 pp. 254-256

2064 See David Criswell, *Controversies in Revelation* Fortress Adonai (Dallas, TX) 2012 for a full debate.

2065 Ruffin, op. cit. pg. 94

2066 Some claim that Clement of Alexandria mentions Nero, but this is an internet myth. Any reading of his work shows he never once even mentions Nero [Clement of Alexandria, "Who is the Rich Man?" *Ante-Nicene Fathers Vol. 2* op. cit. pp. 603-604]

2067 Tertullian, "On Prescription Against Heretics," *Ante-Nicene Fathers Vol. 2* op. cit. pg. 260

2068 Brooks & Winberry, op. cit. pg. 76

2069 Wesley, op. cit. pg. 579

2070 Ibid. pg. 681

2071 Barnes, *Notes - One Volume ed.* op. cit. pg. 1553

2072 Hippolytus, "Refutation of All Heresies," VII.xxiv *Ante-Nicene Fathers Vol. 5* Alexander Roberts & James Donaldson, eds., Charles Scribner (New York, NY) 1886 pg. 115

2073 Ignatius, "Epistle to the Philadelphians," *Ante-Nicene Fathers Vol. 1* op. cit. pg. 71

2074 Clement of Alexandria, *Ante-Nicene Fathers Vol. 2* op. cit. pg. 385

2075 Ignatius, "Epistle to the Philadelphians," *Ante-Nicene Fathers Vol. 1* op. cit. pg. 83

2076 Irenaeus, "Against Heresies," *Ante-Nicene Fathers Vol. 1* op. cit. pg. 352

2077 Barnes, *Notes - One Volume ed.* op. cit. pg. 1560

2078 www.spiritandtruth.org/teaching/Book_of_Revelation/commentary/htm/topics/nicolaitans.html

2079 www.biblestudy.org/basicart/why-does-god-hate-practices-of-the-nicolaitans.html

2080 Johnson, "Revelation," *Expositor's Vol. 12* op. cit. pg. 444

2081 John Gill, "Commentary on the New Testament," Revelation 2:20 E-Sword Software Commentary Series

2082 *Liberty Commentary* op. cit. pg. 754

2083 Johnson, op. cit. pg. 454

2084 George Eldon Ladd, *A Commentary on the Revelation of John* Wm. B. Eerdmans (Grand Rapids, Mich.) 1972 pg. 62

2085 Johnson, "Revelation," *Expositor's Vol. 12* op. cit. pg. 453

2086 H.A. Ironside, *Revelation* Loizeaux Brothers (Neptune, NJ) 1996 ed. pg. 58

2087 George Eldon Ladd, *A Commentary on the Revelation of John* Wm. B. Eerdmans (Grand Rapids, Mich.) 1972 pg. 65

2088 George Eldon Ladd, *A Commentary on the Revelation of John* Wm. B. Eerdmans (Grand Rapids, Mich.) 1972 pg. 65

2089 Johnson, "Revelation," *Expositor's Vol. 12* op. cit. pg.457

2090 Spurgeon, *Treasury Vol. 4* op. cit. pg. 719

2091 Walter Scott, *Exposition of the Revelation of Jesus Christ* Pickering & Inglis (London, England) n.d. pg. 111

2092 *Liberty Commentary* op. cit. pg. 756

2093 Henry Morris, *The Revelation Record* Tyndale House (Wheaton, Ill.) 1983 pg. 76

2094 John Walvoord, "Revelation," *Bible Knowledge* op. cit. pg. 940

2095 Edward Hindson, *The Book of Revelation* AMG (Chattanooga, TN) 2002 pg. 49

2096 Leon Morris, The Revelation of St. John Wm. B. Eerdmans (Grand Rapids, Mich.) 1969 as cited by *Liberty Commentary* op. cit. pg. 758

2097 William Newell, *The Book of Revelation* Moody Press (Chicago, Ill.) n.d. pp. 373-374

2098 George Eldon Ladd, *A Commentary on the Revelation of John* Wm. B. Eerdmans (Grand Rapids, Mich.) 1972 pg. 75

2099 Ibid.

2100 John Walvoord, *The Revelation of Jesus Christ* Moody Press (Chicago, Ill.) 1966 pg. 107

2101 Henry Morris, *The Revelation Record* Tyndale House (Wheaton, Ill.) 1983 pg. 87

2102 Farrar, op. cit. pg. 368

2103 E.W. Bullinger, *Commentary on Revelation* Kregel (Grand Rapids, Mich.) 1984 ed. pg. 219

2104 Wesley, op. cit. pg. 695
2105 Ibid.
2106 Joseph Seiss, The Apocalypse Kregel (Grand Rapids, Mich.) 1900 pg. 103
2107 George Eldon Ladd, *A Commentary on the Revelation of John* Wm. B. Eerdmans (Grand Rapids, Mich.) 1972 pg. 73
2108 Henry Morris, *The Revelation Record* Tyndale House (Wheaton, Ill.) 1983 pg. 90
2109 Robert Mounce, *The Book of Revelation* Wm. B. Eerdmans (Grand Rapids, Mich.) 1977 pg. 135
2110 C. Leonard Woolley, *The Sumerians* W.W. Norton & Co. (New York, NY) 1965 pg. 119
2111 Roux, op. cit. pg. 87
2112 Ibid.
2113 Walvoord, *Revelation* op. cit. pg. 37
2114 Bullinger, op. cit. pg. 192
2115 Ladd, op. cit. pg. 25
2116 Hindson, *Revelation* op. cit. pg. 23
2117 John Nelson Darby, *The Collected Writings of J. N. Darby* Volume 2 Prophetic # 1 Believer's Bookshelf (Sunbury, Penn.) 1971 pg. 196
2118 John Nelson Darby, *The Collected Writings of J. N. Darby* Volume 8 Prophetic # 3 Believer's Bookshelf (Sunbury, Penn.) 1971 pg. 145
2119 Terullian, *Ante-Nicene Fathers Vol. III* op. cit. pp. 384-385
2120 Scott, op. cit. pg. 23
2121 Seiss, op. cit. pg. 27
2122 Morris, op. cit. pg. 37
2123 Ryrie, op. cit. pg. 4
2124 Seiss, op. cit. pg. 116
2125 Aphrahat, *Nicene and Post-Nicene Fathers Second Series Vol. XIII* Philip Schaff, ed., Christian Literature Co. (New York, NY) 1894 pg. 348
2126 John Lightfoot, *The Whole Works of the Rev. John Lightfoot Vol. II* J. F. Dove (London, England) 1822 pg. 322
2127 Hindson, *Revelation* op. cit. pg. 59
2128 Arthur Bloomfield, *The Key to Understanding Revelation* Bethany House (Minneapolis, MN) 1959 pg. 111
2129 Barnes, *Notes - One Volume ed.* op. cit. pg. 1575
2130 Joseph Seiss, The Apocalypse Kregel (Grand Rapids, Mich.) 1900 pg. 108
2131 Wesley, op. cit. pg. 695
2132 Robert Mounce, *The Book of Revelation* Wm. B. Eerdmans (Grand Rapids, Mich.) 1977 pg. 137
2133 George Eldon Ladd, *A Commentary on the Revelation of John* Wm. B. Eerdmans (Grand Rapids, Mich.) 1972 pg. 77
2134 Henry Morris, *The Revelation Record* Tyndale House (Wheaton, Ill.) 1983 pg. 90
2135 E.W. Bullinger, *Commentary on Revelation* Kregel (Grand Rapids, Mich.) 1984 ed. pp. 223-224
2136 Charles Ryrie, *Revelation* Moody Press (Chicago, Ill.) 1996 pg. 44
2137 Edward Hindson, *The Book of Revelation* AMG (Chattanooga, TN) 2002 pg. 59
2138 Tertullian, *Ante-Nicene Fathers Vol. III* op. cit. pg. 682
2139 Farrar, op. cit. pg. 368
2140 All pictures were obtained using valid reuse license.
2141 Criswell, *Rise and Fall* op. cit. pg. 298
2142 Randall Price, *Searching for the Original Bible* Harvest House (Eugene, OR) 2007 pg. 156
2143 Lee Martin McDonald, *The Biblical Canon* Hendrickson Publishers (Peabody, Mass.) 1995
2144 Ibid.
2145 Randall Price, *The Search for the Original Bible* Harvest House (Eugene, OR) 2007 pg. 154
2146 Brian Edwards, *Nothing but the Truth* Evangelical Press (Webster, NY) 2006 ed. pg. 218

2147 Ibid.
2148 www.christian-history.org/muratorian-canon.html
2149 Brian Edwards, *Nothing but the Truth* Evangelical Press (Webster, NY) 2006 ed. pg. 218
2150 www.christian-history.org/muratorian-canon.html
2151 McDonald, op. cit. pg. 314
2152 Ibid. pg. 308
2153 Philip Schaff, *History of the Christian Church Vol. 2* Hendrickson Publishers Peabody, Mass.) 1996 pg.
2154 F.F. Bruce, *The Canon of Scripture* IVP Academic (Downers Grove, Ill.) 1988 pg. 121
2155 The "Jesus Seminar" was a seminar of so-called theologians who met and voted on what portions of the gospels were true and what portions were legends. They called this book the "Five Gospels" and concluded that *only* "love your neighbor as yourself" was legimate, rejecting everything else in the gospels as suspect.
2156 F.F. Bruce, *The Canon of Scripture* IVP Academic (Downers Grove, Ill.) 1988 pg. 144
2157 Edwards, op. cit. pg. 226
2158 J.B. Lightfoot, & J.R. Harmer, *The Apostlic Fathers* Baker Book House (Grand Rapids, Mich.) 1984 pg. 293
2159 Ibid.
2160 Bruce, op. cit. pg. 77
2161 Ibid.
2162 Lightfoot & Harmer, op. cit. pg. 239
2163 Ibid.
2164 J.N.D. Kelly, *The Oxford Dictionary of Popes* Oxford University Press (Oxford, England) 1986 pg. 7
2165 Lightfoot & Harmer, op. cit. pg. 3
2166 J.N.D. Kelly, *The Oxford Dictionary of Popes* Oxford University Press (Oxford, England) 1986 pg. 7
2167 Ibid.
2168 Clement is controversial among Protestants because he is the only early church father who appeals to the authority of bishops, but even this statement is a far cry from the doctrine of papal supremacy expressed later.
2169 Lightfoot & Harmer, op. cit. pg. 215
2170 Ibid.
2171 Bruce, op. cit. pg. 77
2172 Ibid. pg. 166
2173 Ibid. pg. 201
2174 en.wikipedia.org/wiki/Gospel_of_thomas
2175 www.goarch.org/ourfaith/ourfaith9560
2176 Price, op. cit. pg. 113
2177 Ibid.
2178 Nestle & Aland, *Nestle-Aland Novum Tetamentum Graece* op. cit. pp. 685-688
2179 Ibid. pg. 686
2180 Young Kyu Kim, "Paleographical Dating of $\mathfrak{P}^{46}$ to the Later First Century," *Biblica*, lxix (1988) pp. 248-257
2181 Metzger, op. cit. pg. 265
2182 Ibid.
2183 Metzger, op. cit. pg. 38
2184 Kurt & Barbara Aland, *The Text of the New Testament* trans. Erroll Rhodes Wm. B. Eerdmans (Grand Rapids, Mich.) 1989 69
2185 Cf. Metzger, op. cit. pg. 40, footnote 1
2186 Theodore of Mapsuestia, *Ancient Christian Commentary Vol. IV B* op. cit. pg. 395
2187 Ibid & John Foxe, *Acts and Monuments of the Church Vol. 1* Religious Tract Society (London, England) 1860s ed. Pg. 95

2188 Compiled from David Hunt, *In Defense of the Faith* Harvest House (Eugene, OR) 1996 pg. 71 & Price, op. cit. pg. 114

2189 Greenlee, *New Testament Criticism* op. cit. pp. 81-87

2190 Metzger, op. cit. pg. 217

2191 Ibid. pg. 196

2192 Ibid.

2193 Ibid. pg. 187

2194 Ibid. pg. 191

2195 Greenlee, op. cit. pg. 58

2196 It is interesting to note that King James only advocates often attack modern translations for "removing" the word "God." However, the reverse (oς mistaken for θς) also occurs. There is no grand conspiracy to remove God from the Bible. Such attacks are not only frivolous, but the King James only advocate would also be surprised to learn how many times modern translation use the word "God" where it is *missing* from the King James.

2197 Ibid. pg. 196

2198 Cf. Foxe, *Acts and Monuments* op. cit. pg. 95

2199 Price, op. cit. pg. 113

2200   Norman L. Geisler and William E. Nix, *A General Introduction to the Bible*, Moody (Chicago, Ill.) 1986 ed. pp. 366-67

2201 Randall Niles, "Bible Manuscripts," www.allaboutthejourney.org/bible-manuscripts.htm

2202 Ibid.

2203 Sir Robert Anderson, "Bible and Modern Criticism," *The Collected Works of Sir Robert Andreson Vol. II Anderson on Biblical Criticism* Fortress Adonai Press (North Carleston, SC) 2011 pg. 47

2204 Ibid. pg. 48

2205 Ibid. pg. 223

2206 Ibid. pg. 78

2207 See David Criswell, *Controversies in the Pentateuch* Fortress Adonai (Dallas, TX) 2007

WORKS CITED

BOOKS

T.K. Abbott, *Critical & Exegetical Commentary – Epistles to the Ephesians* T & T Clark (Edinburgh, Scotland) 1897

Thomas Abbott, *A Critical and Exegetical Commentary on the Epistles to the Ephesians and to the Colossians* T & T Clark (Edinburgh, Scottland) 1897

Peter Abelard, *Fathers of the Church – Medieval Vol. 12 – Commentary on Romans* Steven Cartwright, trans., Catholic University Press of America (Washington, D.C.) 2011

Kurt & Barbara Aland, ed., *Nestle-Aland NovumTestamentum Graece* United Bible Society (Stuttgart, Germany) 1898

Kurt & Barbara Aland, *The Text of the New Testament* trans. Erroll Rhodes Wm. B. Eerdmans (Grand Rapids, Mich.) 1989

David Allen, *Hebrews* B&H Publishers (Nashville, TN) 2010

David Allen, *Lukan Authorship of Hebrews* B&H Academic (Nashville, TN) 2010

Sir Robert Anderson, *The Bible and Modern Criticism* Pickering & Inglis (London, England) 1907

Sir Robert Anderson, *The Collected Works of Sir Robert Andreson Vol. I Anderson on Prophecy* Fortress Adonai Press (North Carleston, SC) 2011

Sir Robert Anderson, *The Collected Works of Sir Robert Andreson Vol. II Anderson on Biblical Criticism* Fortress Adonai Press (North Carleston, SC) 2011

Sir Robert Anderson, *The Critics Criticized* Pickering & Inglis (London, England) 1904

Robert Anderson, *Forgotten Truths* Pickering & Inglis (London, England)

Thomas Aquinas, *Commentary on the Epistle to the Hebrews* St. Augustine Press (South Bend, ON) 2006

Aristotle, *De Interpretatione* Oxford University Press (Oxford, England) 1975 ed.

Gleason Archer, *Encyclopedia of Bible Difficulties* Zondervan Publishers (Grand Rapids, Mich.) 1982

William Barclay, *The All-Sufficient Christ* Westminister Press (Philadelphia, PN) 1963

William Barclay, *The Letters to the Galatians and Ephesians* Westminister Press (Philadelphia, PN) 1954

William Barclay, *The Letter to the Hebrews* Westminister John Knox Press (Loeisville, KY) 1955 (2002 ed.)

William Barclay, *The Letters of James and Peter* Westminister Press (Philadelphia, PN) 1958

William Barclay, *The Letters of John and Jude* Westminister Press (Philadelphia, PN) 1958

William Barclay, *The Letters to Timothy, Titus, and Philemon* Westminister Press (Philadephia, PN) 1956

Albert Barnes, *Barnes' Notes on Ephesians, Philippians, & Colossians* Harper & Row (New York, NY) 1854

Albert Barnes, *Barnes' Notes on First Epistle of Paul to the Corinthians* Harpers Brothers (New York, NY) 1854

498

Albert Barnes, *Barnes' Notes on Second Epistle of Paul to the Corinthians and Galatians* Harpers Brothers (New York, NY) 1854

Albert Barnes, *Barnes' Notes on the New Testament One Volume ed.* Kregel (Grand Rapids, Mich.) 1962

Donald Barnhouse, *Romans Vol. 1* Wm. B. Eerdmans (Grands Rapids, Mich.) 1952

Donald Barnhouse, *Romans Vol. 2* Wm. B. Eerdmans (Grands Rapids, Mich.) 1952

Donald Barnhouse, *Romans Vol. 3* Wm. B. Eerdmans (Grands Rapids, Mich.) 1952

Donald Barnhouse, *Romans Vol. 4* Wm. B. Eerdmans (Grands Rapids, Mich.) 1952

Donald Barnhouse, *Romans Vol. 5* Wm. B. Eerdmans (Grands Rapids, Mich.) 1952

Donald Barnhouse, *Romans Vol. 6* Wm. B. Eerdmans (Grands Rapids, Mich.) 1952

Donald Barnhouse, *Romans Vol. 7* Wm. B. Eerdmans (Grands Rapids, Mich.) 1952

Donald Barnhouse, *Romans Vol. 8* Wm. B. Eerdmans (Grands Rapids, Mich.) 1952

Donald Barnhouse, *Thessalonians* Zondervan Publishers (Grand Rapids, Mich.) 1977

Karl Barth, *Epistle to the Romans* Oxford (London, England) 1950 ed.

Karl Barth, *The Epislte to the Philippians* John Know Press (Louisville, KT) 2002 ed.

Marcus Barth, *The Broken Wall* Judson Press (Valley Forge, VA) 1959

Ronald Baxter, *Charistmatic Gift of Tongues* Kregel Publishers (Grand Rapids, Mich.) 1981

Ronald Baxter, *Gifts of the Spirit* Kregel Publications (Grand Rapids, Mich.) 1983

Bede the Venerable, *The Commentary on the Seven Catholic Epistles* Cistercian Publishers (Kalamazoo, Mich.) 1985

Ernest Best, *A Commentary on the 1st and 2nd Epistles to the Thessalonians* Hendrickson Publishers (Peabody, Mass.) 1988

E.J. Bicknell, *The 1st and 2nd Epistles to the Thessalonians* Methuen & Co. (London, England) 1932

Charles Bigg, *A Critical and Exegetical Commentary Epistles of St. Peter and St. Jude* T & T Clark (Edinburgh, Scotland) 1978

Allan Bloom, *The Closing of the American Mind* Simon and Schuster (New York, NY) 1987

Arthur Bloomfield, *The Key to Understanding Revelation* Bethany House (Minneapolis, MN) 1959

Arthur Bloomfield, *The Key to Understanding Revelation* Bethany House (Bloomington, MN) 2002 reprint

James Montgomery Boice, *Ephesians* Baker Books (Grand Rapids, Mich.) 1988

James Montgomery Boice, *Foundations of the Christian Faith* InterVarsity Press (Downers Grove, Ill.) 1986

James Montgomery Boice, *The Epistles of John* Zondervan Publishers (Grand Rapids, Mich.) 1978

James Montgomery Boice, *Ephesians* Baker Books (Grand Rapids, Mich.) 1988

James Montgomery Boice, *Philippians* Zondervan Publishers (Grand Rapids, Mich.) 1971

James Montgomery Boice, *Romans Vol. 1* Baker Books (Grand Rapids, Mich.) 1991 ed.

James Montgomery Boice, *Romans Vol. 2* Baker Books (Grand Rapids, Mich.) 1991 ed.

James Montgomery Boice, *Romans Vol. 3* Baker Books (Grand Rapids, Mich.) 1991 ed.

499

James Montgomery Boice, *Romans Vol. 4* Baker Books (Grand Rapids, Mich.) 1991 ed.

A.E. Brooke, *A Critical and Exegetical Commentary on Johannine Epistles* T&T Clark Edinburgh, Scotland) 1912

James Brooks & Carlton Winbery, *Syntax of New Testament Greek* University Press of America (Lanham, MD) 1979

John Brown, *Exposition on the Epistles of the Apostle Paul to the Hebrews Vol. 1* William Oliphant (Edinburgh, Scotland) 1862

John Brown, *Analytical Exposition of the Epistle of Paul to the Romans* William Oliphant (Edinburgh, Scotland) 1857

John Brown, *Expository Discourses on the First Epistle of the Apostle Peter* Robert Carter & Bro. (New York, NY) 1855

Laurence Browne, *Indian Church Commentaries - Acts of the Apostles* Diocesan Press (London, England) 1925

F.F. Bruce, *1 & 2 Corinthians* Oliphants (London, England) 1971

F.F. Bruce, *The Canon of Scripture* IVP Academic (Downers Grove, Ill.) 1988

F.F. Bruce, *The Epistles to the Colossians, to Philemon, and to Ephesians* Wm. B. Eerdmans (Grand Rapids, Mich.) 1984

F.F. Bruce, *The Epistle to the Ephesians* Pickering & Inglis (London, England) 1961

F.F. Bruce, *Epistle to the Galatians – A Commentary on the Greek Text* Wm. B. Eerdmans (Grand Rapids, Mich.) 1982

F.F. Bruce, *The Epistle to the Hebrews* Wm. B. Eerdmans (Grand Rapids, Mich.) 1964

F.F. Bruce, *The Letter of Paul to the Romans* Wm. B. Eerdmans (Grand Rapids, Mich.) 1985

F.F. Bruce, *World Biblical Commentary Vol. 45 1 & 2 Thessalonians* Word Books (Waco, TX) 1982

A.R. Buckland, *St. Paul's 2nd Epistle to the Thessalonians* Union Press (Philadelphia, PN) 1909

E.W. Bullinger, *Commentary on Revelation* Kregel (Grand Rapids, Mich.) 1984 ed.

E.W. Bullinger, *The Great Cloud of Witnesses* Lamp Press (London, England) 1956

Rudolf Bultmann, *The Second Letter to the Corinthians* Augsburg Publishers (Minneapolis, MN) 1985 ed.

Ernest De Witt Burton, *A Critical and Exegetical Commentary on the Epistle to the Galatians* T & T Clark (Edinburgh, Scotland) 1921

John Calvin, *Commentary on 1 John* Crossway Classics (Wheaton, Ill.) 1998 pg. 30

John Calvin, *Commentary on 1, 2 Timothy & Titus* Crossway Books (Wheaton, Ill.) 1998

John Calvin, *Commentaries on the Catholic Epistles* Wm. B. Eerdmans (Grand Rapids, Mich.) 1948

John Calvin, *Commentary on the Epistle to the Hebrews* Wm. B. Eerdmans (Grand Rapids, Mich.) 1949

John Calvin, *Commentary on the Epistle of Paul the Apostle to the Corinthians Vol. 1* Wm. B. Eerdmans (Grand Rapids, Mich.) 1948

John Calvin, *Commentary on the Epistle of Paul the Apostle to the Galatian, Ephesians, Philippians, and Colossians* Wm. B. Eerdmans (Grand Rapids, Mich.) 1965

500

John Calvin, *Commentary on the Epistle of Paul to the Romans* Wm. B. Eerdmans (Grand Rapids, Mich.) 1947

John Calvin, *Commentary on Philippians, Colossians, and Thessalonians* Wm. B. Eerdmans (Grand Rapids, Mich.) 1948 ed.

D.A. Carson, *Showing the Spirit* Baker Book (Grand Rapids, Mich.) 1987

Lewis Sperry Chafer, *The Ephesian Letter* Dunham Publications (Findlay, Ohio) 1953

Lewis Sperry Chafer, *Systematic Theology Vol. IV* Dallas Seminary Press (Dallas, TX) 1948

Kenneth Chafin, *The Communicator's Commentary 1, 2 Corinthians* Lloyd Ogilvie, ed, Word Publishers (Wavo, TX) 1985

Thomas Chalmers, *Lectures on the Epistle of Paul the Apostle to the Romans* Robert Carter & Bro. (New York, NY) 1855

Henry Cook, *The Epistle to the Romans* Carey Press (London, England) 1930

Mal Couch, *A Biblical Theology of the Church* Kregel (Grand Rapids, Mich.) 1999

Mal Couch, ed., *The Fundamentals for the Twenty-First Century* Kregel Publishers (Grand Rapids, Mich.) 2000

Mal Couch, *The Hope of Christ's Return* AMG Publishers (Chattanooga, TN) 2001

David Criswell, *Apostles After Jesus* Fortress Adonai Press (Dallas, TX) 2013

David Criswell, *Controversies in the Acts of the Apostles* Fortress Adonai Press (Dallas, TX) 2013

David Criswell, *Controversies in the Gospels* Fortress Adonai Press (Dallas, TX) 2012

David Criswell, *Controversies in the Pentateuch* Fortress Adonai (Dallas, TX) 2010

David Criswell, *Controversies in the Prophets* Fortress Adonai (Dallas, TX) 2008

David Criswell, *Controversies in Revelation* Fortress Adonai (Dallas, TX) 2007

David Criswell, *Rise and Fall of the Holy Roman Empire* Publish America (Baltimore, MD) 2005

Frederick Danker, *Augsburg Commentary on the N.T. II Corinthians* Augsburg Press (Minneapolis, MN) 1989

John Nelson Darby, *The Collected Writings of J.N. Darby   Prophetic No. 1   Vol. 2* Bible Truth Publishers (Addison, IL) n.d.

John Nelson Darby, *The Collected Writings of J. N. Darby   Volume 2   Prophetic # 1* Believer's Bookshelf (Sunbury, Penn.) 1971

John Nelson Darby, *The Collected Writings of J. N. Darby   Volume 8   Prophetic # 3* Believer's Bookshelf (Sunbury, Penn.) 1971

John Nelson Darby, *Exposition of the Epistle of James* G. Morrish (London, England) n.d.

John Nelson Darby, *Notes on the Epistles to the Corinthians* G. Morrish (London, England) n.d.

John Nelson Darby, *Notes on the Epistle to the Galatians* G. Morrish (London, England) n.d.

John Nelson Darby, *Notes on the Epistles of John* G. Morrish (London, England) n.d.

John Nelson Darby, *Notes from Lectures on the Epistle to the Hebrews* G. Morrish (London, England) n.d.

Benjamin Davidson, *The Analytical Hebrew and Chaldee Lexicon* Zondervan House (Grand Rapids, Mich.) 1848

Franz Delitzsch, *Commentary on the Epistle to the Hebrews* *Vol. 1* Wm. B. Eerdmans (Grand Rapids, Mich.) 1952

Franz Delitzsch, *Commentary on the Epistle to the Hebrews* *Vol. 2* Wm. B. Eerdmans (Grand Rapids, Mich.) 1952

James Dobson, *Hide and Seek* Revell (Ada, MI) 1974

C.H. Dodd, *The Johannine Epistles* Hodler & Stoughtor (London, England) 1946 pg. 27

Roberts & James Donaldson, eds., *Ante-Nicene Fathers* *Vol. 8* Alexander Charles Scribner (New York, NY) 1886

Daniel Dorian, *James : Reformed Expository Commentary* (Phillipsburg, NJ) 2007

James Dunn, *Unity and Diversity in the New Testament* SCM Press (Canterbury, England) 2006

John Eaide, *A Commentary on the Greek Text of the Epistles of Paul to the Thessalonians* James & Klock (Minneapolis, MN) 1877

Brian Edwards, *Nothing but the Truth* Evangelical Press (Webster, NY) 2006 ed.

Jonathan Edwards, *"The Blank Bible" Part 2* Stephen Stein, ed., Yale University Press (New Haven, CT) 2006

Jonathan Edwards, *The Works of Jonathan Edwards* *Vol. 15 Notes on Scriptures* Yale University Press (New Haven, Conn.) 1998

Charles Ellicott, *Commentary on the Epistle of St. Paul to the Thessalonians* Zondervan Publishers (Grand Rapids, Mich.) 1861 (1957 ed.)

Charles Ellicott, *A Critical and Grammatical Commentary on the Pastoral Epistles* Warren Draper (Philadelphia, PN) 1884

Charles Ellicott, *A Critical and Grammatical Commentary on Philippians, Colossians, and Philemon* Warren Draper (Boston, MS) 1876

Charles Elliot, *A Critical and Grammatical Commentary on St. Paul's Epistle to the Galatians* Warren Draper (Andover, CN) 1896

Charles Elliott, *Ephesians* Logmans Green (London, England) 1884

Desiderius Erasmus, *Collected Works of Erasmus, Vol. 42 – Paraphrase on Romans & Galatians* University of Toronto Press (Toronto, Canada) 1984

Desiderius Erasmus, *Collected Works of Erasmus Vol. 43 – Paraphrases on the Epistles to the Corinthians, Ephesians, Philippians, Colossians, and Thessalonians* University of Toronto Press (Toronto, Canada) 2009

Desiderius Erasmus, *Collected Works of Erasmus, Vol. 56 – Annotations on Romans* University of Toronto Press (Toronto, Canada) 1994

Charles Erdman, *The Epistle to the Hebrews* Westminister Press (Philadelphia, PN) 1934

Charles Erdman, *The Pastoral Epistles of Paul* Westminister Press (Philadephia, PN) 1923

Millard Erickson, *Christian Theology* Baker Book House (Grand Rapids, Mich.) 1983

Eusebius, *The Church History*, Paul Meier, trans. Kregel Publishers (Grand Rapids, Mich.) 1999

Patrick Fairbairn, *Commentary on the Pastarol Epistles* Zondervan Publishers (Grand Rapids, Mich.) 1874 (1956 ed.)

Jerry Falwell & Ed Hindson, eds., *Liberty Commentary on the New Testament* Liberty Press (Lynchburg, Virginia) 1978

F.W. Farrar, *The Epistle of Paul the Apostle to the Hebrews* Cambridge (Cambridge, England) 1896

F.W. Farrar, *Texts Explained* F.M. Barton (Cleveland, Oh.) 1899

J.D. Faust, *The Rod* Schoettle Publishing (Hayesville, NC) 2003

Gordon Fee, *1 & 2 Timothy, Titus* Harper & Row (San Francisco, CA) 1984

Gordon Fee, *The First Epistle to the Corinthians* Wm. B. Eerdmans (Grand Rapids, Mich.) 1987

Gordon Fee, *The 1st and 2nd Letters to the Thessalonians* Wm. B. Eerdmans (Grand Rapids, Mich.) 2009

Gordon Fee, *Paul's Letter to the Philippians* Wm. B. Eerdmans (Grand Rapids, Mich.) 1995

G.G. Findlay, *The Epistle of Paul the Apostle to the Thessalonians* Cambridge University (Cambridge, England) 1904

G.G. Findlay, *Expositor's Bible – Ephesians* Armstrong & Sons (New York, NY) 1898

George Findlay, *Fellowship in the Life Eternal* Wm. B. Eerdmans (Grand Rapids, Mich.) 1955

John Foxe, *Acts and Monuments of the Church Vol. 1* Religious Tract Society (London, England) 1860s ed.

James Everett Frame, *A Critical and Exegetical Commentary on the Epistle of St. Paul to the Thessalonians* T & T Clark (Edinburgh, Scotland) 1912

Arno Gaebelein, *God's Masterpiece* Our Hope (New York, NY) 1913

Norman L. Geisler and William E. Nix, *A General Introduction to the Bible*, Moody (Chicago, Ill.) 1986 ed.

Norman Geisler, ed., *Inerrancy* Academic Books (Grand Rapids, Mich.) 1980

Steven Ger, *The Book of Hebrews : Christ is Greater* AMG (Chattanooga, TN) 2009

John H. Gerstner, *A Primer on Free Will* Presbyterian and Reformed Publishing Co., (Phillipsburg, NJ) 1982

William Genenius, *Gesenius' Hebrew and Chaldee Lexicon to the Old Tesament* Samuel Tregelles, trans., Baker Books (Grand Rapids, Mich.) 1847 (1984 ed.)

Gene Getz, *Doing Your Part* Regal Books (Venture, CA) 1984

Gene Getz, *Looking Up When You Feel Down* Regal Books (Ventura, CA) 1985

Gene Getz, *The Measure of a Christian* Regal Books (Venture, CA) 1983

Gene Getz, *Standing Firm* Regal Books (Venture, CA) 1986

Frederic Louis Godet, *Commentary on First Corintians* Kregel Press (Grand Rapids, Mich.) 1977 ed. (1889)

Frederick Louis Godet, *Commentary of Romans* Kregel Publishers (Grand Rapids, Mich.) 1977 ed.

Justo Gonzalez, *Story of Christanity Vol. 1* HarperCollins (San Francisco, CA) 1984 & 2010 eds.

William Gouge, *Commentary on Hebrews* Kregel Publishers (Grand Rapids, Mich.) 1640s (1980 ed.)

Robert Govett, *Govett on 1 John* Conley & Schoettle (Miami Springs, FL) 1985

Robert Govett, *Govett on Ephesians* Conley & Schoettle Publ. (Miami Springs, FL) 1981 ed. (1889)

Robert Govett, *Govett on Galatians* Conley & Schoettle Pub. (Miami Springs, FL) 1981 ed. (1872)

Robert Govett, *Govett on Hebrews* Conley & Schoettle (Miama Springs, FL) 1981

Robert Govett, *Govett on Romans* Conley & Schoettle (Miama Springs, FL) 1981

James Grant, *1 & 2 Thessalonians* Crossway Books (Wheaton, Ill.) 2011

J.P. Greene, *The Pastoral Epistles* S.B.C. (Nashville, TN) 1915

Oliver Greene, *Epistles of John* Gospel Hour (Greenville, SC) 1966

Oliver Greene, *The Epistles of Paul the Apostle to the Thessalonians* Gospel Hour (Greenville, SC) 1964

Oliver Green, *The Epistles of Paul the Apostle to Timothy and Titus* Gospel Hour (Greenville, SC) 1964

J. Harold Greenlee, *An Exegetical Summary of Philippians* SIL International (Dallas, TX) 1992

J. Harold Greenlee, *Introduction to New Testament Textual Criticism* Hendrickson Publishers (Peabody, MS) 1995

Robert Gromacki, *Philippians and Colossians* AMG Press (Chattanooga, TN) 2003

Robert Gromacki, *Stand Bold in Grace* Baker Books (Grand Rapids, Mich.) 1984

Robert Gromacki, *Stand Perfect in Wisdom* Baker Books (Grand Rapids, Mich.) 1981

Robert Gundry, *A Survey of the New Testament* Zondervan Publishers (Grand Rapids, Mich.) 1994

Donald Guthrie, ed., *Galatians* The Attic Press (Greenwood, SC) 1969

Donald Guthrie, *The Pastoral Epistles* Wm. B. Eerdmans (Grand Rapids, Mich.) 1957

Douglas Harink, *1 & 2 Peter* Brazos Press (Grand Rapids, Mich.) 2009

Murray Harris, *Colossians & Philemon* William B. Eerdmans (Grand Rapids, Mich.) 1991

Roy Harrisville, *Augsburg Commentary on N.W. 1 Corinthians* Augsburg Publishers (Minneapolis, MN) 1987

Robert Harvey & Philip Towner, *2 Peter and Jude* InterVarsity Press (Downers Grove, Ill.) 2009

Erik Heen, Philip Krey, eds., *Ancient Christian Commentary on Scripture Vol. X* Intervarsity Press (Downers Grove, Ill.) 2005

William Hendrickson, *New Testament Commentary Exposition of I & II Thessalonians* Baker Books (Grand Rapids, Mich.) 1955

Matthew Henry, *Commentary on the Whole Bible Vol. 6* Hendrickson Publishers (Peabody, Mass.) 1998 ed.

Edward Hindson, *The Book of Revelation* AMG (Chattanooga, TN) 2002

Charles Hodge, *Commentary on 1 & 2 Corinthians* Banner of Truth (Carlisle, PA) 1857

Charles Hodge, *Commentary on the Epistle to the Romans* Wm. B. Eerdmans (Grand Rapids, Mich.) 1886 (1950 ed.)

Charles Hodge, *Ephesians* Crossway Books (Wheaton, Ill.) 1994

Zane Hodges, *The Epistle of James* Grace Evangelical Seminary (Irving, TX) 1994

C.F. Hogg & W.E. Vine, *The Epistles of Paul the Apostle to the Thessalonians* Pickering & Inglis (London, England) 1929

Dave Hunt, *The Cult Explosion* Harvest House (Eugene, OR) 1983

Dave Hunt, *In Defense of the Faith* Harvest House (Eugene, OR) 1996

Dave Hunt and T.A. McMahon, *The Seduction of Christianity* Harvest House (Eugene, OR) 1985

Dave Hunt, *What Love is This?* Loyal Publishing (Sisters, OR) 2002

John Hutchinson, *Exposition of Paul's Epistle to the Philippians* Klock & Klock (Minneapolis, MN) 1887 (1985 ed.)

Thomas Ice & Timothy Demy ed., *When the Trumpet Sounds* Harvest House (Eugene, OR) 1995

H.A. Ironside, *Addresses on the 1st and 2nd Epistles of Thessalonians* Loizeaux Brothers (New York, NY) 1947

H.A. Ironside, *Addresses on the 1st and 2nd Epistles of Timothy, Titus, and Philemon* Loizeaux Brothers (New York, NY) 1947

H.A. Ironside, *Addresses on the Epistles of John and an Exposition of the Epistle of Jude* Loizeaux Brothers (Neptune, NJ) 1931

H.A. Ironside, *Addresses on the Second Epistle to the Corinthians* Loizeaux Brothers (New York, NY) 1938

H.A. Ironside, *Galatians* Loizeaux Brothers (Neptune, NJ) 1941

H.A. Ironside, *In the Heavenlies* Loizeaux Brothers (New York, NY) 1937

H.A. Ironside, *Lectures on the Epistles to the Colossians* Loizeaux Brothers (New York, NY) 1928

H.A. Ironside, *Lectures on the Epistle to the Romans* Loizeaux Brothers (New York, NY) 1927

H.A. Ironside, *Notes on the Epistle of James* Loizeaux Brothers (Neptune, NJ) 1947

H.A. Ironside, *Notes on the Epistles of Peter* Loizeaux Brothers (Neptune, NJ) 1947

H.A. Ironside, *Notes on Philippians* Loizeaux Brothers (New York, NY) 1946

H.A. Ironside, *Revelation* Loizeaux Brothers (Neptune, NJ) 1996 ed.

H.A. Ironside, *Studies in the Epistle to the Hebrews and Epistle to Titus* Loizeaux Brothers (New York, NY) 1932

Flavius Josephus, *The Complete Works of Flavius Josephus* Kregel Publishers (Grand Rapids, Mich.) 1981

Dan Keating, *First and Second Peter, Jude* Baker Academic (Grand Rapids, Mich.) 2011

J.N.D. Kelly, *A Commentary on the Epistles of Peter and of Jude* Harper and Row (New York, NY) 1969

J.N.D. Kelly, *A Commentary on the Pastoral Epistles* Adam and Charles Black (London, England) 1963

J.N.D. Kelly, *The Oxford Dictionary of Popes* Oxford University Press (Oxford, England) 1986

William Kelly, *An Exposition of the Epistle to the Hebrews* T. Weston (London, England) 1905

William Kelly, *An Exposition of the Epistle of John the Apostle* T. Weston (London, England) 1905

William Kelly, *The Epistle of Paul the Apostle to the Thessalonians* F.E. Race (London, England) 1912

William Kelly, *Lectures on Galatians* G. Morrish (London, England) n.d.

William Kelly, *Notes on the 2nd Epistle to the Corinthians* G. Morrish (London, England) 1882

William Kelly, *The Preaching to the Spirits in Prison* Bible Truth Publishers (Oak Park, Ill.) 1970

Homer Kent, *The Pastoral Epistles* Moody (Chicago, Ill.) 1958

Young Kyu Kim, "Paleographical Dating of $\mathfrak{P}^{46}$ to the Later First Century," *Biblica*, lxix (1988)

Woodrow Kroll, *The Book of Romans* AMG Publishers (Chattanooga, TN) 2002

George Eldon Ladd, *A Commentary on the Revelation of John* Wm. B. Eerdmans (Grand Rapids, Mich.) 1972

George Eldon Ladd, *A Theology of the New Testament by George Eldon Ladd* Wm. B. Eerdmans (Grand Rapids, Mich.) 1974

Tim LaHaye, Gen. Ed., *Tim LaHaye Prophecy Study Bible* AMG Publishers (Chattanooga, TN) 2001

Tim LaHaye, Ed Hindson, eds., *The Popular Encyclopedia of Bible Prophecy* Harvest House (Eugene, OR) 2004

G.H. Lang, *The Epistle to the Hebrews* Schoettle Publishing (Hayesville, NC) 1951 (2008 ed.)

Kenneth Scott Latourette, *A History of Christianity Vol. 1* Harper & Row (New York, NY) 1953

C.S. Lewis, *The Screwtape Letters* Collier (New York, NY) 1961

J.B. Lightfoot, & J.R. Harmer, *The Apostlic Fathers* Baker Book House (Grand Rapids, Mich.) 1984

J.B. Lightfoot, *The Epistle of St. Paul to the Galatians* Zondervan Publishers (Grand Rapids, Mich.) 1865 (1957 ed.)

J.B. Lightfoot, *St. Paul's Epistles to the Colossans and to Philemon* MacMillan (London, England) 1875

J.B. Lightfoot, *St. Paul's Epistle to the Philippians* MacMillan (London, England) 1868

John Lightfoot, *The Whole Works of the Rev. John Lightfoot Vol. II* J. F. Dove (London, England) 1822

Robert Lightner, *First, Second, and Third John and Jude* AMG (Chattanooga, TN) 2003

R.C.H. Lenski, *The Interpretation of the Epistle to the Hebrews and Epistle of James* Lutheran Books (Columbus, Oh.) 1938

R.C.H. Lenski, *Interpretation of the Epistles of St. Peter, St. John, and st. Jude* Wartburg Press (Columbus, OH) 1945

R.C.H. Lenski, *The Interpretation of St. Paul's Epistle to the Romans* Wartburg Press (Columbus, Ohio) 1945

R.C.H. Lenski, *The Interpretation of St. Paul's First and Second Epistles to the Corinthians* Wartburg Press (Columbus, Ohio) 1937

R.C.H. Lenski, *Interpretation of the Epistles of St. Peter, St. John, and st. Jude* Wartburg Press (Columbus, OH) 1945

R.C.H. Lenski, *The Interpretation of the Acts of the Apostles* Warburg Press (Columbus, OH) 1944

R.C.H. Lenski, *The Interpretation of St. Paul's Epistle to the Romans* Wartburg Press (Columbus, Ohio) 1945

D. Martin Lloyd-Jones, *Christian Unity Ephesians 4:1-16* Baker Books (Grand Rapids, Mich.) 1980

D. Martin Lloyd-Jones, *Expository Sermons on 2 Peter* Banner of Truth (Carlisle, PN) 1983

D. Martin Lloyd-Jones, *The Life of Joy* Baker Books (Grand Rapids, Mich.) 1989

D. Martin Lloyd-Jones, *Love So Amazing* Baker Books (Grand Rapids, Mich.) 1995

D. Martin Lloyd-Jones, *Romans : An Exposition in Chapter 1* Zondervan Publishers (Grands Rapids, Mich.) 1985

D. Martin Lloyd-Jones, *Romans : An Exposition in Chapter 5* Zondervan Publishers (Grands Rapids, Mich.) 1985

D. Martin Lloyd-Jones, *Romans : An Exposition in Chapter 13* Zondervan Publishers (Grands Rapids, Mich.) 1985

Walter Lock, *A Critical and Exegetical Commentary on the Pastoral Epistles* T & T Clark (London, England) 1924

Walter Lock, *The Epistle to the Ephesians* Westminister Methuen & Co. (London, England) 1929

Rene Lopez, *Roman Unlocked* 21st Century Press (Springfield, MO) 2009

Martin Luther, *Commentary on the Epistle to the Romans* Kregel Publishers (Grand Rapids, Mich.) 1954

Martin Luther, *A Commentary on St. Paul's Epistle to Galatians* Theodore Graebner, trans., Zondervan Publishers (Grand Rapids, Mich.) 1900

Martin Luther, *Complete Works Vol. 18* Concordia House Publishing (St. Louis, MS) 1958

Martin Luther, *Complete Works Vol. 30 The Catholic Epistles* Concordia Publishing (St. Louis, MO) 1967

John MacArthur, *1-3 John* Moody Press (Chicago, Ill.) 2007

John MacArthur, *1 Corinthians* Moody Press (Chicago, Ill.) 1984

John MacArthur, *1 Peter* Moody Press (Chicago, Illl.) 2004

John MacArthur, *1 Timothy* Moody (Chicago, Ill.) 1995

John MacArthur, *2 Timothy* Moody (Chicago, Ill.) 1995

John MacArthur, *2 Peter and Jude* Moody Press (Chicago, Illl.) 2005

John MacArthur, *Colossians and Philemon* Moody Press (Chicago, Ill.) 1992

John MacArthur, *Colossians and Philemon* Moody Press (Chicago, Ill.) 1992

John MacArthur, *Ephesians* Moody Press (Chicago, Ill.) 1986

John MacArthur, *James* Moody Press (Chicago, Ill.) 1998

John MacArthur, *Hebrews* Moody Press (Chicago, Ill.) 1983

John MacArthur, *Liberated for Life* Bible Comm. For Laymn (Glendale, CA) 1976

John MacArthur, *The MacArthur New Testament Commentary Matthew 24-28* Moody Bible Institute (Chicago, Ill.) 1985

John MacArthur, *Philippians* Moody Press (Chicago, Ill.) 2001

John MacArthur, *Romans 1-8* Moody Press (Chicago, Ill.) 1991

John MacArthur, *Romans 9-16* Moody Press (Chicago, Ill.) 1991

Dan McCartney & Charles Clayton, *Let The Reader Understand* BridgePoint Book (Wheaton Ill.) 1994

Lee Martin McDonald, *The Biblical Canon* Hendrickson Publishers (Peabody, Mass.) 1995

Scot McKnight, *The Letter of James* Wm. B. Eerdmans (Grand Rapids, Mich.) 2011

Karl Marx and Frederick Engels, *The Communist Manifesto* Progress Publishers (Moscow, Russia) 1848

Joseph Mede, *The Apostasy of the Latter Times* Macintosh Printer (London, England) 1865 ed.

Bruce Metzger, *The Text of the New Testament* Oxford University (Oxford, England) 1992

Bruce Metzger, *A Textual Commentary on the Greek New Testament* United Bible Society (Stuttgart, German) 1994 ed.

Richard Melick, Jr., *New American Commentary Vol. 32 Philpipians, Colossians, and Philemon* Broadman Press (Nashville, TN) 1991

F.B. Meyer, *The Way Into The Holiest* Fleming Revell (New York, NY) 1893

Heinrich Meyer, *Critical and Exegetical Commentary on the New Testament Romans Vol. 1* T & T Clark (Edinburgh, Scotland) 1873

Heinrich Meyer, *Critical and Exegetical Commentary on the New Testament Romans Vol. 2* T & T Clark (Edinburgh, Scotland) 1873

Heinrich Meyer, *Critical and Exegetical Commentary on the New Testament Vol. VII Galatians* T & T Clark (Edinburgh, Scotland) 1884

Heinrich Meyer, *Critical and Exegeticl Handbook to the Epistles to Philippians and Colossians* T & T Clark (Edinburgh, Scotland) 1898

Stephen R. Miller, *Daniel : New American Commentary Vol. 18* Broadman & Holman (Nashville, TN.) 1994

George Milligan, *St. Paul's Epistles to the Thessalonians* Fleming Revell (Old Tappan, NJ) 1982

R. Milligan, *Epistle to the Hebrews* Chase and Hall Publishers (Cincinatti, Oh.) 1876 pg. 215

Chuck and Nancy Missler, *The Kingdom, Power, and Glory* King's Highway Ministries (Coeur d'Alene, ID) 2007

Dan Mitchell, *Second Corinthians* AMG Publishing (Chattanooga, TN) 2008

Dan Mitchell, *The Book of First Corinthians* AMG Publishers (Chattanooga, TN) 2004

James Moffatt, *A Critical and Exegetical Commentary on the Epistle to the Hebrews* Charles Scribners (New York, NY) 1924 pg. 102

Douglas Moo, *The Letters to the Colossians and to Philemon* Wm. B. Eerdmans (Grand Rapids, Mich.) 2008

Douglas Moo, *The Letter of James* Apollos (Leicester, England) 2000

Douglas Moo, Paul Feinberg, *The Rapture : Pre- Mid- or Posttribulational?* Zondervan (Grand Rapids, Mich.) 1984

Douglas Moo, *Romans – NIV Application Commentary* Zondervan Publ. (Grand Rapids, Mich.) 2000

George Montague, *Catholic Commentary on Sacred Scripture : First Corinthians* Baker Academics (Grand Rapids, Mich.) 2011

George Montague, *First Second Timothy, Titus* Baker Books (Grand Rapids, Mich.) 2008

Samuel Elliot Morison, *The Oxford History of the American People* Oxford Press (New York, NY) 1965

Henry Morris, *The Biblical Basis for Modern Science* Baker Book House (Grand Rapids, Mich.) 1984

Henry Morris, *Men of Science, Men of God* Master Books (El Cajon, CA) 1982

Henry Morris, *The Revelation Record* Tyndale House (Wheaton, Ill.) 1983

Leon Morris, *The Epistle of Paul to the Thessalonians* Wm. B. Eerdmans (Grand Rapids, Mich.) 1958

Leon Morris, *The Epistle to the Romans* Wm. B. Eerdmans (Grands Rapids, Mich.) 1994

Leon Morris, *The Gospel According to Matthew* Wm. Eerdmaans (Grand Rapids, Mich.) 1992

Leon Morris, *The Revelation of St. John* Wm. B. Eerdmans (Grand Rapids, Mich.) 1969

C.F.D. Moule, *The Epistles of Paul the Apostle to Colossians and to Philemon* Cambridge University (Cambridge, England) 1968

H.C.G. Moule, *Studies in Philippians* Kregel Publishers (Grand Rapids, Mich.) 1893 (1977 ed.)

Robert Mounce, *The Book of Revelation* Wm. B. Eerdmans (Grand Rapids, Mich.) 1977

Alexander Nairne, *The Epistle to the Hebrews* Cambridge University Press (Cambridge, MS) 1917

William Newell, *The Book of Revelation* Moody Press (Chicago, Ill.) n.d.

William Newell, *Hebrew : Verse by Verse* Moody Press (Chicago, Ill.) 1947

William Newell, *Lessons on the Epistle of Paul to the Romans* J.I.C. Wilcox, (Toronto, Canada) 1925

Barclay M. Newman, Jr., ed., *A Concise Greek-English Dictionary of the New Testament* United Bible Society (Stuttgart, Germany) 1971

Samuel Ngewa, *1 & 2 Timothy and Titus* Zondervan Publishers (Grand Rapids, Mich.) 2009

George Nickelsburg & James VanderKam, trans., *1 Enoch* Fortress Press (Minneapolis, MN) 2004

Lloyd John Ogilvie, *Let God Love You* Word Books (Waco, TX) 1974

Lloyd John Ogilvie, *Loved and Forgiven* G/L Publications (Glendale, CA) 1977

J. I. Packer, *Evangelism and the Sovereignty of God* InterVarsity Press (Downer's Grove, IL) 1961

J. I. Packer, *Keep in Step with the Spirit* Fleming Revell (Old Tappan, NJ) 1984

J. Dwight Pentecost, *A Faith That Endures* Discovery House (Grand Rapids, Mich.) 1992

J. Dwight Pentecost, *The Joy of Living* Zondervan Publishers (Grand Rapids, Mich.) 1973

Wesley Perschbacher, *Refresh Your Greek* Moody Press (Chicago, Ill.) 1989

David Petersen & Kent Richards, *Interpreting Hebrew Poetry* Fortress Press (Minneapolis, MN) 1992

Richard Phillips, *Hebrew* Presbyterian & Reformed (Philipsburg, NJ) 2006

Albert Pike, *Morals and Dogmas* Freemason Society (Charleston, SC) 1871

Arthur Pink, *The Antichrist* Bible Truth Publishers (Swengel, PA.) 1917

Arthur Pink, *An Exposition of the Gospel of John* Vol 2. I.C. Herendeen (Cleveland, OH) 1924

Arthur Pink, *An Exposition of Hebrews* Baker Books (Grand Rapids, Mich.) 1954

Arthur W. Pink, *The Sovereignty of God* Baker Books (Grand Rapids, Mich.) 1986

Matthew Poole, *A Commentary on the Holy Bible : Vol. III Matthew-Revelation* Hendrickson Publishers (Peabody, Mass.) n.d

Randall Price, *Searching for the Original Bible* Harvest House (Eugene, OR) 2007

Lewis Radford, *The Epistle to the Colossians and the Epistle to Philemon* Methuen & Co. (London, England) 1931

Herman Riddarbas, *The Epistle of Paul to the Churches of Galatia* Wm. B. Eerdmans (Grand Rapids, Mich.) 1953

Archibald Roberston & Alfred Plummer, *A Critical & Exegetical Commentary on First & Second Corinthians* T. & T. Clark (Edinburgh, Scotland) 1911

Marvin Rosenthal, *The Pre-Wrath Rapture of the Church* Thomas Nelson Publishers (Nashville, Tn.) 1990

Georges Roux, *Ancient Iraq* Penguin Books (New York, NY) 1992 ed.

Charles Ryrie, *1ˢᵗ and 2ⁿᵈ Thessalonians* Moody Press (Chicago, Ill.) 1959

Charles Ryrie, *Dispensationalism Today* Moody Pres (Chicago, Ill.) 1965

Charles Ryrie, *Revelation* Moody Press (Chicago, Ill.) 1996

Risto Saarinen, *The Pastoral Epistles with Philemon and Jude* Brazos Press (Grand Rapids, Mich.) 2008

Philip Schaff, *History of the Christian Church Vol. 2* Hendrickson Publishers Peabody, Mass.) 1996

Emil Schurer, *A History of the Jewish People First Div. Vol. II* Hendrickson Publishers (Peabody, Mass.) 1890 (2009 ed.)

Eduard Schweizer, *The Letter to the Colossians* Augsburg (Minneapolis, MN) 1976

C.I. Scofield, *The Epistle to the Galatians* The Gospel Hour (Greenville, SC) 1903

Walter Scott, *Exposition of the Revelation of Jesus Christ* Pickering & Inglis (London, England) n.d.

Joseph Seiss, *The Apocalypse* Kregel (Grand Rapids, Mich.) 1900 (2001 reprint)

D.P. Simpson, ed., *Cassell's Latin Dictionary* MacMillan Press (New York, NY) 1959

R.C. Sproul, *1-2 Peter* Crossway Books (Wheaton, Ill.) 2011

R.C. Sproul, *The Gospel of God : Romans* Christian Focus Publishers (Ross-shire, Great Britain) 1994

R.C. Sproul, *The Purpose of God* Christan Focus Publications (Fearn, Scotland) 1994

Charles Spurgeon, *Exposition of the Doctrine of Grace* Pilgrim Publications (Pasadena TX) n.d.

Charles Spurgeon, *Treasury of the New Testament Volume Three* Zondervan Publishers (Grand Rapids, Mich) 1950

Charles Spurgeon, *Treasury of the New Testament Volume Four* Zondervan Publishers (Grand Rapids, Mich.) 1950

Cornelius Stam, *Commentary on the Pastoral Epistles of Paul the Apostle* Berean Bible Society (Chicago, Ill.) 1983

Thomas Stegman, *Second Corinthians* Baker Academic (Grand Rapids, Mich.) 2009

Charles Swindoll, *Insights on James and 1 & 2 Peter* Zondervan Publishers (Grand Rapids, Mich.) 2010

Charles Swindoll, *Insights in Romans* Zondervan Publishers (Grands Rapids, Mich.) 2010

Charles Talbert, *Paedeia : Ephesians and Colossians* Baker Books (Grand Rapids, Mich.) 2007

Merrill Tenney, *New Testament Survey* William B. Eerdmans (Grand Rapids, Mich.) 1985

Joseph Thayer, *Thayer's Greek-English Lexicon* Baker Book House (Grand Rapids, Mich.) 1977

Alexis de Tocqueville, *Democracy in America* Harper & Row (New York, NY) 1969 ed.

Alexis de Toqueville, *Democracy in America Vol. 2* Perrenial Library (New York, NY) 1966 ed.

R.A. Torrey, *Difficulties in the Bible* Whitaker House (New Kensington, PA) 2003 ed.

M.M.B. Turner, "Spiritual Gifts Then and Now," *Vox Evangelica* No. 15 (1985)

Merrill Unger, *Unger's Bible Dictionary* Moody Press (Chicago, Ill.) 1957

James Ussher, *Annals of the World* Master Books (Green Forest, AR) 2003

Robert van Kampen, *The Sign* Crossway Books (Wheaton, Ill.) 1992

Marius Victorinus, *Marius Victorinus' Commentary on Galatians* Stephen Cooper, trans. Wm. B. Eerdmans (Grand Rapids, Mich.) 2005

Martin Vincent, *A Critical and Exegetical Commentary on the Epistles to the Philippians and to Philemon* T & T Clark (Edinburgh, Scotland) 1897

John Walvoord, *Every Prophecy of the Bible* Chariot Victor Publishing (Colorado Springs, Co.) 1999

John Walvoord, *The Revelation of Jesus Christ* Moody Press (Chicago, Ill.) 1966

John Walvoord, *The Thessalonian Epistles* Dunham Publishing (Findlay, Ohio) 1955

John Walvoord, *Thy Kingdom Come : Matthew* Moody Press (Chicago, Ill.) 1974

John Walvoord, *To Live is Christ* Dunham Publishers (Findlay, Ohio) 1961

John Walvoord, *Triumph in Christ* Moody Press (Chicago, Ill.) 1991

Steve Waterhouse, *Who Wrote Revelation & John's Gospel?* Westcliff Press (Amarillo, TX) 2012

Steven Waterhouse, *Not By Bread Alone* Westcliff Press (Amarillo, TX) 2007

Brooke Westcott, *The Epistle to the Hebrews* Wm. B. Eerdmans (Grand Rapids, Mich.) 1970

Brooke Westcott, *The Epistles of St. John* MacMillian (London, England) 1886

Frederick Westcott, *A Letter to Asia* MacMillan (London, England) 1914

Warren Wiersbe, *Be Alert* Victor Books (Wheaton, Ill.) 1987

Warren Wiersbe, *Be Confident* Victor Books (Wheaton, Ill.) 1982

Warren Wiersbe, *Be Complete* Victor Books (Wheaton, Ill.) 1983

Warren Wiersbe, *Be Encouraged* Victor Books (Wheaton, Ill.) 1988

Warren Wiersbe, *Be Faithful* Victor Books (Wheaton, Ill.) 1987

Warren Wiersbe, *Be Free* Victor Books (Wheaton, Ill.) 1976

Warren Wiersbe, *Be Joyful* Victor Books (Wheaton, Ill.) 1974

Warren Wiersbe, *Be Loyal* Victor Books (Wheaton, Ill.) 1987

Warren Wiersbe, *Be Rich* Victor Books (Wheaton, Ill.) 1977

Warren Wiersbe, *Be Right* Victor Books (Wheaton, Ill.) 1984

Warren Wiersbe, *Be Wise* Victor Books (Wheaton, Ill.) 1984

Peter Williamson, *Catholic Commentary on Scripture : Ephesians* Baker Academics (Grand Rapids, Mich.) 2009

C. Leonard Woolley, *The Sumerians* W.W. Norton & Co. (New York, NY) 1965

Kenneth Wuest, *First Peter in the Greek New Testament* Wm. B. Eerdmans (Grand Rapids, Mich.) 1948

Kenneth Wuest, *In These Last Days* Wm. B. Eerdmans (Grand Rapids, Mich.) 1954

Kenneth Wuest, *Philippians* Wm. B. Eerdmans (Grand Rapids, Mich.) 1942

Richard A. Young, *Intermediate New Testament Greek* Broadman & Holman (Nashville, TN) 1994

REFERENCE WORKS

Kurt & Barbara Aland, eds., *Nestle-Aland NovumTestamentum Graece* United Bible Society (Stuttgart, Germany) 1898

Gerald Bray, ed., *Ancient Christian Commentary on Scripture* Vol. IV A Intervarsity Press (Downers Grove, Ill.) 1988

Gerald Bray, ed., *Ancient Christian Commentary on Scripture* Vol. IV B Intervarsity Press (Downers Grove, Ill.) 1988

Gerald Bray, ed., *Ancient Christian Commentary on Scripture* Vol. VII Intervarsity Press (Downers Grove, Ill.) 1988

Gerald Bray, ed., *Ancient Christian Commentary on Scripture* Vol. X Intervarsity Press (Downers Grove, Ill.) 1988

Gerald Bray, ed., *Ancient Christian Commentary on Scripture* Vol. XI Intervarsity Press (Downers Grove, Ill.) 1988

W.A. Criswell, ed., *Criswell Study Bible* Thomas Nelson (Nashville, TN) 1979

Diagnostic and Statistical Manual of Mental Disorders (DSM-III) American Psychiatric Association (Washington, D.S.) 1987

Frank Gaebelein, ed., *The Expositor's Bible Commentary* Vol. 7 Zondervan Publishers (Grand Rapids, Mich.) 1986

Frank Gaebelein, ed., *The Expositors Bible Commentary* Vol. 8 Zondervan Publishers (Grand Rapids, Mich.) 1986

Frank Gaebelein, ed., *The Expositor's Bible Commentary* Vol. 10 Zondervan Publishers (Grand Rapids, Mich.) 1976

Frank Gaebelein, ed., *The Expositor's Bible Commentary* Vol. 11 Zondervan Publishers (Grand Rapids, Mich.) 1986

Frank Gaebelein, ed., *The Expositor's Bible Commentary* Vol. 12 Zondervan Publishers (Grand Rapids, Mich.) 1986

Alexander Roberts & James Donaldson, eds., *Ante-Nicene Fathers* Vol. I Charles Scribner (New York, NY) 1886

Alexander Roberts & James Donaldson, eds., *Ante-Nicene Fathers* Vol. II Charles Scribner (New York, NY) 1886

Alexander Roberts & James Donaldson, eds., *Ante-Nicene Fathers* Vol. III Charles Scribner (New York, NY) 1886

Alexander Roberts & James Donaldson, eds., *Ante-Nicene Fathers* Vol. IV William B. Eerdmans Publishers (Grand Rapids, Mich.) 1885

Alexander Roberts & James Donaldson, eds., *Ante-Nicene Fathers* Vol. IV Charles Scribner (New York, NY) 1886

Alexander Roberts & James Donaldson, eds., *Ante-Nicene Fathers* Vol. V Charles Scribner (New York, NY) 1886

Alexander Roberts & James Donaldson, eds., *Ante-Nicene Fathers Vol. VI* Charles Scribner (New York, NY) 1886

Alexander Roberts & James Donaldson, eds., *Ante-Nicene Fathers Vol. VII* Charles Scribner (New York, NY) 1886

Alexander Roberts & James Donaldson, eds., *Ante-Nicene Fathers Vol. VIII* Charles Scribner (New York, NY) 1886

Philip Schaff, ed., *Nicene and Post-Nicene Fathers Second Series Vol. XIII* Christian Literature Co. (New York, NY) 1894

John Walvoord & Roy Zuck, eds., *Bible Knowledge Commentary : New Testament* Victor Books (Wheaton, Ill.) 1986

Webster's New World College Dictionary Wiley Publishing (New York, NY) 2004

PERIODICALS

George Guthrie, "The Case for Apollos as the Author of Hebrews," *Faith and Mission Vol. 18 No. 2 Spring 2001*

John Sweigart, "Is There a Departure in 2 Thessalonians 2:3?" *Conservative Theological Journal Vol. 1 No. 15 August 2001*

Dwight Wright, "Homosexuals or Prostitutes," *Vigiliae Christianae* No. 38 (1984)

MISC & WEBSITES

Warwick Aiken, Jr., "The Authorship of the Epistle to the Hebrew," *A Thesis for Dallas Theological Seminary* July 1946

E-Sword Software Commentary Series

Logos Bible Software

Randall Niles, "Bible Manuscripts," www.allaboutthejourney.org/bible-manuscripts.htm

C.I Scofield Reference Bible Online /www.biblestudytools.com/commentaries/scofield-reference-notes/hebrews/hebrews-6.html

Catechism of the Catholic Church ; www.vatican.va/archive/ENG0015/__P5.HTM

biblicaldiscipleship.org/content/relationships-and-bible

en.wikipedia.org/wiki /First_Jewish–Roman_War

en.wikipedia.org/wiki/Gospel_of_thomas

lavistachurchofchrist.org/LVanswers/2011/04-12b.html

thegospelcoalition.org/blogs/justintaylor/2012/02/13/is-god-the-author-of-sin-jonathan-edwards-answer/

www.biblestudy.org/basicart/why-does-god-hate-practices-of-the-nicolaitans.html

www.christian-history.org/muratorian-canon.html

www.earlyjewishwritings.com/testmoses.html

www.facebook.com/groups/scripturally.speaking/

www.goarch.org/ourfaith/ourfaith9560

www.gty.org/Resources/Articles/A189

www.haaretz.com/weekend/week-s-end/in-three-days-you-shall-live-1.218552

www.newble.co.uk/anderson/truths/app5_notes.html

www.rediff.com/movies/report/slide-show-1-rani-when-i-admit-my-children-to-school-i-will-change-my-name/20140625.htm.

www.spiritandtruth.org/teaching/Book_of_Revelation/commentary/htm/topics/nicolaitans.html

www.thebereancall.org/node/1220

www.ingramcontent.com/pod-product-compliance
Lightning Source LLC
Chambersburg PA
CBHW060232100426
42742CB00011B/1515